PERSONALITY
a scientific approach

Elaine Donelson
Michigan State University

GOODYEAR PUBLISHING COMPANY, INC.,
Pacific Palisades, California

This book is dedicated to

Students who teach
and teachers who learn—
especially
Bonnie,
Miriam,
Ellen and Hal—
and to the spirit within them
that enables each of them to be
what they are to me.

0-87620-657-7   10 9 8 7 6 5 4 3

Library of Congress Card Number: 73-2544

PRINTED IN THE UNITED STATES OF AMERICA

Designer: Faith Gertner
Illustrator: Danmark and Michaels Inc.
Text set in Caledonia

CREDITS

The author is very grateful to the publishers, authors, and editors of the
books and journals listed below for permission to reprint material—mainly
tables and figures—from these sources.

Table 2–1: From Schachter, S., Goldman, R., & Gordon, A. Effects of fear,
food deprivation, and obesity on eating. *Journal of Personality and Social
Psychology*, 1968, **10**, 91–97. Copyright 1968 by the American Psychological
Association and reproduced by permission.

Table 2–2: From Schachter, S., & Gross, L. P. Manipulated time and eating
behavior. *Journal of Personality and Social Psychology*, 1968, **10**, 98–106.
Copyright 1968 by the American Psychological Association and reproduced
by permission.

Credits continued at back of book.

CONTENTS

Part

||||| MEASUREMENT PROCESSES

Part

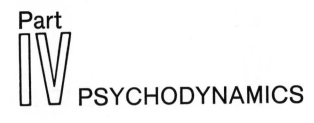

IV PSYCHODYNAMICS

Part V
SOCIAL INFLUENCE

Part VI
DEVELOPMENT OF PERSONALITY

PREFACE

PERSONALITY: A SCIENTIFIC APPROACH is intended for under-graduate courses in personality. It is meant to acquaint the student with what is known about personality, and what has been attempted in the scientific study of personality. The materials for doing this are very rich, for in the last twenty-five years an enormous number of psychologists have examined manifestations of personality in an objective way and presented the results of their experiments to their colleagues.

In an undergraduate text, however, it would not do simply to present the research evidence for study and appraisal. A book that students will read and enjoy must be a great deal more than a catalog of research findings. It must be clearly organized, written in a plain style, and re-lated to the everyday world of those readers. In short, it must integrate the psychologist's scientific objectivity with the reader's need for every-day meaning. If it is to encourage an appreciation of what science can do, it must go beyond reporting the evidence to suggesting what that evidence implies for behavior, and for behavior change.

These goals are not easy to achieve. If I have taken a few steps toward them, I have been helped enormously by those who contributed to the development of this book. Two former teachers—E. Llewelyn Queener and Charlotte Doyle—suggested to me by successful example that text-book writing can be challenging and meaningful. My colleagues at Michigan State University provided helpful readings, skillful advice, and continual support; I am especially grateful to Miriam Burke (now at Earlham College), Lucy Ferguson, Hiram Fitzgerald, Jeanne Gullahorn, John Gullahorn, Gene Jacobson, Lawrence O'Kelly, Albert Rabin, Henry Clay Smith, the late William Stellwagen, and Ellen Strommen. Several of my students at Michigan State also offered help and direction at vari-ous stages: Jackie Fells, Cynthia Haas, Phyllis Leech Heenan, Lorraine Leonowich, Shirley Martinson, and Bonnie Morrison. Many others of-fered kindness and encouragement to their "psych teacher"—whom I hope they also think of as their "friend who teaches psychology."

I am grateful, too, to Fred W. Donelson and Louella T. Donelson for their support throughout this endeavor and for their patience with my often bizarre behavior.

Outside my immediate circle, many people read parts of the manuscript and made invaluable suggestions: Eugene L. Gaier, G. C. Helmstadter, Julian E. Hochberg, Harold J. Johnson, Florence Kaslow, Kenneth Mac-Corquodale, Robert McGinnis, Frank B. McMahon, Edward J. Murray, Myrtle C. Nash, Lita Linzer Schwartz, Harold Stevenson, and Merle B. Turner. My special thanks go to Gardner Lindzey for his support during the early stages of the project.

Finally, I am grateful to the editors, designers, and production specialists at Appleton-Century-Crofts who polished my manuscript and turned it into a book. Those who gave me special help were Jan Buessem and Florence Benjamin, who edited the manuscript; Judi Markowitz, who put my bibliography cards into final form; and Sarah Dike, who handled production of the book.

E.D.

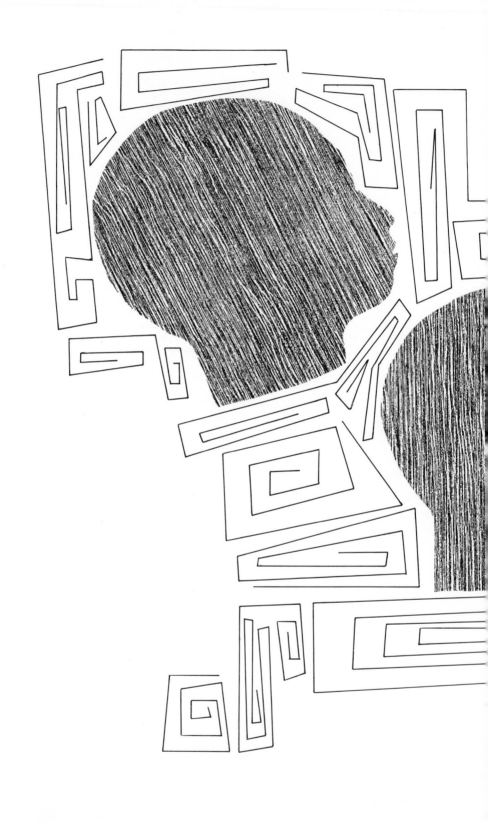

THE SCIENTIFIC PERSPECTIVE

PART I

1

personality
and science

No two people are exactly alike. The biological equipment
with which we enter the world and the environmental
forces which exert themselves upon us, as we grow and
develop, all serve to shape a personality, or individuality,
which is ours alone. The goal of personality psychology is
to understand this individuality. The science of personality
provides the tools for achieving that goal.

SCIENCE OF PERSONALITY

Personality as an *area* of scientific investigation is the study
of individual differences in the behavior of human beings
who are biological organisms which develop and have experiences in physical and social environments. The study
of these individual differences in behavior may be advanced
by a science of behavior which allows for the reasonable
postulation of constructs dealing with the fact that people
think and feel about themselves in ways that control their
overt, observable behavior, and are concomitant with and
responsive to that behavior.

THE ORGANISM IN PERSPECTIVE

The Biological Being and the Social Being

The human being is a biological organism. That is, he is
part of the natural universe of plant and animal life, a
system that in turn is part of the larger physical system.
While the student of personality cannot expect to be an
expert in all these facets of interacting life, he must be sufficiently aware of them to place his individual subject of
study in proper perspective. Without such an awareness,

it is tempting to view the human being as an isolated entity, somehow immune to the implications of being a part of a natural system.

The biological, social, and psychological facets of the individual cannot be separated in any final sense. Nor can the individual be considered apart from his environment. The interactions of the organism—man—with the world are mediated by biological factors. People are contained within bodies, through which they interact with the world. The body is a stimulus to which other people react, and having learned the meanings others attach to his body, the person himself comes to feel proud, ashamed, boastful, or deviant because of his body. The "insides" of the body are equally important as, if not more important than, the outsides. Continual depression may be due to low blood sugar rather than to psychological malaise, but will nonetheless affect interactions with other people. The nervous system influences how we receive and process information about the world and the intensity of our reactions. The body itself is a psychological event which is associated, sometimes as cause, sometimes as effect, sometimes as a concomitant, with our thoughts and feelings, at least some of which, if not all, involve other people in some way. It is a social stimulus and a processor of social stimuli. The biological individual, with feelings, thoughts, and the social needs and behaviors he gradually develops through life, evolves his own characteristics—his individuality—through interaction with both his physical and social environment; his developed characteristics then shape his environment and affect his reaction to its conditions. Climate and soil conditions affect food supply and therefore the adequacy of the nutritional support necessary for physical development and maintenance. Nutritional requirements in turn have implications for the social systems that develop to facilitate individual and group survival. Within the social system in a physical environment, the individual develops, experiences, acts, and *is*.

The differences: their sources. Because the individual is a biological organism growing and experiencing in an environment, both his genetic endowment and his experiences in his environment will shape his behavior. American psychology has not, by and large, attended adequately to the biology of the individual organism. John Watson, the founder of American Behaviorism, was an adamant environmentalist who asserted that if he had complete control of the environment of any infant, he could produce a baker, lawyer, or Indian chief at will. Such a spirit of equality at birth is, of course, consistent with stated American ideals. However, people *do* differ at birth in ways important for their interactions with others and their continually developing behavior patterns (see especially Chapters 14, 19). There is increasing recognition of the biological substrata of all sorts of psychological phenomena, ranging from dreams (Chapter 9), to performance on intellectual tasks (Chapter 10), to emotions (Chapter 14), and even to perception of self (Chapter 12) and adolescent crises (Chapter 21). But we are still a long way from an adequate incorporation of biological variables into psychological understanding. Equality of *opportunity* for personal development is more likely to occur by providing differing experiences for differing people, depending on what is necessary for their *own* optimal functioning, than it is by insisting on exactly the same environment and socialization experiences for all.

Their identification.   Not all facets of the biology or the environmental experience of the organism have recurring or especially interesting effects on behavior. People, as biological and socially experiencing creatures, differ in a variety of ways that are not particularly relevant to the immediate concerns of the psychologist. For instance, in the case of most people, the size of the heart, the number of English royalty in the family tree, or the mean annual temperature of the home town are not dominant determinants of behavior. Consequently, these are not likely to be variables to which a personality scientist will assign a major role in his attempts to understand people.

However, the psychologist must be prepared to consider such apparently irrelevant variables as these when faced with any one person here and now. If Johnny's mother does not let him play tag with other boys because a pediatrician once commented that Johnny has a small heart, then heart size is relevant for Johnny. If Susie goes around bragging to her friends that she has royalty in her family tree, her friends may want to chop it down and see Susie's royal ties broken. A student used to warm weather may find it nearly impossible to make himself leave the warm dormitory of a northern school during the winter months.

These examples of variables which are not relevant to most people but which could be relevant to one person illustrate the difficulties of identifying the variables suitable for the personality psychologist's attention. He must find the right things to look for; he must also find effective questions to ask in order to conceptualize what he sees. He must identify not only the most practical and relevant variables of differences, but also the other variables to which they are related, and the nature of the interrelationships. Further, he must determine what stimulus conditions affect them. This means he must make both R-R (response-response) and S-R (stimulus-response) statements.

The Laws

R-R relationships.   R-R laws are statements of relationships between two responses or, more generally, two subject-located, organismic variables or personal characteristics. They could be called O-O laws (O for organism) just as well. Personality psychologists have a tradition of concern with R-R laws that reflects their interest in existing individual differences. Often, relationships are sought between two responses on "personality tests." Thus, personality psychology has long been identified as a *psychometric* (testing) activity. The identification of a personality with psychometrics was a natural one in that the explicit concern of the early psychometricians was the measurement of individual differences.

However, an R-R statement need not involve two test scores. For example, people who score high on the Taylor Manifest Anxiety Scale (a test) condition more quickly (a behavioral measure) than do those who score low. In fact, there need not be any tests at all involved in R-R laws (e.g., people who spend much of their time watching television do not read many books). R-R statements, or laws, describe existing relationships between responses. An R-R study is also called a differential or correlational study, reflecting the fact that interest is in relationships between existing individual differences that are brought to the situation.

R-R statements are useful insofar as they tell us how two variables are related in one person, or in a group of people. However, the typical correlational study by itself tells us little else. That is, it does not tell us *why* the variables are related, *why* any one person (or group of people) does or does not possess the characteristic we have measured, nor why he has X amount of a characteristic rather than X plus Y amount. Thus, R-R laws alone are not sufficient for understanding human behavior.

S-R relationships. S-R laws relate an observable environmental condition, the stimulus, to observable behavior, a response. Experimental psychologists have long preferred S-R laws. Although the concept of cause is complex, the frequently expressed justification for this preference is that one may make better statements about causation than when one is dealing solely with R-R laws. One has a greater satisfaction of having an answer to "why" when he can state an S-R relationship rather than an R-R one. One can at least say that, given the S, an observable environmental event, the R, is very likely. Personality psychologists are becoming increasingly involved in making the S-R statements, which were once considered the domain of the experimental psychologist, and we shall deal with them frequently in coming chapters.

A United Discipline

Cronbach (1957) has etched the shape of a united discipline as being one concerned with the R-R laws traditionally typical of the personality psychologist as well as with the S-R laws traditionally typical of the experimental psychologist (see also Owens, 1968). Neither approach alone is adequate for the job of explaining human behavior. A response is determined both by the characteristics an individual brings to a situation (including predispositions to respond in the situation) and by the situation itself. The two approaches may be combined into an S-O-R formulation which recognizes that organismic (O) variables influence the effect of the S. As Cronbach states, "We will come to

FIGURE

1–1

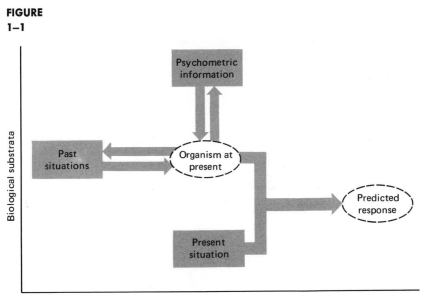

Theoretical Network for United Discipline.

Source: Modified from Cronbach, L. J. The two disciplines of scientific psychology. *American Psychologist,* 1957, 12, 684.

realize that organism and treatment are an inseparable pair and that no psychologist can dismiss one or the other as error variance" (Cronbach, 1957, p. 683). Thus, in an experiment with the college students, examination performance can be understood only in terms of the predispositions the student brings to the exam setting and what he finds in that setting.

Cronbach's relatively simplified diagram (Figure 1–1) indicates the appropriateness of determining relationships between organismic variables (labeled as psychometric information) and the S-R relationships between the stimuli and the observable responses. Notations have been added to his diagram to suggest that behavior, past and present, has a biological base and often occurs in a social setting. The O variables are influenced by the stimuli previously encountered: what we see as the individual here and now is a function of his prior experiences. Any one S-O-R statement is a momentary, static snapshot in a long-range, ongoing S-O-R process. The O is in the statement, from the beginning, at least in terms of biological constitutional differences which shape and direct future experiences, whatever else may be also characteristic of human beings at birth. Thus, a complete picture would look something like that depicted in Figure 1–2. By repeating the S-O-R sequence in the diagram, we have attempted to indicate development and change of the responses, from which we infer development and change in individuality or personality.

FIGURE
1–2

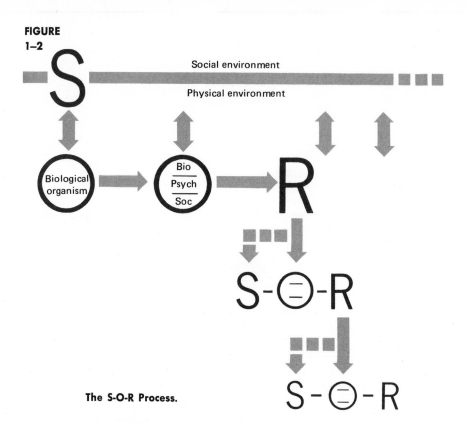

The S-O-R Process.

DEVELOPMENT AND CHANGE

If we describe a person as an aggressive go-getter, one who tackles the world by leaps and bounds, we are *labeling*, not *explaining*. Even when we can see these characteristics in a wide variety of behaviors in diverse situations (individual consistencies) at any particular time in the person's life, we must be able to see also how those habitual modes of behavior developed. Static snapshots in the developmental sequence of people's lives neither exhaustively depict their individuality nor, no matter how thorough, are they evidence of complete and adequate scientific understanding. *A complete science of personality is a science of personality development.*

In order to understand behavior, we must also understand the development of behavior (Carlson, 1971). We must know what factors determine behavior, how to shape the course of development for the best interest of the particular organism, and how to change behavior for the better in ways that would not occur without an intentional intervention in the ongoing developmental sequence. Some psychologists (e.g., Skinner) insist that the ability to change behavior is the most meaningful demonstration of scientific understanding.

Application

The potentiality of behavioral control causes fear in many that nefarious psychologists will manipulate people to their own selfish advantages. What is overlooked is that we are constantly being manipulated and influenced in the normal course of everyday living. Advertising is an easily detectable case in point, but the influences are much more pervasive than this, extending through all of our interpersonal interactions, past and present. The results are not always beneficial to any one individual. A science of behavior is imperative, for it may enable awareness of the influences continually upon us and enable prevention or correction of maladaptive behavior.

Knowledge makes possible a behavioral control that can hopefully be used to ease human suffering. The obvious danger is that this knowledge will be used for less noble ends. One has only to consider the career of an intuitive manipulator of human behavior such as Hitler to realize that the knowledge of how to influence and control behavior may be dangerously used. How and when knowledge of behavior is to be used raises large and important issues, which are not necessarily the same as those surrounding the desirability of knowledge. The profession of psychology is increasingly concerned about professional ethics, but the problems extend throughout society and cannot be shouldered by psychology and other sciences, alone.

It may well be that scientific knowledge is dangerous and scientific methods weak. However, it is not clear that ignorance can cure such faults.

The goal of personality psychology is to advance the understanding of human behavior so that people may, in turn, better understand themselves. The more we know about each other and about ourselves, the less likely we are to fall victim to opportunists, intentional or not, professionals or laymen, who prey on our ignorance and emotional weaknesses, and the more likely we are to develop the potentialities of mankind and those of the individual.

Summary

The human being is a biological creature who experiences and develops within environments which exert both social and physical pressures upon him. He becomes the individual he is through interaction with the elements of the physical and social context within which he lives, and he can be understood only as a distinct part of that context. The goal of the personality psychologist is to gain the capability of grasping individual differences in the behavior of the dynamic, complex human being. He works toward the understanding of the individual. The way in which he defines personality varies greatly with the kind of behaviors he thinks relevant to the study of human beings and with the constructs he uses in conceptualizing the reasons for those behaviors.

Obviously, no one person nor the one discipline of personality psychology can know all that needs to be known about the human being in his environment. With the complexity of the phenomenon of man and the burgeoning of knowledge, the "whole" picture of man becomes truncated into many discrete, incomplete sections. The immediate focus of the personality psychologist is the individual differences in behaviors presumably associated with differences in internal states. To aid him in the task of understanding behavior, the personality psychologist can profit well from the work of other psychological disciplines. In turn, he can serve as a focal point for integrating the knowledge acquired in other disciplines into a coherent picture of the whole, functioning human being.

Experimental psychology offers understanding of basic phenomena of learning, memory, thinking and reasoning, perception, motivation, physiology, and through comparative psychology, a view of man in relation to other animals. The united discipline offered by Cronbach is indicative of the way experimental and personality psychology are becoming increasingly interrelated. Social psychology describes the ways in which people generally interact with others, the dynamics of groups of people and the roles occurring in social organizations, and the ways in which human behavior is responsive to social pressures. The intimacy of the relationship between social and personality psychology is reflected in the fact that the organizational structure of many departments of psychology does not recognize personality as a field distinct from social psychology.

Clinical psychology and personality psychology have a kinship because of their shared interest in achieving understanding of the individual, and because of the early foundations of personality theory laid by practicing therapists. The practicing therapist offers a clinical understanding of personality and personality modification which he develops in his one-to-one interactions with patients. In turn, personality psychology offers the clinician a theoretical formulation of human behavior and associated facts that might prove helpful in dealing with the real-life problems his patients bring to him. Similarly, the personality psychologist may contribute to the industrial psychologist's understanding of man in his work environment, and may, in turn, learn about man in the real-life situation of work, and the influence of experiences in the occupational world on other spheres of life.

Developmental psychology provides the perspective of the developing human being that is necessary for a personality science. Much of the work of developmental psychologists concerns particular age groups (infancy, childhood, adolescence, old age), but with increasing intent to trace the trends of biological and psycho-social development and to mark out the nature of significant events and crucial variables in human development.

The personality psychologist has much to learn from other psychological disciplines, and much to contribute in synthesizing and integrating information from other disciplines into a total view of man. The personality psychologist's ultimate task is to devise a workable, holistic view of the human being within which any one individual may be understood. Thus, personality theory (Chapters 3, 4, 5, 6) tends to be distinguished from other psychological theory in its function as integrative thought which attempts to bring together and organize the diverse findings of specialists in aspects of human functioning.

2
personality as science

The concept of a science of personality may sound alien and even sterile until we realize that the same processes of thought and observation employed by the professional scientist are used by everyone in their daily involvement with people. We are all, in a sense, personality scientists. That is, we attempt to understand the actions of ourselves and others by observing and then thinking, thinking and then observing, in a continual process. More specifically, (1) we observe behavior and the environmental setting in which it occurs; (2) we then ask ourselves questions about the behavior; (3) on the basis of our observations and thoughts, we make generalizations to use in predicting future behavior; finally, (4) we may make inferences about things we cannot see: past experiences of the person we are observing, or his current thoughts, feelings, traits, or abilities.

THE METHOD

Observation

Consider a relatively simple example. Mrs. Brown notices that her husband is acting funny. She asks herself: What do I mean when I label him *funny?* Observing and thinking more carefully, she notices that he is drinking more coffee than usual, chain-smoking, tapping his pencil, cracking his knuckles, biting his fingernails, and, when a neighbor knocks on the door, he jumps out of his chair and starts screaming about continual disturbances and lack of privacy. Thinking further, she notes that this is Thursday evening, and he has just returned from his weekly law school seminar.

Since Mrs. Brown is a patient wife, she doesn't scream back, but stays her distance and wonders what is wrong with him. The strange responses diminish until the following Thursday, when Mr. Brown evidences the same erratic behavior. With continued observation, Mrs. Brown begins to detect a regularity in the occurrence of her husband's eccentric responses; consequently, she makes a *generalization* describing the phenomenon: On Thursday evenings after his seminar, my husband shows a defined set of responses which are not characteristic of him at other times. She may use this generalization to make a *prediction* about future events: The response will occur every Thursday evening after his seminar. So far, all she has done is observe behavior and make a statement about two sets of observable events: the environmental event of the seminar and the subsequent behavior of her husband.

Inference

In addition to relating the two sets of events, Mrs. Brown will probably make inferences based on the events she has observed. In doing this, she uses a *construct*, which is an idea or integrating concept linked to observable events and helping to describe the relationship between events. If Mrs. Brown infers that her husband is anxious on Thursdays, anxiety is a construct which helps her understand his behavior.

If she considers anxiety as an entity, process, or event with physical properties that can be observed with adequate techniques, then the construct of anxiety is a *hypothetical construct*. Thus, if she defines anxiety as a set of physiological responses (e.g., heartbeat, blood pressure, perspiration), her construct is subject to direct verification, though she need not actually measure the physiological responses. In fact, psychologists sometimes postulate physical events for which there are no currently available techniques of measurement.

If she is using the construct of anxiety to describe aspects of her husband which are not themselves directly observable, then her construct of anxiety is an *intervening variable*. An intervening variable is merely an idea and is not subject to direct verification. Unlike the hypothetical construct, an intervening variable has no postulated physical properties or objective existence. One observable concomitant of anxiety may be said to be physiological events, but these themselves are not the anxiety; they are one index of it. One does not see "hurried"; one sees a boy running and assumes "hurried." Similarly, one does not *see* anxiety; one *infers* anxiety.

Construct validation. Neither the scientist nor Mrs. Brown is free to invent constructs willy-nilly. Any construct must be validated: One must give evidence of its usefulness in helping to organize observable events. Because of the importance, and often difficulty, of demonstrating construct validation, later chapters include a formal treatment of some construct validation procedures (Chapters 7, 8).

For the moment, let us note that in the process of validating her construct of anxiety—in demonstrating the usefulness of inferring that her husband is anxious—Mrs. Brown can make a number of hypotheses about antecedents and effects of anxiety as she is using the construct. Her implicit theory about her husband's anxiety might involve social considerations (he dislikes his professor), biological ones (he gets tired in the long class), or factors pertaining to self-esteem (he is afraid of failing).

The more she expands on her ideas about anxiety, the more useful the construct will be in explaining and integrating the events she observes. She may test her ideas by noting whether the behaviors from which she is inferring anxiety occur at other pertinent times—other times when he is with people he dislikes, other times when he gets tired or is afraid of failing in a task. The more predictions she makes and the more they are confirmed, the greater the usefulness, or validity, of her construct and her ideas about it. No one set of conditions or behaviors defines anxiety; many participate in a definition and are integrated by the construct.

THE SCIENTIST

What Makes a Scientist?

So far, we have been discussing thought and observation as they are common to both professional and lay psychologists. What, then, marks the difference between the professional scientist and the layman? The difference lies in the degree to which the professional scientist can and does systematically explore his phenomena rather than in the kind of activity involved. While we all try to explain the world around us, we do not consistently probe for knowledge with the thoroughness and explicitness of the professional scientist.

We take some behavior for granted rather than pause to be curious and ask, "Why . . . ?", and often examine only the unusual to the neglect of the usual. Mrs. Brown asks herself about the unusual "anxious" behavior on Thursdays, but not about why her husband asks for two eggs over lightly on Thursday morning, exactly as he has done every other day they have been married.

We often take a friend's assertion or the supposed expert's explanation as "fact" enough to satisfy our curiosity (appeal to authority). And often our observation and thought processes are implicit rather than explicit, verbalized (at least to ourselves), and examined. Whatever the source of what we believe we know, we do not always feel the necessity for justifying or explaining our conclusions to others.

In contrast, the scientist is curious about the commonplace as well as the unusual (Why is Mr. Brown *not* anxious on Mondays? Why does he always ask for two eggs over lightly, knowing his wife is prepared to fix these for his breakfast?). In pursuit of knowledge about the usual or the unusual, he must *discover* fact and do so by systematic observation. This implies that he must be inventive in the ways in which he looks for empirical evidence and that he must explicitly state his procedures of thinking, his investigation, and the outcome precisely so that others can repeat and retest his efforts.

A Public Activity

Because science is a public venture, the scientist has a great deal of assistance in asking and answering questions, as well as a responsibility to be communicative. The accessibility, through professional publications and informal communications with others, of the knowledge of the past as well as the present, increases the likelihood of a meaningful *cumulative knowledge*. In addition, the scientist often possesses the equipment and the manpower, as well as the public sanction, to make observations not available to the layman. For example, the layman who wants to know how people feel about Brand X would probably have to base his conclusions largely on his own acquaintances and probably would not systematically or thoroughly sample opinion even among those selected people he knows. Further, special equipment is often necessary to test out one's ideas (e.g., a polygraph to measure the physiological responses of anxiety). The behavioral scientist has the techniques, money, and authority to obtain a more representative sample of opinion, and the equipment necessary to observe facets of behavior that are not otherwise easily observable.

Difficulties of the Psychologist

Objective expertise. Psychologists and other social scientists encounter difficulties beyond those that face researchers who deal with nonhuman or inanimate subject matter. The student will feel these problems as he is cast into the role of "psychologist" by friends and relatives who know he is studying psychology.

The psychologist is part of his subject matter. When such an intimate relationship exists between observer and observed, it is often difficult to maintain objectivity and control personal bias in the service of objective thoughts, systematic data collection, and careful interpretation. Everyone, even the scientist, is inclined to see from the perspectives to which he is accustomed, to emphasize what makes sense to him and to derogate what does not. With sciences directly involving human beings, especially matters dealt with by personality psychologists, the tendency to bias in terms of one's own perceptions is tempting; however, this temptation is often recognized, and may then be a source of inspiration.

However, the problem of bias and narrow perspectives is minimized because science is a public enterprise. As a function of its public nature, the thoughts and findings of any one person are subject to the corrective force of scrutiny by others. With continued appraisal, the effects of personal biases are gradually and, it is hoped, totally counterbalanced or eliminated. Nonetheless, it is always legitimate to ask about the extent to which the whole community of scientists (or those nonscientists who evaluate them!) in a given domain may be subjected to a pervasive common bias. The reader is invited to do this while considering the fruits of the science of personality as presented by this author in this text.

Similarly, the layman who discusses his own views and listens openly to those of others may increasingly become less restricted in his view of people. But the layman may escape the careful examination of his views, by himself and by others, more easily than the scientist—often to his own disadvantage more than that of others. Similarly, the layman may surround himself, or check out his conclusions, only with those of a bias similar to and supportive of his own: similar people attract each other and people attracted to each other become more similar (Chapters 13, 18).

Another problem of the psychologist is that many critics expect psychology to have all the answers. They see the social ills and psychological inadequacies that continue to plague our society as signs of psychologists' incompetence or their lack of contact with the realities of the world outside the controlled laboratory. However, the psychologists' aim is to expand to the utmost the knowledge we have about the world as it is and people as they are, though this does include people as they can be. The truth is that psychologists and other social scientists are increasingly involved with the problems of immediate public and practical concern and are continually attempting to focus knowledge on programs of change and improvement. The more painful truth is that much of the accumulated knowledge of the social sciences, incomplete though it often is, has been ignored or unknown. It is hoped that public knowledgeability and receptivity to scientific information will increase, as well as support for continued discovery and application.

FORMAL CHARACTERIZATION OF SCIENCE

Achieving Knowledge

Arguments about whether personality can be studied scientifically are fruitless. Science, because it is a method of dealing with a subject, is not limited by the content of subject matter. Anything can be approached in a scientific way, because science is a way of thinking and doing, a process for converting sensory impressions about the world into organized, scientific knowledge (McGinnis, 1965).

Whether science can provide the answer a person wants when he asks, "What is personality?" is another matter entirely—and so is the question of whether personality *is* in fact being studied scientifically. Science is by definition the one and only route to *scientific* knowledge—but it may or may not be the route to what any one person considers to be the *truth*.

Verifiability

In its simplest form, knowledge is a verifiable (or, conversely, falsifiable) declarative sentence whose logical status can be determined. To be verifiable, it must refer to something objective and be free of personal reference. For example, "The King of the United States is bald," is not a verifiable sentence because there is no King of the United States. In contrast, "The President of the United States is bald," is a verifiable statement. We may verify the sentence by looking at the President's head. If, however, the President's personal assistant makes the statement, "The President of the United States is bald," and then prohibits anyone other than himself from seeing the President, the statement loses its verifiability as it becomes one of personal reference. Science is a public activity. Scientific knowledge is publicly verifiable.

Two Paths to Scientific Knowledge

The process of proceeding from the observable world to scientific knowledge involves the use of two paths: the theoretical and the empirical (Figure 2–1). Both routes require abstractions from the real world, rules of categorization, and rules for the manipulation of terms. But the content and manipulations are vastly different. The theoretical route only gives philosophical knowledge; the empirical route only gives a collection of facts. Together, they may yield scientific knowledge.

FIGURE 2–1

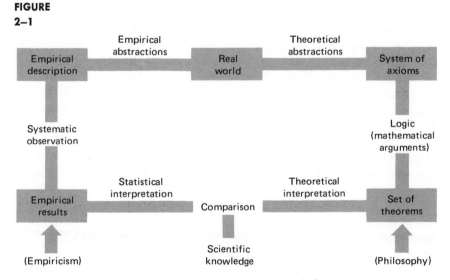

Two Routes in the Process of Attaining Scientific Knowledge.

Source: Modified from McGinnis, R. *Mathematical foundations for social analysis.* Indianapolis: Bobbs-Merrill, 1964. P. 9.

The theoretical. In considering theory, we start with theoretical abstractions or categories of thinking, and basic assumptions which are not directly tested (axioms). The basic assumptions are useful if confirmed theorems are deduced from them. The theorem is logically correct if it is implicit in the assumptions; anyone willing to perform manipulations upon the basic assumptions according to the logical rules of the theory can deduce the theorem. It may be logically correct but not verifiable or confirmed. A theory is not desirable to scientists because of logical elegance or correctness alone. It must also be related to the empirical observation.

The empirical. In the empirical aspect of a question, we again make abstractions and establish categories. We decide on our subject matter; for example, cats, affiliation behaviors, competitive behaviors. We establish categories: black cats, white cats, behaviors of approaching people, behaviors of competing with people. Then, by systematic observation, we determine the way in which our cats or behaviors function. The end result is an empirical statement or fact: black cats lead to disaster; approach behavior is more likely toward people with whom positive experiences are associated. A fact is not knowledge. We have scientific knowledge only when the end result of our observations (the fact) matches a theorem. Let us say, for example, that our theory of cats enabled us to predict that black cats lead to disaster; our theory of affiliation predicted affiliation with positive persons. In both cases, our theorems were verifiable and were empirically confirmed. Thus, the assumptions from which they were derived were useful for making predictions.

It is possible for a theorem to be logically correct but not confirmed. In such a case, we may question the adequacy of the observational procedure, the procedures of logical deduction of the theorem, or the basic assumption from which the theorem was derived. Often, the theorem is simply not complete. The theorem that men will keep lost wallets they find may be a logically correct deduction from an axiom that men are basically selfish. However, people do return lost wallets—at least under some conditions. The theory must specify those conditions if it is to be useful. One of the advantages of research results which do not support a prediction is that they alert us to the fact that further specification is necessary.

Interrelationships of the two paths. Implicit in the example just given is the notion that theory guides observations; what we are thinking tells us what to look for. Also, observation guides theory; what we see can correct our thinking and suggest a revision in our theoretical system. There is continual interplay between theory and observation, continual revision of procedures of observation and the content of conceptualization. Further, theory and observation are linked not only at the end point where a theorem is or is not empirically verified, but also all along the way by the processes of measurement which attempt to translate constructs into observables. To understand this relationship more fully, we turn to the concept of operationism.

Operationism

In our discussion of anxiety as a construct, we mentioned that a construct must be linked to observable events. Establishing a linkage between constructs and observable events is a problem of establishing *rules of correspondence* between constructs and observable events, often seen as a problem of measurement (e.g., McGinnis, 1965; Torgerson, 1958). This process is typically called *operationism*. Operational definitions state the conditions under which a theoretical term is to be used; they link a theoretical construct to observable behavior by an explicit set of observations and measurements. The effect of operational definitions is simply to make our ideas clear by pointing to observable events which help to define them (Feigl, 1945). Without such a translation to observables, others would not know what we are thinking.

In everyday life, friends ask us what we mean by saying that someone is hostile toward us or has an authoritarian attitude. We explain by pointing to the behavior from which we inferred hostility or the authoritarian attitude. Typically, we indicate several things rather than only one. In the case of Mrs. Brown and her anxious husband, his physiological responses are one operational definition of anxiety because they are a factual reference of anxiety which can be observed. The same is true of each of several other responses—coffee drinking, chain-smoking, etc. No *one* operational definition characterizes the construct of anxiety for Mrs. Brown. In fact, if we had only one operational definition, we would not have particular need for the construct. The more manifestations there are of the construct, the more useful it is as an integrating device. All relevant operational definitions help to define the construct.

Originally, operationism maintained that a construct is defined only as the operations used in measuring it (e.g., intelligence is what an intelligence test measures; anxiety is what is measured by the measure of anxiety). Although still held by many psychologists, such a view is quite limited and presents a distorted view of the actual processes of scientific thinking and observation. It does not acknowledge the creative thinking involved in selection of problems to be studied and the determination of what the operational definitions will treat. One who makes an operational definition already has some idea of what he wants to measure. If he would make his implicit thinking explicit, others could follow his reasoning, examine his thoughts, and more easily relate his views and data to their own.

Theory

Obviously, from the vantage point of this book, theoretical statements are vital scientific tools; this is a view typical of personality psychologists, but not one that is undebatable. As such, the role of theory should be closely examined. The equal importance of observation is clear in later chapters.

Organization. Theory organizes the facts of science, and gives focus to our thoughts and observations. Consider the following facts, all methodically gathered by competent researchers:

1. The number of crackers eaten by obese people is not affected by whether they are frightened (expecting strong shock) or have just eaten (Schachter, Goldman, & Gordon, 1968, Table 2–1).
2. When they are in an experiment around dinner time (6:00 P.M.), obese people eat more when the clock is fast than when it is slow (Schachter & Gross, 1968, Table 2–2).
3. Overweight people eat more ice cream than underweight people only when the ice cream tastes good (Nisbett, 1968).
4. Overweight religious Jews are more likely to fast in synagogue on Yom Kipper than are normal-weight religious Jews. The overweight Jews report less discomfort as the hours in synagogue increase than do normal-weight Jews (Goldman, Jaffa, & Schachter, 1968).
5. The more overweight a French flier, the less likely he is to be bothered by the time change he encounters in his flights across time zones (Goldman, Jaffa, & Schachter, 1968).

This would be a rather diverse and apparently meaningless set of facts were it not for the integrating role of theory. What were the researchers attempting to ascertain? One might surmise that their goal was simply to show that fat people do eat a lot. But this is only partially correct. We notice that fat people do not always eat more than do those whose weight is closer to normal. The main concern here was with the roles played by external and internal stimuli in the control of emotions and behavior (see Schachter, 1970). With eating behavior specifically, it has been previously suggested that for normal-weight people, the label "hunger" and amount of food eaten relate directly to internal physiological correlates of food deprivation, while this is not true of those who are overweight. The overweight people may label no internal state as hunger, or label almost any internal arousal as hunger (Bruche, 1961). Compared with normal-weight people, they were predicted to be more responsive to external food-related cues and their eating less related to internal states. Contrasting obese and normal people provided a specific way of investigating the variables of main concern: internal and external stimuli.

The research supported the deductions that obese people's eating is not controlled by internal cues associated with food deprivation as much as is true of normal-weight people. They ate no less when afraid than when not afraid (fear inhibits physiological correlates of food deprivation) and their eating did vary with environmental conditions (e.g., the clock says I should be hungry; the ice cream tastes good; there's no food

TABLE 2–1   Effects of Fear and Preloading on the Eating Behavior of Normal and Obese Subjects

	A. Normal S		B. Obese S	
Condition	N	Average No. of Crackers Eaten	N	Average No. of Crackers Eaten
High fear, full	14	13.78	11	19.64
High fear, empty	11	15.89	10	19.60
Low fear, full	13	16.98	11	17.66
Low fear, empty	10	28.28	11	16.34

SOURCE: Schachter, S., Goldman, R., & Gordon, A. Effects of fear, food, deprivation, and obesity on eating. *Journal of Personality and Social Psychology*, 1968, **10**, 91–97.

TABLE 2–2   Amount Eaten (in Grams) by Subjects, in the Four Conditions

	Time [a]	
Weight	Slow	Fast
Obese	19.9	37.6
Normal	41.5	16.0

[a] The experiment began at 5:00–5:05. At true time 5:40–5:50, the slow clock read 5:25–5:35, the fast clock read 6:10–6:20.

SOURCE: Schachter, S., and Gross, L. P. Manipulated time and eating behavior. *Journal of Personality and Social Psychology*, 1968, **10**, 98–106.

in the synagogue so why be hungry?). In relative contrast, people who are not overweight are more responsive to internal food-related cues than to external cues. They are less likely to eat when they are afraid than when they are not fearful, are less influenced by the taste of the ice cream, are more upset by being in the synagogue whose religious significance does not remove the call of internal hunger cues, and are more disturbed when the time on the clock is not compatible with what their "insides" tell them. Their eating responses are controlled by the appropriate internal cues.

Explanation and Scientific Law

Formal explanation. Implicit in the example just given is the concept that a theory, together with its supporting evidence, provides an explanation by a logical union of scientific laws. That is, "A theory logically binds laws together under the heritage of a common set of postulates and definitions. . . . And it is the deducibility of a law within the theory that constitutes the formal requirements of scientific explanation" (Turner, 1967, p. 252).

The fundamental aim of science is to establish scientific laws (Braithwaite, 1960). Laws always include a generalization, or an assertion about associations between events. In a theoretical context, laws are theorems. From the generalizations, we may infer individual events when the conditions for the application of the law are met. The law itself is not questioned; its range of application is. For example, one would not question the veracity of the law, "Fat people eat a lot," or "Male students take female students to the ball game on Saturday afternoons," but one might well question a statement that the law applies to all fat people at all times or to all male students on all Saturday afternoons. A good theory in which a law is deduced will state the conditions of its applicability. As we shall see, much research is addressed to the problem of specifying the conditions under which a law applies, determining exactly when what response will be made by what people. If no conditions can be found where the law seems to hold, it is not useful.

Cognitive satisfaction. A formal explanation is cognitively satisfying when it is accepted as an explanation about why the event occurred (Turner, 1967). To be accepted, it must appeal to a familiar organization of experience. When terminology and concepts are not familiar, formal explanations can merely be confusing to the questioner, however useful they are to others. For example, the three-year-old child who asks where babies come from will be satisfied with the answer that they come from Mommy's tummy and, should the occasion arise, with feeling the baby move within the mother. An explanation of the biological details of the entire birth process would most likely puzzle the child and not be accepted by him as an explanation. Similarly, a student giving a psychological explanation to his friends may not always be successful in satisfying them using the knowledge that is meaningful to him. In sum, the explanations of science are satisfying to those who know what the scientist is talking about. In many ways, that is what this book is all about, for its aim is to familiarize the student of personality with professional terms and concepts describing behavior, so that the explanations of the researcher and theoretician can become meaningful. This also necessitates a familiarity with the behavior itself, and there is no substitute for one's *own* careful observation. To benefit from a psychology course, the student must, as do the psychologists he studies, relate the abstract to the concrete —the written word about behavior to the behavior itself.

Heurism and economy. A theory should do more than simply organize facts and deduce known scientific laws. It should stimulate additional theorizing and research. The effectiveness of a theory in generating additional efforts is a matter of its heuristic influence. A theory may make a valuable contribution to science by suggesting ideas for research or for other theories, even if those ideas are in opposition to the theory itself. Controversy is healthy and often breeds discovery. To serve a heuristic function, the theory need not be well developed, with explicit structure and deductions: A friend's suggestion that you accompany him to a movie may not be accepted, but it can generate ideas about interesting ways to spend the afternoon. However, a well-developed theory will contain derivations of specific testable theorems. It will also allow economy of research and enable prediction in uninvestigated areas. A deductive system is tested empirically by testing the lowest-level hypothesis of the system (Braithwaite, 1960). Although empirical evidence never *proves* the hypothesis, the evidence may establish the hypothesis as a reasonable one. The direct evidence for lower-level hypotheses provides *indirect evidence* for the higher-level hypothesis from which it was deduced. That is, the observed facts which provide direct evidence for hypothesis P are indirect evidence for hypothesis Q from which P was derived. Furthermore, indirect evidence for hypothesis Q is indirect evidence for *all* hypotheses, other than P, which may be deduced from it.

The fact that a hypothesis can gain indirect support from the evidence about other hypotheses in the system enables us to make predictions about situations which have not been well researched. If we have substantial evidence about hypotheses IIIa and IIIb, we have good reason to expect that IIIc is true also, although we have not tested it directly (Figure 2-2). The confirmation of IIIa also adds to the evidence for IIIb, and vice versa. In short, ". . . any piece of empirical evidence for any part of the system helps towards establishing the whole of the system" (Braithwaite, 1960, p. 18).

Evaluation of Theory

A theory can be evaluated in its own right, regardless of relevant data. A good theory should be both consistent and parsimonious. Two contradictory conclusions should not be implied by, or deduced from, the same system of axioms. For example, a system with the axioms "All men are mortal," and "Writers write forever," would lead to the inconsistent deductions that writers die *and* write forever. A system which asserts that grown men don't cry, and that crying accompanies some emotions, would then have to assert that grown men do not feel those emotions. Parsimony is also a desirable characteristic. There should be as few assumptions as necessary to account for the phenomena under surveillance. Given two theoretical systems which satisfactorily predict the same behaviors, the one using the fewest number of assumptions and constructs is preferable. This principle, called Occam's razor, is applied because it leaves as little as possible in the realm of the untestable. However, one should keep in mind that parsimony is relevant only when two theories predict the same set of behaviors, and this is an infrequent occurrence.

FIGURE
2–2

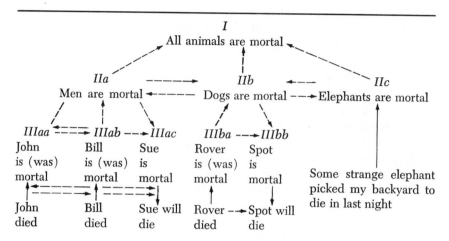

Direct evidence (solid lines) for a lowest level hypothesis (IIIaa, ab, IIIba) is indirect evidence (dashed lines) for the next higher hypothesis (IIa, IIb) from which is was deduced, and for all other lowest level hypotheses (IIIab, IIIbb).

Evidence that men are mortal (IIa) comes from a number of observations of men who have died (III), *and* from observations that other animals have died (IIb, c).

These observations support the generalization that all animals are mortal (I).

Even though we have not observed Sue's death or Spot's death, we have more reason to predict that they will die than if we did not have the theoretical system which provides indirect support for these predictions.

Try your hand at developing a theoretical system:

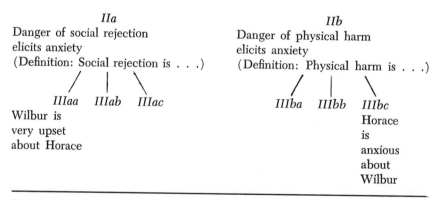

Direct and Indirect Evidence in Theoretical Systems.

Analogy. Models are analogies. They represent the world in an "as if" fashion in order to suggest ways of thinking about empirical events. For example, to expand our thinking about light, we *represent* it as consisting of individual rays. We do not actually *find* light atomized into individual rays, but we find it helpful to consider this so (Toulmin, 1953). Some simplified examples of models are given in Figure 2–3. The modelers do not contend that they have drawn a picture of the real world, but rather that some facet of the world works the same way as the model.

A popular form not depicted is mathematical modeling. In fact, some define a model as a mathematical representation of some aspect of nature (McGinnis, 1965), and mathematical models of learning, perceptual, and social processes are numerous. On the other hand, critics of models often react violently to the suggestion that human processes can be represented by mathematical equations. This reaction is unjustified, for no one defines a person only as a number. However, many psychologists find it convenient and helpful to represent people and psychological events in mathematical systems, because such systems allow greater precision and economy of statements than is possible with verbal statements. Consider the sentence: "The more somebody has done something in the past and gotten something he wanted, the more he'll do the same again." Compare it with a crude mathematical formulation: Response probability = f (prior reinforcement).

A kindred spirit to the mathematical model is the computer model, which has seen service in the domains of economy, weather, city traffic patterns, business and industry, social psychology, and human learning. While computer models have proven their usefulness in many situations, in personality they are yet a portent of things to come. If, in studying real people, we were to construct accurate working models using a computer, we could quickly predict each person's reactions to many different situations. We could see, for example, how much and in what conditions one person will like another; we could "try out" a drastic form of therapy with computer simulation of the person before risking the venture on the person himself; we could discover problems in educational procedures without having to make mistakes with children; and we could use the models to develop interpersonal skills required of teachers, therapists, salesmen, ministers (Loehlin, 1968). The speed of the computer allows rapid simulation of real world events with minimum risks of personal harm. Computer models are also worth consideration because of their usefulness as tools to quickly and efficiently develop, test, and revise effective theories for predicting real world events. An example is given in Table 2–3.

Real and useful. While some modelers are inclined to treat their model as theory, others sharply distinguish between theory and model (Chapanis, 1961; Brodbeck, 1959; Lachman, 1960). The distinction is that a

FIGURE
2–3

Simplified Examples of Models

A. Broadbent's Model of Human Attention. The model is simply a Y tube and a set of balls. The Y stem is narrow enough that only one ball can pass at a time, though branches are wider. A hinged flap at the junction normally hangs down, but it can be moved to close off either branch of the Y. The balls are information about stimuli, the branches are different sensory channels (e.g., eyes, ears), the stem is the response output. If two balls are dropped into the arms at the same time, they will block each other at the junction; this is analogous to what can happen when competing information is given simultaneously over two different channels (Broadbent, 1952; Poulton, 1953). Moving the flap to close off one of the arms is analogous to instructing someone to pay attention only to visual information but to ignore auditory information. Broadbent does not claim that there is a Y in the human being, but using the mechanical model as an analogy is helpful in understanding the more rigorous theory of information processing.

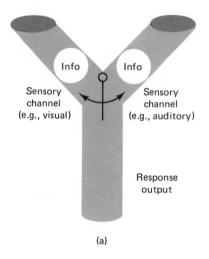

(a)

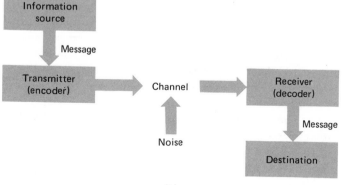

(b)

B. Communications Model. Models such as this appeared in psychology texts long before the birth of modern communication theory, though with words like stimulus, receptor, nerve cell, effector, response (Chapanis, 1961). This model has made us see old problems in new ways. It suggests the roles of both speaker (encoder) and listener (decoder) in effective communications; it provides an explicit place for the "noise" that prevents communication, and suggests that human beings have a channel capacity; that is, there are limits to how much information they can process.

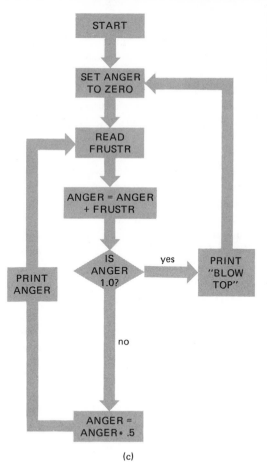

START

SET ANGER TO ZERO

READ FRUSTR

ANGER = ANGER + FRUSTR

IS ANGER 1.0?

yes → PRINT "BLOW TOP"

PRINT ANGER

no

ANGER = ANGER * .5

(c)

C. Computer Model of TEMPER. The language used in programming is succeeded by the translation; diagram represents a flow chart of the computer model.

1. *PROGRAM TEMPER*
   Name of program
2. *ANGER = 0.0*
3. *READ FRUSTR*
   Consider the frustration amount in a stimulus event (an input to the computer)
4. *ANGER = ANGER + FRUSTR*
   Present anger is result of previous anger plus that caused by frustration
5. *IF (ANGER.GGT 1.0), 6, 8*
   A decision point: if the current anger is greater than 1.0, go to step 6; if not, go to step 8. The next step depends on the current state of affairs
6. *PRINT "BLOW TOP"*
   If the anger was greater than 1.0, the computer-personality blows its top, though with less disaster than when a person loses his cool
7. *GO TO 2*
   After blowing its top, the computer-personality returns to step 2, where anger is 0, and awaits further developments (inputs)
8. *ANGER = ANGER*5*
   If the amount of anger after frustration (step 5) was not enough (greater than 1.0) to cause a blowing off, the computer person goes from 5 to 8, where there is a new value of anger, namely half that in step 5 (* means multiply)
9. *PRINT ANGER*
   Amount of anger noted
10. *GO TO 3*
    Start over, see how much frustration in the next event (an input)
11. *END*

Loehlin, J. C. *Computer models of personality.* New York: Random House, 1968. Pp. 12–15.

model is only an analogy while theory is said to state eternal truths. However, an analogy, whether viewed as theory or model, predicts events. Further, by what criteria can even a successful theory generating confirmed deductions be said to embody the *real truth?* Is not a theory itself an analogy, and an analogy a theory (Simon & Newell, 1956)? When the theory, or model, is thought to depict reality, one is led to the often erroneous conclusion that only one view of the phenomenon is appropriate.

If the theory postulates hypothetical constructs, its accuracy in depicting reality can be determined. However, many constructs in personality psychology are intervening variables: they have no postulated physical properties which can be checked directly against the real world. Many theoretical debates, among professionals and students, are about *preferences* for explanation, not about facts. The disagreement does not focus on the "real" explanation or the "real" construct involved, but rather on what theory, model, or construct is most useful in a particular situation for ordering the facts about observable behavior. Often, more than one approach may be useful and, at least for the moment, equally satisfactory. It is only when one's own preference is seen as somehow embodying real truth that questions about reality become a problem. Adherence to a position because of its presumed depiction of real truth is one of several dangers of theory.

Dangers of Theory

There are many differences of opinion regarding the role of theory in psychology. Although its actual and potential usefulness in science has been repeatedly stressed in this chapter, psychological theory is not without its faults. Therefore, some attention should be given to some of the weaknesses inherent in theorizing about personality. These weaknesses are well elucidated by the eminent critic of psychological theory, B. F. Skinner (1950, 1961, 1963).

Skinner does acknowledge two kinds of "theory" which he finds acceptable. First, certain basic assumptions are essential to scientific inquiry. For example, he accepts the theoretical assumption that nature is orderly rather than capricious. Second, he considers all predictions about the outcome of an experiment or statement about previous outcomes as theoretical in the sense that the evidence is never complete. Thus, the statement "Everything that goes up must come down," is theoretical because the possibility cannot be totally excluded that something may someday go up and stay up.

Essentially then, what Skinner questions is the necessity for theories, such as those espoused in this chapter, which appeal to events that take place at some other level of observation, are described in different terms from the behavior itself, and which claim to explain an observed fact. They lead to needless constructs and provide a falsely secure sense of understanding. In psychology, it is true, there are probably many more constructs than are necessary to account for the observed behavior. In addition, these constructs are often ill defined and overlap in unspecified ways.

A pervasive danger, for professional and student, is that of confusing *naming* with *explaining*. We often use a theoretical term to name a behavioral phenomenon and, while not explaining the name, feel satisfied with it. We attribute delinquent behavior to a "disordered personality," without expaining the construct "disordered personality." A mother's sacrifice is said to be explained because of a "maternal instinct," which is not explained. While psychologists are typically more careful than laymen to attempt to explain such labeling and integrating constructs, the temptation is still present to assume explanation with the name. There is a comfort in having labels.

Such "explaining" by naming amounts to assuming implicitly a little man, a homunculus, inside and controlling people, just as a puppeteer's hand within the puppet causes his movements. Such "explanation" is really a contemporary form of primitive animism. To "explain" one's unusual behavior with "I wasn't myself today" (a different homunculus is on duty?) is logically no different from the ancient view that man is sometimes possessed by evil spirits. The primitive thinking is not made sophisticated and explanatory by breaking the little man into bits and pieces to deal with his wishes, motives, and feelings, bit by bit. We say that a man works because he wishes to get a paycheck which will provide for a new car that the neighbors will admire. However, we are not explaining the wish until we identify it as a response itself which is related to antecedent or concomitant environmental events. Without showing the intervening concepts as responses—anchoring the intervening variable on the antecedent as well as on the consequent side—we are making only after-the-fact explanations which are not really explanations at all. "The objection is not that these things are mental, but that they offer no real explanation and stand in the way of a more effective analysis" (Skinner, 1963, p. 951).

Flights from the Laboratory

Concomitant with his castigation of psychological theory is Skinner's insistence that the proper activity of the psychologist is stating empirical laws relating observable events, without needless attempts to make inferences about internal characteristics of the organism. Skinner regards the activities of many psychologists as flights from the laboratory, escapes from their business of observing behavior.

Some fly to inner man by appealing to psychic processes (typically through intervening variables and the homunculus just discussed) or to physiological processes which are left at the level of unverified hypothetical constructs or are not treated as responses themselves. The study of behavior is acceptable in its own right and need not be studied with an aim toward reducing it to physiological events. Skinner also sees the use of mathematical models and postulate systems as flights away from behavioral observation. He asserts that mathematical models will be appropriate only when the data have been gathered and ordered; until that time, they are constructed with little regard for the fundamental dimensions of the reality of behavior.

Perhaps the most difficult flight to admit and abort is the flight to real people. Real life has its appeal. A boring lecture is brought to· life by a case history of a real person. And, for most of us, it is gratifying to be helpful to specific others whom we can actually see being helped by our own efforts and to feel that we are working toward solutions of important, immediately existing social problems. Nevertheless, Skinner holds that by spending energies and talents helping our fellow man on a one-to-one basis, we are missing the delayed but larger gratification possible by contributing to the greater scientific understanding which may have sweeping benefits for all mankind. He cites the example of Albert Schweitzer—a brilliant man who earned the gratitude of thousands because he dedicated his life to helping his fellow man, one by one. Skinner asks, if he had worked as energetically in a laboratory of tropical medicine, could he not have made discoveries which would have helped not thousands but literally billions of people? Though each person will have a different answer to such a question when applied to himself, it is a problem worth pondering.

SUMMARY

Theories, as Skinner argues, can be an escape from the real world of behavior. But they can also be effective agents in helping to understand people. Certainly, the personality theories discussed in the following chapters (Chapters 3–6) must be approached with caution and with possible restrictions in mind. The content of these theories can lure the novice into believing he can understand, explain, and correct any behavior exhibited by himself or by his friends because he can make interpretative theoretical statements. In addition, the global personality theories, given the description in this chapter, are deficient as formal theories. They should be viewed more as theoretical orientations than as formally sophisticated scientific theories. The logical structure and the implicit reasoning by which deductions are made are often only intuitive and implicit. Their relation to fact is not always clear, nor are they always consistent, parsimonious, or verifiable. They are not completely susceptible to specific empirical tests and research does not, often cannot, clearly demonstrate any consistent usefulness of one theory over another. Many theoretical explanations of specific events are drawn from a multitude of constructs available for post-hoc explanations, but these are not always precise or definitive enough for prediction or clear elimination of alternative explanations. We hope that coming generations of professionals, now students, will do better.

Why, then, bother with personality theories? First, in spite of their lack of formal elegance, they have had a large heuristic influence in personality research, as well as in the more traditionally experimental areas of learning and perception. Much research can be better appreciated with an understanding of basic concepts delineated by the theorists and when approached within the broad unifying perspectives they offer. Their deficiencies are in large part due to their attempt to make broad swaths through the range of behavior (a molar approach) rather than contenting themselves with careful in-depth delineation of a small aspect of behavior (a molecular approach). This kind of deficiency is also the source of their strength, inspiration, and richness in grappling with the complicated phenomenon of man searching to find himself and then to understand himself, to understand himself and then to find himself.

In short, the prime value of personality theories is their representation of the insights of sensitive observers of human nature; these insights, in turn, can be a catalyst in thinking about what it means to be a human being. They can generate ideas and stimulate curiosity for the student as they have for psychologists. The focus of the curiosity can be subjects of formal psychological research. It can also be the individual reader himself.

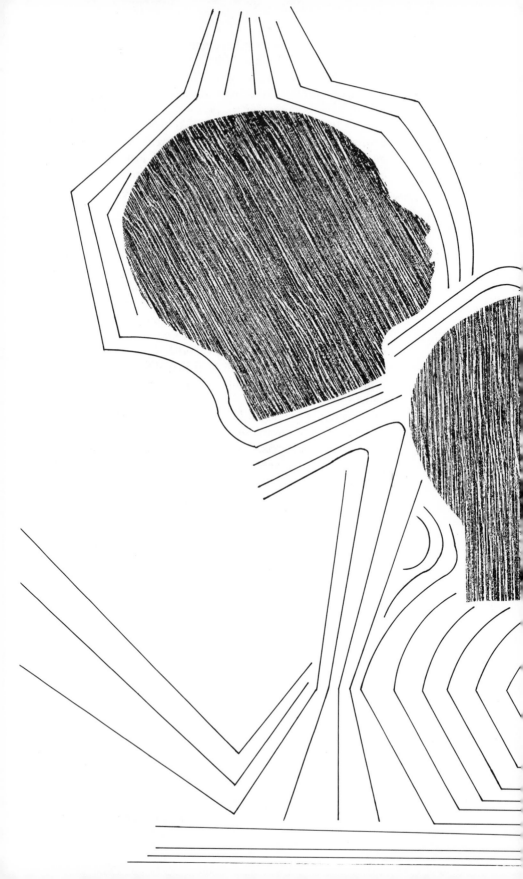

THEORETICAL ORIENTATIONS TO PERSONALITY

PART

3
freudian personality theory

If asked what name first comes to mind when psychology is mentioned, most of us would say Sigmund Freud. Although the intricacies of his theories may not be generally understood, the impact of his thought is obvious, not only in the work and writing of psychoanalysts and other professionals, but also in everyday language. How often do we speak of Freudian slips? How many times have we heard of or made reference to ego, unconscious, phallic symbols, or the Oedipus complex? At some time or other we have probably indulged in a bit of amateur Freudian analysis without being aware of its theoretical roots: We decide that Joe has too much conscience; Jane has a weak ego; Jim is too impulsive, and he does not think before he acts.

Sigmund Freud (1856–1939) developed a body of concepts around which much of our understanding of personality has grown. He postulated that people can be understood only if we know their inner thoughts and feelings and recognize that these are shaped by past experience. He saw man not merely as a product of his conscious action and experience but as a complex organism functioning with degrees of awareness; not just as a one-dimensional creature, but as a many-faceted being in which the components of id, ego, and superego struggle. While many laymen are inclined to equate Freud's theory with sex theory, his overall view of behavior was too broad to justify this label. Freud did emphasize sexuality as a strong force in behavior, but he did not, as many assume, attribute all aspects of behavior to sex.

In the first part of this chapter, we will examine Freud's psychoanalytic theory of personality structure and development. In the second part, we will explore his views of psychoanalytic psychotherapy.

PERSONALITY STRUCTURE

During the latter part of the nineteenth century, scientists assumed that events, including behavior, were determined, but they saw the determinants as outside forces of nature acting upon the individual. Psychiatrists of the day dismissed patients' symptoms, whether a headache or paralysis, as trifles, indicative perhaps of problems but of no significance themselves—just as natural scientists dismissed the pattern of movement exhibited by a leaf falling from a tree as determined but hardly worthy of scientific examination.

With his concept of *psychic determinism* Freud took scientific determinism *inside* the person. He assumed that all thoughts and feelings, all behavior, and all symptoms were determined by inner psychic causes, dynamic forces within a person. One's behavior, therefore, could be understood as meaningful—by the psychologist and by the individual himself—when its underlying continuity and logic were revealed, and this was not likely to be discovered through the use of a psychology of consciousness alone, as was typical at the time when Freud began his work.

Freud postulated that personality is made up of three coexistent parts (id, ego, and superego) and that behavior is influenced by three levels of consciousness (conscious, preconscious, and unconscious).

The Three Layers of Consciousness

The *conscious* consists of those thoughts and feelings of which we are aware, anything that we are thinking or feeling at the moment. Your conscious thoughts at this time are—or should be—related to the material you are reading and your reactions to it.

Preconscious mental events are those easily accessible to consciousness, even though they are not on one's mind at the moment. Right now, for instance, you are not thinking of your high school graduation, but you easily could (and doubtless did when it was suggested). As attention fluctuates, there is a constant interchange between conscious and preconscious thought.

The third layer, the *unconscious,* contains material of which we are largely unaware. Some of it—the transmission of nerve impulses, for example—is not of direct interest to the personality psychologist. What is important here is the area that constituted Freud's primary concern, the *dynamic unconscious,* or those mental events and feelings that are "held down" and can come to consciousness only with difficulty. It is this material which "must be inferred, discovered, and translated into conscious form" (Freud, 1963, p. 38).

Freud used the analogy of an iceberg to explain the relative parts played by layers of consciousness: The exposed tip of the iceberg represents the conscious; the part that appears and disappears with the movement of the water represents the preconscious; and the large mass hidden from view beneath the water represents the unconscious.

Material of the dynamic unconscious is subject to *repression,* which operates automatically and without conscious intent. It is not a passive forgetting, but an active, dynamic process of holding down certain mental events and keeping them from becoming conscious. Preconscious material, although not at the moment a part of consciousness, is not being dynamically held down. For example, the event of Sue's first date is in her preconscious: She can remember the name of the boy she went out with; she can recall the movie they saw; and, if she tries hard enough, she can even remember the color and design of the dress she wore—even though she has not consciously considered these events for several years. However, several aspects of her first sexual experience, which occurred much more recently, cannot be recalled at will. A frightening and bewildering encounter with a young man she did not like, although physically harmless, was so upsetting and alarming to Sue that she told no one about it and deliberately pushed it out of her thoughts. She can no longer recall the young man's words; nor can she recall the fact that she encouraged, by flirtation, his action. In other words, she repressed the event.

Although the unconscious cannot be examined directly, it can be detected expressing itself in conscious content and behavior, especially when the rational, logical functions of conscious processes work less effectively than usual to censor the expression.

Evidence of the unconscious. Freud pointed to the many little oddities of everyday behavior—the "psychopathology of everyday life"—as evidence of the unconscious. "Freudian slips," such as slips of the tongue, are well known. It is often obvious that a person who made a "mistake" in his speech did in fact say what he felt, although he did not intend to reveal his thoughts. Consider the individual who greets an unwelcome guest with "I'm so glad you could leave."

Proponents of psychic determinism claim that superficially meaningless events such as mislaying objects, forgetting familiar names, forgetting to do an errand, misreading words, and accidental self-injury are indicative of the unconscious. These phenomena (called *parapraxes*) "are not accidents; they are serious mental acts; they have their meaning; they arise through the concurrence of two different intentions" (Freud, 1949, p. 41). We intend to forget, to hurt, to express, but we intend also to hide such desires from ourselves and others.

Are we to conclude, then, that all our mistakes and lapses are meaningful? Freud's answer is equivocal: "We do not maintain—and for our purposes do not need to maintain—that every single mistake which occurs has a meaning, although I think that probable" (Freud, 1949, p. 54).

Other evidence of unconscious processes can be found in our dreams. Freud maintained that dreams often reveal long-suppressed wishes and repressed anxieties. However, the interpretation of dreams is not necessarily limited to the obvious content; one cannot safely conclude, having dreamt of being chased down an endless, dark corridor by a raging dog, that he has repressed a fear of being chased by a dog. The dog may be a *symbol* for something else of which the dreamer is fearful.

The type of symbol provides a link between the two levels—according to Freud—of our dreaming. The *manifest content* of dreams—the events and images we remember from our dreams and use in recounting them—are merely the façade behind which lies the real meaning, or *latent content*. Freud believed that a direct, undisguised expression of forbidden needs or intensely anxiety-provoking material in dreams would be so upsetting that the sleeper would awaken. Thus, the successful disguise of such conflicts protects the period of sleep, while allowing some release of repressed material.

The dream of the dog chase, referred to above, might be explained as a depiction of feelings about sexual intercourse. The aggressive dog in the dark hall may symbolize a penis in the vaginal canal, suggesting that the dreamer, male or female, may want and/or fear intercourse. How does the dream end? The dreamer's assumption about the conclusion, if the dream were interrupted, would itself reflect unconscious feelings.

Modern dream research has shown that dreams do serve some necessary functions, but, as we shall see in Chapter 9, Freud's explanation for their occurrence and his symbolic interpretation are not universally accepted.

The Three Components of Personality

The basic components of personality structure, the id, ego, and superego, are mental systems which become fairly stabilized with experience (Freud, 1962, 1963, 1964). They develop from habitual mental processes which have been repeated often enough to become a structure, just as flowing water (a process) becomes a river, that is, a stable part (structure) of the landscape.

The id. The id (literally, *the it*) is the original component of personality, a repository for all that is inherited and fixed in the constitution. It contains the instincts and thus is the source of all energy required for personality functioning.

Id is raw, uncontrolled drive. It follows no morality and recognizes no reality other than itself. This element of personality is impulsive and irrational and takes no account of the realistic consequences of its actions. It is concerned only with immediate need satisfaction; in other words, the id operates on the *pleasure principle*, its only goal being the satisfaction of instinctual needs. It seeks to satisfy these needs by *primary process activities*. The primary process can work as a reflex mechanism: Just as the eye blinks to keep out dust, when provided the stimulus, the id automatically prompts a search for an object to fulfill sexual needs, an outlet for anger, an expression for anxiety, and so on.

A more psychologically important form of the primary process is *wish-fulfillment*, namely, the formation of a mental image of the object which will reduce tension. The infant who has learned that mother's breast is associated with hunger reduction literally has an image of her breast. Daydreams, night dreams, and hallucinations illustrate wish-fulfillment in adults. Adults, like the infant, may find such images of the desired object or event satisfying, but normal adults are likely to remind themselves that their reveries are only wishful thinking and not objectively real. They are able to do this because of ego processes not well developed in the infant.

Ego. The wish-fulfillment acceptable in the subjective reality of the id obviously cannot ensure survival in the objective world. The development of the ego from the id is an adaptive maneuver which helps to preserve the individual, for the ego serves as an intermediary between the id and the external world and can attend to the task of self-preservation and id gratification in realistic and effective ways. This adaptive functioning is possible because the ego operates by realistic thinking (the *secondary process*) in obedience to the *reality principle*. While the id contains only passions, the ego represents reason and common sense and has contact with external reality. Thus, the ego is capable of *reality testing*, by which it distinguishes between subjective and objective reality, between images only in the mind and things in the external world. When the subjective reality is not matched by an external reality, the ego can plan and take actions toward obtaining the objectively real goal.

The ego develops from the id to serve the id. It tries to prohibit satisfaction obtained exclusively through wish-fulfillment, but it does not attempt to prohibit id gratification altogether. Rather, the ego seeks to maximize realistic satisfaction, which often implies inhibition and delay of immediate gratification. The ego makes decisions about which goal to pursue when and in what ways and often will forego pursuit of a specific id demand in order to avoid a damaging punishment or to achieve a more desirable goal.

As the child grows, the ego increasingly develops the cognitive abilities of planning, perceiving, learning, remembering, setting goals, making decisions—all ways of dealing with the external world and all necessary for effective adult functioning. However, this is certainly not to say that id functioning is absent in adults.

Id impulse to eat—image of hamburger $\quad\Big|\Big|\quad$ Realistic Ego
$\uparrow$ $\qquad\qquad\qquad\qquad\qquad\qquad\quad\Big|\Big|\quad$ decision making:
inhibit
$|$
Ego: I really am hungry; I had better eat if I want to keep going all night. So stop just imagining and get something to eat.

Or

Id impulse to eat—image of hamburger $\Big|\Big|$ Realistic Ego:

Ego: I really am hungry; I had better eat if I want to keep going all night. But I'll be able to relax and enjoy eating more if I can get another chapter out of the way first. And by then, some of my friends may be taking a break too, and I can see them for a while. So stop thinking about food and finish the next chapter.

Or

Id impulse to eat—image of hamburger $\Big|\Big|$ Realistic Ego:

Ego: Yeah, I think I am hungry, but I've been using that a lot lately as an excuse to stop studying. I'm getting fat, spending too much money, and not getting my work done. OK, think about eating for a minute, then get back to work.

The superego. Even with a beginning ego, the child is not completely able to attain instinctual satisfaction and avoid punishment because much of his life is controlled by other people, typically his parents, who are following rules or standards of behavior unknown to the child. The development of the superego is an adaptive function by which these rules and standards of the external world, as communicated by the parents, are *taken into* the ego and become internalized as a part of the child's reality—a component of his own personality. At this point the child's parents will not have to tell him not to go outside without any clothes on; his superego will tell him. If he violates a standard, he will punish himself by experiencing guilt (the conscience). If he adheres to a standard, he will reward himself through his feelings of pride (ego ideal).

A person's superego performs the same functions that the important people in the external world previously performed: ". . . it observes the ego, gives it orders, corrects it and threatens it with punishments, exactly like parents whose place it has taken" (Freud, 1963, p. 121).

Because the child internalizes the parental standards as he *perceives* them to be and because his cognitive development is incomplete, he does not always obtain an accurate picture of what his parents actually think. Often, therefore, the standards internalized by the child are likely to be more severe and extreme than those actually held by the parents. Another danger in superego development is that the child may be at odds with society simply because the parental standards are not those of the majority of society. The child whose parents approve of going outside without clothes will be in conflict with a society that takes a dim view of public nudity.

Interrelationships of components. The id asks, "Is it pleasurable?" The ego asks, "Is it realistic?" The superego asks, "Is it moral?"

While the ego is not in basic conflict with the id's demands for pleasure, the superego *does* often conflict with the id. It attempts to persuade the ego to abandon the id's pleasure principle, to strive for perfection, and to pursue moralistic goals. Like the id, the superego is irrational and unrealistic in its demands. The ego, for the sake of internal stability, must find ways of reconciling the conflicting demands while maintaining its own integrity and keeping sufficient energy to negotiate with the outside world.

It should be obvious, then, why *ego strength* is Freud's central measure of mental health, and is a dominant concept even for neo- and non-Freudian psychologists. If the ego must use all of its energy to hold the id and superego forces in check, it will have little left for effective interaction with the world upon which the whole personality is dependent for survival. If it overindulges the id's demands, it is subject to pangs of conscience. If it indulges the superego to the exclusion of the id, the result may be a severe pathology in which the id withdraws the energy invested in the ego. Mental health is not achieved by the neglect of the id.

Fortunately, most people have enough ego strength to enable the id, ego, and superego systems to work together harmoniously so that it is difficult to attribute any one behavior to any one system. These people find a reasonable amount of drive satisfactions in ways which do not bring superego censure and yet are not so demanding or unrealistic as to incapacitate them in their relations with the external world or to prevent them from working toward long-range goals.

The crucial role played by the ego is also evident in the relationships between the layers of consciousness and the structure of personality. In the normal adult the id is confined to the unconscious, while both the ego and superego span all three layers of consciousness. It is in the id that the biological energy becomes the *psychic energy* necessary for all psychic functions. But in normal adult functioning only consciousness controls action, so the id and its instincts can influence behavior only through the ego (or in some cases the superego). Although we can describe role and function, we cannot establish absolute dividing lines between the id, ego, and superego, nor between the levels of consciousness. Psychic life is not a matter of discrete independent entities. Freud indicates in the goals of his treatment method that he thought it difficult, *but not impossible,* for unconscious material to become preconscious. Some material may be permanently held down, but other repressed material may slip out and emerge in a form disguised to meet ego, or superego, "approval."

PERSONALITY DYNAMICS

We have spoken of the energy of the instincts of the id, some of which is captured by the ego and superego, and of the energy used in repression. It is through his *instinct theory* that Freud attempted to unify or relate the physical and the psychological life into a coherent whole, and to depict the purposefulness and motivation as well as the conflict and variety of human life (Freud, 1957, 1959, 1962, 1963). By means which Freud himself admitted that he did not understand (and which he considered outside the scope of psychology), the biological energy of the body is somehow transformed into *psychic energy* through the id and its instincts. All psychological activities—all observable behaviors as well as all thoughts and feelings—require energy. The goal of all activities is the discharge of energy, or *tension reduction.* Freud was a biological theorist who conscientiously attempted to trace mental processes and social behaviors to biological bases.

Freud suggested that there is a limited amount of energy, and energy used in one way cannot be simultaneously used in another way (his economic concept)—just as most of us cannot read and watch television at the same time. *Psychodynamics* is a matter of how the energy is distributed and used. Psychological development is a matter of coming to channel energy in habitual ways.

Motivating Forces

Instinctual drives, or simply instincts, are the motivating forces of behavior, and the purpose of all behavior is to reduce drive tension. (Freud used the German, *Trieb,* meaning moving force or urge, a concept more similar to our current concept of drive than to that of instincts.) An instinct is a psychological representation of internal bodily stimulation; in other words, our body has a need which is felt psychologically as a wish and an impulse to action. If, for example, our body needs food, then we have an impulse to eat. As the intensity of the physical need increases, the impetus or force of the impulse increases too. The aim of all instincts is to reduce tension by satisfying the need. Exactly how an individual strives for instinctual satisfaction—the action he takes and the specific objects involved—depends upon his experience and is, therefore, an important source of individual differences.

Life instincts and death instincts. Admitting insufficient knowledge to enable a listing of all biological needs, Freud classified instincts on the basis of their functions: most generally, working for life or working for death. The life instincts, *Eros,* contribute to the perpetuation of the individual and of the species. The energy by which Eros works is *libido.* Hunger and thirst gratification, for example, function to preserve the individual, and sex gratification functions to perpetuate the species.

Freud's thinking about the death, or destructive, instincts (*Thanatos*) was not as clearly nor as completely presented as was his thinking about life instincts. The only aspect of death instincts he elaborated on was aggression, the death instinct turned outward. He saw death instincts as strong, biologically rooted competitors of the life instincts, and this competition represents the basis for an inherent *internal* conflict in the nature of man. He literally meant that there is a push toward death, the ultimate tension-free condition. The goal of all life is death.

From instinct to action. Instinctual drives provide only the energy for psychological activities, they are not preprogrammed sets of responses. What the person comes to do with instinctual energy is a result of his learning experiences. The process that intervenes between the impetus of an instinct and the object toward which it becomes directed is *cathexis,* or the channeling of the raw, uncontrolled id energy toward specific activities and objects, including people, things, parts of one's body, thought processes, feelings, attitudes, behavior patterns, and so on. To cathect something is to invest energy in it. Without the process of cathexis, we would have energy but would not know what to do with it. Without the process of cathexis, the hungry infant would not seek his mother's breast; the hungry adult would not eat.

Because cathexis patterns develop with experience, behaviors associated with any given instinct may vary greatly from person to person or within one person from time to time. There are natural objects and actions associated with instinctual satisfaction (e.g., eating food when hungry), but often natural objects may be considered inappropriate, or be unavailable temporarily or permanently (e.g., objects to satisfy sexual needs). Cathexis patterns must be learned through experience.

PERSONALITY DEVELOPMENT

Freud's theory of personality is a developmental one which details the individual's attempts to adapt to the problems of his life. We have discussed some of Freud's views of development in terms of the emergence of personality components and the acquisition of cathexis. Freud's theory of *psychosexual development* integrates these facets of personality in an overall view of the dynamics of a complete person growing from an asocial and impulsive infant to, hopefully, a mature, social, and controlled adult.

Freud's developmental theory is a *stage theory,* according to which each individual is assumed to pass through set stages of life. Freud defined these stages with reference to *oral, anal,* and *genital* body regions and the associated sex instincts. Because of the universality of instincts, Freud felt that the stages and the nature of development were universal and inherent in the human condition, but later Freudian psychologists, aware of the evidence of cultural variability, have been inclined to view personality development as culturally as well as biologically determined. Similarly, Freud's view that personality was fairly well fixed by about age six is considered by many to be an exaggeration.

However, it is reasonable to consider the experiences at each stage as providing the child's first encounters with certain kinds of problems in dealing with himself and with others (Baldwin, 1967). The ways in which he learns to handle the problems may serve as prototypes for meeting similar problems later in life.

Ideally, the child progresses through each stage without undue stress or strain. However, the thoughts, actions, and feelings characteristic of each stage are invested with some libidinal energy. The mature adult is a blend of characteristics of all developmental phases, with perhaps slightly greater cathexis for, and therefore greater emphasis on, one particular stage. The stage with the greatest cathexes defines adult character types and provides the basis for some forms of psychopathology.

Progress from one stage to another requires the child to relinquish the security which comes from having developed habitual ways of behaving and from having learned how others will react to him. There must be a venture into the unknown of the next stage; new ways of behaving and a new set of others' expectations must be learned. Typically, the shift is made with only slight anxiety, and only a moderate amount of feeling is left directed to the former stage.

However, taking the next step, moving to the next stage, may in some cases be fraught with unusual anxiety, and the child is relatively *fixated* at the previous stage. *Fixation* may be caused by either overindulgence or underindulgence of the needs of a particular stage. The parents may make it so comfortable for the child at one stage that giving it up is more painful than it otherwise would be. On the other hand, if there has been insufficient gratification of the child's needs and demands, he may be inclined to linger. Freud also acknowledged that constitutional factors may encourage fixation at a given stage.

Fixation is seldom total; the child eventually forsakes the old for the new, though traits developed in the fixated stage may be more evident in his adult personality than those of other stages. But adults often express their childish traits in socially accepted behavior; while the child at the oral stage sucks the nipple, an adult may smoke a pipe.

Oral and Anal Stages

Although Freud did consider birth a significant psychic event, he did not elaborate upon it to the same extent as did some of his followers. The first stage he focused on was the oral stage of development, in which the area of the mouth is the main source of pleasure, and feeding is the main function. The infant enjoys mouthing and sucking and other oral stimulation.

In understanding his behavior, we must remember that the infant's only personality component is the id. His cognitive development is minimal. He cannot distinguish between himself and the world of external reality; *he* is his whole world. Consequently, he develops a sense of omnipotence, he feels that he has a magic control over the world. This characteristic is called *primary narcissism*. Of course, in actuality the infant is dependent upon the world; thus, this phase is termed the *oral dependency* stage.

If the person looking after the baby satisfies the child's needs, the seeds of optimism, trust, and confidence—sometimes, indeed, overoptimism and gullibility—are sown; if, on the other hand, there is inadequate attention to his needs, then pessimism, pervasive distrust, and despair may be the eventual results.

The main object of gratification in the oral stage is food; food is equated with love. Because of the immature state of cognition, the *love object* is not recognized as having an existence apart from the infant; it exists only for his gratification. The love object (food) is to be consumed, and it disappears with consumption. Freud labeled this relationship with the loved object *incorporation*. Adults fixated at an oral stage may display this attitude toward their love objects—other people are seen as existing only for their own pleasure and are discarded after they contributed to the egocentric's gratification. Equating food and love is also seen in those people, notably mothers, who insist on overfeeding their kin.

In the later part of the oral stage, the child may feel aggressive in response to the frustration of weaning. Although his world is still egocentric, he is beginning to realize that other people can annoy him and that he can annoy others. The adult characteristics of "biting" sarcasm and argumentativeness have their roots in this oral-sadistic stage.

The anal region next becomes the chief center of pleasure and of interpersonal focus. Release of fecal material is tension reducing and, therefore, even adults may associate the anal area with pleasure. Because of this pleasure and because of parents' concern with bowel training, feces become valuable possessions for the child.

In bowel training, the child faces the first stringent demand for *impulse control* in conformity with societal rules. At this stage, the child has matured sufficiently in cognition, muscular control, and locomotor abilities to be relatively autonomous in the face of parental demands; he must decide whether to use his autonomy in conformity or rebellion. If he produces feces at the appropriate time and place, he pleases his parents and learns that loving is giving. But he may punish his parents by rebelling, by withholding (hoarding) his feces or releasing them inappropriately. Thus, generosity, productivity, and creativity, as well as miserliness and hoarding, have anal roots.

If the child is not sure of his ability to follow the established rules, he may become overly inhibited ("psychologically constipated") and unable to do anything without clear signs of how to behave; he will lack spontaneity and will not be able to trust his own impulses. The overly autonomous child, in contrast, is defiant and refuses whatever is requested. He is stubborn, rebellious, and contemptuous of rules. Shame and shyness may also have their basis in this stage of experience if the child is ridiculed.

The ideal outcome is a balance between the two extremes: autonomy without defiance, submission to rules without inhibition of spontaneity or loss of autonomy. In other words, the parents' task in this stage of socialization is to make the child comfortable with the rules he has to follow;

they must help him be able to be himself without the necessity of rebelling in order to assert himself.

At this stage, too, the child views loved people as possessions. Although he now realizes that the external world exists apart from him, he is still egocentric. People are cherished, but they exist for him alone. He regards loving as both giving to a loved object and owning the loved object. Anal features of our culture are expressed in such statements as "She stole my man," or "I'm not going to share my wife!" In fact, anal experiences help to maintain a monogamous marriage system.

Phallic Stage

In about the fourth year, the phallic stage (or early genital stage) emerges. The pleasurableness of the genitals becomes a focal concern in interpersonal relations, and sexual interest increases. Now people are seen as people, separate from the child himself, but their purpose is to please. The orientation is still egocentric, and the relationship with loved ones is exploitative.

During this time, children show curiosity about and interest in sexual activities and the relationship between their parents. They may have witnessed their parents' intercourse (the primal scene). Even if this has not occurred, they may pick up many subtle cues about the fact that their parents' relationship with each other is somehow special and different from their relationship with their children.

It is also at this time that major differences in the development of males and females begin. Because of constitutional anatomical differences between the sexes, the nature of the problems faced by boys and girls differs, and so, therefore, do the methods of their resolution and their effects on the adult personalities of men and women. For Freud, masculine or feminine traits are *not* innately associated with special organs; basic human trends are *bisexual*. However, personality develops out of the relationship between biological needs and the environmental possibilities for fulfillment. Thus, personality development is sex-differentiated because of differences in the genital organs. "After all, the anatomical distinction must express itself in psychical consequences" (Freud, 1964, p. 124).

Male development: from love to anxiety. Children of both sexes look to the person who takes care of them—in our society, usually their mother —to provide them with pleasure. Thus, when a boy begins to find that his genitals are a source of pleasure, it is natural that he should look to his mother to provide him with genital gratifications. "By her care of the child's body, she becomes his first seducer" (Freud, 1963, p. 90).

According to Freud, a little boy literally wants to have intercourse with his mother, although this is not to say that he realizes the mechanics or significance of intercourse. Mother is likely to reject her son's sexual overtures, while she accepts those of the father, who thus becomes a rival

—and a powerful one at that—and the target of hostile feelings. This, then, is the *Oedipal* situation, named for the mythical King Oedipus who unknowingly killed his father and married his mother. While the child fears retaliation by the powerful rival, the father is often making things worse by exerting pressure on the boy to become a "little man" instead of a "Mama's boy."

The unfulfilled longings for the mother combined with the fear of the father elicit *castration anxiety,* a fear that the father will deprive the boy of his genitals, or specifically, his penis. This fear seems ridiculous to adults, but childhood anxieties tend to be extreme and irrational. The penis is a valued object and the source of the dangerous stimulation. Consequently, what could be more reasonable than the father's retaliation by removal of this valued object? The anxiety about possible loss of the penis is so intense that the son represses his longing for his mother and identifies with the father, thus resolving the Oedipal problem. Without the (conscious) desire for mother, there is no reason to fear castration. Through an identification with the father, he may not only protect himself from the feared adult, but may also share the father's power. This mechanism is often called *identification with the aggressor,* or *defensive identification.*

Identification with the father marks the beginning of the development of the superego, for this identification facilitates the child's internalization of parental standards of behavior, including those requiring him to exhibit masculine behavior. The libidinal energy formerly directed toward the mother and the aggressive energy directed toward the father become re-cathected and provide the energy for the superego.

In sum, the Oedipal situation proceeds and is closed by castration anxiety. The inappropriate love for the mother must be avoided if the boy is to avoid the powerlessness of castration. Male development proceeds from the pleasures of love to the burden of anxiety.

Female development: from anxiety to love. Freud admitted that he was unsure about females and once remarked, "What does a woman want? My God, what does she want?" The answer he suggested with both hesitancy and boldness was that essentially she wants a penis. Like the boy, the girl is said to value the penis; consequently, upon discovering that she does not have the desired object, she experiences feelings of penis envy. She feels inferior and wounded in her self-love because of her stunted penis (the clitoris); this sense of inferiority extends to her whole self. This lack of a penis is blamed on the mother, who has already castrated her daughter or has inadequately provided for her. In addition, the mother is devalued because of her own lack of a penis. Thus, the girl, ". . . repudiates her love for her mother and at the same time not infrequently represses a good part of her sexual impulses in general" (Freud, 1964, p. 126).

The child's own sense of deficiency and her repudiation of love for the mother motivates a search for a new love object without the deficiency, namely, the father. For the girl, the castration anxiety prepares for the Oedipus complex instead of destroying it, as in the case of the boy. However, the girl also wants her mother's continuing love and fears the loss of it if she continues to be a rival for her father's attention. Fear of mother's retaliation and loss of her love are overcome by repressing the love for the father and identifying with the mother; thus, she avoids losing her mother's love and is also able to enjoy the father. The girl's identification with the mother as a warm positive object is the prototype of what is often called *anaclitic (dependent) identification*. However, because of fear of the mother as a rival, some *defensive identification* occurs also. (Both anaclitic and defensive identification processes actually occur among children of either sex and with both parents; seldom is either parent entirely a positive or a negative figure.)

The anxiety about the Oedipal situation is not so intense for the girl as for the boy, and the matter not so much in need of a definite, complete resolution. Neither the repression of the desire for the opposite sex parent nor the identification with the same sex parent is as complete for the girl as for the boy. Thus, there is less energy freed for superego formation in the case of the girl than in that of the boy, and the adult woman will continue to show signs of penis envy and depreciation of herself and other females, perhaps with an underlying hostility toward males. If her desire for a penis is in fact transformed to a desire for pregnancy and birth, her femininity, according to Freud, is a true and mature one; unfortunately, he was not at all helpful in elucidating how this transformation is to occur.

Is Freud to blame? Freud's theory of women, sketchy though it be, is offensive to many and can easily seem quite ridiculous. He is often blamed for women's "problems," and the merit of his theory is neglected because of what seems the ridiculous concept of penis envy. Had Freud possessed the knowledge available today (though still very incomplete) about constitutional differences between men and women, perhaps he would not have emphasized the penis as the primary physical factor associated with sex differences. (He did, however, suggest other constitutional factors in both boys and girls which are involved in their shifting the identificatory balance between the mother and the father.)

Freud must be given credit for trying to explain the phenomena he observed (phenomena *not* of his own creation) within the overall theoretical framework, which was heavily based on biological factors. Today, as in Freud's time, there *are* differences between the personality styles and life styles of men in general and women in general, and the traits and activities more typical of women than of men have been generally less valued, as increasing numbers of works document (e.g., Donelson & Gullahorn, 1973a; Bardwick, 1971; Sherman, 1971).

Latency

Following the resolution of the Oedipus complex and the beginning of superego development, the child enters the latency stage, usually around the time he enters the first grade. Psychic life now is relatively stable; there is little conflict and there are no new kinds of interpersonal problems. The changes that occur are merely a matter of elaboration and growth of the structures and processes established in early years. Relationships outside the home are explored, and the child is given occasion to practice social skills and sex roles. The superego becomes more principled, and concepts (e.g., honesty) rather than rules about specific behaviors (e.g., "Don't steal bubble gum") guide behavior.

Adolescence: Genital Stage

Freud saw adolescence as a reactivation of the sexual urges repressed during the phallic stage, with the important difference being that nonincestuous objects are now available. However, the choice of love objects and the nature of the love relations may be colored by early experiences in the family. Another important change is that the adolescent is less egocentric than the child; his love relations may now be tender and altruistic rather than selfish and pleasure-oriented.

The task during the genital stage is to integrate and fuse the separate, discrete, *organ pleasures,* or expressions of partial instincts, which were previously enjoyed in the oral, anal, and phallic stages, toward the orgasm that mature, healthy adults experience in the sex act. Sexual life goes through phases, as the caterpillar turns into the butterfly. "The turning point . . . is the subordination of all the sexual component instincts under the primacy of the genital zone" (Freud, 1952, p. 337) and the use of sexuality for reproduction.

Vestiges of the desire to incorporate (oral stage), to possess (anal stage), or to exploit for pleasure (phallic stage) may play their roles in the adolescent's attainment of the pleasure of the orgasm. Puberty brings a repetition of prior sex conflicts which must be resolved; instinctual demands must now be accepted without fear; and dependence upon parents must be ended. "From the time of puberty onward the human individual must devote himself to the great task of *freeing himself from the parents;* and only after this detachment is accomplished can he cease to be a child and so become a member of the social community" (Freud, 1949, p. 295).

The fully genital person is Freud's ideal of the mature human being who seems to have the best of all traits and the worst of none.

PERSONALITY DEFENSES

Anxiety is a painful emotional experience, a response of the ego to stimulation it cannot control (Freud, 1936). It is a *conscious* experience, although the reason for it may be unconscious. To cope with this painful experience, the ego often uses defense mechanisms—techniques to disguise, distort, or falsify internal or external reality.

The Nature of Anxiety

For Freud and many other psychologists, anxiety and fear are synonymous. For the layman, fear usually implies a response to a realistic external danger. Freud called this response *reality anxiety*, or *objective anxiety* (Freud, 1964): The house really is on fire. The car really is skidding on the ice. The notice from the boss really does say "You're fired."

Neurotic anxiety is fear that the instincts will get out of control and possibly lead to physical punishment or loss of love. Neurotic anxiety may be shown in a *free-floating apprehension* (a generalized, undirected anxiety); in a *phobia* (an extreme irrational fear) about an object associated with the threatening instinct; or in a panic behavior, in which prohibited impulses are acted out in mild form (e.g., shouting abusively) or extreme form (e.g., going berserk and shooting people).

Moral anxiety is fear of the superego. Acting, or even thinking, in ways counter to the internalized standards (e.g., lusting after your neighbor's spouse) elicits self-punishing guilt or shame. Both neurotic and moral anxiety have their base in reality anxiety. The person was at one time punished by others for allowing id impulses to go unchecked and for violation of standards of behavior which he later internalized.

Anxiety is adaptive in that it is a recognition of a real external or internal danger. Although it is a painful state, it enables avoidance of a larger pain; therefore, if it is limited to a short danger signal it can be useful. (Long-lasting anxiety, however, may be harmful.) With experience, the ego learns to protect itself from anxiety by responding quickly with actions to remove or avoid the danger (Freud, 1924). The ego may respond to signal anxiety by taking effective problem-solving routes to reduce external dangers: If, for example, you receive a note telling you that you are fired, you go out and look for another job. On the other hand, the ego may use defense mechanisms to protect itself from anxiety.

Defense Mechanisms

Defensiveness, according to Freud, is an essential part of the normal personality. Even a strong ego cannot tolerate conscious acknowledgment of all the perils of the world or all the individual's own imperfections. However, a healthy ego is fairly judicious in its choice and timing of defenses: it neither excessively distorts huge chunks of reality nor consistently distorts in the same way; in other words, it does not use the same defenses for all problems. Often, too, the healthy ego can overcome the defenses when it needs to.

Defenses become maladaptive when they are extreme in frequency or intensity. The more the defensiveness, the more reality is distorted and the more energy is expended. The more rigidly defenses are established as habitual modes of functioning, the less flexibility the ego has in adapting to reality and the more difficult it becomes to correct the situation.

Rigid defenses prohibit reality testing and are self-perpetuating. The realistic danger that originally elicited the defense may disappear with time, so that the defense is no longer necessary; but the ego cannot detect this because the defense disguises or avoids facing the reality that is no longer dangerous.

Theorists have suggested a number of defense mechanisms (A. Freud, 1936; Fenichel, 1945); some of the more common processes are discussed here.

Repression. As we noted before, repression is an active, dynamic process of holding down. It serves to keep an impulse, idea, or feeling from becoming conscious. Very painful, anxiety-provoking material—the Oedipus complex, for example—is repressed. Anxiety is reduced or completely avoided by preventing the forbidden thought from becoming conscious. That which is repressed is contained in the id.

Some repressed material may be returned to a conscious level by psychoanalytic treatment. This is necessary if the individual is to be able to deal realistically with the thoughts he has repressed.

Repression should not be confused with *suppression,* which is a voluntary refusal to act on an impulse or a conscious attempt to prevent material from maintaining a place in awareness. To say, "I won't let myself think about how angry I am," is to suppress. Not to be at all aware of anger is to repress. Because repressed elements may act like magnets pulling other elements toward them, we may not only become unaware of angry feelings for a specific person, but of all angry feelings.

Denial. Some individuals simply deny the existence of an anxiety-provoking element. For example, a parent may deny the reality that his child has died even when confronted with the evidence that this is so. While denying the death of a loved one is a common initial reaction, continued denial is neither common nor healthy. Denial is a primitive and unadaptive mechanism in that it so drastically distorts reality that the individual can neither cope with nor recognize it.

Displacement. As an example of object displacement, consider a small child fondling his genitals. This is a sexual (specifically, genital) instinct; the action is manipulation; the object is the penis. The activity is natural, but suppose this child's mother does not approve of it. Fearing her punishment, the child changes to playing with his toes. This activity will be partially successful in reducing tension in an acceptable way. But after he gets to college, the young man's roommate considers this toe-fingering behavior strange indeed, and makes his feelings known. The individual has to displace again, so he constantly plays with his pencils. The source and the actions are always the same, and the aim is always gratification. The object has merely been changed to give the appearance of innocence; in other words, the object attachment has been successively shunted in acceptable directions. Freudians are able to explain, in a similar fashion, all manner of behaviors as object displacement of sexual drives.

In displacement, the activities used in approaching satisfaction are often more appropriate for gratification of another instinct. If, instead of engaging in a sexual behavior (such as manipulation), the individual eats, the object involved—food—is one appropriate for eating, not sex. When substitution is habitual, the behavior is termed an *instinct derivative.* Thus, playing with pencils or eating could become derivatives of the sex instinct. Collecting china and reading cookbooks could become derivatives of the hunger instinct. In this manner, Freudians can explain hobbies, values, occupational interests, as instinct derivatives. When a displacement is socially valued, it is called *sublimation,* the only truly healthy defense, and the one that makes civilization possible.

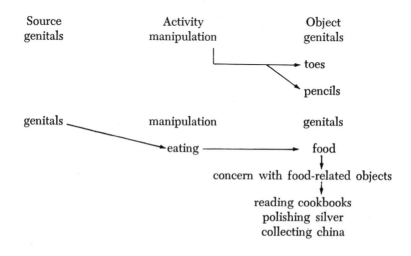

Regression. Freud used the analogy of an army to describe his concept of regression. As the army advances, it leaves a few soldiers behind at each campsite or strategic point. When the army later encounters frustration or defeat at the hands of the enemy, it retreats to an area of relative safety, most likely the encampment with the greatest number of reserve soldiers and supplies, and, therefore, security.

When an adult encounters problems, he may regress to a former stage of development which, to him, means security. The stage to which he regresses is likely to be one at which he had fixated. Except in extreme pathological cases regression is not total. For example, a person may regress to the anal stage and become very defiant of authority or attempt to win love by giving presents. However, unless he is very sick, regression may occur only in certain selected areas of thinking and behaving. He may rebel only against his boss, or may give presents only to his wife, but he is likely to retain bowel control. Or, he may have elimination problems but exhibit no other sudden or extreme anal characteristics.

Projection. Attributing characteristics to other people or things on the basis of one's own characteristics is called projection. If aggression violates one's superego standards, he may attribute this unacceptable feeling to other people and think, "They're out to get me." The effect of projection is to transform neurotic or moral anxiety into reality anxiety. This substitutes a lesser danger for a greater one, and thereby reduces anxiety, since the ego can deal more readily with external than with internal danger. It also allows expression of the impulse in a disguised form. If "they're out to get me," it is justifiable to attack them in "self-defense." In this way, the person avoids feeling guilty and also expresses his aggression.

Identification. Identification occurs when we feel that we are *like* another person or that we *are* another person. The person with whom we identify may be someone we admire—a famous athlete, for example—or someone we fear. Identification with an admired person enhances self-esteem, while identification with a feared person reduces anxiety. This latter type of identification occurs in the Oedipal situation: The son, fearing his father, identifies with him in self-defense, taking on some of the father's characteristics in the process.

Reaction formation. Reaction formation is the mechanism of unconsciously replacing an undesirable feeling or trait with a desirable one. While one is often in the position of giving excessive thanks for a present he knows he does not like, this is not reaction formation, because he was conscious that he disliked the gift. However, suppose the object in question was one he could not "admit to himself" that he disliked—his mother, for example. He might show excessive devotion to her, just as he gave excessive thanks for the gift. Reaction formations are likely to be more intense and persistent than are expressions of genuine emotions. Further, avoidance of real feelings by reaction formation may help accomplish a forbidden aim: The parent whose love for his child is a reaction against rejection of the child may achieve at least a psychological destruction of the child by his or her constant overprotection, or "smothering love."

Closely related to reaction formation are the mechanisms of *undoing* and *atonement.* One attempts to cancel out the effect of impulses to unacceptable or anxiety-producing actions, even if those impulses have not been acted upon. Thus, the rejecting mother's compulsive behaviors in caring for her child may also be atonement for the unconsciously felt rejection.

Intellectualization. This defense is a somewhat peculiar one in that it involves an apparent facing of the anxiety material. (It is also one which may easily become the "psychology major's defense.") An individual faces his problems or wishes as they are, but in a coldly intellectual way—without feeling their significance. He defends against the impact of the feelings by pretending to deal with them through the gimmick of intellectual labels, sometimes used correctly, sometimes with only superficial insight. The intellectualizer has the satisfaction of being able to say, "I know myself; I'm facing my problems," but the *feelings* involved are not faced. An exciting or disturbing event may be calmly discussed and analyzed, but the appropriate affect may be repressed, displaced, or isolated, only to burst forth inappropriately at a later time. A frequent manifestation of intellectualization and *isolation* occurs in the separation of the physical and tender components of sexuality, accompanied by "enlightened" pronouncements about sexuality.

Intellectualization is often confused with *rationalization*. With rationalization, feelings and behavior become permissible to the realistic, rational ego (and to other people who hear the excuse) because they are given a rational justification, but this justification is not correct. It is simply an explanation that seems logical. A student is rationalizing if he says that he cut a class in order to clear his head so that he could study better when his true reason is that he hates the teacher, fears failure, feels guilty because of lack of preparation, or wants to indulge himself with a movie. He is intellectualizing if he acknowledges that the reason is, for example, fear of failure, but he talks about the fear without feeling and actively grappling with the problem.

PSYCHOANALYTIC THERAPY

The goals and techniques Freud used to attempt to change personality through psychotherapy reflect his assumptions about the nature and development of personality. Freud's aim in therapy was to increase the ability of the ego to deal effectively with internal and external conflicts. The change he envisioned was in the position of the ego in relation to the demands of the id, superego, and reality. Freud's insistence on recovering repressed memories and dealing with repressed ideas and emotions is still apparent in present-day psychoanalysis (and other therapies as well) in the general principles of insight and feeling.

Achieving insight requires uncovering unconscious material, which, in turn, requires a building up of the ego to enable it to face the material without being overwhelmed. Psychoanalytic treatment includes both the analysis of ego defenses and the analysis of hidden materials of the id; it attempts to correct an ego deficiency and to bring a part of the id into consciousness. The ego may resist the change and the attendant restructuring and thus the individual may view the analyst with hostility. Overcoming this initial resistance is a crucial first step. Before change can occur, the ego must have a sufficient understanding of reality and the value of more effective dealings with it. Freud did not claim his therapy to be of use in treating psychotics because of the impoverished state of their ego.

Practitioners of Psychoanalysis

A psychologist may be a devoted follower of Freud and be psychoanalytically oriented in his work, whether this be research, teaching, or therapy. However, he is not for that reason a *psychoanalyst* or a *psychiatrist*. A psychiatrist is a medical doctor with a specialty in psychiatry. A psychoanalyst is typically a psychiatrist who has had extensive training at a psychoanalytic school. As part of his training, he undergoes didactic (teaching) analysis. Analytic schools sometimes accept candidates from professions other than medicine, usually from the social sciences, but these *lay analysts* are relatively rare (although Freud himself did not consider medical training necessary for psychoanalysts). Psychologists, of course, are not all therapists, nor are all therapists psychologists.

PSYCHOANALYTIC TECHNIQUE

If the goal of psychoanalysis is to help the individual recognize, verbalize, and cope with his internal and external conflicts, how is this goal reached? How do psychoanalysts actually go about uncovering unconscious material and aiding a person in strengthening his ego?

Freud maintained that actual psychoanalytic sessions cannot be demonstrated since their effectiveness depends exclusively on the privacy and trust of a one-to-one, therapist-to-patient encounter. An observer would destroy this intimate communication. Freud's own description of the psychoanalytic technique emphasizes the importance of this relationship:

> In psychoanalytic treatment nothing happens but an exchange of words between the patient and the physician. The patient talks, tells of his past experiences and present impressions, complains, and expresses his wishes and his emotions. The physician listens, attempts to direct the patient's thought-processes, reminds him, forces his attention in certain directions, gives him explanations and observes the reactions of understanding or denial thus evoked.*

Through analysis of ego defenses, slips of the tongue, "accidental" mistakes and omissions, and dream material, the therapist can help his patient understand the forces at work in his personality. Unconscious material can often be revealed through the technique of *free association,* and further enlightenment can be accomplished through *transference* and *interpretative comment.*

* Freud. S. *A general introduction to psychoanalysis.* New York: Perma Books, 1949. P. 19.

Free Association

Freud was originally led to his concept of the unconscious by the memories articulated by hypnotized patients. However, the applicability of hypnosis as a technique for studying the unconscious was limited because only a small number of people could be put into a deep hypnotic state, and the effectiveness of hypnotic treatment greatly depended on the patient-therapist relationship (Freud, 1959). Freud evolved the free-association technique to replace hypnosis as a major tool in studying unconscious content. He considered the technique so innovative and important as to warrant coining a new name: psycho-analysis!

The rule of free association is to describe the flow of consciousness with complete honesty, reporting all ideas as they occur even if they seem disagreeable, nonsensical, or irrelevant. This is not as simple as it sounds. Try to speak each thought as it enters your mind for the next two minutes. You should have no conscious intention of either revealing or hiding your secrets. Nor should you deliberately withhold a thought because it is repugnant to you or because it may be distasteful to someone else (in the case of psychoanalysis, the listening therapist).

Sometimes an unintentional block occurs in free association. The patient may feel that his mind is blank, that his thoughts are jumping around too quickly for him to get hold of them, or he may intentionally withhold something. If resistances, conscious or unconscious, do not continue too long, they may be instructive; they suggest that the train of association was about to reach dangerous territory. What a person does *not* say can tell us as much about him as what he does say. Even in everyday conversation, people avoid topics that they consider unpleasant, and if you notice at which point a friend habitually changes the subject, or has a strange gap in what he is saying, you will know something about the things that bother him.

Transference

Transference refers to the seemingly irrational emotional aspects of the relationship between the patient and therapist. The patient often reacts to the therapist in ways that appear inappropriate to the situation. However, the reactions are useful in that they may reflect the patient's feelings about another person—mother, lover, rival, sister—in another situation. The patient transfers his feelings about the other person to the analyst, who psychologically *is* the other person. In some extreme cases, the patient actually sees the analyst as his mother or lover.

These irrational aspects of the emotional relationship between therapist and patient can serve an extremely useful purpose in any psychotherapy. Indeed, if transference does not arise naturally, the analyst may take steps to induce it.

In transference, the patient relives an interpersonal conflict; he "produces before us with plastic clarity an important part of his life history . . . as though he were acting it in front of us instead of reporting it to us" (Freud, 1963, p. 68). The value here lies in the fact that he does this in a protective situation in which the therapist may help to correct the prior experience. If the patient had an immature, punitive father, then the therapist, who is more objective and understanding, could play the part of a "good father." In this way, the feelings about the early experiences which inhibited development can be expressed and corrected, and personality growth can continue.

Transference can also occur outside the therapeutic situation, toward someone other than a therapist. Many interpersonal difficulties may be due to transference: One person's feelings toward the other may be inappropriate, or he may have unjustified expectations of the other, because he is reacting to the person as if he were someone else. The other person may, in response, become confused and be goaded to extreme actions in an attempt to be known as he is.

Interpretation

Another therapeutic tool is interpretative comment, with which the analyst provides a major integration of the therapy techniques. The therapist points out the patient's feelings and attitudes, he clarifies the reasons for these feelings, and he directs the patient's thoughts to the implications of his feelings and behaviors. This sounds like a technique that is easily used; however, it is actually one of the most difficult to use effectively (Freud, 1963).

In making interpretative comment, the analyst must evaluate problems of current interest to the patient and carefully time his comments so that the patient may assimilate a new insight. Although the analyst may have arrived at an interpretation of some aspect of the patient's problems early in therapy, the patient may not have been ready then to accept the comments and to deal with them in an appropriate fashion. Without preparation, he may ignore the interpretation, or violently resist it; this can hinder progress or block it altogether. The analyst must provide some support and must time his interpretative comment so that the patient may feel secure enough to relax his defenses and get closer to the basic conflicts, realizing that his conflicts may be more manageable than he had believed them to be. Further, the interpretation must not result solely in intellectual acknowledgment of its accuracy. A "cure" will not evolve merely from intellectualization about the problems and their background. There must also be an emotional involvement of the patient; that is, he must *abreact*. While intellectual insight by itself can act as a resistance against cure, abreaction without insight gives only small relief and, in some cases, may even be dangerous. People must integrate thinking and feeling.

A Critique of Freudian Theory

The attention we have given to Freud's ideas is a fitting acknowledgment of his many "firsts" in providing fundamental concepts for studying personality. Freudian terminology is pervasive in psychology, even affecting those who do not consider themselves Freudians. Many basic concepts of psychodynamics and adjustment are elaborations on or modifications of the principles he articulated.

Many psychologists feel that Freud erred in the extremity of his positions more than in their content. Much behavior doubtless reflects defensive maneuvers to avoid or reduce anxiety, but this is probably not true of all behavior. Tension reduction is a powerful motivator of behavior, but humans also behave to increase stimulation and excitement. Further, the defense mechanisms Freud considered necessarily unconscious probably need not be so. While psychologists agree with Freud on the important function of dreams, they have questioned the reason given for their occurrence and the façade he claimed they present. Freud's conception of the stages of human development have been criticized as being too rigid, and he seems to have virtually ignored the influence of cultural variation. Thus, in the view of many theoreticians, he placed too much importance on early childhood experiences as exclusive determinants of personality and gave too little attention to the continuous process of personality development. Freud is seen as having exaggerated the role of sex in determining behavior; most psychologists seem to feel that we do have problems and conflicts that are not sexually based. Modern behaviorists have disputed his insistence that all symptoms reflect an underlying problem that must be uncovered if there is to be relief. Finally, evidence does not demonstrate conclusively the effectiveness of psychoanalytic therapy, and certainly not a superiority over other therapies.

In fairness to Freud, it must be admitted that these comments are made on the basis of continued expansion within personality theory and empirical evidence which has been collected, for the most part, since his death. And much of the theory has developed and the data been collected because Freud originally raised the issues! It is absurd to criticize him for failure to revise his theory on the basis of research he inspired. In view of the evidence with which he worked, Sigmund Freud did a remarkable job of depicting and trying to explain complex human phenomena within a single theoretical system.

A major strength of Freud's theory lies in the fact that he tried to understand so many important kinds of questions about human behavior. He attempted to explain phenomena as far-ranging as the mind of the infant and the existence of civilization, the nature of complex thought and the social effects of the biology of sex. Thus far, no other theorist has been so comprehensive in his efforts, nor so influential in his impact on psychological thought.

4
freudian
descendants

Sigmund Freud's influence on personality psychology has been so immense that we would not be far in error if we were to list all personality psychologists as Freudian descendants. However, as was mentioned before, not all current psychologists nor all Freudian disciples agree that his contributions have been uniformly valid. Jung, Adler, Fromm, Horney, Sullivan, and the ego psychologists are all strongly identified with Freudian theory, either by close personal association with Freud or by strong dependence upon his thought. All, however, have modified traditional Freudian theory in an attempt to correct what they perceived as biases or deficiencies in Freud's contributions.

Notable in their work relative to Freud is minimal emphasis on sex and, to some extent, aggression as chief determinants of human behavior, and in increased attention to social-cultural factors in normal and pathological behavior. Another relative modification in Freudian thinking is found in the descendants' interest in the wholeness and the essential soundness of personality, as expressed in their concepts of self and the associated notions of the striving to fulfillment as a governing life motive. As Carl Jung stated, ". . . I prefer to look at man in the light of what in him is healthy and sound . . ." (Jung, 1933a, p. 117).

CARL JUNG: ANALYTICAL PSYCHOLOGY

Carl Jung (1875–1961) was an early associate of Freud, but severed relations with him in 1912 to establish his own theory of *analytical psychology*. To Freud's biological and deterministic emphasis, Jung added a deep sense of social-cultural history and a consideration of man's orientation toward the future. Although he did not disagree with the importance of biology in Freud's theory, Jung conceived sexual energy as only one form of *libido*, the creative life force. Jung saw life as a purposive venture in which man moves forward with aspirations and goals (a teleological perspective).

Pervasive in Jung's thinking is the assumption that, if the self is to be attained, opposing aspects of personality should be equally developed and integrated into a balanced whole. Full attainment of self is the goal of our struggle through life.

Introversion and Extraversion

Our everyday use of the terms introversion and extraversion have much in common with Jung's use, but Jung did not limit their applicability to social behavior as we do when we decide that John is an introvert because he would rather eat by himself than join in a group in the cafeteria, or that Mary is an extravert because she gives two or three large, noisy parties every month. For Jung, introversion and extraversion are *attitudes* of the personality, the basic stance of the person toward the world and toward himself (Jung, 1923, 1928, 1933b). When a state of introversion or extraversion is habitual with a person, he is an introverted or extraverted *type*.

An introverted type demonstrates hesitating, reflective, defensive, and reticent behavior, while the extravert has an open and ready disposition, is at ease in any situation, forms attachments quickly, and ventures confidently into unknown situations. In the introvert, the libido (life force) is directed toward the self rather than the outside world; in the extravert, the libido is turned outward.

Most people are neither entirely introverted nor entirely extraverted, although one tendency is usually dominant. But the greater one tendency is on the conscious level, the greater the opposite tendency is on the unconscious level. The unconscious attitude may occasionally break through in a crude form (as when the shy typist tells a vulgar story at the office party) which, while embarrassing or startling, need not be deeply disturbing to the "normal" personality. In its pathological form, however, such a breakthrough can have disastrous consequences (as when the quiet, retiring young man picks up a gun and shoots a dozen people).

We can often see awkward breakthroughs in normal behavior. For example, the typical extravert tries to be alone for a while and is very uncomfortable doing so, or becomes very moody and selfish when he insists on staying with people but would be better off being alone. Or, the introverted and perhaps overly studious "square" tries to tell a joke or become a real "swinger" at a party but just does not have the savoir faire to bring it off because his tendencies toward extraversion have not been well developed and differentiated.

Jung thought that there are hereditary predispositions toward introversion or extraversion. However, the environment may frequently shape an individual in ways contrary to his natural attitude. Also, whether the submerged attitude is natural or not, it may burst forth in later years with dramatic—perhaps neurotic or even psychotic—effects, as discussed above. Jung thought these breakthroughs to be due more to the over-whelming buildup of the unconscious attitude than to the biological changes that occur as people age. Jung attributed special blame, in treating maladjustments of the adolescent and the young adult, to the conflict between a person's natural bent and environmental pressure.

Psychological Functions

Introversion and extraversion are terms used to describe the direction our life force takes; psychological functions refer to the way in which we approach the world (Jung, 1923, 1933a, 1933b). Jung described four functions, two of which are rational (*thinking* and *feeling*), and two irrational (*sensation* and *intuition*).

Rational functions. The rational functions, thinking and feeling, are modes of *judgment* by which we try to make sense of the world. *Thinking* is a process of making conceptual connections between events or objects; *feeling* is a process of giving subjective value to objects or events, and it provides experiences of pleasure, pain, anger, fear, and so on. If we analyze the "Mona Lisa" in terms of its place in art history or its similarity to other Florentine paintings, we are thinking; if we look at it and say, "How beautiful!" we are feeling.

Irrational functions. The irrational functions, sensation and intuition, are modes of *apprehension* based on the perception of the concrete rather than the abstract which is dealt with by rational functions. Jung used the term irrational quite literally, namely, to denote an absence of the rational. Sensation and intuition, then, are irrational in that they deal with an object or event as it is presented rather than as it is responded to intellectually or emotionally.

The sensation function is the reality function. Concerned with the present, it yields concrete facts about the world and tells us what an object or event realistically is. A person with sensation as the dominant function sees the "Mona Lisa" as a photograph would depict it—as a painting of a woman.

Intuition is the function which unconsciously transmits perceptions. We apprehend the world by way of unconscious processes, by going beyond facts, thought, feeling, and ideas. We go beyond the data given and deal with the potential of an object or event. In this case, the "Mona Lisa" might stimulate a related, fanciful vision of our own.

Combinations. In Jung's actualized person, each function would be equally well developed. However, in most people one function usually dominates. The most highly developed function, the *superior* one, plays the dominant role in conscious actions; an *auxiliary* function, usually of the pair opposite to that of the superior function, takes over when the superior cannot operate. Thus, in Jungian terms, a person may be described as a thinking-sensation type or as a feeling-intuition type (Figure 4–1). The least obvious and well-developed, or *inferior* function, is repressed and dominates in the unconscious, expressing itself in compensatory dreams and fantasies, and it too has an auxiliary function, typically from the other pair.

Both the introvert and the extravert may have any combination of dominant-auxiliary functions. For example, prophets and spiritual leaders may be seen as dominated by intuition and feeling, but they can be active extraverts like Billy Graham, or meditative introverts like the Eastern gurus. A creative scientist, with thinking and intuition superior, may be an introvert who, seeing beyond the immediate, is content to spend large amounts of time in his laboratory working on the possibilities he sees. He may need the help of a thinking-sensation type to perfect the details for instrumenting these possibilities, to translate the insight about what is potential into the workable techniques of the actual. An extravert would be helpful in soliciting public approval and financial support for the scientific work.

The Collective Unconscious

Jung's concept of *personal unconscious* is similar to Freud's concept of the unconscious in that it consists of experiences in the life of the in-

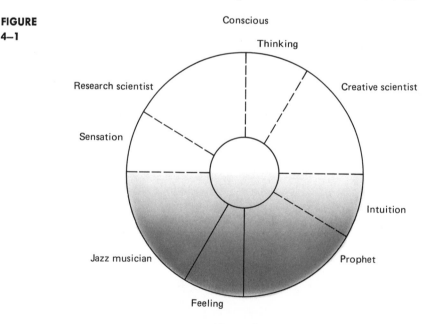

FIGURE
4–1

Jung's Four Functions, Shown with Thinking as Superior Function.

Source: From Jacobi, I. *The psychology of C. G. Jung*, 1959.

THEORETICAL ORIENTATIONS TO PERSONALITY

dividual which have been repressed or have had little impact. Thus, its contents vary greatly from person to person. Jung, however, thought that there is another aspect of the unconscious which is shared by all human beings. This he called the *collective unconscious.*

The shared past. Due to a common evolutionary background, all humans have essentially the same brain structure in which is recorded ancestral experiences extending over millions of years. "This psychic life is the mind of our ancient ancestors, the way in which they thought and felt, the way in which they conceived of life and the world, of gods and human beings" (Jung, 1939, p. 24). Upon this foundation, which determines the individual life in invisible ways, all acquired structures of personality are erected. Although we do not inherit the actual memories of our ancestors, we do inherit *predispositions* to respond as our ancestors did.

Archetypes and behavior patterns. The components of the inherited reaction system are *archetypes,* also called symbolic or mythological images, and behavior patterns (Jung, 1939, 1959). An archetype is a universal idea which is elicited by current objects and experiences and influences behavior. Because all humans have had mothers, each child has a mother archetype, elicited by his own mother, and a predisposition to react to her in a way influenced by the archetype. Some archetypes may never be elicited; some need very little personal experience to emerge as important influences. A predisposition to fear snakes may not become apparent if we do not encounter snakes; the idea of a Supreme Being may emerge without any formal religious instruction.

Even if one rejects Jung's hypotheses about archetypes, one can—indeed, must—deal with the important personality dynamics he expressed in archetypal terms. Among the more important of his archetypes are the *persona,* the *soul,* and the *self,* which help to define the crucial importance of coming to terms with all of our human potentials and predispositions. In coming to understand ourselves, we must recognize that these forces are frequently in opposition.

Persona

Jung used the archetype of persona (literally, mask) to relate the concepts of roles to deeper aspects of personality (1923). The persona evolves through experiences with other people which elicit man's inherited predisposition to assume a role; it is the mask worn in social interactions. Our persona presents to others an image of who and what we are, although the image may or may not express our true selves. While we may be offended by the idea of playing roles, assuming that masking our real feelings and thoughts is dishonest, Jung suggested that the persona is a *necessity* for social living. He felt that constant exposure may be as unbearable to the person himself as to those forced to deal with him.

This point was vividly illustrated in a case cited by a Jungian therapist (Wickes, 1938) of a young man whose ideal was complete frankness. He expressed his reactions, thoughts, opinions, and feelings honestly and openly at all times. One night he dreamed of being at a social gathering where people were trying to avoid an uncouth monster—a turtle without its shell. With the help of the therapist, he came to realize that he was the monster of the dream, a man without a mask being like a turtle without a shell. Other people were disgusted with his rudeness rather than appreciative of his candor.

Too much "shell" is a more typical problem. When a person becomes exclusively identified with the role or roles he plays, his inherent potential can be smothered. An individual may be a fine doctor, a charming hostess, an effective politician, but will not be a real human being if the expression of his real self is neglected. There is the danger, too, that the unexpressed aspects of a person's nature will grow to unmanageable proportions in the unconscious and burst uncontrollably into consciousness.

The introvert finds it particularly difficult to change his mask as the occasion demands. Thus, he frequently finds himself in situations where his sole persona is uncomfortable and inappropriate. As other people react only to that mask and he identifies with it, he comes to wonder who he really is, and to ask, "Who am I?" In contrast, the extravert changes his persona as easily as his dress. He is not a hypocrite; he is just sensitive to the social demands of a situation because of his awareness of the outside world. Whereas the response of the introvert is directed inward, the reaction of the extravert is directed outward, thereby enabling him to decide what actions and words are appropriate to various situations and people. He is able to select a proper role and feel comfortable with it. The extravert lawyer may argue learnedly in front of the jury, entertain charmingly at a cocktail party, respond tenderly to his wife, and romp joyfully with his children, never feeling awkward in any of these roles. But if he identifies with the ever-changing masks, the extravert, too, comes to wonder who he really is, and to ask, "Who am I?" The question is particularly likely when a major mask is stripped away by failure or rejection. The extravert may then seek an answer in yet another mask or look inward at his own emptiness.

Soul

The outer character is the persona; the inner character is the soul. As with other aspects of personality, these are reciprocally related, the soul containing all the human qualities lacking in the persona: if the persona is intellectual, the soul is sentimental; if the persona is masculine, the soul is feminine. How one relates to his own soul images influences his relationships with actual other persons, and his relationships with others affect the development of his soul images. The soul of the scientist permits an understanding of the poet; the soul of the man permits an understanding of a woman. If the scientist does not establish good relations with the poet, or the man with the women he encounters, those parts of himself will be perverted and may come to dominate his unconscious. With distortions or lack of acceptance of those elements in one's self, there follow distortions in interpersonal relationships, as one, for example, responds to the other in the way he feels about himself.

The impact of Jung's insight on this matter can usually be readily felt by honestly examining the characteristics of people for whom we have intense feelings of attraction or rejection (see Putney & Putney, 1964). What strongly attracts you in another is a valued part of yourself that you have not recognized. What you strongly reject may reflect a devalued part of yourself you have not acknowledged, or your own envy at the other's success in the development of a trait you would like to see developed in yourself. In either case, you are probably not seeing the other person as he in fact is; you are projecting your own soul images onto him. With actualization, one can have more effective relations with others because one can see, and be, himself as he is. This occurs with the achievement of selfhood.

Self

The self is an archetype (expressed chiefly through the symbol of a circle, a perfect whole) that leads man to search for the wholeness of complete development of all aspects of personality. Although all of life is a striving toward the self-actualization of wholeness, the goal is rarely accomplished, and Jung felt that, in most cases, it is not even approached until middle age, as all personality components have only then had time and opportunity to develop. With the emergence of self, we have a point of unity which stabilizes and brings together all aspects of personality.

Apart from the development discussed above, selfhood is often approached through deep religious experience. In fact, Jung developed the concept in his studies of the religions of the Orient which aim for unity of self with the world.

Jung's Influence

Jung's influence outside psychology, particularly in religion and literature, has been considerable. But most psychologists focus on a small part of his contribution: his typology (based on introversion-extraversion and the functions), and his concept of the collective unconscious. While Jung's typology is gaining increased attention from researchers (e.g., Briggs & Myers, 1957; Eysenck, 1947, Chapter 8), they still largely reject his view of the collective unconscious, mainly because of the mystical context in which it seems imbedded rather than because serious consideration has shown that it cannot be used. He has been given little credit for his insights about self-actualization and goal direction, even by those later theorists (Chapter 6) whose thoughts are most similar to his own. Jung attempted to place man in a cultural-social perspective and concentrated on man's striving to become actualized, his efforts to achieve a harmonious integration of internal and external forces and a whole, healthy personality. Jung's ideas merit close attention from any serious student of psychology.

ALFRED ADLER: INDIVIDUAL PSYCHOLOGY

Alfred Adler (1870–1937), a Viennese psychiatrist, was initially a close friend and follower of Freud, but he gradually deviated from Freudian doctrine. Although few psychologists today consider themselves Adlerians, Adler did pave the way for social-psychological theorizing within a Freudian framework, and his direct impact is still felt through the journal he founded (*The International Journal of Individual Psychology*) and the work of his students.

Adler's theory is direct, easily understandable, and optimistic. According to Adler, man is a unique, generally conscious, whole individual who is motivated by inherent social urges and who creates experiences to fulfill his style of life. Any one part of the personality is an integral part of the whole organism, and any one individual is inextricably intertwined with all other individuals as a part of society. Adler's *individual psychology*, then, is a psychology of man's relation to man.

Striving

The unified, whole organism is determined by one dynamic force of which all other drives or motives are only aspects. In his earliest view, Adler (1908) maintained that aggression, rather than sexuality (as Freud then asserted), was the important governing motive. Both Freud and Adler noticed that frequently women prefer to be men, and that men were concerned with being "real men" (Ansbacher, 1965). Adler labeled this phenomenon the *masculine protest,* and he attributed it to a lust for the power of masculinity. Both men and women engage in the masculine protest as a form of overcompensation for feelings of inadequacy and inferiority (Adler, 1910). Thus, *will to power* came to be seen as the key motive of life.

Superiority. Adler later came to see the general concept of striving for superiority as the governing aspect of personality development. This superiority is not one of social distinction, prestige, leadership, or control over people. Instead, it does have much in common with Jung's concept of self-actualization: a perfect completion, a subjectively conceived success. Adler's superiority is a superiority of self. Man attempts to master himself, to be competent, to be complete, to be perfect. The striving for this superiority is innate; it is anchored in the structure of life itself, and is an attempt to compensate for inferiority. Inferiority is the force which pushes man to strive; superiority is the goal toward which his striving aims.

Inferiority. The inferiority which first intrigued Adler was *organ inferiority:* a stutterer, such as Demosthenes, becomes a great orator; a physical weakling, such as Theodore Roosevelt, becomes a Rough Rider. Later, Adler thought that any *feeling* of inferiority, real or imagined, leads to a sense of incompleteness which, in turn, contributes to the striving for the superiority and perfection of self.

Social Interest

Each person has a different conception of exactly what perfection of self is and how this should be attained. However, for all normal people, the specific goals required for attaining the larger one of superiority are *social goals* (Adler, 1930, 1964). Only neurotics strive solely for self-esteem, power, or self-aggrandizement; healthy people try to find concrete ways to work toward helping society attain the goal of perfection (Hall & Lindzey, 1971). Social usefulness was Adler's criterion of mental health. Social interest is an innate potential in man.

The Creative Self

In spite of Freud's originality in attending to every word and action of his patients, he was a conservative scientist in that he believed the inner psychological world, revealed by words and actions, to be ultimately determined by objective causes from the past, and in that he felt that mental disorders were caused by forces beyond the individual's control (Ansbacher, 1964, 1965). In contrast, Adler proclaimed that the inner world of the individual is not objectively caused but is *created* by the individual himself. Adler believed that the individual uses his hereditary and environmental equipment in striving for the goal of success which he creates in response to these objective factors: "We fashion our own experiences. Everyone determines how and what he will experience" (Adler, 1957, p. 20).

Style of life. The creative self shapes personality toward goals along its own style of life, and when experiences are not found which will aid in fulfilling the unique life style, the self attempts to create them. If the style of life proves to be ineffective, symptoms develop to safeguard self-esteem and provide excuses for failure. Thus, the neurotic is likely to accuse others of not having done enough for him. Adler believed mental disorders to be essentially mistaken ways of living, or faulty life styles. Consequently, the task of therapy is to understand life style and replace the neurotic's big mistakes in living with the little mistakes of a nearly normal person.

Adler's Influence

Adler's theory was very appealing to the laymen of his time because it was a commonsense approach, which kept technical terms at a minimum, and because it was optimistic. It is easier for a person to understand himself as having inferiority feelings that he wants to overcome and as being a unique, creative organism than it is for him to cope with the concept of himself as a combination of ego, id, and superego and as a battleground of conflicting impulses. The theorizing is of increasing appeal to many modern students for much the same reason. Robert White (1957) maintains that Adler's ideas have become accepted clinical common sense. Of particular interest in contemporary psychological thought is White's notion of competence motivation, which is an elaboration of Adler's concept of striving for superiority. Adler himself concluded that there may be more sophisticated theories than his, but none which would bring greater gain to all people (Adler, 1964).

Adler was a forerunner of our present community mental health programs (Papanek, 1965). He helped to create over thirty child guidance clinics associated with the public schools of Vienna, and he led a large-scale adult education effort to inform the public of the social principles of mental health (Ansbacher, 1964).

ERICH FROMM: HUMANISTIC PSYCHOANALYSIS

The psychology of Erich Fromm (1900–   ) is essentially an attempt to humanize psychoanalysis by applying Freudian thinking to man as a social being in a social setting. The result is often closer to social philosophy than psychology. At the same time, Fromm aims for the perspective attempted by Jung in that he sees mankind in the context of all nature; hence, his writings reveal a deep respect and sympathy for the animal called man.

The Nature of Man

According to Fromm, "Man may be defined as the animal that can say 'I,' that can be aware of himself as a separate entity" (Fromm, 1955, p. 62). Man is aware that he is free from nature but, at the same time, that he is also part of it and helpless before it (an existential dichotomy). The experience of separateness is the source of all man's anxiety. He is anxious about the aloneness he has as a special creature of nature and, simultaneously, searching for satisfactions of needs he has as a creature of nature (Fromm, 1941, 1955). Man needs to relate to other people, and he must also transcend his state of being a passive creature. He must feel rootedness in the world, must have an identity (feel that "I am I") and a frame of orientation which provides a stable way of understanding the world, a philosophy of life.

Love

If man is to escape the anxiety of his aloneness and satisfy his needs in productive ways which allow him to achieve self-integrity, he must accept his freedom as an individual and realize his inborn capacities for imagination, reason, and love (1947, 1955).

Reason enables him to grasp the essence of an object, while love enables him to overcome the barrier separating him from that object or another person and to comprehend that object or person. "Love is union with somebody, or something, outside oneself, under the conditions of retaining the separateness and integrity of one's own self" (Fromm, 1955, p. 37). With love, man can escape the anxiety of isolation while he maintains his individuality and achieves a self-integrity; indeed, Fromm contends that self-integrity is impossible without love.

The Escape from Freedom

Fromm (1941) is concerned that man is taking unproductive routes in trying to escape the anxiety of aloneness; he is trying to "escape from freedom" rather than use his freedom to develop his human capacities. Lacking the courage and self-confidence to fulfill himself as an individual, man is succumbing to the pressures of society to forfeit his freedom and uniqueness. Thus, man is denying the potentialities which are his.

Fromm's idea is that society rejects and punishes the individual who attempts to become himself. Just as primitive man was helpless before natural forces, so modern man is helpless before the social forces he has himself created.

Fromm's Influence

Fromm's psychology stresses the potentiality of man with his distinctly human qualities of love and reason. He sees our society as a "sick" one in that man must struggle against society, and even revise it, if he is to fulfill his basic psychological needs in productive ways. Fromm's (and Horney's) emphasis on the role of society in personality development has helped to stimulate consideration of social variables within psychoanalytic theory. In addition, he has contributed an ethical interpretation of psychological issues.

KAREN HORNEY: SOCIOLOGICAL NEO-FREUDIANISM

Although she viewed herself as definitely within the Freudian framework, Karen Horney (1885–1952) saw fallacies in Freud's mechanistic and biological orientation and particularly objected to his emphasis on sex as an important basis for neurotic development. Her association with Fromm increased her interest in the influence of cultural factors on personality development, and she ultimately contended that neuroses are generated by cultural factors, specifically disturbances in human relationships.

In contrast to Freud, she emphasized continual adaptation to life situations, particularly interpersonal ones, and believed that "a man can change and go on changing as long as he lives" (Horney, 1943, p. 19). Like Jung, Adler, and Fromm, she believed in the importance of personal actualization, but she thought that the conditions of human life are such that full realization of our capacities is usually not attained. In defining neurosis as any deviation from the achievement of the rare goal of fulfilling human potentiality, she therefore includes us all when she discusses neurotics!

Basic Anxiety

Horney believed the primary condition for the development of neuroses to be *basic anxiety,* the feeling the child has of being isolated and helpless in a potentially hostile world. Children who are secure in an environment that provides love, acceptance, and appreciation can handle realistic hardships, but children who feel isolated, at the mercy of a cold, hostile environment unconsciously develop neurotic strategies for handling the anxiety they feel (Horney, 1939). When these strategies become compulsive ways of dealing with events and relationships, they attain the status of *neurotic needs,* or *neurotic drives.* Horney (1942) saw the neurotic needs according to three general interpersonal orientations:

1. Moving *toward* people.
2. Moving *against* people.
3. Moving *away from* people.

In the normal person, the three strategies are compatible and spontaneous moves which complement one another. In the neurotic, however, the strategies become compulsive devices used to keep basic anxiety at a minimum. The neurotic follows a strategy even when it is not appropriate; it pervades his entire personality and encompasses his relations to himself and to life in general. Horney also listed ten specific neurotic needs.

1. *The neurotic need for affection and approval.* Indiscriminate need to please others and be approved of by others; opinion of others rather than of self more important; dread of self-assertion and the hostility of others.

2. *The neurotic need for a "partner" who will take over one's life.* Over-value of love because it is supposed to solve all problems; dread of being deserted; search for partner who is to fulfill all expectations.

3. *The neurotic need to restrict one's life within narrow borders.* Necessity to be inconspicuous, undemanding, and contented with little; modesty and belittling of existing potentials; dread of making demands or having expansive wishes.

4. *The neurotic need for power, prestige, and possession.* Craving for domination over others; disrespect for individuality, dignity, and feelings of others; devotion to a cause; adoration of strength, contempt for weakness; dread of helplessness and uncontrollable situations.

    4a. *The neurotic need to control self and others through reason and foresight* (traits common to people too inhibited to exert power directly). Denial of power of emotions; belief in power of intelligence, reason, foresight, and prediction; dread of stupidity and of recognizing limitations of reason; feelings of superiority because of foresight.

    4b. *The neurotic need to believe in the omnipotence of will* (a type of introversion in detached people for whom direct exertion of power means too much contact with others). Belief in magic power of will; restriction of wishes and withdrawing of interest to avoid dread of failure; feeling of desolation with wishes frustrated; dread of recognition of limitations of sheer will.

5. *The neurotic need to exploit others.* Pride in skills of exploitation; value of others based on degree of susceptibility to exploitation; dread of being exploited and thus reduced to level of stupidity.

6. *The neurotic need for social recognition or prestige.* Evaluation of self dependent on nature of public acceptance; all things evaluated in terms of prestige; dread of humiliation.

7. *The neurotic need for personal admiration.* Need to be admired for imagined rather than actual self; value of self dependent on living up to image and on others' admiration; inflated self-image (narcissism); dread of humiliation.

8. *The neurotic ambition for personal achievement.* Evaluation of self dependent on being the best; need to surpass others in activities rather than in self-presentation or actual self; driving of self to achieve, and striving marked by anxiety; destructive tendencies to defeat others; dread of failure.

9. *The neurotic need for self-sufficiency and independence.* Dread of needing others, closeness, love, or being tied down; security only with distance and separateness.

10. *The neurotic need for perfection and unassailability.* Driving for perfection, self-recriminations about possible flaws; superiority feelings because of perfection; dread of mistakes, criticism, reproaches.*

Because they are irrational and compulsive, the neurotic strategies are not likely to bring interpersonal success. Their failure often intensifies

* Horney, K. *Self-analysis.* New York: W. W. Norton, 1942. Pp. 54–60. Also see Horney, K. *New ways in psychoanalysis.* New York, W. W. Norton, 1939.

the very need or anxiety which generated the behavior, and a *vicious circle* emerges. New conflicts are generated, additional steps are necessary to overcome them, and those steps lead to additional conflict. The neurotic's attempts to meet his needs are often inappropriate for a particular situation and, even when appropriate in content, are compulsive, intense, irrational, and likely to meet with disappointment.

Anxiety
↓
Excessive need for affection, including demands for exclusive and unconditional love
↓
Feelings of rebuff when demands are not met
↓
Hostility
↓
Need to repress hostility because of fear of losing affection
↓
Tension of diffuse rage
↓
Increased anxiety
↓
Increased need for reassurance *

Horney's Influence

Like Fromm, Horney emphasized the social and cultural factors which influence individual behavior, and, also like Fromm, she had an essentially humanistic attitude. She was an expert clinician with great influence on psychotherapeutic practice.

HARRY STACK SULLIVAN: INTERPERSONAL THEORY OF PSYCHIATRY

The most distinctive features in the theory of Harry Stack Sullivan (1892–1949) are the heavy emphasis upon social interaction and the concomitant minimization of the importance of biological determinants. The biological needs have their influence through social relationships. Sullivan believed that social relationships are the most important factor in understanding personality development, and even went so far as to define personality as the "relatively enduring pattern of recurrent interpersonal situations which characterize a human life" (Sullivan, 1953, p. 111). To understand an individual, therefore, we would begin, not with the person himself, but with his relationships with others.

* Adapted from Horney, K. *The neurotic personality of our time.* New York: W. W. Norton, 1937. Pp. 137 ff.

The Significant Other

Personality, according to Sullivan, is not fixed at an early age, but may change any time new interpersonal relations arise. The first social relationship of the child is with the mother; she is the *significant other*. Although the infant cannot speak, he does respond empathetically to her. (*Empathy* is nonverbal communication.) When the mother's mood is negative, the child experiences the tension of anxiety.

The Self-System

The *self-system* is formed from experiences with significant others, particularly experiences with the mother. It comes into being because of the child's need to avoid anxiety. He learns that he can avoid anxiety by controlling his behavior to conform to his parents' wishes; thus, the self-system approves of some behaviors (the good-me) and forbids others (the bad-me).

The self-system, as guardian of security, becomes inflated and dissociated from the rest of personality; it is protected from criticism and prevents objective judgments of a person's own behavior. Although it functions to reduce anxiety, the self-system does interfere with the ability to live effectively with others. It is both necessary and unfortunate.

Sullivan's Influence

While many of the Freudian descendants considered social factors important, only Sullivan developed a relatively systematic and comprehensive theory of personality development in terms of social relationships as the basic units. His emphasis on interpersonal relationships has been very influential in later psychological thinking, particularly in social and developmental psychology.

EGO PSYCHOLOGY

For Freud, the ego, although the "executive" of personality, was generally subservient to the id in that it developed to serve the wishes of the id and operated on energy captured from the id. The id and its instincts were seen to express the purpose of life. The resulting picture of man is analogous to a seething cauldron, for man is "bubbling" with impulses and conflict. All behavior strives to keep the "cauldron from boiling over"; all behavior, therefore, is ultimately defensive.

The ego psychologists—Erik Erikson, David Rapaport, Heinz Hartmann, Rudolph Loewenstein, and Ernst Kris—do not reject Freud's drive theory (as did Adler and Horney, for example), but they do object to the Freudian dependence of the ego on the id.

Ego Autonomy

The ego psychologists find it difficult to see all the activities of the ego as defensive, made necessary by internal conflict or conflict with the environment. Even in Freudian theory, the ego is responsible for higher-order cognitive planning and interaction with the world, as well as for the more mundane realities such as deciding between scrambled or fried eggs for breakfast and remembering to put gas in the car. The ego perceives, learns, remembers, thinks, and acts, and, according to ego psychologists, often performs these functions *without* the causal conflict and dependence on id assumed by Freud. Thus, Hartmann proposed "that we adopt the provisional term *conflict-free ego sphere*" (Hartmann, 1958, p. 8) to describe functions that occur without mental conflict.

Thus, ego psychologists distinguish between *ego defensive functions*, which reduce anxiety and resolve conflict, as Freud suggested, and *ego autonomous functions*, which serve for nonconflicting interactions with the world.

The ego is independent of the id both in origin and in function; in other words, it is characterized by *primary autonomy*. The ego has its own source of energy, and both the id and the ego are present in undifferentiated form at birth. However, drawing on Freudian theory, these psychologists contend that the ego captures additional energy from the id to use in defensive functions. This energy, originally used for defensive purposes, may later become neutralized and be available for nondefensive use (Rapaport, 1951). Adaptive habits and defenses may persist and become relatively autonomous. Thus, the ego also has *secondary autonomy*. Primary autonomous functions originate in and persist in the conflict-free ego sphere; secondary autonomous functions born of conflict come to function in the conflict-free sphere.

Ego, Id, and Environment

Just as ego autonomy frees man from being dependent on the id, the ego's autonomy from the environment serves to prevent man's complete dependence upon the external world and his experiences in it. We are not slaves to environmental stimuli. On the basis of our internal needs, values, and identity, we can select the features of the environment to which we will respond, and we can modify and postpone reaction to external events.

The ego's capacity for autonomy from the id ensures the capacity for autonomy from the environment, and vice-versa: The capacity to relate to reality prevents servitude to drives, and the strength of drives prevents servitude to the environment (Rapaport, 1958). The ego is slave to neither id nor environment, but is an autonomous, decision-making pivotal point between them. This idea has much in common with Jung's notion of balance of introversion and extraversion; energy is not exclusively directed inward or outward.

Ego Identity: Erik Erikson

Erik Erikson (1950, 1956, 1959) believes that each individual progresses through built-in stages of ego development, defined in terms of the way he resolves the crises or social encounters typical of each stage. In Erikson's works, the early years are no longer of almost exclusive importance; here, adult development takes on meaning.

Erikson sees the developing human as a rational and logical creature who realistically attempts to make decisions and cope with problems. The ego becomes "a concept denoting man's capacity to unify his experiences and his action in an adaptive manner . . . [with] roots in social organization" (Erikson, 1963, p. 15).

The growing individual gradually develops an identity, a characteristic Erikson sees as arising from the ego rather than the superego. This ego identity is the only safeguard against the anarchy of drives (biological determinants), on the one hand, and the autocracy of conscience (social determinants), on the other (Erikson, 1963). If the protective ego identity is lost, the adult is at the mercy of his prior childhood conflicts and the overconscientiousness which resulted from inequality with his parents.

Identity is both a social and an individual concept. The growing child must at every step experience a sense of reality from his individual way of mastering experience: "ego identity gains real strength only from . . . recognition of real accomplishment—i.e., of achievement that has meaning in its culture" (Erikson, 1963, pp. 235–236).

Influence of Ego Psychology

While the ego psychologists' modification of Freudian theory is slight, its effect is radical—with implications that have only begun to be explored. Man is depicted by the ego psychologists as retaining the vibrancy and intensity of the biological world of impulses, but he is not a victim of his biology. He is responsive to the demands of external reality, and he is an effective participant in social interactions; however, he is not a puppet in the hands of others and is not helpless in the face of reality. He is a social individual who experiences his individual existence.

SUMMARY

The Freudian descendants start from a basic Freudian approach and modify it in distinctive ways to emphasize the role of cultural factors, social relationships, social needs, and movement toward self-actualization in personality development. They provide a psychoanalytic correction to Freud's biological and deterministic emphasis, as well as a theoretical link between Freud and the fulfillment theorists (Chapter 6), who have captured attention in recent years. They assign to man the rational awareness and social consciousness that man believes he possesses. In doing so, they attempt to preserve, with varying degrees of success, the physical potency and aliveness of man, the biological creature.

5

learning theory
and behavior therapy

FOUNDATION CONCEPTS

A Point of View

"Learning theory" is, strictly speaking, a misnomer. There is not one learning theory; there are many. However, within these many theories is a relatively common core of assumptions, intent, procedures, and concepts. What we shall be concerned with initially is learning theory as a perspective, a way of analyzing behavior, and then we shall apply learning theory perspectives to conflict and therapy.

Learning, behavior, and personality. When people talk about personality theory, most are likely to have in mind the kind of thinking typical of the theorists discussed in Chapters 3, 4, and 6, often with the implication that those personality theorists are to be considered in relative *contrast* to learning theorists. As will become evident, the distinction is a useful, though sometimes confusing one for crudely pointing to differences in approaches to the study of human behavior, but the distinction should not be overdramatized. Learning theorists themselves see no incompatibility between the study of personality and the study of learning, and there are increasing attempts to apply concepts from the learning laboratory to issues of interest to personality psychologists, and vice versa. In spite of the increasing rapprochement, the fields of learning and personality arise from separate traditions and are characterized by differences in orientation that still impair communication between descendants of the two traditions.

The empty organism strategy. Learning theorists assume that the human being, like other living creatures, must be considered an initially empty organism until science is able to prove otherwise. Their claim is that the behavior of the organism is determined by antecedent stimulus events. This approach reduces any tendency to attribute to the organism characteristics that are unnecessary or irrelevant to understanding the behavior. The earliest proponent of this idea was John Watson, the founder of American Behaviorism, who maintained that the proper concern of psychology is behavior. So radical was this claim that the psychological establishment of his time reacted as if he had told them to abandon their whole function and to dispose of their only useful tools in studying man. The only internal characteristics Watson could allow as legitimate considerations in the science of behavior were simple neurological structures, specific innate reflexes, and simple innate emotional patterns from which more complex behaviors developed. To many his approach sounded simpleminded, but he was expressing a commitment to a strategy that had been successful in other sciences: the study of simple phenomena in which there are clues that facilitate the study of more complex phenomena.

B. F. Skinner is the current, more sophisticated spokesman for the necessity to limit one's study to observable events. Other, less severe behaviorists from the learning laboratory have been more willing to postulate events *inside* the organism. For example, the behavior theory of Clark Hull contains concepts of drive and incentive motivation—an explicit allowance for internal events. However, learning behaviorists are parsimonious with their constructs. These are postulated much more carefully and cautiously than in the work of Freud, for example, and employed only when they are shown to be necessary to account for behavior. When constructs are used, they are carefully and tightly related to observables. Treatment variance (Chapter 1) is still the dominant concern, with consideration given to the individual, organismic variance only when necessary to improve prediction.

Generality of Behavioral Laws

Animal research. Behaviorists are more likely than other theorists to make an *explicit* assumption that behavior laws are general, controlling human beings and species. Animal research, then, is relevant to humans and has the advantage that the environments and the genetic history of the animals can be carefully controlled. Thus, one is in a better position to specify the organism's characteristics and the antecedent and current conditions associated with behavior. Complete explanations of human behavior may require concepts beyond those necessary to explain the behavior of other animals, but such concepts should be cautiously introduced. It is very possible that more of our behavior than we care to admit can be explained in the simple terms we think sufficient to explain rat behavior. Our concept of man as the apex of the evolutionary scale sometimes causes us to lose sight of the fact that he does have a *place* in the evolutionary scale. In Fromm's terms, man is the animal that can say I, but is a creature of nature nevertheless. We may expect, then, that laws derived from laboratory animals should also apply to human beings, although often in complex interaction with laws more distinctly human.

Human laboratory research. Generalizing from laboratory research with humans to behavior outside the laboratory is also a problem (in fact, a problem even for research done in naturalistic settings, Chapter 7). The psychologist doing research in a laboratory is accused of dealing with only simple behaviors in simple situations. The accusation is justified, for he does simplify. However, a researcher must start somewhere, and a logical place to begin is with a simple segment of behavior (Lundin, 1963). When an experimenter does attain a "simple" situation it means that his definition of the phenomena has been sufficiently successful to permit the essential features to stand out, providing a simple result as the product of his own complex thinking. Curiously, people who criticize generalizations from controlled laboratory situations are very likely to generalize from behavior in one complex, uncontrolled situation to another complex, uncontrolled situation (Farber, 1964). Certainly, real life behavior results from a combination of several variables. This means that the researcher must continually study combinations of many variables and many kinds of subjects, not that he should abandon the laboratory.

CONDITIONING CONCEPTS

Classical Conditioning

Our current conceptions of conditioning rely heavily on the pioneering work of a Russian physiologist, Ivan Pavlov (1848–1936). In the process of investigating the digestive processes of dogs, Pavlov noted that his dogs salivated as they heard the food cart rattling down the hall. Certainly this response to cues about the approach of food was not peculiar to Pavlov's animals. But Pavlov was curious about the usual as well as the unusual (Chapter 2) and, in trying to understand this everyday phenomenon, developed the essential concepts of classical conditioning.

Requirements. Classical conditioning requires an unconditioned stimulus (UCS) which reliably *elicits* an unconditioned response (UCR). The ability of the UCS to elicit the response is not dependent upon anything that occurs in the current situation. The response may be innate, such as salivation (the UCR) to food (the UCS), or it may have been previously acquired. The UCS is the eliciter; the response is an *elicited* response. If another stimulus, the conditioned stimulus (CS), is presented in temporal and spatial contiguity with the UCS, it may acquire the property of being able to elicit a conditioned response (CR) which it did not elicit before the pairing. The ability of the CS to elicit the CR is *conditional* upon its pairing with the UCS. The effectiveness of the procedure of pairing one stimulus with another is described by the *contiguity principle:* If an originally ineffective stimulus is paired with an effective stimulus, it becomes able to elicit a response which it did not previously elicit.

The stimuli. Generally, the greater the contiguity between the stimuli, the better the conditioning, although long delays are possible, particularly with human beings who "fill in" the time to make a connection between the CS and UCS. Several forms of pairing of the UCS and CS are effective in obtaining conditioning (Figure 5–1). The only requirement is that the CS not begin after the UCS appears. If the CS follows the UCS, the procedure is backward conditioning, which is difficult, perhaps impossible to obtain (Kimble, 1961, p. 48).

As was said above, the CS is an ineffective or neutral stimulus in that it does not initially evoke the UCR or the CR before being paired with the UCS. However, the designation "neutral" is relative, for rarely does an objective change in the environment that is noticeable by a subject elicit *no* response. Pavlov called the initial response to the CS a what-is-it reflex, an orienting reflex, or orienting response (OR). The OR is an indication that the organism noticed the CS, a condition obviously necessary for conditioning to occur. The OR, particularly defined in physiological terms, has acquired significance on its own as a measure of attention (Sokolov, 1963). People differ widely in the magnitude of the OR, and those with relatively large ORs show better conditioning than do those with smaller ORs (Maltzman & Raskin, 1965).

Response strength. The time during which the two stimuli are paired and the CR comes to be given to the CS is the period of *acquisition* of a response. During this time, response strength is increased: The greater the number of pairings, the stronger the response. Conversely, *extinction* occurs when the UCS is withheld, when the CS is repeatedly presented *without* the UCS. During extinction, the strength of the response decreases. (We shall see, however, that extinction does not always occur when the subject is deprived of the UCS.)

Response strength is a construct measured in several ways, not all of which are relevant for all responses. The measures typically used are (a) *probability* of the response occurring prior to the UCS (percent of trials on which a subject gives a CR, or percent of subjects giving a CR); (b) *latency* of the response (time from onset of the CS to onset of the CR); (c) the *magnitude* and vigor of the response (e.g., how much saliva, how strong a knee-jerk); (d) *resistance* to extinction (how many times the CS has to be presented without the UCS before the response is not given.

Two other phenomena that reflect response strength are *spontaneous recovery* and *relearning.* After the response has first been extinguished

FIGURE
5–1

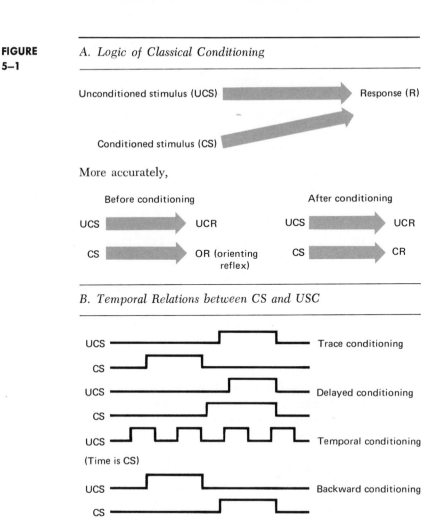

A. *Logic of Classical Conditioning*

Unconditioned stimulus (UCS) → Response (R)

Conditioned stimulus (CS)

More accurately,

Before conditioning

UCS → UCR

CS → OR (orienting reflex)

After conditioning

UCS → UCR

CS → CR

B. *Temporal Relations between CS and USC*

UCS / CS — Trace conditioning

UCS / CS — Delayed conditioning

UCS — Temporal conditioning
(Time is CS)

UCS / CS — Backward conditioning

Time

Classical Conditioning Paradigm.
Increased height of line representing each stimulus indicates the stimulus comes on; decreased height indicates the stimulus goes off.

Source: Kimble, 1961, p. 48.

(this being defined by a set number of trials on which the CS is presented and the CR does not occur), it may spontaneously appear again, though with decreasing strength over time. The probability of spontaneous recovery, as well as the time required for it to become unlikely, increase with the strength of the initial response. After extinction, additional pairing of the CS and UCS constitutes relearning: The stronger the original response strength, the fewer trials required for relearning to an established criterion. Both spontaneous recovery and relearning reflect the fact that even after extinction, the response is not completely "gone." Although the measures are not perfectly correlated, we may think of them as generally measuring the same construct, response strength.

Little Albert: an example of classical conditioning. Little Albert was an infant who, like most infants, was not afraid of white rats, but was afraid of sudden loud noises. Watson and Rayner (1920) took advantage of these facts and used classical conditioning procedures to induce the first experimental neurosis in humans (an experiment that today would be considered unethical). Specifically, they demonstrated the acquisition and transfer of phobic responses. (A phobia is a strong, irrational fear.) As Albert was playing with the rat (CS), the experimenters clanged an iron bar (UCS) behind him. A fear response (UCR) was high in Albert's *innate hierarchy of responses:* Elicitation of the fear response was not dependent upon prior conditioning, and was very likely to be given to the noise. With repeated pairings of the noise and the rat, Albert came to show signs of fear in response to the rat alone. Fear came to be the dominant response in his *acquired hierarchy of responses* to the stimulus rat: The response was dependent upon conditioning rather than being an innate reaction.

Further observation of little Albert's responses illustrated another basic principle of conditioning, *stimulus generalization:* A response given to one stimulus, called the original stimulus, is also likely to be given to stimuli similar to it; the more similar the new stimulus to the original one, the greater the response strength to the generalized stimulus. Little Albert's fear generalized to objects resembling the white rat, such as a white rabbit, cotton, a fur coat, and the experimenter's hair (Figure 5–2). These other objects had never been paired with the loud noise;

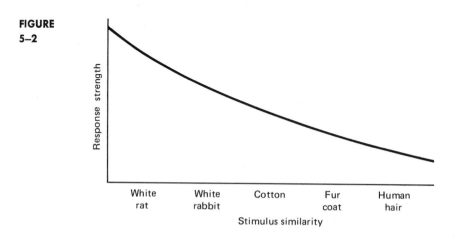

FIGURE 5–2

Response strength

White rat | White rabbit | Cotton | Fur coat | Human hair

Stimulus similarity

Theoretical Generalization Gradient for Little Albert's Acquired Phobia of a White Rat.

however, because of their similarity to the rat, they elicited fear responses. Someone who did not know of Albert's conditioning history might well question his fear of a fur coat. Knowing the history, we can more easily understand his behavior. While ours has probably not been a laboratory experience, many of our seemingly irrational fears may well have such a history of conditioning processes.

Let us fabricate upon the example to present one more basic principle, *higher order conditioning*. It is not necessary that the UCS be one which *innately* elicits the response; it is required only that the UCS *reliably* elicits a response. Once a CS becomes a conditioned eliciter, it may function as a UCS in additional conditioning. After conditioning, if the white rat (UCS) had been paired with a carrot (CS), the carrot would have become effective in eliciting the fear response. Would not the response extinguish if the rat were continually presented without the noise? With relatively nonemotional responses, it is necessary to occasionally pair the old CS (the new UCS) with the old UCS. However, strong emotional responses are amazingly, sometimes disastrously, resistant to extinction.

There are, of course, objects resembling the new CS, the carrot, and stimulus generalization may affect Albert's response to these (Figure 5–3). Given stimulus generalization and higher order conditioning, the

FIGURE 5–3

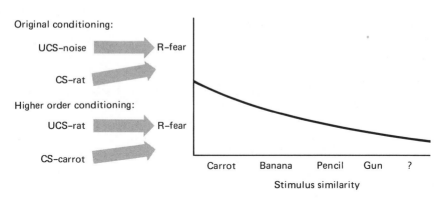

Theoretical Case of Higher Order Conditioning for Little Albert's Acquired Phobia of a White Rat, with Generalization to a new CS.

response may be given to a complex variety of stimulus conditions bearing no readily apparent relation to the original stimulus—unless one can detail the conditioning history. Notice that Little Albert's phobia is analyzed only in terms of classical conditioning, with no reference to any deep-seated psychological problems the boy may have had. According to the behaviorist, a complete conditioning history is all that is needed to understand Albert's phobic behavior.

Instrumental Conditioning

The other major paradigm of conditioning that plays a crucial role in learning theory is instrumental, or operant, conditioning, pioneered by E. L. Thorndike and elaborately developed by Skinner and his followers.

Effect learning. In instrumental conditioning, the starting place is a response. The eliciting stimulus, if there is one, is irrelevant; it matters only that the response is *emitted*. After the response occurs, the reinforcing stimulus is presented: $R - - - - S_+$. The relationship between the instrumental response and the reinforcement may be highly arbitrary and dependent upon the whims of those people (or machines!) in the environment who control the reinforcement. A frequent technique in the investigation of principles of instrumental conditioning is to have water or food pellets automatically delivered to rats or pigeons in return for their pressing a lever or button in a Skinner box. The results are said to occur because of the reinforcement principle, or the empirical *Law of Effect:* The presentation of a positive reinforcing stimulus following a response strengthens the response. Response strength has the same kind of meaning as it does in classical conditioning, but it is most likely to be measured by response frequency. Note that the reinforcing stimulus occurs *after* the response. The response is *instrumental* in bringing about the reinforcement; the organism *operates* on the environment. In classical conditioning, the UCS occurs regardless of the organism's response; the organism simply responds to the stimulus presented. Thus, the two conditioning paradigms are also called operant and respondent conditioning, and the responses manipulated in the two paradigms are called operants and respondents (Skinner, 1935, 1937).

Cooperation. Human beings may not live in a Skinner box, but they do live in a reinforcing community which controls behavior by presenting reinforcement contingent upon behavior. The relevance of instrumental principles to complex social behaviors was indicated by a laboratory study in which jelly bean reinforcers were given contingent upon the joint occurrence of the responses of *two* children (Azrin & Lindsley, 1956).

Ten teams of two children each, seven to twelve years of age, played a game using an apparatus that could not be operated by one individual alone. The children were on opposite sides of a table with three holes and a stylus in front of each child (see Figure 5–4). A wire screen across the table prevented each child from manipulating the other child's stylus. The children were instructed that they could play the game of putting their stylus in the holes in front of them and that sometimes jelly beans would drop in a cup. If the two styli were placed in opposite holes within 0.04 seconds of each other (a cooperative response), a jelly bean (reinforcing stimulus) fell into the cup accessible to both children. During the first fifteen minutes, the reinforcement period, every cooperative response

FIGURE
5–4

Apparatus Used for the Reinforcement of Cooperation between Childen.

Source: Azrin, N. H., & Lindsley, O. R. The reinforcement of cooperation between children. *Journal of Abnormal and Social Psychology*, 1956, 52, 100–102.

was reinforced. During the second fifteen-minute period, the extinction period, cooperative responses were not reinforced. Then, cooperative responses were again reinforced.

All teams of children learned to cooperate in the first ten minutes, although they had been given no specific instructions to do so. The median number of cooperative responses (per three-minute periods) increased during the reinforcement period (from 5.5 to 18.5). When reinforcement was withheld, the rate of cooperative responding dropped (to 1.5 at the end of extinction). Response rate increased again during the second reinforcement period (to 17.5). Notice that no mention has been made about what the children were thinking or whether they were "nice" children. The results are explained by reference only to events in the environment in which the behavior occurs. *Rats* also may be taught to cooperate with other rats to obtain food and avoid shock (Daniel, 1942).

Shaping. When an experimenter wants a response not already in the organism's repertory, he starts with those responses already exhibited by the subject and then reinforces any kind of response close to the desired one. He reinforces responses increasingly similar to the desired reaction, progressively withholding reinforcement for the kinds of responses previously reinforced. The process is somewhat like the parlor game in which the person who is "it" is told that he is hot or cold as he explores various portions of the room in an effort to find the target object. He progresses from being cold, to warm, to hot. In behavioral terms, the subject gets reinforcement as he moves toward the "correct" behavior. Reinforcement is given only for closer and closer approximations to the desired behavior; by *shaping*, or *successive approximations*, the correct response is developed. Therefore, the kinds of responses that may be controlled are vastly extensive and dependent upon reinforcement contingencies. A parent may shape a child successively to more mature responses, from sucking a milk bottle to eating peas with a fork, from asking mother to put on clothes to putting them on himself. However, with shaping, as with other conditioning techniques, the kinds of responses that may be controlled are restricted by the capabilities of the organism. The six-month-old child does not have the motor capability to handle a fork efficiently enough to use it to eat peas.

Reinforcement Schedules

Varieties. We might expect that conditioning would be better if reinforcement were given every time a response occurs (regular, or continuous reinforcement) rather than only some of the time. Response strength does increase quickly with continuous reinforcement. However, conditioning is more efficient on partial (or intermittent, or discontinuous) reinforcement schedules. After the response has been built up by regular reinforcement schedules, it may be maintained at high rates by shifting to partial reinforcement, and it is more resistant to extinction if only some responses have been reinforced. The phenomenon is called the *partial reinforcement effect.* Naturally occurring human behavior is more likely to be on an intermittent than a continuous schedule. For instance, does the reinforcing stimulus "Thank you" follow your every good deed? Concomitantly, many of our behaviors are highly resistant to extinction; our "personality" consists of many habitual responses which do not require constant reinforcement in order to be maintained.

Partial reinforcement may be given on one of four basic kinds of reinforcement schedules (Figure 5–5). On a *fixed ratio* schedule, reinforcement is given for every X number of responses: On a 4:1 schedule, for example, the organism gets one reinforcement after every four responses. A motivated organism responds rapidly at first; as conditioning continues, it tends to pause after reinforcement, and then to increase its response rate as it gets closer to the response to be reinforced (the fourth).

With *fixed interval* schedules, the number of reinforcements is specified with respect to time: On a 4:1 schedule, one reinforcement is given every

**FIGURE
5–5**

	FIXED _Reinforcement predictable_	VARIABLE _Reinforcement not predictable_
RATIO _Reinforcement based on number of responses_	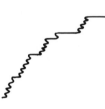	
	Reinforcement for every X responses. Frequency of pause after reinforcement increases as number of reinforcements increases, due to satiation for reinforcer. Examples: Piece-work, being paid on basis of number of units produced. Getting a final grade whenever you turn in two termpapers.	Reinforcement for every X responses, on the average. Highest, most steady rate. Pauses after reinforcement eliminated by change from fixed to variable schedule, so time of reinforcement not predictable. Examples: Gambling, fishing. Interesting lecture on the average of every ten times you go to class, but you can't predict exactly when.
INTERVAL _Reinforcement based on time intervals, not controlled by organism_		
	Reinforcement every X time units. Fairly gradual positive acceleration of response rate as time for reinforcement approaches. Pauses after reinforcement lengthen, the responses become more precisely timed. Example: Turning on TV set for favorite program—one well-timed response is sufficient to get the program.	Reinforcement every X time units, on the average. Fairly constant rate. Pauses eliminated because time for reinforcement varies. Examples: Teacher reinforcing student expression of ideas. If you like commercials, turning TV set on to see if by chance one is on.

Partial Reinforcement Schedules.

four time units (usually minutes), provided the organism responds by this time. This schedule produces a "scalloped" curve. There is little responding immediately after reinforcement, and then rapid responding occurs as the time for reinforcement comes near. The organism comes to respond very carefully, immediately *before* the "correct" time, and then rest immediately after reinforcement.

Both ratio and interval schedules may be *variable* instead of fixed: Reinforcement is given on the average for every X responses, or every X time units. Response rate is much steadier, and the curves are smoother, because the organism does not "know" exactly when reinforcement will occur. Response rates are generally higher on ratio (fixed or variable) schedules than on interval schedules because the organism itself controls the reinforcement: Reinforcement is contingent only upon the organism's responses rather than on its responses *and* time.

An example of partial reinforcement. Brackbill (1958) demonstrated the partial reinforcement effect on the smiling of three-and-a-half to four-and-a-half month old infants. During the initial, operant, period of eight five-minute intervals, the experimenter stood motionless and expressionless, with her face fifteen inches above the infant. They smiled less than three times per time interval. During the reinforcement phase, the experimenter reinforced an infant's smile by smiling, speaking softly, jostling, patting, and picking up and holding the infant for about thirty seconds. Some infants continued receiving reinforcement for every smile; others were maintained on a regular schedule for ten intervals, and then worked up progressively through 2:1, 3:1, to a 4:1 variable ratio schedule. During the extinction phase, infants were observed for thirteen five-minute intervals without reinforcement, as in the operant period.

The infants who had partial reinforcement smiled more during extinction than did those who had been continuously reinforced (Figure 5–6). This was true in spite of the fact that the partial reinforcement group had the same number of acquisition trials as the regularly reinforced group, and thus received a smaller number of reinforcements. Notice that there is no reference to making the babies happier. Perhaps the babies were happy because the experimenter was attending to them; perhaps those on the partial schedules had enough reinforcement to know that they wanted more. It is sufficient to say that the probability of a response (smiling) increased when reinforcement (experimenter's attention) was contingent upon it, and response rate was more resistant to extinction after partial reinforcement than after continuous reinforcement.

Discrimination

Although the instrumental response is not elicited by a stimulus, the response may be brought under stimulus control. In the presence of a *discriminative stimulus*, S^D (for example, a green light, rather than just any light, or a two-tone bell rather than just any bell), the response is

FIGURE
5–6

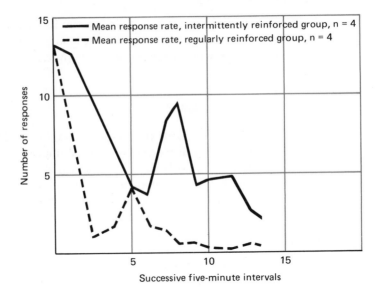

Response during Extinction Period.

Noncumulative curves showing mean rates of smiling response during extinction period.

Source: Brackbill, Y. Extinction of the smiling response in infants as a function of reinforcement schedule. *Child Development,* 1958, 29, 115–124.

followed by the reinforcer. The response is not followed by a reinforcer when performed in the presence of other stimuli (without S^D), each of which is called S-delta (S^Δ) to indicate a difference of the S from S^D. The organism acquires stimulus discrimination and learns to respond only in the presence of S^D.

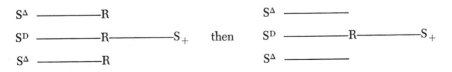

Thus, a pigeon can come to respond with pecking only in the presence of a green light, S^D, rather than when just any light is on. For humans, verbal instructions and emotional expressions provide important clues about internal states of another person and about the kinds of responses likely to be reinforced. (However, a strict Skinnerian would find reference to the internal feeling state useless.) When a friend is smiling (S^D), the response of asking a favor is more likely to be followed by reinforcement than when he is frowning and hurrying (S^Δ).

Much behavior consists of a *chain* of responses. The S^D for a response is often a response-produced cue. One response may produce, or be, the stimulus for the next. Reading the last sentence on a page is a response which is also the S^D for turning the page, which in turn is the S^D for

LEARNING THEORY AND BEHAVIOR THERAPY

continuing to read. Each response in a chain is a cue for another response. Through reinforcement and practice, separate response units are grouped into larger units, and the whole chain of behavior proceeds smoothly and often without thought.

Classical, Instrumental, or Both?

Whether or not there are different processes of learning underlying the effectiveness of classical and instrumental conditioning in modifying responses is a controversial issue beyond our current needs or purposes. In spite of the usually helpful distinctions between procedures, a purely instrumental or classical conditioning situation is logically impossible (Kimble, 1961). Because reinforcement for a response occurs in some situation, the situational cues become conditioned stimuli associated with the reinforcing stimulus. Similarly, a CR may have instrumental consequences which affect the reinforcing value of the stimulus that follows. For example, Albert's acquired fear response to the white rat, discussed above, could function as an instrumental response to scare the rat away, or might eventually lead Albert to avoid all situations in which the rat might appear. Although either the instrumental or the classical features of a situation are often prominent, it is important to remember the effects of both kinds of conditioning and to look for both the instrumental and classical conditioning features in an analysis of complex behavior.

Combinations

Secondary and generalized reinforcers. The intimacy of the operation of the contiguity principle and the law of effect is easily seen in complex chained behavior, discussed above. The effectiveness of a reinforcer spreads backwards to responses and stimuli which have preceded it, so that discriminative stimuli acquire *secondary reinforcing* properties. Thus, poker chips may become secondary reinforcers for chimpanzees by association of the chips with food (classical conditioning), and chimps will work (an instrumental response) at a task for which the chip is the reward (Wolfe, 1936; Cowles, 1937). Consider, for example, a six-year-old chimp named Moos (Keller, 1954).

Moos first observed the experimenter insert a white poker chip into the slot of a vending machine and receive a grape. Moos himself quickly performed this feat and then learned (with only ten errors out of eighty choices) to select a white chip (S^D) rather than a brass chip (S^Δ) which did not work in the vending machine. He also learned to operate an apparatus (lifting a lever) in order to obtain the white chip. The chip was an S^D for the response of operating the vending machine *and* was the secondary reinforcer for the lever pushing.

The first response established (using the vending machine) is the one that produces the reinforcer (grape). Because of the backward spread of the effect of reinforcement, the S^D comes to reinforce the response

$S^\triangle$ brass chip

R ——————S^D white chip——————R————S_+ grape

Work to get S^D Put chip in vending machine

which produced it. The first response in the chain may be far removed in time, and in apparent relevance, from the primary reinforcer at the end of the chain; yet it is controlled by this.

Complex human behaviors are behavior chains developed from primary reinforcers and these come to be heavily dependent upon *generalized reinforcers*. Generalized reinforcers are built up from associations with more than one kind of primary reinforcement and are capable of reinforcing a variety of responses whose initial dependence on the primary reinforcement is not always clear. Money, attention, approval, affection, or even the submission or dominance of another person are examples. Favorable report cards, diplomas, trophies, and our name in the newspaper may acquire reinforcing value and control our behavior. "They are usually not the immediate occasions for primary reinforcement, but they lead us down the road thereto!" (Keller, 1954, p. 30).

Fear reduction. The combination of contiguity and effect principles in *escaping* rather than approaching an acquired reinforcer is shown in a famous experiment by Neal Miller (1951). Rats were put in a white compartment of an experimental cage and shocked through the floor; they quickly learned to run to the non-electrified black compartment of the cage when the dividing door was raised. After ten trials, Miller stopped giving shock. The rats continued to run to the black compartment. By the contiguity principle, the cues (CS) in the white box acquired the ability to elicit fear (CR). The fear motivated the acquisition of new responses. The rats learned to turn a wheel and later to press a bar to lower the door to the safe box. Reduction of the acquired fear instrumentally reinforced the responses necessary for escape.

UCS-shock ——— CR fear   R escape CS ———S_+ fear reduction

CS-white

The rats' instrumental escape might be called defensive behavior which originally was an adaptive way of escaping externally induced pain. However, the strength of the "defensive" response prevented them from "reality-testing" to see if the environmental threat was still present. Thus, they used energy in unnecessary escape behaviors which would appear very irrational and maladaptive if their reinforcement history were not known. Doubtless, many human habits of thinking and acting have similar bases.

In Miller's experiment, the rats acquired the escape response while the realistic threat was still present. Additional work showed that the escape response may be acquired *after* the objective danger is removed (Brown

& Jacobs, 1949). Shock and a tone-light CS were paired while the experimental rats were kept in one end of a box; control rats had only the CS. When the CS was presented *alone* and a door raised to allow entry to the other end of the box, the experimental animals ran much more quickly to the other end than did the control animals (Figure 5–7).

Generalizing to human experiences, this experiment suggests that acquired fear may motivate the development of defensive maneuvers when there is no current realistic basis for the fear. The child may have to endure mother's spanking (and probably his fear of loss of love) while she is scolding him; later he may develop defenses to escape the anxiety elicited by mother's criticism (CS) or, by generalization, any hint of criticism from a sweetheart.

Similarities

Conditioning phenomena. Not only do classical and instrumental conditioning both play a part in complex behaviors, but they also share many phenomena in common. In both procedures, a critical stimulus is required; the amount of the stimulus and number of presentations affects response strength; and withholding the UCS or reinforcing stimulus can produce extinction. However, even after extinction procedures, the response is not eliminated, as shown by spontaneous recovery and relearning. In both paradigms, formerly neutral stimuli acquire secondary properties by association with other stimuli, and stimulus generalization occurs.

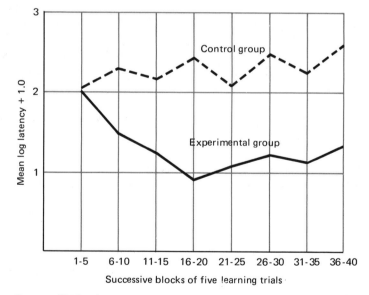

FIGURE 5–7

Fear as Motivation.

Source: Brown, J. S., & Jacobs, A. The role of fear in the motivation and acquisition of responses. *Journal of Experimental Psychology,* 1949, 39, 747–759.

FIGURE
5–8

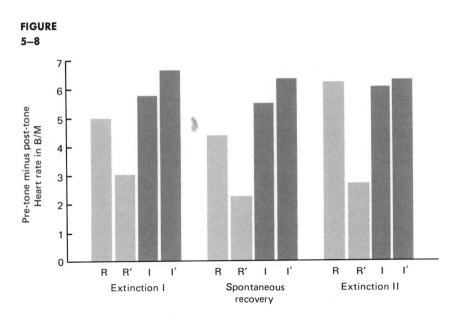

Partial Reinforcement in Classical Conditioning.

Resistance to extinction of regularly and irregularly reinforced groups. Response strength of the first five trials (labeled R or I) is compared with response strength of the last five trials (R' or I') for the indicated phases.

Source: Notterman, J. M., Schoenfeld, W. N., & Bersh, P. J. Partial reinforcement and conditioned heart rate response in human subjects, *Science,* 1952, 115, 77–79.

Although they are not often recognized (Kimble, 1961), partial reinforcement effects occur with classical conditioning as well as with instrumental conditioning (Notterman, Schoenfeld, & Bersh, 1952). Figure 5–8 illustrates an experiment in which heart rate conditioning was compared for subjects on a partial reinforcement schedule and those on a continuous one. There were six phases of the experiment: determination of change in basal heart rate in response to a CS-tone, conditioning, extinction I, spontaneous recovery, reconditioning, and extinction II; during non-conditioning phases, the tone was presented alone. One group had five conditioning trials on which a shock (UCS) was paired with the CS-tone; seven CS-only trials were given for the intermittent reinforcement subjects. Another group had the same number of tone-shock combinations, but no tone-only trials during the conditioning phases. Heart rate changes *were* conditioned on the intermittent schedule, and the changes were more resistant to extinction than on a regular schedule.

Responses. Classical and instrumental conditioning have traditionally been said to be distinguished on the basis of the kinds of responses they can modify and control (Kimble, 1961; Rescorola & Solomon, 1967). Classical conditioning procedures have been thought appropriate for involun-

FIGURE
5–9

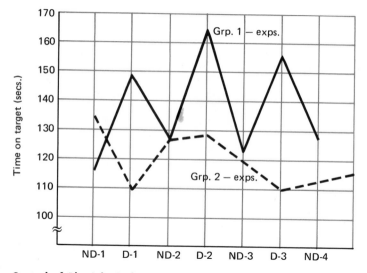

Control of Physiological Responses.

Total time in six-beat target area of groups receiving feedback.

ND: No display of heart rate.
 D: Display of heart rate.
Group 1 subjects were told the display was of heart rate, while Group 2 subjects were not told the display was of heart rate.

Source: Lang, P. J., Sroufe, L. A., & Hastings, J. E. Effects of feedback and instructional set on the control of cardiac-rate variability. *Journal of Experimental Psychology,* 1967, 75, 425–431.

tary responses of which the organism has no awareness; these are generally responses of the autonomic nervous system involved in emotional behavior (Chapter 14). They do not operate on the environment; they simply respond to it. In contrast, instrumental procedures have been considered applicable only to voluntary motor responses with which the organism can "knowingly" and voluntarily act upon the environment; they cannot modify the unconscious, involuntary responses. However, this distinction has become clouded. Physiological responses (galvanic skin response, heart rate, brain waves) have been instrumentally controlled, and there is some indication that they may be voluntarily controlled (Kimmel, 1967; Donelson, 1966; Kamiaya, 1972). Although the role of awareness of the response is not yet clear in either case, it seems that feedback providing information about the response does facilitate the control.

Subjects who were told to try to keep their physiological responses constant, particularly their heart rate, were more successful when they had an external display of their heart rate than when they did not (Lang, Sroufe, & Hastings, 1967). Control subjects were also told to try to keep their heart rate constant and watched a display of the rate. However, they were not told that the meter was displaying their heart rate. During the display periods, their variability was not as low (measured by the time their heart rate was within six beats per minute of their average rate) as that of the subjects who knew they were watching their own heart rate on the meter (Figure 5–9).

In either the instrumental or voluntary control studies, it is possible that the change of autonomic responses was mediated by changes in voluntarily controlled skeletal-muscular responses: Muscular tension, such as clenching the fist, can increase heart rate. However, responses can be instrumentally controlled when skeletal mediation is virtually impossible. This is shown by studies with animals who have been given curare, a drug which paralyzes muscles.

Rats so completely curarized that they had to be kept alive by artificial respiration learned to speed up or slow down their heart rate when shock avoidance or termination was contingent upon the heart rate change (DiCara & Miller, 1968). The acquired visceral responses of heart rate change were at least partially under the control of discriminative stimuli. The changes were greatest for trials (five seconds) on which there was a signal (tone or light) that shock would come if heart rate did not change, and least with a signal (light or tone) of a safe trial, on which no shock was impending, regardless of heart rate (Figure 5–10). Changes on blank trials (five seconds not preceded by any signal) were intermediate. Further, heart rate changes acquired under curare can be re-

FIGURE 5–10

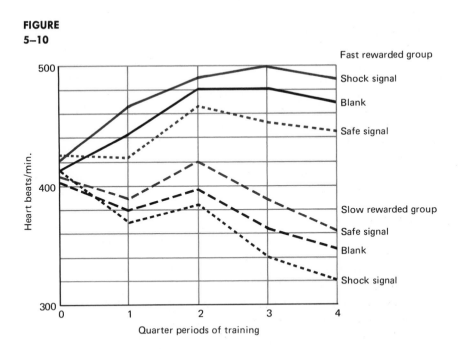

Heart Rate Changes during Avoidance Training.

Source: DiCara, L. V., & Miller, N. E. Changes in heart rate instrumentally learned by curarized rats as avoidance response. *Journal of Comparative and Physiological Psychology*, 1968, 65, 8–12.

tained over three months and transfer to noncurarized states (DiCara & Miller, 1968; DiCara & Weiss, 1969).

Such work has many immediate practical implications for the treatment of psychosomatic disorders, in which physical malfunctioning has a psychological rather than a physical origin. The susceptibility of glandular and visceral responses to instrumental conditioning procedures opens up the possibility that psychosomatic symptoms may be learned as escape or avoidance procedures and may be altered by specific reinforcement of changes in a helpful direction (Miller & Weiss, 1969).

Reinforcers

Tension Reduction. Thus far we have spoken rather easily of reinforcers as those kinds of events which increase response strength. What is the nature of the events? Many learning psychologists have long maintained that reinforcement is essentially a matter of what Freud called tension reduction or instinctual gratification (Hilgard, 1956). While they are likely to call it drive reduction, they have in mind the same process Freud was considering, namely, satisfaction of physiological needs. Most primary reinforcers are said to be those which reduce homeostatic needs such as hunger, thirst, and pain-avoidance, or they reduce sex drive or any strong stimulus (Miller, 1951). In other words, they have innate reinforcing properties. Consequently, much of the research on reinforcers has focused on these needs and has employed animals, whose needs are easier to manipulate than are those of humans. All other reinforcers are traditionally said to be secondary reinforcers which derive their reinforcing value from primary reinforcers. However, the fact that such need reduction is reinforcing does not prove that *all* reinforcers reduce needs as we now conceive them. In fact, we have probably only begun to discover innate reinforcers, so little do we know about the biology of the human being.

First, the very assumption that tension reduction is a necessarily satisfying state of affairs is questionable. This is dramatically shown in *sensory deprivation* experiments in which stimulation, and therefore tension, is minimal. College males were offered $20 for every day they would spend in a soundproof room, on a foam rubber bed, wearing translucent goggles, gloves, cardboard cuffs around their arms, and resting their head on a U-shaped pillow (Bexton, Heron, & Scott, 1954). They merely had to remain for five days to earn $100. Such a state of low stimulation (and the promise of $100) should have been pleasing. However, few subjects could stay more than two or three days. While in isolation they found it difficult to sleep or think, they had hallucinations and became panicked, and they did poorly on intelligence tests. After leaving the room, they were disoriented, fatigued, and experienced feelings of nausea for up to twenty-four hours.

Second, the tension reduction value of some events demonstrated to be reinforcing is hard to detect. Electrical stimulation of certain parts of the brain has been found to be reinforcing, and saccharine, which has no nutritive value, has also been used for reinforcement (Sheffield & Roby, 1950; see also Chapter 10).

Third, some events which *increase* tension are reinforcing, even though tension reduction would also be reinforcing. Sexually inexperienced male rats ran increasingly faster down a runway to receptive female rats, although copulation is interrupted before ejaculation. The sexual activities are reinforcing although they are associated with tension increase without reduction by ejaculation and although the activities have not previously been associated with ejaculation (Sheffield, Wulff, & Backer, 1951).

Both humans and other animals seek out experiences which increase rather than decrease tension. They find playing, manipulating things, exploring new areas, and seeing new sights to be reinforcing (Hunt, 1965; Fiske & Maddi, 1961; Berlyne, 1960). Rats learn to distinguish between white and black arms of a T-maze for the reward of a chance to explore a more interesting maze. They will leave their comfortable nests and cross an electrified grid to get to a maze filled with novel objects (Nissen, 1930). Humans prefer to look at novel, complex figures rather than at familiar or simple ones (Berlyne, 1960). Monkeys work for hours to unscramble mechanical puzzles without any apparent reinforcer other than the activity itself (Harlow, 1950). Monkeys in an enclosed box (a Butler-box) learned to discriminate between panels of different colors when the only reward was that the panel of the "correct" color opened so that they could see into another room for thirty seconds (Butler, 1953).

Exploratory, manipulatory, and curiosity motives do not appear to be derived from association with primary reinforcers that reduce primary drives as typically conceived. They are called *intrinsically motivated* behaviors in that the reinforcement is intrinsic to the activity. With drive reduction behaviors, reinforcement is *extrinsic* to the activity; there is an external object involved. Intrinsically motivated activities may bring an extrinsic reward, but that reward is not necessary to instigate or maintain the behavior. The behaviors themselves are satisfying, or reinforcing, and do not serve needs typically considered homeostatic needs.

However, it may well be that these behaviors are necessary homeostatic functions. It has been suggested that the nervous system "needs" to process information (Hunt, 1965) or, more generally, that a moderate amount of stimulation is required for normal development and functioning of the brain and central nervous system (Lindsley, 1951; Hebb, 1955). Stimulation is required for development and thereby for adjustment to the environment. The brain, like the stomach, may have needs of its own. With such a view, it is no longer necessary to struggle to see the intrinsic behaviors as derivatives of desires for food, drink, or sex, as did Freud and many learning theorists. It becomes more possible to conceive of the basis for needs such as growth and knowledge which the fulfillment theorists postulate (Chapter 6); man the biological organism can also be—and must be—man the inquirer, the explorer, the knower.

Punishment. Reinforcers are not all positive events which are approached by the subject. A punishment is a noxious stimulus which the subject would presumably escape or avoid if given a choice (Solomon, 1964). Punishment affects response strength by decreasing the tendency to respond, while positive reinforcement increases the tendency to respond. Punishment teaches the subject what not to do. However, punishment does not eliminate the response; it only *suppresses* the response. "Neither punishment, nor any other technique, serves to eliminate a response after it has been established" (Church, 1969, p. 111). Mild stimuli may have no effect at all; fairly unpleasant stimuli may temporarily reduce response rate, but the response returns when punishment is omitted. If the punishment is intense enough to affect the behavior so that for all practical purposes the response is "gone," the punishment can result in undesirable emotional side effects by inducing anxiety and perhaps inhibiting too many behaviors.

Children whose parents were strict, severe disciplinarians were found to be better behaved than were those with less punitive parents, but they were also less curious, sociable, and spontaneous (Baldwin, 1948). Negative emotional effects resulting from intense punishment at early ages are consistent with Freudian theory. Experimental inducement of neurosis in animals shows the effectiveness of severe punishment in producing neurotic behaviors in cats, dogs, monkeys, and rats (Masserman, 1943; Gantt, 1944; Brady, 1958; Maier, 1949; Wolpe, 1952).

However, punishment need not be intense to be effective—and may not necessarily lead to neurosis if it is severe (Solomon, 1964). Punishment is an effective training technique if a new, desirable behavior occurs and is rewarded during the time of temporary suppression of the undesirable behavior. Rats were trained to take one route in a maze with food at the end, and then were given mild shock for taking that route (Whiting & Mowrer, 1943). They quickly learned to follow a new route and never used the old one again. Dogs swatted with a newspaper for urinating inside the house will cause no problems if they are allowed to develop the response of using the outdoors. One would expect that a mild scolding from a teacher for a poor term paper might be effective if it is accompanied by suggestions on how to do better.

Under some conditions, punishment can be used to increase response probability (Brown, 1969; Church, 1969). The punishment can operate as a secondary reinforcer if it is presented along with *positive* reinforcement during training (Holz & Azrin, 1961).

It is possible to become accustomed to punishment (Church, 1969). Prior exposure to at first short-term or mild punishment, which has gradually increased in length or intensity, reduces the effectiveness of later long-duration punishment in suppressing behavior. For example, after rats were trained to press a lever for food, some of them received occasional shock, the duration of which increased from .15 seconds to 1.0 seconds over eight punishment sessions (Church, 1969). Then all rats received shocks lasting 3.0 seconds. Those rats with the previous experience with shock were less affected by the long shock than were those without the experience (Figure 5–11).

Parents who find themselves using punishment to no avail may have to attribute this to their own carelessness as reinforcing agents. If in the early stages of the child's development of the response (whether baby talk or painting the dog with shaving cream), they combined mild punishment with appreciation of "cuteness," they will find that when they get tired of the cuteness, their punishment, even if stronger, will be to no avail. Or if they progress from mild annoyance and punishment to sterner disciplines, they are similarly ineffective. Masochism in adults may well have such roots. Punishment has acquired positive value, has become neutral, or has become more or less a way of life.

The neurotic's vicious circle (Horney, Chapter 4) is a case of self-punitive behavior (Mowrer, 1947). Remember that neurotic behavior leads one into problems which in turn intensify the neurotic behavior. Rats trained to escape shock by running to a nonelectrified region at the other end of a straight alley continued to run for many trials after the shock was no longer present at their starting point, but was still present in the mid-section of the maze they had to cross (Brown, 1969).

Mowrer's (1947) interpretation of this vicious circle is still the most acceptable explanation (Brown, 1969). The rat runs because he is afraid,

FIGURE 5–11

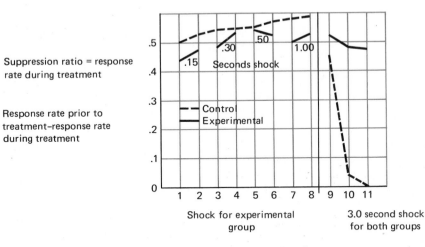

Suppression ratio = response rate during treatment

Response rate prior to treatment–response rate during treatment

Shock for experimental group

3.0 second shock for both groups

Punishment session

Effects of Prior Exposure to Punishment.
Mean suppression ratio of subjects with punishment of gradually increasing duration (Experimental) or no prior exposure to shock (Control). Both groups received the same punishment condition on Sessions 9 through 11.

Source: Church, R. M. Response suppression. In B. A. Campbell & R. M. Church (Eds.), *Punishment and aversive behavior.* New York: Appleton-Century-Crofts, 1969. Pp. 111–156.

and he is afraid because he is punished when he runs. Because of pairing of the shock and environmental cues during training, fear is elicited by the environmental cues and motivates running to a safe place. The running is reinforced by the fear reduction occurring in the safe goal box. Encountering shock in the runway (although it is on the way from one safe place to another) strengthens the fear-arousing properties of the whole situation. The human in such a situation might say, "See, I was right; there is shock in here to be afraid of."

APPLICATIONS AND ISSUES

Conflict

Miller and Dollard (1941, 1950; Miller, 1944) have written extensive translations of Freudian theory into learning theory terms and principles. According to these lay analysts, personality dynamics is largely a matter of the relative strengths of responses in hierarchies of responses to particular stimuli and stimuli similar to them. Personality change is thus a matter of manipulating response strengths.

This approach has been criticized for adding little to psychoanalytic theory while robbing the theory of its richness (Rappaport, 1953). However, many theorists consider the treatment effective in its definition, through the use of learning theory terminology and principles, of an underlying logic of psychoanalytic theory. As an immediate example of their thinking, we shall consider Miller and Dollard's approach to displacement and conflict, an approach which has shown itself amenable to a wide variety of specific applications.

Displacement. Displacement (substituting one response or target stimulus for another) may occur because action toward the original object is prevented by absence of the object or by conflict; the explanation of the second case is an extension from that of the first. Both cases are understood by use of the key concept of stimulus similarity: Response strength generalizes from the original stimulus to similar stimuli.

In order to study displacement of aggression, Miller (1948) developed aggression in rats by making the offset of a shock (through the floor of their cage) contingent upon one of two rats hitting the other. Strength of the aggressive response was then measured by the frequency of hitting without any further use of shock. Even when shock was discontinued, the rats continued to hit each other, and they "preferred" hitting each other when another object, a doll, was present. Although response strength toward the original object was stronger than toward other objects, the rats did tend to strike a doll placed in the cage when there was no other rat present (Figure 5–12). When a rat trained in this form of aggression was in the cage without either a rat or a doll, he struck the walls of the cage. Offhand, a doll does not seem particularly like a rat,

FIGURE
5–12

Displacement of Aggression.
When the two rats were placed in the apparatus along with the doll, they struck at each other as soon as the electric shock was turned on; when placed into the apparatus one at a time, they struck at the doll.

Source: Miller, N. E. Theory and experiment relating psychoanalytic displacement of stimulus-response generalization. *Journal of Abnormal and Social Psychology*, 1948, 43, 155–178.

nor a wall like a doll, but the doll, like the rat, is a standing object in the cage, and the wall is a "thing" present as well as part of the stimulus situation in which the aggressive response was practiced. Displacement of aggression is not limited to the behavior of animals. For instance, a man who has just lost a business deal may speak angrily to his secretary. A child who is angry with his mother may kick a toy or hit a playmate.

Displacement of aggression is the mechanism that has been suggested for the *scapegoat theory of prejudice*. During an experiment concerning minority groups, the frustration suffered by young boys because of an annoying experimenter (who quickly left the scene!) affected their initially positive attitudes toward Mexicans and Japanese (Miller & Bugelski, 1948). The minority groups, though symbolically presented in the experimental situation, were similar enough to elicit a detectable amount of undeserved aggression; in other words, they were scapegoats.

Although aggression is a frequent target for analysis (by Freudians and learning theorists), other behaviors may be displaced as well. Darlington and Macker (1955) found displacement of altruistic behavior resulting from guilt about not having gone to the aid of a deserving person in need of help. In what was described as an experiment in co-operation (each subject could add extra points to the other subject's psychology grade by doing well on the experimental tasks), the subject was made to think that she had earned only two points for the other subject (a male stooge who had previously described his career and the health of his pregnant wife as dependent on a few extra points in psychology). Thus, experimental subjects were led to experience guilt because they had not helped another, deserving person. Subjects in a control group thought the male stooge did not need the extra points anyway. After the experiment, the experimental (guilty) subjects showed displaced altruism by being more willing to donate blood to the local blood bank than were the control (not guilty) subjects.

Conflict and displacement. Displacement may also occur when there is conflict about the behavior. And conflict is in its own right a pervasive phenomenon. How many activities or people do you judge in only a positive or only a negative way? Probably few. It is generally the case that an avoidance tendency conflicts with an approach tendency. We want to do something with respect to a person or object, but there is reason to inhibit the behavior. The avoidance gradient may be attributed to current anxiety due to prior punishment for the behavior, or to the fear of retribution from a powerful other person. Often, the approach tendency is somewhat akin to the id tendencies of Freudian theory, and the avoidance tendency reflects ego or superego restraints or inhibitory anxiety about the desire for the approach behavior. Both the approach and avoidance tendencies generalize.

Miller assumes that the avoidance gradient is steeper than the approach gradient; the strength of the avoidance response decreases more quickly with decreases in stimulus similarity than does that of the approach response (Figure 5-13). (Although this assumption leads to useful and verified predictions, the rationale is not clear.) Conflict is greatest when two competing response tendencies are at exactly equal strength, and it decreases as the difference between the response tendencies increases. The more similar objects are to the original one, the greater the drive reduction and the more likely and more "satisfying" is displacement to those objects. However, the inhibitory tendency also elicited by similar stimuli is relatively high for highly similar objects and reduces the likelihood of approaching them. The point of *most likely displacement* is the point at which the net differences between the approach and avoidance gradients is greatest. Miller's predictions agree with those of Freud:

FIGURE

5–13

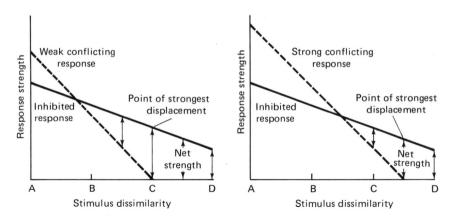

Point of Displacement.

It can be seen that displaced responses can occur and that the strongest displaced response will be expected at an intermediate point: C in the diagram on the left. Increasing the strength of the conflicting response weakens the strongest displaced response and causes it to be elicited by less similar stimuli, those between C and D in the diagram to the right. Although straight lines were used in order to simplify these diagrams, the deductions are not dependent upon the assumption of linearity.

Source: Miller, N. E. Theory and experiment relating psychoanalytic displacement to stimulus-response generalization. *Journal of Abnormal and Social Psychology,* 1948, 43, 155–178.

Displacement due to conflict is most likely to be directed toward an object of intermediate similarity to the original object rather than one of very high or very low similarity.

The height of the gradients varies with response strength and the associated drive. Although the avoidance gradient is steeper than the approach gradient, it may be higher at all points of similarity, or lower at all points.

Varieties of conflict. Conflict analysis is appropriate for almost all of the situations we are likely to have in mind when we say, "I'm in conflict about . . ." or, "I don't know what to do." The conflicts discussed so far are *approach-avoidance* conflicts. The subject has reason, or drive, to engage in a behavior, as well as a tendency to be anxious about it or to avoid it. The conflict is difficult to resolve because no matter what the individual does, he is pulled to the point of maximum conflict (Brown, 1957). As he moves toward the desirable goal, he hits the conflict point. If he manages further movement toward the goal, anxiety increases and causes retreat back to the conflict point. If he moves away from the goal, the increased *net* difference between the approach and avoidance tendency causes him to move back to the conflict point. Because of its self-balancing nature, such a conflict cannot be resolved unless the heights of the gradients are markedly changed.

With an *avoidance-avoidance* conflict, the person is caught between two unpleasant alternatives. To move away from one undesirable alternative, he must move toward another: A person may have a severe toothache, but at the same time he may have an overwhelming fear of going to the dentist. Avoidance-avoidance conflicts are particularly difficult to resolve. Every movement in one direction arouses anxiety and sends the person back to the conflict point. He is caught in the middle, and may "freeze" at that point, becoming unable to move, physically or psychologically; or he may fall victim to conflict-induced anxiety.

An individual who is caught in an *approach-approach* conflict wants to possess two mutually exclusive alternatives. This type of conflict tends to be self-resolving and is not likely to be disturbing. As movement in one direction begins, the appeal of the alternative increases and conflict decreases. Even when one is precisely between the two choices, a slight change in stimulus conditions or momentary personal dispositions will start movement toward one or the other of the goals. A young man's conflict about calling two equally desirable girls for a date on the same night may be broken because the phone number of one is easily available, or because one answers the phone when the other does not.

If we think carefully about these kinds of conflicts we can see that we will often find ourselves in situations which are actually *double approach-avoidance* conflicts because many of our choices are between two or more acts or objects which both have obvious desirable and undesirable features. To approach one is to gain its disadvantages as well as its advantages and at the same time to avoid the advantages as well as the disadvantages of the alternative. A man's commitment to one woman means that he will have to endure her faults as well as profit from her desirable features while missing the charm as well as escaping the faults of her rival. Such conflicts are the most difficult to resolve, perhaps because the avoidance-avoidance features become so dominant (Miller, 1944), or perhaps because there are so many factors to weigh.

The problem of personality change entails an analysis of the dimensions of the conflict and manipulation of the response hierarchies to increase the likelihood of desirable behaviors which were formerly inhibited or to increase the likelihood of the inhibition of undesirable behaviors which were formerly performed.

Thoughts and verbalizations. Dollard and Miller (1950) draw extensively on their basic conflict theory in explaining covert responses (thoughts, feelings) as well as overt responses. Resistance in free association may be thought of as hitting the conflict point when approaching symbolic material which represents threat. Repression is a not-thinking response which reduces or helps one avoid anxiety. One learns to not-think about an object or event that elicits anxiety and by generalization, to avoid thinking of related material. If anxiety about having sexual thoughts about one's mother is intense enough (the avoidance gradient very high), the repression to avoid anxiety may generalize to other females as well.

Murray (1954, 1962; Auld & Murray, 1955) used conflict theory in analyzing the verbal content of psychotherapy sessions. In one study, he content-analyzed statements made by a twenty-four-year-old male patient by classifying them as to whether they were hostile or defensive statements, and whether they were directed to his mother, his aunt, or other people. In the permissiveness of the therapy situation, the patient became able to "let loose" and express his feelings: The total number of defensive statements decreased and the number of hostile statements increased. However, as predicted by psychoanalytic theory, the expression of hostility toward the mother increasingly elicited anxiety and therefore defense against the hostile thoughts. In approaching full expression of his feelings about her, the patient hit the conflict point and blocked further expressions of feelings about her. Hostility for the mother was displaced to an aunt; as this, too, began to raise anxiety and defense, hostility was displaced even further, to other people (Figure 5–14).

Thus, the Miller and Dollard approach represents one way of analyzing personality dynamics and change in S-R terminology. The recent behavior therapy movement has extended the realm of the learning psychologist

FIGURE 5–14

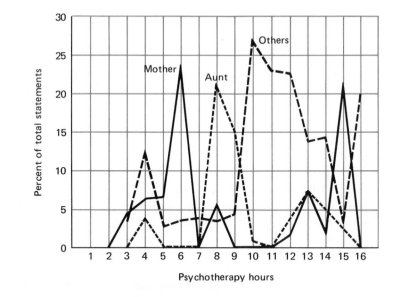

Analysis of Hostility Statements.
Hostility statements referring to mother, aunt, and others—general throughout therapy.

Source: Murray, E. J. A case study in a behavioral analysis of psychotherapy. Journal of Abnormal and Social Psychology, 1954, 49, 305–310.

more dramatically into personality psychology, with a radical departure from the conventional thinking of personality theorists as epitomized in Freudian theory.

BEHAVIOR THERAPY

From the laboratory of the learning psychologist with his rats and pigeons have come innovative and effective techniques of therapy. The development of normal (e.g., cooperation, smiling) and abnormal (e.g., phobic) habits can be explained in terms of learning theory; by the application of learning theory they can be modified. Behavior therapists generally assume, contrary to Freud, that there is no need to delve into underlying causes and no need to ponder at length about the unconscious symbolic significance of symptoms (Eysenck, 1959). *The problem is the symptom itself; the task is to remove the symptom.* Freud's contention, which is still adhered to by conventional psychotherapists, was that removal of the symptom without attention to the cause of the symptom would result in *symptom substitution,* the appearance of another symptom caused by the untreated problem. Behavior therapists maintain that this is not so, that it is useless to postulate or worry about hidden causes, to analyze dreams, to induce transference, to plummet into past experiences for hints of what might be going on in the unconscious, or to clarify feelings in order to enable free growth.

Systematic Desensitization

Joseph Wolpe (1958) brought to current attention a form of behavior therapy called systematic desensitization. When his initial faith in Freud became seriously shaken, he turned first to Pavlov, then to Hull, and finally to studies of experimental neurosis which suggested to him a method of therapy based on learning theory, and a serious alternative to conventional psychotherapies.

After depriving cats of food for twenty hours, Wolpe (1952) put them into an experimental cage in which they were alerted to the presence of food by the sound of a buzzer and then were shocked before they could reach the food. The cats quickly developed neurotic behavior—restlessness, clawing, butting the roof of the cage with their heads—and refused to eat in the cage, even after three days of starvation. These responses generalized to other rooms in the laboratory, and the animals exhibited their neurotic behavior and refused to eat in any area that was similar to the experimental room in terms of light, noise, and furnishings.

When the cats were confined to their cage for several hours each day without shock, their neurotic reactions did not diminish. Because of this, Wolpe reasoned that anxiety and eating are reciprocally inhibitory: The occurrence of one inhibits the occurrence of the other. Finding a room

(Room D) in the laboratory that was somewhat dissimilar to the experimental room (Room A), Wolpe was able to get his cats to eat—Room D elicited little anxiety and, therefore, eating was possible.

After strengthening the eating response in Room D, Wolpe gradually moved the cats to Room C. He was able to do this because (1) the eating response generalized to other rooms and (2) the inhibition of anxiety that occurred in Room D also generalized to other rooms. As a result of these two processes, the cats, after having eaten for a while in Room D, became able to eat in Room C. The experience in Room D had weakened the anxiety elicited by Room C and strengthened the tendency to eat in Room C so that eating there was now possible. Similarly, the cats became able to eat in Room B, and finally in Room A—the cats were cured. They were *systematically desensitized* to the anxiety stimuli. If Wolpe had been too eager to undo the neurosis he caused and had jumped immediately from Room D to A, the change would not have been accomplished. The anxiety-evoking stimuli must be *gradually* introduced so that the response incompatible with anxiety *always* has greater strength than the anxiety response.

On the basis of his observations, Wolpe formulated the *principle of reciprocal inhibition:* If a response antagonistic to anxiety can be made to occur in the presence of anxiety-evoking stimuli so that it is accompanied by a complete or partial suppression of the anxiety responses, the bond between these stimuli and the anxiety responses will be weakened. Notice that the process is not simply one of extinction, and remember that extinction is not particularly effective in eliminating emotional responses. Systematic desensitization demands building up a positive response to replace the negative one of anxiety.

Desensitization in humans. Mary Cover Jones (1924) managed to cure rat phobia in Peter (a patient similar to a slightly older Albert) by the same kind of process Wolpe later systematized into a formal therapy technique; by bringing a rat progressively closer to Peter while he was eating, Jones was able to cure his phobia. However, in working with humans, therapists are more likely to use anxiety-inhibiting responses such as assertion, sex, or, especially, relaxation (instead of hunger) in order to effect a "cure." Since most people do not really know how to relax, the patient is given relaxation training, often with the aid of hypnosis. When he can relax, he begins working through his *anxiety hierarchy*, analogous to the cats' progressing from Room D to Room A. The patient himself constructs a list of thoughts, situations, and feelings that make him anxious, ordering the list from the least bothersome to the most bothersome. Someone intensely afraid of fire might begin with the apparently simple situation of seeing a book of matches on a table, or perhaps even walking by a firehouse. Seeing a fireplace without a protective screen might be an intermediate item on the list, and thinking of a burning house the most anxiety-producing item on the list. A snake phobic's hierarchy might begin with seeing wires coiled on the floor or reading the word snake, and progress up to stepping on a snake in the woods.

While in a relaxed state, the patient imagines the lowest item on his hierarchy. If he feels the slightest twinge of anxiety, he raises his hand and is told by the therapist to stop thinking and relax. The relaxation response must remain dominant. As he becomes able to think of the lowest item without any anxiety, he moves up to the next item. Just as hunger remained dominant over anxiety in Wolpe's cats as they progressed through the rooms, in the human patient relaxation must be dominant over anxiety as he moves through his hierarchy. Progressively, he comes to be able to think calmly about the most frightening item on his list. Relaxation replaces anxiety as the response given to the formerly anxiety-eliciting cues. Notice that the technique involves the subject's cognitive activities, such as imagining, thinking, feeling (Weitzman, 1968).

Effectiveness of desensitization. Wolpe (1958) reported that almost 90 percent of 210 neurotic patients he had seen over nine years of private practice were either apparently cured or much improved. The average number of interviews required was 31, with two-thirds of the patients having fewer than 40 sessions. Other practicing therapists report 86 percent of 408 patients on whom the techniques had been used were cured; 78 percent of all 408 patients were cured by behavior therapy (Lazarus, 1963). The overall cure rate for conventional psychotherapy, including psychoanalysis, is about two-thirds, which is the same as the rate of *spontaneous remission* of symptoms, the rate of cure without therapeutic intervention (Eysenck, 1961). Wolpe contends that the cures attained in other therapies, as well as spontaneous remissions, are due to the accidental occurrence of systematic desensitization procedures.

Laboratory evidence of desensitization. Findings from laboratory studies of the effectiveness of desensitization have been overwhelmingly positive (Paul, 1969; Marks & Gelder, 1968). In a pioneering experimental study of behavior therapy, Lang and Lazovik (1963) demonstrated effective treatment of snake phobics with relaxation training and desensitization. Subjects were college students who reported intense fear of snakes on a questionnaire and in an interview, and showed strong avoidance when actually confronted with a live, nonpoisonous snake. During the training procedure (five sessions of forty-five minutes), the experimental subjects constructed an anxiety hierarchy of twenty situations involving snakes and were trained in relaxation. Control subjects were not given relaxation or desensitization training but were tested for fear of snakes in the same ways as were the experimental subjects (Table 5–1). Subjective ratings of fear were reduced more for experimental subjects than for control subjects, and more experimental subjects held or touched a snake during the avoidance tests.

The experimental subjects who completed more than fifteen of the

TABLE 5–1 Number of Subjects Who Held or Touched the Snake during Avoidance Tests

Group	N	Test 1 *	Relaxation Training	Test 2	Desensitization	Test 3
Experimental						
E_1	8	1	yes	1	yes	5
E_2	5	no	yes	1	yes	2
Control						
C_1	5	0	no	0	no	0
C_2	6	no	no	1	no	2
$E_1 + E_2$	13			2		7
$C_1 + C_2$	11			1		2

* One experimental and one control group did not have the initial testing with the snake to enable the detection of any effect the initial test might have had on later avoidance tests, relaxation training, or desensitization. Both experimental groups but neither control group had relaxation training and desensitization.

SOURCE: Adapted from Lang, P. J., and Lazovik, A. D. Experimental desensitization of a phobia. *Journal of Abnormal and Social Psychology*, 1963, **66**, 519–525.

twenty items of their hierarchy had greater change in their ratings of fear than did those who completed fewer than fifteen items (Table 5–2). The gains of the experimental relative to the control subjects were maintained *or increased* at a six-month follow up. There was no evidence of symptom substitution as predicted by Freudians who insist that the underlying conflict must be uncovered.

Crucial variables. The effectiveness of the desensitization procedures seems due mainly to the patient's gradual exposure to the phobic object rather than to other features of the situation, such as learning to relax, having contact with and attention from a therapist, or becoming convinced that the phobic object is not really dangerous. Patients who had training in relaxation but not desensitization during interviews with a therapist did not improve, while those given desensitization did (Lang, Lazovik, & Reynolds, 1965). Subjects afraid of public speaking did not improve if they were given short-term (five hours) conventional therapy or had no contact with a therapist, but did improve with systematic desensitization (Paul, 1966). Lang (1968; Lang, Melamed, & Hart, 1970) reports good results with subjects treated by a computer that presents subjects with relaxation instructions and takes them through the hierarchy (recorded on magnetic tape and automatically presented). In studies of students who feared snakes, Crowder and Thornton (1970) found that desensitization with a therapist was no more effective than with programmed fantasy, whereby subjects progressed by themselves

TABLE 5–2 Changes in the Fear Survey Schedule (FSS) following Desensitization Therapy for Subjects Who Completed More Than 15 Hierarchy Items, for Those Who Completed Less Than 15, and for the Mann-Whitney U Test

NUMBER OF HIERARCHY ITEMS SUCCESSFULLY COMPLETED	PRETHERAPY	POSTTHERAPY	DIFFERENCE	U
Fear survey schedule (FSS)				
More than 15 [a]	2.34	1.85	.49	4.5 *
Less than 15 [b]	3.21	3.20	.01	
FSS-subject's rating of snake fear				
More than 15 [a]	6.71	4.14	2.57	3.0 **
Less than 15 [b]	6.67	6.67	0.00	

[a] $N = 7$
[b] $N = 6$
* $p < .02$ (probability less than 2 out of 100 that difference due to chance)
** $p < .01$ (probability less than 1 out of 100 that difference due to chance)
FSS is a list of 50 phobias, each of which is rated by the subjects on a 7-point scale.
SOURCE: Lang, P. J., & Lazovik, A. D. Experimental desensitization of a phobia. *Journal of Abnormal and Social Psychology*, 1963, **66**, 519–525.

through their hierarchy items which were written on 3 × 5 cards. They also showed that desensitization is not due to convincing the subject that snakes are actually harmless; subjects who read about snakes (bibliotherapy) instead of having regular desensitization or programmed fantasy did not improve (Table 5–3).

Range of application. Wolpe's technique has been criticized as applicable only to relatively simple neurotic behaviors, particularly phobias; however, Wolpe (1968; Wolpe & Lazarus, 1968) contends that a behavioristic analysis of any kind of neurosis can establish clear-cut stimulus antecedents of all neurotic reactions and give the case a phobic-like appearance. For example, general anxiety neurosis is but a collection of specific phobias which, together with higher-order conditioning and generalization, result in the subject's being afraid of nearly everything he encounters. The neurosis is a simple one if there is only one set of maladaptive responses to one obvious family of stimuli; these take a median of 11.5 sessions for cure. In more complex neuroses, there are several families of stimuli involved so that longer time is needed for desensitization: Wolpe reports a median of 29 sessions for complex neuroses.

THEORETICAL ORIENTATIONS TO PERSONALITY

TABLE 5–3   Improvement in Snake Phobia in Three Conditions

	GAIN IN SNAKE APPROACH BEHAVIOR, AVERAGE	NUMBER SUBJECTS WHO TOUCHED SNAKE AFTER TREATMENT
Systematic Desensitization (N = 10)	3.5 feet	10
Programmed Fantasy (N = 10)	3.7 feet	8
Bibliotherapy (N = 9)	1.0 feet	2

For both measures, the Systematic Desensitization and Programmed Fantasy groups were significantly better than the Bibliotherapy group, but were not different from each other.

SOURCE: Adapted from Crowder, J. E., & Thornton, D. W. Effects of systematic desensitization, programmed fantasy, and bibliotherapy on reduction of fear. Paper presented at the 1969 Midwestern Psychological Association Convention, Chicago, Illinois.

Observation of Others

Another behavioristic technique involves simply having the subject watch others who do not have his problem (Bandura, 1969; Krasner, 1971). (More extensive consideration of observational learning phenomena is given in Chapter 18.) In spite of equivocal results with phobic children and neurotic cats in earlier years (Jones, 1924; Masserman, 1943), recent experiments with *vicarious extinction* of children's fears have had encouraging outcomes (Bandura, Grusec, & Menlove, 1967). Twenty-four boys and twenty-four girls, ranging from three to five years, were selected by the parents' rating of their children's fear of dogs, and by the children's performance in a sequence of tasks in which they were asked to make increasingly intimate interactions with a dog (from walking up to the playpen in which the dog was enclosed to climbing in the pen and staying there alone with the dog). Children in modeling conditions observed a peer model approach a cocker spaniel, progressing from making verbal responses and petting the dog on the first session to climbing in the playpen, petting, hugging, and feeding the dog in the last two sessions. Children in control groups did not see the model interacting with the dog.

After observation of a model's successful interaction with the dog, 67 percent of the children were able to be confined in the playpen with the dog while all observers were absent from the room; only 33 percent of children in control groups did so. When subjects were eliminated who had initially shown very weak avoidance of the dog, the difference between control and modeling groups was even more pronounced (55 percent versus 13 percent). Further, more children in the modeling conditions (42 percent) than in the control group (12 percent) stayed alone with a strange dog as well as the familiar dog.

In a similar study, the interactions of the model with the dogs were presented on *film* (Bandura & Menlove, 1968). Children who saw either one or several models dealing with a dog without fear showed greater approach to dogs than they had before seeing the filmed models. Those who had seen several models instead of only one became even bolder in their own approach to dogs a month later than they had been immediately after the exposure to the nonfearful model (Figure 5–15).

Operant Techniques

Skinnerian principles, as well as the classical conditioning principles of Hull and Pavlov, have been effectively applied to pathological problems (Krasner, 1971). For Skinner, the problem of therapy is simply one of changing the reinforcing environment so that adequate behaviors are

FIGURE 5–15

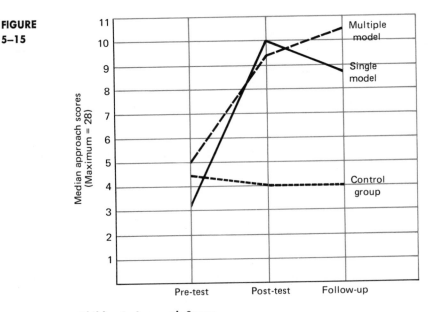

Children's Approach Scores.
Approach scores were determined from the child's performance on a graded series of 14 performance tasks in which he was required to engage in increasingly intimate interactions with a dog (e.g., petting, feeding). Two points were given for fully executing a task, spontaneously or willingly, and 1 point given for performing it minimally with hesitancy and reluctance (e.g., 2 points for playing with the dog while alone with her, 1 point for staying in the room alone with the dog but avoiding contact). Follow-up was one month after the posttreatment measurement.

Source: Bandura, A., & Menlove, F. L. Factors determining vicarious extinction of avoidance behavior through symbolic modeling. *Journal of Personality and Social Psychology*, 1968, 8, 99–108.

developed and maintained, and inadequate behaviors extinguished. A psychotic woman who wore excessive clothing (several dresses, sweaters, coats) was treated by making the reward of eating contingent upon increasing amounts of weight loss; the easiest way for her to weigh in at the proper poundage was to take off some of her clothes (Ayllon, 1963). Psychotics who had long required feeding by a nurse came to eat by themselves when they had to in order to get food. Patients typically tardy for meals became quite prompt when the time between the dinner bell and the closing of the dining room doors was progressively shortened. Schizophrenics who had not communicated for years carried on conversations and played ping-pong before meals when social behavior was required for admittance to the dining hall.

In some hospitals, *token economies* have been established in which patients are given tokens for adaptive behavior and may use the tokens to eat, to have a softer bed, or to gain ground privileges (Allyon & Azrin, 1968). They receive tokens for talking to each other, improving their personal appearance, cleaning up their rooms, and other pro-social behaviors: The rate of these behaviors increases as predicted from operant principles.

Techniques used with delinquents. Teenage male delinquents (an average of 1.4 years on probation) are likewise susceptible to operant techniques (Schwitzgebel, 1967). During the research interviews, for which the subjects were paid, one group received positive consequences (verbal praise, gifts, extra money) for making positive statements of concern about other people (e.g., "Joe is a good guy") and for prompt arrival at the interviews. Another group received positive reinforcement for socially desirable *nonverbal* behaviors (tact, politeness, honesty). Group I, the group that was reinforced for promptness, showed less tardiness than the other group (Figure 5–16) and a greater increase in the number of positive statements. When both groups took part in a game situation, the group that had previously been reinforced for desirable nonverbal behaviors had a greater increase in their reports of the number of good things they could think of to do.

Techniques used with autistic children. Lovaas (1967, 1968) has been engaged in a dramatic program of applying behavior therapy techniques to autistic children. One characteristic of some of these children is that they typically speak very little. Because one of the reasons for the lack of adequate speech is lack of imitation, development of an imitation response is a reasonable beginning for therapeutic change.

Mute children were given food when they imitated a sound made by an adult (Lovaas, Berberich, Perloff, & Schaeffer, 1966). The fact that the imitation was under reinforcement control was shown by a decline in imitation responses during test sessions in which food was given independent of imitative responses. After training, imitation itself had reinforcing properties. The imitation of Norwegian words (which the children

FIGURE
5–16

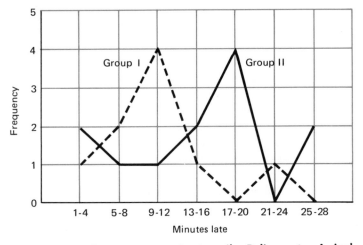

Reinforcement for Promptness in Juvenile Delinquents: Arrival Discrepancies.

Group I was reinforced for statements of concern about other people and for dependable and prompt arrival at work (N = 9). Group II was reinforced for socially desirable nonverbal behavior giving evidence of tact or employability; negative consequences for hostile (negative) statements about people.

Source: Schwitzgebel, R. L. Short-term operant conditioning of adolescent offenders on socially relevant variables. *Journal of Abnormal Psychology*, 1967, 72, 134–142.

could not pronounce at first) improved over trials in the absence of food reinforcement for imitation. The only reinforcement was for imitation of occasional English words interspersed among the Norwegian.

Thus, it appears that the reinforcement became intrinsic to the general response of imitation; consequently, the children should be able to acquire *new* behaviors on the basis of imitation. In the second phase of the verbal training program, children who had been taught to imitate speech, along with other autistic children who were echolalic (who parrot other people), were trained to speak appropriately by making reinforcement contingent upon *correct* descriptions of the environment ("This is a chair") and correct motor responses to verbal instructions ("Sit down") rather than imitation (mere repetition of "What is this?" "Sit down"). The children *learned to learn.* "There is no question that the training procedures we have employed can establish very complex, and very abstract speech in these children who have never spoken, or have used speech inadequately" (Lovaas, 1968, p. 117). Lovaas maintains that the children do not learn a simple restricted set of words; they become able to generate sentences on their own and respond appropriately to new combinations of words.

In spite of the obvious success to date, Lovaas is not under the impression that the problems of autistic children are solved. He mentions, in particular, a case of a little boy who explained that he was making crazy faces to scare away a school task that was difficult for him. "I see this as a conceptual problem for us, since I don't see how this interaction could be handled within reinforcement therapy. It demands empathy" (Lovaas, 1968, p. 119).

Implications

The results of behavior therapy techniques are impressive. Behavior highly resistant to other forms of therapy may be changed by techniques of behavior modifications, and symptom substitution does not seem to occur. When behaviors and feelings other than those which were the target of the therapy are affected, the consequences are more likely to be positive than negative ones. This is not to say that behavior therapy is universally effective or that other techniques are without effect. Nor does it necessarily mean that a person is nothing but a collection of overt behaviors which are automatically associated with environmental events without mediation by the internal feeling states of the organism—a view that humanistic students and skeptical clinicians are likely to attribute unfairly to behavior therapists. Most learning theorists are probably willing to admit that feeling changes occur along with outward behavioral modification and are of importance, and they can concede, without damage to the *concrete* effectiveness of the techniques, that learning theory has not yet provided a complete explanation of personality development and change (Weitzman, 1968).

The Effects of Behavior

At a more immediate practical level, think of some behavioral problems you have, such as eating too much, staying up too late, biting your nails, shyness, bad study habits, impatience with your roommate. Perhaps you have all of these habits and are tempted to describe yourself as an anxiety neurotic! According to the behaviorist, "neuroses" are collections of maladaptive behaviors. A psychoanalyst might attribute them to displaced sexual drive; a Rogerian (Chapter 6) might speculate about incongruence between self and experience. Perhaps the assertions of each of these theorists are in some sense correct. However, consider the impact of the behavior itself. If this could be modified to your satisfaction, the change would not be without a variety of effects: You would be pleased not to have the annoying behavior, and you would be freed from a number of unpleasant consequences of the behavior. The mere fact of being somewhat happier with yourself is no small accomplishment. Probably you would also experience a number of other good results stemming directly from the behavior change. Many of these are of interpersonal significance. With more sleep, less food, better grades, less nervousness, more patience and comfort with people, your behavior will be more pleasing to others, and you will be more likely to receive the approval and other positive reinforcements that people can provide. "The symptom removal does more than just remove the symptom; it is the occasion for the acquisition of new socially acceptable behavior" (Neuringer, 1970, p. 7).

Of course, the more severe the behavior problem, the more dramatic the consequences of change. Consider, for example, the effects of changing the behavior of the person who responds with violent head twitching or stuttering when faced with other people, the child who attacks other children, the hospital patient who hides in the bathroom. A change in any of these maladaptive behaviors would have widespread consequences in terms of the reactions of other people and of the person's view of himself. People respond to their own behavior, and they approach or avoid, interpret and evaluate other people on the basis of behavior. Behavior change has implications far beyond the simple fact of the specific change itself.

Dehumanization?

The efficacy of behavior modification techniques is frequently disputed on the basis that people are unethically being dehumanized, being made into things to be manipulated. One aspect of the issue concerns the appropriateness of the aversive stimuli that are sometimes used to modify an undesirable behavior. Electrical shock can be painful; but we must decide whether it is worse than the pain that must be endured because of the symptom. Is it better for a child to bite off his fingers (literally!) than to receive a few electric shocks to stop the finger-biting response? Is it better for the autistic child to ignore all social stimulation than to endure punishment until he learns to escape this by the response of physically going to other people?

While the behavior therapist is accused of treating people like objects and "controlling" them in dehumanizing ways, the fact is that everyone is under the control of other people—parents, teachers, friends, platoon sergeants, news media, and textbook authors. Presumably, most of us will never be completely controlled by any one person or group of persons because of the *many* sources of control which compete for attention, and because we can influence those who influence us. Of all those who regulate behavior, the behavior therapist should probably arouse the *least* fear. He differs from the other controllers in that he makes an *explicit admission* that he is attempting to control; he gives systematic thought to the determination of the appropriateness of the desired behaviors and the most effective ways of control; and he is usually assuming the controlling position at the *explicit request* of the controllee. When he exerts control over someone who has not himself asked for it, that someone is likely to be a patient put in the hospital by others who were otherwise ineffective in exercising influence on his behavior. The controller also knows very well that he cannot exert complete control—the person brings with him a reinforcement history that may set limits on the extent of change possible, and he lives in a social environment in which others are also shaping his behavior. And the subject can himself control the controller.

Paradoxically, the effects of the behavior modifier's control are the diametric opposite of brainwashing, constriction, and dehumanization because of the effects of the behavioral change:

> Once the behavior is changed (either through symptom elimination or building in increased competence), the person is now *free* to explore his world further; he is *free* to consider new possibilities. Behavior modification opens up . . . a whole new world of possible reinforcements that were previously closed off to him because of the presence of the symptom or symptoms (Neuringer, 1970).

SUMMARY

Freud's picture of man stressed the unconscious forces that shape behavior, the biological foundations of personality, and the intricate defenses against anxiety that are the basis of personality structure and dynamics. Man is a deterministic product of his body and his society, the battleground on which society, particularly his parents, struggle against biological instincts. The dominant view of man on the part of learning theorists has not been radically different; what it has added has been a workable language for describing behavior and a theory of how behavior is acquired, which is a detail Freud did not attend to with utmost concern. What this view has taken away is some of the Freudian sense of mystery and intrigue, the drama of psychodynamics.

Freud essentially started from the internal mental activity of man; learning theory started from the external, observable behavior. Nevertheless, learning theorists share with Freud a deterministic view, for they portray the ways man *reacts* to environmental events—ways of which he is not always immediately aware, and ways he or others do not always consider rational.

Behavior therapists have found that by manipulating the immediate environment (the stimulus) accompanying these reactions (responses) and by reinforcing or punishing the reactions, they can change or modify the behavior of humans and other animals. Through the use of techniques such as systematic desensitization, observation of others, and operant conditioning, behavior therapists have effected behavior changes in neurotics, psychotics, delinquents, and autistic children. Using methods based on the work of learning theorists—Watson, Pavlov, Skinner, Hull, and Dollard and Miller—the therapists have shown that behavior therapy *works,* whether on modifying a fear of snakes and dogs or on changing the asocial behavior of schizophrenics.

There are, of course, many unresolved or unexplored issues, and behavior therapy, like its parent behaviorism, is still growing. It has been predicted that the behavior therapy movement will go further inside the organism, by relating physiological functioning to behavior change processes, and further outward to the variables of the social environment (Krasner, 1971). In the coming years, we are likely to see also an increasing rapprochement with other theoretical approaches and therapy techniques. Consideration of the current behavior therapy movement can make us aware of the conditioning principles that operate continually in our everyday social environment. Probably all of us could attend more effectively than we do to the punitive or reinforcing effect of our behavior on the behavior of others, and we could become more aware of the ways in which we allow our own behavior to be controlled by the behavior of others.

6

the third force: fulfillment theory

Freudian theorists contend that behavior results from personality, which in turn is determined by past needs and experiences. Learning theorists, too, take a deterministic view of personality, but with a slightly different twist: Personality is behavior which is learned. In direct opposition are several more recent theorists who maintain that personality is a unique force, not a product of preceding forces. The past is a burden to be lifted, not an explanation of the person as he is. In their approach and their concepts these theorists are similar to the Freudian descendants.

Gordon Allport, Carl Rogers, and Abraham Maslow, discussed in this chapter, are proponents of what Maslow called the "third force" in psychology, the other forces being Freudian psychoanalysis (Chapter 3) and learning theory or behaviorism (Chapter 5). These men, and others within this general orientation, wear a variety of labels whose subtle differences in meaning will not concern us here; they are called fulfillment theorists, phenomenologists, actualizers, self-theorists, existentialists, organismic theorists, and field theorists. They all tend to share a view of man as being a unique, dynamic whole, capable of self-awareness and self-direction. Because exponents of the third force emphasize freedom and maintain that man needs to find meaning and values if he is to achieve fulfillment as a human being, their writing often appears to be the work of philosophers rather than psychologists.

FROM VIEW TO APPLICATION

In an effort to clarify the views of the Freudians, learning theorists, and fulfillment theorists, we will consider a specific personality and then anticipate, superficially, the approach that each of the three schools might take.

119

John R., twenty-three years old, has been to four doctors seeking a cure for his persistent headaches. A perfectionist, a chronic worrier, John feels that the doctors are probably right when they cite strain and nervous tension as the cause of his pains. John lives with his widowed mother who competes with his job and his friends for his attention. She invents frequent crises to keep him at home in the evenings, and on occasion she has demanded that he stay home during the day to help with some "emergency." Although John suspects that most of his mother's problems are fabricated, he has been unable to refuse her demands.

His job is going badly because he cannot turn in his sales reports on time and because he can seldom meet his monthly sales quota. His reports are late because he doesn't want to hand them to the manager until they are "just right." By the time he fills out the forms, tears them up, and fills them out again and again, the deadline is passed. His fear of less-than-perfect performance in dealing with customers makes him appear incompetent, and the customer soon looks for a more knowledgeable salesman. He feels inferior to his fellow workers, and they, sensing this, make him the target of jokes and the victim of harmless but demoralizing pranks.

John knows that he is a bad salesman. Although he is unhappy in his job, he is terrified at the prospect of being fired. He had thought about going on to graduate school and into teaching after college, as his father had done, but his childhood was filled with his mother's complaints about lack of money and her indictments of his father as a failure. The starting salary and the future offered by the sales job looked good, and John accepted it.

The Freudian Approach

A strict Freudian would study separate aspects of John R.: his id, ego, and superego; his mind and body; his past and present. Among his many considerations, he might then ask the following questions.

Is John's ego strength impaired because of a strong superego that suppresses the id? Could his inhibitions and perfectionism be indications of an anal fixation? Does he suffer guilt because of his repressed identification with his father? What are the implications of his relationship with his mother?

Freudian descendants. Adler, Fromm, Horney, and especially Jung modified Freud's views to include an appreciation of man's capacity for self-awareness, and, in Jung's words, "self-actualization." Their ideas (Chapter 4) are clearly the forerunners of fulfillment theory. That these theorists are not usually viewed in this context probably reflects the fact that they often evoke an aura of Freudianism that is not compatible with the intent of the third force. However, the convergence of their and the fulfillment theorists' views is remarkable considering the divergent backgrounds and sources of data.

The Learning Theory Approach

A learning theorist, like the Freudian, would examine "pieces" of John R., for he would attempt to separate what John is from what he does, what he feels from how he acts. Because the learning theorist treats symptoms rather than cause, he would attempt to deal with the behavior that John exhibits rather than with the internal reasons for that behavior.

Using the various learning theory strategies presented in Chapter 5, try to anticipate which of John's behaviors the learning theorist might want to modify, how he would go about it, and what kind of reinforcement might be possible.

Fulfillment Orientation

Third-force psychologists take a *holistic* view of man: They would look at John R. as a *whole* being. This orientation springs from their acceptance of organismic theory (Goldstein, 1939, 1963), which developed as a reaction against the split of the organism into mind and body, and the further division of the mind into discrete particles such as sensations, feelings, and images. Instead, the emphasis is upon unity, integration, consistency, and organization as the natural, normal state of the organism. Organismic theory demands attention to the body as well as to the "psyche," the union of the body and psyche forming an organismic whole.

Rather than trying to catalog his past and his behavior, third-force psychologists would attempt to understand how John R. views himself and his world. This method draws upon phenomenology, the philosophical system developed by Husserl, who grounded physical reality upon the self, contended that one must study experience as it is presented to the individual. It would be important to a fulfillment theorist that John try to experience himself and his environment as they are, rather than as theories, beliefs, conventions, or value systems attempt to make them appear. Consequently, the theorist would help John R. to realize that his life does not have to be restricted by past experience or current environment. Each individual has responsibility and opportunity for self-direction here and now, and it is up to him how he chooses to live his life.

John R. can choose to spend his time blaming his disappointments and psychic pains on the past and on current external determinants, or he may choose to change himself, refuse to be a victim, and exercise what he feels is free will to control his own life. He is mistreated by others only as he chooses to let others mistreat him. He feels inferior only because he gives other people the right to make him feel inferior.

Two Roads to Fulfillment

Although third-force psychologists agree in emphasizing the positive and in viewing man as a complete unity of mind and body, they differ in exactly how they characterize the fulfilled person and in how they conceive the *life force* that directs growth.

Perfection Version

For the *perfection theorist,* ideals and values, which are not necessarily inherent, determine the direction of fulfillment. The life force is the tendency to strive for that which will make life ideal or complete, and this may require compensation for functional or genetic deficiencies (Maddi, 1972). Ideals and values concerning the best mode of living determine the nature of fulfillment. Perfection is sought even when it requires personal struggle.

One of the most avid and effective spokesmen for perfection theory was Gordon Allport, whose ideas are discussed below. It should be noted, however, that although Fromm and Adler were presented as Freudian descendants, they are also fulfillment theorists. In fact, Adler may be considered the purest example of the perfection view.

Actualization Version

Actualization theorists share with perfection theorists the view that fulfillment is the goal of life toward which we strive, but they believe that fulfillment follows a course inherently determined by what could be described as a genetic blueprint. Thus, actualization theorists, such as Carl Rogers and Abraham Maslow, are essentially biological theorists, but ones who do a very effective job of relating to the postulated biological foundation some of the most noble features man has attributed to himself. They maintain that fulfillment follows a genetically determined course and that the life force directing growth is "the tendency to express to an ever greater degree the capabilities, potentialities, or talents based in one's genetic constitution . . ." (Maddi, 1972, p. 85). Carl Jung comes close to being an actualization theorist in this respect, although he also emphasized the struggle of striving for selfhood.

GORDON ALLPORT

Gordon Allport (1897–1967) was an avid and effective proponent of man's individuality and uniqueness. He thought that although people in a particular culture may share certain patterns of behavior, no one person is exactly the same as another:

> How, in dealing with a concrete person, can we expect to understand, predict, control, unless we know the individual pattern and not merely the universal tendencies of the human mind-in-general? (A man who wishes to please his wife with a Christmas gift does less well if he relies on his knowledge of feminine psychology in general than if he knows the individual desires and tastes of his wife.) *

* Allport, G. *Letters from Jenny.* New York: Harcourt Brace Jovanovich, 1965. P. 159.

The theorist who emphasizes uniqueness is in a difficult position for formulating a theory applicable to many people. Allport, like other fulfillment theorists, nonetheless proceeds to make assumptions and depict ways of functioning he thinks typical of or relevant to many people, while allowing for uniqueness in manner of expression.

Basic Assumptions

Allport's (1955, 1961) basic assumptions about mature adults illustrate his belief in the self-directing and growing nature of people as unique beings. In fact, these assumptions serve well to characterize the dominant views of other fulfillment theorists as well.

People are proactive rather than reactive. This concept may be seen to characterize a focal point of difference between fulfillment theorists and other psychologists. It asserts essentially that man's natural functioning is as an *Origin* of his own behavior rather than as a *Pawn* of external circumstances (see deCharms, 1968; Chapter 12 of this book). Man initiates action (pro-acts); he is not just a passive victim who responds (re-acts) to the environment. According to many psychologists using traditional Freudian or behavioristic concepts, behavior is an attempt to adapt to the environment and is determined more by the environment than by the person himself. Allport agrees that the environment does set restrictions on the range of behavioral possibilities, but the limits are wide and leave considerable latitude to the individual within which he may choose his behavior: We can manipulate the world, rather than be manipulated by it.

People function rationally. The mature, healthy person is a rational being, governed by consciously determined plans and intentions. This view is in contrast to that of Freud, who believed that behavior is largely unconsciously motivated and in the service of primitive impulses; even the realistic, rational ego functions on energy captured from the irrational id and came into existence to attain pleasures for the id.

Because of his assumption of rational functioning, Allport felt that consideration of unconscious and irrational motives is unnecessary, except in trying to understand the behavior of children and the mentally ill. Allport considered self-report information both sufficient for, and necessary to, an understanding of normal adult behavior. People know themselves, and the psychologist can work more efficiently by simply asking his subject to describe himself rather than by using elaborate, disguised methods of personality measurement. An investigation of a person should begin with questions as to what he is trying to do in his life and what he is trying to be. It is no wonder, then, that the test Allport developed, the Allport-Vernon Study of Values (1931), is a self-report measure of values.

People are future-oriented. The key to our behavior is what we plan for the future and what we are trying to do here and now, not what we have done or what has been done to us in the past. Personality development, therefore, is to be understood in terms of the *becoming* of psychological *growth*. Further, since growth and future planning often imply an increase in tension, Allport's view of behavioral goals, in contrast to that of Freud, is not one of tension reduction.

Considering that choices for future action are not determined by the satisfaction (and subsequent tension reduction) attained through actions of the past we then see that future orientation also implies the relative divorce of the present from the past. Allport deals with this separation in his concept of *functional autonomy*. A behavior may have been initiated because it was instrumental in one's achievement of a desired goal; however, it may come to function autonomously or independently of the former need—the behavior becomes valued in and of itself, although the goal for which it was originally designed has since been attained or is no longer relevant. A young man walks to work each morning because he is saving every penny he can to buy a boat for weekend sailing. After three years, he has enough money to buy the boat, but he continues to walk to work and to pinch pennies because these behaviors have become valued for their own sake. Functionally autonomous motives are *historically* associated with the need that instigated them, but they are *functionally* independent of that need. The dispositions we retain as autonomous ones are likely to be those most expressive of the self. In this way, the interests, values, and even the total life styles of mature people develop. The extent to which motives are functionally autonomous is one important measure of maturity.

People are psychologically organized, complex, and unique. Because of man's psychological organization and complexity, he must be viewed as a whole. By attempting to divide him into separate parts, one misses the *purposiveness* characterizing his organization, a purposiveness that is psychological. Certainly, ideas and feelings have a physiological substrate, but they are genuine and important determiners of behavior as real, psychological events. Their reduction to instinctual energy, as was conceived by Freud, is not necessary.

Allport believed that each human being is unique and that no individual can be understood merely by reference to or by comparison with other species or other humans (Allport does, however, cite experiments with rats in support of his functional autonomy concept). Because each person is relatively unique, Allport (1961, 1962) felt that psychologists should focus on the individual (*idiographic* or *morphogenic approach*) rather than on descriptions about "people in general" (*nomothetic* or *dimensional approach*). He maintained that while both kinds of information are appropriate in psychology, American psychology, in particular, has allowed the nomothetic methods to dominate, when it is the idiographic approach which will lead to better prediction and understanding. We must use methods which *reveal* rather than *conceal* a person's individuality.

The assumptions about human nature are actually the characteristics of the *propriate* functioning of mature adults. In spite of his emphasis, Allport did recognize, as doubtless any theorist must, that humans, along with other animals, have biological and survival needs. However, his opinion of these needs is reflected in the disparaging term he selected to identify the functioning of behaviors in their service: *opportunistic*. Much more to Allport's liking are propriate functions, which reflect psychological considerations that are expressive of the self. Development is a matter of changing from the opportunistic functioning of the child to the propriate functioning of the mature adult.

Opportunistic functioning. Opportunistic functioning, the opposite of propriate functioning, is biological, reactive, past-oriented, and often irrational. Opportunistic behavior is dependent upon the external environment, which can either satisfy or frustrate our needs; hence, we have little control over this aspect of behavior.

When a biological need is aroused, the organism relies on past habits which have been successful in satisfying the needs and contributing to survival; the aim of the acquired habits is, of course, need or tension reduction. Opportunistic functions are characteristic of children, the mentally ill, and animals. Thus, where the immature or abnormal are involved, Allport actually agrees with Freud's description of behavior. However, since opportunistic functions work only for the satisfaction of biological needs and do not involve psychological considerations of values and philosophical principles of life, they are of little relevance to Allport's concern with the nature of the healthy adult.

Propriate functions. Allport was more intrigued with the propriate functions that express the self, or *proprium:* that "warm, central, private region of our life" (1961, p. 110). Self is phenomenologically what the person believes himself to be.

Although Allport maintained that "it is much easier to feel the self than to define the self" (1961, p. 127), he did list seven aspects of selfhood or propriate functions (Table 6-1) which he believed to comprise the "me" as felt and known. They are propriate aspects of personality, aspects contributing to inward unity, which are brought together by the self, or proprium. Life is a developmental process in which functioning is guided by the need to express the proprium. The effects of previous opportunistic functioning may be seen in the form of personal dispositions or traits which initially may have been opportunistic habits, but are retained as functionally autonomous ones because they are expressive of the developing proprium. They are, for the most part, functionally autonomous of their opportunistic origins.

Because of the vast difference in character between opportunistic and propriate functioning, Allport is one psychologist who assumes a discon-

TABLE 6–1   Allport's Seven Aspects of Selfhood

FIRST THREE YEARS OF LIFE	
1. Sense of bodily self	"Our sensations and our movements feed us with constant awareness that I am I" (1961, p. 114) "The bodily sense remains a lifelong anchor for our self-awareness" (1961, p. 114)
2. Sense of continuing self-identity	"It is the actions of the other to which he differentially adjusts that force upon a child the realization that he is not the other, but a being in his own right" (1955–1960, p. 44) "By hearing his name repeatedly, the child gradually sees himself as a distinct and recurrent point of reference. . . . Our name is warm and central, a symbol of our whole being" (1961, pp. 115, 117)
3. Self-esteem (or Ego-enhancement)	". . . the most notorious property of the proprium . . . its unabashed self-seeking . . . we are endowed by nature with the impulses of self-assertion and with the emotions of self-satisfaction and pride" (1955–1960, p. 44) "To him (the child around age two) it seems safer to resist any adult proposal in advance, as a protection to dawning self-esteem. . . . Some adults seem to have preserved the childish trait of negativism" (1961, p. 119) "Their solicitations have a heavily biological quality and seem to be contained within the organism itself" (1955–1960, p. 43)
AGES FOUR TO SIX	
4. Extension of self (or Ego-extension)	"A child . . . who identifies with his parent is definitely extending his sense of self, as he does likewise through his love for pets, dolls, or other possessions" (1955–1960, p. 45) ". . . soon the process of learning brings with it a high regard for possessions, for loved objects, and later, for ideal causes and loyalties. . . . A mark of maturity seems to be the range and extent of one's feeling of self-involvement in abstract ideals" (1955–1960, p. 45)
5. Self-image	". . . the way (one) regards his present abilities, status, and roles; and what he would like to become, his *aspirations* for himself" (1955–1960, p. 47) ". . . intentions, goals, sense of moral responsibility, and self-knowledge . . ." (1961, p. 123)

TABLE 6–1   Allport's Seven Aspects of Selfhood (continued)

AGES SIX TO TWELVE	
6. *Self as rational coper*	"Objective knowledge fascinates him, and the question 'Why?' is always on his lips" (1961, p. 124)
	"Previously he *thought,* but now he *thinks* about thinking. . . . They now fully know that the self is a thinker . . ." (1961, p. 124)
ADOLESCENCE	
7. *Propriate striving*	". . . in adolescence long-range purposes and distant goals add a new dimension to the sense of selfhood. . . . In order to be normal, an adolescent, and especially an adult, needs a defining objective, a line of promise" (1961, p. 126)
	". . . however beset by conflicts, it makes for unification of personality" (1955–1960, p. 50)

tinuity of development, and a qualitative (as opposed to quantitative) difference between the functioning of children and adults, the immature or sick and the mature or healthy.

Allport's Influence

What impact have Allport's ideas had? On the negative side, we find that his theory has not been effective in generating research (although he was an active researcher himself), and it has been criticized on a number of grounds: failure to provide an adequate account of the mechanism of functional autonomy; neglect of the sociocultural determinants of behavior; the practical difficulties of doing research from the assumption of uniqueness of every person; and the assumption of discontinuity between normal and abnormal, infant and adult, animal and human (Hall & Lindzey, 1970).

On the positive side, Allport has been an effective bridge between the personality psychology of the clinic and the traditions of academia. In spite of his aversion to basic Freudian tenets as applied to mature, healthy adults, Allport has become a popular theorist among psychoanalysts; his emphasis upon active propriate (ego) functions and functional autonomy is compatible with recent concerns in ego psychology. Allport's work is responsible for much of the current renewed interest in concepts of self, the ego, and the nature of healthy maturity.

His emphasis upon conscious behavior determinants, while at one time novel, is gaining recognition as a valid approach to understanding people.

Similarly, his pleas for the study of single cases have facilitated tolerance, sometimes acceptance, of the individual case as a legitimate method of psychological research.

CARL ROGERS

Carl Rogers (1902–) is an undisputed optimist who maintains that man is basically good. In many ways Rogers is in distinct opposition to Freud, but the impact of Freudian thinking on Rogers' position is clear to the thoughtful reader.

Basic Assumptions

Rogers believes that with the proper environment, any individual will develop into a cooperative, healthy, mature person. The selfishness, destructiveness, and cruelty that do occur among nations and individuals are *distortions,* rather than expressions, of man's true nature. If people were basically selfish and competitive, as Freud maintained, behavior destructive of others would be accompanied by constructive behavior toward the self. However, the mistreatment of others that occurs with maladjustment is usually associated with self-destructive attitudes and behavior. People who like themselves, as they should, also like others.

Antagonism and competition between people may usually be resolved by facing misunderstandings honestly and by trying to see things from the other's point of view. The disagreements that may persist will be ones which are respected rather than ones which lead to misunderstandings and conflicts.

The total person reacts to total experience. The *organism* (the total individual) is an organized whole which reacts to the *phenomenal field* (the totality of experience) to meet its needs, the most basic of which is the motive to actualize, maintain, and enhance itself (Rogers, 1951). The phenomenal field consists of conscious and unconscious events, and the organism may react to both aspects of experience.

"The organism reacts to the field as it is experienced and perceived" (Rogers, 1951, p. 484). To understand an individual, we must see his behavior from the internal frame of reference of the individual himself. If a young woman is depressed on the eve of her mother's arrival for a week-end visit, Rogers would not issue judgments in terms of cultural values (one *should* value mothers) or in terms of his own frame of reference (*I* enjoy my mother's visits). Rather, he would try to understand this young woman's experience of her mother—her perception of her mother, the feelings she has about her mother—and help the woman to be able to know and accurately express her feelings.

Actualization is inherent. The life of the organism is directed and characterized by an inherent actualizing tendency, "the biological pressure to fulfill the genetic blueprint, whatever the difficulty created by the environment" (Maddi, 1972, p. 93). Fulfillment of this blueprint or pattern (i.e., being what we are), rather than tension reduction, is the goal of the actualizing tendency.

The actualizing tendency is selective, directional, and constructive (Rogers, 1963). It does not call for the fulfillment of all potential, such as that for nausea, pain, and self-destruction. Man shares the actualizing tendency with all the rest of life, animals and plants alike, but he sometimes blocks the natural unfolding of the inherent potential for growth.

The specific content of the genetic blueprint varies among all living things; therefore, Rogers can give little hint about its specific content. However, he has quite dramatically illustrated the persistence of the growth tendency and its pervasiveness throughout life:

> During a vacation weekend some months ago I was standing on a headland overlooking one of the rugged coves which dot the coastline of northern California. Several large rock outcroppings were at the mouth of the cove, and these received the full force of the great Pacific combers which, beating upon them, broke into mountains of spray before surging into the cliff-lined shore. As I watched the waves breaking over these large rocks in the distance, I noticed, with surprise, what appeared to be tiny palm trees on the rocks, no more than two or three feet high, taking the pounding of the breakers. Through my binoculars I saw that these were some type of seaweed, with a slender "trunk" topped off with a head of leaves. As one examined a specimen in the interval between the waves it seemed clear that this fragile, erect, top-heavy plant would be utterly crushed and broken by the next breaker. When the wave crunched down upon it, the trunk bent almost flat, the leaves were whipped into a straight line by the torrent of the water, yet the moment the wave had passed, here was the plant again, erect, tough, resilient. It seemed incredible that it was able to take this incessant pounding hour after hour, day after day, week after week, perhaps, for all I know, year after year, and all the time nourishing itself, extending its domain, reproducing itself; in short, maintaining and enhancing itself in this process which, in our shorthand, we call growth. Here in this palmlike seaweed was the tenacity of life, the forward thrust of life, the ability to push into an incredibly hostile environment and not only to hold its own, but to adapt, develop, become itself.*

A distinct psychological offshoot of this basic actualizing tendency is the self-actualizing tendency, a pressure to behave, develop, and experience in a way consistent with the view of self. It differs from the fundamental actualizing tendency only in that the self is specifically involved (Figure 6-1).

* Rogers, C. R. The actualizing tendency in relation to "motives" and to consciousness. In M. R. Jones (Ed.), *Nebraska symposium on motivation*. Lincoln: University of Nebraska Press, 1963. Pp. 1-2.

FIGURE
6–1

Actualizing Tendency
Self-Actualizing Tendency, a psychological offshoot. "Pressure to behave, develop, to experience in a way consistent with view of self."

Specialized expressions | Need for positive regard, from other
└─Need for self-regard
"He becomes his own significant social other."

The Actualizing Tendency.

The Self: Its Nature and Expression

The self is our conscious perception of "I" or "me" and embodies our perceptions of the relationship of I or me to other people and to our environment (Rogers, 1951, 1957, 1959). Consequently, the self is a part of the phenomenal field, for it develops from interaction with the environment; it has perceptions about the values of others and often introjects them. People attempt to behave in ways consistent with their perceptions of self. The self-actualizing tendency is, therefore, a push to *experience* ourselves in the same way we consciously view self, to be what we think we are.

Regard. Two other specialized expressions of the actualizing tendency are the *need for positive regard* and the *need for self-regard* (Rogers, 1959, 1961, 1963). Early in infancy, we begin to develop a concept of self through interaction with the environment and particularly with "significant" other people. As awareness of self emerges, so too does a need for the approval and love of others. Whether this need for positive regard is inherent or learned is irrelevant to Rogers, for he maintains that the tendency in human beings to be satisfied by the approval of others and be frustrated by their disapproval is universal.

Because of the association of self-experience with the satisfaction or frustration of the need for positive regard, the growing child comes to feel a need to regard himself positively, to approve of himself. That is, he experiences a need for *self*-regard and, as a result, self-approval becomes satisfying, and self-disapproval frustrating. Thus, the child comes to be the monitor and evaluator of his own behavior: "He becomes in a sense his own significant social other" (Rogers, 1959, p. 224). However, the standards he uses are those he perceives others using in their evaluation of him.

Incongruence. Our potentialities are genetically shaped and come to include all that we experience as a total organism. In contrast, our self-concept is a product of our association with others; it is formed on the basis of the perceived evaluations of other people. Thus, there is a possibility for a discrepancy, or *incongruence,* between our organism and our concept of self. A person may try to ignore aspects of his potentialities and his organismic experiences in order to conform to his self-concept. A client in Rogerian therapy remarked, "I've always tried to be what the others thought I should be, but now I'm wondering whether I shouldn't just see that I am what I am" (Rogers, 1947, p. 363).

Discrepancies such as the one mentioned above may result when other people fail the individual by holding *conditional positive regard* (Rogers, 1959, 1961, 1963), in other words, by determining precise standards and accepting, valuing, and respecting the individual only when he conforms to the rules. Positive regard from others is *conditional* upon a person's doing and being what others want and expect; as result, the individual comes to hold *conditions of worth* for himself (which serve somewhat the same function as Freud's superego). In order to achieve self-approval, he must meet the conditions of worth evolved in interaction with other people; to do this, he must distort or blot out something of who he is and what he feels. This is a matter of defensiveness.

Defensiveness. Rogers, like Freud, postulates defense mechanisms as serving to minimize or avoid anxiety (Rogers, 1959). Organismic experiences incongruent with the self-structure (and its incorporated conditions of worth) are threatening to the self. Were they accurately expressed in awareness, the self-concept would not be consistent, conditions of worth would be violated, and the need for self-regard frustrated: A state of anxiety would exist. The process of defense can prevent these events by selective perception, *distortion*, and/or *denial* of awareness of the experiences, keeping the total conscious perception of experience consistent with the self-structure and conditions of worth.

Whereas Freud felt that some defenses can be helpful, Rogers maintains that defenses result in rigid and inaccurate perceptions and thus serve as crippling restrictions on self-actualization. They prevent us from truly knowing ourselves and expressing all our potential. Thus, personality is divided. This is, according to Rogers (1963), the basic estrangement in man. Although not theoretically necessary, this condition tends to be the rule rather than the exception, so pervasive are conditional regard of others and the rigidity of malfitting conditions of worth. The estrangement is a perverse channeling of some of the actualizing tendency into behaviors which do not actualize. The self and organismic functioning are dissociated, and we are not "in tune with ourselves." Consequently, we become self-defeating, unhappy, divided. Man is wiser than his intellect, but he has lost trust in his experiencing and has only partial glimpses, if any, of the truth present in his own experience: "The tragic condition of man is that he has lost confidence in his own nonconscious inner directions" (Rogers, 1963, p. 21).

Congruence. While this tragic condition of estrangement from ourselves can be avoided, it does not seem likely, nor is it frequent. Congruence is possible when there is *unconditional positive regard* from others, when there are no conditions of worth. Self-regard is unconditional and the needs for positive regard and self-regard are not at variance with organismic experiencing. There is no need to be defensive about what we are and feel ourselves to be.

Unconditional positive regard does not require that *no* restrictions be placed on a child's behavior. A child must learn certain rules of behavior, but when he breaks those rules, and perhaps is punished, he can be helped to see that it is his *action* that is disapproved, not his total self or his feelings. In an argument over who is to play with a favorite toy, Billy delivers his little brother a quick kick before Mother arrives on the scene. Mother can communicate, "Your behavior is bad," rather than "You are bad." According to Rogers (1959), the attitude of the mother suggests, "I can understand how satisfying it feels to you to kick your brother and it is all right for you to have those feelings. But I have feelings too, and I feel distressed when he is hurt. So I will not let you kick him anymore. Both of us can have our own feelings." Thus, Billy might sometimes choose the satisfaction of kicking his brother and sometimes that of pleasing his mother. The important aspect of this situation is that Billy need not disown either kind of satisfaction or dissatisfaction. He can choose which experiences to act on. Thus, as an adult, he may not act destructively to those who annoy him, but he can accept his aggressive feelings about them.

The fully functioning person. With such acceptance from others and acceptance of self, one can know and be himself and become a fully functioning person. Probably the most basic characteristic of the mature, adjusted, fully functioning or congruent person is that he is *open to experience.* He has no need for defenses and is, therefore, able to listen to himself and to experience what is going on within him. "He is free to live his feelings subjectively, as they exist in him, and also free to be aware of these feelings" (Rogers, 1961, p. 188). He is open to feelings of fear, discouragement, and pain, and to attitudes of courage, tenderness, and awe. He is comfortable with himself and accepting of his unflattering characteristics as well as his flattering qualities. He can "let go" and live fully in the moment (*existential living*), with confidence that he will choose correctly if he listens to himself (*organismic trust*). The fully functioning person experiences himself as choosing freely from behavioral alternatives with a sense of power and mastery of himself and, all in all, is *creative (experiential freedom)*.

Personality Change in Interpersonal Relationships

If one is unfortunate enough to have grown up with conditions of worth and lack of complete acceptance of himself and his feelings—which is typical—he is not necessarily destined to live at a less than fully functioning level. Rogers maintains that personality can change and develop whenever one person has an impact on another.

Such impact and freeing of personality for full development is by no means limited to the formal psychotherapeutic situation. However, Rogers' theory of personality, theory of therapy, and experiences as a therapist, like those of Freud, are all closely related. Both view the therapeutic interview as uniquely valuable for providing data about people: "We are admitted freely into the backstage of the person's living where we can observe from within some of the dramas of internal change" (Rogers, 1947, p. 359). In turn, the views of therapy reflect theories of what people are and conceptions of the nature of the ideal course of development. Rogers' client-centered therapy is an attempt to provide an atmosphere in which the stumbling blocks previously placed in the individual's path of natural growth are removed (Rogers, 1951, 1959, 1961, 1962, 1963).

Client-centered therapy. The therapist need not control or manipulate the therapeutic process, nor should he resort to elaborate techniques to understand the patient. What the person says about himself reveals his personality. Diagnostic testing and a deep search for the unconscious or for past determinants of behavior give little information about how the person experiences himself here and now. The therapist attempts to understand the client as the client sees himself, to see the perspective of the client's phenomenal field. Each person has the capability of solving his own problems and the role of the therapist is to aid the person in realizing his potential strength. He assists the client in recognizing and accepting the feelings he has been denying in awareness. To do this, the therapist often acts as a mirror in which the client may view himself.

> **Client:** I feel as though my mother is always watching me and criticizing what I do. It gets me all stirred up inside.
> **Counselor:** You resent her criticism. (Rogers, 1951 [1965 paperback edition, p. 28])

If the therapist's statement is made with the attitude and tone appropriate for saying, "You are sitting on my hat," he does little good. The response must be made from an attitude of empathy so that the client's reaction shows increased awareness, such as, "Yes, I do feel that way, and I see it a little more clearly now that you have put it in somewhat different terms."

In short, the client comes to know his feelings and can revise the concept of self to assimilate and include them. Once he is freed from the estrangement caused by his denial of aspects of himself, he is free to experience himself as complete and as better able to grow.

Figures 6–2 and 6–3 illustrate the changes in a hypothetical individual's personality following successful psychotherapy. The person living at a less than fully functioning level has, in order to achieve a self-concept acceptable to himself, distorted a portion of the phenomenal field and come to perceive this as part of his own experience. Further, this person, whose self-concept necessitates distorted perception, will not admit to

**FIGURE
6–2**

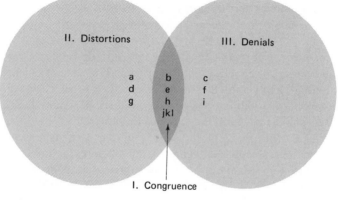

Total Personality in a State of Psychological Tension.

Elements before therapy

a. I am inadequate with mechanical things, and this is one sign of my general inadequacy (an introjected concept and its value taken from parents).

   The experience was "My parents regard me as inadequate mechanically." The distorted symbolization is "I am inadequate mechanically." The reason for the distortion is to guard against losing "I am loved by my parents." Thus, I want to be acceptable to my parents and so I must experience myself as being the sort of person they think I am.

b. I experience failure in dealing with mechanical apparatus. Direct experiences which have occurred are assimilated into structure of self because they are consistent with it.

c. Experience of succeeding with a difficult mechanical task. The person cannot experience success in mechanical operations because that is inconsistent with self-structure. It may be impossible to completely deny the experience, since the evidence is clear. However, the experience may be distorted, "It was just luck . . . I couldn't do it again," into congruence with self, and could in distorted form take its place in Area II. But the actual experience is denied to awareness and remains in Area III.

d. "I feel nothing but hatred for my father, and I am morally right in feeling this." (mother had been deserted by husband, so the individual introjects her feeling and value as if it were based on her own experience.)

e. I have experienced dislike for my father in my contacts with him. (There was firsthand experience of dissatisfying association with father; the experience is congruent with the self-structure and assimilated into it.)

f. Experience of positive feelings for father. (There were some satisfying experiences, but they are denied to awareness because of their inconsistency with self-structure and are admitted into consciousness only in distorted ways: "I like my father in some ways and this is shameful."

j. Other people think of me as tall.

k. I experience myself as tall.

l. Rarely do I find myself shorter than others. The attitudes of others are perceived as such and not as my own experience. My evidence of tallness is acceptable to me; the occasional contradictory evidence is always accepted.

FIGURE
6–3

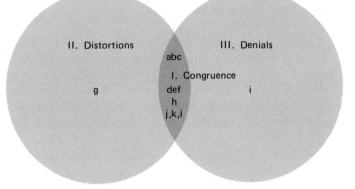

Total Personality after Successful Psychotherapy.

Elements after successful psychotherapy

a. I realize my parents felt I was inadequate in mechanical things and that this had a negative value for them.

b. My own experience confirms this evaluation in a number of ways.

c. But I do have some competency in this field—experience has been admitted to awareness and organized into the self-structure. *a* is no longer seen in a distorted way, but is perceived as the attitude of others.

d. I understand that my mother hates my father and expects me to do the same.

e. I dislike my father in some ways for some things.

f. I like my father in some ways for some things; the experience of both like and dislike are an acceptable part of me.

* g, h, i, are left unchanged to represent the fact that therapy never achieves a complete congruence of self.

Source: Adapted from Rogers, 1951. Pp. 524–531.

his awareness certain experiences because they are inconsistent with his self-structure. Thus, self-structure necessitates distortion (II) and experiences incompatible with self-concept lead to denial (III). However, the segment of experience that is not at variance with the concept of self and self-in-relationship is in the area of congruency (I), where there is no need for defensive action. It is this area that the client and therapist illustrated in the diagrams seek to expand.

Essential conditions. What occurs in successful psychotherapy is probably unusual for the client; otherwise, he would not need to seek there what the professional therapist can give him. However, Rogers sees this situation as only one instance of therapeutic interpersonal relationships. Friends, husbands, wives—even students and teachers—may all be very effective therapists. In fact, any meaningful relationship can be therapeutic, for the essential conditions for successful therapy are in many ways the conditions for a meaningful relationship between *any* two people. They include the therapist's *unconditional positive regard* for the client, his communicated *empathic understanding*, and his own *congruence* or genuineness (Rogers, 1962).

Unconditional positive regard for the client as a respected individual enables a decrease in the client's conditions of worth which evolved because of, and were reinforced by, those who held conditional regard. This attitude enables the free exploration and acceptance of feelings. In a relationship with someone who is warm and accepting and does not make judgments, defenses can be set aside and the client can explore those feelings he had previously distorted or denied. He can establish unconditional self-regard as he comes to know and accept himself. The barriers to growth are no longer necessary, and the individual is free to know and to be what he is.

The therapist with empathic understanding can "be with" the client and experience the client's private, phenomenal world as if it were his own. The typical "understanding" most of us have is likely to be an outside, inadequate awareness in which the other is judged and analyzed in terms of our own frame of reference: "I know what is wrong with you," rather than, "I understand what you feel." It is rare to find someone who is capable of, or even interested in, seeing us as we see ourselves rather than rebuking us for not seeing as they see.

Perhaps the most crucial requirement is that the therapist himself have a high degree of congruence. The greater the congruence of *one* person, the greater the improvement in psychological functioning and satisfaction of *both* participants in *any* interpersonal relationship. As a congruent and self-accepting person, the therapist is free to allow the client to be himself, to give unconditional regard, and to try to see from the client's frame of reference without feeling that his own is in jeopardy. The fully functioning person does not need the artificial support of agreement or conformity by another. He does not try to force his personal values on the other, but instead can help the other to discover his own values. As an experiencing and self-accepting person, he is free to meet the client on a person-to-person basis, without a façade. It is easy to trust a person who, we feel, is being what he is rather than playing a role or operating from behind a mask.

Even if the therapist's feelings are ones of annoyance, boredom, or even dislike, Rogers suggests that it is better for him to be "real" than to put up a façade. A counselor persistently bored with a client owes it to the relationship to share the response and to *own* the feeling. In sharing this feeling, "*I* am bored," there can be a deepening of the relationship. In contrast, an evaluation of the client by "*You* are boring," can be of harm. Frequently in social relations we translate *our* own feelings, "I feel . . ." into evaluative judgments of the other, "You are. . . ."

Rogers is not under the impression that these are necessarily all of the essential conditions, nor does he state that they are necessarily effective for all kinds of helping relationships. However, his strong affirmation of these conditions is obvious:

If I can create a relationship characterized on my part:

by a genuineness and transparency, in which I am my real feelings;

by a warm acceptance of and prizing of the other person as a separate individual;

by a sensitive ability to see his world and himself as he sees them;

Then the other individual in the relationship:

will experience and understand aspects of himself which previously he has repressed;

will find himself becoming better integrated, more able to function effectively;

will become more similar to the person he would like to be;

will be more self-directing and self-confident;

will become more a person, more unique and more self-expressive;

will be more understanding, more acceptant of others;

will be able to cope with the problems of life more adequately and more comfortably.

I believe that this statement holds whether I am speaking of my relationship with a client, with a group of students or staff members, with my family or children. It seems to me that we have here a general hypothesis which offers exciting possibilities for the development of creative, adaptive, autonomous persons (Rogers, 1961).

Rogers' Influence

The chief criticism typical of Rogers' self theory is that it is based on a naïve phenomenology (Hall & Lindzey, 1970 ; Pervin, 1970). Self-reports cannot tell the whole story; the person may intend to deceive his listener or may simply not know the whole truth about himself. Rogers' reply is that the client's conscious statements are reports about his phenomenal world which, in turn, guides his behavior. Further, Rogers explicitly recognizes that the person has experiences which are denied expression because they are inconsistent with the self-image. Thus, Rogers cannot be said to have totally neglected the unconscious, though he has not clearly considered how unconscious forces are related to the conscious phenomenal field. Nor has he specified how self-experience congruency is to be measured. Whether man is inherently good, as Rogers claims, and whether Rogerian analysis can uncover all the unconscious experiences, are other kinds of important questions which are not easily answered.

Nevertheless, Rogers has opened up psychotherapy and the nature of self as areas of meaningful research (Chapter 12). Just as important, his contributions have extended far beyond the confines of the field of psychology. His approach to counseling has influenced the professional activities of clergymen, businessmen, and teachers. Recently, he has been actively engaged in sharing with encounter groups what he has learned from individual therapy and research about personality change, acting in these groups as a facilitator to promote increased effectiveness in the interpersonal communication of already well-functioning people.

ABRAHAM MASLOW

Abraham Maslow (1908–1970), an actualization theorist, believed that man's nature includes not only his anatomy but also his most basic needs, desires, and psychological capacities (Maslow, 1943, 1954). His theory is a blend of influence from personality and experimental psychology positions and from sociology and psychoanalysis. He derived his observations about human behavior from normal and highly creative people and had no hesitancy about attempting to capture the essence of their dynamics without the aid of rigorous experimentation.

Level of Needs

Maslow actually presents a variation on the fulfillment theme in that he postulated two kinds of needs or motives rather than only one: a survival tendency and an actualizing tendency (Maddi, 1972). The needs within these tendencies are called basic or deficiency (or deprivation) needs (Maslow, 1955, 1962, 1970). Needs are hierarchically arranged (Figure 6–4) and a later need cannot emerge as an important behavioral de-

**FIGURE
6–4**

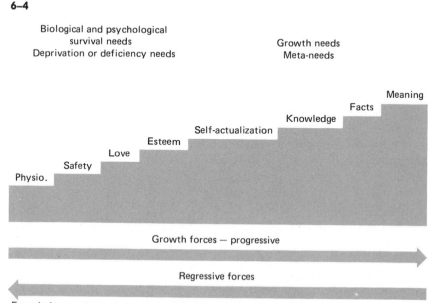

Hierarchical Arrangement of Needs.

terminant until all lower needs are relatively satisfied. Only after earlier needs have declined in importance and require less than full attention can we progress to the next need level. The earlier the need appears, the more physiological and less psychological it is. The actualizing tendency can be vigorously expressed only when the survival tendency is satisfied.

At the first level are *physiological* needs, the most prepotent of all (need for food, shelter, warmth). If such needs are not satisfied, other needs may not emerge: A starving man acts only to get food. One of culture's main functions is to eliminate the frequency of physiological emergencies. At the second level are *safety* needs, evidenced in the avoidance of the new and unfamiliar and search for the familiar. Science, religion, and philosophies may be used to organize the universe into meaningful and familiar wholes to meet safety needs: Adults strive for jobs with tenure and are preoccupied with insurance and savings. *Love* needs, at the next level, include needs for love, affection, and belongingness. If these needs are relatively satisfied, needs for *esteem*—from self and from others—can emerge. We need firmly based feelings of prestige, recognition, appreciation, and a feeling of importance (a theme ignored by Freud, but emphasized by Adler).

The best known need in Maslow's hierarchy is the need for *self-actualization,* the desire to become what we are, to be everything we are capable of becoming: "What a man can be, he must be" (Maslow, 1943, p. 382). Maslow sees true self-actualization as a rare condition.

The final need man experiences, if the others have been relatively satisfied, is a *cognitive* need, the *need to know and to understand.* We need to seek out the facts, to know rather than remain ignorant, and then to understand the meaning of the facts. At this level, our knowledge and understanding do not spring from the deficiency of the safety-need level. Similarly, we can eventually be capable of experiencing an unneeded love for the being of another person, which is quite different from a selfish love due to our own deficiencies. In the earlier stage of development, love is needed; in the other case, it is not related to personal deprivation and therefore is capable of unlimited growth and enjoyment.

Growth and Regressive Forces

Growth is the inherent set of forces which bring a person toward self-actualization (Maslow, 1954, 1955, 1956, 1962, 1970). Through growth, we learn our particular aptitudes, what we really like, and what our tastes and capacities are. Growth is spontaneous, delightful, and natural, free from the necessity of intentional or purposeful straining toward a goal: We grow because we like to grow.

However, if growth is so natural, why do not all people fully grow and progress through the hierarchy? Maslow attributes this to a deeply imbedded existential dilemma basic to the nature of every human being. We have not only growth forces, but regressive influences as well, leading us to cling to safety and defensiveness out of fear, to hang on to the past. Because of regressive forces, we are afraid to take chances of jeopardizing what we already have, afraid of independence and separateness, afraid of growth. Meanwhile, growth forces impel us forward.

Life is a series of choice points. We repeatedly have to choose to go ahead or to stay back. The inherent dilemma is not a problem if we can choose on the basis of our *own* subjective delight, for when we are truly free, we will usually choose in the direction of growth. Neurotic people are likely to make the wrong choices; even when they know what they want, they do not have the *courage* to choose correctly.

We may lose the ability to experience the delight of growth if we are forced to choose between the approval of others and our own growth desires. The choice here is between others and self rather than between two strictly personal needs. For example, since safety is a basic need, and if the only way to fulfill it is to win the approval of others, our choice is likely to be for safety (compare with Rogers and Fromm). It should be noted, though, that healthy people seem able to detach themselves from an unhealthy environment and live by inner laws; it is *inner* freedom they have, and *self*-approval they seek.

Summary

Third-force psychologists insist that man must be described as he is. He must be viewed as a whole, unique individual, not analyzed in separate pieces or in terms of other men or animals. It is his own view of himself and his environment that will lead us to an understanding of his personality. Delving into his past, his unconscious wishes, and others' evaluations of his behavior can only interfere with an awareness of the phenomena that make him what he is.

Man is capable of self-awareness, and through self-awareness can become self-actualizing, can strive and grow toward fulfillment.

Third-force proponents maintain that psychology should not present merely an external view of man, for what man wants is personal understanding. Psychology should, according to these theorists, help man to find meaning and significance in life. This view has evoked intense responses from students, laymen, and a growing core of academically trained psychologists who have found their training in statistical rigor insufficient for their job of helping people. The strong reactions from such a variety of people are, in themselves, sufficient reason for psychology to pay close attention to this approach to the study of man.

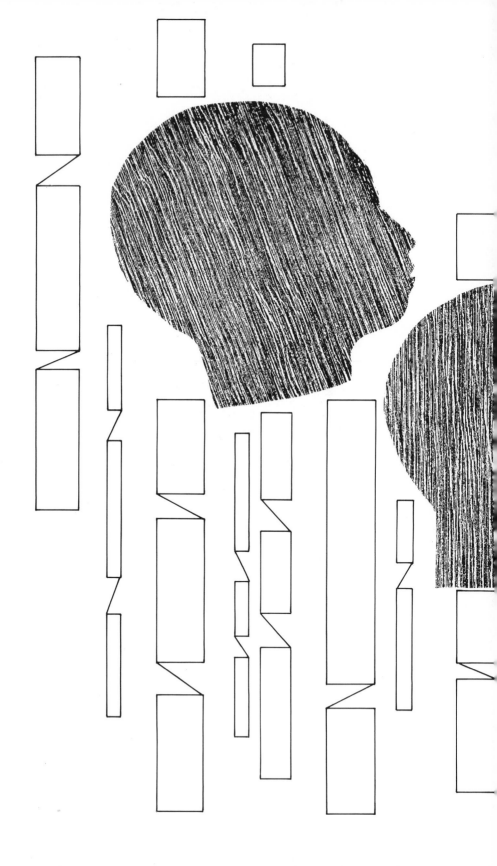

MEASUREMENT PROCESSES

PART III

7
systematic observation as measurement and assessment

The scientist who studies personality is seldom a white-coated technician surrounded by the gleaming paraphernalia of the laboratory. He is, however, one who not only thinks about human behavior, but also observes it in systematic ways.

The attention of previous chapters has been on some theories of personality representing dominant perspectives within which people think about human beings. However, theories alone cannot produce scientific knowledge. By themselves, theoretical constructs and hypotheses are empty, and must be given content. They must be related to observable events by rules of correspondence or by measurement procedures which give empirical content to theory (Chapters 2, 8). Empirical categories and systematic observation procedures constitute the empirical route to observed fact. The systematic observation procedures often are used without any particular regard to a formally and explicitly stated theory, although it is unlikely that they are used without any guiding thoughts on the part of the observer.

The systematic observation procedures discussed in this chapter are just what their label implies: relatively systematic ways of observing behavior. Observational techniques are by no means under the sole proprietorship of the professional scientist, however. They bear strong resemblance to the procedures used by laymen in the normal course of obtaining information about people. The greatest difference lies in the fact that while the layman often uses these procedures intuitively and thus without an awareness of their pitfalls or their advantages, the scientist uses them intentionally and in preplanned ways for clearly stated purposes.

Observational Strategies

There are many observational strategies for research and many ways of classifying them. The crucial determinant underlying one popular classification is the degree of control the researcher has over what the subjects experience (Scott & Wertheimer, 1962; Hyman, 1964). The amount of control usually is least in naturalistic studies and greatest in experiments. Compared with other methods, experimental control has been typically thought to represent a more advanced stage in the understanding of a behavioral phenomenon and the relevant constructs. However, all research strategies have their distinctive and necessary functions. All are capable of contributing to the development of understanding when they are done by competent observers who carefully report what they observe and under what conditions; consequently, their presentation states the range of applicability of the conclusions, and claims no more than is warranted by the data.

Each person is like all other persons, like some other persons, and like nobody else in the world. Any observational strategy may be helpful in coming to understand all people, some people, or the idiosyncratic organization and dynamics of one individual. As we shall see, the researcher's task is often to determine what the research tells us about whom.

Naturalistic Observation

The term *naturalistic observation* is used for those methods of observation which involve minimal disturbance by the observer of the subjects' naturally occurring behavior in their more or less typical environment. In other words, while gathering data, the observer tries to interfere as little as possible with the subjects. He simply observes. Naturalistic observation is the major strategy of behavior ecologists, who seek simply to describe the natural behavior units and their occurrence in natural settings (Barker, 1963; Willems & Raush, 1969; Weick, 1968). Watching students in the dormitory could provide naturalistic data about how students tend to behave with each other outside the classroom or research laboratory, particularly if the observer were another student who looked as if he "belonged" there.

The most representative and complete information about a person's behavior may be obtained by *tailing*, throughout a comparatively prolonged time period, as a private detective might do, and as psychologists did to describe the activities of a young boy in the natural habitat of his hometown (Barker & Wright, 1951). Lovers and friends frequently use much the same technique. However, smaller samples of behavior are more typical for research purposes.

Situational samples are chosen because they are distinctive in some way or maximize the chances of observing the behavior of interest. An investigator interested in children's excitability might select Christmas week as a relevant situation in which to observe his subjects; one interested in performance under stress could choose to observe college students during exam week.

In contrast, *representative samples* are taken over a variety of predetermined time periods distributed to provide a more representative sample of behavior. The kind of behavior sample observed affects the kind of conclusions that can be drawn. "He spends more time in shopping centers than in the library" could be a misleading statement about a student if the observations had been made during the Christmas season and the conclusions not specified for that situation. It could be a valid generalization if the observations had been representatively distributed throughout the year. Failure to take account of the situation of observation and the degree of situational specificity or representativeness is a common error in laymen's observational procedures, as the student draws conclusions about the professor only from observing him in a book-lined office, or about another student he observes only in the classroom or the library.

Situational testing. When the researcher needs to manipulate the environment in some way to observe a behavior of interest, he makes a *contrived* observation. For example, arranging to have the college dean call off exams could allow a contrived observation of behavior in unusual circumstances. Situational testing is a form of contrived observation for the purpose of individual personality assessment. The subject is placed in a situation which closely resembles a "real-life" situation, but which has been structured to elicit various specific behaviors of immediate interest (Anastasia, 1968; Kleinmuntz, 1967).

Although they have been used for a long time (e.g., Hartshorne & May, 1928), situational tests became popular during World War II. A task assigned to the Office of Strategic Services (OSS) was to select men for military intelligence work (Murray & MacKinnon, 1946; OSS Assessment Staff, 1948). During a three-day session of intensive training, candidates lived in small groups under the observation of the assessment staff. In addition to aptitude and projective tests, the groups were given situational tests adapted from German and British military psychology. One task was to construct, with the assistance of two helpers, a five-foot cube from wooden poles, blocks, and pegs. The helpers were actually psychologists assigned to play obstructing roles. They did so well in frustrating the candidates that no subject was able to complete the cube.

Situational tests should be related as closely as possible to the criterion situation, that is, the real-life situation which is intended to be tested (Cronbach, 1960). For example, a young man who considers it essential that his future wife be socially poised and a good cook might give his girl friend a situational test in which she must prepare and preside at a formal dinner party. Although the results of the test situation may be more precise than her response to the simple question, "Can you cook and entertain?" the test is still not the actual situation of performing those functions as a wife. The young woman's skills may improve as she practices at being a cook and party-giver—or they may deteriorate as she becomes bored with such tasks.

Behavior rating scales. Whatever the observational strategy chosen, the researcher must translate his observations into a readily understandable language which permits the observed behavior to be recorded and quantified. In view of the almost infinite number of possible observations in the natural setting, this is often more of a problem for naturalistic observations than for laboratory research. One frequently used language is the rating scale, which specifies the kinds of responses to be looked for or the judgments to be made about the person, and asks for ratings on the degree of a particular characteristic shown. Verbal definitions of the points on the scale help to enable a consistent interpretation of the meaning of the ratings on the characteristics. Such scales allow relatively easy quantification of behavior and permit a comparison between subjects (*normative measurement*) or between different situations or times for the same subject (*ipsative measurement*).

Rating scales are often designed for a specific research or practical purpose, but there are some scales available for general use. An important example is the Wittenborn Psychiatric Rating Scale (Wittenborn, 1955), which may be used quickly and easily by nonprofessional personnel in reporting the behavior of psychiatric patients at different times. The scale permits an actual description of the patient's behavior, rather than simply placing it in a diagnostic category, which seldom reflects the complexity of the behavior and does not allow for noting behavior change. Improvement may be detected and assessed; the psychologist can say not just that "He is better today," but can state exactly how the patient's behavior has changed and relate the behavior change to environmental circumstances. Such scales may, of course, be effectively used in many settings, such as in assessing the effect of various teacher styles on children who are disciplinary problems.

Peer ratings. A highly reliable observational procedure is to obtain judgments or behavior ratings by the subject's peers who observe him in natural environments. The typically high effectiveness of the technique is probably due in part to the fact that a *large* number of observers are reporting on the basis of observations of the subject's *typical* behavior in his natural environment (Anastasia, 1968). Of greater importance may be the fact that the measurements are determined by the people with whom the subject interacts in his everyday activities, instead of by an intruding psychologist. An outside observer might consider the behavior of a subject to be mature and self-sufficient. The people who actually interact with the subject may consider the same behavior a manifestation of snobbishness or shyness. The judgments of the peers are likely to be much more important in the ongoing life of the subject and thus more helpful in the understanding of his social world.

Peers may be asked to make behavior ratings of each other on a number of traits or, with the *peer nomination technique,* to "nominate" peers who fit provided descriptions, nominating either all the group members who fit the description or those for whom it is most or least characteristic (e.g., "He always wants to be the center of attention"). With children, instructions are often in the form of "Guess who is being described." These are examples of *sociometric* measurements, which also include techniques for describing the group itself (Moreno, 1953). One may detect and depict the social structure of the group, in terms of friendship, for example, and see subgroups of people who like each other, those accepted but peripheral, and isolates not chosen by anyone.

Laboratory Observations

Although naturalistic observations have unquestionable advantages, they do not easily allow the same precision and efficiency that are possible in the laboratory. For laboratory studies, the researcher may select the number and kinds of subjects he wants, and he may expose them to situations of his own choosing. For example, the researcher who is interested in how people react to emergencies does not have to sit on the street corner waiting for an accident to occur. He can arrange to produce in the laboratory what appears to the subject to be an accident. By creating the situation and selecting his subjects, he can have control over at least some of the variables he thinks relevant and can obtain greater precision than is possible in naturalistic observations (Scott & Wertheimer, 1962). However, the logic of the research designs discussed here can sometimes be applied in naturalistic settings, as will be seen in certain examples discussed later in the chapter.

Experimental method. When using an experimental design, a researcher tries to create differences in responses by exposing the subjects of an experimental group to certain selected critical conditions, called the experimental treatment (independent variable), before or during the measurement of the responses (dependent variable). The observed behavior is said to be dependent upon or to vary with the independent variable. The aim of an experiment is to make a statement about the relationship between the stimulus and the response, to attribute variability in behavior to the treatment (Chapter 1). *Organismic variance* is error variance in the experiment; it is due to unspecified differences between subjects rather than to the specified experimental treatment. In a research program with an exclusively experimental strategy, the researcher attempts to continually reduce organismic variance and increasingly specify experimental treatments as accounting for the responses of his subjects. In order to establish a definite relation between the observed responses of the experimental group and the manipulated stimuli, he must have a *control group* which does not receive the experimental treatment, and the responses of the experimental group must differ from those of the control group.

Research findings may establish the *fact* of a relationship or the *function* relating two variables. For example, if the researcher discovers that a class which was told the final examination will be extremely difficult obtains lower grades than does another class which was told nothing of the difficulty of the examination, then he has established the fact that there is a relationship between performance and the anxiety he presumably induced. However, he has not established the nature of the relationship. He cannot be certain, for instance, that every increase in anxiety is associated with a given decrease in performance. This can be known only by establishing the function relating the two variables, and requires using several levels of the variables—say, using several classes, each given a different statement regarding the level of difficulty of the impending examination. In this example, the overall relationship between anxiety and performance is, in fact, curvilinear rather than linear (Chapter 15).

Whether fact or function is established, how can the researcher say that anxiety is responsible for the response differences on the examination? He could make a *manipulation check* to see that the instructions about difficulty were effective in inducing anxiety. But how would he know that variables other than anxiety were not responsible for the results, even assuming equal instructor effectiveness in the classes? Did the students in the experimental classes happen to be of lower ability than those in the control classes; did they have less interest in course content, less sensitivity to cues about what would be asked on the exam, or less trust in the instructor who told them about exam difficulty? Even if the researcher knew the classes were equated or matched on aptitude, there are still many other variables which might be relevant; it is often impractical to try to account for all variables that may be relevant, and we do not know how many variables are possibly relevant. The research in this example could *not* be an experiment *unless* the students had been randomly assigned to classes, rather than having been allowed to choose their classes or been placed in a class according to a nonrandom procedure, such as alphabetically.

Random assignment of subjects is a critical ingredient of the pure experimental design. It is a necessary condition (though not a sufficient requirement, as we shall see) if the researcher is to claim that the group differences in the observed behavior are attributable to the treatments he provided. The random assignment is an attempt to assure that there is no variable consistently associated with differences in the dependent variable other than the experimental conditions manipulated by the researchers. Each subject must have an equal chance of assignment to any given condition so that groups differ only in the experimental treatment they have received. Of course, any one subject is bound to differ from any or all of the other subjects on other variables, but the groups should not be different in the net effect of the characteristics they bring to the situation. The larger the groups (and the more expensive the research), the more valid is the claim that they do not differ in systematic ways.

The logic of experimentation may be applied in naturalistic settings outside the confines of a laboratory and have particularly been used in naturalistic studies of altruistic behavior. For example, subjects who had been made to "feel good" by having been given cookies while studying in the library or by finding a dime in a public phone, were more likely to respond positively to a request for help than were control subjects who had not been given the pleasant experiences (Isen & Levin, 1972). Although the researchers did have control over the independent variable (cookies, dime), this (unlike control of subjects' assignment to experimental or control groups) is not a necessary factor in experimental design.

A researcher might, for example, do a field experiment testing the relative effect of rural and urban environments on the mental health of immigrants by randomly assigning the immigrants to various geographical areas differing in degree of urbanization (Scott & Wertheimer, 1962). He could not have control over the actual living conditions of the subjects, as he often does in a laboratory model. However, the random assignment of subjects enables a statement that the observed differences are due to the external conditions the immigrants encountered rather than to any pre-existing characteristics of the subjects. Psychologists, particularly ecological psychologists, are becoming aware of the opportunities for field experimentation and are employing the experimental technique developed in the laboratory in their observation of subjects in their natural environments.

Differential and mixed designs. Obviously, the psychologist using experimental designs can make useful statements, but he is in some danger that the statements will apply only to the mythical "average person" described by the group mean if he does not take account of existing personality differences. In *differential investigations* or studies, the researcher is assessing existing differences among subjects rather than trying to create differences experimentally. He studies what is "given" to him or brought to him by the subjects, looking for relationships between subject-located variables rather than between a treatment and a response. A researcher using this experimental design may eventually be able to state the fact of a relationship between specific variables, or may report the function involved in their association. This design may be used in field as well as laboratory research. Examples of statements from differential research are: Homosexuals show greater pupil dilation to pictures of same-sex than to different-sex people (Hess, Seltzer, & Shlein, 1965); people who assume life is a game of skill (internal-external locus of control variable) are more likely to believe the Warren report than are those who think life a game of chance (Hamsher, Geller, & Rotter, 1968); only children or firstborn children are more likely to be college students than are later-borns.

A *mixed design* combines features of the experimental and differential designs; it enables the researcher to detect whether different kinds of people react differently to an experimental treatment. Males and females (sex is a differential variable) react differently to instructions (experimental variable) designed to increase performance (Chapter 10). Subjects low in confidence about a task ability do more poorly when someone is watching than they do without an audience, but the audience variable has no effect on subjects high in confidence about the task (Shrauger, 1972). Part of the challenge of personality research is to discover what subject variables can profitably be considered in conjunction with what treatment variables. Biographical variables (e.g., birth order) and the psychological tests discussed in the next chapter provide subject classifications that are frequently used. Other variables of current concern (Sarason & Smith, 1971; Singer & Singer, 1972) and ones mentioned frequently in later chapters are trait anxiety, self-esteem, internal-external locus of control, sensitizing-repressing defenses, and other cognitive styles.

The advantage of differential and mixed designs is also the source of their chief deficiency: lack of random assignment of subjects, which eliminates studying the effects of individual variations. When studying individuals, one does not know what other variables are associated with the one assessed, and the other variables may be more strongly related to the behavior of interest than is the variable being measured. Thus, some psychologists contend that experimental designs are ultimately superior. Rather than study the effects of anxiety or self-esteem, say, by measuring existing individual differences on those variables, one should experimentally induce anxiety or high or low self-esteem. However, it is currently impossible or unethical to induce subject differences on some variables, such as birth order or absence of the father from the home.

More important, as long as people *do* differ, as is certainly the case, differential and mixed designs will have a proper and necessary place in psychology; in fact, these kinds of studies have been urged as a necessary corrective to the current increase in praise for experimentalism in personality psychology (Singer & Singer, 1972; Carlson, 1971). "One can study persons in experimental situations—but one cannot 'study personality experimentally'" (Carlson, 1971, p. 213).

DATA INTERPRETATION

While making observations and collecting data are fairly easily accomplished, interpreting the findings is more difficult. A friend says, "No, I don't want to go to the movies with you." Why did he say that? To interpret his statement accurately, we need much more information than the fact that he made the statement. Was it just a careless remark, or does it in fact tell us something important? Perhaps he does not like movies. Or, he likes movies, but tonight is not the night. We might conclude that he does not like us or that he likes us and movies, but not the two together. Perhaps he thought we really did not want to go and a refusal on his part was the proper and sensitive thing.

When he observes a subject, the researcher is more likely than the layman to collect data systematically, but the problems of interpretation are much the same. He too needs to know if the statement was a random reaction or a reliable answer that carries information and, if the latter, what the response tells him. And he needs to worry about the possibility that the response is not an accurate, direct reflection of those dispositions he is trying to measure. While some of the problems mentioned here are usually more acute with laboratory observations, they can plague the field researcher as well.

Reliability and Validity

Before we spend much time and energy trying to interpret our data, we want to be sure that it is reliable. It would be unusual if, for example, the means of two or more groups were exactly the same in any given study. However, is the variation due to chance, or is this a reliable difference which we can count on, one that we will observe again in similar groups and similar conditions? While the observed association between two variables is seldom perfect, we must determine whether there is a significant relation between them. One test of this is by a replication (repetition) of the observation. The reliability of the data may also be estimated by statistical techniques which allow the analyst to state the confidence with which he can say that the results are or are not due to chance. By convention, results whose probability of occurrence by chance alone is less than 5 in 100 repetitions of the research are called statistically significant ($p < .05$). To have a statistically significant result is to be able to say that "I have a 5 percent chance of being wrong in my statement that what I observed is a reliable observation." However, such statistical information does not by itself prove a point nor assure that the result has any practical or theoretical significance; reliance upon statistical criteria may become excessive (Bakan, 1966; LaFarge, 1967; Lykken, 1968; Sprott & Kalbfleisch, 1965), since statistics themselves do not tell the researcher what the results mean.

If a researcher has reliable results, he must also state the conditions of their validity. The results probably are not due to chance, but are they due to the variables he claims or to other, confounding variables? This is a matter of internal validity (Campbell, 1957; Campbell & Stanley, 1963, 1966). Random assignment of subjects, as previously discussed, helps rule out the influence of confounding variables associated with the subjects themselves, but there are other sources of error as well, particularly in incomplete research designs covering an extended period of time.

If a reliable result is safely attributable to a given variable in one instance of observation, in what other kinds of instances can we expect to observe the same result? That is, what is the degree of *representativeness* or *generality* of the results? Is the outcome valid only for these particular people in these particular circumstances? This is a matter of the external validity of the observation. Unfortunately, design features which increase internal validity are likely to lower external validity, and vice versa. The more control the researcher has over the situation and the better able he is to specify the operating variables, the more likely it is that the observation is not highly generalizable. Theoretically, we should first define the population of interest, then randomly select people from the group, so that we may eventually generalize to that population. In practice, the reverse tactic is common: We study whoever is available and then worry about defining whom they represent—or, worse yet, we forget that we must define the population and talk as if we have a universal finding.

Because of subject availability, American psychology is dominantly the psychology of the middle-class white, male, young adult who takes psychology courses and participates in research because of interest, because of a course requirement, or because of the lure of extra credit for the course grade. Certainly, trying to understand such subjects is a challenging and worthwhile goal. However, there is little reason to suspect that they are representative of mankind. Indeed, they are not even representative of young adults, or college students, or Americans in general. Nor are studies during this period in life necessarily helpful for understanding those same persons as they grow older. Intrapersonal and interpersonal dynamics do become consolidated and restructured during and after college years (Constantinople, 1969; White, 1966).

Just as subjects should be randomly selected from the population about which we make generalizations, so too should the stimulus conditions be representative samples of the subjects' typical experiences if generalizations are to be made about life outside the laboratory (Brunswick, 1947). However, research conditions are often devised because of their facility rather than because they are central to understanding the phenomenon of concern. Friendship is an obvious area in which there is precise experimental research which does not illuminate the development and power or even the nature of friendship (Strommen, 1973; Carlson, 1971). In studies of interpersonal attraction, strangers are brought together for approximately an hour, during which time they may be allowed to see each other or may only be given *false* information about one another; their attraction is often measured by their ratings of each other on the forms the psychologist provides. The results of such studies are uncontaminated by prior contact between the participants, but the results are also likely to remain uncontaminated by friendship (Strommen, 1973). Factors which contribute to a good first impression are not necessarily the same as those which sustain a continuing relationship, even when the relationship is only a few weeks or months old (see Newcomb, 1961; Rosenfeld & Jackson, 1965; Halverson & Shore, 1969). For example, extraverts may be preferred as more rewarding friends during short-term, ongoing interaction, while the certainty and stability attributed to introverts may be preferred for a long-term relationship (Hendrick & Brown, 1971).

Construct Validity

Construct validity becomes a salient issue when we wish to go beyond the data as immediately given and formulate and defend an interpretation of the data in terms of a construct. We wish to do more than say, "When I did this, the subjects did that." We want to make inferences about the meaning associated with the behavior. To do this, we must first make inferences about constructs, and show them to be valid or useful (review example, Chapter 2).

Defining a construct and establishing its validity in regard to the related observational procedures requires an elaboration of the *nomological network* in which it occurs (Cronbach & Meehl, 1955). The nomological network consists of the relationships between constructs (theoretical system), between observable behaviors (empirical system), and between constructs and observable events (measurement system). In order to elaborate the network, one must establish these relationships. Typically, the researcher may predict a diversity of behaviors as being related to the construct. In fact, if there were only one kind of response of interest and one environmental condition concomitant with it, we would not need the construct. Thus, no one piece of evidence is sufficient for establishing construct validity, and almost any kind of evidence can be used to contribute to, or detract from, construct validity.

As an example, consider a construct of recent research interest, delay of gratification (see Mischel, 1971). Mischel first noticed that two different groups of people living in close proximity (blacks and East Indians on the island of Trinidad) agreed in seeing themselves as different from one another in terms of delay of gratification. To confirm this naturalistic observation, he devised the procedure of offering children a choice between an immediate small reward (e.g., a small candy bar) or a delayed larger reward (e.g., a larger candy bar next week), and continued to establish a theoretical and empirical network about the construct, although the theoretical predictions were not derived from any one explicit formal theory.

Ability to postpone gratification (impulse control, ego strength, will power) is clinically considered an important correlate of maturity and adjustment. Thus, the fact that the behavioral measure of the construct accurately differentiated among seven-, eight-, and nine-year-old children contributes to construct validation by the *known groups* method: that is, groups expected to differ on the measure do differ (Cronbach & Meehl, 1955). Observation of an increase, over time, in these same children's capacity for delay of gratification would be a validation of the construct by the *change over occasions* strategy. (In the case of some constructs, it is of course possible that one might predict that changes should *not* be observed; e.g., a measure of emotional adjustment should not necessarily be affected by taking a physics course.)

Constructs that are theoretically related should have measures that are empirically related. Mischel reasoned that delay of gratification requires trust, specifically in the person who is making promises of the later, greater reward. Such trust is also probably a basic ingredient of social responsibility. Thus, Mischel predicted and found a relationship between his measure of delay of gratification and scores on a questionnaire of social responsibility, which had itself received previous validation. A greater number of delinquent than nondelinquent children chose an immediate smaller reward, and, among the delinquent children, those preferring the delayed reward had higher social responsibility scores. While all three measures (delinquency, questionnaire, choice test) were correlated, the relation was far from perfect; they are not all measures of exactly the same thing. If the social responsibility scores were very highly correlated with the delay of gratification measure, one would question the value or necessity of two different constructs. Moderate and low, positive and negative relationships can all contribute to construct validity.

Mischel extended the network and found, for example, that children who chose to wait for rewards also tended to cheat less, to yield to temptation more slowly, to be more concerned about achievement; there were also relationships between the behavior and the children's sociocultural and rearing conditions (e.g., presence of father in the home), and between behavior and intelligence. Certain rearing antecedents seemed likely either to facilitate or impair the development of trust. For example, the group Mischel originally observed on Trinidad had a history of past experiences in which promises of future rewards had been broken, and the culture was one in which selecting the immediate gratification was modeled and extensively rewarded.

In this country, more black students (56 percent) chose a delayed reward from a black experimenter than from a white experimenter (33 percent), apparently because they were less trusting of the white experimenter (Strickland, 1972). This suggests that if subjects in an experiment were given experiences which increased the trustworthiness of the particular experimenter, there would be an increased probability that they would choose to wait to receive a larger reward from the experimenter; this would be using an *experiment* to contribute to construct validity (a specific form of change over occasions method). Similarly, after observing a model choose a delayed or an immediate reward, children altered their preferences to be consistent with those of the model.

However, the researcher is seldom fortunate enough to find that all of his predictions about all the measures are confirmed. When they are, he may suspect the adequacy of the measuring instruments or the definitions of the construct. Mischel found that although predictions were generally confirmed, the people on the island of Trinidad who had a marked preference for immediate reward would nevertheless save money, make elaborate preparations, and forego immediate gratification in order to plan ahead for the future rewards of annual feasts, religious events, and carnival celebrations. The capacity for delay in these cases may be a very different phenomenon from that of some other kind of delay studied. Or, the same construct may be applicable but, in this case, the anticipated reward and the confidence that the reward will materialize are probably much greater than usual.

Observation and Reactivity

A significant problem in interpreting the meaning of observation is simply that in measuring a phenomenon one is changing it. Observation itself is a variable that limits validity. The very act of measurement negates the possibility of observing the phenomenon as it would have occurred had it not been observed (Heinsenberg, 1958). For instance, our knowledge of a cell's being alive may depend on our knowledge of its molecular structure; to know its structure, we may have to destroy the cell. "It is, therefore, logically possible that life precludes the complete determination of its underlying physiochemical nature" (Lana, 1969, p. 121).

Just as the biologist removes living tissue from its typical environment in order to subject it to the reactive measurement available with the microscope, the psychologist attempts to isolate behavior for analysis in his laboratory. In so doing, he is observing in an artificial environment what may well be atypical behavior. He observes in restricted and contrived situations in order to gain precision and control, but he must face the fact that with this gain, he runs the risk of making more and more precise statements about behaviors that matter less and less to the fully functioning human being.

Although the subjects' awareness of being tested or observed need not affect their responses, this awareness is likely to be a factor in many situations (a *reactive response*). An example of the reactivity of observation is the series of studies done at the Hawthorne plant of the Western Electric Company to determine the effects on production of various working conditions such as illumination, temperature, hours of work, rest periods, wage rates, and so on (Roethlisberger & Dickson, 1939). The production of the experimental group of workers increased no matter what working condition was manipulated. This phenomenon, called the *Hawthorne effect*, was attributed to the fact that the workers felt honored at being chosen for the experiment and believed that they were working together for the benefit of the rest of the employees. The fact that their behavior was being measured changed not only the magnitude of the dependent variable (the production rate), but also the nature of the social situation itself.

Test sensitization. Reactivity can be a particularly acute problem when it seems necessary to pretest the subjects before observing a specific behavior or before administering an experimental treatment. The initial measurement process may make a subject more sensitive to later experiences (Sechrest, 1968). For example, subjects who were given an attitude questionnaire about prejudice before seeing a movie on the topic responded differently to the movie and the post-movie questionnaire than did subjects who were not given the pretest (Campbell, 1957). A pretest must be considered part of the experimental treatment.

The value of pretesting is that it can increase the precision of measurement by allowing the researcher to evaluate individual differences in the amount of change from pretest to posttest. The problem of deciding between the advantages and disadvantages of pretesting can be avoided by the use of the *Solomon four-group design* in which there are two experimental groups and two control groups; one of each type of group has had the pretest while the other has not, and subjects have been randomly assigned to all groups (Solomon, 1949). In this way, the researcher may assess any test sensitization, ascertain the state of subjects before the treatment, and draw conclusions about what subjects were most or least influenced by the treatment. Unfortunately, most researchers are likely to choose randomization *or* pretesting rather than go to the expense of the four-group design.

Experimenter Effects

In our everyday observation, we are often guilty of seeing only what we want to see, and perhaps of behaving in subtle ways that lead others to behave as we expect them to. So too can the scientist fall victim to the disease of distortion, despite his attempts at objectivity (Rosenthal, 1966, 1969). Errors in interpretation are annoying and distracting, but are susceptible to correction when they are made public. More serious are those artificialities and distortions that creep into the data during the observation process itself and are hidden from public view.

In research, as in testing settings (Chapter 8), data collection implies a social interaction. The behavior of the subject has been shown to be affected by the behavior and perceived characteristics of the experimenter, and vice-versa (Rosenthal, 1966, 1969; Sechrest, 1968; Sattler, 1970). For example, experimenters have been found to prolong the data collection interaction with subjects of the opposite sex (Rosenthal, 1967; Shapiro, 1966), and female subjects are treated more protectively by their experimenters than are males (Rosenthal, 1966, 1967). Experimenters high on need for approval tend to behave so as to gain the approval of their subjects. A researcher's mood was even related to subjects' physiological responses: On the researcher's "bad day," the subjects' heart rate showed greater acceleration than on a "good day" (Malmo, Boag, & Smith, 1957). The presence of a black investigator has been shown to decrease the amount of anti-black prejudice reported by whites (Summers & Hammonds, 1966). The subject may also use the experimenter as a model and show highly similar behavior, or use him as a negative reference point and show an inverse relationship (Silverman, Shulman, & Wiesenthal, 1972).

A common experimenter effect is experimenter expectancies. Robert Merton (1948) used the term *self-fulfilling prophecy* to describe the phenomenon in which the behavior of the "prophet" is such that it makes the predicted event more likely to occur. The self-fulfilling prophecy can easily occur in the classroom (Rosenthal & Jacobson, 1968), sometimes with unfortunate consequences. If a teacher assumes, on the basis of tests, social class, or prejudice, that a child (or a whole class) is not very bright and will not perform well, the child probably will not do as well as he would otherwise. In ways not completely understood, the teacher's attitude and behavior communicate the assessment of a particular child to that child and he fulfills the teacher's "prophecy" by doing poorly. The teacher's expectations for the class also affect his own teaching efforts; a teacher aims to teach more when he expects favorable performance from the class than when his expectations are unfavorable. Fortunately, the phenomenon also works in positive ways; randomly chosen students from whom teachers were told to expect intellectual growth did fulfill the prophecy by showing greater IQ gains over the year than did control students. The effect may be partially attributable to the greater attention and praise given by the teacher to the students thought to be gifted than to the control students (Rubovits & Maehr, 1971).

Demand Characteristics

Subjects' expectancies also contribute error to research finding. When psychologists do research involving human subjects, they are dealing with sentient and uniquely motivated organisms. People think. Doing experiments with people has been compared to performing chemistry experiments with dirty test tubes (Silverman & Shulman, 1970). The contaminants are the needs, motives, and role expectancies of the experimental subjects themselves. However, when one is studying dirty test tubes, he must do research with them, and he can choose either to try to ignore the contaminants or to recognize their effect and try to understand them as part of the subject. Thus, some psychologists are trying to understand subject expectancies about the research situation.

For the human subject, an experiment is a problem-solving situation in which he tries to figure out an appropriate behavioral sequence or role (Orne, 1962, 1969, 1970). "By singling out an individual to be tested . . . the experimenter forces upon the subject a role-defining decision—What kind of person should I be as I answer these questions or do these tasks?" (Webb et al., 1966, p. 16). At some level, the subject tries to determine the true purpose of the research and, often, to respond in ways that support the hypothesis he thinks is being tested: He tries to play the role of a good subject. The behavior selected may be considered, upon later reflection, to be dishonest or atypical, but the subject need not have felt deceptive in the situation itself; the "faking" was not done with intentional awareness.

Demand characteristics are those cues which govern the subject's perception and communicate to him what is expected and what the experimenter hopes to find; therefore, they shape the role the subject tries to play (Orne, 1969). In a sensory deprivation experiment, for example, the presence of a "panic button" to be pressed in order to ask for release from the situation is a demand characteristic to which the subject may react, "I am expected to be upset by the situation." In this example, the subject is actively attempting to respond appropriately to the totality of the situation.

However, cooperation with the demand characteristics to support the assumed hypothesis is not the only reaction available to a demand-aware subject, particularly when a behavior with potentially negative implications is being tested (Silverman & Shulman, 1970; Page & Scheidt, 1971; Rosenberg, 1969). Where there is a conflict between favorable self-presentation and cooperating with the hypothesis, "looking good" will be the stronger motive (Sigall, Aronson, & Vanhoose, 1970). However, subjects do come to different conclusions about what makes them look good (Page & Scheidt, 1971). "Demand awareness and evaluation apprehension may be viewed as complementary processes that together describe the *social nature of the psychological experiment* from the subject's point of view" (Page & Scheidt, 1971, p. 304; italics added).

Deception. Psychologists, particularly those doing personality and social psychology research, sometimes deceive the subjects about the purpose of the study, the apparatus, the treatment procedure, or the performance of other subjects; or they may mislead the subjects in regard to the subjects' own behavior and characteristics. The ethical issues involved in such deception in experiments have been increasingly discussed (Stricker, Messick, & Jackson, 1969; Kelman, 1965, 1967; Baumrind, 1964; Milgram, 1964; McGuire, 1969). While the psychologists engaged in deception may ordinarily be decent people, ". . . we seem to forget that the experimenter-subject relationship—whatever else it is—is a *real* inter-human relationship, in which we have responsibility toward the subject as another human being whose dignity we must preserve (Kelman, 1967, p. 5). By institutionalizing the use of deception in experiments, psychologists may be contributing to the increasing societal pressure to treat man as an object to be manipulated, leading him to view himself as an object.

In addition to the ethical implications of his behavior, the effectiveness of the psychologist's deception in gaining useful scientific information has been questioned (Simons & Piliavin, 1972; Carlson, 1971; Kelman, 1967; Stricker, Messick, & Jackson, 1969; Schultz, 1969). As knowledge of misleading tactics becomes more widespread, we can expect subjects to have a tendency to be suspicious of all psychological experiments (Argyris, 1968; Ring, 1967; Allen, 1966). Participation in a prior study using deception may arouse disbelief about a later study, although the disbelief need not generalize unless the two studies have something in common (Brock & Brock, 1966).

Among the immediate consequences of deception for research effectiveness, the most serious is that it increases the difficulty of interpreting the meaning of the results. When deception is used, the situation is likely to be more ambiguous than is usually the case, since information about the situation is withheld and false reasons are substituted. This arouses suspicion and probably makes the subjects more likely to try to figure out for themselves what is going on. Some subjects try to do a good job of following instructions even though they are suspicious (Holmes, 1967; Fillenbaum, 1966); however, other subjects *over-compensate* in their attempts to be honest and actually show behavior opposite to what would otherwise occur without their suspicion (Allen, 1966), an occasional reaction exhibited by experimenters offered payment for "good results" (Rosenthal, 1961).

Thus, all in all, deception increases the difficulty of knowing what the subject is thinking and what he is responding to. Not only is the researcher behaving unethically, but he is also losing the scientific value he rationalizes to be the justification for his behavior. The researcher loses control of the situation and is unable to specify the stimulus associated with the responses he observes. Not all personality and psychological research studies use deceptive techniques. However, the ethical and scientific problems are acute enough to warrant concern and public and professional sensitivity.

Unobtrusive Measurement

In the face of problems posed by deception, reactivity, test sensitization, experimenter effects, and demand characteristics, some psychologists have urged the discovery and use of unobtrusive or nonreactive measures, which do not affect the response dispositions being assessed (Webb et al., 1966). Thus, in many ways, we have come full cycle, trying to gain some of the benefits of naturalistic observation. Observing nonverbal information, such as expressive movement, speech patterns, postures, distances maintained between people (e.g., Duncan, 1968, 1972; Mehrabian, 1969; Sechrest, 1968) are considered unobtrusive measures. For example, introversion and anticipated stress in a social interaction increased the linear distance assumed between people (Leipold, 1963).

With other, more distinctively unobtrusive measures, the person himself need not be present while his responses are being measured. A reactive measure of preferences among museum exhibits would be to ask subjects (museum visitors) which exhibit they most preferred, and would be subject to a great deal of bias in reports; an unobtrusive measure would be to observe the wear of the floor tiles or carpet (behavior traces) in front of the exhibits after the visitors have gone. Assessment by means of archival measures or other factual information gathered without the person's awareness can also be useful. The diagnosis of schizophrenia was related negatively to the measure of number of activities in high school as determined by yearbooks (Barthell & Holmes, 1968). Graffiti may be analyzed to index sex attitudes or other topics of current concern. A very simple unobtrusive study provided some information on the relationship between political sentiment (during the 1968 presidential elections) and obeying the law that probably could not have been attained through direct obtrusive means (Wrightsman, 1969). Political sentiment was assessed by the bumper stickers on cars in parking lots; lawfulness was operationalized as the presence of a required $15 automobile tax stamp on the car. A correlation between political preference and lawfulness was detected. Simply to have asked subjects about their political preferences and respect for the law would have been to take an extremely reactive measurement. While unobtrusive measures cannot totally replace all other forms of observation, their potential should be seriously considered and pursued.

THE INDIVIDUAL

Case Studies, N = 1

The essential feature of a case study is that $N = 1$, though the unit of analysis may be an individual, a social unit such as a group or culture, or a particular event (such as a natural disaster). In practice, case studies are most frequently in-depth descriptions of a single individual used for purposes of individual assessment, particularly in service professions such as psychotherapy, social work, and medicine. Those who prepare case histories do so to assist in the immediate and very practical goal of understanding one person. (We all implicitly make case studies of people we know well.) Case studies may also serve useful roles in the development of scientific understanding if their chief limitation is recognized: lack of generalizability. With just one subject, we cannot know the extent to which people differ in the observed behavior and cannot comment upon the general applicability of the findings—we do not know how much we know. Lack of control is often associated with this problem, though it need not be; that is, case studies can effectively be used in conjunction with experimental observations.

Case studies do have a firm, though largely unrecognized, place in psychology, including the experimental areas of learning and perception (Dukes, 1965; Davidson & Costello, 1969). "A few studies, each in impact like the single pebble which starts an avalanche, have been the impetus for major developments in research and theory. Others, more like missing pieces from nearly finished jigsaw puzzles, have provided timely data on various controversies" (Dukes, 1965, p. 76).

Case studies provide valuable descriptions of complex theoretical ideas or techniques, uncommon events, and events which require unusual time and effort to observe. Because so few true cases of multiple personality have been recorded (only about 86), the detailed study of Eve White (and Eve Black and Jane) was particularly valuable (Thigpen & Cleckley, 1954).

Case studies may be used in combinations to provide survey information or to establish a data pool (Barry, Bacon, & Child, 1957; Escalona & Heider, 1959). At the simplest level, we may count the number of cases in which a given theoretical prediction was or was not confirmed (a beginning step toward measurement that Freud did not take, Chapter 3). More complex analysis is possible through content analysis (Chapter 8). The *critical incident technique* (Flanagan, 1954) is a promising method of obtaining exploratory survey information on aspects of behavior not yet studied intensively. Observers report particularly meaningful experiences or events (such as examples of very satisfactory or unsatisfactory on-the-job behavior).

Currently, a single case study cannot confirm a point of view. It can, however, *challenge* a view. This is because the typical scientific law is stated in the form "All A is B" rather than in the form "No C is D." The law can never be proved conclusively because all cases cannot be observed, but it can be challenged by one negative incidence. For example, learning to understand language had been hypothesized to depend upon hearing oneself speak. A description of a boy who was congenitally unable to talk but who could nevertheless understand language successfully challenged this view (Lenneberg, 1962).

Necessity? The Person in Personality Research

In spite of the demonstrated usefulness of the case study approach, it is not used as much as it could be and, perhaps, must be if we are to find the person in personality research (Carlson, 1971). Perhaps most important, the case study is a suitable vehicle for discovering and discussing the naturally functioning, complex individual who is, after all, the target of personality psychology (White, 1966). Conventional research procedures typically study slices of personality, one at a time, and these slices may be arbitrary behavior segments which do not correspond very well with natural behavior units. What is relevant to understanding the nonexistent perfectly average person may be irrelevant to the ubiquitous nonaverage person. Many important details of a person are best seen in terms of his own particular life, not in terms of group generalizations. For example, analysis of Theodore Dreiser's novel, *A Gallery of Women*, resulted in trait dimensions which were highly related to Dreiser's own life, and these were *not* trait dimensions which could be recast readily into the kind of structure which typically emerges from aggregate *group* data (Rosenberg & Jones, 1972).

Studies of single cases may be used to put the pieces together or to generate and test hypotheses about behavior principles pertaining to specific people, or hypotheses about the organization and dynamics of people generally. Studies of one or two traits at a time cannot lead to principles of personality organization, nor can an hour's observation define principles of personality change. Single case histories are susceptible to quantitative analysis rigorous enough to please the most adamant of measurement fanatics. Baldwin (1942) analyzed letters written over an eleven-year period by Jenny, an unhappy old lady (see Allport, Chapter 5). Nunnaly (1955) used the Q method to study changes in the self-concept of Miss Sun. Osgood and Luria (1954), using the semantic differential technique (Chapter 8), mapped the semantic space of the three personalities of Eve as they changed with therapy.

Although Skinnerians and humanists are not usually in agreement on how to approach the study and treatment of human beings, they do agree on the value of the single case in the study of personality. Skinner has maintained essentially that there is no variability between people— when we know enough to specify all the relevant conditions for the observations. Behavioral laws are general: Two people in exactly the same situation (which implies the same genetic make-up and the same life history) would behave the same. Bonner, the humanist, says: "Like Skinner and others, we should have greater confidence in the 'intensive concentration on the single case'. . . . A sound psychology of personality can be built on the study of a single case. We believe that a detailed knowledge of the traits of single individuals can increase psychology's predictive power" (Bonner, 1965, p. 30).

SUMMARY

The psychologist has a large assortment of observational strategies, techniques, and concepts of data interpretation at his disposal. He can observe his subjects in their natural habitat, contrive observations in field research, find out how the subjects are seen by their peers, or bring subjects into the laboratory where he may measure their behavior under constant, controlled conditions. By moving into the laboratory, he gains the capability of making more precise statements about what variables are operating to affect the behavior, but he also encounters there the problem of making observations in an increasingly artificial environment and the risk of concentrating on segments of personality which may not be important, or valid, in the subjects' natural life.

The fact that the researcher is observing and measuring may change the phenomenon he is studying, and his own expectations will influence what he observes. His problems are complicated because he is dealing with subjects who think and who try to understand and respond in ways they consider desirable and appropriate to the situation they are in. The use of deceptive tactics in manipulating the subject to behave as the researcher expects may result in a loss of aspects of the researcher's scientific precision.

The challenge, for professional and layman alike, is to determine the meaning of observations and to put together pieces of information in order to understand a complex human being. The case study can play a vital role in this endeavor.

8
personality measurement through testing

Can personality be measured? No, not strictly speaking. We cannot measure individuals themselves or "personality," for measurement is the assignment of numbers according to rules, and we cannot put numbers on a personality. However, we can measure properties of an individual, his behavior, the descriptions provided by others, and the responses he makes on personality tests. Similarly, we cannot measure the concept "book," but we can measure the properties of a specific book, such as its weight and thickness, which help to define what we mean when using the term "book" (Torgerson, 1958). Thus, any measurement of personality is indirect in that it is a measure of selected manifestations of personality as a construct, a measurement of some of the observable features and actions from which we make inferences about the construct of personality (Chapter 2). As with the book, measurements of the properties can help to define what we mean by the construct, "personality."

In the previous chapter, we looked at some techniques for the systematic observation of behavior and some of the problems in interpreting the observations. In this chapter we shall do much the same, with the difference that we are observing responses elicited under the specific conditions of psychological testing, and our techniques are those of personality assessment. Psychological tests, such as those discussed in this chapter, are often the basis for subject classification in the differential and mixed designs discussed in the previous chapter. We shall raise questions about how one knows what he should be trying to observe and measure, and about the most effective role of the human observer in the assessment of individuals.

Measurement Techniques:
Information and Requirements

Scale Properties

Whatever observation or assessment procedure is used, there must be numbers assigned in systematic ways if there is to be a measurement process relating theory and observation. The sensitivity of the measurement scale is simply a matter of how much information about the properties of the behavior is contained in the numbers representing those properties; this information is, in turn, limited by the sensitivity of the observations themselves.

The easiest measurement scale to construct and use is a *nominal scale.* It provides a quick and very crude way of assigning people (or other objects or events) to discrete, discontinuous categories; names, nonsense syllables, or Sanskrit characters serve as well as numbers in labeling these categories. In regard to the property in question, nominal statements denote or reflect only the relationship of equality among the objects, people, or events with a shared name, and lack of equality with objects of a different name. One does or does not fall into a given category; if the former, the object, person, or event is like all others who are also in that category and unlike all others who are not. Thus, nominal measurement is essentially a typology. It is the crude measurement of the two-level differential study discussed previously (Chapter 7). Nominal distinctions can be useful if they are followed quickly by attempts to determine and measure the underlying variables that should be of concern and if they are recognized as *not* noting similarities on *all* properties of the objects. "Males solve mechanical problems quickly and females do not" is a useful nominal statement, but it tells us little about males and females or about problem solution. For example, measurement of socialization variables concerning amount of prior encouragement and experience with such problems is likely to tell us more about problem solution and to encourage research aimed at detecting and accounting for the fact that some females are better than some males on the task. Nominal statements do not contain much information and easily lead to an oversimplified, sometimes erroneous view (some logicians refuse to consider nominal scales to be true measurement scales, e.g., Torgerson, 1958). They are, however, ubiquitous.

Other measurement scales enable more precise and accurate statements than do nominal scales; they carry more information and are necessary aspects of functional designs (Chapter 7). *Ordinal scales* reflect rank order as well as equality among the properties of the objects, events, or people measured. *Interval scales* permit, in addition, statements about the distance between any two objects measured. If an interval scale has a natural origin (a zero point), it is a *ratio scale.* Unfortunately, this scale is rare in psychology. Because we have not defined zero intelligence or zero aggressiveness, we cannot make statements that one person is twice as intelligent or one-fourth as aggressive as another; often we can say only that John is less intelligent or more aggressive than Mary.

Whether we are professional psychologists or laymen trying to make sense of the world and the people in it, we can escape the crudeness of nominal thinking only by increasing the precision of what we think and try to see. Our thoughts may be so crude that we think and see only that "this person is a college senior and that person is a college freshman" (nominal), or that "college seniors have had more years of schooling than have college freshmen" (ordinal). At a more sophisticated level, we might think, "The difference between the level of education of college seniors and that of sophomores is the same as the difference between the level of education of juniors and that of freshmen" (interval). With even greater precision, we might consider that "First-semester college freshmen have had only one-eighth of the formal college education that second-semester seniors have had and one-sixth of what second semester juniors have had" (ratio).

As the complexity of thought and observation increases, so too does the complexity of the measurement system possible, and necessary, to relate the two; consequently, we are dealing here with more information. In this way, measurement systems function as a language with which we describe and think about the world.

Testing and Measurement

The meanings of testing, measurement, and assessment overlap but are not synonymous (Tyler, 1963). Tests are simply standardized situations designed to elicit samples of behavior. Their dominant use is in assessing an individual for the immediate, practical purpose of making appropriate decisions affecting him (e.g., counseling, therapy, job assignment); but they are also invaluable tools in personality research, which seeks to establish general laws descriptive of human behavior.

Some tests do not result in numerical scores and, consequently, are not measuring devices. However, they may provide information considered useful for personality assessment. We shall be particularly concerned here with tests as measuring instruments, although we will note assessment procedures which lack the benefit of quantification.

Measurement: Reliability and Validity

A test, or any observation procedure, must have the logical properties of reliability and validity if it is to be useful. We must be able to count on it (reliability) to do a job (validity). Measurement error reduces both reliability and validity.

Reliability statistics are estimates of the extent to which individual differences in test scores are attributable to true differences in the characteristics. *Correlation coefficients* are often used to evaluate reliability. The further the correlation is from 1.00, the less closely associated are two sets of numbers and the more irrelevant factors have influenced the scores, thus increasing measurement error and reducing the likelihood of the test's producing consistent results. Test reliability is expected to be in the .80's. Specific ways in which reliability may be estimated are shown in Table 8–1.

The degree to which a test is able to achieve clearly stated aims indicates its *validity* (APA, 1966, pp. 12–14). Unless a test meets its goal and does the job, the fact that it is measuring something consistently is not impressive. A test can be reliable without being valid, but it cannot be valid without being reliable. However, since tests are used for many purposes, the kind of information required to establish test validity varies.

Construct validity. The most important function of tests in contributing to scientific understanding is the measurement of theoretical constructs (Chapters 2, 7). Tests can be part of the nomological network which establishes construct validity. Concomitantly, in order to use a test to best advantage, we must know the construct of which it is a relevant measure; every use of the test can give evidence which contributes to, or detracts from, its construct validity. To know something about the construct validity of a test is to know what it measures, how it works, what other constructs, tests, and facts it is related to, and how. The name of a test is not necessarily a help in determining what it measures, nor is a construct necessarily defined by a test bearing its name. In fact, two tests with the same label, such as "achievement anxiety," may measure very different constructs.

However, in the case of some tests, construct validity is not necessary. All that matters is criterion validity; in other words, it has been shown empirically that the test results are associated with a specific criterion behavior of interest. Construct validity becomes important when one asks what is being measured by this test so that it can predict, say, who will do well in college. The more elaborate the nomological network, the more meaning there is in the construct and the more we know about what the test is measuring or why some people score higher than others on it.

SELECTED TEST PROCEDURES

In any testing situation, two or more people are interacting. The examiner may be immediately involved and be the one who will make a decision about the subject (e.g., a potential employer, a mental health expert), or he may be an instrument gathering information to be used by others. Whatever the situation, he may be influenced by biases, preconceptions, or moods (Chapter 7). The subject, too, receives and processes information, and his responses may be colored by his reaction to the examiner or by what he perceives to be his proper role, by doubts

TABLE 8–1 Techniques for Measuring Reliability

TESTING SESSIONS REQUIRED	TEST FORMS REQUIRED	
	One	Two
One	*Split-half reliability.* Two scores are obtained for each individual by dividing the test into comparable halves. Also called a measure of internal consistency. Test is usually split into odd and even items rather than first and second halves. Other things being equal, the longer the test, the more reliable it will be; we get a more adequate measure with a larger sample of behavior. Error is due to fluctuations in performance from one set of items to another, content sampling. *Scorer or inter-judge reliability.* Two scores are obtained for each individual by having one test scored by two (or more) scorers or judges. Relevant for tests without highly standardized procedures and routine scoring, when much is left to the judgment of the scorer, such as projective tests and some tests of creativity. Error is due to differences between the scorers.	*Alternate form, immediate, reliability.* Two scores for each individual from two forms of the same test given in the same session. Error is due to fluctuations in performance from one set of items to another, to content sampling (not to fluctuations over time, time sampling. Alternate forms should contain the same number of items, expressed in the same form and covering the same type of content, with equal range and level of difficulty. Reduces but does not eliminate practice effects.
Two	*Test-retest reliability.* Two scores are obtained for each individual by repeating the test on a second occasion. Reliability is specific to the time interval, and decreases as the interval lengthens. The shorter the interval, the more likely inconsistencies in scores are due to intervening events, which do not necessarily affect all subjects equally. Practice also produces varying amounts of improvement on the re-test scores. A measure of temporal stability; error is due to time sampling, fluctuations over time.	*Alternate form, delayed, reliability.* Two scores for each individual from two forms of the same test, administered in different sessions. Measures both temporal stability and consistency of response to different item samples, both of which are important for many purposes; error is due to time sampling and to content sampling.

SOURCE: Adapted from Anastasi, A. *Psychological testing* (3rd ed.). New York: Macmillan, 1968. Pp. 78–89.

and suspicions arising from prior situations in which deceptive techniques had been used, or by what he considers the intended use of this particular test. Both the examiner and the subject thus may be sources of measurement error with any testing procedure, but tests differ in the relative extent to which there is likely to be error (and therefore reduced reliability and validity) attributable to subject and examiner (Table 8–2).

Self-Report Techniques

The interview. The interview involves a face-to-face encounter between two (or more) people. In an *unstructured interview,* conversation can develop naturally with minimum constraint and pressure upon either participant (Kleinmuntz, 1967). The interviewer may have some basic questions which he must ask, but he is free to choose his method of obtaining the answers and free to explore facets of the issue not explicitly called for. A skillful interviewer may obtain all the information he needs while the respondent is relatively at ease and perhaps not worrying about what information the interviewer is gathering or its potential use. However, since the situation is not standardized, this apparently advantageous freedom may also be the source of problems. Because each respondent encounters a different interviewing situation, comparison between respondents is difficult and there is no clear base line against which to compare any one person. In contrast, the *structured interview* is more nearly equal for all respondents because the interviewer tries to use the

TABLE 8–2   Classification of Measurement Techniques

		Extent to which success is dependent upon the examiner as a part of the measuring instrument in collecting, scoring, interpreting the data	
		High	*Low*
Success of test, dependent upon subject's apparent intent or willingness to reveal or conceal specific information about himself	*High*	Interviews	Self-report personality inventories, paper-and-pencil tests, questionnaires Intelligence tests Interest inventories Value measurement
	Low	Projective techniques	Situational tests Biological measurements Behavior in laboratory Tailing techniques, behavioral sampling, natural situations Sociometric measurements

same kinds of questions for each interview and may, in fact, work from an interview schedule of questions. However, the restrictions of the structure may interfere with open communication and prevent a relaxed atmosphere so that the interview becomes an inquisition.

Generally, the less structured the interview, the less reliability and validity it is likely to have (Kleinmuntz, 1967); in both the structured and unstructured interview, the results are highly dependent upon both the subject and the administrator. The subject may behave in uncharacteristic and misleading ways because of his anxiety and his expectations. He may alter his behavior in order to present a positive impression or may withhold information that he feels would contribute to a negative assessment of his abilities, traits, interpersonal skills, or whatever is being evaluated.

The *halo effect* is a dominant way in which the interviewer can contribute error in the results of the interview: He has, or develops, a favorable or unfavorable reaction to the subject on the basis of one characteristic and this reaction then influences his interaction with the subject and his judgment of other characteristics. For instance, an interviewer's fondness for blond people, or for people who answer his first question as he himself would have done, may lead him to an unjustifiably favorable impression of a subject who conforms to these preferences. Such biases in interviewer judgments may be minimized by the experience of the interviewer, by the use of structured interviews, and by explicit, well-defined rating scales according to which the interviewer evaluates the subject (Chapter 7).

Rating scales also enable quantification and thus extend the value of the interview for scientific research. Similarly, the value of the interview, particularly for research, is furthered by the use of *content analysis,* whereby verbal behavior is coded and quantified. For example, classification of a client's statements revealing defensiveness and hostility toward various family members during several therapeutic interviews showed systematic changes supporting Miller's theory about conflict and displacement (Murray, 1954, 1962; Chapter 5).

In spite of the possibility of poor results, the interview will undoubtedly continue to be a prime technique, in practical situations, for making decisions about people and their behavior. One may hope that the interviewer is aware of the pitfalls as well as the advantages of this method of assessment. As a research tool, its potential is increasingly recognized.

Self-report inventories. Self-report tests, inventories, or personality scales are usually paper-and-pencil tests consisting of statements to which the subject reacts in terms of their applicability to him. As with interviews, the success of the procedure is often highly dependent upon the subject's intent and ability to provide information about himself, but unlike the usual interview, the self-report test is much less susceptible to errors made by the examiner. The subject typically fills out a form, and the examiner need not necessarily be with the subject during the testing itself. There is, however, usually some interaction between examiner and subject which may affect test results, as will be seen later in the chapter. Responses are scored against a standard answer key, so that the examiner's interpretation of the subject's behavior during testing does not affect test scores (though observation of the subject's behavior might be useful for some kinds of interpretation of the test scores). Thus, the self-report inventories are sometimes arbitrarily called "objective" tests.

Although the administration and scoring of self-report inventories are relatively straightforward, the use and interpretation of the test results are very much under the control of the examiner and reflect some fundamental assumptions about the meaning of test scores and, indeed, that of behavior in general. Self-report test results, or any behavior for that matter, may be used as *signs* from which to make psychometric inferences about traits or other characteristics of the subject that are not directly observable (constructs). The test responses are not of particular interest in and of themselves; their value is that they are signs or manifestations associated with nontest behavior (Loevinger, 1957). For example, the test responses may be considered a sign of the subject's *self-concept*, a true description of the way he sees himself; a sign of his *public self-concept*, how he wants others to see him (Cronbach, 1960); or a sign of the traits which actually are descriptive of him. Self-reports, accurate or inaccurate, may be also used as signs for *dynamic interpretation* in which clinical judgment is used, not so much to infer a specific trait as to build a complete picture of the underlying psychodynamics.

In contrast to these approaches to test use and interpretation is the procedure of viewing the test responses as a *sample* of behavior important in and of itself (e.g., Mischel, 1968, 1971). Test responses are to be observed and understood without reference to internal causes or conditions. Assumptions about the insight or intent of the subject or about the accuracy of his self-view are irrelevant. Untrue statements may be as useful as true ones if relationships have been empirically established between the test responses and other behavior or other observable events, and the test user need not worry about trying to decide which is which. Construct and content validity are irrelevant because there is no meaning assumed to exist apart from the responses themselves. Empirical, or criterion, validity is the only appropriate benchmark for evaluating the test. This position is, of course, the application to psychological testing of the strict empirical approach typified by Skinner (Chapter 5). The MMPI is the prototype of this approach to test development.

MMPI. The Minnesota Multiphasic Personality Inventory, commonly called the MMPI or the Mult, is one of the most frequently used and thoroughly researched of all test instruments. It is a 550-item true-false test on which the subject is required to indicate whether a wide variety of statements are applicable to himself. The test items range from social interests to attitudes to physical and mental health.

The MMPI was developed by J. Charnley McKinley and Starke R.

Hathaway at the University of Minnesota to differentiate groups of psychiatric patients (criterion groups) from samples of normal people (control groups). Each scale score (Table 8–3) represents the degree of similarity between the subject's answers and those answers that served to discriminate between each specific psychiatric group and normal samples. An item which schizophrenic patients answered differently from the normals is keyed on the Schizophrenia Scale. There are no attempts to understand why one group should answer True and another False. "Thus, if a hypochondriac says that he has 'many headaches' the fact of interest is that he *says* this" (Meehl, 1945, p. 9). The development and interpretation of the MMPI have centered on actuarial or strictly empirical information. The test responses are considered samples of behavior important in their own right rather than signs from which internal events are to be inferred. With a precise application of the MMPI, all that matters is the fact that response differences between groups were empirically shown. Curiously, however, MMPI researchers have come to be concerned with formulating constructs about characteristics underlying different responses and have shifted their attention to problems of developing construct validity: What does it mean about a person when he says he has many headaches or when he has a high score in depression? (Hathaway, 1960)

Profile analysis, which takes account of the total pattern of scores on all scales, is common in clinical use of the MMPI (Figure 8–1). The interpretation of a high score on one scale varies with the scores on the other scales. Empirically developed codebooks providing interpretations of major profile patterns and data from groups of subjects can be efficient indicators of underlying processes obscured by unreliability of individual profiles (Goldberg, 1972).

In spite of its popularity, the MMPI is not without fault in terms of the reliability of some scales and the adequacy of the criterion groups used in validating the scales (Anastasia, 1968; Kleinmuntz, 1967). Some criterion groups were quite small, and the use of the diagnostic categories within which the groups were differentiated fluctuates widely so that the criterion itself has low reliability. A major value of the MMPI remains that it has served as an important prototype for actuarial test construction, and has provided a large and continually used pool of items, about which there is extensive data. Items from this pool have been used in a large number (perhaps 300) of special MMPI scales and new tests (Butcher, 1969). Special scales have been derived to measure, for example, defensiveness, anxiety, repression, delinquency, ego strength, and the potential for committing violent crimes (Little & Fischer, 1958; Welsh, 1956; Hathaway & Monachesi, 1963; Barron, 1953; Megargee, 1971). Prominent tests using items drawn from the MMPI pool include the CPI, MAS, and R-S scales.

CPI. The California Psychological Inventory, or CPI (Gough, 1957, 1968), is one of the most comprehensive and well-constructed personality

TABLE 8–3   Validity and Clinical Scales of the MMPI

Scale	Sample item	Interpretation
?	No sample. Score is the number of items marked in the "cannot say" category	One of four validity scales; a high score indicates evasiveness.
L	I get angry sometimes. (False)	Second validity scale. High scores from people trying to present themselves in a favorable light.
F	Everything tastes the same. (True)	Third validity scale. High scores suggest carelessness, confusion, or an attempt to fake bad.
K	I have very few fears compared to my friends. (False)	Last validity scale. High score suggests defensive test-taking attitude. Excessively low scores may indicate lack of ability to deny symptoms, over-openness.
1. Hs Hypochondria	I wake up fresh and rested most mornings. (False)	High scorers described as cynical, defeatist, and crabby.
2. D Depression	At times I am full of energy. (False)	High scorers tend to be shy, despondent, and distressed.
3. Hy Hysteria	I have never had a fainting spell. (False)	High scorers tend to complain of multiple symptoms.
4. Pd Psychopathic deviate	I like school. (False)	Some high scorers are adventurous, courageous, generous.
5. MF Masculinity-femininity	I like mechanics magazines. (False)	High scoring males described as aesthetic and sensitive; high scoring females described as rebellious, unrealistic, and indecisive.
6. Pa Paranoia	I am happy most of the time. (False)	High scorers described as shrewd, guarded, worrisome.
7. Pt Psychoasthenia	I am certainly lacking in self-confidence. (True)	Fearful, rigid, anxious and worrisome.
8. Sc Schizophrenia	I believe I am a condemned person. (True)	Withdrawn, unusual.
9. Ma Hypomania	I am an important person. (True)	Sociable, energetic, impulsive.
10. Si Social Introversion	I enjoy social gatherings just to be with people. (False)	High scorers described as modest, shy, and self-effacing. Low scorers described as sociable, colorful, and ambitious.

True or False responses noted for the items indicate the scored direction of each item.

SOURCE: Kleinmuntz, B. *Personality measurement.* Homewood, Ill.: Dorsey, 1967. P. 220.

FIGURE 8–1

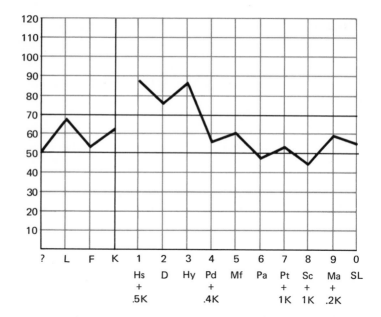

MMPI Profile, Illustrating the Conversion V Code.

Scales 1 and 3 are higher than Scale 2, giving a V-shaped profile frequently associated with conversion hysteria, in which somatic complaints are combined with emotional immaturity, dependency, and a tendency to evade problems. When Scales 1, 2, and 3 are elevated (above 70), the profile is referred to as the neurotic triad. If Scales 1 and 3 are higher than Scale 2, it is the conversion V. Scores are plotted in terms of standard scores with a mean of 50 and a standard deviation of 10 (determined from original control sample of approximately 700 people). Scores higher than 70 (2 standard deviations above the mean) are generally considered indicative of pathological deviations, though the clinical significance of a score may vary from one scale to another.

Source: Adapted from Anastasi, 1968.

inventories available and has the notable advantage of having been standardized on normal populations (Anastasia, 1968; Kleinmuntz, 1967). About half of its 480 items are from the MMPI. The items for eleven of the eighteen scales were selected using external criteria such as course grades, social class, participation in extracurricular activities, and ratings by the subject's peers.

MAS. The Taylor Manifest Anxiety Scale (MAS or MA) was developed to select subjects for learning experiments (Taylor, 1953). However, the items were chosen to correspond to a standard definition of chronic anxiety (Cameron, 1947), and the test is correlated with other measures of anxiety in predictable ways (Kleinmuntz, 1967; Byrne, 1966). It is frequently used in research as a measure of anxiety as a trait (Chapter 15).

R-S scale. The Repressor-Sensitizer (R-S) scale provides an improved measure of the same kind of dimension rated by the MMPI Hysteria and Psychasthenia scales (Byrne, 1961, 1964). A low score indicates the dominant use of repression, denial, blocking, or avoiding as defense mechanisms. A high score (sensitizer) indicates the use of sensitizing defenses such as reaction formation, isolation, intellectualization, rumination, obsession, compulsion, or projection. The repressor has much in common with Freud's phallic character, and the sensitizer is very like the Freudian anal character (Chapter 3). Because of the greater anxiety manifest with the sensitizing defenses than with the repressing defenses, the R-S scale correlates highly with the MAS (Joy, 1963).

Although the tests previously discussed (and others mentioned later in the chapter) use the item format in which the respondent indicates agreement or disagreement, or degree of applicability to himself, other techniques are also used in self-reports, often to specifically determine self-concept. Among the more frequently used and flexible formats are the Adjective Check List, the Q-sort, the semantic differential technique, and the Rep Test. In each case, the specific content of test stimuli is often varied for a particular research and applied purpose, but there are standard forms available with some reliability and validity information.

Adjective check lists. With adjective check lists, the subject simply checks those adjectives he considers characteristically descriptive of himself or applicable to himself as he feels at the moment. Often a researcher constructs a list for a specific purpose. Frequently used and researched lists include the Nowlis Mood Inventory (Nowlis & Nowlis, 1956) and Gough's Adjective Check List, or ACL (Gough, 1960; Gough & Heilbrun, 1965). In the latter format, responses to 300 adjectives may be scored for twenty-four scales, some of which were empirically validated.

Q-sort. With the Q-sort technique, the subject is asked to sort cards containing statements such as "I am a responsible person," or "I am shy," into piles ranging from "most characteristic" to "least characteristic" of himself (Butler & Haigh, 1954; Block, 1961) and based, for example, on his perception of his real self. He must, however, place a specified number of cards in each pile to produce a normal distribution (Stephenson, 1953). In addition, the subject is often asked to sort the cards under other instructions, for example, to indicate what or how he would like to be (ideal self), how he thinks others see him (social self), how he thinks any other specific person (parent, wife, teacher) sees him or wants him to be, how he perceives others, or how he perceives fantasied states or people. The technique became especially popular with its use by Rogerians to assess the effectiveness of psychotherapy (Rogers & Dymond, 1954). The following list provides samples of Q-sort statements. Items 1–9 are positive, reflecting good adjustment if the subject says, "Like me." Items 10–19 are negative, reflecting good adjustment if the subject says, "Unlike me."

1. I make strong demands on myself.
2. I am a responsible person.
3. I usually like people.
4. I express my emotions freely.
5. I can usually live comfortably with people around me.
6. I am optimistic.
7. I am sexually attractive.
8. I am intelligent.
9. I understand myself.
10. I put on a false front.
11. I often feel humiliated.
12. I doubt my sexual powers.
13. I feel helpless.
14. I am disorganized.
15. I am shy.
16. I am no one. Nothing seems to be me.
17. I have to protect myself with excuses, with rationalizing.
18. I dislike my own sexuality.
19. I am unreliable.*

Semantic differential technique. Osgood et al. (1957) developed the semantic differential technique for use in the study of meaning, but it has become a valuable tool in personality assessment. The subject rates a concept (e.g., my mother, myself, home) on a series of seven-point scales of bipolar adjectives. Osgood found three major factors underlying the ratings: *evaluation* (good-bad, valuable-worthless, clean-dirty), *potency* (strong-weak, large-small, heavy-light), and *activity* (active-passive, fast-slow, sharp-dull). The similarity of meaning of any two concepts for an individual, or similarities among groups of people may be compared.

Rep. The Role Construct Repertory Test (RCRT or Rep Test), developed by George Kelly (1955), requires the subject to produce the constructs he used in responding to events and people. The subject is given a list of personal roles (e.g., my best friend, my mother, my favorite teacher) and is asked to state how any two of them are alike but different from the third. With this technique, the personality researcher can determine the dimensions that are of importance to the subject (his constructs) and the number of dimensions he uses in his perception of others (cognitive complexity, Chapter 13).

Evaluation of self-report inventories. A test developer needs to determine that his test has satisfactory reliability and validity before it becomes

* One hundred statements were taken from therapy protocols and two clinical psychologists judged each statement with respect to whether a well-adjusted person should indicate it was like or unlike him. Twenty-six items were eliminated as irrelevant; new psychologists judged the remaining statements, with high agreement (Butler & Haigh, 1954; Dymond, 1954). Subjects sort the cards "to describe yourself as you see yourself today" (self-sort), and "to describe your ideal person—the person you would most like within yourself to be" (ideal sort).

widely used for research or assessment purposes. What constitutes adequate reliability and validity varies with the purpose of the test and is often subject to debate and dispute. However, even when the reliability and validity are judged adequate by professional standards, the test can often produce misleading results and be the basis for ill-formed decisions about a particular person. There has been recent public and professional attention to the use and misuse of psychological tests, as well there should be (see Goodstein & Lanyon, 1971; American Psychological Association, 1965). The problems, however, are not necessarily with the tests themselves, but with the often untrained people who administer and interpret the tests. These comments are applicable to all testing procedures but are particularly pertinent to self-report inventories because of the relative ease with which they can be administered and scored, and therefore used and misused.

Reliability and validity of tests are specific to the population on which the tests were established and the conditions under which they were developed. Failure to use the test in the ways for which it has known reliability and validity is a dominant form of misuse of tests. A test reliable and valid for predicting psychological adjustment over a three-month interval, as judged by agreement with a clinical psychologist's assessment from extensive interviews, might not be valid for a ten-year period. It might be valid for college sophomores but not for middle-aged dog breeders. It might predict loyalty to friends but not number of friends. Measures of intellectual abilities adequate for middle-class populations are often inadequate for lower-class populations, and attempts to develop culture-free tests not sensitive to these population differences have not thus far been outstandingly successful (Anastasi, 1968; Hess, 1970).

Thus, the relevant question is not, "Which is the best test of adjustment or intelligence?" but "Who is to take the test?" "Who is to use the results of the test?" "For what specific purpose will the results be used?" Human judgment is often necessary to determine whether the test is adequate to do the desired job in any specific case for any particular person or group of persons.

However, even adequately developed tests, properly selected and used, do not have perfect validity, do not represent an infallible route to the truth about a person. All tests have at least some measurement error. The typical usefulness of a particular set of test results may be lowered by peculiarities of the specific condition of testing and the effect of a particular examiner-subject interaction—complexities of testing which are discussed later. In many research situations, test administration is adequately controlled, and lack of perfect validity of tests need not be a problem. However, faulty test administration and lack of perfect validity can be problems when practical decisions are to be made about a particular individual. It would not be warranted, for example, to label a black child emotionally disturbed or mentally retarded on the basis of a conventional test administered to him by a white examiner in a crowded room at the end of a frustrating school day. No major decision about a person should be based on the results of one test or on the opinion of one examiner. Final decisions should be made by people, not by tests alone (Tyler, 1963; Forehand, 1964).

Projective Methods

Projective techniques have long been favorites in clinical psychodiagnostic work because they elicit complex responses presumably indicative of unconscious material (Gleser, 1963; Lindzey, 1961). They are multidimensional and typically interpreted clinically in terms of a holistic analysis to capture a picture of the *complete* individual. The test stimuli are deliberately ambiguous or incomplete in order to allow the subject freedom to respond without being aware of how his responses will be analyzed and without being constrained by the reality of the stimulus content. This situation allows him more freedom to project.

The projection involved is not necessarily defensive. Freud spoke of the defense of projection, but he also used the term very broadly to refer to the projections of ideational processes which are used to shape the outer world (Freud, 1919). It is the concept in this broader sense that provides the rationale for projective techniques, although the development of specific test stimuli and scoring systems have seldom been particularly tied to specific Freudian hypotheses. In fact, a dominant problem of projective tests is that for the most part they have not been well placed in any theoretical context (Lindzey, 1961; Rabin, 1968).

Actually, any test may be used projectively, just as a test typically used projectively may be used otherwise, as a sample of behavior, as a self-concept measure, or as a means for inferring a particular trait. The variety of projective techniques is indicated in the following list (classification schema from Lindzey, 1961).

1. *Association Techniques.* *Rorschach:* Stimuli are inkblots to which the subject provides associations by describing what he sees (see text).

   Word Association: Stimuli are words presented one at a time, orally or visually; subject is to respond with the first word that comes to mind. May be scored for response latency (time from presentation of stimulus word to response) or response deviancy (how unusual that associative response is in a defined population). Long latency and deviant responses indicate a problem area.

   Chain Association: Word association modified so that subject gives more than one response to a stimulus word.

2. *Construction Techniques.* *TAT:* Stimuli are ambiguous pictures; subject constructs a story (see text).

   Modifications of the TAT:

   Children's Apperception Test (CAT): Ten pictures of animals in human situations, designed to elicit stories related to Freud's theory of psychological development.

Thompson Modification of TAT (T-TAT): Stimuli are pictures of blacks rather than whites; more productive than TAT in eliciting stories from black college students, though this result not consistently found.

Auditory Apperception Test (AAT): Stimuli are ten sets of three sound situations about which the subject is to create a story using the sounds.

Michigan Picture Test: Sixteen TAT-like pictures, developed to investigate the emotional reactions of children aged eight to fourteen years; highly explicit and quantitative scoring system: responses analyzed on a tension index, direction of force, and verb tense. Has good standardization, norms, but validity evidence weak.

Iowa Picture Interpretation Test (IPIT): A multiple-choice modification of the TAT, four alternative interpretations provided for each card, subjects rank alternatives; choices intended to represent anxiety, hostility, achievement, blandness. Moderately high reliability, but scanty normative data and lack of demonstrated validity. Easily fakable.

Blacky Test: Stimuli are cartoons of a dog, Blacky, and his dog family. Devised especially to test Freudian theory of psychosexual development, used on adults as well as children. Subject constructs a story. Reliability, validity, and normative data inadequate, though research continues to improve the test. A female version of the cartoons has been developed.

3. *Completion Techniques. Sentence Completion:* Test stimuli are sentence stems, e.g., "My mother is a person who . . ." Stems often constructed for the particular population of interest, though some standard forms are available. Clinicians do not often score them quantitatively, but for research purposes, responses are often scored on dimensions such as intensity of affect, conflicts, level of adjustment.

Rosenzweig Picture Frustration Study: Stimuli are a series of cartoon drawings in which one of two characters is the victim of some frustrating circumstance; one person makes a statement, the subject is to fill in what he thinks the victim would say in the situation. Scored in terms of direction of aggression (intra-, extra-, or impunitive) and the specific type of reaction. Relatively objective scoring and norms available on many special groups.

4. *Ordering Techniques. Horn-Tompkins Picture Arrangement Test:* Test stimuli are sets of drawings which the subject arranges to tell a story.

Picture Arrangement Test: A subtest from the Wechsler Adult Intelligence Scale or from the Wechsler Intelligence Scale for Children is often used in projective fashion.

5. *Expressive Techniques. Draw a Person Test (DAP):* The subject is asked to draw a person on a blank sheet of paper. After the first figure is drawn, he may be asked to draw a person of the opposite sex, and then may be asked to tell a story about each of the persons. Scoring is usually a qualitative analysis of characteristics of the figures, e.g., relative size of male and female figures is said to reveal facets of sex identification; attention is also given to omission of body parts, disproportions, erasures, symmetry or asymmetry. Evidence is weak.

Variations on Drawing: *Draw a family, Draw-a-Person-Quality* scale (scored on an artistic scale), and the *House-Tree-Person (HTP)* scale.

6. *Spontaneous* drawings, paintings, verbal material not requested for the specific purposes of testing may also be analyzed for projective information. Scoring may be a qualitative analysis, or more objective content analysis.

Inkblot tests. The *Rorschach Inkblot Test* was developed by Hermann Rorschach (1921) for the diagnostic evaluation of personality as a whole, in contrast with previous use of inkblot procedures to measure specific imaginative and cognitive functions of personality (Rabin, 1968). On the basis of tests administered to psychiatric groups, mental defectives, normals, artists, and scholars, Rorschach selected ten inkblot cards (five with some color and five black and white) and developed a scoring system that differentiated among the groups.

The subject is shown the inkblot cards one at a time and is asked to describe his impression of each card (free association phase), for example, ". . . looks like a bat or a butterfly," or "That resembles two women bending toward each other." After the subject has responded to each card, the examiner asks him questions about his responses (the inquiry phase) to clarify exactly what the subject had in mind. Often, he scores responses in the categories of content (e.g., human, animal, nature, abstract concepts, etc.), location (what part of the card—the whole blot, a large detail, or a small portion of it—gave rise to the response), and determinants (the formal qualities of the blot influencing the response—shape, color, shading in the blot, and degree of movement attributed). Whether a subject interprets blots in terms of humans, animals, or objects, whether he responds strongly to black and white blots or to colored blots, whether he reacts to the whole blot or only to a part of it, as well as his explanations of his interpretations, are all elements influential in the examiner's analysis.

The empirical validity of the Rorschach as commonly used is doubtful at best (Zubin, Eron, & Schumer, 1965; Suinn & Oskamp, 1969). Nevertheless, it is a popular test among clinicians, perhaps because the testing situation is an interpersonal one. The Rorschach is being considered by some psychologists as a variant of an interview, in which examiner and subject are engaged in a personal exchange (Masling, 1960; Sarason, 1972). Attention is then drawn to characteristics such as speech fluency, emotional expressiveness, attempted reliance on the examiner, and so on.

The use of content analysis rating scales of the Rorschach interview, as for other interviews, permits collection of quantifiable data on connotative aspects of responses that go neglected in conventional scoring. Reference to a roaring, ferocious lion and to a tiny mouse would both be rated equally in conventional scoring (animal responses), but the emotional connotations are quite different. The Rorschach can be clinically useful when viewed and evaluated as ". . . simply a standard interview behind the veil of inkblots" (Zubin, Eron, & Sultan, 1956, p. 780).

The *Holtzman Inkblot Technique* or HIT (Holtzman, 1958a, b, 1959; Holtzman et al., 1961, 1963) provides a larger number of more varied cards (forty-five rather than ten) than does the Rorschach, and it has a more reliable and comprehensive scoring system. On the Rorschach, the subject is encouraged to respond freely to each card and to provide as many responses as he wishes. He may say that a blot looks like a bat or a butterfly, for instance, and add later, during inquiry, that it also resembles a girl's hair ornament or a flying monster. On the Holtzman, the subject is restricted to *one* response for each card. This makes comparison scoring easier; individual differences can be assessed on the basis of empirical scales. However, many clinicians claim that responses of diagnostic significance may not be the first to be voiced, and therefore the Holtzman technique may prevent responses that provide valid clues to important psychodynamics.

The HIT is much less affected by situational factors, and the examiner is not considered as important a factor in determining test results as with the Rorschach (Molish, 1972). Compared with the Rorschach, the HIT has definite psychometric advantages in its use of parallel forms, in its standardization, and in its reliability (Buros, 1970).

TAT. The Thematic Apperception Test (TAT), developed by Henry Murray and his colleagues (Murray, 1943; Morgan & Murray, 1938), is the only other projective test that approaches the Rorschach in amount of use and research generated. The subject is shown relatively ambiguous pictures selected from paintings, drawings, and magazine illustrations and is asked to make up a story to go with each picture. The examiner rarely uses all of the thirty pictures for any single subject; typically, he selects ten to fifteen pictures or a blank card for which the subject is required to imagine a picture and describe it.

The subject is asked to tell what is going on in each scene, what the characters are thinking and feeling, and what the outcome of the action will be. Thus, the subject is required to engage in fantasy (primary process), but to do so in a relatively organized manner (secondary process). The statements of the story are symbolic, taking their meaning from the emotions, but they are organized by the intellect (Henry, 1956).

The TAT was originally developed within the context of Murray's personality theory and thus was directed toward the discovery of internal motivators of behavior (needs) and real or imaginary environmental determinants (presses) which facilitate or interfere with need satisfaction. The interpreter must first determine the "hero" of the subject's story, with whom the subject presumably identifies, and then analyze the story content to discover the hero's needs and presses. Murray's list of needs has been more extensively used than has his nonquantitative scoring system for the TAT.

There is great variation in means of interpreting the TAT, and each clinician is likely to evolve his own methods. One simple procedure is the *inspection technique:*

> It is frequently helpful merely to read through the stories, treating them as meaningful psychological communications; one

simply underlines anything that seems significant, specific, or unique. When an experienced examiner rereads the stories a second time, he can, almost without effort, find a repetitive pattern running through them, or he can find facets of different stories falling together into a meaningful whole.*

When the judges are thoroughly trained with a specific, carefully defined scoring system, interjudge reliability (agreement between scorers) can be quite high. However, the use of idiosyncratic and nonstandardized methods is more common, making estimates of reliability difficult. Reliability tends to be low when the typically less structured, global analyses are made. Empirical evidence of validity is minimal at best. For example, the TAT has not differentiated among patients of separate psychiatric categories and, in fact, normal subjects have been misclassified as seriously disturbed (Little & Shneidman, 1959).

However, the TAT has increasingly recognized research possibilities in terms of examiner-subject interactions, stimulus properties, and the relationship between fantasy and behavior (Buros, 1970). Its use to the researcher is not challenged (Fisher, 1967; Molish, 1972).

Evaluation of projective tests. Projective techniques have not lived up to their promise (Zubin, Eron, & Schumer, 1965; Molish, 1972). In fact, diagnostic testing in general is declining, and projective techniques are being deemphasized in many clinical training programs, as the practice of clinical psychology changes (Molish, 1969).

Although projective tests are assumed to measure relatively enduring personality characteristics, there is frequent marked measurement error due to instructional sets, examiner characteristics, the subject's perception of the testing situation, and the subject's verbal ability (Anastasia, 1968). Careful research attention is being increasingly given to such variables (Molish, 1972). For individual diagnosis, the examiner needs extensive information about the circumstances in which the test responses were obtained and the aptitude and background of the subject, if he is to interpret them meaningfully.

The usefulness of projective techniques is very difficult to assess. The approach to interpreting scores on a projective test is often configural, taking account (often intuitively) of the complex patterns of responses and interrelationships of traits. When there is no anxiety or fear of punishment about the expression of aggression, for example, evidence of aggressiveness in projective measures is positively associated with aggressive behavior (Mussen & Naylor, 1954; Pittluck, 1950). If there is anxiety or fear about the expression of aggression, no relationship is expected between the specific isolated test scores relevant to aggression and actual behavior. However, complex experimental designs are needed to show

---

* Bellak, L. *The T.A.T. and C.A.T. in clinical use.* (2nd ed.) New York: Grune & Stratton, 1971. P. 66.

that the lack of relationships between test scores and behavior is not due to the test's failure to detect aggressiveness.

When experienced clinicians are allowed to examine projective test protocols in their own way, their evaluations of the subjects match independently determined case history evaluations to a degree that is significantly better than chance similarity (Anastasia, 1968). However, the relationships are generally low and there is little agreement among personality evaluations based on different projective techniques and among clinicians using different techniques.

Some adherents of projective techniques are trying seriously to make them into tests in the strict sense by giving refined attention to the nature of the stimulus, to greater objectivity in scoring, to new theoretical models, to the effect of examiner-subject interaction, and to variables of the experimental situation in general (Molish, 1972; Masling, 1966). Other adherents maintain that projective instruments are of value as clinical tools in the process of clinical interpretation, although their efficiency certainly varies with the skill of the examiner (Murstein, 1968).

So far, the greatest weakness and the greatest advantage of projective techniques lie in the sensitivity of observation and effectiveness in information processing and understanding of the human being who uses them —which, when you come to think of it, is also true of any other test or observational strategy. Thus, increasing research attention is being given to processes of clinical inference and judgment (Bieri et al., 1966; Goldberg, 1968, 1970; Loehlin, 1968). "Psychologists who have been interested in the study of 'persons' and their problems remain convinced of the significant contribution projective techniques can continue to make to the understanding of personality dynamics and in the study of human problems" (Rabin, 1968, p. 16).

Factor Analytic Methods

The decision about what a personality test should attempt to measure is often based on theoretical considerations or on existing convention in ways of thinking about people. For instance, the Blacky Test (Blum, 1950) was derived from Freudian theory of castration anxiety; the MMPI was developed to predict membership in commonly used psychiatric categories. Projective stimuli or inventory items are selected empirically or theoretically to measure predetermined dimensions. However, there is no guarantee that either current theory or current common sense will be particularly effective in leading the way to those dimensions of personality that are most useful to consider.

Factor analytic techniques can be effective aids for the development of both theory and tests by providing an empirical determination of parsimonious ways in which to conceptualize properties of behavior. They can suggest what a test or theory should be about, namely the empirically discovered "common themes" or factors underlying a variety of responses.

The central function of factor analysis is to account statistically for the pattern of relationships observed between responses. It "reduces" a large number of observations to a smaller number of factors by finding an underlying order among many observations. The beginning point for analysis is a table of correlation coefficients which provide an index of the strength of the relationship between each pair of many variables measured. When there are few variables, few observations, we can often visually detect a pattern of relationships. However, when there are many variables, ordering or accounting for the relationships among the observed measures would not be possible visually.

The logic of factor analysis is illustrated by the problem of relating a variety of physical measurements (perimeter, surface area of two sides, surface area of five sides, volume, etc.) of many boxes (Thurstone, 1947). If we factor analyze the physical measurements, we will extract dimensions of height, width, and depth, the factors statistically underlying the more specific observations. Each box has a score (or loading) on each factor. With knowledge of the scores of any one box on these three factors, we may describe the box and, if we wish, determine any of the other properties of size known to be relevant to the factors. If we then factor analyze the factor scores themselves, we would get one or more second-order factors, perhaps a general size factor.

With personality measurements, however, we do not always know ahead of time exactly what factors to look for or what factors are there to be found—we do not know the x, y, and z, or the basic dimensions. Thus, factor analysis can serve a more useful function than that of demonstrating the existence of predicted factors (although it may do that also). There are what seem to be a limitless number of possible personality measures—ratings by other people, self-ratings on test items, any kind of physical or social fact. Must we use all possible information at any one time to assess a person? Is there any order among the separate pieces of information? We can analyze information about individual differences on many variables at once and come up with personality factors (analogous to height, width, and depth) that describe an individual or group. Having established our factors, we can select those items, tests, and behaviors that most heavily contribute to the factor definitions. By adding and deleting items, we can move toward a purer and more efficient measure of the factors than would be possible if we continued to use all of the items from which the factors originally evolved.

For example, factor analytic studies of the MMPI indicate that some of the clinical scales are not pure measures of a factor in that they measure more than one factor, so some items should be regrouped or discarded.

The empirically derived factors have the advantage of being clearly defined in terms of specific measurements, for example, "Factor A is x amount of Test 3, y amount of Test 5, and z amount of Test 10, and is unrelated to the other tests; Factor B has x amount of Tests 4 and 6 and is unrelated to everything else." Similarly, higher-order factors, resulting from a factor analysis of factor scores, are defined by the loadings of the first-order factors.

We cannot, of course, extract a factor if no relevant data were included; we could not extract a color factor in the box example because we had no information about color (unless perhaps color happened to be associated with some of the physical dimensions). Thus, personality researchers like to include a wide variety of measures, although logically they cannot claim to have sampled all kinds of measures possibly relevant to all factors that may actually exist or be meaningful theoretical ones to use in trying to understand human behavior.

Prominent theorists who base their concepts on factor analysis are Raymond Cattell and Hans Eysenck. Although these men make different mathematical assumptions about performing factor analysis and often collect very different kinds of data, there is a significance in the similarities in their views about the most important factors in conceptualizing personality.

Raymond Cattell. Cattell's (1950, 1957) theory is a trait theory in which trait is a "mental structure" inferred from observed behavior to account for regularity or consistency in behavior, across situations and over time.

Cattell distinguishes between *surface traits,* a cluster of characteristics or behaviors that seem to go together, and *source traits,* characteristics which represent underlying variables that determine surface manifestations. According to Cattell, the latter are the basic building blocks of personality, the "real structural influences underlying personality" (Cattell, 1950, p. 27). These can be discovered only with factor analysis. Thus, Cattell is one factor analyst who assumes that factors are real entities rather than merely statistical conveniences.

In searching for source traits of personality, Cattell has used three kinds of data:

1. L-data: life data from actual records of the person's behavior, such as school records and ratings by people who know the individual in real life settings.
2. Q-data: information from self-rating questionnaires containing the person's own statements about his behavior.
3. T-data: data from objective tests gathered in laboratory tasks other than those using paper-and-pencil questionnaires.

A similar factor structure emerges, in various age and national groups, from L- and Q-data, but different factors emerge from the T-data. Cattell developed the Sixteen Personality Factor Questionnaire, 16PF, to measure those main personality factors that were reasonably well established in L- and Q-data. Factor analysis of scores on the sixteen factors measured by the test reveal two general second-order factors behind the 16PF scores, namely adjustment-anxiety and introversion-extraversion. Further, a correspondence between T-data factors and these higher-order factors has been found.

Cattell's second-order anxiety factor is defined by low ego strength, guilt proneness, shyness, and suspiciousness. The introversion-extraversion factor is defined by traits of being happy-go-lucky, imaginative, outgoing, and venturesome. These factors are very similar to two of those independently developed by Eysenck.

Hans Eysenck. Eysenck claims three personality factors, or factors of temperament: introversion-extraversion, neuroticism, and psychoticism (1947, 1952, 1960, 1961, 1967). Intelligence, as a factor, interacts with each in complex ways. Psychoticism is defined in terms of measures of loss of contact with reality and failure of ego functions (e.g., poor consciousness, memory loss, lack of fluency). Eysenck's attention has been directed mainly toward neuroticism and introversion-extraversion, and he developed the Eysenck Personality Inventory, EPI (an improved version of the original Maudsley Personality Inventory, MPI) to measure these traits. Neuroticism is a factor of stability-instability, or emotional overresponsiveness and reactivity of the autonomic nervous system. The characteristics associated with the introversion-extraversion factor are very similar to those associated with Jung's (Chapter 3) concepts, namely outgoing, impulsive, uninhibited, sociable tendencies in the extravert versus quiet, retiring, introspective tendencies in the introvert.

However, it is important to note that Eysenck's dimension was statistically derived without preconceptions about Jungian theory, and has the advantage of being defined quantitatively by the kinds of measures employed. Notice also the similarity between Eysenck's factors and Cattell's second-order factors. Like Jung and Cattell, Eysenck suggests, with supporting data, genetic influences in introversion-extraversion as well as in neuroticism (Chapter 14).

Unlike Cattell, Eysenck does not think that factor analysis by itself can point to real personality processes or structures. The factors may denote such reality, but other techniques are necessary to verify what the factors indicate. Accordingly, Eysenck engages in research to develop and to try to support a theory explaining the factors he finds. On the basis of theory and research, Eysenck postulates that the introversion-extraversion dimension is basically one of the balance of cortical excitatory and inhibitory potentials. The introvert has greater excitatory relative to inhibitory cortical potential than does the extravert. The balance of cortical potentials affects, among other things, conditionability, with quick and efficient conditionability associated with introversion and slow, inefficient conditioning associated with extraversion. In part because of his conditioning efficiency the introvert becomes "oversocialized": he overlearns impulse control (compare with Freud's anal character), is very persistent and reliable, and has high levels of aspiration.

Eysenck has used a variety of measures and experimental techniques to support his theory, including drug studies in which the excitatory/inhibitory balance is experimentally manipulated by administration of drugs. Notice that for Eysenck and Cattell, measures other than the standard form of personality testing have vital roles in personality assessment.

Putting Some Pieces Together

The personality pyramid. There are various kinds of factors that may evolve from a factor analysis, each of which may be thought analogous to a "layer" or personality "structure" in a theoretical pyramid. When units of a lower order (e.g., habits, surface traits) tend to occur together, a construct of a higher order is suggested (e.g., trait, source trait). As the scope of each construct *increases,* the predictability of a specific response *decreases.* For example, if we know only that a person is an introvert (higher-order construct), we cannot predict as safely that he will condition quickly (lower-order unit) as we could if we had observed him in a conditioning situation. If all we wanted to know about a person was his conditioning rate, we would be better off measuring that and only that. However, personality is much more than conditioning—or any other system of responding for that matter. Knowing that the subject is an introvert does increase the range of things we can say about him with a fair degree of accuracy overall and allow greater understanding of his mode of functioning. According to Eysenck's theory, the introvert is more likely than the extravert to condition quickly, to be persistent, to be distractible, and so on.

The generality and, therefore, presumed scientific significance, of the statements that we can make will increase with higher levels. This thinking is analogous to the use of constructs and deductive systems (Chapter 2). No one response defines the construct (source trait or type), but all together define the construct; theoretical deductions are made from the construct to the observable behavior which defines it. Any one specific response is subject to a number of influences, but overall there is a predisposition toward particular kinds of responses.

Consensus? As suggested by the content of the pyramid example, there is reasonable consensus on the importance of introversion-extraversion as a major concept for understanding personality, and on the importance of the less clear-cut factor of stability-instability, or emotionality. These are factors found by contemporary researchers other than Eysenck and Cattell (e.g., Vernon, 1964) and have a long tradition in Western attempts to conceptualize personality. Eysenck (1963) has pointed out the similarity between the fourfold classification provided by these two factors and the ancient Greek classification of personality on the basis of body fluids, and he has also suggested the similarities of the dimensions with other psychological concepts. While there is no claim here that these factors are *the* basic dimensions of personality or are sufficient for exhaustively defining personality, their recurrence through time and from a variety of observational strategies and conceptual frameworks suggests their importance and usefulness in working toward a parsimonious theoretical understanding of basic personality structure and processes.

The specific ways in which any one investigator or theorist studies introversion-extraversion certainly vary; thus, with our current information, at least, generalizing from one specific index of introversion-extraversion to another is hazardous (Carrigan, 1960). Any one response, on a personality test or otherwise, is subject to a number of influences. However, quantitative approaches suggest that there may be some common factor much like the trait hypothesized by Eysenck and Cattell, and construct validation work is promising (Guilford & Zimmerman, 1956; Gale, 1969). There is some reason to see the introversion-extraversion dimension as roughly correlated with the use of sensitization and repressing defenses—defense styles which are discussed in later chapters—as is emotionality, an approximation of the stability (or neuroticism) factor. The repeated appearance of these two factors may reflect the fact that they are basically factors of the *direction of behavior* (introversion-extraversion) and the *intensity or controllability of intensity of behavior* (stability-instability). Direction and intensity of behavior would seem to be rather fundamental in any classification of any kind of behavior in any theoretical or empirical system (Chapter 10).

COMPLEXITIES IN TESTING

As we discussed in Chapter 7, any response is influenced by the predispositions brought to the situation by the subject and by the examiner, and by the subject's interpretation of the situation and reaction to the examiner. A response on a test is simply a response which, like any other, is subject to a variety of influences that can increase the measurement error of a test. Neglect of this fact can lead to erroneous conclusions and surround psychological testing with an unwarranted aura of omniscient infallibility as instruments for automatically uncovering what a person "really" is.

Situational Determinants and Examiner Effects

Test stimuli occur in an interpersonal situation and cannot in any complete sense be considered the *only* stimuli responsible for a response. The context in which the test is given, the examiner's characteristics, the prior activities of the subject, and the test responses themselves have all been shown to influence responses on projective instruments (Sechrest, 1968; Rabin, 1968). Scores on intelligence tests are also affected by procedural, situational, and interpersonal variables (Sattler & Theye, 1967). Unfortunately, minor changes in intelligence test procedures are more likely to affect special subgroups; for example, discouragement affects children more than college students, and subjects high in test anxiety are more susceptible to impaired performance than are those low in test anxiety.

Similarly, the performance of blacks varies greatly with situational variables (Katz, 1970; Sattler, 1970). Black subjects generally obtain lower scores on intelligence tests with a white examiner than with a black examiner. When a digit-symbol task was presented to Southern blacks as an intelligence test, those who had a black experimenter did slightly better than they had done when the test was presented as a measure of eye-hand coordination; subjects who had a white experimenter showed impaired performance under the intelligence test instructions (Figure 8–2; Katz, Roberts, & Robinson, 1963, 1965).

Even relatively experienced examiners can be influenced by their interaction with the subject (Masling, 1959). Subjects (actually accomplices) who interacted warmly with the administrator of an intelligence test (communicated respect and liking for him, and responded freely to his questions) scored significantly higher on the test than did accomplices who acted coldly disinterested. Examiners were more lenient in scoring the answers of the warm subject than the cold, and during testing used more reinforcing comments and gave more opportunity for the subject to clarify or correct responses. Some of the examiners even emphasized that

FIGURE 8–2

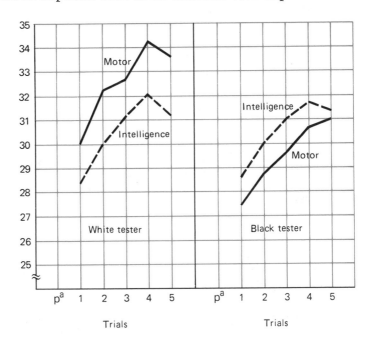

Situational and Examiner Effects on Test Results.

Mean digit-symbol scores on five one-minute trials of the hard task for black subjects who had a white or a black experimenter and motor-test or intelligence-test instructions (N = 23 for every group).

[a] Last trial of pretest.

Source: Katz, I., Roberts, S. O., & Robinson, J. M. Effects of task difficulty, race of administrator, and instructions on digit-symbol performance of Negroes. *Journal of Personality and Social Psychology*, 1965, 2, 53–59.

the disinterested behavior was "sick." The more experienced examiners were just as biased by the interaction as the interviewers who had less experience. The differences in examiners' experience, though small, were more marked than differences due to the interaction with the subject. However, the lesson remains: Human experimenters are not objective automatons.

Some writers suggest that the confounding effects of the test examiner can be eliminated by the use of machines to administer tests (Kintz et al., 1965), but others maintain that the examiner is not just a reader of test items (Sattler & Theye, 1967). He can establish a relationship which enables the subject to perform effectively; he can evaluate the subject's motivational level and, if need be, modify the subject's attitude or at least report that the subject was not trying his best. If the examiner knows what to do to maximize each subject's performance, then perhaps humans are the answer to all our testing problems. However, to use them effectively, we need to know the specific examiner characteristics and behavior that influence specific groups of subjects behaving in defined situations.

Response Styles of the Subject

Response styles are tendencies to respond to test stimuli in given ways, irrespective of the content of the item. While these styles have been discussed most often with respect to paper-and-pencil tests, the problem seems also applicable to other tests, including projectives, A subject may have a tendency to mark true rather than false, to agree rather than to disagree (yeah-saying or acquiescence), to choose an alternative in a favorite physical location on a multiple-choice test (position bias), to be unusually defensive (e.g., as measured by the MMPI K scale), or to present himself in a positive manner (social desirability). Although the exact nature and extent of the contribution of response styles to test scores is often debatable, and they may determine the answer chosen only when the subject is in doubt, they can lower the test validity (Block, 1971; Bentler, Jackson, & Messick, 1971, 1972; Rorer, 1965).

While some test constructors attempt to minimize or control for the contribution of response styles to test scores, others attempt to use response styles as meaningful information (Couch & Keniston, 1960). A dominant example is *social desirability (SD)*, a tendency to endorse socially desirable responses to indicate that one behaves in conventionally acceptable ways. The probability of attributing traits to oneself is positively related with the judged desirability of the item (Edwards, 1953b). Of course, people sometimes deliberately fake desirable responses, but of more interest is SD as a form of unconscious faking, a well-learned tendency to "put up a good front."

The Edwards Personal Preference Schedule, EPPS, uses a *forced choice technique* in which the subject is forced to choose on each item between two statements equated for social desirability (Edwards, 1953a, 1957, 1959). It is a measure of Murray's needs based on a rational or content validity; items were selected because they seemed relevant to the need as defined. While the test controls for SD, the subject often feels that he is forced to choose between two alternatives of equal applicability or inapplicability to himself. It is somewhat like being asked, "Have you stopped beating your wife?"

In contrast to the approach of trying to control for SD is the approach of trying to measure it as a meaningful variable in and of itself (Edwards, 1957, 1961, 1970; Crowne & Marlowe, 1964). Why do some people show the SD style more than others? If we know that someone typically tries to put on a good front, we can either be annoyed with him, as test examiner or personal acquaintance, or we can realize that we have some information about him. People who score high on the Marlowe-Crowne SD scale are likely to be more conforming, conventional, cautious, and persuasible, and to show less deviant behavior than are those low in SD; they seem to have strong needs for self-protection, avoidance of criticism, social conformity, and social approval. The person unusually low on SD may be expressing a need for attention or sympathy. The characteristics of the high SD scorers also tend to apply to people high in the tendency to assume that others are similar to them (Chapter 13), and to those likely to be conformers (Chapter 17).

Clinical and Statistical Decision Making

In many situations, the information provided by tests is processed subjectively: Someone uses the information to make a prediction about a subject. In the clinical setting, the decision making often involves predicting the appropriate diagnosis of the patient and his responsiveness to various forms of treatment. The decision process is subjective and idiosyncratic. The justification for the clinician's decision is his "clinical intuition," his insight, his hunch, his experience, and his human understanding. The complexities of the human mind notwithstanding, the human does *not* always do a very good job at the often lengthy ordeal of processing information and making decisions. In initiating the famous *clinical versus actuarial debate,* Meehl characterized the clinician as "a costly middleman who might better be eliminated" (Meehl, 1956, p. 271). He concluded that predictions made actuarially from the MMPI were equal or superior to those made by a clinician, and that the clinical diagnostician should be replaced by clerks using mechanical, statistical formulas and "cookbooks" of personality descriptions (Meehl, 1954, 1965). Meehl was not suggesting doing away with clinicians; his plan was to free them from a time-consuming job they cannot do particularly well in order to give them more time to use their skills in therapy and research. Nevertheless, clinicians complained of ". . . a vague feeling that a fast one has been put over on them. . . . Meehl has actually sold the clinical approach up the river" (Holt, 1958, p. 1).

Clinicians and other defenders of human judgment take heart, however, from Sawyer's (1966) conclusions of his analysis of forty-five studies which used as criteria diverse behavioral outcomes, including grades in training programs, rating of improvement in therapy, parole violation, retention as a co-pilot, and even the number of children a couple had twenty years later (Table 8–6). Consistent with Meehl's conclusions, the mechanical (statistical) mode of combining data to make predictions always proved equal or superior to the clinical mode. However, Sawyer distinguished between measurement and prediction. Before they can become the source of prediction, data must be gathered. The effectiveness of human judgment is more apparent when this distinction is made. The best method of predicting criterion behavior was found to be a composite procedure involving a statistical, mechanical analysis of data which had been collected mechanically *and* data which had been collected clinically. Adding the results of clinical judgment to the mechanically collected data improved predictive accuracy. "This suggests that the clinician may be able to contribute most not by direct prediction, but rather by providing, in objective form, judgments to be combined me-

TABLE 8–4   Summary of Conclusions from Forty-Five Clinical-Statistical Studies

MODE OF DATA COLLECTION	MODE OF DATA COMBINATION			
	Clinical		*Mechanical*	
Clinical	1. Pure clinical	20%	2. Trait ratings	43%
Mechanical	3. Profile interpretation	38%	4. Pure statistical	63%
Both	5. Clinical composite	26%	6. Mechanical composite	75%
Either or both[a]	7. Clinical synthesis	50%	8. Mechanical synthesis	75%

Within each mode of data collection, the mechanical mode of combination is superior, by margins of 23, 25, 49, and 25 percent. Within each mode of data combination, the clinical mode of collection by itself is inferior, by margins ranging from 6 to 32 percent. With the exception of one method, the difference between modes of combination depends very little upon the mode of collection, and vice versa (no interaction). The exception to the low interaction is the clinical composite; it is about 24 percent lower than the other seven values would indicate in the absence of interaction. When combination is mechanical, it is better to have both kinds of data than either alone; but when combination is clinical, having both kinds is little better than having only clinically collected data and not as good as having only mechanically collected data. Neither synthesis appears promising.

Note: In each cell is the percentage of the comparisons in which the method surpassed, plus one-half the percentage of the comparisons in which it equalled, the other method.

[a] Plus, for the clinical synthesis, the prediction of Method 2, 4, or 6; or, for the mechanical synthesis, the prediction of Method 1, 3, or 5.

SOURCE: Sawyer, J. Measurement *and* prediction, clinical *and* statistical. *Psychological Bulletin*, 1966, 66, 178–200.

chanically" (Sawyer, 1966, p. 193). Clinical skills may contribute by assessing characteristics that would not otherwise be considered in the prediction.

The Sensitive Observer

The value of the sensitive human observer and the superiority of clinical judgment over actuarial methods in some circumstances were demonstrated in a study comparing the effectiveness of an actuarial method with that of highly skilled clinicians in differentiating between male homosexuals and heterosexuals on the basis of TAT protocols (Lindzey, 1965). The clinicians and an actuarial method developed for a college sample were approximately equally accurate when applied to that sample. However, the same actuarial method was totally ineffective when applied to a different group, namely, a prison population. That the clinicians could move successfully into a new population while the statistical method collapsed is evidence of the clinicians' pragmatic superiority in dealing with new populations for which actuarial methods have not been developed (Meehl, 1965). The clinicians were able to detect significant signs relevant in the new population that had not been incorporated into the actuarial formulas calculated for the old population. In very primitive areas of psychological measurement, there is no substitute for the human observer. In fact, he is always present: "Although the efforts of psychologists to dehumanize—more positively, to 'objectify'—the process of data collection have been many and ingenious, it remains true that behind every validity coefficient or network of justifying concepts and operations, there lurks, at some point, an observer, hopefully, a sensitive and unbiased observer" (Lindzey, 1965, p. 17).

Summary

With any observational strategy, including that of testing, the assignment of numbers is necessary for measurement. The simplest and least precise, but frequently used, measurement scale is the nominal scale. Precision and information increase as the scale reflects equality and rank order (ordinal scale) and the distance between the objects or people being measured (interval scale). Ratio scales require a zero point and are therefore currently rare in psychology.

Any test, or other observational strategy, must have reliability and validity: We must be able to depend on it to do a stated job. Most important for scientific understanding is that a test have construct validity, that there be a sufficient body of research and theory concerning the test and the construct measured to enable us to know what is being measured.

One dominant class of assessment techniques consists of self-reports, including the interview and self-report inventories. Interview reliability and validity tend to be low, although they can be improved by structuring the interview and by using rating scales and content analysis, which also extend their research usefulness. Test scores may be viewed as providing signs from which inferences are made about personal characteristics not directly observable, or they may serve as samples of behavior shown to be empirically related to other observable behaviors and events. The MMPI is the most frequently used inventory and has been the prototype of the actuarial or empirical development and use of tests.

Projective tests have been popular because of the assumption that they tap fundamental unconscious characteristics. However, they have not lived up to their promise; current efforts are directed toward improving their reliability and validity as tests on the one hand, and, on the other, toward considering them as tools for use by skilled clinicians.

No test, self-report or projective, is infallible: All have some measurement error at best, and all can be misused. Any test is at least somewhat subject to distortion by both the subject and the examiner and by the interaction of the two persons, although tests differ in their susceptibility to such influences. Attempts may be made to control subjects' response styles such as acquiescence, social desirability, and defensiveness, or these may be measured as meaningful variables in their own right.

Factor analytic methods can be used in developing tests and theories because they enable detection of patterns of relationships among a great number of responses. They have provided an important basis for the theories and tests of Cattell and Eysenck, both of whom, along with others, find the factors of introversion-extraversion and stability-instability to be particularly significant.

Although the human being is not as effective as are well-established statistical methods for processing large amounts of complex information, he is irreplaceable as an observer and as judge and evaluator; he always has responsibility for deciding what tests to develop, for evaluating their suitability, and for directing their use.

PSYCHODYNAMICS

PART IV

9

fantasy

When King Nebuchadnezzar had a puzzling dream, he assembled his magicians and sorcerers and announced, "If you do not tell me both the dream and interpretation, you shall be torn in pieces and your houses shall be made into a dunghill."

If we no longer believe that kingdoms rise and fall on the strength of a dream, Nebuchadnezzar's ultimatum will seem unreasonable; however, it does illustrate the ancient roots of man's preoccupation with his dreams. Whether we believe with the Freudians that dreams are the disguised, symbolic fulfillment of repressed wishes, or whether we share with pre-Christian man the suspicion, or hope, that dreams might well be omens sent by the gods, we are all intrigued with these excursions into fantasy. We are fascinated with the potential of dreams and daydreams to provide clues about how the mind works in solving problems and expressing feelings—sometimes in touch with what others recognize as reality, sometimes not. An exploration of this inner world may show us the ultimate futility of trying to make sharp distinctions between thinking and feeling, between mind and body, and in fact between reality and unreality.

"Why do I have nightmares?" the young child asks. And while we may be able to attribute his dream of hostile tigers to an overdose of pizza at bedtime, we cannot so easily answer our own questions about the implications of dreams. What do dreams tell us about ourselves? How are dreams related to personality?

Although clinicians have speculated extensively about the role of fantasy in personality functioning, psychology has only recently begun to give it serious and systematic research attention. One of the reasons for the neglect has been the tendency of modern Western man to define reality only in terms of the external and physical world to the neglect of the internal and the intangible (Dement, 1965). The sleep world is dismissed as a biological necessity, but its psychological contents are unreal and therefore unimportant; day-dreaming is the pursuit of the idle.

Yet much of our time is spent in sleep and in waking fantasy, and research has shown that these internal experiences not only are real and meaningful ones, but can actually make more effective our relations with the external world.

With the development and skillful use of equipment to measure the contents and results of our internal experiences, we can come closer to an understanding of how dreams and personality are related.

ASLEEP AND DREAMING

What Is a Dream?

Suppose you are asked to take part in an experiment. The researcher explains that you will fall asleep, and within about an hour after going to sleep you will experience a series of changes: (1) Your eyes will begin to move rapidly. (2) A sudden relaxation of head and neck muscles may be accompanied by twitching facial muscles, smiling, frowning, sucking, and grinding of teeth. (3) Blood pressure, heart rate, and respiration will fluctuate erratically. (4) Brain temperature will rise. (5) In males, full or partial penile erection will occur.

It all sounds rather frightening, if not dangerous, and a decision to take part in such an experiment might take some thinking. But perhaps the decision would be made less difficult if the researcher were to go on to explain that the conditions described above are experienced by every human being—indeed, by most mammals—during 20 to 25 percent of the adult's sleeping hours, that these strange, "abnormal" conditions are likely to signal the occurrence of a dream (Murray, 1965; Witkin & Lewis, 1967a).

The definition and measurement of dreams involves relatively new procedures. As with many discoveries, the initial observation that such body changes during sleep might be related to dreams was accidental. E. Aserinsky, while watching sleeping infants in the sleep laboratory of Nathaniel Kleitman at the University of Chicago, noticed a rhythm in the infants' sleep behavior: periods of rapid eye movements (REMs) and of general body movement alternated with periods of quiescence and non-REMs (NREMs). Later, REMs were found related to dream reports and to fluctuations in brain waves and were measured by electrical recordings of brain waves and eye muscles.

REM Time Is Dream Time

How can we substantiate the claim that REMs are related to dreams? The simplest approach is to waken a sleeper during an REM or NREM period and ask him whether he was dreaming. Investigators are consistent in showing a higher number of dream reports from REM awakening (about 85 percent) than from NREM awakening (Dement, 1965). This is *not* to say that there is no mental activity during NREM sleep. The brain is never inactive, although the nature of its activity varies. Images may occur during NREM stages, but the reports of mental activity during these periods are likely to be of a plotless, mundane nature. The mental activity that most of us call dreams is more characteristic of REM sleep.

In order to know when to wake a sleeping subject to question him about his dream activity, the dream researcher must know when the subject is experiencing REM sleep. The most reliable indicator of REM sleep is the depth of sleep as measured by an electroencephalogram (EEG), a recording of the electrical activity of the brain. Sleep progresses through four stages: from Stage 1 sleep, in which the EEG records small, rapid brain waves, indicating light sleep, to Stage 4 sleep, with its large, slow waves indicating deep sleep.

REMs—and therefore dreams—occur during periods of Stage 1 sleep. Once the REMs begin, it is very difficult to waken the sleeper. This presents us with a strange, contradictory set of circumstances: This period of difficult arousal comes during the time that the brain wave pattern indicates that the subject is in his *lightest* sleep. In other words, the sleeper is most difficult to awake at the very time that the EEG recording tells us that he is, physiologically, closest to being awake! Because of this apparent contradiction, REM sleep has been labeled the *paradoxical sleep period* (or Stage 5, or Stage 1–REM).

Young adults experience about five to seven REM periods per night; the length of the periods increases and the time between them decreases through the sleep period—the longer we sleep, the longer and more frequently we dream. An experiment was conducted in which rewards were promised to subjects if they could increase their length of dreaming time by sheer will, but they were unable to do so (Taylor, 1971).

But how do we really know that REM time is dream time? Is it possible that dreams might be merely easier to remember at REM awakenings? This does not seem to be the case (Dement and Kleitman, 1957a). There seems to be a strong relationship between the duration and content of dream reports and the duration and patterns of the preceding REMs. And subjects' estimates of the length of a dream and the number of words that occur in their reports of a dream are both proportional to the length of the REM period prior to the awakening.

Research with animals also supports the contention that dreams occur during REM periods. When rhesus monkeys were trained to press a bar every time an image was flashed on a screen, researchers found that during sleep, with the onset of REMs, the monkeys flared their nostrils, grimaced, yelped, and suddenly began to press the bar (Vaughan, 1965). Since they were isolated from sound, light, and other stimuli, they presumably "saw" images during these periods. In other words, they were dreaming.

Dream Recall

Everyone dreams. To be able to make such an unqualified statement about the nature of human behavior is refreshing, but it does leave us with a problem. How do we account for Aunt Mary, a truthful, humorless woman, clearly unaddled by drink or senility, who maintains solemnly that she does not dream? Or for our own lack of an interesting dream to share every morning?

Many people simply do not recall the dreams they have, and probably few of us recall all of our dreams. In some cases, people label as "thought" what others would call dreams, and do not differentiate well between waking and sleeping mental activity. In particular, young children, poor sleepers, and some mentally ill people often have difficulty telling the difference between dreams and waking states (Vaughan, 1965).

In general, subjects who claim to have few dreams are found to have as many REM periods as those who report a high dream rate (Antrobus et al., 1964). They report a dream at least half the time they are wakened during a REM period (Goodenough, 1967). For best dream recall, a sleeper should be awakened during or very shortly after a REM period. Five to ten minutes after REM activity ceases, a dream cannot be recalled easily.

Some differences in dream recall may be due in part to methods of awakening and the associated physiological states at the time recall of mental activity is attempted. The frequency and quality of dream reports by nonrecallers improved when a loud awakening bell was abruptly sounded rather than when a soft one gradually became loud (Goodenough et al., 1965). Perhaps the soft, gradual wakening gives the nonrecallers a chance to repress their dreams before complete awakening. For subjects high in dream reports, on the other hand, almost any kind of awakening from REM sleep produced a dream report.

Some people, however, consistently report thinking rather than dreaming, regardless of method of awakening (Lewis et al., 1966). These people, though rare, have one-third fewer eye movements per unit time in REM sleep than do reporters. It has been suggested that they lack self-involvement in waking and in dreaming (Goodenough, 1967). Lack of dream recall associated with a report that nothing was going on, that one was dreaming but cannot remember the content, or that one was awake and thinking rather than asleep and dreaming may be explainable in different ways.

There is some reason to suggest a high incidence of dream repression in low recallers. Although the evidence is not clear cut, research tends to support the clinical suspicion that high recallers show more overt, manifest anxiety and relative underuse of repressive kinds of defense mechanisms (see Cohen, 1970). Nonrecallers, on the other hand, seem relatively nonanxious and use repression and other avoidance techniques to meet situations and feelings that could otherwise lead to experienced anxiety. This is not to say that they are without pressures and conflicts; rather, they tend to rely on repression and avoidance techniques to avoid experiencing anxiety. The fact that some nonrecallers have more frequent eye movements during a shorter period of time has been seen as indicative of their attempted avoidance even while the dream is going on (Antrobus et al., 1964). An inability to recall dreams, then, may reflect an unwillingness to admit conflicts even to oneself, or simply a fear of knowing oneself. Such a person might also be one who finds it easy to consider dreams to be foolish nonsense! Minimal use of avoidance defensive techniques may lead to more experienced anxiety, but also enables more self-knowledge and potential self-control and self-acceptance.

Dream Deprivation

Freud called dreams the "guardians of sleep" because they provide a disguised fulfillment of unconscious wishes that might otherwise interfere with sleep. Contemporary research does suggest that people need to dream, although not necessarily for the reasons Freud suggested.

To study the effects of dream deprivation, researchers have awakened subjects at the beginning of REM periods over a period of several nights. After four to seven nights of dream deprivation, subjects typically show some disturbance of ego functions: irritability and hostility, along with problems in motor coordination, memory, concentration, startle reaction, and the sense of time (summarized by Fisher, 1967).

Could these reactions be due merely to repeated awakenings and lost sleep? The investigators were careful to provide the necessary control information by awakening the subjects the same number of times during nondeprivation phases (usually on other nights) only during NREMs and keeping them awake for the same amount of time as they had been kept awake during the REM interruption phase. The disturbed reactions are related to REM deprivation specifically, and not to sleep deprivation without REM deprivation.

Dream recovery. Further evidence of a need to dream is provided by the fact that we make up our lost REM time. On progressive nights of a deprivation experiment, more and more awakenings are necessary because REMs occur more and more often (a *recovery phenomenon*). A subject who requires seven awakenings to prevent REMs the first night might require as many as thirty by the fifth deprivation night (Dement, 1960). After several nights of REM deprivation, subjects who are allowed to sleep without interruption experience marked increase in REM time. REM sleep in the first undisturbed night after three to seven deprivation nights increases by about 40 percent above the usual amount of REM sleep. As the number of deprivation nights increases to eight, fifteen, and sixteen, the increase in REM time grows to 72, 120, and 160 percent.

To make sure that the recovery phenomenon is related only to REM deprivation, rather than to deprivation of sleep in general, researchers have experimented with NREM deprivation. They have found that subjects experience no increase in dream time as a result of NREM deprivation.

Other animals also show both the emotional changes accompanying REM deprivation and the recovery phenomenon (Murray, 1965). Cats become depressed and lethargic; if deprivation is prolonged, they show abnormal sexuality, hunger, and restlessness. When REM sleep is prohibited for prolonged periods, some cats are unable to make it up, become psychotic, and die.

Mental activity. There are individual differences in the quantity and quality of REM recovery. There is some reason to suppose that the differences may be due to differences in the need and occurrence of the kind of primary process activity typical of many dreaming states. This hypothesis is based on a study showing that at least for small amounts of deprivation (half a night), REM recovery is related to the kind of mental activity which takes the place of sleeping dreams (Cartwright & Monroe, 1968). When subjects were required to repeat a series of digits backward and forward upon being awakened from a REM, the REM recovery phenomenon occurred in the subsequent nondeprivation phase. However, when they reported the ongoing dream activities or other fantasies upon being awakened, there was no such consistent pressure for additional REM time in the nondeprivation period.

These results suggest that primary process activities may be a critical feature of REM time. Continued study of individual differences in tolerance of dream loss may help to answer questions of dream functions in the normal and abnormal balancing of reality-oriented and nonreality-oriented thought.

Need for NREM sleep. Are we to conclude, then, that we sleep only in order to dream? No, not at all. Although REM sleep seems necessary, the need for NREM sleep seems even more important.

During the first night of uninterrupted sleep, after complete sleep deprivation for 60 to 108 hours, subjects increased their Stage 4 sleep and correspondingly decreased their REM time; REM time then increased during subsequent nights (Williams et al., 1964; Berger & Oswald, 1962). Prolonged and complete sleep deprivation has also been shown to result in psychotic-like behavior in some people (Kleitman, 1963). Apparently, all stages of sleep are essential to our psychological and physical health.

THE FUNCTION OF DREAMS

Why people need to dream is still an unanswered question. The answers may have important implications for understanding biological rhythms as well as the psychological requirements for sound functioning. Indeed, understanding dreams may be one way of seeing the intricate interweaving of our biological and psychological lives and the futility of trying to separate the two.

Biological Bases

Some researchers have pointed to the regularity of REM time as suggesting that basic biological processes can account for the necessity of dreaming (Ullman, 1958a, b; Snyder, 1963; Berger, 1969). One theory maintains that REM periods reflect anxiety about survival and that they developed on an evolutionary basis to facilitate vigilance and orientation to the environment (Ullman, 1958a, 1958b). Organisms living in potentially hostile environments would be more likely to survive if they could avoid long periods of sleep and inattentiveness to the environment in which their predators might be stalking them. However, the theory does not account for the increasing length of the REM periods as the night progresses, or for the fact that in some species the auditory threshold during REM sleep is *increased* rather than decreased as would be expected if the REM period has survival value (Adey, Kodo, & Rhodes, 1963).

Stimulation. The most parsimonious and clear theory about dream occurrence maintains that dreams are part of a homeostatic process whereby the organism maintains an optimal level of cortical stimulation (Ephron & Carrington, 1966). As depth of sleep increases, cortical activity falls below the optimum. The brain corrects for this by stimulating itself. Thus, the fact that REM time increases as sleep continues through the night can be attributed to the increasing need for corrective stimulation as the night progresses.

This view can also incorporate the fact that sleep problems, such as nightmares, occur during Stage 4 sleep rather than in REM sleep. If organisms have anxiety about survival during sleep, it should be during the stages of deepest sleep when they are most vulnerable. The physiological states suggesting stress do occur during Stage 4, as do sleepwalking episodes, with signs of fear ranging from mild anxiety to a terror state in which heart rate is doubled. Nightmares and enuresis in children and adults takes place during NREM sleep or upon being awakened from NREM sleep, and abrupt awakenings from NREM sleep provide a wide range of bizarre, disorganized reactions.

A compatible speculation maintains that the increased neuronal activity and vascular flow in the brain during REM sleep may be essential for normal growth of the central nervous tissue (Roffwarg, Dement, & Fisher, 1964). REM periods account for 50 percent of the neonate's total sleep time. They may be a built-in stimulating system that "prepares" the central nervous system for the later influx of sensory input from the external world. The rather sharp reduction of REM time around three to four years of age may be related to the emergence of repression as an important defense mechanism.

CONTENT OF DREAMS

The initiation and maintenance of REMs as a biological rhythm or necessity does not preclude the possibility that the mental content during those times is also important and perhaps necessary. Before considering the matter of what dream interpretation can tell us about the value of dreams, we must first consider the source of the manifest images of dreams. For Freud, of course, the manifest content serves to hide the latent content, lest the dreamer awake. Modern efforts continue to try to understand the source and meaning of the images of the manifest content as potentially important for themselves.

Manifest Images

Stimuli before and during sleep. Freud postulated that preconscious perceptions are a main source of images of the manifest dream content: objects and events encountered during the day, but not intentionally or consciously seen, are perceived preconsciously and become a main source of images in the manifest dream content. This claim has been called the *Poetzl phenomenon* because of the apparent experimental demonstration of it by a Viennese physician, Otto Poetzl (1908). Although some current researchers still accept the validity of the Poetzl phenomenon (Fisher, 1960; Shervin & Loborsky, 1958; Giddan, 1967; Foulkes, 1966), careful research suggests that this claim is unwarranted (Johnson & Erikson, 1961). The burden of proof lies on those who claim preconscious perception as an important source of dream images.

Nor is there clear evidence that stimuli and activities immediately before sleep are a dominant source of dream images. Only 5 percent of dream reports could be traced to films shown to subjects immediately before going to sleep (Foulkes & Rechtschaffen, 1964), although some researchers using symbolic interpretation of dream elements claim evidence of the effect of movies preceding sleep in dreams (Witkin & Lewis, 1967b).

Better supported by evidence is the contention that stimuli occurring during sleep are incorporated into dreams (see Tart, 1965). They do not cause a dream to occur, but often are incorporated into an ongoing dream. Tones, lights, drops of water have been shown to affect dream content, with tactile stimuli being the most effective (Dement & Wolpert, 1958). Visual material presented to dreaming subjects whose eyes were taped open did not influence dream content (Rechtschaffen & Foulkes, 1965), nor did internal stimuli associated with thirst (Bokert, 1965).

There are some suggestions that dream time is favorable for telepathic communication, with images and thoughts of a waking "sender" being incorporated into the dreams of the sleeping "receiver" (Ullman & Krippner, 1970).

Reflections of life. What we dream about is probably what we know about. The images of our dreams are drawn from the waking world we attend to. The images that are persistent parts of our waking life are the main source of those used in our sleeping life; it is not necessary to assume preconscious perception of them nor that we were exposed to them specifically immediately before sleep. (Erik Erikson found that the manifest content of dreams often reflects the life style of the dreamer [Knight & Friedman, 1954].) This claim has implications for dream interpretation but it is not to say that we necessarily assemble the images in dreams in the ways in which they appear in waking life nor that we cannot use the images in expression of thoughts and feelings we may not clearly express to ourselves in waking life.

Sex differences. The easiest way of illustrating the lack of a mysterious separation between manifest content of dreams and what may be thought of as the manifest content of waking life is to point to sex differences in manifest dream content. The differences are generally consistent with the differences observed in waking life in terms of the general life styles of men and women, the things of concern to women in general and men in general, and the resulting environmental imagery (Hall & Van de Castle, 1966; Van de Castle, 1970).

Women have more people in their dreams than do men, and they are likely to be familiar people such as other family members. For men, they are others identified on the basis of their occupational status. Women pay more attention to clothing, jewelry, and physical descriptions of people and are concerned with household objects and flowers. Men are more interested in cars, tools, weapons, and money. Women make more esthetic and moral judgments than men, who are apt to identify things in terms of size, speed, intensity. Men have more physical aggressiveness in dreams; women have more subtle aggression and are sensitive to possible rejection. Men describe more dreams involving overt sex, physical activities, and failure or success. Women's dreams are more concerned with verbal activity and emotional reactions, and they have dreams set in familiar indoor places, whereas men's are in unfamiliar outdoor areas (Van de Castle, 1970).

More specifically, during menstruation, women tend to dream of destruction, red and pink colors, the human body, and unfriendly men. During the last trimester of pregnancy, they dream more about their unborn babies and their own mothers than about their husbands (Van de Castle, 1970).

Hypnosis. Although it does not work well with all subjects, posthypnotic suggestion may be the most powerful method for the experimental study of dream content, such that researchers can more successfully find the sources of dream content by manipulation of conditions (see Tart, 1965). The subject is given suggestions about dream content during hypnotic trance and instructions to forget that he has been given the suggestions (posthypnotic amnesia). The suggestions can influence the content of dreams occurring during later natural sleep. Dreams occurring during the hypnotic trance also offer an opportunity for understanding cognitive activities of thinking, fantasy, hallucinations, and dreaming.

Functions of Dream Content

Whatever the source of dream imagery and the biological requirements of REM time, we still have the question of what the dream content may mean. What can our dreams tell us about ourselves, other than the kinds of things we do and notice in waking life, which we know anyway? What can dreams do to help us in later waking states? We go to bed angry about an argument and have conflict-ridden dreams which may help us understand how we feel. We have a dream of a warm encounter with a friend and carry the pleasant feeling into our daytime relations with the person. We fall asleep after struggling unsuccessfully to balance a check-book, and in a dream we find a mistake in subtraction.

Often our dreams seem to be a direct reflection of the problems and conflicts—and pleasures—of the day. At other times, they may be confusing, frightening, and seem to be totally unrelated to our experience. What is the meaning of these nighttime fantasies and their function in our ongoing life? Is it to inform, to prophesy, to reflect, to relieve? The specific content of dreams probably serves as important a role in our lives as does the REM time; it may even be a physiological necessity. Dreams as psychological content probably do serve some useful function simply by occurring, but there are many views about why (see Murray, 1965; Breger, 1967; Snyder, 1967; Foulkes, 1966).

Safety-valve theories. For Freud, as for some contemporary psychologists, the important function—and perhaps necessity—of dreams is to be understood in terms of their content. Dreams can give disguised expression to conflicts and unfulfilled wishes and permit some wish-fulfillment gratification. They thus serve as a "psychic safety valve" through which we can blow off steam, as it were, and express in sleeping fantasy what we cannot feel free to let out in waking activities.

A modern elaboration of the Freudian view proposes that total dream time is a balance between the pressures of instinctual drives and the adequacy of the defensive and controlling forces of the ego (Fisher and Dement, 1963). The safety valve view does not have strong empirical support at this time, although the suggestion of the importance of primary process activity is consistent with it.

Problem-solving theories. Another theory about dream content is that its function is basically a problem-solving one. Dreams allow conflicts to be *resolved* as well as expressed (Breger, 1967). By dream expression of current problems, along with the memories about former problems more available in dreams than in waking states, the dreamer may be able to better formulate the problem and to arrive at a solution. (Thus, in a dream, one solves the problem of the unbalanced checkbook.)

There are many reports, not all of them well documented, of creative inspiration occurring in dreams (Krippner & Hughes, 1970). Artists, writers, scientists, and philosophers have been inspired by dreams or solved problems in their dreams. Goethe, Blake, Shelley, Tolstoy, Poe, Robert Louis Stevenson, Mozart, Schumann—all used dream material in their writing and music. Niels Bohr, the physicist, conceived the model of the atom in a dream he had as a student. When Elias Howe had difficulty making his sewing machine work, he dreamed he had been captured by savages and would die by their spears if he did not produce a working machine. As the savages approached with their spears raised, he noticed that the spears had eye-shaped holes near their tips. He awakened and realized that the eye of his sewing machine needle should be near the point. Once he repositioned the eye, the sewing machine worked.

DREAM INTERPRETATION

Closely related to the possible psychological functions of dreams in terms of dream content is the still debated matter of the "real" meaning of dreams—how are dreams to be interpreted? Should they be?

The Symbolic Approach

Freud maintained that the real meaning of dreams can become clear only when the symbolism of the manifest content is analyzed. In fact, were the latent content (the real meaning) not successfully disguised in the symbolic form of the manifest content, the dreamer would awake, and dreams then could not perform their function of guarding sleep by being the "safety valve."

To oversimplify for the sake of illustration, consider a dream about a young woman who steals a pen from a young man. A Freudian analyst would look on the pen as a phallic symbol and the action of stealing as a disguised wish to castrate the male and have a penis for herself. The dream permits expression of the envy and wish-fulfillment through symbolic action that the dreamer would be hesitant to express while awake.

Such symbolic interpretation is provocative, and probably worth more than a casual musing. The use of symbols can also be given a straightforward learning theory interpretation through the principle of stimulus generalization (Chapter 5). A response elicited by an object or event also tends to be elicited by similar objects or events. This is true both for response tendencies of thinking about them (an approach gradient) and for response tendencies to be anxious about them or to avoid thinking about them (avoidance gradient), and the avoidance gradient falls off more quickly than the approach gradient. Thus, we may be inhibited from thinking about the real object but not about a similar, "symbolic" one. In addition, thoughts inhibited in waking life may not be inhibited in sleeping life with its greater distance from (external) reality.

However, the symbolic approach can easily get out of hand and lead to much ambiguity and confusion, and, in the extreme, to almost any post hoc and ad hoc interpretation one cares to offer, for whatever the reason, Freudian or otherwise. Over how wide a range do we extend the generalization? What are the essential dimensions of a stimulus along which generalization to other stimuli will occur? When is an image exactly what it appears to be rather than a symbol of something else?

Although a knife is similar in shape to a penis, it is also similar in physical characteristics to a nail file, a fence post, a screwdriver, a radio antenna. It is conceptually similar to a fork because of the association of both with eating. When one dreams of a knife, is the knife a symbol of a penis, or of one of the other objects also similar to it? Is the dreamer really dreaming of sexual activities, eating, cleaning fish, building fences, or listening to a radio?

At the other extreme is what can be called a random-generation approach to dream interpretation. The images of dreams are randomly determined and therefore meaningless nonsense. The situation is somewhat like that in which a monkey with a typewriter somehow puts together letters that form somewhat intelligible words or phrases but that have no known relevance to the activities, experiences, or feelings of the monkey. Which key the monkey strikes may have some potentially demonstrable determinants, but probably not ones that are relevant to symbolic communication as we now understand it.

Both the extreme Freudian symbolic approach and the extreme random model seem to violate some intuitive common sense. A middle-ground approach seems a more reasonable one, particularly as expressed in the cognitive theory of Calvin Hall.

The Cognitive Approach

Freud's contention that the manifest dream content *hides* the real meaning of dreams has been particularly called into question. For example, Carl Jung believed that the manifest dream content presents a true picture of the subjective state: "Perhaps we may call the dream a facade, but we must remember that the fronts of most houses by no means trick or deceive us, but, on the contrary, follow the plan of the building and often betray its inner arrangement . . ." (Jung, 1956, p. 12).

Calvin Hall (1966; Hall & Van de Castle, 1966) is currently a leading spokesman for a cognitive approach to dream interpretation which emphasizes dreaming as a function of the ego and attends to the manifest content as important in its own right. He lists four specific criticisms of

Freud's view that the symbols in the manifest dream content *hide* the meaning of the latent content. First, the same subject can report some dreams that have frankly overt sexual content and some that would seem to a Freudian to be full of symbols designed to hide the sexual content. Why should a person at one time feel the need to hide his sexual meaning, and at another time reveal it in full force? Second, many people who have no training in Freudian symbolism or dream interpretation are capable of examining the manifest content of their own dreams and giving sexual interpretations. Why should the dream hide a meaning a person can arrive at anyway without the help of a trained therapist? Third, centuries before Freud, slang, figures of speech, and profanity employed "Freudian symbolism" for the penis (e.g., rod, gun, pistol). Fourth, why need there be so many symbols for the same referent?

Hall does not deny the meaningfulness of dream content or symbols. But, he maintains, the symbols *enhance* meaning rather than *disguise* it:

> The function of dreaming as we have said many times is to reveal what is in the person's mind, not to conceal it. Dreams may appear enigmatic because they contain symbols, but these symbols are nothing more than pictorial metaphors, and like the verbal metaphor of waking life their intention is to clarify rather than to obscure thought. What is the difference between a person awake exclaiming, "he's a majestic individual," and a person asleep conjuring up the image of a king? There is no difference except in the medium of expression (Hall, 1966, p. 215).

"Any clear headed person should be able to interpret dreams" (1966, p. 85). The cardinal rule for dream interpretation, according to Hall, is to understand that a dream is a creation of the dreamer's mind, a projection or screen play about what the dreamer thinks about himself and the world. The subjective reality depicted in the dream may not correspond with objective reality, but it is an accurate picture of the reality that appears to the dreamer, even though it is not always clearly presented in conscious form during the day.

Our dreams are very personal conceptions and can reveal how we see ourselves, other people, and the world, how we feel about our impulses and the obstacles in the way of their gratification. While some feelings and experiences are general enough that a common symbol may be used by a number of people, most symbols are unique to the person using them. Thus, because of differences in experience and conception, one person may see a cow as a warm nurturant creature, while another may see it as a dumb but necessary beast. To interpret a man's dream in which his mother appears as a cow, we would have to know his personal conception of a cow.

Whether we prefer Freud's symbolic approach to dream interpretation or whether we find Hall's cognitive theory a more reasonable explanation, we can discover, through a study of our dream life, helpful clues about our attitudes, our anxieties, our defenses, our needs—in short, our personalities. Much the same can be said about the waking fantasy of daydreams.

AWAKE AND DREAMING

Is Daydreaming Normal?

It is sometimes difficult to avoid forming an image of a daydreamer as an unhappy, maladjusted person living in a world of his own particular—and perhaps peculiar—invention. "You're daydreaming" is more often an accusation than a neutral observation or a statement of praise. The most widespread view of fantasy is the psychoanalytic one that fantasy grows out of a frustrated impulse and serves a defensive or cathartic function (A. Freud, 1937). But daydreaming is pathological only if it is used improperly. Daydreaming is a "neutral skill" which may be used for the "adaptive enrichment of the life of otherwise ordinary persons" (Singer, 1966, p. 187), or it may be a manifestation of attempted escape, self-dissatisfaction, or evasion of responsibility.

In trying to relate daydreaming to emotional stability, we must take account of the content of daydreams as well as their frequency, and of the implications of the self-awareness that seems to underlie the use of daydreams.

Does Everyone Daydream?

Not everyone, but almost everyone, reports daydreaming. Most of us do in fact daydream, in that we spend time attending to matters other than those presented by our immediate environment. The currently accepted definition of daydreaming is any shift of attention away from an ongoing task or event in the external environment toward a response to some internal stimulus (Singer, 1966). In a culture as oriented to the external and tangible world as ours, it is curious—and perhaps relieving—that so many people spend some time each day in responding to thoughts not triggered by the external world. Considering what can be gained by daydreaming, perhaps we know what we are doing by "rebelling" in this way. If the words of a famous science-fiction writer, an expert in fantasy, are to be believed, "The ability to 'fantasize' is the ability to survive" (Bradbury, 1968, p. 28). We know better than our culture.

Daydreaming is in fact much more common than most people realize (Schaffer & Shoben, 1956; Singer, 1966). The development of the General Daydreaming Scale by Jerome Singer and his associates has helped to provide reliable quantification of daydream frequency and content, and its use thus far has enabled some beginning information about daydream frequency and content.

Using this instrument, 96 percent of a sample of college-educated adults, aged nineteen to fifty years, reported some daydreaming every day (Singer & McCraven, 1961). Daydreaming was found to occur chiefly when alone, most often before falling asleep, and least often in the morning, during meals, and during sexual activity.

The frequency of daydreaming reached its maximum between ages eighteen and twenty-nine and decreased to the lowest frequency in the forty to forty-nine-year-old group, the oldest group in this sample. The decline with age may be due to decreasing time for solitude and the narrowing of concerns to current and near future situations.

Although some daydreaming content was wish-fulfillment in the traditional sense, the dominant content seemed to involve practical concerns with life situations. There was a high frequency of planning for future actions, particularly interpersonal contacts.

Preparation for Daydreaming

How often we daydream, and about what, differs greatly from one person to another, for reasons not yet clearly specified. So far, there is reason to suggest that people who daydream more often than others have had both the need and the occasion to practice daydreaming skills, and have received indirect encouragement through socialization pressures that encourage impulse inhibition and self-control, relative to pressures for action in the external environment (Singer, 1961, 1966; Singer & McCraven, 1962).

For example, the child who daydreams frequently is more often the oldest or only child, or has fewer older siblings than does the child who daydreams very little. Thus, the frequent daydreamer probably had more privacy for the practice of self-generated play and daydreaming skills. Further, the attention he received from parents was often along fantasy lines, such as storytelling and fantasy games. The tendency for frequent daydreaming may, then, be associated with early opportunity for solitary activities, and for free exploration and play, together with parental encouragement of fantasy activities.

Functions and Content of Daydreams

What good is daydreaming? With dreams of the day as of the night, exploration of the internal world through fantasies definitely has some potential assets. Whether or not fantasy is necessary for survival, daydreams can serve some very useful functions in our otherwise humdrum lives. In the reality of our fantasy, we have the advantage of a free mind. We can use daydreams to help to compensate for an unpleasant or boring environment, we can become more effective in interacting with the environment, we can seek gratification and catharsis, and perhaps most important, we can extend our self-awareness.

Daydreaming as compensation for environmental deficiencies. The occurrence of daydreaming, *regardless of content,* may have beneficial effects in environments that are monotonous or otherwise stressful. In daydreaming the mind may wander from the immediate external environment. No matter how bound the body, the mind can be free.

Daydreaming is a frequent occurrence in sensory deprivation studies, in which the experimenter prohibits as much visual, auditory, and tactile stimulation as possible. People who are highly predisposed to daydream are less disturbed by an anticipated shock than those with a lesser predisposition to daydream (Rowe, 1963). Hungry subjects who engage in fantasy (relevant or irrelevant to hunger) experience time as passing more quickly than hungry subjects whose attention is held by nonfantasy tasks (Moore, cited by Singer, 1966).

The internal stimulation provided by daydreaming can actually *help* to maintain alertness and improve attentiveness to an environment that provides minimal and monotonous stimulation. For example, in a ninety-minute task, one group of subjects was asked to count from one to nine repeatedly, while another group was asked to talk spontaneously and to free-associate (daydream). Both groups also had to perform a *vigilance task,* detecting when a flashing light was brighter than usual (Antrobus, 1963). Those whose thoughts were severely restricted by the repeated counting showed irritability and discomfort, and took frequent naps. At those times when they were awake and alert, the restricted group was more accurate in detecting the brighter signal than the other group, but their frequent drowsiness impaired overall performance. Those subjects who were encouraged to vary their thoughts were able to maintain a higher average level of performance.

Thus, daydreams can provide internal stimulation that can compensate for external stress or boredom. This suggested function of daydreams has much in common with the homeostatic view of nocturnal dreams.

Daydreaming and interaction with environment. The content of daydreams often allows us to compensate for our own deficiencies and work toward effective interaction with external reality. Within our own inner reality we may prepare for negotiations with outer reality and find occasional solace from its pressures.

Daydreaming may help us to recognize and clarify problems, and also to solve them. Actual or possible aspects of a situation are considered, plans of action are rehearsed, and their outcomes can be anticipated. The dangers and the pleasures of "what if . . ." may be faced in privacy before we perform in view of others. In daydreams, we may also make a leisurely review of past conflicts and stressful situations, in order to understand the situation better than we could when the immediate pressures of the moment were upon us: "Oh, so that's what was wrong . . . ," "I could have said. . . ."

One specific kind of problem that seems to be dealt with in daydreams is very basic: finding out who we are, how we want to be viewed by ourselves and others, and what we can do to be viewed that way. With mental role-playing, we can get a look at ourselves as we want to be, or think we should be, and we can practice being that. This may have the side benefit of increasing self-esteem.

One investigator predicted that if daydreams served to enhance one's self-perceptions, then men and women would report fantasy material relevant to the enhancement of their masculine and feminine strivings, that each sex would report dreams accentuating its own idealized sex-role image: Cultural stereotypes of masculine and feminine behavior are mirrored in daydreams (Wagman, 1967). The prediction was by and large confirmed.

Consistent with stereotypes, male students reported a high incidence of assertive, sexual, heroic and self-aggrandizing daydreams, while women reported a higher frequency of passive, affiliative, narcissistic, oral, and physical attractiveness daydreams. Unexpectedly, women daydreamed more often of practical and planning activities than did men!

Gratifications available in daydreams. Daydreams may help to provide gratifications, such as increased self-esteem, that we cannot always find in external reality. Daydreams are also frequently used to provide some gratification, role-playing, and problem-solving about other activities of concern—namely, success and sex. Ours is an achieving society, with achievement typically defined in terms of vocations, money, applause, intellectual skills (Chapter 10). Both men and women undergraduates report a high frequency of daydreams about accomplishing a mental feat, achieving vocational success, obtaining money or possessions, gaining applause for ability or daring (Shaffer & Shoben, 1956; Wagman, 1967).

For both men and women, daydreams about sexual gratification tend to be popular, and elicit strong emotional reactions (Shaffer & Shoben, 1956; Seeman, 1948). However, men and women do differ markedly in the *style* of their sexual fantasies, in ways consistent with their socialization experiences (Barclay, 1973). The sexual fantasies of college men reflect training to be sexually aggressive and forward; they find the visual aspects of sexual behavior more interesting than the emotional aspects and report highly visual imagery with many specific details about the partner. For young college women, the fantasies are vivid, but they are more involved with their own emotional responses than with the details of their partners, who are likely to be familiar men, as they are in night dreams. The fantasies are much more diffuse and "romantic."

Catharsis. One kind of fantasy gratification is provided by catharsis. Catharsis is thought to "drain off" and reduce the need for further expression of a motive or emotion; this hypothesis dates back to Aristotle and appears again in Freudian theory. For Freud, the infant's hallucinations of the object that would satisfy a drive result in partial drive reduction, in that the need to satisfy the drive is reduced.

Our current interest is in how indirect expression of feelings can replace direct—and socially unacceptable—expressions. Subjects in an experiment were insulted in order to arouse aggression. Then they spent ten minutes either daydreaming, writing TAT stories (an induced rather than a spontaneous fantasy), or working on a judgment task (Pytkowicz, Wagner, & Sarason, 1967). Subjects who had an opportunity for fantasy following the insult showed a cathartic effect; when required to complete a questionnaire, they expressed less hostility toward the experimenter and experimental situation than did the insulted subjects who did not have a chance for fantasy.

More important, the cathartic effect was much stronger for high daydream frequency subjects than for those with a low daydream frequency. This supports the contention that subjects who daydream often have learned better to use fantasy activity as an adaptive mechanism in coping with stress.

However, high daydream subjects may pay a price for the advantages they purchase with their daydreaming skills. Aggression was not discharged in fantasy, but was displaced onto the self. No subject reported hostile or anxious daydreams, and there was little relationship between reported hostility and aggressive themes in the TAT stories. Insulted high daydream subjects who had been given the chance for fantasy had increased hostility with self as the object. Fantasy following frustration can facilitate the internalization of anger. While the daydreamer may reap the rewards of impulse inhibition, he may also have to pay the price of having more negative feelings about himself. And perhaps even the high frequency daydreamer may be inhibited in the use of fantasy for gratification or catharsis.

Inhibition in Fantasy

It is pleasant to think that in our fantasy we are free of all the restrictions of the world, free to find compensation and solution for whatever problems and lack of gratification we experience in external reality. Unfortunately, however, much of the potential freedom of our own internal world is unused; we can be almost as inhibited in our internal private reality as in our external public one. The rules of those around us become incorporated as our own—an idea well articulated by Freud with his concept of superego and by Rogers with his concept of conditions of worth. Thus, we carry around with us the inhibitions taught us by others.

Some of the inhibitions are against the free-wheeling thought possible in fantasy, or against fantasy itself. Society, through its pressures in favor of external reality, often inhibits our ability to "let loose" and use fantasy well, freely, and without guilt. Our daydreams can be as monotonously rational, orderly, logical as our contacts with external reality are so often forced to be.

In our society, sexual as well as aggressive feelings and behavior are particularly likely to be punished by others, resulting in anxiety that can inhibit not only behavior but often the fantasies that could be useful in providing gratification or catharsis. We learn not only "Don't do that," but also "Don't even think of doing that!" Some people reach a point where they cannot freely feel the sexual or aggressive feelings that are their own, even in the fantasy world that should be most freely and openly their own, where a person may know and be himself.

We come to avoid anxiety by not thinking about themes that have been disapproved by others, even in our world of fantasy. The following experiment featured induced rather than spontaneous fantasy, but it illustrates the same inhibition that can go on in spontaneous fantasy. Male students were shown pictures of attractive nude females (the aroused, experimental group), under the guise of providing ratings of body types (Clark, 1952; Clark & Sensibar, 1956). Other students were shown landscape scenes (neutral, control group). Contrary to the general prediction of increased imagery relevant to a motivation after arousal of the motive, the experimental subjects who had looked at the females showed less *sexual* imagery in TAT stories given after the exposure than subjects who had seen the landscapes. The reduced amount of sexual fantasy in the aroused group suggested an active inhibition of sexual fantasy to levels below normal, rather than lack of arousal of sexual interest. Avoidance of sexual imagery was an attempt to avoid or reduce guilt or fear about the sexual fantasies they were tempted to have.

This reasoning was supported by results from subjects who had been drinking at fraternity beer parties when participating in the experiment. Consistent with the hypothesis that alcohol reduces anxiety and guilt, the males shown the sexual slides after they had been drinking revealed more manifest sex content in TAT stories than did the control subjects shown the neutral pictures, and the beer-aroused group had more overt sexual imagery than either class group. Sexual interest increased by exposure to the pictures was not expressed in manifest form in the TAT stories unless the aroused subjects had been drinking!

It is easy to focus on gratification or catharsis, or on inhibition about sex and aggression in fantasy. It is much harder to grasp the pervasiveness with which inhibitions can occur and inhibit self-awareness generally.

Self-Awareness

The profile of the frequent daydreamer is similar to the picture of the person who easily recalls his night dreams. Overall, the frequent daydreamers tend to be self-aware: They tend to recall more night dreams, have lower scores on lie and repression scales and more manifest anxiety (Singer and Schonbar, 1961; Wagman, 1967b). Certainly there are differences in type of content of daydreams and these must be taken into account in relating daydreaming to personality variables or maladjustment (Singer & Antrobus, 1963). Only some frequent daydreamers show signs of neurotic or disturbed patterns; those who limit their fantasy activity to fearful thoughts and somatic preoccupations are the ones likely to show evidence of clinical manifestations of neurosis. By and large, frequent daydreamers are not neurotic or disturbed.

Rather, frequent daydreamers are probably people who are ". . . willing to see themselves in temporal or spatial perspective and to engage in some form of imaginative living" (Singer, 1966, p. 75). Underlying the different types of daydreams seems to be a pattern of self-awareness and introspection. At one end of this dimension are fantastic, fanciful daydreams; at the other is more controlled or orderly, objective material. The fanciful daydreamers tend to be curious about people and their motives; the orderly daydreamers tend to be curious about natural events or the physical world. Both extremes reflect responsiveness to internally initiated cognitive experiences.

Daydreaming, then, is one means of implementing curiosity. It is an internal exploration of thoughts and feelings which can be used adaptively to increase awareness and understanding of the real world of self and the real world of other people. In both cases, one generates and further responds to his own experiences. But the internal activity is not completely free from external prohibitions. Even those among us who often daydream cannot be sure that they have explored to the utmost their potential for knowledge and understanding of themselves or of the world they live in.

Summary

Dreams have puzzled and fascinated man since ancient times. Theories of dreaming and interpretations of dreams have sprung up through the years and have varied among cultures, but only recently has man been able to define and measure this part of his fantasy life. By using the EEG to detect the various stages of sleep and by waking subjects during or immediately after REM sleep, researchers have proved that we tend to dream during REM time. We have learned not only that everyone dreams but, through experiments in REM deprivation, that everyone needs to dream.

Although research on dreams is proceeding rapidly, there has been more modest work, but work of equal potential importance, on daydreams. Daydreaming has been found to be a much more common activity than we had previously realized, and, when not used in extreme, it can help us compensate for and interact with our environment. It can extend our self-awareness, supply gratification, and provide an outlet for anxiety and stress.

Because our culture dictates that only the external is real, we can easily neglect exploring the potential of our internal world. By doing so, we limit the extent to which both daydreams and night dreams can lead to heightened self-awareness.

10

motivation: biological and social

Motivation is difficult to study because there is no way of actually getting inside a person. We can see what happens to a person and we can see how he behaves, but we cannot directly observe what goes on between a stimulus and the response. At the human level at least, it is difficult to see how the questions about personality differ from those about motivation. In both cases, there is an assumption that internal, organismic processes must be inferred to explain individual differences in responses which are not readily apparent from a careful description of the current objective situation.

Thus, our discussion of motivation will serve to illustrate several kinds of principles and issues involved in thinking about people and trying to understand why they behave the way they do. The most pervasively important principle is that *the human being is a psychobiological organism which grows, experiences, and behaves in an environment.* There are biological determinants of behavior and determinants from current and past situations.

Some questions raised in considering the role of motivation in personality center on the role of situational relative to personal determinants of behavior, biological relative to experiential factors, the nature of what is reinforcing or pleasant for what person in what circumstance, and, indeed, whether or not the concept of motivation is a necessary or useful one. A recurring problem is to *explain* behavior rather than to merely name it or to assert, after the fact, that intervening, motivational, mechanisms have occurred.

We will look first at foundation concepts for approaching the study of motivation and then at achievement and affiliation as two important examples of human motivation. Finally, we will raise some theoretical questions about the role of motivation in understanding human behavior.

FUNDAMENTAL CONCEPTS OF MOTIVATION

A complete understanding of behavior requires comprehension of the impetus or energy for behavior and the direction of behavior. A related concern is that of the maintenance and change of behavior. Accordingly, three kinds of properties have been attributed to the motives which are conceptualized as intervening between the objectively immediate stimuli and the response: A motive *energizes* behavior, a motive *directs* behavior, and motive reduction is positively *reinforcing*. Theorists differ about which property or combination of properties should be emphasized.

The Energy of Behavior

Arousal positions. Arousal theorists are concerned with the energy or intensity of behavior, focusing on the fact that behavior requires an activation or arousal (Duffy, 1941, 1949, 1951; Malmo, 1957, 1958). The importance of the intensive dimension of behavior is recognized by Freudians (psychic energy) and learning theorists (Hullian generalized drive) alike, though with differing theoretical rationales. Arousal is best viewed as a construct (an intervening variable, Chapter 2) with many kinds of behavioral manifestations. It is most often defined with respect to biological activity (see Hokanson, 1969), and sometimes defined as the biological activity itself (hypothetical construct, Chapter 2).

The physiological indices of arousal are themselves responses which are correlates or antecedents of other more easily observable responses. The usual indices of arousal are physiological response systems under the control of the somatic nervous system, the central nervous system, and the autonomic nervous system. Muscle tension is measured with surface electrodes which pick up electrical activity of muscle groups; tension increases as arousal increases. The pattern of firing of nerve cells in the brain (CNS activity) varies with arousal level (Jasper, 1958). The form of brain waves, measured by EEGs, changes with depth of sleep and with amount of alertness in waking states (Chapter 9).

Indices of autonomic nervous system (ANS) activity, as was mentioned above, are frequently used arousal measures. With low arousal, the parasympathetic branch of the ANS is dominant, while with high arousal, the sympathetic nervous system is increasingly innervated, mobilizing the organism for vigorous action—for fight or flight. Increases in rate and variability of heartbeat, blood pressure, and respiration are ANS indices of arousal, as is an increase in skin conductance (SC) of electricity (or decrease in skin resistance, SR). As with most constructs, the response measures do not correlate perfectly, and people differ in which is their most sensitive measure—some people are heart rate responders, some skin responders, and so on (Lacey, 1956).

In all cases of measurement of arousal, it is important to keep in mind that the arousal being measured is internal arousal, which may not be obvious overtly; for example, one can be very aroused and tense while sitting still (as in the dentist's waiting room), or very relaxed while moving (when taking a stroll or swimming).

Arousal reflects the intensity of behavior, or, alternately, the interest or incentive value of the stimulus conditions. For example, muscle tension increase was greater when subjects were offered financial reward for performing a laboratory task than when they were led to believe that they were simply helping the experimenter to calibrate his machinery (Stennet, 1957). When subjects listened to a detective story for the first time, muscle tension increased from the beginning to the climax of the story, and the amount of increase was lower on successive repetitions of the story. Thus, arousal is an objective measure of the motivation value of the stimulus, and of the concomitant drive or energy level of the responding organism.

The construct of arousal refers to a characteristic of the organism, but, like any construct, to be useful it must be linked to observable events. Arousal is associated with observable environmental conditions, as in the cases just mentioned. It is also linked to behavior, as will be discussed later (Chapter 15). Briefly, there is a curvilinear relationship between arousal and performance effectiveness, shown by evidence from human behavior as well as that of other animals. For any task, there is an optimum arousal level at which performance is maximal; below that level, the organism is not "warmed up," and above that level, the organism is "too motivated." We will also see arousal as a concomitant of emotionality and anxiety (Chapters 14, 15).

Energy and Direction of Behavior

Homeostatic concepts. While arousal theorists are concerned only with the energy of behavior, other theorists attempt to account for the energy component and the directional component of behavior simultaneously. The nature of the source and the content of the arousal are associated intimately with the direction of behavior; how and why an organism is aroused affects what he does. The term *homeostasis* refers to the relatively constant steady states maintained by physiological processes, and homeostatic concepts have provided a pervasive backdrop for the development of many theoretical positions not explicitly identified as homeostatic theories.

Behavior is a regulatory process which enables correction of internal imbalances by transaction with the environment. Disequilibrium activates behavior directed toward the specific objects which will restore an equilibrium. However, the homeostasis principle requires only that *a* state of equilibrium is attained, not necessarily a *prior* state of equilibrium or a state of no tension. Reflexes maintain balance within the organism: A sneeze or cough exhumes a foreign body from the nasal passage or the throat; scar tissue forms over cuts; the central nervous system prepares the organism for emergency action; salt is craved when there is a salt deficiency (even to the point where humans will drink urine to maintain salt balance—ourondypsia). When a motive or drive is aroused, behavior occurs which serves to reduce the disequilibrium; the response that occurs is likely to be a response which has been effective previously in reducing the disequilibrium, that is, a response that was reinforced. The Freudian theory of tension reduction as the goal of behavior, and the learning theory views of drive reduction as essential for learning, are basically homeostatic positions. In both traditions, it is maintained that a person learns which behavior directed toward what object will reduce the motive and restore equilibrium.

How can homeostasis account for nonroutine activities which seem to disturb equilibrium, such as dangerous sports or working to the point of exhaustion? The homeostatic explanation for the explorer who exposes himself to discomforts and dangers, for example, is that he has built up a perception of himself as an exploring person and he can maintain equilibrium only by engaging in the activity he perceives as appropriate for him. Thus, the homeostatic position is one which is difficult to disavow because it can "explain" behavior after the fact only by asserting the existence of a search for an equilibrium. This is a weakness which can be corrected by careful specification of the conditions under which disequilibrium and equilibrium will occur.

Ethology

In spite of many attempts to exorcise instinct theory from the body of science, particularly by American behaviorists whose orientation reflects an extreme environmental determinism, it remains viable, and is, in modern ethology (the science of behavior) of increasing contemporary interest and recognized value (e.g., Moltz, 1965; Nash, 1970; Ratner, 1973). Unlike the instinctivists at the turn of the century (e.g., McDougall, 1908) who essentially bypassed problems of explanation by merely labeling behavior as instinctual (even not stealing apples from one's own orchard was attributed to a specific instinct; Murray, 1964), contemporary workers analyze *species-specific behaviors* (such as caretaking of the young, courting and mating, aggression) into component responses and the *sign stimuli* which elicit them.

The sign stimuli are often characteristics or behaviors of another species member. For example, a red spot on the bill of the adult herring gull releases pecking of that spot by the young chick; the pecking releases a regurgitation response of the parent, and the chick has his supper. Other stimuli tend to be ignored as the sign stimulus is attended to and responded to: Perception is selective. A male stickleback fish courts a female with a swollen abdomen (in which she is carrying eggs for potential fertilization), and he will also court a cardboard model if it has the important swollen abdomen. Other fish characteristics are irrelevant if the sign stimulus is present. While the instinctual responses typically function to ensure survival in the animal's natural environment, sign stimuli can elicit the response when encountered outside the typical context and in inappropriate circumstances, as seen with the responses directed toward models.

For Konrad Lorenz (1943, 1950, 1958, 1966), an instinctual act has its own energy (reaction-specific energy) in the central nervous system, which is released by an innate releasing mechanism (IRM) activated by the sign stimulus. The energy increases sensitivity to the appropriate stimuli. In this sense, the energy is directed, and the behavior instigated is homeostatic. If the sign stimulus is not encountered, the sensitivity may build up until complete or partial acts are performed in the absence of a releasing stimulus (vacuum activities) or are directed in inappropriate ways or toward inappropriate objects (displacement). If a goose does not make the appropriate display responses, which are sign stimuli for the gander, the male displaces from sexual responses to nest building. (Notice the similarity to Freud's concept of displacement.)

Current treatments emphasize the *interaction* of environmental with genetically based determinants. An instinct does not necessarily imply a fixed, immutable behavior pattern, present at birth, which occurs independently of the environment in which the organism experiences and reacts (Fletcher, 1966): An instinct is actually an inherited tendency to develop certain behaviors. In the natural environment, some behaviors are highly likely to be developed and to have reinforcing and survival value. However, modifiability of instinctive behavior and the capacity for intelligent control are themselves inherited features on which species differ and various instinctual behaviors are differentially suspectible to modification. A strict dichotomy between heredity and experience—between innate and acquired behavior patterns—is not warranted, nor is a dichotomy between intelligence—or reason—and instincts.

Relatively permanent changes in instinctual behaviors can occur because of the organism's susceptibility to early experiences and domestication. Early failures to learn can block the occurrence of responses. Monkeys reared without the typical exposure to mothers or peers failed to respond to sign stimuli associated with sexual behavior or with care of their young (Harlow, 1961; Chapter 19). Or, responses may be directed toward inappropriate objects which had been present during early critical periods. Birds made courting responses to people, boxes, or shoes if the stimuli had been present in early life; a male peacock raised in the reptile house of a zoo totally ignored, for the rest of its life, the prettiest of peahens and made advances only to giant tortoises (De Ropp, 1969).

Domestication, too, can affect the stimulus and response elements of feeding, sex, fighting, nesting, and care of the young. Domestication implies controlling the species' environment and mating so that the new, domesticated species is different from the original, natural species (Ratner, 1973). The effects of domestication are generally to increase the plasticity of stimuli and responses, so that a wider range of stimuli elicits a response and a wider range of responses is produced. However, the effects of domestication may also be to select our survival mechanisms. For example, turkeys bred to have large breasts—for the benefit of humans who purchase them for holiday feasts—cannot mate successfully without help because of the interference of the large breasts with the mating act.

Human ethology. The idea that there are species-specific behaviors which are characteristic of humans must be taken seriously, although it is difficult to set forth clear instances of instinctual behaviors in man (Ratner, 1973; Nash, 1970; Fletcher, 1966). With humans, modifiability of instinctive behaviors noted among other animals reaches a high degree, and experience in learning and intelligent control play a greater part in altering the innate patterns. The long infancy and the protracted immaturity in man make possible the greater plasticity of behavior. Details of behavior common to all species members may be modified by culture, just as the responses of other animals are modified by experience. This is not to deny the importance of attempting to uncover the basic instinctual patterns. The apparent absence of universal sign stimuli and fixed responses may merely reflect the susceptibility of humans to the dynamic properties of the species-specific behaviors.

Human beings share with their fellow animals a similarity of basic skeletal structure which has persisted over geological periods, and they may well share instinctual determinants of behavior as well. There are observations suggesting that odors, facial expressions, postures, and vocalizations act as sign stimuli and fixed responses for many humans. Parental nurturant behavior is easily elicited by the sign stimuli of a kewpie doll configuration (e.g., short face, large forehead, protruding cheeks, and maladjusted limb movements—characteristics made salient in dolls, babies in the movies, and pets). Women who adjust perfectly ordered hair and men who stroke their beards may be illustrating displacement activities in conflict situations, a form of skin-care instinct. A steady, fixed stare elicits a feeling of distinct discomfort. Angularity is a recurrent feature in masks of devils and witches and elicits avoidance response, while roundness of eyes and facial characteristics elicit approach and sexual responses (Barclay, 1971). Sign stimuli such as penis, breast, and buttocks have important functions in human social and sexual behavior (Wickler, 1967; Barclay, 1973).

Ethological theory and research are likely to prove especially revealing in the study of aggressive behavior. Animals other than man not only respond to sign stimuli which activate aggressive responses; they also have stimuli which inhibit the aggression once the victor is established but before mortal harm occurs to either combatant. When one contestant begins to lose, he assumes a surrender posture which inhibits continued fighting to the death; for example, a dog lies on his back to expose the belly. Lorenz (1943, 1958, 1966) speculates that the invention of artificial weapons has disturbed the natural equilibrium in man; sign stimuli which might inhibit lethal aggression cannot be detected by the operators of control panels which activate long-distance artillery.

"It is hardly likely that, of all the species in existence, man alone is born with no such instinctual heritage" (Fletcher, 1966, p. 21). Thus, there is more to be gained by facing the possibility and perhaps profiting from the knowledge than by denying it. To the extent that man is becoming a new, domesticated species, he may be improving on nature, or he may be interfering with nature's attempts to ensure his survival.

Direction of Behavior

Hedonism. Hedonism is one of the earliest and most basic explanations of motivation, attending to the direction of behavior to the neglect of the energy of behavior. Man acts to seek pleasure and to avoid pain. This is a popular view with laymen, and one with a notable intellectual ancestry, having roots in ancient Greek thought and finding major spokesmen among English philosophers. One of the latter, Herbert Spencer, linked hedonism to evolutionary concepts by maintaining that behaviors which produce pleasure are also likely to contribute to survival, whereas pain frequently signals that survival is threatened (see Hokanson, 1969). Spencer also anticipated current views of reinforcement by suggesting that responses are performed because they have in the past been effective in attaining pleasure and avoiding pain.

More recently, P. T. Young's (1947, 1955, 1961) research with rats revealed that needed foods are usually enjoyable foods (and thus chosen in free preference situations), so that bodily need and positive affect are positively correlated. It is, though, an imperfect correlation because of the influence of habit on food palatability.

Psychologists have been discontent with traditional hedonistic conceptions, as with homeostatic ones, because of their dependence on unobservable experiences of pleasure, or equilibrium, and the inability to predict. Affective processes are inferred from the behavior which affect is postulated to explain: If a rat drank a non-nutritive saccharine solution instead of a nutritive one, it was because he liked it. If a person is observed to engage in behaviors that others consider lead to pain, the hedonist can only assert that the state is pleasant for the one behaving. Behavior is explained after the fact without independent evidence of the pleasurable affect.

Recent physiological studies showing the existence of reward mechanisms apparently independent from conventional conceptions of drive reduction have opened the way for a new hedonistic theory of motivation (Hokanson, 1969; Olds & Olds, 1965; Miller, 1959). There are "pleasure centers" in the brain (in the forward part of the hypothalamus and related parts of the limbic system) which, when stimulated by electrical current, can maintain behavior at extremely high rates. Rats, cats, and monkeys will press a lever—up to 5000 times an hour—if the press is followed by an electrical stimulation to the pleasure center. Some studies using human subjects, typically patients with neurological, physical, or psychiatric disorders, suggest that humans have similar brain centers. Electrical self-stimulation of apparent pleasure centers is associated with a considerable symptom relief: increased alertness, better memory, improved psychomotor activity, elimination of depression and anxiety, and relief of some pain. An eleven-year-old epileptic boy became animated, optimistic, and sociable during periods of stimulation, in contrast to his typical flat affect and uncommunicativeness.

There also seems to be a "punishing" area (in parts of the limbic system further to the rear of the brain). Animals learned to turn a wheel to terminate stimulation in this area, and learned to avoid shock when a tone warned that the current was about to be turned on (Miller, 1959).

Thus, there seems to be an actual physical basis for hedonistic experiences which is not dependent upon primary, biological needs. However, brain stimulation interacts with those physiological needs—some points in the rewarding brain area are more effective when animals are food deprived, and others when animals have been given sex hormones. Animals, probably including man, have hedonistic physiological structures, but the hedonism has survival value in that when there is a need or altered body condition, the locus of pleasure shifts in accordance with that need. Thus, appropriate pleasure is sought to restore homeostatic balance. Probably many instinctual behavior patterns serve hedonistic and homeostatic functions.

Although the major foundation concepts of motivation outlined in this section appear to be quite different, they are not necessarily incompatible positions. Behavior is energized and usually directed. Through evolution, nature seems to have done a remarkable job in ensuring that life perpetuates itself but is capable of individual variation from one animal to another and of modifiability within any one animal. Automatic responses combine with intelligence and reason, innate mechanisms combine with environmental experiences, survival intermixes with pleasure. Although much of the work on these foundation concepts of motivation has been done with animals other than humans, and deals with relatively basic biological needs, the assumptions of the approaches appear to be appropriate as a background against which human behavior can be understood.

Social Motivation

Man, like other species, is a *biological organism* existing and attempting to survive in a *social environment,* with other members of his own species and with other species. However, he is in many ways a domesticated species, and his behavior has a great deal of plasticity. While this allows for what man considers advancement over nature, it allows for distortions in natural expressions and disturbances we may not yet have begun to realize. The means possessed by man for physical survival and the conditions he sees as necessary for psychological survival depend to a considerable extent upon other people, and his views of what is necessary or appropriate for working toward either kind of survival are shaped by experiences with other people.

Although the basic goals of competence in dealing with the environment and affiliation with other species members are shared with other animals, they appear on frequently cited lists of social motivation, perhaps reflecting their susceptibility to modification by experiences, and lists of human motivation, perhaps reflecting man's self-centered assumption that he alone has such concerns. Both competence and affiliation motivation can have survival value, but in man they sometimes take debilitating forms and interfere with survival tendencies, perhaps because of the interference of domestication and because of distortions which are induced by cultural experiences. The direct expression of competence or affiliative behaviors can become inhibited or overly intensified by socialization experiences, as we come to strive for satisfaction in inappropriate ways or aim toward inappropriate goals.

People do what they think they have to do in order to get what they think they want. Competence and affiliative goals are prominent, if not the dominant, examples of important goals, and the motivational systems supporting the concerns are central in personality dynamics. (Other conventional motivational systems—dependency, aggression, and sexuality—are discussed in later chapters.) Because of the influence of social experience on these motives, people differ markedly in the extent to which the goals become important to them and in the ways in which they do or do not directly express behavior obviously relevant to these goals. The direct expression of any motive may be inhibited and one motive may be served through an expression considered typical of another motive system. Because of vast differences in experiences which shape the development and expression of competence and affiliation motives, variability of relevant behavior is striking, particularly differences between males and females. With these motives, as with others, the context in which the behavior does or does not occur and the perceived outcome of a given course of action must be taken into account to understand the behavior. Our perceptions of a situation and of the likely outcome of a given course of action are shaped by prior experiences in such situations and by our own self-view of what is appropriate; such perceptions vary greatly with sex-role related experiences.

Thus, in discussing achievement, we will be considering particularly the situational variables which affect motive arousal and concomitant responses, and the influence of sex roles. In addition, we will look at the question of the appropriateness of thinking of motives as properties internal to the organism, the relative effects of intrinsic and extrinsic reinforcers, and the interaction of motive systems.

ACHIEVEMENT

The aspect of competence motivation most frequently researched and discussed centers around achievement; other manifestations of competence motivation include curiosity, exploration, and manipulation of objects (White, 1959). Achievement motivation is a motivation to compete with a standard of excellence, or the desire to accomplish something difficult, to master objects, people, or ideas, and to do so as rapidly and as independently as possible (Murray, 1938; McClelland et al., 1953).

Doing well is a goal. Obviously, there are many ways of doing well, but the broad areas within which achievement and mastery are particularly likely to be noted and studied are those which reflect dominantly white middle-class male values: academic achievement, education, intellectual competence, occupational status and prestige, and, to some extent, the financial rewards for occupational success. Although this is a relatively narrow view of achievement motivation, and achievement motivation is only one aspect of competence motivation, this view of achievement is relevant to large segments of society and has been thoroughly researched, at least with white males.

Measurement and Correlates

Need for achievement has often been measured by content scoring of stories subjects tell in response to TAT-like pictures. Subjects typically are informed that they are in a study of creative imagination, and are sometimes asked specific questions about the pictures: (1) What is happening? (2) What has led up to this situation? (3) What is being thought? (4) What will happen? McClelland and Atkinson (1948) first demonstrated that the procedure is effective in measuring human motives by analyzing stories told under conditions of food deprivation (one, four, or sixteen hours). As the number of hours of food deprivation increased, and thereby the intensity of the hunger motive, the frequency of themes related to food deprivation increased for pictures relevant to food deprivation. McClelland and his associates then proceeded to demonstrate the validity of using the technique in the measurement of achievement motivation (McClelland et al., 1953; McClelland, 1961; Atkinson et al., 1958).

The stories are scored for the imagery of goal-directed fantasy or thema expressive of competition with a standard of excellence. With relatively objective scoring systems and training of judges, there can be relatively high inter-judge and intra-judge reliability. Motive arousal may be accomplished by instructions about the meaning of an experimental task, or by feedback about performance—all of which serve to make achievement an appropriate concern in the measurement situation. For example, arousing instructions may consist of having the experimenter describe experimental tasks as measures of general intelligence and leadership ability used to select important government leaders. A group given these instructions about the tasks being performed was compared with a group given instructions designed to minimize the relevance of achievement motivation—these people were told that the experimenter was just interested in getting some information about the test—and with a group given neutral instructions to do their best. Achievement motivation scores obtained by the TAT procedure immediately after the tasks were related to the amount of achievement motivation presumably aroused by the instructions.

After demonstrating the usefulness of the TAT-like procedure in measuring achievement motivation, McClelland and his associates then assessed individual differences in achievement motivation and investigated correlates of achievement motivation (see McClelland et al., 1953; McClelland, 1961; Atkinson et al., 1958; Heckhausen, 1967; Birney, 1968). The problem in relating achievement motivation to achieving behavior is complicated by the fact that there are many ways of achieving, and the need for achievement is only one of many factors that affect accomplishment (McClelland et al., 1953; Heckhausen, 1967). Nevertheless, there are some predictable broad patterns. Achievement scores are related to peer ratings of achievement and community service shown by the subject, and to occupational status, education, social class, and intelligence.

More interesting are relationships between achievement motivation and *change* of intelligence test scores. In a sample of middle-class children of the upper range of intelligence (average IQ above 120), the measured intelligence of those high in need for achievement *increased* between ages six and fifteen. In contrast, for those low in achievement motivation, IQ scores stayed the same or decreased (Kagan & Moss, 1959). Students who are high in achievement motivation generally do better in grade school and college, although in selected college samples the picture is often confusing (Heckhausen, 1967). High-achievement-oriented students are likely to have better grades even when intelligence differences are controlled by statistical techniques, or when the samples studied are very much alike in intelligence. However, college students in an honors program had *lower* average achievement motivation scores than did average performers of equal aptitude; those low in achievement motivation when they entered college had higher grades at the end of their first semester than those with higher scores (Cole, Jacobs, & Zubok, 1962). McClelland (1953, 1961) suggested that high grades often reflect skill in following directions and producing the solutions found by others, while the high-need-for-achievement person wants to solve problems set by himself rather than those set for him by others.

There does seem to be a physiological correlate of achievement motivation and related behavior, namely uric acid, the end product of purine metabolism in man (Mueller, Kasl, Brooks, & Cobb, 1970). People with high levels of drive, leadership, and upward social mobility tend to have higher uric acid levels. However, the mechanisms relating the physiological index and behavior are not clear, and there is yet no reason to conclude that the uric acid level has a causal influence on motivation and behavior.

Components of Achievement Motivation

Hope of success. The total motivation to achieve has been conceived as composed of both a motive to succeed (Ms) and a motive to avoid failure (Maf), or a hope of success (HS) and a fear of failure (HF)

(Murray, 1938; McClelland et al., 1953; Atkinson, 1957, 1964; Heck-hausen, 1967). Within this context, a motive is a disposition to strive for certain kinds of satisfactions and a capacity for finding satisfaction in attaining a certain class of incentives (Atkinson, 1966). Someone with a high hope of success strives for the satisfying feeling of pride; someone with a high fear of failure strives for the satisfaction of avoiding shame at failure. The tendency to act upon the basis of either is influenced not only by the strength of the other and the situational factors affecting their arousal, but also by the perceived outcomes of attempting a specific task in a specific situation. For example, no matter how strong the motivation to succeed, there is little reason to try if *expectancy* of a desired consequence (e.g., success) or the *incentive* to attain it are too low.

The ideal high-need-for-achievement person, and the kind most frequently studied in the laboratory, is one who has a strong hope of success and a weak fear of failure. Such a person prefers tasks of intermediate difficulty (perceived probability of success about .3 to .5). Medium risks are most relevant to the need to demonstrate excellence because of one's own ability. If success is assured because of the ease of the task, the incentive is low. A person does not succeed because of his own efforts, but because the task is simple; thus there is little to be gained with success. On the other hand, if the task is very difficult, the expectancy of success is very low; the person will probably fail regardless of his abilities, so the task is irrelevant to the need to demonstrate competence.

Thus, behavior is not a function of the motive alone, but of the perceived outcome of the relevant behavior. For the motive to achieve to be aroused in performance of a task, the individual must also consider himself responsible for the outcome and have explicit knowledge of the results so that success or failure may be clearly and adequately assessed and be interpreted as due to his own efforts (McClelland, 1961). People who differ in level of achievement motivation also differ in the characteristic manner of accounting for the causes of the outcomes; the high-level achiever more often attributes success or failure to the personal effort expended than do the intermediate or low achievers (Kukla, 1972).

The theoretical model predicting preference for medium risks has received substantial support in laboratory situations, particularly with male subjects (see Birney, 1968). Further, McClelland has pointed out that businessmen who are high in achievement motivation tend to take medium risks in business ventures more often than they take extremely high or low risks; high-achievement-motivation males tend to like occupations involving risk, including business, more than do those who are low in achievement motivation. High-achievement-motivation scorers choose to work on and work longer at tasks described to them as being of medium difficulty than on very easy or very difficult tasks. They have moderate and realistic levels of aspiration.

The preference for moderate risks is present as early as kindergarten years. In one study, children could choose the distance they stood from a peg in a ring toss game; the probability of success varied inversely with the distance from the peg (McClelland, 1958a). The children above the median in achievement motivation tended to concentrate their throws in the middle distance ranges, from twenty to forty inches, where there was a moderate probability of success. Of the eleven throws made standing as close to the peg as one could get (four inches), ten were made by low-achievement-motivation children. Of the eleven throws made from five to seven feet, ten were made by the low-achievement-motivation children. Thus, high-achievement-motivation children took moderate risks while those lower in motivation were either very safe or very speculative. The same pattern of results tends to occur with college populations.

Fear of failure. Why might someone prefer extremely safe or extremely speculative risks? We can begin to understand these preferences when we take account of the motive to avoid failure—the fear of failure (measured by anxiety tests or projective techniques). One may be very desirous of success (high on the motive to approach success) but also very afraid of failure (high on the motive to avoid failure), which may inhibit achievement efforts that would otherwise occur. When motives to approach success and avoid failure are equal, there is maximum conflict, and, typically, achievement tasks are not voluntarily approached. When hope of success is higher than fear of failure, then preference for intermediate risks occurs, as previously discussed. When fear of failure is greater than hope of success, then the very easy or very difficult tasks are preferred. A person can avoid failure by taking the easy task, but there is no cause for shame in failing at a very difficult task. Tasks of intermediate difficulty are avoided because failure is a definite possibility and would be indicative of an individual's own deficient abilities (Karabenick & Youseef, 1968).

In daily functioning, we have predispositions to evaluate our own probability of success or failure; seldom do we have a psychologist around telling us the supposed measured difficulty of a task. We often estimate our probability of success and do so with systematic biases (Ryckman, Gold, & Rodda, 1971; Ryckman & Rodda, 1971; Karabenick, 1972). Females tend to underestimate their abilities, whereas males overestimate their adequacy, even when the actual abilities are equal. Men generally feel a greater sense of personal capacity and adequacy than do women. Women's lower perceived adequacy is observable in lower confidence, lower levels of aspiration, and greater expectancy of failure (Bennett & Cohen, 1959; Crandall, Katkovsky, & Preston, 1962). Compared with males, females are also more likely to assume greater personal responsibility for their failures relative to their successes.

Social Roles and Achievement

Behavior does not occur in a vacuum; task success does not necessarily bring social success. Some people are expected to fail, and their acceptance is contingent upon failure—just as some people are expected to succeed and their acceptance is contingent upon their successes (Klinger & McNelly, 1969).

Many differences in achievement behavior may be attributable to social roles, for social status governs the responses appropriate in particular circumstances (Klinger, 1966; Klinger & McNelly, 1969). People prefer and strive hardest in task situations consonant with self-perceptions and avoid situations and behavior that are inappropriate to their role. While the sex-role system is obviously a dominant role system governing much behavior, as discussed in the next sections, this is certainly not the only one. As we stated above, people do what they think they have to in order to get what they think they want. If they believe that failure will bring the social acceptance they want, they fail with pleasure —and perhaps with some effort. Subjects assigned a high status in a research group tried to succeed, but low-status subjects attempted to lower their performance level (Burnstein & Zajonc, 1965).

It has been suggested that women are strongly motivated by a fear of success (Horner, 1968, 1972). Achievement situations are competitive ones which may be viewed as sublimated forms of aggressive behavior. Aggression (or simply competition and assertiveness) is seen as a masculine trait; consequently, a female who is successful in competitive situations, especially with males, is viewed as behaving masculinely rather than in a role-appropriate way. This increases her anxiety about her perceived femininity and sexual identity. A woman may inhibit strivings for academic excellence and achievement efforts in competitive situations and avoid vocational success in typically male professions. In short, she simply expects that success will bring social censure, or she is uncomfortable with role-inappropriate behaviors. Achievement-directed behavior is thwarted by anxiety over the negative consequences expected to follow the otherwise desired success. Achievement-oriented women with high fear of success pay a price of impaired performance and feelings of frustration, hostility, aggression, bitterness, and confusion (Horner, 1968, 1972). For males in our culture, on the other hand, social roles prescribe achievement as relevant, and concomitant socialization encourages the development of hope of success to a high degree and the development of the other component hopes and fears of failure to a lesser extent.

Role relevance and rewards. For a motive to be engaged and to affect behavior, the situation must be one which is relevant to the person's own view of what constitutes success. Social roles are an important, though not the only, source of self-definitions of appropriateness. Typically, females have been taught to channel their striving for excellence into role-appropriate realms, and their achievement motivation is engaged by situations different from those relevant to males.

In conditions encouraging concerns about a woman's traditional role rather than about intelligence or leadership, women college students responded with greater achievement thema to pictures containing female figures than to pictures with male figures (French & Lesser, 1964). Similarly, conditions which make social acceptability a salient issue engage women's achievement motivation while they do not affect that of males; female students who thought that they were very popular or unpopular (analogous to task success or failure which engages male achievement motivation) showed increased achievement scores, while males were not affected by the perceived acceptance or rejection by other students (Field, 1951).

However, in the case of many women, conventional achievement in terms of intelligence, general competence, education, and occupational success is relevant indeed. Achieving female college students (in the top quarter on academic averages), for whom conventional arousing instructions are relevant, showed increased achievement imagery to pictures of females but not to pictures of males under the arousal conditions (Lesser, Krawitz, & Packard, 1963). In contrast, the underachievers (equal intelligence to the first group but in the bottom quarter on academic averages) responded to the arousing instructions with achievement imagery to male pictures but not to female pictures.

Motive and behavior. Achievement motivation is not necessarily correlated with differences in actual achievement behavior. As we discussed above, expectancy and incentive must be at optimum levels. Girls and women may have fairly high levels of achievement motivation which are not allowed direct expression in achievement-related behavior. The *perceived* appropriateness of achievement affects the relationship between motivation and behavior. Girls and women with high achievement motivation associated a traditional orientation toward women's roles with reduced actual achievement (grades) and reduced plans for further education compared to the attainment and goals of those with more liberalized or contemporary views of what is appropriate for women (Houts & Entwisle, 1968; Lipman-Blumen, 1972). However, these same women who are interested in realizing their own potential or who are planning to enter previously masculine career fields do not differ from those with a traditional sex-role orientation in general happiness, nor in romantic and platonic relations with men (Gump, 1972; Tangri, 1972). The more liberal women tend to have higher ego-strength and be more autonomous, individualistic, and motivated by internally imposed demands, all valuable characteristics necessary to withstand the social role pressure and to "buck the system."

The fear of failure experienced by some women has a more direct effect on their behavior than is true for men. A young boy must strive in spite of his fear, while girls afraid of achievement situations are allowed to avoid achievement situations. Thus, fear of failure and withdrawal from achievement situations are relatively stable from six to fourteen years of age for girls, but not for boys (Kagan & Moss, 1962). Similarly, anxiety is associated with lower academic achievement more strongly in girls than in boys; middle-class girls are most highly concerned about school achievement and suffer the greatest detrimental effects from anxiety (Phillips, 1962). It is as if the girls are allowed the temporary psychodynamic luxury of letting their anxieties about achievement get away from them, while males cannot afford to allow this to occur. Or, the role patterns of American females permit failure stress to override other effects in the impairment of their performance (Klinger & McNelly, 1969).

If the inhibitions on active achievement striving seemed highly limited to an educational setting, the obvious answer would be to keep women out of educational activities for their own good. However, the fear of failure can easily be a pervasive fear applicable to a variety of behaviors and will show in apprehensions about *any* position of responsibility and mean loss of confidence in decisions about the family and major purchases, and anxiety in social situations in which a person fears negative judgments (Kagan & Moss, 1952). A woman's fear of failure can generalize to interfere with her effectiveness in performing the traditional feminine role of household manager, caretaker of the children, and partner of her husband—all roles which require competence, a trait that has traditionally been seen as appropriate to the male but not to the female. Thus, even *the fulfillment of traditional roles can be inhibited by traditional role-appropriate prescriptions.*

Development and Change

The social setting. The development of achievement motivation and behavior has been shown to be shaped by social influences attributable to three sources: (1) cultural environment; (2) racial, religious, and ethnic background; and (3) the socioeconomic class of the family. Cultures vary in the general level of stress on achievement, and groups within cultures vary in the intensity of their demands for achievement and in the specific forms of achievement behavior which they are likely to encourage and reward (McClelland & Friedman, 1952; McClelland, 1951, 1961). Religious orientations which stress individualism and high standards in education encourage achievement motivation (Heckhausen, 1967; McClelland, 1961). However, social class seems to have a more potent and consistent effect than does religion. The middle-class family with orientations toward upward social mobility provides the optimum situation for development of future-oriented achievement motivation (Heckhausen, 1967). Achievement behavior in children is positively correlated with parents' education (a frequently used indication of social class), particularly when the children become adults (Kagan & Moss, 1962). Upper-class families are more likely to be concerned with the continuation of their status symbols than with acquiring new goals. Lower-class families are likely to see achievement, by conventional standards, as impossible or as irrelevant to them.

Social class variation in achievement motivation and behavior is likely due to the values and goals instilled in the child and to the expectations others hold for him as well as to the patterns of reinforcement for specific behaviors. Adults, parents, and teachers typically expect upper- and middle-class children to do well in school, go to college, and enter high-status occupations (Kahl, 1957). In view of the effects of the perceived expectations of others on performance (see Chapter 7), it is no wonder that the lower-class children do not see academic performance and college as relevant to them. Thus, subcultural differences in achievement, particularly academic achievement, seem to be perpetuated; the attainments of one generation affect the values, aspirations, and eventual attainments of the next. (This theme is explored in other ways in Chapter 16.)

Early parental influences. Parents are instrumental in mediating social group influences; parents may facilitate the development of achievement motivation by the home environment they provide the child. Middle-class homes are particularly likely to offer books, adult discussions, supervised television, and other opportunities to engage in intellectual pursuits, as well as "educational" toys and games. Parents also serve as models for the child (Chapter 18). In their own behavior they set standards observable by the child, and they behave with respect to those standards in ways discernible to the child. In other words, parents hold expectations and evaluative attitudes for their children that are the same as those they apply to themselves and to their own achievement (Katkovsky, Preston, & Crandall, 1964a, 1964b). Parents interfere with the child's activities in order to transfer their own attitudes to him.

Parents also provide their children, typically their sons, with direct encouragement and reinforcement for independence and achievement striving and performance. Mothers of elementary school boys with high achievement motivation stressed independence training more than did mothers of low-achievement boys, and they gave frequent and intense rewards of physical affection for the boys' meeting demands placed on them and for their spontaneous efforts at being independent (Winterbottom, 1958). Both mothers and fathers of high-need-for-achievement boys have higher aspirations and expectations for their son's performance; in turn, the boys did perform better and asked for help less frequently than did low-achievement boys (Rosen & D'Andrade, 1959).

All in all, the direct teaching role seems to be performed by the mother; she rewards desirable behaviors and punishes undesirable ones (Heckhausen, 1967). The father is a warm and suitable model whom the son imitates while he develops his own independence. If the father interferes with his son's activities or exerts too much pressure for achievement (as is likely in the upper classes), it is difficult for the son to imitate the father's values, and the son becomes dependent and low in achievement motivation (Strodbeck, 1958; Bradburn, 1963).

Similarly, the mother has been shown important in the development of fear-of-failure motivation in boys (Teevan & McGhee, 1972). If she has expectations of independence and achievement behaviors or if she has encouraged these but did not reward satisfactory behavior or did punish unsatisfactory behavior in independence and achievement situations, the boy is likely to develop a negative attitude toward achievement concerns and a high-fear-of-failure motivation rather than a positive attitude and high-hope-of-success motivation.

Girls, too, may develop high achievement motivation because of the parental encouragement for independence and achievement. However, thus far in our society, this has not been frequent. Girls relative to boys are likely *not* to develop achievement motivation; they receive less encouragement for independence, more parental protectiveness, and less pressure for establishing an identity separate from mother, and thus they do not develop adequate skills or confidence, but rather maintain dependence on others (Hoffman, 1972). Much of the achievement behavior that does develop in girls is motivated by a desire to please; if the achievement behavior comes into conflict with affiliation, as previously discussed, achievement is likely to be sacrificed, or anxiety is likely to result.

Change in achievement motivation and behavior. In view of the relevance of achievement motivation to behaviors valued in our society, some attempts have been made to increase the achievement motivation of those people with initially low orientation toward accomplishment. Counseling and training programs with students and adults have indicated some effectiveness. An eight-week period of counseling which focused on behaviors similar to the categories in McClelland's fantasy scoring for need for achievement did produce an increase in over-all grade averages, although this effect was not produced in the self-improvement course from which the subjects were drawn (Burris, 1958). A training program for under-achieving high school boys (IQ above 120 but grades below C) resulted in improved school grades (Kolb, 1965). The training program was designed to teach the students the characteristics of a highly motivated person. Improvement was shown one-and-a-half years later in students from higher social class; there was no improvement in the grades of lower-class students or in control boys who did not receive the training. The differential effect for social class may be reflecting the reinforcement the higher-social-class boys received at home and from peers relative to that received by the lower-class boys. Results with other behaviors have shown that special training programs are ineffective if the new behavior is not supported and reinforced by the social community the subject enters after leaving the training situation.

McClelland (1964c, 1965a) has attempted to raise the achievement motivation of businessmen in India and Mexico. His program includes training in achievement fantasy, goal-setting and risk-taking in achievement-related tasks, and role-playing people with high achievement standards. Preliminary data indicate change in the proportion of subjects who show unusual entrepreneurial activities such as an unusual promotion or raise, or the establishment of a new business (McClelland, 1965). Within four years, the percentage of businessmen in the training group showing unusual entrepreneurial activities rose from 27 percent to 67 percent (n = 30). The comparable figures for a control group were 18 percent and 27 percent (n = 11).

The extensive focus on achievement motivation and the accompanying sex differences should not be taken to mean that very high achievement motivation and the conventional male pattern with respect to it are necessarily ideal and to be sought by one and all. Preoccupation with achievement goals can blot out consideration of the effect on others of one's work and its meaning in the larger social scheme. The diffusion of achievement needs in women may allow greater flexibility in responding to the possibilities of life offered at different stages of the life cycle. "A *richer life* may be available to women *because* they do not *single-mindedly* pursue academic or professional goals" (Hoffman, 1972, p. 150; italics added).

AFFILIATION

Why do we affiliate with one another? What satisfactions do we find in being with others? In what situations are we most likely to seek these satisfactions? Certainly, there is survival value in the infant's attachment to the mother that quickly becomes established, and this dependency forms the basic social background from which adult affiliation can develop (Chapter 19). There may well be other survival mechanisms served by adult affiliative behavior in ways we do not yet realize, mechanisms not only for survival of the species, but for the individual as well.

Among the important values of affiliation are the fact that other people provide information and the fact that people serve as stress reducers. Other facets of affiliative behavior, including some of its developmental correlates and the problems (as well as the advantages) imposed by association with others, are recurrent themes in later chapters (Chapters 16–22). It is important to remember that, as with achievement motivation, people differ in the degree to which an affiliative motive is developed and the ways in which it is expressed.

Information and Stress Reduction

Researchers employing social comparison theory (Festinger, 1954a) hypothesize that people have a need to evaluate themselves, their opinions, abilities, and emotions, and this need for self-evaluation often can be met only by comparison with other people, who must be somewhat similar to oneself on the matter in question. For many areas of judgment, there is no real criterion other than the consensus of other people. For example, we tend to be attracted to people with similar attitudes; the similarity can reassure us of the validity of our own attitude (Clore & Byrne, 1971).

Stanley Schachter (1959) predicted that we will approach other people if we find them to be relevant others from whom we can obtain information with which to evaluate ourselves. Schachter also predicted that anxiety increases affiliation tendencies. There is some evidence that when people are isolated (e.g., sea voyagers, prisoners, castaways, hermits), survival is most likely for those who recognize their sense of loneliness and attempt to maintain contact with their former world by thinking of people or even hallucinating about them, conversing with nonhuman or imaginary companions, keeping diaries, or engaging in other mental exercises (Haggard, 1964). Thus, Schachter predicted that affiliative behavior would be particularly likely under anxiety-inducing conditions when a person has the opportunity to associate with another who is thought to be in a similar emotional state.

Schachter found that subjects (female college students) chose to wait with others more often when they were expecting to be shocked in a coming experimental session (anxiety arousal) than when they did not expect such anxiety-provoking conditions. "Misery loves company." However, misery does not love just any kind of company; it loves only that company in similar misery. In the Schachter study, other subjects waiting for a different experiment—expecting a different state—were not approached. Such results are much more marked for firstborn children than for later-born ones. Of firstborn female subjects, 80 percent chose to wait with others prior to being shocked, while only 31 percent of later-borns did so.

Other kinds of studies show the importance of affiliation in order to gain information. Having information about one's own abilities or opinions reduced desire to affiliate with others (Singer & Shockley, 1965; Radloff, 1961; Gerard & Rabbie, 1961), as did seeing an understandable educational film relative to a confusing one (Byrne & Clore, 1967).

Association with other members of the species, particularly familiar ones, does reduce fear, even though the danger itself is not necessarily reduced by the presence of others. This has been shown with rats and monkeys, and with children and soldiers during wartime (Latané, 1968; Latané & Glass, 1968; Mason, 1960; Burlingham & Freud, 1943; Marshall, 1951; Bovard, 1959). Subjects who worked on frustrating (actually insoluble) tasks in the presence of a friend who was working on another task, were significantly less aroused than were subjects who performed with a stranger or performed alone (Kissel, 1965). The presence of a stranger in fact increased the stress for those subjects who were high in test anxiety and need for affiliation. A friend may elicit positive feelings which compete with and minimize stress reactions, as seems to be the case with a child's response to his mother when confronted with anxiety-inducing novelty (Chapter 19).

Affiliation Avoidance

An aroused motive is not always directly expressed in observable behavior. As with achievement motivation, affiliation motivation may not be reflected in behavior if the subject does not expect that his behavior will be instrumental in satisfying the need. There is little reason for us to act affiliatively if we expect rejection. Affiliative behavior is a function of both affiliation motivation and the expectancy of successful affiliation in the specific situation.

For subjects who were high in their expectancy of having a positive interaction in a small group, need for affiliation (measured by a TAT procedure) was correlated with frequency of positive social responses in the group session (Fishman, 1966). The subjects were college women who lived in a small dormitory and were acquainted prior to the study; expectancy of successful affiliation in the group was inferred from sociometric ratings by each subject of the friendliness and likeability of the dormitory acquaintances who were to be in the research group discussion with her. For those who had low expectations for the group, there was no relationship between the motive strength and the response frequency. A person may have high affiliative needs but will not behave positively toward others if he does not expect that they will behave positively toward him. Thus, perhaps one should be cautious in criticism of people who do not behave positively toward him; he may not be giving them signals that their positive responses would be returned. Similarly, anxieties, guilt, or fear of inappropriate behavior may inhibit affiliation with others (Brehm & Behar, 1966; Sarnoff & Zimbardo, 1961).

Birth Order, Achievement, and Affiliation

Birth order influences both achievement and affiliation behaviors and needs (Ferguson, 1970; Nash, 1970; Sampson, 1965; Warren, 1966; Lenneborg, 1968). This is due in large part to the variation in the patterns of parent-child interactions associated with number of children and also to the fact of the presence or absence of siblings. (However, physiological explanations are not completely ruled out; there is a possibility of differences in the intrauterine environment and in the birth process itself, which can vary with number of prior pregnancies.)

In many ways, parents "practice" on their firstborns; they are inexperienced with the job of parenthood and unsure about how to deal with an infant or child. They may be more extreme and inconsistent in their dealings with the child. All of this may increase the likelihood that the firstborn, or only child, will be more anxious than he would have been otherwise. One result of the anxiety is an increased approach to the parents for reassurance and anxiety reduction. Thus, the child becomes more in need of affiliation and more used to approaching other people than if he were a later-born. This is especially true of female children. Firstborns respond in a more affiliative manner than later-borns when made anxious or uncertain about their emotional reactions or opinions (Sampson, 1965). Also, parents have more time to respond to the child's approach than they would if there were other children needing attention.

The undivided parental attention often provided the first, or only, child is also likely to allow parental encouragement in the child's development of adult-like behaviors and values and in his mastery of developmental skills. Thus, the child may also become an achiever and may attempt to gain or increase parental approval by this achievement. If other children appear on the scene, the firstborn may intensify achievement efforts to win the parental approval he feels he has lost. Firstborns are also more intelligent than those born later, attend college more frequently than predicted on a chance basis, and do better in college than those in other ordinal positions.

The effects of birth order and sex on affiliative behavior were shown in a naturalistic study during the 1965 power failure (Zucker, Manosevitz, & Lanyon, 1968). In this blackout in the northeastern states, people were deprived of information and separated from their families and friends. Additionally, many people in New York City were physically uncomfortable and uncertain about the events of the immediate future. The researchers collected data from people gathered in the major bus terminal in Manhattan and in a midtown hotel, both of which had some emergency lighting. About 70 percent of the people from whom information was requested cooperated and completed a questionnaire about birth order, anxiety about the blackout, and their preferences about being with others. The researchers also noted whether the subject was actually affiliating with someone or was alone before he was approached to participate in the research. Both male and female firstborns tended to be more anxious, as predicted. However, while female firstborns responded to their anxiety by actually affiliating with others, the males showed the opposite reaction—firstborn men preferred to be alone. Subjects who were behaving as predicted reported less anxiety than those behaving counter to the predictions. Higher anxiety and being alone may be a life-long pattern for firstborn males. They are not encouraged to admit anxiety in stressful situations or to approach others for comfort.

MOTIVES OR RESPONSES?

Perhaps the most basic and often debated issue permeating the topics of achievement and affiliation motivation, or any of the other kinds of motivations discussed in later chapters, is simply the question of whether the concept of motivation is a necessary and useful one for understanding behavior. That is, is it more meaningful to think of a motive energizing and directing behavior or to think simply of observable stimuli controlling the behavior of an active organism? If a motive is a useful concept for *understanding* behavior, does a motive necessarily *cause* the behavior?

Some psychologists claim that motivation is an unnecessary and misleading concept, as is the concept of a trait. Apparent inconsistencies between traits or motives attributed to a person and his behavior supposedly illustrate the limited utility of such concepts. For example, if a shy person is sometimes outgoing, or if someone high in achievement motivation does not necessarily strive persistently to master any task given him, then, it is suggested, we are forced to throw out the whole concept of describing a person or his behavior in terms of traits or motivation. Behavior would have to be explained as a function of the current situation and its similarity to situations in which a given response has been reinforced previously. Some people have been reinforced for achievement efforts more than others—and have been reinforced in some situations and not in other circumstances. Women are not low in achievement motivation; they just have not been reinforced for effective achievement behavior in many situations. Nor is men's affiliative motivation inhibited; they have just not been reinforced for admitting anxiety and acting affiliatively.

Similarly, the thoughts, verbal expressions, and fantasy measures often used as indices of a motive may be seen simply as responses in and of themselves rather than as being indicative of an internal state of inferred affairs which precede or cause the behavior (Klinger, 1966). There is some reason to contend that tendencies to respond in fantasy and in actual striving are two classes of responses traceable to environmental conditions and not requiring a construct of achievement motivation for explanation. Other psychologists who accept the usefulness of a concept of motivation also point out that thoughts are themselves responses which, while they may precede action, may also occur concomitantly with the action or even after it (de Charms, 1968; Chapter 17).

However, people do differ in the frequency and intensity of achievement and affiliative responses in ways that can be summarized or integrated by the concept of a motive as an intervening variable. To use the concept of motivation is not necessarily to invoke a mysterious causative factor which is unexplained or unlinked to observable events. People differ in the extent to which given kinds of events, whether task success or association with other people, become important goals to them, and in their perceptions of what they can or cannot do to attain the goals. People high in achievement motivation do not work on just any task and may not strive at all in conventional ways if they expect task failure or social failure for their efforts. Certainly, behavior varies with the situation because of the variations in a person's perceptions of what the outcome of any given response in that situation will be. The situation is interpreted by the individual in terms of what goal states are attainable, their desirability to him relative to other events, and the likelihood of his attaining them by a given course of action. Perhaps one of the most important, though neglected, of the specific components implied by the concept of motive in this sense is the disposition to see *possibilities* for gratifying a motive or attaining a goal, particularly in ambiguous situations, that is, the predisposition to make a situation relevant to a motive whenever possible (Veroff, 1965; de Charms, 1968). Thus, in an interpersonal setting where ideas are discussed, an individual can approach the situation with a set to achieve (to perform well in an intellectual discussion), to affiliate (to establish effective ties with the people there or to win their approval), or perhaps to influence others (to argue and change the views of those present).

Intrinsic and Extrinsic Reinforcement

An important issue for one who speaks of motives involves the nature of reinforcement associated with behavior. If the reinforcement is intrinsic, one engages in the behavior for the sake of the behavior and natural goal in themselves: "I just like to. . . ." If the reinforcement is extrinsic, one engages in the behavior because of the external reinforcement that can be gained: "I do it in order to get. . . ."

Achievement for approval or for achievement? Is reinforcement for achievement behavior intrinsic in the striving for and demonstration of excellence itself, or is the behavior developed and maintained by events extrinsic to the acts themselves? (Although achievement motive is often defined conceptually as intrinsically motivated, it is often inferred operationally from striving for extrinsic goals.) Do we strive for excellence for excellence's sake, or do we hope to gain something else because of excellence? The external events may be concrete ones—good grades or raise in salary—or they may be the social reinforcement of pleasing an important other person or being accepted and loved. In any case, when operating because of extrinsic motivation, we strive in order to get something besides self-judged success in the task at hand.

At one extreme is the view that all achievement behavior is or has been directed toward the goal of attaining approval and avoiding disapproval (Crandall, 1963). Thus, achievement behavior is in the service of affiliation needs. Achievement-related behavior differs from other means of seeking approval only in that it involves specifically the demonstration of competence against a standard of excellence. The approval of others may be given directly and immediately—"I'm proud of you"—or may be anticipated in the future or internalized from the past. In this extreme view, it is emphasized that even when the current evaluation is internal—"I'm proud of myself"—it is derived from rewards that originally were extrinsic. In short, we are concerned about achievement because other people have offered rewards for achievement.

At the other extreme is the view that the relevant reinforcement is intrinsically located and defined with respect to success and failure itself rather than dependent upon the approval or disapproval of others, experienced in the past or anticipated in the future. Robert White (1959, 1960), an Adlerian, views competence as an intrinsic motive and not a secondary one in the service of other needs such as affiliation or aggression. Organisms, particularly humans, have a need to deal more and more effectively with their environments; mastery, akin to achievement, is one specific aspect of the general effectance or competence motivation. Achieving against a realistic standard of excellence is a challenge, a test of our competence in dealing with the environment. No other reward than the perception of competence or feeling of efficacy is necessary to maintain achievement striving. Achievement is valued for itself.

It is likely that some people are more extrinsically motivated and look for external reward more often than others, and that some are more persistent in working for the intrinsic reward of self-judged mastery of a task. Probably both intrinsic and extrinsic rewards play their roles in the development and maintenance of achievement motivation and behavior. McClelland's (1943, 1958a, 1958b) view seems to be that children naturally have self-initiated demands and expectations for mastery in the environment (intrinsic component), but that a strong need to achieve requires external demands and rewards from other people (extrinsic component).

Obviously, other people sometimes withhold approval or even punish the naturally occurring behavior, and their standards may be internalized and accepted by the individual as his own. When extrinsic rewards are withheld, the individual may persist, with some personal strain, because of intrinsic reinforcement, or he may find other ways of expressing the motivation while receiving some external rewards; for example, women who espouse traditional sex-role ideology for themselves express competence through affiliative and domestic concerns; men may channel affiliative concerns into achievement behavior. The person most comfortable with himself and with his social environment is likely to be one who acts because of intrinsic or self-located motivation but who also receives some extrinsic rewards in the process. He is rewarded by others for being and doing what he wants.

Affiliation for affiliation's sake? If we had an extreme extrinsic motivational set to affiliation, we would affiliate only because of the reinforcers that other people control—food, water, better grades, job promotions, money. For some people, this seems an applicable view; they literally use other people in the attainment of other than affiliative ends.

In the extreme intrinsic view of affiliation, the act of affiliation itself is reinforcing, irrespective of who the other is and what he provides. The state of being with another is satisfying: "I just enjoy people." Notice that this set, similar to the extreme extrinsic set, ignores the distinctiveness of the other person.

The genuinely maturing person probably become increasingly discerning and discriminating in his choice of people with whom to affiliate, because of increasing self-knowledge of his own psychological needs (including perhaps a need to give to others) and because of knowledge of the kinds of people who can meet those needs. Affiliative choices are made on the basis of the properties of the particular other person as the other person is or appears to be. The reinforcement is in the act of affiliation itself as well as in the qualities of the other person.

Thus, for both achievement and affiliation, there may be components intrinsic and extrinsic to the specific motive and behavior. We strive or affiliate because we like to, but we are likely to obtain other reinforcers in the process. While we may have internal standards of excellence, we are not likely to ignore completely the reactions of other people who comprise our social reality; while we may value others for themselves, we are not likely to continue associations with others who provide no rewards for us. Mature, healthy behavior is likely to be a function of both kinds of reinforcers.

Summary

While some psychologists claim that the concept of motivation is useless and that only observable stimuli and responses should be considered, others do find motivation useful for explaining the energy or direction of behavior, or both. Arousal theorists view motivation in terms of the intensity of behavior. Those representing the homeostatic position explain behavior as a regulatory process which attempts to reduce the disequilibrium which occurs when a motive is aroused. Ethologists analyze behavior in terms of the specific responses in behavior systems and the sign stimuli which elicit them. They point to the stimulus functions of other species members and the influence of experience on the manifestations of instinctually-based responses, and they encourage a search for the effective sign stimuli involved in human behavior. Hedonistic theories of motivation are based on the assumption that man acts to seek pleasure and to avoid pain. Events which are pleasurable are often those which are homeostatic and contribute to survival, but what is pleasurable is also subject to the effects of experience. Such motivational positions form a broad backdrop against which we can view human behavior.

Account must be taken of an individual's perceptions of himself and his situation, and his view of the possible outcomes and their relative desirability to him. Behavior is a function of both the motive strength and the expectancy of success in the specific situation, as perceived by the individual. The individual's perceptions and related behavioral skills and dispositions are heavily influenced by birth order and sex-role related socialization, which may intensify or dampen the development of the motive strength that would otherwise occur. Fear of failure and fear of success are particularly likely to develop in women and can inhibit achievement-related behavior, while the traditional male socialization encourages the confidence, independence, and perceived appropriateness of achievement that increase hope of success. Anxiety and desire for information and anxiety reduction instigate affiliative responses, but women are likely to feel more freedom to act affiliatively than are men.

Both achievement and affiliative behavior can be intrinsically or extrinsically reinforcing. Some people are probably more extrinsically or intrinsically motivated than others for their achievement or affiliative behaviors. In the mature person, both kinds of reinforcement usually occur jointly.

11

perception

"Whether beautiful or ugly or just conveniently at hand, the world of experience is produced by the man who experiences it" (Neisser, 1967, p. 3). Perception is the process by which we obtain information about the world (Gibson, 1969). On the basis of this information, we react to and interact with our environment. When confronted with the same environment, we differ greatly in what we notice in that environment and how we interpret and react to it. Thus, in understanding a person, we must take into account the fact that the phenomenal world in which he is acting and experiencing may not be the same as that of other people living in the same physical world. The focus of this chapter will be mainly on certain principles of perception as seen in the perception of nonsocial objects. The following two chapters deal with perception of self and others. However, the concepts discussed here will recur in many contexts, for it is our perceptions of self and environment which provide the substrata for all of the thoughts, feelings, and overt behavior that help to define who we are.

PERCEPTUAL PRINCIPLES

Frequently, the same stimulus evokes very different responses in different people, or in the same person at different times. Correlatively, perceptions are less often completely veridical (realistic) than we realize. "Seeing is believing" is true to the extent that we tend to believe that what we see is real, and seen by others as well. However, we often see with systematic and predictable error. As a wise man once said to his bride, "There are three sides to this argument, your side, my side, and the correct side." The wisdom of this statement may be seen in the basic perceptual work done in the laboratory with simple stimuli, but the principles are far reaching.

Limitations in Perception

Cautions from vision. Vision provides some obvious examples of why we should be cautious about concluding that we have a faithful picture of reality. First, our perceptions are reactions to, and elaborations upon, the stimuli as immediately given. The physical stimuli for visual experiences are not the colors red, green, blue; nor are they rectangles and circles. The physical stimulus for vision is *electromagnetic energy.* Electromagnetic energy becomes a red bicycle lying in the middle of an asphalt street a block away because of what happens inside of us; parts of what we perceive "always come . . . out of our own head" (William James, 1890).

Second, we do not respond perceptually to all events in the environment. Under normal conditions, we can experience light only if the lengths of electromagnetic waves are within a relatively narrow band of the spectrum (Figure 11–1). Variations in the electromagnetic spectrum of which we have no visual awareness can nevertheless influence us, and can be used and measured (e.g., X rays, radio communications). Our awareness of the environment is further limited by how we direct attention to events which are physiologically detectable. Many differences in responses are due to differences in selection of what aspects of a situation receive our attention.

Third, even when we mean to attend to certain aspects of a situation, there will always be some stimulus information that does not "get through." Although the eye is a beautifully built, complex mechanism,

**FIGURE
11–1**

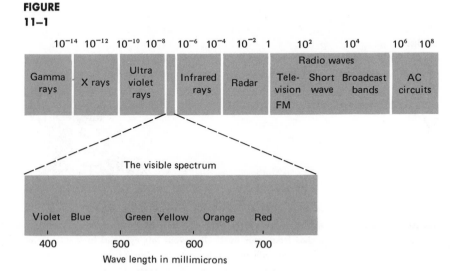

The Electromagnetic Spectrum.
The visible portion is shown enlarged in the lower part of the figure.

Source: After Chapanis, A., Garner, W. R., & Morgan, C. T., 1949.

it has a necessary defect. There is a *blind spot* where the nerve fibers from the retina converge to form the optic nerve leading back to the central nervous system. If the eye were a camera, there would be a blank spot in every picture. Without the optic nerve, the picture would not be developed. While we may sincerely deny its existence, the blind spot is there nonetheless (Figure 11–2). It is not typically noticed because, as with many imperfections, we learn to adjust for it; we "fill in" the gap in accordance with the information we do have. Also, there is no long-lasting blockage of any one part of the environment because the eyes continually shift.

Similarly, defense mechanisms are psychological "blind spots" which may cause one to fill in parts of reality that are blocked, and which, when overused, can lead to relatively permanent blockages of selected aspects of the environment. Much of the lack of complete veridicality of perceptions is fairly general across people, as shown in basic distortions.

Distortions in Perceptions

Typically, perceptions are not entirely accurate representations of objects of the environment. The phenomena specifically classed as illusions are really only very prominent and dramatic examples of the lack of complete veridicality, for most perceptions contain some distortions or illusions. In Figure 11–3, the stimulus configurations inducing illusions are such that the viewer can easily recognize the distortion of his experience. Many distortions in perceptual processes are more subtle.

FIGURE 11–2

X

The Blind Spot.
Hold this page fourteen inches from your eyes, close your left eye and look directly at the cross with your right eye. If you still see the head to the right of the cross, move the page slightly closer or farther away, until the head disappears. You cannot see it because the light from it is striking your blind spot.

Source: Kendler, H. H. *Basic psychology.* New York: Appleton-Century-Crofts, 1968.

FIGURE
11–3

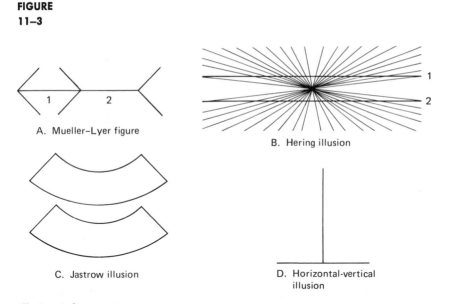

A. Mueller–Lyer figure

B. Hering illusion

C. Jastrow illusion

D. Horizontal-vertical
illusion

Illusion Inducement.
A. Segments (1) and (2) are the same size. B. The two horizontal lines are parallel, the distance between (1) and (2) being the same all the way across the figure. C. The two crescents are the same size. D. The horizontal and vertical lines are exactly the same length.

Source: Hochberg, J. E. Perception. Englewood Cliffs, N.J.: Prentice-Hall, 1964. P. 54.

Perceptual constancies. Perceptions are typically a compromise between the sensory image itself and what is known about the object. Within limits, there is a tendency to see objects as remaining relatively constant irrespective of the changes in the actual image on the retina of the eye. The sensory image of a table viewed from an angle is a trapezoid, but we perceive the table as a rectangle (shape constancy). We do not perceive a person walking toward us as growing up as he gets closer (size constancy). A white cow in the shade is seen as a white cow even though she may reflect no more light than a black cow in the sun (brightness constancy). Constancies are not uniformly perfect, of course, and should be thought of as *relative constancies.* We do see an object moving away from us as becoming slightly smaller, but our perceptions tend to correspond more closely with the object as we have previously known it than with the current sensory image. Thus, a large part of the constancy effect is learned (Gibson, 1969), as shown by differences between children and adults (Figure 11–4). Constancies with social stimuli are frequent. The effect of first impressions on the interpretation of information later received about a person is a constancy effect. When a person makes a poor first impression, the degree to which he must change before he is perceived as having become more acceptable

FIGURE

11–4

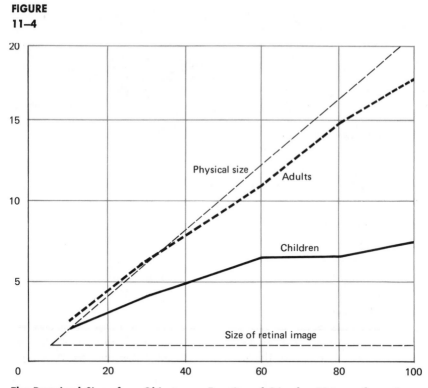

The Perceived Size of an Object as a Function of Stimulus Distance for a Group of Adults and a Group of Eight-Year-Old Children.

The size of the test object was adjusted so that it always projected a retinal image of a constant size. The horizontal broken line indicates the size of the retinal image projected by the test objects at the different distances, while the oblique broken line indicates the physical size of the test objects at the different distances. The adults' judgments were close to the physical size of the test objects at all distances. In contrast, the children's judgments approximated physical size only at the shortest distance. With increasing distances, their estimates became more removed from the physical size and closer to the retinal size.

Source: After Zeigler & Leibowitz, 1957.

than he was is as much a problem for the constant perceiver as for the unhappy acquaintance struggling to smooth his rough edges.

Multiple stimuli. The perception of a stimulus depends in part on the context in which it is encountered, including the other stimuli with which it occurs and preceding perceptions. Gray is gray. But if the gray is on a blue background, it is experienced as having a yellowish tinge (yellow is the complement of blue). This is *simultaneous contrast:* The perception of one color depends upon other colors in the stimulus field. If we look first at red and then at yellow, the yellow appears greenish. This is *successive contrast:* The perception of one color depends upon preceding perceptions. The similar phenomenon of *aftereffects* occurs with the perception of shapes, motion, and haptic space (the space we know of through the sense of touch). A line that initially seemed to be curved appears less so and the straight appears crooked (Figure 11–5).

When the same stimulus is continuously received, there is a change in the perceptual experience of that stimulus. This is *adaptation*. A stimulus at the adaptation level (AL) is one which evokes no response or a neutral one. We adapt to the slightly cold or hot water of the bath so that it is experienced as about right rather than as too cold or too hot. An AL becomes a reference point for the perception of other stimuli. When we come in from the cold, a sixty-eight-degree room is warm; when we come in on a hot summer day, the room is cool at the same temperature. A related concept is that of the *difference threshold*, the amount of change (in brightness, color, movement, weight, etc.) in a single stimulus, or the difference between two stimuli that is necessary for the detection of the difference. The change necessary for the perception of difference is called a *just noticeable difference* (JND). It varies as a function of the level of the first stimulus with which the second stimulus is compared. Generally, the greater the value of the initial stimulus (i.e., the more intense), the greater the difference necessary for detection

FIGURE 11–5

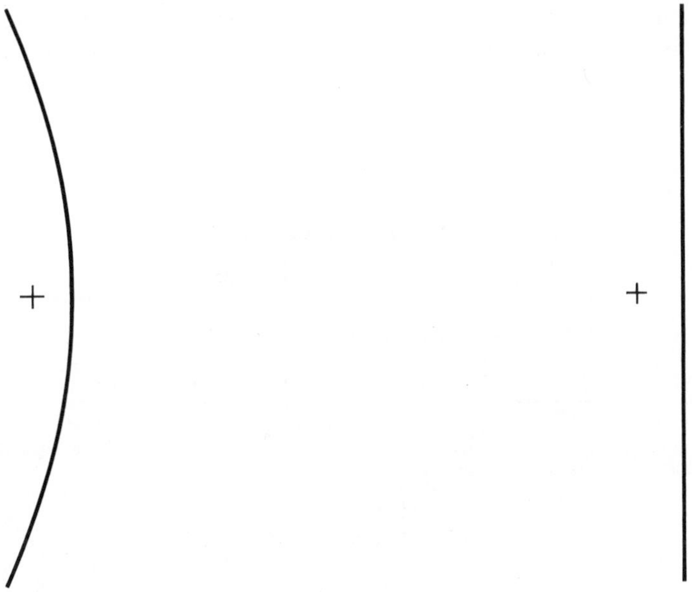

A Demonstration of a Visual Figural Aftereffect.
Fixate the cross near the left figure for several seconds, then shift the page so that the right figure is in the same visual field as the left had been. Fixating the cross by the right figure, observe the apparent curvature of the straight line.

Source: Underwood, B. J. *Experimental psychology.* New York: Appleton-Century-Crofts, 1966. P. 104.

(Figure 11–6). Thus, a gain of five pounds will be less noticeable on a fat person than on a skinny one.

Perceptual sensitivity. The smaller the difference threshold and the more sensitive one is to the attribute, the more highly differentiated his perception with respect to that attribute. Although there are probably some built-in limitations on some difference thresholds, most of us have room to achieve greater differentiation on many dimensions of judgment. We may acquire some sophistication about art and learn to respond differentially to stimuli which were not initially perceived as different. Similarly, many people who claim to be tone-deaf may be trained to achieve a greater sensitivity to tones and become able to differentiate among them; differences between tones become effective stimuli. Perceptual discrimination is a function of experience with the stimulus and the distinctiveness of the stimulus.

Hopefully, we move toward being able to respond to subtle differences between people or between the slightly shifting moods of a close friend, and develop perceptual and cognitive differentiations which enable us to notice and appreciate subtle distinctions between concepts and ideas (compare with the concept of measurement scales, Chapter 8). Unfortunately, many people who do not hesitate to admit that they are not accurate judges of tones or colors may insist that they are good judges of people, though their perceptual sensitivity may be equally undeveloped in all areas.

FIGURE
11–6

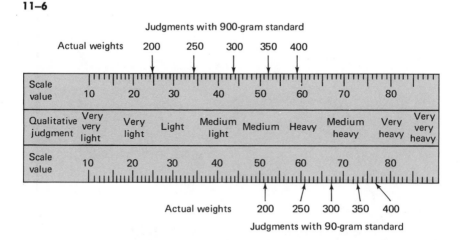

Subjective Scales of Weight Developed by Subjects in Cases Where the Standard Weight Was Very Heavy (Upper Scale) or Very Light (Lower Scale).
Results like this are sometimes said to indicate that the standard weight "anchors" the scale.

Source: Constructed from data obtained by Helson, 1948.

Perceiving Complex Stimuli

Attention. Perception is selective. Out of the innumerable stimuli to which the sensory organs are exposed at any one time, some are attended to, some are not. As William James stated, ". . . each of us literally chooses, by his way of attending to things, what sort of a universe he shall appear to himself to inhabit" (James, 1890, p. 402). The stimuli in the field vary from those clearly perceived in the focus of attention to those dimly perceived in the margin of attention, to those completely outside the attention field. Attention constantly shifts, so that what is in focus at one moment may become marginal or entirely outside the field at the next moment. The determinants of attention are roughly divisible into the two general classes of external and internal factors.

Among the external factors are (1) intensity and size, (2) contrast or change (including novelty), (3) repetition, and (4) movement. A shout is more attention demanding than is the normal speaking voice; a full-page advertisement is more likely to be noticed than is a smaller one. Intensity or size is a particularly potent determiner when we enter any new setting. Both the onset and offset of stimuli are attention arousing because of the contrast they provide. We may not notice the ticking of a clock, but we do note the contrast when the clock is suddenly *not* ticking. Similarly, a word printed in ALL CAPITALS is noticed quickly because of its contrast with the small letters. A repeated stimulus has a better chance of catching us when our attention is not solidly on other stimuli. Moving neon signs demand attention over static ones. These same principles of attention are applicable to a social event, such as going to a party of unfamiliar people. The principles of attention suggest that the first people we notice are the largest or loudest; the one female in a room of males, or the one man in a clerical collar; the set of triplets, each one of which calls attention to the other; or the hostess darting across the room.

Internal determiners of attention may also operate: motives, set, and expectancy. A poor student goaded to the party by his hunger motive rather than his affiliative motive would probably spot the food before he noticed the people. A student more in need of academic than nutritionary help would be more attuned to the cues of academic success such as a Phi Beta Kappa key dangling from the key chain of another party goer. If one attends a party expecting to see a friend, no matter how unattention-arousing he might be otherwise, the friend is quickly noticed. Or, if one is set to expect that an attractive member of the opposite sex will make overtures, any reasonably seductive behavior will be noticed quickly.

Perceptual organization. Closely related to the determiners of attention are the Gestalt principles of perceptual organization. We do not typically see arrays of disconnected and unrelated objects. We see things and also see relationships between things. The most basic organizational tendency is the perception of *figure and ground.* The figure stands out against the diffuse background and has form while the ground is formless. The figure and ground are sometimes easily reversible (Figure 11–7), but more often the relation is stable. A picture (figure) hangs on the wall (background); the wall does not stand behind a picture. A lovely girl poised on a diving board is seen as a figure against the ground of other pool-side activities. In music, chords are the ground against which the figure of the melody is heard. A person's general postural stance is ground against which we see the figure of his finer movements and gestures; his facial physiognomy is a ground against which the tenseness and position of facial musculature are evaluated.

Another organizational tendency is to group objects. Objects *near* each other are perceived as a group, as are *similar* objects. We also tend to group objects which form a *symmetrical organization* or have a *continuous direction.* Perceptions of human groupings or belongingness seem to be organized by the same principles as are the perceptual groupings of nonhuman objects (Heider, 1958).

We also seek *closure* by filling in gaps in the stimuli received so that a whole object is perceived. This principle has been encountered in the previous discussion of the blind spot. Figure 11–8a is seen as a circle and not simply as a series of short lines, nor as a series of blank spaces. Moreover, missing information is often filled in, in accordance with *expectations.* Whether the dots in Figure 11–8b are perceived as the letter B or as the number 13 may be manipulated by the warning to expect a letter or a number. The stimulus is just a series of splotches which are perceptually closed by the perceiver to form a meaningful unit. Closure is one principle responsible for stereotypes. We pick up some limited cues about a person, such as his skin color, the shape of his nose, or eyes, cues for sex, or the sign on the door of his business. We automati-

FIGURE
11–7

Figure Ground Perception.
Is it a vase or two faces in profile?

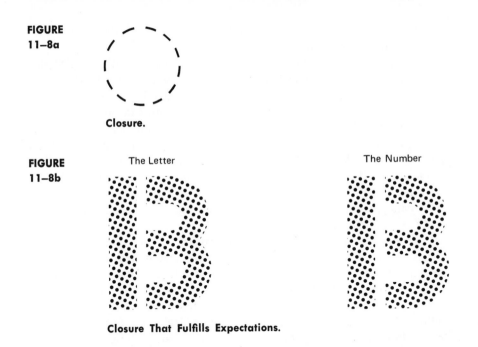

FIGURE 11–8a

Closure.

FIGURE 11–8b

The Letter

The Number

Closure That Fulfills Expectations.

cally proceed from this limited information to more complete impressions of the whole person. Thus, the closure principle is economical, it often permits us to respond appropriately even when we have minimal information about a person or situation. For instance, if a man has an M.D. after his name, we may assume that when we visit his office we may very well have to take our clothes off and be subjected to a great deal of pushing and probing, but we do not have to worry about a sexual attack. The dangers of stereotypes, of course, are that too often we respond too quickly and too finally to a small sample of cues which may be irrelevant to the understanding of the particular person with whom we are dealing (Chapter 13).

Anchoring Effects

Assimilation and contrast. The perceptual concepts of adaptation level and anchors were initially developed in the perception laboratory but have come to be important tools for understanding the processes of making social judgments and those of attitude change (Helson, 1948, 1964; Bieri et al., 1966). Judgments are made with respect to the AL (adaptation level), which is determined by the stimuli being judged, by other aspects of the situation in which judgment is made, and by internal stimuli or predispositions, such as attitudes, traits, or simply an internal frame of reference. Any one of these kinds of stimuli may function as *anchors*. An anchor is a stimulus which exerts a large influence on the judgment of other stimuli. Analogous to the anchor of nautical terms, the anchoring stimulus is relatively fixed in one place and serves as a point of reference. An extreme anchor shifts the AL toward the anchor and thereby affects judgments.

The exact nature of the effect of an anchor varies with the distance between the stimulus being judged and the anchor itself (Sherif & Hovland, 1961). A stimulus close to an anchor is judged more similar to the anchor than it really is (assimilation), and a stimulus far away is judged more different than it really is (contrast). For example, judgments about other people's attitudes are made with respect to the anchor of one's *own* attitudes. The greater the discrepancy between one's own position on an issue and another position, the more extreme and unlike one's own the other position appears to be (contrast). When there is only a small discrepancy, the other statement is judged more like one's own than it really is (assimilation).

The effect of one's own attitude as an anchor is influenced by the extremity of the attitude, the degree of involvement with the issue, and the stimuli in the immediate environment (Bieri, 1968; Eagly, 1967; Atkins & Bieri, 1968; Markley, 1971). In an experiment, subjects who were in favor of, against, or neutral about fraternities judged the favorability of the stand represented by statements about fraternities, presented three at a time (Atkins, 1966). Each group of three statements consisted of two extremely pro or extremely con statements functioning as context anchors, and one moderate, mid-range statement. The subject's own attitudes served as anchors initially; that is, both pro and con subjects judged moderate statements about fraternities to be very similar to their own attitudes. However, the effect of the context anchors became more dominant on later trials and the effects of the subjects' own attitudes diminished.

Perspectives. An individual's perspective may be characterized by the extremity of the stimuli which anchor end categories of a dimension of judgment. An important objective of education is to teach people to use a common perspective when discussing issues or describing their world (Volkmann, 1951). For example, when learning to use a set of labels, such as those ranging from "very pro-black" to "very anti-black," people anchor the extreme categories with specific beliefs, feelings, and policies about blacks. Some may define "very pro-black" as absolute equality whereas others may define it as black supremacy. The two will have difficulty communicating unless they are careful to make their anchor positions explicit.

While some end anchors result from habits of thinking, others may be *externally* imposed and thereby influence the content of one's own attitude (Ostrom & Upshaw, 1968). The following example illustrates this fact: Subjects read a case history about a man convicted of making bomb threats; they were then asked to rate how stern or lenient they would be as judges sentencing this man to prison, and to write a paragraph explaining the degree of sternness in their recommendations. After this commitment to their initial self-rating, the subjects were given an externally imposed perspective; half were told that the legal range of sentences was from one to thirty years, the others were told it was from one to five years. They then stated the actual number of years and months they would sentence the offender to prison if they were in a position to impose punishment.

Subjects given a wide perspective advocated more years imprisonment than did those given the narrow perspective (Figure 11-9). The difference was largest for those who initially rated themselves toward the stern end of the scale; this was expected since the lower anchor (one year) was the same in both conditions, with variation confined to the upper anchor (five or thirty years). The specific social evaluations we make about what is proper are influenced by general personal dispositions (e.g., "the legal limit"). Sometimes we have objective information about what is possible. More often, the range of alternatives we take into account reflects the range of direct or vicarious experiences we have had and our openness to them, and these vary greatly from individual to individual.

Other research has also shown that the penalty options available have a strong effect on whether the verdict is guilty or not guilty (Vidmar, 1972). Jurors (simulated) having a moderate penalty option seldom

FIGURE 11–9

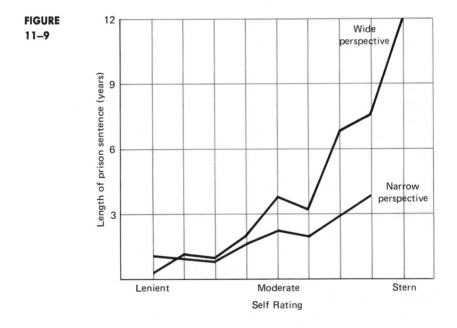

Length of Advocated Prison Sentence as a Function of Perspective Condition and Original Self-Rating.

Source: From Ostrom, T. M., & Upshaw, H. S., 1968, p. 231.

chose a verdict of not guilty (average 6 percent), whereas over half of those with only a severe penalty option chose not guilty. Obviously, our perceptual judgments of social stimuli as well as nonsocial ones are formulated in terms of other stimuli than those directly associated with the stimulus target per se.

DIFFERENCES IN PERCEPTUAL HABITS

People come to "see" the same world in different ways because of differential environment conditions in which they grow and act, and because of constitutional foundations of sensory mechanisms. Many stable differences in perceptual responses arise from differential familiarity with the objects to which one is being exposed, from learning what is salient or important to notice, and, of course, from how one comes to interpret the information received. There is selective attention and variation in interpreting what is attended to in the world. Some differences in perceptual habits are relatively general through a culture. Other differences reflect individual styles of perception and ways of dealing with needs and anxiety.

Cultural Differences in Perception

Cultures differ in the kind of objects present in their environment, with resulting differences in basic perceptual phenomena. Studies of geometric illusions have generally confirmed the "carpentered world hypothesis" (Segall, Campbell, & Herskovits, 1963, 1966; Campbell, 1964). This hypothesis states that individuals who live in a squared-off world of right angles learn to introduce corrections when they see angles in perspective (see shape constancy) and are consequently more susceptible to some illusions. European subjects showed a significantly greater effect on the Müller-Lyer illusion than did tribal people whose housing was almost entirely of rounded shapes. Degree of familiarity with angular objects is also cited as the reason for differences in the perception of the Ames (1951) rotating window under nonoptimal conditions for the illusionary effect (Allport & Pettigrew, 1957). The Ames window is a rotating trapezoid proportioned so that when viewed with one eye from twenty feet, the perception is of a window swaying back and forth. Under optimal conditions for the illusion, there was no difference in the perceptions reported by South African Zulus in villages and those reported by urban Zulus or Europeans. Apparently the stimulation in the illusion is too compelling to be overridden by cultural familiarity effects. However, under conditions not optimum for obtaining the effect, the illusion was seen more frequently by the urban subjects, both Zulus and Europeans, than by villagers. Notice that the cultural influence is not sufficient for completely overcoming the basic effect. The cultural differences are a figure against a background of the basic perceptual phenomena. Much the same may be said for individual differences against the background of cultural differences.

Cultures differ also in the kinds of events and the kinds of discriminations that are salient in their environment. When bullfight and baseball pictures were simultaneously presented, Mexican subjects reported seeing the bullfight first, while American subjects reported the baseball pictures first (Bagby, 1957). Notice that neither group of subjects reported seeing something that was not there; they differed in which part of the total stimulus field first captured their attention. The method used was the *binocular rivalry* technique whereby different stimuli are presented to each eye with a stereoscope apparatus so that neither stimulus can be seen by the other eye; the dependent variable is which of the two stimuli is reported first or remains the dominant image.

A frequent concomitant of the importance of a kind of event is a high level of perceptual discrimination about the event. The Eskimo language, compared to American English, has a large variety of words for snow. We cannot say that the Eskimos necessarily see snow differently from the way we do, but they do have more precise labels for dealing with snow, that is, a more complex cognitive system for thinking and talking about snow. This principle applies also to social stimuli. For instance, suggesting to Trobriand Islanders that two brothers resemble each other is a social indiscretion, although to an American they both look like their father. Do the Trobriand Islanders actually see the brothers as different or do they just elaborate on the differences that others neglect as unimportant? One reviewer concluded that they "fail to note any resemblance because they do not want or expect to find it" (Klineberg, 1954, p. 205). The number of distinctions made about people (cognitive complexity) will also be discussed later on as an important dimension of social perception (Chapter 13).

Differences in Cognitive Style

A cognitive style is a person's relatively consistent way of perceiving, thinking, remembering, and problem solving. The two cognitive styles chosen for discussion here, global analytic and leveler-sharpener, are both measurable by perceptual tasks and have a variety of correlates in diverse aspects of personality functioning, including defense mechanisms.

Global-analytic cognition. Witkin (1965, 1969; Witkin et al., 1954, 1962) distinguished between people on the basis of the extent to which they were dependent upon the perceptual field for making judgments, or were independent and actively and analytically oriented toward the world. Dependency upon the perceptual field is one aspect of the construct of global versus analytical style of cognitive functioning. Field dependence-independence is measured by space orientation tests which ascertain the extent of reliance on the external visual field relative to reliance on self-located cues. The Rod and Frame Test (RFT) is the best known measure. The subject is in a dark room and has the task of adjusting an illuminated rod to the vertical position while the illuminated frame in which the rod is located is systematically tilted at various angles. The subject needs to ignore the distracting field of external stimuli (the frame) to make a judgment of verticality. That is, he must deal with the field analytically, differentiating an item (the rod) from the configuration of stimuli in which it occurs. Subjects who are relatively accurate in making vertical settings are said to be field independent. Those who are less accurate, presumably being more influenced by the field, are field dependent.

Perception is considered global when a person is dependent on the perceptual field for making judgments. Perception is considered articulated or analytical when the person is able to perceive items as discrete from the background when the field is structured (analysis) and able to impose structure and perceive a field as organized when the field has little inherent structure (Witkin, 1969).

The global-analytical construct seems particularly related to the degree of activity of the individual in dealing with the environment and the extent of differentiation in views of the environment, self, and others. These orientations seem to be diverse expressions of an underlying process of development toward greater psychological complexity (Witkin, 1969). Analytical functioning is associated with a greater degree of psychological differentiation; global with less differentiation. Global people are generally more dependent on the external environment. They tend to see themselves as fused with others and with the world around them. They are likely to change their feelings and attitudes in the direction suggested by others, to have less differentiated concepts about themselves, and to tell TAT stories in which the central character is unassertive in dealing with problems. Analytic people who are relatively articulate are better at insight problems which require taking an item out of the context in which it is presented and restructuring the problem material (Karp, 1963), and better on those measures of intelligence tests which require separating an item from a context. Males tend to be more field-independent than females, though the difference is small compared to the range of differences within each sex.

Also, people at the global end of the global-analytic continuum are likely to use primitive defense mechanisms such as massive repression and primitive denial, which involve a relatively indiscriminate "turning away" from current stimuli and memory of past experiences, and comparatively nonspecific ways of functioning as opposed to more analytic mechanisms such as intellectualization and isolation.

Age and intelligence are both correlated with field independence and perceptual differentiation. With increased age, there is increased experience with an environment consisting of objects which actually are different and separable, and consequently, increased ability to deal actively with the environment and to experience oneself as a structured self segregated from it. With the sense of self as a separate identity, there is an internal frame of reference for viewing, interpreting, and dealing with the world as an autonomous agent. In turn, this facilitates articulation of the immediately present environment. However, within this developmental trend, there is marked relative stability of individual differences (Witkin, Goodenough, & Karp, 1967). Those who are relatively global at age eight are relatively global at age twenty-two, compared to others of equal age.

Socialization experiences which foster separate functioning are also associated with development of an articulated cognitive style (Witkin, 1969). Mothers of articulated children were themselves more differentiated than were mothers of global children. They tended to have greater self-assurance, self-realization, more personal values and standards of their own, and felt free to encourage the child to develop an independent sense of himself and the world. They encouraged an appropriate sexual role and a separate identity in their children, and encouraged an acceleration in independence of action which would meet the child's needs.

Mothers of the less differentiated children seemed to lack definition of their own roles as wives and mothers, lacked clarity about implementing their plans for working toward goals, and had little awareness of their children as separate persons. Mothers of infants who were later measured as less differentiated tended to lack perception of distress in the infant, to disregard the infant's need because of their own mood or needs at the time, and to use the same techniques of comforting (e.g., putting the infant to breast, picking the infant up), whatever the cause of the infant distress. Their own anxieties and wishes prevented them from making an accurate differentiation of signs of distress and responding to the infant as a person separate from mother.

Although there are consistent socialization patterns associated with global-articulated functioning, this fact does not necessarily mean that there are no genetic contributions to the dimension. Because of genetic determinants of responsiveness, the infant himself may "encourage" a mother to react one way rather than another (Chapter 19). Biological differences between infants may encourage different child-rearing practices by mothers. According to our cultural stereotypes, men are expected to be independent and women to be dependent and socially oriented. Consistently, mothers do tend to place greater emphasis on social training for their daughters than for their sons, and are more accepting of independence and assertiveness in their sons than in their daughters.

The Leveler-Sharpener Dimension

The leveler-sharpener dimension is one of several investigated by ego psychologists who are giving increased attention to the adaptive, nondefensive, conflict-free aspects of ego functioning (Chapter 4). Their concern is with the consistent modes of thinking and perceiving (cognitive controls) which may function independently of needs to deal with anxiety, though these may also function defensively (Gardner, 1962; Klein, 1954).

Measures. Two related measures of the general leveler-sharpener dimension are perceptual-change tasks and the Stroop test. With perceptual-change tasks, subjects are given stimuli in fine gradations and asked to report when they detect that the stimulus has changed, such as when a square has become bigger. Levelers tend to assimilate new stimuli to a dominant cognitive structure and are therefore less aware of the differences between the old and the new (Holzman & Gardner, 1959). Sharpeners, on the other hand, are more aware of changes and make sharper distinctions between stimulus situations; they tend to respond to small differences and exaggerate change. Thus, levelers show a "lag" before they give evidence of reacting to stimulus change; sharpeners react to change quickly.

The Stroop Color Naming Test requires the subject simply to name colors. The trick is that on the test card, color names are printed in colors different from the color named. The word "green" may be printed in yellow ink, or "red" printed in blue ink. The subject must ignore the word "green" or "red" and say "yellow" or "blue." The student may get the feel of the difficulty of this task by making a miniature Stroop test with a red and black pencil. The measure of performance is the length of time it takes the subject to complete calling the colors on the card, usually corrected by the time taken on control cards, when the subject names the hues of color patches and reads color names printed in black ink.

Those who do well on the test card are levelers—low-interference or flexible control subjects—for they are able to "level out" or smooth the stimulus configuration, showing a flexible control. They can ignore the difference between the two kinds of stimuli and assimilate the word names into the background of the colors themselves. Those who do less well are called sharpeners, also called high-interference or constricted control subjects. They sharpen the stimulus elements and are aware of the difference between the two kinds of stimuli, showing a constricted control. Although they do well on problems requiring careful attention to detail (e.g., perceptual-change tasks), they do poorly on those which are facilitated by ignoring part of the stimulus configuration, such as the Stroop test. Obviously, the kind of control that is more effective depends on what the situation requires.

Sharpeners tend to have a persistent focus on a critical stimulus. Concomitant with this, they seem to be generally characterized by constriction in perception and in thinking, and this tendency to constrict is exaggerated under conditions of need deprivation (Klein, 1954, 1959). For example, when they are thirsty, they concentrate on a picture of an ice-cream soda in the middle of a stimulus disc to the neglect of the letters and figures in the periphery. In free association, they give many more associations close in meaning to the stimulus word, and, when thirsty, have more intrusions of thirst-related words into their associations to a neutral word, such as house, than is true of levelers. Levelers are more attentive to the peripheral stimuli than to the central elements of both visual and verbal stimuli.

INTERNAL DETERMINANTS OF PERCEPTUAL RESPONSES

Need or Reality Bound?

Is perception in the service of one's unconscious needs, tensions, conflicts, and id impulses as the Freudian position implies? Or, are our perceptions conscious ones which are the realistic, knowledgeable responses of a rational being to events which in fact *are?* Are we bound by needs or bound by reality? Whether one wishes to emphasize the *internal determinants* of perceptual responses, such as physiological needs, motivations, values, and anxieties, or to focus on reality and conscious determinants, is largely a matter of personal preference. In normal conditions, internal determinants, conscious or unconscious, control perceptual responses only when they can do so without a marked violation of reality. That is, we see what we want to see—perhaps an unconscious wanting—only when we will not feel foolish for doing so. This is possible when (1) the stimulus material is relevant to the internal state, and (2) there is a tendency for perceptual error anyway, or (3) when the reality of the situation is unclear because of the ambiguity or complexity inherent in the situation or because one has minimal information about it.

Physiological needs. Needs can influence perceptual reports when the stimuli have a clear relation to the motivational state (Pastore, 1949; Saugstad, 1966, 1967). The effect of food deprivation (four to sixteen hours) on TAT stories was most marked in responses to a stimulus card which contained a clear picture of food-related objects, such as meat (Atkinson & McClelland, 1948). More generally, most people would feel rather ridiculous talking about food when shown a picture of a library, and indeed, they are likely not to have had positive reinforcement for thinking of food as they approach a library for a long afternoon's work. Similarly, sexual arousal level and accessibility of a judged stimulus object (a prospective date) affected the perception of the attractiveness and receptivity of a stimulus person (Stephan, Berscheid, & Walster, 1971; Epstein & Smith, 1957).

In studies making more direct use of perceptual techniques, the deprivation effects were clearest in those in which the stimuli were clearly presented pictures of obviously need-satisfying objects (Gilchrist & Nesberg, 1952). Increasing need (hunger or thirst) was associated with increasing error in memory estimates of the brightness of slides of objects relevant to that need. The error of overestimating the brightness level of slides increased as the hours of deprivation increased, and decreased after the need was satisfied (Figure 11–10). Control subjects not deprived also overestimated the brightness of critical pictures (a constant perceptual error), but their error did not increase over time. Notice that there was a tendency for perceptual error (overestimation), as shown by the error of the control group, and that the estimates of brightness were made from memory.

Values. Values too influence perceptual responses. The values may be relatively enduring ones or may be experimentally created in the research situation. Lambert, Solomon, and Watson (1949) used a procedure similar to that used with monkeys (Chapter 5) to create a positive value of a poker chip. For some children, a poker chip became a secondary reinforcer because it could be used to get candy; control children received candy directly, without the mediation of the poker chip. They were rewarded, with the chip or with candy, for turning a crank on a toy apparatus. After ten days of training, all children estimated the size of a poker chip by adjusting a disc of light to match the size of the chip being held by the experimenter while the child made

FIGURE 11–10

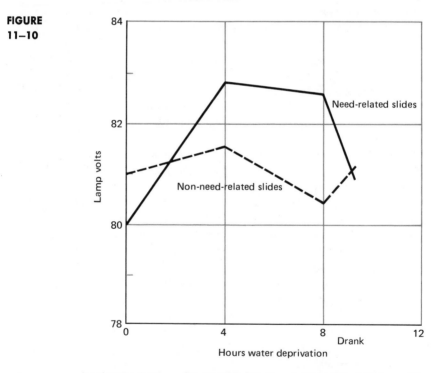

Luminence Settings for Need-Related and Nonrelated Slides with Increasing Thirst and after Drinking.

Source: Gilchrist, J. C., & Nesberg, L. S. Need and perceptual change in need-related objects. *Journal of Experimental Psychology*, 1952, 44, 369–376.

the estimate. Children for whom the chip had been associated with the candy reinforcer did increase their size estimate of the chip over their estimate before the training. Those for whom the chip had not been paired with candy did not give different estimates from what they had given before training. The group differences disappeared after an extinction session (no reward for crank turning) and again appeared after additional reinforcement trials the following day (Figure 11-11).

The perceptual response of size estimation was controlled by the experimental reinforcement contingencies. However, the effect was quite small and the control group also had a tendency to overestimate the chip size. Similarly, children from poor families overestimated the size of more valuable (and larger) coins to a greater extent than did those from more affluent families (Bruner & Goodman, 1947), but both children and adults have a tendency to overestimate large discs, whether or not they are coins (Carter & Scholler, 1949).

Although the results of studies of values in perception are not totally consistent and the magnitude of the effects is small, most of the evidence indicates that when there is a tendency for an error, the positive value of the stimulus has some effect on emphasizing the error, especially when the judgments are made from memory (Forgus, 1966). Perceptions are influenced by needs and values, but the "distortion" is kept within bounds by the characteristics of the stimulus—by reality.

Defenses. Another body of personality and perception research has dealt extensively with emotional, anxiety-arousing stimuli expected to elicit defense mechanisms (see Minard, 1965; Eriksen, 1963, 1966; Eriksen & Pierce, 1968). Defense mechanisms have in common the characteristic of in some way denying or distorting reality (Chapter 3). Again, there are limits in the amount of distortion that can occur as a function of internal states; the stimulus, as we have been taught to define it realistically, exerts control over the perceptual response. When there is no reasonable doubt about what the stimulus is, most of us forego defense protection and "see it as it is." However, in many complex real-life situations, there is always some lurking ambiguity which defenses may be used to resolve and clarify.

In the experimental laboratory, defenses are often studied by presenting visual material (e.g., slides of words or scenes) with a tachistoscope (T-scope), a slide projector which allows for fine control of illumination and exposure duration. Recognition thresholds are measured as the amount of illumination or duration necessary for a correct report of the stimulus—how much information the subject has to have before recognizing the stimulus for what it is. In early research, the stimuli were "dirty" words (e.g., McGinnies, 1949). Subjects who took longer to report the dirty words than neutral ones were said to show perceptual defense; those who reported the dirty words more quickly than neutral ones were showing perceptual vigilance. Although these early experiments were criticized on a number of grounds (Howes & Solomon, 1950,

FIGURE

11–11

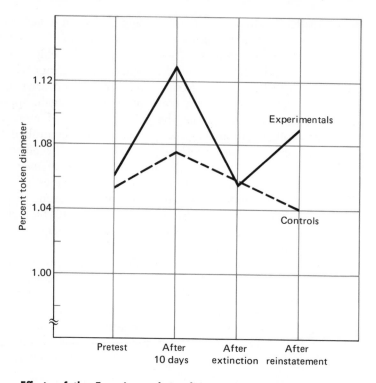

Effects of the Experimental Conditions upon Children's Estimates of the Diameter of a Token When These Estimates Are Taken as Percents of the True Diameter.

Source: From Lambert, W. W., Solomon, R. L., & Watson, P. D. Reinforcement and extinction as factors in size estimation. *Journal of Experimental Psychology,* 1949, 39, 637–641.

1951), later research has been more adequate in helping to understand the perceptual vehicle for defenses and individual differences in perceptual defense phenomena.

People differ in what is anxiety provoking for them, so defensive reactions are not general to specific material. For instance, not all people are upset by "dirty" words; if dirty words are not disturbing to them, the threshold for reporting taboo words will not differ from the threshold for neutral words. The stimulus material must be relevant to the internal state if it is to evoke a response differentiating one person from another. Defenses do not operate independently of the stimulus situation.

Defense styles. People also differ in the ways in which they react to material which is anxiety provoking for them. Subjects independently assessed as inclined to use repressive defenses show perceptual defense for material independently determined to be anxiety provoking for them but not for material not threatening to them. People who favor sensitization defenses show perceptual vigilance for material independently determined to be anxiety provoking for them but not for neutral stimuli.

Individual differences have also been demonstrated for material to which anxiety has presumably been experimentally attached. The success/failure technique is a frequent one; the typical college student subject is assumed to become anxious when an experimenter makes him think that he has failed on an experimental task, but subjects differ in how they react to the anxiety induced. Repressors (R-S scale) led to think that they had failed on an anagram word task later had significantly higher thresholds for the task words than did a group of sensitizers who had also been told that they had failed (Tempone, 1962). Repressors and sensitizers who had experienced success did not differ from each other in recognition thresholds for the task words, nor did the experimental treatment or defense groups differ in recognition of neutral words. Similar findings were reported with a carbon-copy technique, with which subjects start with the last, most illegible carbon copy of the stimulus materials and work up toward the most legible until they make a correct report (Cowen & Beier, 1950).

Unconscious Perception?

Some people recognize stimuli that are anxiety provoking more quickly than they recognize neutral stimuli; others seem to avoid recognition of anxiety stimuli as long as realistically possible. Why? The *subception* explanation attributes the defense phenomena to a process by which a discrimination is made when the subject is unable to make a correct conscious discrimination (Lazarus & McCleary, 1951). Unconscious processes are assumed to have greater capacity for perceiving, learning, and remembering than conscious ones. They can therefore screen, or censor out, material that is unacceptable or anxiety provoking to the conscious mind. They enable a person to "see *before* he sees." While most professional psychologists are no longer sympathetic with the subception explanation, it remains a popular misconception. Studies presented as evidence for subception of anxiety stimuli have been soundly criticized for methodological inadequacies (Eriksen, 1960). Careful consideration leads to the clear conclusion that "at present there is no convincing evidence that the human organism can discriminate or differentially respond to external stimuli that are at an intensity level too low to elicit a discriminated verbal report. In other words, a verbal report is as sensitive an indicator of perception as any other response that has been studied" (Eriksen, 1960, p. 298). Unconscious perception, often measured by galvanic skin response (GSR), is *not* superior to conscious perception, measured by verbal report. Also, remember the Poetzl phenomenon (Chapter 9).

Stimuli labeled *subliminal* (below threshold for conscious detection) often do convey some information. However, the stimuli in studies claiming to demonstrate subliminal perception were, in part or whole, *supraliminal*, as measured by the simple device of asking subjects what they saw instead of assuming that their threshold for detection of stimulation was below an average level. We often hear comments such as "I unconsciously knew that . . ." or "Some part of me saw . . ." Although unconscious perception is implied by these comments, more careful observation is likely to show that the response was made to aspects of the stimulus situation which were in fact *above* threshold and were at the time *consciously* perceived. Their significance may not have been realized at the time they were perceived, or perhaps no decision was made then to act upon them. After-the-fact reflection may have led the person to assume other features of the situation which were present but were not consciously perceived. When dealing with people we know well and with familiar situations, we do not need many cues to be able to figure out what is going on or what is about to happen. Thus, the usual claim for unconscious perception is most likely the result of well-made inferences from consciously perceived cues.

The following example should demonstrate the fact that *supra*liminal rather than *sub*liminal stimuli control perceptual reports (Weiner & Schiller, 1960). Subjects were shocked during the presentation of critical words until a conditioned GSR to the words was established. Then a variety of words was presented at short durations. Some of the words were semantically related to the previously shocked words: *Boat* is semantically related to *ship*. Others were structurally related: *Shop* is structurally related to *ship*. If a subject responds to the partial cues he consciously perceives (those above threshold), he should initially see greater similarity between the originally shocked words and those structurally related to them; greater generalized GSRs should occur to structurally similar words. If the subject is able to perceive the whole word unconsciously, he should show greater, or at least equal, GSR generalization to the semantically related words: The meaning of *boat* is closer to the meaning of *ship* than is the meaning of *shop*. If unconscious perceptual processes are to have a protective effect, the meaning of a stimulus must be determined. The results showed that when subjects incorrectly identified the complete words under conditions insufficient for complete detection of the words, GSR responsiveness was greater to the words structurally related than to those semantically related to the previously shocked words. Further, there was a decrease in GSR measures to the structurally similar words as the exposure duration increased, and the amount of conscious identification possible thereby increased. The pattern of incorrect verbal guessing also showed that the subjects seemed to be responding verbally as well as autonomically to the perception of the portions of the stimuli they could see.

A theory of unconscious perception cannot explain the perceptual defense phenomena. This does *not* mean that those phenomena we casually call unconscious do not exist. They do. Understanding them is necessary for any complete understanding of psychodynamics. What is at issue is *why* and *how* they occur. To answer simply, "It's the unconscious," does not add to an understanding of the phenomena and often distracts from determined efforts to find answers.

Reinforcement of Perceptual Responses

A more comprehensive and adequate explanation of the unconscious phenomena is a reinforcement explanation (Eriksen, 1963, 1966; Eriksen & Pierce, 1968). It is essentially an extension of Miller and Dollard's formulation of defense mechanisms as covert responses which follow the same laws of learning as do overt responses. Covert responses, thoughts, memories, and images function in the same ways as do overt responses, and are subject to the same laws of learning and reinforcement. A person learns to think of something in the same way as he learns to do something. Similarly, not-thinking is a response and one learns to avoid some thoughts. It is important to notice that in this explanation perceptual defense phenomena are attributed to perceptual responses rather than to the ways in which the stimulation is received and processed.

Responses to partial cues. In everyday life, events are often too complex for us to attend to all aspects of the situation or we are simply not given complete or clear information about what others are, for example, thinking or feeling. The situation in the typical perceptual defense study is much the same. In both cases, we "fill in" the missing information in accordance with habits and expectations built from prior experiences. We associate to what we do perceive, a special mechanism by which the closure principle works. Perceptual-recognition experiments measure the associative strength of associative responses to partial and indefinite cues. To any stimulus configuration, one has a variety of acceptable responses. The response which occurs, whether overtly reported or not, is determined by reinforcement history. Responses that have in the past been followed by positive reinforcement should be elicited more quickly from restricted cues than would responses which in the past have been punished. The probability of thinking those thoughts which have been accompanied by anxiety will be relatively low in the thought hierarchy of a repressor, while the probability of thinking and reporting those thoughts previously associated with pleasant experiences or anxiety avoidance will be relatively high. The kinds of thoughts which have positive or negative experiences associated with them vary from person to person. As more and more information is presented (the clarity of the stimulus increases because of increased illumination or exposure time, for example), the scope of the hierarchy of realistically acceptable responses to the available cues decreases. When the stimulus is clear, it is reported even if it might evoke some anxiety. Thus, if the subject has a low probability of giving the response that corresponds to the stimulus chosen by the experimenter, there appears to be a perceptual distortion resulting from the superior unconscious processes of perceptual discrimination. It is, however, simply the result of prior reinforcement upon response probability (Figure 11–12).

Notice that it is when the stimulus information is incomplete or ambiguous that defense occurs. We have not been punished in such cases for reporting in accordance with defensive needs. By denial, the repressor may avoid the anxiety that would come with the admission of the presence of anxiety-evoking material. Because the sensitizer deals with anxiety by facing problem material, he has anxiety-related ideas high in his hierarchy of responses, and reports them quickly, even though he sees no more of the stimulus than does his repressing counterpart. Both the sensitizer and repressor respond to what they consciously see; it is their response hierarchy that is responsible for the "censor" behind the "defense." The subject need not feel that he is searching for acceptable perceptual responses to fragmentary or ambiguous stimuli. The response may be immediate and automatic. Although awareness seems to be necessary for *acquiring* a response, it is not necessary for the *performance* of the response. The performance of a defensive response may be said to be "unconscious" in some loose sense. The defense is simply a well-learned response to consciously perceived stimuli.

Modifying the thought hierarchy. The reinforcement explanation assumes that thoughts follow the same laws of reinforcement as do overt responses. This assumption was experimentally validated in a word association study (Eriksen & Kuethe, 1956). Subjects were asked to give word associations to fifteen stimulus words, repeated for several trials. Regardless of what responses the subject initially gave to each of five

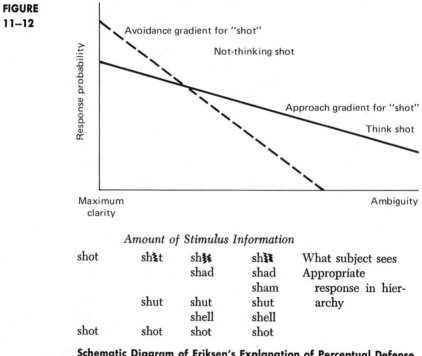

FIGURE 11–12

Amount of Stimulus Information

shot	sh⋮t	sh⋮	sh⋮	What subject sees
		shad	shad	Appropriate
			sham	response in hier-
	shut	shut	shut	archy
		shell	shell	
shot	shot	shot	shot	

Schematic Diagram of Eriksen's Explanation of Perceptual Defense, for Repression.

words chosen as "critical" for that subject, he was shocked on the first trial and on all other trials on which he again gave the response initially given. Thus, the subject's existing dominant response to the critical words, but not to the neutral words, was followed by shock. The probability of reporting the responses originally given to the critical words did in fact decline markedly over trials, while the probability of repeating the responses originally given to neutral words showed only the small decline to be expected in a repeated word association task (Figure 11–13).

One might suggest that perhaps the subjects' first thought was their original one, but since they knew that they would get shocked for saying it they thought of something else to say (a criticism of intentional response suppression). However, although the experimenters were not able to observe directly what the subjects were thinking, they were able to take measures which indicated that the thoughts themselves were being manipulated rather than only the verbal responses from which thoughts were inferred. One source of such evidence was that the subjects reported, after the testing was over, that after they caught on that some responses were being shocked, they had to stop and think of another word to say. However, giving another response came to be automatic so that they did *not* have to stop and search. The reaction time for responding to critical words markedly increased in the middle trials, consistent with subjects' reports that they did in fact initially continue to have the original thought and thus had to look for another response. The fact that the reaction time to critical words decreased until it was no different from that to neutral words prohibits concluding that such a process continued (Figure 11–14). Rather, it is more consistent with assuming that the thought itself had been changed; there was no time for the original thought to occur and to be replaced in the verbal report by another response.

Acquisition of defense styles. We learn to be anxious about some ideas but not others. In addition, we learn how to deal with anxiety. Contingencies in the environment affect the defense style that develops. Perceptual defense may be learned when responding to a threatening stimulus is punished and responding to other stimuli is not punished. This perceptual defense may then be reinforced by punishment avoidance (Dulaney, 1957). People come to use the kind of defense which avoids punishment; whether that is a repressive or a sensitizing defense depends upon the environmental reinforcement contingencies. If punishment follows recognition of threatening material but is avoided by turning away from that material, avoidance mechanisms develop. If punishment can be avoided by a rapid and accurate detection of threatening material, but is likely to follow lack of correct recognition, sensitization is more likely. Sensitizing subjects have reported restrictive home backgrounds (Byrne, 1964). In a punitive home, rapid spotting of problem areas can facilitate an avoidance of punishment. If parents

FIGURE
11–13

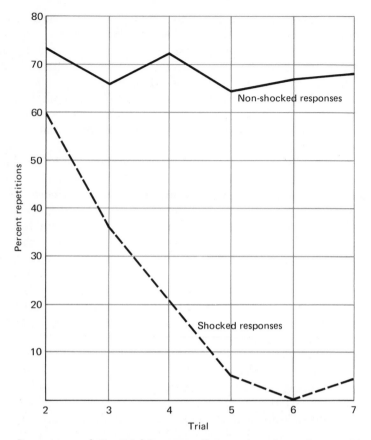

Percentages of First-Trial Responses Repeated on Succeeding Trials as a Function of Punishment.

Source: Adapted from Eriksen, C. W., and Kuethe, J. L. Avoidance conditioning of verbal behavior without awareness: A paradigm of repression. *Journal of Abnormal and Social Psychology,* 1956, 53, 203–209.

are severely restrictive and punitive about aggression, the child will likely become quickly attuned to his own aggressive impulses and to cues of impending aggression generally. It is important to him to be vigilant to his impulses so he can check them and avoid punishment. Thus, his way of dealing with anxiety about aggression comes to be that of excessive concern and worrying about it. Similarly, a child in a restrictive home may be extra alert to the cues of his parents' behavior which may signal that they are in a "bad mood" and likely to censure him if he is not careful. Repressors, in contrast to sensitizers, reported permissiveness and acceptance in their childhood homes. It is not clear that punishment would necessarily have followed recognition of threatening material, but at least there is less need in a permissive home to be on the lookout for problem areas.

This is not to say that defenses are entirely a matter of reinforcement contingencies. It is very possible that there are genetic determinants as

**FIGURE
11–14**

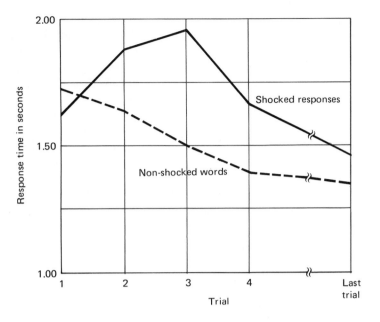

Reaction Times to Critical and Noncritical Stimuli as a Function of Trials.

Source: Same as Figure 11–13.

well as environmental ones. People may differ innately in the extent and nature of emotional responsiveness and perhaps therefore in the defenses which are necessary or effective in controlling anxiety (Chapter 14). Also, the pervasive effects of cognitive styles in non-conflict areas is suggestive of an underlying predisposition to develop one mode of defense over the other. It is unlikely that people are exactly alike at birth in the probability that they will acquire repressing or sensitizing defenses, or any other kind of response for that matter.

Summary

Perceptions of the world, whether the relatively simple ones of the experimental psychologist's laboratory or the more complex ones of the ongoing world of people and social acts, are seldom totally veridical ones responsive only to the objective properties of one stimulus. We attend to some events and not to others; we distort, impose order, and see in organized ways. The perception of any one stimulus is a function of the other stimuli that occur in the perceptual field with it and those previously exposed. Stimuli are judged with respect to reference points, or anchors, provided by the immediate situation and interacting with those which tend to be habitual with the perceiver himself. Individual, and cultural, differences occur as a function of experience with environmental objects and events to be perceived, and also by the importance of attending to and making discriminations about aspects of the environment. There are relatively stable and pervasive perceptual styles, perhaps with genetic bases, certainly with experiential antecedents, which function to differentially direct attention to some aspects of the environment to the relative neglect of other aspects. These perceptual styles are not specific to defense against anxiety, but are apparent in defense styles. They include modes of functioning which reflect a passive global orientation in dealing with the perceptual field or a more active and independent one, and a tendency to assimilate new material into old, to minimize discrepancies between stimuli with conflicting information, or a tendency to exaggerate differences.

Thus, part of what we see always comes out of our own heads. We differ in the content of our past experiences and in the specific ways and the extent to which our needs, values, and interests lead us to select from available stimuli and to interpret what we see. Our overt responses are often not valid as direct indications of our actual perceptions. Previous punishment for a given perceptual report may prevent our admitting to the perception, and we can come to develop a response tendency to interpret our environment in ways that seem most likely to avoid punishment. For some people this means that they quickly detect potentially problem material in the environment, while others develop the tendency to try to avoid recognition of anxiety material. As we shall see in the following chapters, this fact has important implications for perceptions of self and of others.

12

perception of self

Who are you? Other people may think that they know you, and may in fact know well many details of your life and your behavior, your parents, friends, habits, and moods. They may even be able to predict your behavior better than you care to admit. But do they for that reason know you? Some of the objective facts of your life and your behavior may not make much sense, and may lead others to erroneous conclusions and predictions if they do not know of your own feelings and perceptions about yourself. Our views of self do not always match the views others have of us, yet it is in large part through interactions with others that our views of self develop, and it is often because of our self-view that we act in ways that are sometimes confusing, sometimes understandable to others.

CONCEPTS OF SELF

Some theorists view self in terms of a process: knowing, doing, perceiving, acting. Others view it as an internal "object" about which one has feelings and attitudes, thoughts and valuations. Many contemporary views of self stem from William James (1890), who considered self to be the "empirical me," the sum total of all a man calls his, including his body, his characteristics and abilities, his material possessions, his occupation, hobbies, friends, enemies, and so on. Whatever theory is chosen, it has seemed meaningful to discuss as components of self our *self-concept*, or what we think and feel about ourselves, and our *ideal self*, or what we want to be. Favorability of view of self, that is, general level of self-regard or self-esteem, is often measured by the number of positive things a person says about himself, the lack of discrepancy between self-concept and ideal self, or by other measures of self-acceptance and worthiness.

No one is born with a fully formed self-concept. It develops as we experience approval and criticism, success and failure; it grows with our perception of the world around us—our family, our friends, our place in society; it matures as our bodies mature and we evaluate our physical, social, and emotional characteristics. Although the self-concept is resistant to change, we modify our view of self as we continually have evaluative experiences and social interactions, as we gain more information about ourselves, and as we do in fact change. As we become more mature, hopefully we develop an internal locus of self-definition rather than one dependent entirely upon other people, and we also achieve the feeling that we are in control of our lives.

Often there are inconsistencies between what we think we are, what we want for ourselves, and what important other people think of us and want us to be (see Rogers, Chapter 6). We take advantage of many mechanisms for maintaining consistent views of the self and for minimizing disturbing inconsistencies. A young man who really wants to be a professional athlete may attempt to deny this wish if his family has strongly encouraged a view of him as one who is best fit to be a scholarly professor. He may be aware of the inconsistency between his attempts to become a scholarly professor and what he wants, or he may so thoroughly incorporate the standards of his parents that he must defensively block out of awareness his own desires, if he is to have a favorable view of himself. Consistency and favorability of view may be realistic or they may be defensive; a very positive self-view is often made possible by such defensiveness.

Influences on the Self-Concept

Evaluative experiences with other people are considered the most important contributors to the self-concept. Through the atmosphere they create in the home and through the values they endorse, the parents provide the first evaluative experiences for the child: The child comes to regard himself as he thinks his parents do.

The family atmosphere. Rogers maintained that the self develops from the perceived approval and disapproval of other people, and that unconditional positive regard is necessary for the development of a positive, accepting view of self (Chapter 6). Consistent with his hypothesis, the attitudes and evaluations of self by children and college students are correlated with their reports of their parents' attitudes toward them (see Wylie, 1961, 1968; McCandless, 1970). Maladjusted children perceive conflicting views between their parents and have conflicting views about themselves. Rewards and punishments help to communicate to the child his parents' perceptions of him. Male college students reported positive concepts about themselves on those traits which they also reported had been rewarded by parents and other significant people in their childhood; they had lower views of themselves and anxiety about those traits which had been punished or not rewarded (Child, Frank, & Storm, 1956). Reward, however, is not a magic act which automatically results in a positive outcome. When parental reward systems stress the child's *objective* success rather than the intrinsic value of the child himself, negative results are likely (Ausubel et al., 1954). The child must feel accepted and valued for *himself*. It is not necessarily the specific actions of the parents that are important, but the total climate in the family which influences the child's perceptions of his parents and of their intentions toward and feelings about him.

This point was supported by an extensive study of the *self-esteem* of ten- to twelve-year-old boys (Coopersmith, 1967, 1968). Self-esteem is the positive evaluation the individual makes about himself and customarily maintains; it is a personal judgment of worthiness. Compared to boys who had low self-esteem, those boys of high self-esteem were more assertive, competent, independent, and creative; they had an internal locus of evaluation, and were held in high esteem by others.

Three conditions appeared to be important to the development of high self-esteem: (1) total or nearly total acceptance of the child by his parents; (2) clearly defined and enforced limits on behavior; and (3) respect and latitude for the child's individual action within the defined limits (Coopersmith, 1967). Mothers of boys with high self-esteem had closer and more loving relationships with their sons and showed interest which the boy interpreted as a sign that he was significant and worthy of concern. The rights and opinions of the boy were respected within a clearly stated and enforced role system. In contrast, the parents of low self-esteem boys seemed autocratic and rejecting; guidelines for the boys' behavior were ambiguous and inconsistently reinforced; harsh punishment alternated with extreme permissiveness. A family background of instability and conflict, and of inconsistent or extreme disciplinary practices, was also reported by those of a large sample of Navy men who had a low self-valuation (Gunderson, 1965).

Stereotypes. Cultural stereotypes learned inside and outside the home influence the level of favorability of the self-concept as well as some of its specific content. The essence of stereotyping is that large numbers of people are "telling" a person, directly or through mass media, who they think he is and what is expected of him. Stereotypes are obvious for classifications of people by sex, race, religion, and national origin, although we are not yet able to specify what effect stereotypes have on self-concepts for the members of all such groups.

There has been some research on the self-concept of women and blacks. A less favorable stereotype of "women in general" than of "men in general" has been confirmed by research with a variety of techniques and subject ages (see Wylie, 1968; Donelson, 1973a, b). Neither males nor females are particularly happy with sex-role pressures, however, and both groups see themselves as less masculine or feminine, respectively, than the cultural ideal held up them. Both males and females attribute more socially desirable descriptions to males than to females, and there are some suggestions that the bias against women is stronger in females than in males. The child labels himself as male or female sometimes as early as two years of age, and has a fairly accurate though not necessarily comprehensive knowledge about the content of sex-role stereotypes at least by the age of six (Kohlberg, 1966; and Chapter 21). The girl's unfavorable view of the female stereotype and her acceptance of it as personally relevant seem to increase rather steadily from about age eight (Lynn, 1959).

Even though girls tend to accept the less favored stereotype, and to go through a period during middle childhood in which feminine behavior is to some extent rejected (the tomboy stage that many girls pass through), girls do not necessarily have lower self-esteem than boys (Wylie, 1968; Donelson, 1973a). In fact, before they enter high school the self-esteem of girls is higher than that of boys; in high school, the self-esteem of boys increases to the level of that of girls. The higher self-esteem of girls, despite the culturally less favorable stereotype, is probably attributable to the greater ease with which they receive rewards and praise during this period in the school environment, which is more favorable to girls' predispositions and abilities at this age, than to boys'. For women of college age and older, the picture is ambiguous at best. While women describe themselves relatively consistently with the stereotype, evidence at hand does not support the view that they deprecate themselves as persons, have a negative rather than a positive self-concept, or have "no self-esteem."

However, it is certainly true that compared with men, women have lower self-esteem in that they consistently underestimate their abilities, have lower aspirations relative to their abilities, are more likely to assume personal responsibility for their failures relative to their successes, and generally do not have the confidence and internal locus of self-definition that men do (Donelson, 1973a, b; Donelson & Gullahorn, 1973b; Gullahorn, 1973). (No known facts support the idea that such sex differences are inherent; the generalities describe the way things are now.)

The picture is not necessarily more rosy for the professional woman than for the housewife, although the career-minded college woman and the professional woman are likely to have greater ability than their comparable male colleagues and to have greater personal autonomy and self-definition than their female counterparts, both of which can stand them in good stead (Gullahorn, 1973).

One reason so many women can be as happy as they are while accepting the less favorable stereotype is that the social evaluations of what is desirable (and even mentally healthy!) are masculinized definitions. While knowing and accepting these definitions, the woman is nonetheless being what she has been told through the role system that she is supposed to be. Both girls and boys strive to be competent in being what they think they are supposed to be (Kohlberg, 1966; Chapter 21), and the woman receives reinforcement from others for conforming to the traditional female role, just as the man is rewarded for conforming to the masculine role. However, some mental-health data suggest that women pay a large price for their conformity (Chapter 21).

There has been even less work about the effects of stereotypes on the self-concept of blacks, but the existing evidence is not encouraging. The effect of the negative stereotype and adoption of it as personally relevant seem more persistent and extreme for blacks than for females. Children have racial awareness as early as age two or three. At very young ages, black children selected a black doll rather than a white one when asked to select the one that "looks bad" *and* when asked to select the one that "looks like you" (Clark & Clark, 1958). At least in the past, children of both races preferred and identified with whites. Although self-concepts are influenced by socioeconomic status and residence areas, which vary between blacks as between whites, ". . . there still seems to be little doubt that the American Negro holds relatively negative self-valuations" (Dreger & Miller, 1968, p. 33).

However, again, for both blacks and women, to say that they have no self-esteem is unwarranted, though certainly their lives would be at least somewhat smoother if they did not have to contend with the stereotyped expectations applied to them. It has been suggested that the fundamental reason each can escape the complete self-negation and lack of esteem one would expect from the stereotypes is that in the very early years, during which a central core of self-esteem is established, the child is mainly exposed to the immediate family, in which he or she can be accepted even if black or female (Baughman, 1971, 1972; Bardwick, 1971; Donelson, 1973a). Although a person may know the stereotypes and react when they are made salient, the negative expectations that prevail outside the family are largely irrelevant in the day-to-day interactions within the family. The stereotypes later encountered in the outside world have their effect, but that effect occurs against a background of self-esteem and self-valuation developed in earlier years with supportive others.

Both women and blacks have had some protection for their self-esteem in that they can with some realistic basis see lack of success as a result of the social system rather than of their own inadequacies. Recent activities within the black movement and some developing ones in the women's movement provide mutual support for the members in fighting stereotypes and discovering personal realities. That each group has survived thus far as well as it has, with enough stamina and ability to formulate and support such movements, is testimony to the adaptiveness of the human organism in hostile environments, a facet of life that current psychology has not yet satisfactorily explored.

Continuing influences. Although there seems to be a strong core of consistency, perceptions of self do shift with new experiences from which a person can gain information about who he is and how he is seen by others. A person may see himself continually reflected in the reactions of others, and the reflected appraisals contribute to the "looking glass self."

An increase of self-esteem is typical of winners in political elections, and decreases of esteem typical of the losers (Ziller et al., 1969). In experimental situations, subjects have changed their concepts of themselves with respect to their masculinity or oral communication ability, for example, when given information from a supposed expert that their former views were inaccurate (see Gergen, 1971). Change is more likely when the other person providing information about self is seen as an expert about people generally, in the specific area of evaluation, or about oneself in particular. Change is also more likely if the other person is *personalistic;* that is, he is sincere, uncalculating, and attuned to the person himself as an individual. We are more responsive to the views of people who know us and whom we know we can trust to be honest.

Personality characteristics and self-definition also shift in the direction of occupational stereotypes (see Secord & Backman, 1964). For example, as medical training progressed, an increasing proportion of medical students reported that they felt more like doctors than like students in dealing with patients, and more like doctors when interacting with patients than when interacting with other people.

Some of the expectations and evaluations by others are attendant upon age, a variable whose effects have been clearly acknowledged only in older populations. Self-acceptance increases steadily from age twenty to the fifties, and then declines (Bloom, 1961). The increase is likely due to a person's having solved many problems until some stability of life has been achieved. Because of societal concepts about old age, aging presents acute problems of adjustment that understandably foster a lowered self-concept (Chapter 21).

Consistency of Self and Experience

There is continual fluid development of the self-concept with new and continuing experiences, but there is also a tendency to resist change and to avoid inconsistency between information and the view of self. The tendency to maintain the existing self-concept and seek experiences consistent with it helps to determine the situations we encounter, the specific people we seek out, and the way we respond to them. Perception and other cognitive processes are used to maintain consistency between self-concept and experience.

Social experience. We tend to be attracted to those people and social situations which provide confirming, usually positive information about ourselves and our views of the world (see Berscheid & Walster, 1969; Byrne, 1969; Newcomb, 1941). In *congruent situations,* we get reinforcement for being who we are and for thinking as we do. The perception of congruence is "easier" when it is realistic. Others are liked best when they not only are *perceived* as having congruent views about each other and about other matters, but when they actually *do* have congruent views. However, in the face of inconsistency with the views of important others or of minimal information, the perception of consistency between self and others may be attained by distortions. Misperceptions of other people's views tend to be in the direction of creating a greater correspondence between how we see ourselves and how we think others see us. Our preference is for other people to have views consistent with our own and views of us which are positive. We like best those who evaluate us positively, but the positive evaluation is much more effective in producing liking when it is congruent with our own evaluation.

What if views of self are not positive ones? Views of self do fluctuate with ongoing experiences, and some people have relatively persistently unfavorable feelings about themselves. Most of us are not under the impression that we are totally perfect in all aspects of our personality functioning and performance and desirability to others. When we do not have a positive view of self, will we like and choose association with those who have a more positive view of us than we ourselves do (positivity position)? Or will we seek out those who have a view consistent with our own even when that view is negative (consistency position)? Will we choose others who also seem to be low in status and acceptability, or those who seem to be more positive people? There is evidence both ways. Consistency as well as positivity is desirable. Positive responses from others and association with positive people are most desirable, but the preference is kept within bounds by the reality of what we know about ourselves (consistency) and by the anticipation of future outcomes.

When there is a good chance of rejection or failure in interacting with a desirable other person, low-self-esteem people choose to approach someone of lesser attractiveness than do high-self-esteem subjects (Kiesler & Baral, 1970; Murstein, 1972). This is a realistic choice, in that rejection by the more desirable other is felt to be likely. However, when people of low self-esteem can be convinced that they are accepted and positively valued, they are more responsive to the acceptance of others than are those of higher self-esteem. College women whose self-esteem had been lowered temporarily by experimental manipulation had a greater valuation of a male confederate who had asked them for a date than did those women whose esteem had been experimentally increased (Walster, 1965).

All in all, low-self-esteem people seem to have a strong need to have the acceptance and approval of others and a strong positive reaction to those they perceive as likely to meet the need. The problem is that they expect rejection and are distrustful of others who seem to have a positive view of them or are more desirable than they. "How can he possibly like me?" they ask themselves, and they require more clear-cut evidence of acceptance by the other (Jacobs, Berscheid, & Walster, 1971). Considering the natural ambiguity of social interactions, in which positive things are said because of social courtesy and ulterior motives, it is not unrealistic for the person of low self-esteem to be distrustful of others' apparent acceptance of him (they are not personalistic). If we consider the roots of self-concept in previous interpersonal interaction and reactions to the self-deprecatory behavior of low-self-esteem people, we can understand that they are likely to have experienced previous rejection and that they feel they will encounter it again. It is easy to see a self-perpetuating pattern.

The pressure to face reality is reflected, too, in the fact that people prefer other people's evaluations of them to be low and consistent with their own when inconsistency or inaccuracy can lead to the later negative outcome of having the accepted falsity revealed. When subjects were induced to evaluate negatively their ability on a task of "social sensitivity," they preferred others who negatively evaluated them *if* they thought the experimenter would later announce correct answers in front of the group (Jones & Pine, 1968). Even though it may be inconsistent, people want positive reactions from others when they can get away with it, but are willing to forego immediate but inaccurate approval to avoid loss of face at a later time.

Mechanisms for maintaining consistency. When we are given information, often negative information, that differs from our view of self, many coping mechanisms are available to help maintain consistency, and they are used increasingly as the extent of the discrepancy increases. People may fail to believe a negative evaluation, distort it in a favorable manner, or discredit, dislike, or avoid another person who makes the unfavorable evaluation (Edlow & Kiesler, 1966; Harvey, Kelley, & Shapiro, 1957). People also selectively recall information given by others to reduce the amount of discrepancy from their own view or to reduce the unfavorability of information given by others. Similar principles operate in responding to others; for example, we remember more about people we like than about people we dislike (McLaughlin, 1971), and we have relatively more dislike for people with inconsistent traits (when we are aware of the inconsistency) than for those with only consistent ones (Hendrick, 1972).

Situational factors and personal habits in dealing with the inconsistent or unfavorable information determine which kinds of coping responses, if any, occur. For example, subjects took a variety of tests and were later given fictitious ratings supposedly made by a graduate student whose ability to interpret personality tests was being evaluated (Hamilton, 1969). After examining the graduate student's reports, which rated the subjects more unfavorably than they had rated themselves by varying amounts, the subjects again rated themselves, evaluated the graduate student's competence, and reported what they recalled of the graduate student's evaluations. Change of own view (conformity), rejection of the graduate student, and devaluation of the testing instrument all increased as discrepancy of the false information from self-view increased. However, subjects differed in the kind of response to inconsistency they used, and the amount of under-recall of the discrepancy varied with the subjects' need to appear socially desirable. A week after receiving the evaluations, the subjects' primary response mode was under-recall of the amount of discrepancy. Apparently, under-recall of the discrepancy becomes easier with time, and thus the need for other coping responses decreases.

Other evidence also indicates that subjects' self-esteem and amount of consistency influence reactions to discrepant information. Subjects who have inconsistent views of themselves are more susceptible to the influence of others than are those who are highly consistent (Gergen & Morse, 1967). There is generally a greater resistance in accepting unfavorable information when the information is about oneself than when it is about others. However, high-self-esteem people, and males in general, protect themselves against unfavorable evaluations better than those with less self-esteem and females in general (Eagly, 1967; Eagly & Whitehead, 1972). They resist negative (false) information and accept positive (false) information more than do subjects of low self-esteem, a reaction which does not occur when the same information is presented as being about someone else rather than about the subject himself (Eagly & Whitehead, 1972). If we have a consistent and positive view of self, rejection of discrepant or unfavorable information may be realistic, but it may also be unrealistic and result from or necessitate defensiveness.

Self-Perception and Adjustment

What do we mean when we speak of Jane as being well adjusted and of Frank as being poorly adjusted? If we were to compare Jane with Frank, we might find that Jane seems to be "comfortable" with herself, with others, and with her environment, while Frank expresses dissatisfaction with his performance, his accomplishments, and his relationship to the world around him. Jane disapproves of some things about herself, but she nonetheless accepts herself, the good and the bad. Although we all have moments of dissatisfaction—we perform poorly on an examination, or we behave awkwardly in a social situation—we can consider ourselves well adjusted if, in general, we see our actions, accomplishments, and relationships as coming relatively close to what we want them to be. In other words, our self-concept does not deviate too far or too often from our ideal self; and we are not so severely threatened by perceived deviations that we have to deny or distort our failures. We are self-accepting, but not complacent.

One of the benefits of adjustment and a favorable view of self is meaningful relationships with other people. Rogers and other theorists have maintained that a person who accepts himself will accept others (Rogers, 1951; Adler, 1926; Horney, 1939; Fromm, 1947). In fact, Rogers attributes behavior which is interpersonally destructive to lack of self-acceptance. Empirically, there is typically a positive correlation between acceptance of self and of others (Omwake, 1954; Suinn, 1961; Medinnus & Curtis, 1963).

Another benefit of adjustment is academic achievement. A variety of evidence with subjects from different age groups and ability ranges demonstrates that achievement is related to adjustment and view of self (see

Hamachek, 1971). Underachievers—children and college students who do not achieve academically as well as their ability suggests that they should—are generally less well adjusted, have relatively negative self-concepts, see themseves as less adequate and less acceptable to others, and feel more criticized, rejected, and isolated than do students of equal ability who are not underachievers. The association between positive self-view and achievement, and between negative self-view and underachievement, can begin as early as kindergarten, and is generally stronger for boys than for girls, perhaps because males experience greater cultural pressure for success than do females.

Self-view as a student, like self-view in general, is responsive to the specific views of significant other people. An extensive study of the academic performance of about 800 college freshmen illustrates some of the complexities of self-perceptions and the continuing influence of parents (Wyer, 1965). Parents as well as students served as subjects. Overall, there was a general tendency for academic effectiveness (measured by first-term grades relative to aptitude scores) to be related to self-acceptance (measured as the difference between the actual and the ideal self), and to mothers' and fathers' acceptance of their sons or daughters. And the more agreement there was between the parents about the child, the more academically effective the child was. However, there was an important qualification in these trends: acceptance by the mother was not significantly related to the academic effectiveness of female students. The sex differences with respect to mothers' acceptance may indicate that college daughters did not consider the mother to be a significant other in the academic area. Another explanation may be that mothers encourage sons in behavior related to academic pursuits and accept them contingent upon academic achievement; in contrast, mothers may give their daughters neither positive nor negative reinforcement for academic effectiveness, or inconsistent reinforcement (compare with sex differences in achievement motivation, Chapter 10).

Which comes first, self-acceptance and adjustment, or academic effectiveness? A change in one facilitates a change in the other, positively or negatively. In experimental situations, subjects who think they are failing tend to stop trying, and success tends to increase confidence, effort, and the likelihood of future successes. However, the problem is complicated for people of low self-esteem. Subjects certain of their low esteem relative to a given task did not show improvement in later performance after a success—they avoided continued success (Marecek & Mettee, 1972). Oddly, however, they accepted the success if they saw it as due to luck rather than to their own abilities, and they improved after the success attributed to luck. Believing in failure may guarantee failure, a self-fulfilling prophecy.

More than a positive self-concept is necessary for achievement, of course, and not all students see academic achievement as important in their view of self. Nonacademic performance (in arts or athletics, for example) may be more salient for them, and therefore a support for a positive view of self. However, the effect of self-views on performance in areas relevant to the self-concept cannot be denied.

Defensiveness. Acknowledging and dealing with all possible discrepancies and all available negative information with which we are confronted would probably be intolerable. However, the self-concept must include some relatively negative material if we are responsive to reality without distortion—if we recognize our internal and external worlds for what they are. For most people, an extremely high opinion of self is an unrealistic one, purchased with repression and denial that block acknowledgment of the negative aspects of self (Chorodokoff, 1964). The self-acceptance of mature adjustment implies recognition of the bad with the good. An extremely favorable view of self, and a very low discrepancy between self-concept and ideal self, may be as indicative of maladjustment as are unfavorable views and a very large discrepancy.

Students who perceive little difference between self-concept and ideal self tend to be high on measures of defensiveness, unwillingness to admit to undesirable traits, and denial of traits and feelings that are adverse (Block & Thomas, 1955). They seem to emphasize social appropriateness over interpersonal intimacy and wish to control expressiveness and spontaneity while being accepted and popular. On the other hand, an overabundance of negative comments and feelings about self, resulting in a high self-ideal discrepancy, could reflect an extreme use of sensitizing defenses and overavoidance of repressive defenses. Students with very high discrepancy scores have been shown to have tendencies to project and to feel that others are against them. They seem to be confused, overly introspective, and despairing; they have unrealistic and contradictory aspirations, and are seeking a feeling of personal integrity. In either case, there is distortion and denial of realistic aspects of self. In contrast, the students with moderate discrepancies are more reasonable and accepting of themselves. They have problems but do not despair nor deny. They want more of what they positively value and less of what they negatively value. They accept the ambiguity of emotions and have comfortable relations with other people. They see themselves realistically and accept reality.

Thus, realistically oriented people are able to recognize and admit their own shortcomings, but they are also aware of their strengths. When we accept ourselves, we need not deny either the negative or the positive.

The Individiual and His Self-Concept

Is a person's self-concept nothing but a "looking glass self" in which other people's views are reflected as one's own? Is it a concept dictated by others? Not necessarily. Certainly the self-concept is derived in interaction with other people, and their views of us and our feelings of success and failure with them are leading contributors to the self-concept. However, self-concept can be individualized and personally derived, and subject to some change at a person's own initiative.

The individual himself spontaneously operates on the information he has and generates novel concepts based on it (Kohlberg, 1966; Chapter 21). A person's view of himself is not likely to be just a collection of the views, expectations, and desires of others, although for some people this is almost the case. Nor are we totally dependent on others for information. We can observe our own behavior, even if it is not reacted to specifically and explicitly by others. We have the opportunity to notice our own behavior and—just as others do—to form opinions about the kind of person who behaves in such a way (Bem, 1966, 1968). Similarly, we can observe in ourselves feelings and thoughts not always easily accessible to others, and we can derive views about self based on these thoughts and feelings. Both internal and external responses can function as stimuli for extending self-knowledge and evolving self-definition. We have access to more of this information than does any other one person. Whether or not we use it is another question.

Concepts about self may guide behavior, and recognition of behavior may stimulate us to formulate new aspects of the concept or to revise old ones. A change in either self-concept or behavior may effect a change in the other. Successful psychotherapy is usually seen as changing behavior by changing internal conditions, including self-concept. Changing behavior can also lead to a change of self-concept. Marked changes in a person's privately held self-concept can occur as a result of the public presentation of a very positive image of self (Gergen, 1965). Thus, behavior therapy programs intended only to change behavior may produce a change in self-view.

Neither conventional psychotherapy nor behavior modification is always necessary for a person to modify his own behavior and self-view. We have many avenues for attaining self-knowledge and changing ourselves that do not necessarily involve others, though other people can be invaluable assistants. While we may all want to extend our knowledge and change some aspect of our self or behavior to attain greater consistency or favorability, we need also to confront the possibility of limitations in our self-view.

Knowledge of self is likely to be incomplete. We probably are many things we do not realize. There is information available to us in our observable behavior and in our thoughts, feelings, and fantasies that we do not always detect and integrate into self-view, and we may be unnecessarily complacent in accepting undesirable or inconsistent behaviors and feelings. Failure to attain complete self-knowledge and desirable change may be due to defensiveness, acknowledged fear, neglect, or simply the complexity of what any person is. There may be inherent limitations on complete self-knowledge, and, as long as we live with other people, on the extent to which we can be free of their views. We may also be inherently limited in self-knowledge and dependent upon other people for information about ourselves simply because so much of what we are is other people and can be known best by them. A paradox. We cannot see ourselves from their perspectives. Part of what we are is how we affect others. Their "I" can react to us as our own "I" cannot. Their eyes can see ours, while our own eyes cannot see themselves. They can see our body, as well as observe our behavior, better than we ourselves can, but maturity demands a clear perception of external and internal self.

BODY AND SELF

Concepts of the body both help to form the total perception of self and are formed by it. The body separates us from the rest of the world while being the instrument with which we interact with the world. Through actions and concepts of body, the self and the tangible environment interact. The effectiveness of that interaction depends partly on the favorability of self-view and partly on the extent to which we have a sense of separateness from the environment.

Awareness of our body as our own and as an entity apart from others is a critical ingredient in the initiation of self-awareness and in the continuing development of components of self-concept (Schilder, 1950). The body is part *of* the perceptual field of physical objects but apart *from* them, just as a person is part of a social field of other selves, but is apart from them. Without the sense of body as separate from other objects, without the sense of self as internally defined apart from other selves, there is no comfortable self; there is only others-as-self, or no self.

Body Types

Physical makeup is related to personality. It influences self-concept, and affects other people's assessment of us. We all have images of our bodies and an ideal of what our bodies should look like, and deviation of the actual from the ideal can be quite unpleasant.

Behaviors and traits associated with body types, together with the general cultural approval of certain physical characteristics, can affect the discrepancy between self-concept and ideal self and can induce behavior inconsistent with our internal feelings. For instance, a woman who is nervous and miserable because she is greatly overweight may feel compelled to act the part of the easygoing clown because of others' expectation that a fat person be jolly. Or the short, frail young man may incorporate into his ideal self the cultural ideal of the male as tall, strong, and athletic. People who have trouble accepting their bodies often have trouble accepting their selves (e.g., Secord & Jourard, 1953).

Social reactions to body types are extremely consistent across races, social classes, and age groups. Before they are old enough to know or pronounce the labels for body types, young children report general evaluations of body types consistent with the assessment rendered across our culture (See McCandless, 1970; Hamachek, 1971). *Mesomorphic* characteristics (athletic, muscular, hard, rectangular) consistently elicit positive evaluations, e.g., success, popular, self-sufficient. *Endomorphic* characteristics (soft, flabby, spherical) consistently evoke the most negative set of expectations. The *ectomorph* (thin, lightly muscled, fragile, linear) tends to be seen as more socially acceptable than the endomorph but vulnerable and self-punishing.

Children as young as six describe mesomorphic silhouettes as aggressive, outgoing, active, having leadership skills, while they see the endomorphic silhouettes as socially offensive and delinquent; the ectomorphic silhouettes are considered by children to be nervous and shy (Staffieri, 1967). From a group of silhouettes of the major body types, children are able to pick with considerable accuracy the one they themselves most resemble, and they pick a mesomorphic silhouette as the one they would most like to resemble. They know what they look like, and they apparently know which body type elicits the most positive reactions in others.

In turn, self-views consistent with cultural stereotypes of the body, and with ideals, tend to develop. Endomorphic children are less popular in school, know that they are unpopular, and tend to reject their body image. High self-esteem and general self-confidence tend to be associated with the ideal mesomorphic physique, in both males and females. More males than females, however, tend to be mesomorphic (Bardwick, 1971).

There are also cultural ideals for other aspects of physical attractiveness. For females, the ideal body is described in terms of the proportions of bust, waist, and hips (35-24-35 inches, respectively). Girls like their own dimensions if they coincide with the ideal, but dislike them increasingly as they deviate from the ideal. Males want to be tall, and large in the shoulders and chest. Cultural expectations for male physique are more clear and firm than for female bodies. In turn, psychological correlates of body build and physical development tend to be more variable in girls than in boys. Perhaps this reflects the fact that girls are judged in terms of how they *look* and boys in terms of how they *perform* (Hamachek, 1971). Thus, girls can make greater use of external trappings of cosmetics, dress, and padding, and may compensate for big hips by having a pretty face.

Body Types and Psychological Traits

Why is there a culturally agreed-upon response to the major body types and one so salient that young children have already started responding to it in evaluating themselves? It is significant that body physiques are associated not only with *view* of self, but with *actual* personality traits, temperament, and behavior patterns which correspond somewhat to the kinds of expectations held (Sheldon, 1954; Hall & Lindzey, 1970; McCandless, 1970). Roughly speaking, mesomorphs tend to be socially desirable, pleasant, successful extraverts; ectomorphs tend to be aloof and worrying introverts; and endomorphs tend to be selfish, pleasure-seeking, and somewhat antisocial. Preschooler mesomorphs were rated by their teachers as dominating, assertive, energetic, open to expression, and fearless; ectomorphs were considered aloof, cautious, hesitating, tense, and somber (Walker, 1962).

Are the relations among body types, stereotypes, self-image, and personality traits inherent in our biology? Or are they just a result of arbitrary cultural assumptions? Stated so strongly, either alternative is an oversimplification. The associations between body type and psychological characteristics may result partially from the operation of biological factors, so that body characteristics might tend to occur along with psychological attributes as consequences of the same factor. The relationship is then noted and elaborated in socially shared stereotypes.

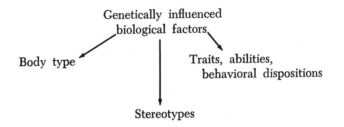

On the other hand, environmental influences including stereotypes, rather than a biological source, may tend to produce behavioral tendencies and shape the body type simultaneously.

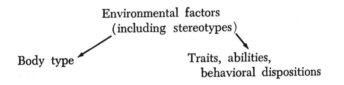

It is likely, however, that the relationships among body types, traits, self-views, and stereotypes are due to complex interactions of genetic and environmental factors.

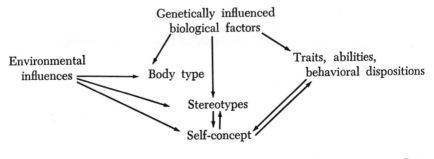

To different degrees, genetic factors predispose the development of some traits and behaviors in a particular environment, with implications for many of the experiences of the person in that environment (Chapter 14). Inherent associations between body types and at least some traits may be responsible for the origin of social stereotypes, which then support the association, intensify it, and elaborate around the central core of biological influence. As with other stereotypes, it is unlikely that the stereotypes about body types developed with *no* basis in reality, but it is equally unlikely that in current form they are clear mirrors of reality and thus reflect how things *must* be. For instance, the frail ectomorph may not have a strong predisposition for athletic activities or extraverted behavior. Because of the way he is inclined to be *and* because of the expectations held for him, he is not likely to experience athletic success nor the success of being outgoing and assertive in interpersonal relationships. In an environment in which being an athlete and an assertive extravert are socially desirable, he may accumulate negative experiences and miss out on positive ones. The mesomorph, on the other hand, may have an inherent predisposition toward the development of traits which the environment applauds.

The ectomorph and the mesomorph thus live in very different social worlds, shaped by some responsiveness to the individual's own predispositions and the stereotyped expectations. The expectations of others are further intensified by the self-fulfilling prophecy: Because we respond to what others tell us we are, we expect that of ourselves and become that.

Body-Object Relations

Perceptions of the body are an appropriate focal point for the general study of a person's view of himself in relation to external objects (Freud, 1962; Piaget, 1952; Witkin, 1965). Specifically, perceptions of the body as a physical entity are a correlate of cognitive maturity. The mature, healthy adult experiences himself as separate from the rest of the world. He is an object apart from other objects, just as he is a self apart from other selves. This sense of separateness implies or requires a sense of body barrier or definiteness of the body boundary.

A sense of separateness has been measured in experimental situations in which the subject is placed in a tilted chair and is asked to adjust a rod to the position of his own body as well as to the apparent vertical (Wapner & Werner, 1965, Figure 12–1). The sense of body-object separateness is inferred from the subject's degree of exaggeration of difference between himself and the vertical; the disparity between apparent vertical and apparent body position increases with age. The greater the exaggeration and disparity, the greater the body articulation and sense of separateness.

Body articulation is seen by Witkin (1969; Witkin et al., 1954, 1962; Wapner & Werner, 1965) in the broad context of psychological differen-

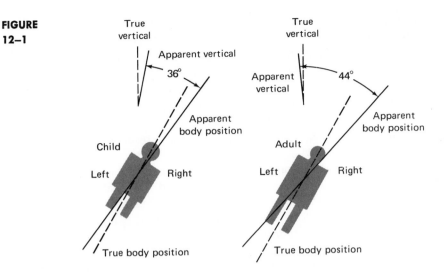

FIGURE 12-1

True vertical

Apparent vertical

36°

Apparent body position

Child

Left   Right

True body position

True vertical

Apparent vertical

44°

Apparent body position

Adult

Left   Right

True body position

30° right body tilt

Diagrammatic Representation of Apparent Vertical and Apparent Body Position for 30° Right Body Tilt in Child and Adult.

Source: Wapner, S., & Werner, H. An experimental approach to body perception from the organismic-developmental point of view. In Wapner, S., & Werner, H. (Eds.), *The body percept.* New York: Random House, 1965.

tiation (Chapter 11). Degree of inner psychological structure is assumed to be correlated with body articulation and with field independence. Ability to separate body from field is unlikely if the bounded body is only an undifferentiated blob, an empty jar. Generally, people with articulated body concepts are more field-independent and analytical in their cognitive style. The body concept guides and organizes perception and is inferred from perception.

A chief measure of body boundary is a "barrier score" derived from inkblot responses that emphasize protective, containing, decorative, or covering functions such as a cave with rock walls, a woman in a costume, or a vase (Fisher & Cleveland, 1965, 1968; Fisher, 1970). People with definite boundaries, shown on projective tests, report more sensations from the boundary regions of the body (skin and muscles), while those with vague boundaries report more internal sensations (stomach and heart) than external ones.

Definiteness of body boundaries appears correlated with cognitive development. It is less firm in schizophrenics and in children, as well as in normal adults under a drug such as LSD, than it is in adults under non-drug conditions (Wapner & Werner, 1965). The association of a firm body boundary with maturity is supported by the fact that the more definite the boundary, the greater the independence and individuality and the greater the likelihood of autonomous action, high achievement motivation, persistent striving toward goals, effective communication with others, and strong interpersonal relations (Fisher & Cleveland, 1968).

It has been suggested that a person with clear-cut boundaries has learned during socialization to focus attention on musculature because of its importance in voluntary and active cooperation with the outside world. It is also true, however, that those with firm boundaries are more responsive physiologically in the external regions of the body rather than the internal. Whether the attentiveness or the responsiveness comes first is impossible to say.

Psychological development is accompanied by an awareness of body and self as separate from the rest of the world. The mature adult accepts himself and feels himself to be a distinct entity separate from the environment. However, man is constantly immersed in a field of other entities, linked to them by relationships that often blur distinctions. And, as noted later, there is reason to suppose that losing one's sense of self can be a concomitant of being intrinsically motivated, a state generally assumed likely with the maturity of self-actualization.

CAUSALITY AND CONTROL

The individual exists in a matrix of other people, objects, and events, and many of his relationships with other people and things in the environment are viewed in terms of causation and control. So strong is the tendency to think in terms of causation that causative motivation has been found to be easily attributed to inanimate objects (Michotte, 1954; Heider & Simmel, 1944). Instead of reporting the observable contingencies and saying, "The big square moved until it touched the little one and then the little one moved," subjects say, "The big square chased the little one and made it move." More generally, we expect answers to our questions "Why . . . ?" to be answered by statements of causation. "Why does man wage war?" "Because he is greedy and aggressive." "Why does John avoid Sally?" "Because she makes him feel uncomfortable." Similarly, we are quick to assign responsibility, particularly when things go wrong. "Who is responsible for this mess?" "It's all his fault. He caused the confusion." Much informal social discussion at home and at work is concerned with attempts to infer relative power so that one may supposedly know who made whom feel and do what.

Development of the concept of causation is not well understood (compare Piaget, 1930; de Charms, 1968). Certainly a child learns to see contingencies between his behavior and what happens to him, and he learns how to produce some of the effects he wants by manipulating his own behavior. He also comes to recognize that sometimes stronger and more powerful agents than he act so that he cannot get what he wants. He makes inferences about the internal or external locus of causality for his own and others' behavior, and he develops general expectations about his own causative powers compared to those of others. Whether we generally view ourselves as the cause of what we do and of what happens to us, or as objects subject to the control of outside forces, has important implications for our behavior and for our view of ourselves and what we attain in the world.

Generalized Expectancies

Rotter has maintained that on the basis of prior experience, we develop "a generalized attitude, belief, or expectancy regarding the nature of the causal relationships between one's own behavior and its consequences" (1966, p. 2). A history of experiences in which outcomes are seen to be outside one's own personal control because they are not contingent upon one's own behavior, but are subject to chance or the whims of others, can build into a generalized expectancy of *external control*. The opposite—a history of experiences in which outcomes are perceived as the result of one's own behavior—can develop into a generalized expectancy of *internal control*. If a person believes in external control, then what happens after he responds has little effect on his expectations about the future, or on his behavior, for one cannot predict outcomes anyway: "I got a reward once, but it was just an accident." Thus, reinforcement has little effect when the situation in which it occurs is seen as a chance one of external control. If a person believes in internal control, a reward for his behavior strengthens the expectancy of future rewards for similar behavior and increases the likelihood of the behavior. The effect of reinforcement is mediated by the person's assumptions about whether there are stable rules or contingencies in the world such that his own behavior makes a difference in what happens to him (see Rotter, 1966; Lefcourt, 1966, 1972).

The internal-external scale. The Internal-External Scale (I-E) measures individual differences in beliefs, not preferences, about the nature of the world and expectations about how reinforcement is controlled. Subjects who believe in internal control see life as a game of *skill* and depict themselves as goal-directed and striving to overcome hardships. In contrast, subjects who believe in external control see life as a matter of *chance* and portray themselves as suffering, anxious, and less concerned with achievement itself than with their affective responses to failure. Those who score as internal are more vigilant and observant; they attempt to gain information about the world and take action to change it; they assume responsibility for what happens to them, even when blaming environmental distractions would be realistic; and they perform better when they can attain knowledge of the correctness of their response by self-discovery, rather than being told by someone else (see Rotter, 1966; Lefcourt, 1966, 1972; Sarason & Smith, 1971; Phares, Wilson, & Klyver, 1971; Baron & Ganz, 1971).

Self-reliance is implicit in the initiative of people who perceive reinforcement as contingent upon their own behavior. But, although initiative and self-reliance may often lead to positive outcomes, they can also lead a person to overlook the possibility of help from outside sources. For instance, in an experimental situation, subjects who believed in internal control preferred to make their own decisions in games, even though their partners were presented as being more successful on the tasks than they (Julian & Katz, 1968). This was true for a chance task of predicting the next number drawn out of a hat and for a skill task of judging which of two words were synonyms or antonyms. Why these subjects preferred self-determining strategies even under chance conditions is not clear. Although the I-E scale has not been found to be related to intelligence, subjects who favor internal control may have strong feelings of competence and so rely on themselves even though it would be more effective to look to others for guidance.

Class and race differences. Groups whose control over the environment is small because of class or race tend to expect external control more than those with greater power. Within racial groups, class adds a second handicap to create the greatest expectancy of external rather than internal control (Lefcourt, 1966). Black prison inmates had greater expectancy of external control than did white inmates; also, blacks had lower levels of aspiration on experimental tasks (Lefcourt & Ladwing, 1965). Blacks reported greater expectancy that one cannot control his fate (powerlessness) and greater expectancy that socially unapproved behavior is required to achieve goals (normlessness). The lack of motivation that others often attribute to lower classes and to blacks may, then, be due to disbelief in the effectiveness of effort, a disbelief derived in previous interactions with those who in fact have controlled reinforcement.

Learned helplessness. The development of a generalized expectation of external control may be a defensive explanation of one's own failures, or it may be a realistic view of the way things are. The feeling that others control our actions and outcomes can develop because we *are* relatively helpless, as in the case of social groups that do exercise little power. This can also occur when parents respond to an infant as an object they own rather than as an independent person, when teachers ignore the requests of students, when management simply issues orders rather than listening to workers, or when a friend assumes without asking that a person is going to do something or go somewhere because the friend wants him to. Repeated experience in external control situations can lead people to assume that they cannot control what happens to them in any situation, at any point in life.

Dogs that could not escape electric shock failed to learn to avoid shock when the contingencies were changed so that avoidance was possible—they had learned to be helpless (Seligmen, Maier, & Solomon, 1969). Similar results occur with humans who "give up" and do not try because they feel that they have no control when they do (Thorton & Jacobs, 1971). This is not to say that the reality of the situation in which a person finds himself is not without influence over his behavior. However, in relatively unstructured situations, where the amount of a person's own control is ambiguous—a situation that is common in real life—generalized expectancies are likely to play an important role in the inferences a person makes about the source of causation (Feather, 1967). Those who have had extensive experience in not having internal control see themselves as victims when they need not be. Victims of their previous noncontingent environment, they become victims of their perceptions of themselves as helpless beings when the "rules of the game" have changed and their perceptions are no longer true.

Personal Causation

De Charms (1968) has suggested an approach to motivation which maintains that human beings like to see themselves as causes. Behavior we feel to be freely chosen is attractive in its own right, regardless of the specific goal that may be attained by the behavior:

> Man's primary motivational propensity is to be effective in producing changes in his environment. Man strives to be a causal agent, to be the primary locus of causation for, or the origin of, his behavior; he strives for personal causation. . . . A man is not a stone, for he is a direct source of energy; nor is he a machine, for the direction of the behavior resulting from his energy comes entirely from within him. Rather, man is the origin of his behavior (de Charms, 1968, pp. 269, 271).

Whenever a person experiences himself to be the locus of causality for his own behavior, he is *intrinsically motivated;* if he perceives the locus of causality to be outside himself, he is *extrinsically motivated.* In one case, he is the origin; in the other, he is a pawn. A person feels more like an origin under some circumstances and more like a pawn in others. An origin attributes changes in his environment to himself and to his personal behavior. A pawn feels that he and his behavior are determined by forces residing in others or in the physical environment; he feels powerless and ineffective.

When a person is in an extrinsically motivated state, he is a pawn who does what he does only in order to gain an externally mediated reward (Koch, 1956). In the extreme, such a person may feel depressed, drowsy, guilty about purposelessness, and generally ineffective and separated from his values. He is highly aware of himself and the awareness is not pleasant: "My self-image constricts into a small, desiccated thing" (Koch, 1956, p. 67). When a person is in an intrinsically motivated state, he feels a total involvement of self and a lack of anxiety or threat within a free state of commitment not confined by self-consciousness. Paradoxically, it is when one is most unaware of himself that self is showing itself to best advantage. The self-image diminishes in importance and as a separate entity; the distinction between self and the task at hand becomes irrelevant. In some sense, you *are* the task. The arrow shoots itself; the term paper writes itself. One is most an origin when his sense of separateness is most irrelevant, relaxed, or obliterated. Satisfaction is derived from the feeling of personal causation, whether recognized by anyone else or not. Confidence accompanies loss of self-consciousness.

To carry this loss of self too far is to run the risk of getting completely lost. But without a diminution of self-awareness, we are victims of external reward systems and can only work and live in ways calculated to reduce tension, anxiety, and guilt and to obtain rewards doled out by those whom we have pleased. To be free to interact with the environment without fear of becoming engulfed by it, a person must develop the sense of self as a coherent entity separate from the environment and from the expectations of others. With such a self, one may effectively lose it. The distinction between self and environment, self and others, becomes meaningless or nonexistent.

SUMMARY

The study of self, perhaps more than any other area of personality research, is a study of paradoxes and unresolved issues. Part of who we are is other people. Self is all that is ours, but it results from and guides our interactions with other people.

Although a negative self-concept indicates maladjustment, an extremely positive self-concept may be attained and maintained by defensive denial of reality. Those who are optimally adjusted have a positive view of self but at the same time are willing to be self-critical; because of acceptance of self, there is no need to deny the negative, and freedom to accept self provides freedom to accept others.

Self-awareness, acceptance, and a feeling of being generally in control of oneself are characteristics of the mature, healthy adult, and the perception of body as articulated within the environment is a concomitant of these characteristics. A sense of separateness and of body boundaries is essential to the awareness of self as apart from and a part of the external world.

While defining our place in the environment, we become concerned about causation and control and develop generalized expectancies about the degree to which what happens to us occurs because of our own behavior. A perception of external control can develop from defensive denial of our own inefficiency, or from a realistic appraisal of fact, as seen in the examples of racial or social groups of low social power. But learned helplessness can prevent us from seeing that a current situation does have reliable contingencies so that our own behavior can now make a difference in what happens to us.

A perception of control as internal can lead to gaining information and taking action, but it can also be an unjustified denial of the fact that we are not always in direct control of what happens to us and a stubborn insistence on self-reliance when that is inappropriate.

Perhaps the paradox of self and the relation of self and others indicates that man has not yet come to grips with what it means to have self, to be self, to be related to self and environment. Or perhaps it indicates that while a person is an individual, unique and separate, he is also a member of a social community. One cannot easily separate the figure of individuality from the ground of other people. To do so implies that one is a threatened pawn rather than a secure origin.

13

perception of others

In Chapter 12, we were concerned with the perceptions people have of themselves. Here, we will look at a closely related set of phenomena—the perceptions people have of others. One person's perceptions of another person can often be as revealing of the attitudes and values of the viewer as they are instructive about the person being perceived. The perception of other people is complicated, compared to the perception of nonhuman objects, in that in perceiving another person we are making inferences about events or characteristics which are inside that person rather than responding only to what is directly observable. We attribute traits, feelings, and motivations to others. Thus, person perception involves going beyond the data immediately given in an attempt to obtain knowledge about the other person. In the process of going beyond the data, and even in selecting the data to pay attention to, our own theories, expectations, and needs strongly enter in. Part of what we see always comes out of our own heads. "A major task in life is to achieve increasing success in our perception of one another" (Allport, 1961, p. 522).

THE PERCEIVER: THE FRAMEWORK OF PERCEPTIONS

The form—and some of the content—of one's perceptions is determined by his *implicit personality theory,* the set of ideas and expectations a person uses in judging others (Bruner & Tagiuri, 1954; Cattell, 1955; Smith, 1966). Although we generally are only vaguely aware of the theory and do not attempt to test it systematically, it guides our judgment processes and interpersonal behavior; it influences what we look for, what sense we make out of what we find, and what we assume to be true without any obvious reason. Partly because of the nature of person perception, and partly because of implicit theories, we jump easily from the data about another person to an assumption of knowledge about him. Our theory may not be valid, but it gives us a conviction of knowing what a person is. Instead of recognizing and admitting that we see only a strong jaw and piercing eyes, we are convinced that we see a ruthless person. "We do not normally separate the facts we have observed about a person from the inferences we make from the facts. They are interwoven and the result of the interweaving is, for us, what the person *is*" (Smith, 1966, p. 42).

Personal construct systems may be assessed by the Role Construct Repertory Test, or Rep Test (Bonarious, 1965; Bieri, 1966). In this test the subject lists people he knows who fit such roles as mother, liked teacher, disliked neighbor, father, and boss. The subject then indicates which two roles are alike in some way, and different in some way from a third role. For instance, mother and boss may be alike in that they are tense, and they may both differ from father, who is easygoing. Tense-easygoing, therefore, is a functional personal construct for the subject. Another procedure, which illustrates the rationale of the theory, is to ask subjects for descriptions of other people and to note the dimensions they use (Sarbin, 1954; Hastorf, Richardson & Dornbusch, 1958). The examiner observes the ways in which people describe other people, in order to assess their personal constructs. Free response descriptions can be analyzed to determine the trait dimensions that are highly related to the viewer's life dimensions that do not emerge from group data (Rosenberg & Jones, 1972).

A person's questions about others also reveal important personal constructs. People tend to ask for some kinds of information rather than others and to organize their judgments along dimensions that serve to integrate specific judgments and to generate others. When the viewer receives information relevant to a dominant construct, this information strengthens the impression; if the information is not relevant, the impression is vague (Secord & Backman, 1964). The mother who asks her daughter whether the daughter's suitor is rich will not feel that she knows him if she does not get that information. Once she knows the young man's economic value, she will be likely to assume that she also knows his status on other dimensions she considers to be related to wealth. She might assume that a man who is rich is also well mannered and well educated. This trait correlation—the technique of assuming the existence of other traits or conditions based on the knowledge of one trait—greatly influences our perceptions of others.

Trait Correlation

No doubt most people, given some information about one trait, go on to make conclusions about other traits, even if these conclusions are not justified by available data. Given information about psychological traits, such as generosity and warmth, some people will confidently make assumptions about a person's physical appearance. These assumptions about how traits are related to each other serve to regularize reality and to clarify and define our impressions of another person. If we know that a person is sociable, we are likely to think of him as warm and unlikely to assume that he is humorless and irritable. (This is sometimes called a logical error.) In fact, we may resist acknowledging traits we consider to be inconsistent with the impression we have formed.

Are some traits more likely than others to influence our general impression of a person? Solomon Asch (1946) found the warm-cold dimension to be central in providing an organization for the total impression. For example, a person described by a list with the word "warm" in it was described by subjects as generous, happy, good-natured, humorous, and humane. Given the *same* list with "cold" instead of "warm" in it, subjects described the person as ungenerous, unhappy, irritable, humorless, and ruthless. Asch maintained that any one trait changes the meaning of other traits with which it occurs; impressions are integrated wholes, Gestalts, which cannot be understood as simply the sum of separate traits.

Not all psychologists agree that the meaning of one trait changes the meaning of other traits, but they do agree that traits seem to "go together" along such broad dimensions as good-bad, hard-soft, warm-cold. For example, someone who is considered reliable, honest, helpful, sincere, and sociable (good), is unlikely to be considered dishonest, unsociable, humorless, or irresponsible (bad) (Rosenberg, Nelson, & Vivekananthan, 1968). Someone who is perceived as persistent, scientific, determined, and skillful (hard) is unlikely to be seen also as wasteful, unintelligent, frivolous, warm, good-natured, and humorous (soft).

Some conclusions about what traits are associated with what other traits may result from unwarranted and unchecked assumptions. However, a good many inferences may be accurate descriptions of reality. If we decide that John is kind because we have observed him to be considerate, we may be assuming that "good" traits go together; on the other hand, our judgment may also be a realistic description of John's traits (Peabody, 1967). The problem is that it is often difficult to distinguish between an assumption that happens to be correct and one that is based on *evidence* that it is correct. Unfortunately, we seldom examine our implicit personality theory for the accuracy of its assumptions. And the validity of our assumptions about what goes with what is a crucial element in accurate perception of others.

Cognitive Complexity

Some people judge others by rather simple concepts of what people are and do. Others indulge in much more complex analysis, and differentiate much more finely among various personality traits. The degree of cognitive complexity or differentiation can be measured by the number of constructs a person uses or the number of distinctions he makes in judging people (Bieri, 1955, 1968; Crockett, 1965). It may be assessed by the number of constructs used in free descriptions of a person, by similarity of ratings given in the Rep Test, or by other measures of cognitive differentiation.

Cognitively complex people typically have more sophisticated and accurate perceptions of others than do the cognitively simple (e.g., Bieri, 1955). Many people differ from others in gross and obvious ways, but often the differences are very subtle. The cognitively complex person is better able to detect such differences among people, including differences between himself and others, and is more able to integrate specific bits of information about a person into a coherent, whole impression. As a result, he can make more accurate predictions about another person. There are limits on this generalization, of course; as we shall see, people are not only different from each other, they are also similar to each other, and a person who reacts in a very complex way may be inaccurate because he is assuming more differences than are warranted (Wegner, 1971).

Cognitively complex people are more able than the less complex to detect, use, and integrate contradictory information into a coherent impression. In one study, for example, subject groups that scored high and low on cognitive complexity were asked to evaluate a person on the basis of tape-recorded descriptions (Mayo & Crockett, 1964). The first four descriptions presented positive traits (considerate, intelligent, humorous, well liked) or negative ones (immature, bad-tempered, dishonest, sarcastic). After recording their impressions, the two groups of subjects heard the opposite kind of trait emphasized, positive or negative. Both groups—those high and those low in cognitive complexity—changed their impressions after receiving the second set of descriptions. However, the low-complexity subjects showed a *recency effect:* Their final impression was disproportionately influenced by the description they heard last. The subjects higher in cognitive complexity integrated the two kinds of information, using both the positive and negative traits equally in forming their impression. It is not clear whether the more complex subjects were less bothered by the inconsistency between the positive and negative traits, whether they were better able to resolve the inconsistency, or whether they were better able to accept and tolerate it as a natural consequence of responding to people as the complex, sometimes contradictory beings that they are.

Subjects low in cognitive complexity are likely to categorize people into two groups—good and bad, or desirable and undesirable—while the cognitively complex subjects tend to avoid narrow judgment based on such absolutes (Campbell, 1960; Scott, 1963). Cognitive complexity, with this tendency to avoid absolutes and the willingness to attempt to reconcile contradictory information, seems to depend upon interaction between an individual's existing cognitive organization and his experiences with events and people.

Experience

There is some reason to suspect that the degree of cognitive complexity a person exhibits may be relatively the same in many different general judgment situations on different matters (Bieri, 1968). However, others things being equal, differences in cognitive complexity are to be expected because some matters are more important and better known to some people than to others. If a person is not interested in racing cars and never pays attention to them, the judgments and distinctions he makes about racing cars are likely to be very few and simple: "Some racing cars are faster than others." In the same way, our abilities to respond to other people vary depending on the importance we place on other people in general and on these people in particular, and on how often we interact with them (Crockett, 1965). Our ability to judge others complexly rather than simply is limited if we lack experience with others or are not interested in them. Without interested interaction, we will be unable to make accurate distinctions about people that lead to a perception of them as unique and complex individuals. We will be confined to assessments that simply categorize others as good-bad, yellow-black, or like-unlike ourselves.

THE PERCEIVER AND THE PERCEIVED: THE CONTENT OF PERCEPTIONS

Perceptions of others are jointly determined by the perceiver and by the person who is the object of his attention. The perceiver brings to any situation some predispositions that lead him to notice some traits and not others, to organize his impressions in characteristic ways, and to make many or few distinctions among people. The content of impressions is influenced also by the object-person as he is and as he appears to be, and by all the other information available about him, including that provided by the situation in which he is encountered and by his apparent relationships with other people. Since the content of impressions is determined by both the perceiver and the perceived, the accuracy of this content depends on how the perceptions of the perceiver match with the facts of the perceived. Accuracy is possible because there *are* associations between traits and between nonverbal features and internal characteristics which do exist and can be known and incorporated into our attempts to understand another person.

Same and Different

Perhaps the most important kind of assumption we make about another person is whether he can be classed as "the same as" or "different from" ourselves or other specific groups of people.

The extent to which people are assumed to be the same as or different from self or from other specified people is central to the relationship of any two people. Our assumptions about similarity influence the content of many interpersonal judgments, and they help to determine what traits we see as related to each other. Thus, the assumption of similarity or dissimilarity is important in influencing the accuracy of an impression. The assumption of similarity may be due to basic judgmental processes, reasonable and sometimes valid guesses about the way people are, assumptions about trait correlation, or attempts to reduce anxiety about deviation.

The assumption of similarity. In judging others on the basis of their similarity to us, we are setting ourselves up as the standard against which others are measured (Tagiuri, 1969). This results in *assimilation* and *contrast* (Chapter 11); that is, we generally overestimate similarity with those who are most like ourselves (assimilation) and underestimate similarity with those who are least like us (contrast). If we perceive a few characteristics in common with ourselves, we assume many more; if we perceive a few dissimilarities, we assume additional ones (Smith, 1966). College students, for example, assume too much similarity with others of the same sex and too little with those of the opposite sex (Livensparger, 1965).

Different people have different views about others' similarity or dissimilarity to themselves. Extreme views in either direction produce inaccurate perceptions of others (Chance & Meaders, 1960). People who make such extreme assumptions appear to be made anxious by social deviance. Those subjects who, on personality test items, assumed a great deal of similarity between themselves and target persons they heard in a taped interview had a strong need for security and predictability in interpersonal relations, attempted to meet this need by complying with the expectations of others, and had tendencies toward dependency and conformity to the constraints others impose. They attempted to increase security feelings by seeing themselves and others as being close to socially accepted norms. The subjects who were unusually low in assuming similarity seemed to use a reaction-formation mechanism in handling anxiety about conformity problems. They were nonconforming, impatient with authority and custom, not inclined to plan or accept schedules, and preferred aggressive behavior; they seemed, in short, to value a picture of themselves as deviating from cultural norms.

Which are the most socially sensitive people? Neither. Both extreme groups err, by assuming too much or too little similarity. But even though we must be aware of the pitfalls in making extreme assumptions, we must also recognize that the assumptions of similarity can be well used. If we ask ourselves, "How would I react?" or "How would I feel in this situation?" we can often increase our understanding of the behavior of others. When only a little information is available about another person, the assumption of similarity can be a useful beginning for understanding him. People tend to like and associate with others who are similar to themselves, and people who associate with each other tend to become more similar than they were initially (see Berscheid & Walster, 1969; Byrne, 1969; Newcomb, 1941). The chief problem with the assumption of similarity comes in knowing with whom it may be used, to what extent, and about what characteristics.

Stereotypes

A stereotype is an automatic assumption of similarity among other people or groups of people who may or may not be seen as similar to oneself. Because a person shares one characteristic with others, he is assumed to share other characteristics with them. A generalization about the group is applied to the individual. If we assume that a person is intelligent because he wears glasses or has a high forehead, we are using a stereotype to pass judgment on him.

Females, students, teachers, garbage collectors, interior decorators, members of any racial, national, political, or religious group—all have been subjected to stereotyping. Powerful stereotypes are often linked with physical features that can easily be observable in members of the group; strong stereotypes may also be linked to the context in which group members are typically encountered. Membership in the group is readily noted and stereotypes applied and perpetuated, even though the person belongs to the group because he possesses a physical feature that is of no particular importance to the person himself, and, if we but knew it, often gives us incorrect information about him.

Stereotyping is frowned upon by social scientists and laymen alike. The word conjures up images of spiteful prejudice or, at best, careless pre-judgment. Indeed, stereotypes are often both negative and inaccurate, and some writers restrict the word to this meaning (see Brigham, 1971). Some stereotypes, however, can be accurate and valuable aids in making predictions about people. There *are* similarities among members of a group which differentiate them from other groups of people, whether the people are doctors or lawyers, college or high school students, Americans or Frenchmen, Democrats or Republicans, or aggressive and passive children. It is part of the business of social science to discover similarities among groups of people. To the extent that we know what these similarities are, we can use them to advantage in forming impressions.

There are, however, three basic pitfalls in the use of stereotypes (see Smith, 1966). First is the simple but important fact that the stereotypes the layman uses are often invalid; he does not test the generalizations inherent in his own implicit personality theory, either by his own observation of people or by scientific information. In fact, he is likely to be unaware of the role of generalizations in his perception of people.

Second, stereotypes are often self-perpetuating and highly resistant to change. This may be partly because they are extremely well-learned ways of thinking. They easily prompt selectivity and distortion in perception so that we see and remember only information which is consistent with the stereotype. Thus, even when we have the opportunity to test our stereotypes against the facts, we do not necessarily profit from the observation. Similarly, simply giving people scientific information that contradicts their stereotypes can be amazingly ineffective in correcting them.

Third, even when the stereotype is accurate for a group as a whole ("on the average"), it may not be valid for a particular member of that group, and certainly it is unlikely to be sufficient for attaining any sort of complete understanding of that person. Accuracy in the use of stereotypes may be improved by making judgments on the basis of *multiple* group membership. What would we expect, for instance, of an attractive female civil engineer whose hobbies are playing the cello and baking angel-food cakes? If we rely only on stereotypes about attractive females, or about civil engineers, or cellists, or cooks, chances are that our predictions about this woman would not be very accurate. When we consider her membership in several groups, we get a more accurate picture.

This method of "pooling" has been shown to be effective in improving interpersonal sensitivity (Wakeley, 1961). Subjects were instructed to note all the groups to which a person belonged, to select from a list of familiar people those whose characteristics most closely match the person in question, and to assume that the person would think and behave like the average person of the matched pool. Ability to profit from such a method is probably related to how many distinctions among people the perceiver is able and willing to make (cognitive complexity), as well as to how much information the perceiver has about the members of the various relevant groups, and how accurate this information is.

Thus, stereotyped generalizations may be useful in understanding others, *if* they are based on accurate information, *if* they do not force the perception of a particular person to be consistent with expectations, and *if* multiple group membership is taken into account. "All people use stereotypes. Since they do, one step toward accuracy would be to practice organizing and using stereotypes effectively" (Smith, 1966, p. 145).

Implications of Deviance

Assumptions about one person's similarity to others and about the similarity of people within a group are used in developing impressions of others. However, people often deviate from what is expected of them, whatever the basis for the expectation. A frequent effect of deviance from expectations is a pressure to conform; failure to conform often elicits rejection or mistreatment. This is particularly obvious when the others are different from the way we are, but it occurs also when they do not conform to any kind of expectation.

When another person is very different from ourselves or from what we consider average or "normal" for the group he belongs to, he is called deviant. All of us have had at least a few experiences of temporary deviance. Any perceived deviation from normal appearance, experience, or behavior is stigmatizing and can easily give rise to "friendly" teasing, physical avoidance, or censure and mistreatment on the part of the perceiver. Studies of important groups of deviates—criminals, members of some ethnic and religious groups, the mentally ill, the physically handicapped, and even the nonconformist in contrived research settings—emphasize that the deviate is often mistreated. Although deliberate mistreatment may be prevented and the desire for mistreatment denied, the urge to punish the deviate may be expressed in subtle ways not easy for the perceiver to detect (Farina, Holland, & Ring, 1966; Farina, Chapnick, & Chapnick, 1972).

Why should deviates be perceived negatively and be mistreated? The answer is not clear, although it seems likely that mechanisms for anxiety reduction are involved. When faced with what one considers an undesirable deviance, one can convince himself that he lives in a just and predictable world by seeing the deviate as deserving negative responses. When one is deviant because of membership in a special group, the mistreatment can be rationalized on the basis of disapproval of the content of deviance—the particular traits, behaviors, and attitudes stereotypically assumed for the group: "People like that deserve punishment!"

There is also reason to believe that the mere *fact* of deviance rather than the actual *content* of deviance calls forth negative reactions; that is, the simple fact that a person is "different," "not average" may be enough to bring about rejection, regardless of the precise way in which the person is deviant. To explore this possibility, Freedman and Doob (1968) experimentally induced a "contentless deviance" by telling subjects that one among them was different from most people of their age and sex, without telling them exactly how. Subjects took a battery of personality tests selected to be ambiguous enough that the subjects could not know what they were revealing about themselves. False feedback sheets gave the supposed scores of each person in the group (Figures 13–1, 13–2).

One striking example of the effect of perceived deviance was shown by a study in which subjects selected other subjects to receive a punishment or a reward. The subjects chose among four other group members to select one for an additional experimental procedure in which punishment (shock) would be given for noncreative responses, or extra pay (and no shock) would be given for making an additional contribution to the experiment. Subjects who had been made to think that they were deviant themselves picked subjects they thought to be deviant in a similar way (i.e., deviant on the same personality test) to receive rewards, and avoided choosing similar "deviants" to receive punishment. Those who had been led to see themselves as about average were inclined to select deviants for the shock condition but not for the reward task (Table 13–1). It is not difficult to imagine real-life parallels.

Conversely, mistreatment at the hands of oneself or another person encourages the perception of negative characteristics that justify the punishment. Even when the other person is recognized initially as a victim of impersonal fate who is suffering through no unworthy action of his own, the need to believe in a just world may lead one to convince

FIGURE
13–1

THEMATIC APPERCEPTION TEST	
Score	*Percent of general population receiving this score*
0–5	1
6–9	2
10–12	2
13–15	10
16–20	29
21–24	25
25–27	18
28–30	8
31–33	3
34–40	2
Person in current group	*Score*
A	25
B	3
C	22
D	24
E	23

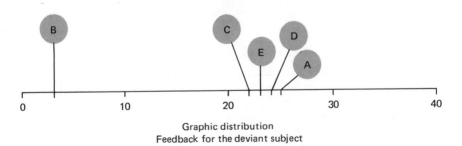

Graphic distribution
Feedback for the deviant subject

Sample of Feedback Scores for Female Deviant Subjects.

Source: Freedman, J. L., & Doob, A. N. *Deviancy: The psychology of being different.* New York: Academic Press, 1968. P. 20.

himself that the victim really is an undesirable person who deserves to suffer (Lerner & Simmons, 1966; Lerner, 1971; Reagan, 1971). Derogation of the victim to maintain a view of the world as just serves a defensive function (Walster, 1967; Shaw & Skolnick, 1971): "The world is just and fair, orderly and predictable, so I need not worry about being a potential victim myself."

Thus, perception of deviance brings about mistreatment and derogation of the victim, which of course justifies further mistreatment and derogation in a potential vicious circle (see Berscheid & Walster, 1969; Kiesler & Kiesler, 1967). The one responsible for mistreating another may be a

FIGURE

13–2

THEMATIC APPERCEPTION TEST	
Score	*Percent receiving this score*
0–5	1
6–9	2
10–12	2
13–15	10
16–20	29
21–24	25
25–27	18
28–30	8
31–33	3
34–40	2
Person	*Score*
A	25
B	24
C	21
D	22
E	23

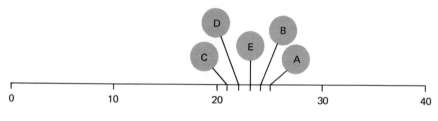

Graphic distribution
Feedback for the nondeviant subject

Sample of Feedback Scores for Nondeviant Subjects.

Source: Freedman, J. L., & Doob, A. N. *Deviancy: The psychology of being different.* New York: Academic Press, 1968. P. 21.

seemingly impersonal fate, or it may be oneself. One changes perception of the other to justify one's own behavior (Glass, 1964; Strickland, 1958). Fortunately, one's own behavior toward another can be positive rather than negative, and one's view of the other can be altered accordingly, in the positive direction, to justify the positive behavior (Schopler & Compere, 1971). The perceiver is part of the stimulus. That our perceptions of others are influenced by the needs of our own self-perceptions is shown, too, in the phenomena of projection.

PSYCHODYNAMICS

TABLE 13–1   Mean Rank of Deviants in Choice for Shock and Reward

Subject	CHOICE			
	Shock	Reward		
Similar deviants	2.82	1.27	t = 4.08	p. < .01
Different deviants	2.09	1.73		
Nondeviants	1.09	2.18	t = 2.52	p. < .05

N = 11 in each cell. A rank of 1 was assigned when a deviant was the first choice, 2 for second choice, 3 for third, 4 for last choice; the lower the score, the greater the preference for a deviant for the job.

SOURCE: Freedman, J. L., and Doob, A. N. *Deviancy: The psychology of being different.* New York: Academic Press, 1968. P. 97.

Projection

Our reactions to others are also influenced by anxiety that is produced, not by them or the deviance we perceive in them, but by seeing in ourselves a trait we consider undesirable and often one we feel makes us deviant. Attributing traits to other people on the basis of our own is projection, a defense meant to reduce or avoid anxiety.

Attributive projection, in particular, is attributing to others the same trait one possesses himself (Holmes, 1968). It may be seen as a special case of assuming similarity, particularly when the traits involved are likely to be negatively evaluated and anxiety-inducing. A young man, for example, is given seemingly indisputable evidence that he has homosexual tendencies (Bramel, 1962, 1963). If he has a negative view of homosexuality, and if his self-esteem is relatively high, he can handle the problem of thinking he has homosexual tendencies by assuming that others whom he likes, values, and respects, have them, too.

This phenomenon has been analyzed within the framework of cognitive dissonance theory (Glass, 1968a, 1968b). Festinger (1957) maintains that when two cognitions are inconsistent, a negative tension state of dissonance is generated; the person then attempts to reduce the tension by changing one or the other of the cognitions or coming to perceive them as unrelated to each other. If the young man felt that homosexuality was a negative attribute, but had low self-esteem, there would not be much dissonance. The cognition, "I have a negative trait," is not inconsistent with the cognition, "I'm not a very worthy person anyway." The new information would provide just one more bit of data about his unworthiness, consistent with all the data he thinks he has already gathered. On the other hand, if he had high self-esteem, the cognitions about his (negative) homosexual traits would be highly dissonant with his cognitions about himself. Thus, it is the high-self-esteem people who experience dissonance with negative information and thus need to protect themselves against the information; and, as discussed in the previous chapter, high-esteem people generally protect themselves better than do low-esteem people.

Dissonance theory further predicts—correctly—that the targets for projection will be other people who are liked, valued, and respected—friends, members of one's own reference group, or other people seen as similar to oneself in some ways (Holmes, 1968). Negative traits are projected onto liked and respected persons or peers rather than disliked or out-group persons, and this may enable the person to re-evaluate the trait or convince himself that he does not deviate from his reference group (Holmes, 1968, 1971; Bramel, 1962, 1963; Secord, Backman, & Eachus, 1964; Endlow & Kiesler, 1966). Attributing the trait to negatively valued persons would only confirm the fact that homosexuality is bad and increase the dissonance. If the trait is seen as characteristic of a valued other, then the trait must not be so bad after all, so dissonance between high self-esteem cognitions and knowledge of possession of the trait is reduced: "I'm not so bad—he's that way too!" Further, attributing a negative trait to a positive other can help change the perception of the trait, making it more positive (Secord, Backman, & Eachus, 1964): "If he's that way too, it can't be as bad as I thought." Projection, then, offers a double protection.

There is no evidence, however, to suggest that projection is unconscious, and there is some question whether attributive projection serves a defensive function by reducing anxiety (Holmes & Houston, 1971). Although projection may not be an unconsciously operating defense mechanism which reduces anxiety, it *is* a mechanism of interpersonal perception whereby one assumes similarity with important others about a trait one considers negatively.

Complementary projection is attributing to someone else a trait different from a trait which the person himself has (Holmes, 1968). Thus, it is a special case of assumption of dissimilarity. It also is assumed to be a defense mechanism, although no evidence shows that it functions unconsciously. When a different trait is projected, it is likely to be a complement of one's own trait of concern. Seeing the complement in someone else helps to justify or explain one's own feelings: "Why am I scared? Because he is threatening and dangerous." It helps to make the world make sense. It can be seen as reducing uncertainty about one's own feelings: "He's so frightening—no wonder I'm scared!" Like attributive projection, complementary projection can be seen as reducing dissonance: "I am scared," though inconsistent with the cognition, "There is nothing to be afraid of," is highly consistent with the cognition, "He is threatening and dangerous." In fact, Murray's (1933) early informal demonstration of complementary projection spurred the development of the TAT (Chapter 8). After his daughter and her slumber-party guests had been frightened by playing the game "Murder," they saw people in photographs as more frightening than before. In more systematic studies, college students frightened by electric shock rated another person as aggressive or dangerous (Feshbach & Singer, 1957; Hornberger, 1960). Such projection may also be used in supporting an expectancy of external control (Chapter 12): "I'm failing in what I do, but it is the system's fault, not my own."

As modes of thinking, both attributive and complementary projection may have a realistic basis. People—particularly among one's own reference group and friends—are similar in many ways, and our own responses are often reasonable ones in light of the behavior of another—dangerous people do elicit fright; when one is frightened, it is not necessarily unreasonable to assume that others are dangerous. However, like many habits with a realistic beginning, they can become unrealistic (Chapters 5, 12, 14).

Nonverbal Cues in Person Perception

Often we receive verbal information about a person from him or from a third party, and from that we develop perceptions that fit our assumptions about trait correlations, similarity, and deviance. However, there is some evidence that trait descriptions themselves are relatively uninformative and may not well elucidate the natural process of perception formation (Rodin, 1972). In any case the starting point for finding terms that appropriately describe a person is usually someone's observation of the person himself as a physical entity in some sort of situation: What does Florence look like? Where is she? What is she doing?

Cue selection and interpretation. Some of the nonverbal stimuli about a person are features he can control—dress, neatness, weight, posture, gestures, expressions. Others are relatively immutable features he cannot control—the structure of his face or body. Psychological traits are inferred from both kinds of cues, sometimes validly, sometimes not. How the perceiver selects from the multitude of cues available and responds to them is influenced by the content of his personal constructs, their complexity, and how they are organized. He is likely to be most attentive to those cues he deems relevant to his personal constructs, and he will make inferences from them that fit his assumptions about the meaning of the cues.

Cue selection and interpretation are often automatic, used without examination or justification. Often we can only say, "Something about him makes me distrust him," or "There is something likable about her." Students who judged photographs were confident about their ratings of both physiognomic and personality traits of the people portrayed. Specifically, some men were seen as hostile, boorish, quick-tempered, sly, and conceited—those who had dark complexions, coarse, oily skin, heavy eyebrows, and straight mouths. Certain features not only captured the attention of the observer, but were also assumed to have psychological meaning. But the student subjects were unable to give more than vague statements justifying their ratings of the personality traits (Stritch & Secord, 1956).

Many nonverbal cues are available that people do not use, either because they cannot detect them or tell them from other cues or because they do not realize their relevance (Figure 13–2). On the other hand, people often respond to cues that are irrelevant to the trait or state inferred, or they interpret the meaning of the cue incorrectly (Figure 13–4). Judges did well in agreeing with each other about the intelligence of a person in a photograph, and about the leadership qualities, sociability, and state of physical fatigue of speakers, but their ratings were not associated with actual measures of the person seen and heard (Kramer, 1963; Davitz, 1964). However, when people agree with each other about the meaning of the nonverbal properties of another person, or when one important judge responds consistently, whatever cue is responded to is important for social interaction *simply because people respond to it*. The perceivers are interacting with the target person on the basis of what they think he is, not what he actually is.

There are many components of nonverbal communication, including body movements and posture, voice quality, speech habits, smell, skin sensitivity, preferred amount of space between people, direction of gaze, dress, and cosmetics (Duncan, 1969; Argyle, 1967). All of these components may carry information about the person's general characteristics or momentary state and may be used by a perceiver in reacting to him.

FIGURE 13–3

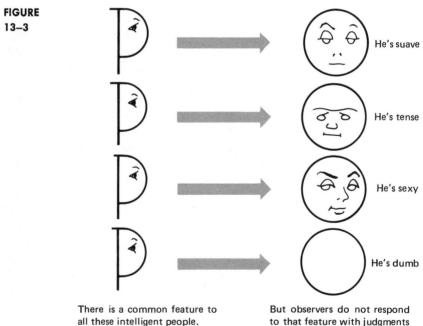

There is a common feature to all these intelligent people.

But observers do not respond to that feature with judgments that P is intelligent. Perhaps they show attributive (or complementary) projection?

Variety of Judgment Responses to Intelligence.

FIGURE
13–4

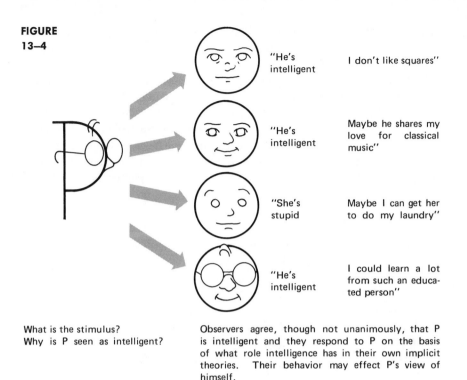

	"He's intelligent"	I don't like squares"
	"He's intelligent"	Maybe he shares my love for classical music"
	"She's stupid	Maybe I can get her to do my laundry"
	"He's intelligent	I could learn a lot from such an educated person"

What is the stimulus?
Why is P seen as intelligent?

Observers agree, though not unanimously, that P is intelligent and they respond to P on the basis of what role intelligence has in their own implicit theories. Their behavior may effect P's view of himself.

Role of Perceived Intelligence in Response to One Person.

P may be intelligent—or he may not be.

There *are* fairly reliable associations between such external cues and internal states which can be detected and well used by the sensitive observer. Here we will focus on nonverbal cues in the expression of emotion, for there are both inherent and acquired associations between the external cues and the internal states.

Emotional expression. The use of nonverbal cues in making inferences about another person's internal attributes is perhaps most obvious with emotions. Recognition of emotions is often fairly accurate, partly because it is very important in daily life to draw the correct inference about emotions (Singer & Singer, 1972). Often, in interpersonal interaction, it is much more crucial to know what a person is feeling at the moment—say, depressed—than to know his characteristic traits—for example, that he is usually warm, humorous, sociable.

A great many cues—voice, hands, body movements, posture, head orientation, and facial expressions—convey information about the nature and intensity of emotional states (Ekman & Friesen, 1968; Kramer, 1963). Emotional facial expressions, particularly, are fairly easy to classify. A simple classification (Figure 13–5; Schlosberg, 1952, 1954) has three dimensions: pleasantness-unpleasantness, the most important; attention-rejection; and activation.

The common associations between expression and emotion exist because of both biological factors and learning experiences. The human face is "wired" to present a series of emotions and these extend across cultural groups, although there are some important cultural differences (Izard, 1971). Further, the number of fundamental emotions is limited, and the closer a feeling is to the pure form—pure happiness, pure anger, pure fear —the greater the chance of recognition even when a picture is used. Facial

FIGURE
13–5

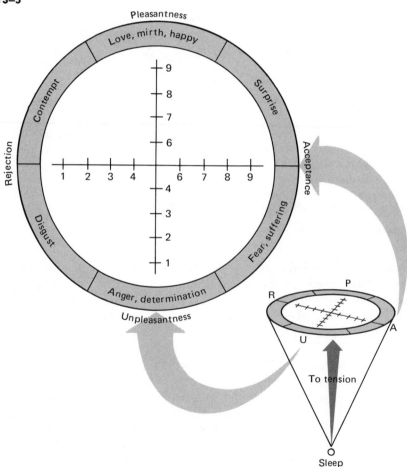

Model of Feeling.
The three-dimensional model of feeling hypothesized by Schlosberg and its relation to names given to feelings, such as surprise and disgust.

Source: After Schlosberg, H., 1954.

PSYCHODYNAMICS

expressions of some basic emotions—happiness, anger, sadness, disgust, surprise, fear—were judged about the same by Caucasian and Oriental subjects; and people from preliterate cultures were also capable of identifying the same fundamental emotions (Ekman et al., 1969; Ekman & Friesen, 1971).

These inherent, seemingly universal associations between expressions and emotions seem to extend even to people who have had little opportunity to observe facial expressions. Blind people who have not had the opportunity to observe the expressions of others still express emotions much as sighted people do. However, blind people have a more limited range of emotional expressions and their expressions are likely to be relatively gross and lacking the fine details of the person who has observed emotional expressions in others. Similarly, monkeys reared in isolation were inadequate both as senders and as receivers of emotional expressions when given the chance to communicate with another monkey not similarly deprived (Miller, 1967).

Because particular expressions are likely to accompany particular feelings, an assumption of similarity may be accurate. It certainly is if two people had had relatively similar experiences. It has been hypothesized that emotions provide a common basis of subjective experiences and expressive behaviors, and these tend to generate labels or symptoms with universal meaning (Izard, 1971). We may assume that the internal state associated with an observable expression is much the same in others as in ourselves. Curiously, if we have been trained to inhibit our own emotional displays, we may be more sensitive to these displays in others than if we had not learned to control the expression of our emotions (Lanzetta & Kleck, 1970). Our attention has been called to the association between expression and emotion, though in a negative way.

It is likely, too, that we can know the feelings of another person because we actually experience some of the same physiological sensations and accompanying emotions while observing him. For example, people respond with increased physiological arousal to the perceived stress of another (Chapter 14). More subtly, some evidence indicates that we may know the feelings of another person because of a slight imitation of the other's movements and posture (Gellhorn, 1968). If we know our own feelings, we can know those of another person.

With emotional expressions, as with body types, both biological attributes and cultural assumptions are likely to influence the use and interpretation of nonverbal cues, and both make possible accurate inferences from these cues. Accuracy of responding to nonverbal cues can also be enhanced by taking account of the physical properties not only of the person himself, but also of the context in which the person is encountered. In fact, knowing the context increases the accuracy of recognition of emotions (Frijda, 1970; Tagiuri, 1969).

Context of observation. The context in which a person is observed influences what we notice about him, and it is likely to offer some information about him and his attitudes (Heider, 1958; Kelley, 1967). What we think we need to know and what we think we do know about a person standing in front of a classroom will be quite different from the inferences we will make about that same person when we encounter him at a lively party. And the mere fact that he is encountered in one place or the other (or both) tells us something about him.

Part of the information we derive from the context of observation comes from the *sequence* in which events occur (Tagiuri, 1969). If we observe a boy crying and then hitting his playmate, our interpretation of his crying will be different than if we saw the boy hit his playmate and then begin to cry. What we see in the playmate will also contribute to our interpretation of the boy's behavior. Even with schematic drawings, an expression on one face is interpreted partly according to the expressions on another face in the picture (Figure 13–6; Cline, 1956). Any one stimulus is part of a configuration of stimuli which influences the perception. Any one person is a part of a social configuration, even if the only other person immediately present is the observer himself. With person perception, the perceiver himself is a part of the perceived. This contributes to the difficulties of achieving and maintaining accuracy, but it can contribute to accuracy.

PERCEPTION: ACCURACY OF IMPRESSION

To interact pleasantly and effectively with other people, to develop friendships and an intimate knowledge of another person, we need to improve our ability to form relatively accurate impressions of others. It is the mutual accuracy of perception that enables communication (Chapter 16).

Accuracy: Who, When, and What?

From a wealth of cues available about a person, we select some for interpretation and quickly go beyond the data to make inferences shaped by our personal constructs, cognitive complexity, assumptions, and anxiety. We do not always carefully consider or test our assumptions against facts. We may attend to some cues rather than to others which are potentially more useful, and we may arrive at our conclusions by careless intuitive jumps. Can such conclusions be accurate? We like to think that they are. We like to suppose that we are "good judges of character" and glibly assert, "I know human nature." Allport (1961) has suggested that the "good judge" must have breadth of personal experience, intelligence, cognitive complexity, self-insight, social skills, and good adjustment. He is probably correct that such characteristics contribute to accuracy of interpersonal perceptions. However, there is little evidence of any unitary general ability to judge all kinds of people in all kinds of situations (see Tagiuri, 1969). Some people may be better judges in some situations than

**FIGURE
13–6**

Smiling-Frowning

Subjects' ratings of smiling face (in relation to frowning face): Wants to be helpful, friendly, peace-making; enjoyment not from misfortune of another, but from an external event.

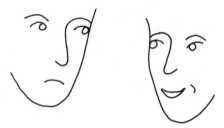

Glum-Smiling

Subjects' ratings of smiling face (in relation to glum face): Dominant, vicious bully, strong enough to defeat the other and sadistic in enjoyment of the victory.

Perception of Faces.

Source: Cline, M. G. The influence of social context on the perception of faces. *Journal of Personality,* 1956, 25, 142–158. P. 146.

others, but their ability is likely to be based on a combination of many abilities relevant to understanding others in a particular case, rather than on a unitary ability or process. Some people may be extraordinarily good judges in many circumstances, but they are rare in the usual research populations of judges, or simply have not been discovered by current techniques.

Thus, a person who believes that his perceptions are always accurate is likely to have an inaccurate perception of his own abilities. And sometimes when our impressions of others are correct, the accuracy is fortuitous, rather than the product of great sensitivity: biases happen to match the actual characteristics of other people. And we may be consistently right about other people if we associate only with those about whom we can be consistently right—people very like ourselves.

What does it mean to be right about another person? The obvious reply is that we end up with knowledge of the other person as he *is*. However, what he is cannot always be easily defined. We can elicit the response from another that we have correctly understood him and have made contact with him, a condition reflected in his statement that "You understand me" or "We understand each other." Why do both of us assume understanding? Because we think we have what amounts to a good theory about the other, usually an implicit theory. Like a formal theory, the implicit personality theory, about other people generally or about a specific person, may be evaluated in terms of its adequacy in accounting for known facts and in making correct predictions about events unknown to us or to the person himself, including future events. Prediction of future behavior in unfamiliar circumstances is a particularly stringent test of understanding that most of us would fail, even for ourselves or someone very close to us.

Self-reports by the perceived person are sometimes suitable criteria for evaluating the correctness of our predictions: "Yes, I do tend to be that way." "Yes, I have been thinking about dropping out of school." While it might seem that such self-reports supply the most direct support of the correctness of our perceptions, they are limited by the completeness and accuracy of the other person's self-knowledge and, of course, by his willingness and ability to share that knowledge honestly.

An outside observer can often see a pattern in behavior and a meaning behind the pattern that is not easy for the person himself to detect (Chapter 12): "Hey, you're right! I never thought of it that way before! I just can't stand Professor Snodgrass." The self-reports are themselves responses to be accounted for and predicted. The person might, of course, deny hostility toward Professor Snodgrass (and the denial itself would be predicted in an effective theory), but the assumption that he is hostile may do an excellent job of predicting his behavior; it is a workable assumption about how he construes the world. It helps us to understand and predict his behavior. In smoothly functioning interactions, predictions and their confirmations are scarcely noticed. Their absence in unsuccessful relationships are more obvious: "I just don't know what to expect of you anymore. . . . I never know how you're going to feel. . . . I just don't understand you!" We do not know how he is seeing himself, us, or the rest of the world.

Accuracy: How?

By continuously observing one person, we may be able to formulate enough descriptive laws to predict his behavior with reasonable accuracy in a variety of situations. Some psychologists say that prediction is all that matters. However, without knowing how the other person sees the world, most of us would be unable to select, among the multitude of cues, those significant ones to which he is responding. Nor would we know why he responds to them as he does. To know another person requires knowing how he construes the world, including himself, even though he himself may not be able to articulate his view. This is easiest when he construes the world in the same way we do. This similarity certainly facilitates prediction, and some degree of similarity appears to be a necessity for any relationship that rests on understanding and communication.

A similarity strong enough to nurture casual interactions with another person usually results from the simple fact of sharing some physiological characteristic and from growing and experiencing in similar social environments. Members of a culture share "world views," or norms, which in many ways are broadly shared personality theories (Chapter 16). People growing in similar environments may each *observe* a common reality and independently incorporate knowledge of that reality into their individual construct systems. They become aware of biologically inherent and culturally induced associations; they observe the way people are in their social context and formulate expectations for others on that basis. They are also explicitly taught what cues are to be considered relevant and what interpretations to make of them. Cultures evolve agreed-upon meanings for behavior ("Nice boys don't do that!"), physical characteristics ("Fat people are jolly"), and expression ("He's scowling because he is angry"), and these meanings are passed on from generation to generation.

This is not to say that common learning in a common culture and the sharing of experiences provide exactly the same construct system and the same world view for any two people. If that were the case, this chapter would not be as necessary as it is.

Subcultures—cultures within cultures—provide markedly different worlds and, often, markedly different assumptions about people (Chapter 16). Even within a subculture, no two people, even identical twins, can see the world from exactly the same perspective. One can never enter the physical or psychological "skin" of another.

Along with interest, experience, many personal constructs, and cognitive complexity, learning to understand others means learning to understand ourselves. And just as acceptance of others requires acceptance of self, so does knowledge of others require knowledge of self.

SUMMARY

Detection of relevant cues and knowledge of their meaning are the ingredients of effective perception of others. The key is to pay attention, to be willing to learn, and to be in tune with social reality and with self.

The first step in improving perception of others is to examine the structure and content of our personal construct system. Some potentially useful cues to the personality of others are neglected because they are not relevant to our own constructs, and some are misused because of erroneous assumptions about their meanings.

Cognitive simplicity narrows the range of things we can know about another person and increases the likelihood of perceiving him in simple and absolute terms which ignore his complexity. We must learn when to assume that others are similar to ourselves and when they are not, and we must be careful to make use of stereotypes only when they are based on accurate generalizations and to take into account the multiple group membership of the person being assessed. Knowledge of others can also be improved when we are attentive to their emotional expressions and when we are accurately aware of our own expressions and emotions.

Accuracy of perception can be facilitated by observation and by similarities of culture and experience; however, no two people ever have exactly the same feelings, attitudes, and views. Perception is complicated by inaccurate self-awareness on the part of the perceiver and the perceived.

Knowledge of others requires a sufficient similarity for psychological contact, but the commonality can never be complete if the two people are to remain separate, distinct individuals—a deficiency that perhaps can be partially amended by our having enough security of self to move in the other's phenomenal field, to try to see things from his perspective, to use his assumptions about what he thinks he knows.

14

emotions

Human emotions run the gamut from ecstasy to despair. They enable us to enjoy the most rewarding and positive of human experiences, and to suffer the most abysmal of human dejection. Elaborate defenses are often used to control the intensity of emotional experience or to direct the intensity to more pleasurable ends.

Where do emotions come from? Are we born with specific patterns of emotional response, or do we acquire these responses through experience and interaction in a social environment? What are emotions? Are they the bodily changes that make our hands feel clammy and our hearts race faster, or are they perceptions and thoughts of ourselves and the environment? The issues of whether emotions are innate or acquired, and whether they are best defined in terms of physical events or cognitive processes, are basic to the study of emotional experience. Emotions, like other kinds of behavior, have their antecedents and concomitants in both biological factors and social experiences. Furthermore, both the physiological systems of the body and the higher cognitive processes of perception and thinking are responsive to environmental events and affect attempts to express and control emotional reactions. We will look first at the ways in which particular emotional experiences and individual differences in emotionality may be said to be innate and acquired, and then at the ways in which mind and body interact to determine emotional experiences.

FOUNDATIONS OF EMOTIONAL BEHAVIOR

A person's general emotional level and the likelihood of his experiencing particular emotions are the results of the interplay between his genetic makeup and experiences in the world. We will see this first in terms of genetic foundations of individual differences in emotionality and then in terms of the developmental phenomena which are relatively common among people. Attention is given to innate contributions to specific classes of responses—e.g., aggression, love—in Chapters 10, 19, and 20.

Genetic Foundations of Differences in Emotionality

Twin studies. It is clear that emotions, like other aspects of personality, have a genetic basis, but exactly how the genes have their effects is not certain (see Mansosevitz, Lindzey, & Thiessen, 1969; Lindzey, Loehlin, Mansosevitz, & Thiessen, 1971). In experimental work with nonhuman animals, selective breeding is the main method by which genetic components of emotionality are investigated. Animals that display extremes of a particular characteristic are bred with each other to produce offspring who reliably show the same extreme characteristic, such as high or low emotionality, exploration in novel environments, or the deviant motor behavior of crouching and freezing or going into convulsions.

Selective breeding has not been used to study human genetics, for obvious reasons. Instead, genetic components in human behavior are usually estimated from studies of twins. Correlations between scores for a given characteristic, or a *concordance* rate stating the likelihood that one twin has a given characteristic when the other does, may be determined for a sample of twins. Differences between the indices for sets of fraternal twins and those for sets of identical twins provide a rough but useful measure of the relative contribution of genetic and environmental factors affecting the characteristic. The greater the index for the identical twins compared to the fraternal twins, the greater the genetic contribution. This is because identical twins come from the same zygote and therefore have exactly the same genetic makeup; genotypes are identical. They are monozygotic (MZ). Fraternal twins are dizygotic (DZ); they develop from two different zygotes and are no more genotypically similar than any two siblings. On the average, fraternal twins share about 50 percent of their genes (Gottesman, 1966). The DZ twins provide a measure for controlling environmental influence in that, like MZ twins, they share birth rank, parents' age and experience, family circumstances at birth, etc.

The genetic components of normal and abnormal human behavior are greater than usually imagined, and they affect a wide variety of characteristics ranging from intelligence and abilities, to interests, values, and personality traits. Identical twins tend to exhibit greater similarities in their scores on personality and interest measures than pairs of same-sex fraternal twins; the overall correlation for identical twins is about .46 versus about .28 for fraternal pairs (Lindzey, Loehlin, Mansosevitz, & Thiessen, 1971). There are also strong genetic components in at least some neurotic disorders and the functional psychotic classifications of schizophrenia, manic-depression, and involutional melancholia. The evidence does not result from the circumstance of the twins having been reared by a disturbed parent, or having grown up in a common environment. The frequency of schizophrenia among adults who had been adopted at birth from hospitalized schizophrenic mothers and reared by normal mothers was about as great as the frequency expected among children reared by a schizophrenic mother. Concordance rates are still high even when twins are reared apart for at least five years.

Those who argue against the evidence of genetic contributions to human functioning contend that the higher correlations of personality and interest test scores for MZ twins than for DZ twins is due to the fact that MZ twins are more likely to be treated alike. It is true that mothers perceive the personalities of MZ twins to be more alike than the personalities of DZ twins (Scarr, 1966). However, this may well be because they *are* more alike. Surprisingly, many parents do not know whether their twins are identical or fraternal or are wrong in what they think. Comparisons of twins correctly and incorrectly classified by their parents showed that the parental treatment of twins is more a function of the degree of the twins' *actual* genetic relatedness than of parental beliefs about whether they are identical or fraternal. Differences between DZ twins (on needs for affiliation and change, anxiety, social maturity) were greater than differences between MZ twins, regardless of the correctness of parental diagnosis. There are obviously genetic influences in human behavior that cannot be explained away by appealing to common experiences in a common environment. This is not to say that genes have their effect regardless of a person's experiences in an environment or that they alone determine behavior.

Genetic and environmental influences. There are no genes for behavior; the genes affect behavior through enzymes, hormones, neurons. Genetic predispositions influence an organism's reaction to environmental experiences, making some reactions more likely than others. In turn, experiences influence the extent to which genetic predispositions are developed and overtly manifested. If a child has a genetic predisposition to be easily irritated by frustration, for example, and also is muscular and agile enough to be victorious in physical combat with would-be frustrators, a generalized response of aggression is likely to develop. Because of his genetic predisposition, he is likely to feel aggressive often and to receive reinforcement for acting aggressively. As he grows, the physical aggressiveness is likely to be increasingly discouraged and may then give way to social aggressiveness—he becomes a "real go-getter," admired for his assertiveness in business, politics, etc. Needless to say, the adult personality would be very different if the aggressive behavior failed to overcome frustration or if it brought punishment and more frustration (more likely for females than for males). Moreover, the genetic predisposition might never become obvious in an environment which contained no frustrators or which encouraged overcoming frustration by other than aggressive means.

With human emotions generally, processes of the autonomic nervous system and cortical functioning are likely to be important genetically influenced factors which affect broad classes of emotional patterns. These are predisposing factors rather than exclusive and exhaustively determining ones. People may differ in their genetic predisposition to be conditioned or to resist conditioning (Chapter 8, Eysenck). Some quickly acquire strong conditioned responses that resist extinction, while others slowly acquire responses that are weak and easy to extinguish. Much of the variation in emotional responses in general, and anxiety responses in particular, is probably due to genetic contributions to the responsiveness of the autonomic nervous system in conjunction with the predisposition to form and retain conditioned emotional responses. However, a person genetically inclined to be overreactive and to develop conditioned anxiety may never show any prolonged or acute adjustment problems if the environment does not provide much stress for him. On the other hand, someone with a low susceptibility to conditioning may develop transient or prolonged neurotic or psychotic symptoms if his environment is temporarily or typically a very stressful one. Even a very stable person may "break" if the stress of the environment is intense enough. For some disorders, the genetic contribution is so pervasive that the disorder is very likely to develop no matter what amount of stress exists in the environment. By and large, however, genetic contributions to neurotic and psychotic behavior, as well as normal behavior, should be thought of as predisposing factors. For instance, if there is schizophrenia in your immediate family, you will not necessarily develop schizophrenic symptoms. If you encounter a particularly stressful situation, however, you are more likely to become schizophrenic than someone without schizophrenia in his background. There are probably genetic contributions to sensitizing-repressing styles, but these do not by themselves dictate that a person will need to develop these defenses in extreme forms. And they do not dictate what specific kinds of events one will consider threatening and need to defend against.

Maturation and Emotionality

The complex interaction between genetic factors and environmental experiences is further shown by the simple fact that it takes time for emotions and the accompanying behavior to develop. During this time, the organism is maturing physiologically, and the person is continuing to have experiences in the environment. Because of this ongoing development and interaction with the world, emotions become differentiated and spontaneous fears emerge.

Emotional differentiation. Evidence for a variety of emotions in newborn infants is meager. It has been popular to claim, since the early work of John Watson, that complex emotions are acquired by conditioning from the unlearned bases of three primary, innate, emotional reactions, namely, rage, fear, and love. However, the emotional reactions of newborn infants are apparently much simpler than that (see Munn, 1965). Observers agree in attributing certain emotions to young infants—pain, love, joy, etc. This agreement among the adults apparently reflects their shared interpretations of the *stimulus* conditions rather than differences in the infants' *behavior*. When observers did not know what the stimulus for the infants' response had been, they disagreed more than they agreed about the interpretation of the response. Agreement among observers of infants is likely to reflect consensus about what they *expect* to be experienced in a given situation rather than a consensus based on a response to the infants themselves.

The startle pattern seems to be the only unlearned response of emotional significance that appears in normal infants and adults. Emotions appear to be differentiated from an initial base of the generalized excitement and gross motor reactions of the startle response. From such a primitive response, other responses likely to be called "emotional" are differentiated, both by genetically determined maturation processes and by learning in interaction with others. Two types of responses occurring at a very primitive level are the withdrawal response, which appears to be accompanied by unpleasant feelings and sympathetic discharge of the nervous system, and the reflex response, which leads to increased contact with the stimulus, such as sucking and a thrust toward another object (Gellhorn, 1968).

One schema of emotional differentiation suggested by a study of infants is shown in Figure 14–1 (Bridges, 1932). However, the timing and exact classification of emotions given should not by any means be

**FIGURE
14–1**

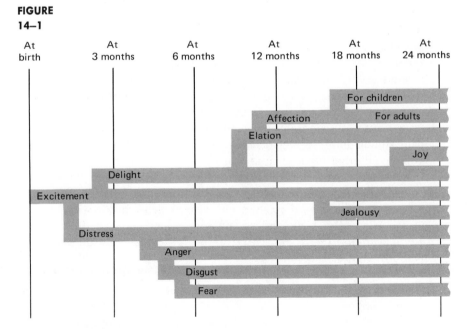

Emotional Differentiation in Early Childhood.

Source: From Bridges, K. M. B. Emotional development in early infancy. *Child Development,* 1932, 3, 340.

taken as proven. The significance of the schema is that it explicitly indicates that an increasing number of emotions may be inferred reliably from the growing infants' increasingly differentiated motor and expressive responses. The observable responses themselves are differentiated. What the infant experiences is anybody's guess. The smile appears extremely early in life and closely resembles the smile of the mature person. However, infant smiles are evoked by minimal stimulation of a variety of forms, even scolding. Crying does not accompany distress alone. However, mothers can discriminate between crying which signals a distress to be responded to immediately and crying which is not distressed (Wolff, 1969). Infant responses come to be progressively differentiated and appropriate (by adult definition) as a function of the reinforcement that adults provide, within the limits of the infant's capacities to discriminate environmental events and to respond in interaction with the environment. Adults observe the environmental situation in which the infant responses occur, make inferences about the infant's feelings, and act upon their interpretation. Adult reactions initially help shape the infant's behavior and, later, the cognitive interpretations the child makes of his own behavior, his internal feeling states, and the events he encounters in the environment.

Spontaneous fears. Although the responses of others help develop and shape the infant's behavioral repertoire, emotional reactions not present at birth may develop as a result of maturation, with little if any help from environmental reinforcement. The similarity in emotional expressions across cultures and between blind and sighted people suggests an unlearned basis for some physical patterns of expression which are not present at birth (Chapter 13.) Maturation may be responsible for the increased ability of various stimulating conditions to arouse emotional responses and expressions as the child grows older. Physical and cognitive development enables an increasing sensitivity to the environment and thus a greater susceptibility to emotional stimuli. Watson argued that innate stimuli for fear include only loud noise, sudden loss of support, and pain; all other fears, such as fear of darkness, water, animals, strangers, were said to be due to conditioning from the base of these three. Although long accepted, such a view is too simple. Others claim that there are at least several spontaneous fears which *emerge* with maturation occurring after birth and are *not* dependent upon conditioning for their appearance (see Gray, 1971; Hebb, 1946, 1949). Controlled observations suggest that fears of novelty, snakes, the dark, and of inert, mutilated, or dismembered bodies are likely to be spontaneous in humans and chimpanzees. For example, in all species studied, strange objects and strange members of the species elicit fear (Bronson, 1968). However, wide individual differences were found among six-month-old children in how predisposed they were to fear novelty. And for boys, but not girls, the differences at six months of age were predictive of fear reactions through the eight years of the study (Bronson, 1970).

PSYCHODYNAMICS

Some fears, of course, can diminish, or one may simply learn effective ways of living with them. Emotional reactions to body mutilation or major surgery are strongest on first exposure to them (after sufficient maturation). Who faints in the operating room, the new medical student or the experienced surgeon?

Direct conditioning cannot be the explanation of the fear of such scenes and avoidance of them. However, maturation and experience are necessary for the development of spontaneous fears. Although fear of novelty and strangeness emerges in all species, the fear can occur only after the organism is mature enough to detect the difference between the familiar and the novel and has had experiences with objects, mother or otherwise, which can become familiar. Fear of strangers thus depends on experience, but is a fear which emerges rather than one which is specifically conditioned. Should fear of strangers be attributed to heredity or to environment? Obviously, the distinction easily becomes meaningless.

MIND-BODY INTERACTIONS

Even though some genetically determined factors are involved in emotional behavior and experiences, can we say that emotion is simply a physical event? A central problem in attempting to define and understand emotion has been to specify the relationships between mind and body, ideation and physiology, or in cruder but equally effective terms, the thought or feeling and the "gut" reaction.

For some psychologists, a body change is an emotion. For others, a body change leads to a cognitive reaction which is the emotion. Thus, one research tradition centers on a search for specific physiological bases of emotions, particularly for different patterns of body responses associated with different emotions. Another approach attempts to specify explicitly the role of mental events which interact with physiological ones in determining emotional experiences (see Arnold, 1970). The various generalized definitions of emotion are shown below.*

1. Emotion is a noncortical event; consciousness of emotion is a mental event which depends upon the prior bodily event.
   a. Emotion is a vasomotor disturbance (Lange).

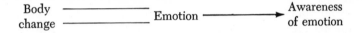

Body change ——————— Emotion ——————→ Awareness of emotion

* Suggested by definitions given by Wenger, M. A. A., Jones, F. N., & Jones, M. H. *Physiological psychology.* New York: Henry Holt and Company, 1956. Pp. 340–342.

2. Emotion is a mental event which depends in part upon other bodily events.
   a. Emotion is a mental event which depends upon changes in the hypothalamus which have been initiated by an appropriate stimulus (the Cannon and Bard thalamic theory).

Hypothalamic change ⟨ Mental event ——————— Emotion / Other bodily changes

   b. Emotion is a mental event, the feeling of changes occurring in the viscera and the skeletal muscles. The changes have been initiated directly by perception of an appropriate stimulus (James).

Body change ——————→ Perception, feeling of body change ————— Emotion

In this chapter, we will explore the second approach, a modern derivation and elaboration of the physiological and phenomenological perspective of William James (1890). James contended that an emotion is the result of a sequence: (1) A person perceives an exciting fact in the environment; (2) his body reacts because of innate reasons or prior conditioning; and (3) he perceives the body change. Perception of the change is the emotion for James. Body change precedes and is the controlling stimulus of the subjective thinking and feeling reaction. One does not cry because he feels sad, but feels sad because he cries. One is afraid of a bear because he notices a body reaction, perhaps running, after he has seen the bear. Freud also had a physiological and phenomenological emphasis compatible with that of James: Anxiety is the conscious, painful response of the ego to stimulation it cannot control, namely, the stimulation of internal body activity or arousal. In this physiological-phenomenological perspective, similarities and differences in the emotions of individuals can be attributed to physiological reactivity and cognitive activity. Both kinds of components of emotions may be affected by hereditary factors and by environment. However, before we delve into the interacting sequence of body activity and cognitive events in determining emotions, we should look at the physiological responses associated with some specific emotions.

Physiological Response Patterns

There is no doubt that emotions have extensive and varied physiological concomitants (see Glass, 1967; Gellhorn, 1968; Arnold, 1970; Di Giusto, Cairncross, & King, 1971). Brain structures play crucial roles, particularly the hypothalamus, the reticular formation, and the cortex itself. Body chemicals associated with the functions of such structures are equally relevant in understanding emotions. A prominent factor in emotionality is the balance of the hormones epinephrine (adrenalin) and norepinephrine (noradrenalin). These are related to mood, particularly to states of anger and fear. Drugs which affect mood change the level of these hormones in the brain, reducing norepinephrine and producing depression, or increasing it and producing elation, euphoria, and hyperactivity.

Fear and anger. The unfortunate subject of an early study had an accident which had closed his throat (Wolf & Wolff, 1942). The opening which was made to permit direct feeding to the stomach also allowed direct observation of the stomach. When the subject was worried or fearful, his stomach reflected his emotional state: Stomach motility and digestive secretion were inhibited. In contrast, when the subject was angry or resentful, stomach motility and acid secretion were increased. The rest of the body showed parallel reactions—thus the "red face of anger" and the "pale face of fear." Since these early observations, more sophisticated studies have found compatible response patterns suggesting that anxiety or fear is associated with epinephrine reactions (Martin, 1961; Breggin, 1964). The physiological responses during anger are not so clear, sometimes appearing to be a norepinephrine-like pattern, and sometimes to be a mixed epinephrine and norepinephrine pattern.

An important study showing different patterns during anger and fear was done by Albert Ax (1955), who experimentally induced these emotions. In the fear manipulation, the volunteer subjects were unexpectedly shocked; the experimenter expressed surprise and then alarm at the shocks and became very excited about what he portrayed as a dangerous short circuit in the high-voltage equipment wired to the subject. A dummy piece of apparatus suddenly sent sparks flying around. After five minutes the experimenter assured the subject that the malfunction had been corrected and that all was safe.

For the anger manipulation, the experimenter's assistant was described as an emergency substitute who had been fired previously for incompetence and arrogance. During the experiment, his behavior was designed to make clear to the subject that the firing was deserved; he interrupted the procedures, criticized the subjects and the experimenter, and was generally obnoxious. Because of this clever (and, by current standards, unethical) experiment, and others, many psychologists leaped too quickly to the overgeneralization that there are different physiological bases for each distinct emotion. Differences in response patterns are often subtle ones and the overall results are often due more to idiosyncratic physiological responses of the subjects (organismic variation) than to the environmental conditions and assumed emotional states (treatment variation).

Nonetheless, the evidence does point to the biological underpinnings of emotions and the evolutionary adaptation of which man is the heir. The hormones epinephrine and norepinephrine are well suited to promote survival in the situations in which their secretion is likely to be increased. Epinephrine has a general energizing effect, facilitating the activity of the organs stimulated by the sympathetic branch of the autonomic nervous system. It puts the organism on an emergency status, preparing it for the muscular exertion and endurance required to escape a fear-inducing situation or to overcome it, to fight or to fly. It constricts the blood vessels of the body cavity (stomach, intestines), dilates the vessels of the heart, brain, and skeletal muscles, speeds up the heart, and increases heart output; systolic blood pressure is increased because of the increased intensity of the heart contraction. The effects of norepinephrine seem to be more limited, and less is known about them. One important property of norepinephrine is that it leads to an increase in systolic blood pressure by causing a contraction of the peripheral blood vessels rather than by increasing heart output. Thus, it serves to reduce the acute effects of hemorrhage that might otherwise occur under attack, when the outcome is unavoidable and muscular activity would be useless—a situation in which anger or rage would also be likely (Kety, 1967).

Furthermore, which hormone dominates—epinephrine or norepinephrine—may be related to individual differences in reacting to stress (Funkenstein, 1955). Psychoanalytically, "anger-out," rage, lashing out at the environment are patterns of early stages of development when the child is relatively helpless and vulnerable to attack. Emotional control, and the internalization of anger which this implies ("anger-in"), is considered a more advanced reaction. Associated with the anger-in reaction are fear and passivity with respect to the environment. As the person grows older, the ratio between the two hormones does shift to a greater dominance by epinephrine. However, hormone ratios do differ among adults, as do their emotional patterns. During the tense period when medical students were awaiting decisions about internship applications, those who experienced the anger-in response of being depressed or angry at themselves showed a characteristic epinephrine dominance. In contrast, those who experienced the anger-out response of being angry at other people showed norepinephrine dominance.

The body changes controlled by epinephrine and norepinephrine enhance chances of survival when physical attack is an issue. However, civilized man must often inhibit the motor activity and physical expressiveness for which his body has prepared him and must endure the consequences of internalizing his anger or of symbolically lashing out at others. In some individuals, psychosomatic disorders develop when psychological needs are not met or emotional expressions must be inhibited or distorted.

Psychosomatic disorders. The association of different patterns of body responses with different patterns of emotionality and psychological adjustment is evident in psychosomatic disorders. *Psychosomatic disorders* are those in which actual bodily damage has presumably been caused by psychological factors rather than by biological ones. They are to be carefully distinguished from conversion hysterical reactions, in which body symptoms, such as paralysis or blindness, appear without any initial actual tissue damage or physiological reason for the symptom. The psychosomatic disorders also introduce the notion that subjective feelings, thoughts, and experiences have consequences for body functioning. A case in point is provided by comparing the feelings of patients suffering from hives to the feelings of those with hypertension (Grahm, 1962). The characteristic emotional attitude of patients with hives is to feel unfairly treated and unable to do anything about it. The attitude of the hypertensive patient is to feel susceptible to attack and to be on the alert at all times. Hives usually brings increased skin temperature, whereas greater (diastolic) blood pressure accompanies hypertension. The highly specific body patterns characteristic of the two disorders were successfully manipulated by suggesting to hypnotized subjects that they had the attitudes of patients with either hives or hypertension. The physiological changes in temperature and blood pressure were as predicted, with no changes occurring in other presumably unrelated measures, such as heart and respiratory rate. Other "suggested" emotions have also been shown to lead to consistent autonomic patterns.

With ulcers, too, there is a strong association between reactions to emotional problems and physiological factors. Gastrointestinal ulcers develop when there is a high level of pepsinogen (enzyme in gastric juices) secretions and a characteristic pattern of emotional reactions. In a study of over two thousand army inductees, everyone found to have a gastrointestinal ulcer was also in the upper 15 percent of the subject pool as to the level of pepsinogen in his blood (Weiner et al., 1957). The hypersecretors (oversecretors) and the hyposecretors (undersecretors) could also be identified on the basis of twenty criteria from personality tests. The two extreme groups on pepsinogen differed in the kinds of anxieties and conflicts they experienced rather than in their level of general psychological adjustment. The hypersecretors, prone to ulcers, generally had strong feelings of dependency upon others and a need to be compliant and passive in relations with authority figures. Psychoanalytically, their needs were generally oral in nature, as shown in terms of wishing to be fed, leaning on others, and seeking close bodily contact with others. When their attempts to find external support failed, the resulting anger and frustration could not be expressed lest it lead to loss of the source of the supply of their needs. In contrast, subjects with low concentrations of pepsinogen had strong needs to express hostile impulses and a greater capacity for the overt expression of anger. They had fewer problems about dependency on external sources of supply and support, were more narcissistic, and had greater protective defenses against anxiety. Oddly enough, they gave more verbal reports of bodily complaints than the hypersecretors.

In sum, it is fairly clear that an intimate relationship exists between physiological responses and some emotions or specific kinds of emotional problems and attitudes. Fear and anger are associated with different response patterns of the autonomic nervous system, and psychosomatic disorders occur with characteristic sets of emotional needs. Which comes first, the physiological pattern or the subjective reaction and psychological attitudes? Does a feeling of fear elicit an epinephrine response or does the increased epinephrine lead to fear? Exact specification of the sequence of events is not possible. Genetically determined predispositions in body responses may make it highly likely that a kind of psychological attitude or emotional orientation to the world will develop. Alternatively, repeated experiences which shape emotional attitudes may influence the characteristic physiological reaction. In addition, there may be different kinds of resolutions to this issue for different emotional patterns and perhaps for different people. In any case, emotional experiences and behavior exhibit a variety that has not yet been accounted for on a purely physiological basis. Very likely, there are limits set by physiological factors on the kinds of emotions possible for particular people to experience in given situations. Within these limits, the specific emotion is determined by cognitive factors and individual experiences (Gellhorn, 1968). The role of cognitive factors is currently most clearly seen within the tradition that conceptualizes the biological foundations of emotions in terms of general arousal rather than of specific physiological patterns of responses.

Arousal and Cognition

The other dominant approach to emotions more explicitly views emotions as an interacting sequence of body activity and cognitive events. A jukebox provides a useful analogy for introducing the theoretical and empirical approach that has developed within this tradition, a modern version of the James approach (Mandler, 1962). What do you do with a jukebox? First, you activate it by inserting a coin, and then you make a selection. The activation of the machine is a necessary condition for producing any desired sound, but by itself it is not enough. Conversely, pushing the selection button without having inserted the money is futile; making the selection is a necessary but not a sufficient condition for hearing the music. For emotions, too, both an activation and a selection process are necessary; neither alone is sufficient. There must be both a body activation or arousal, and an interpretation or labeling of the arousal. The body must "get going," just as the jukebox must. In addition, there must be "direction" to the energy. The direction is a matter of interpreting the arousal as emotional or not, and, if emotional, as one specific emotion rather than another. For the jukebox analogy to hold further, there would have to be a separate money slot for each selection, because with emotions, the same event may trigger both the activation and the selection process (Figure 14–2). The activation or arousal necessary for an emotion is conceptualized in terms of intensity, as indicated by changes in the autonomic, central, and somatic nervous systems. No attempt is made to determine different physiological bases for different emotions. The working assumption is that differences between emotions are due largely to differences in the cognitive labels about the body change. Thus, as with James's model, a bodily event is the controlling event for an emotion. However, there need not be a different body state associated with different emotions. Research has shown the necessity both of arousal and of cognitive labels for the bodily state if a "full" emotion is to be experienced.

Necessity of arousal. That arousal is necessary to the experiencing of an emotion is shown by both experimental and naturalistic evidence of variations in intensity of experience with variations in arousal level (see Schachter, 1966, 1967; Schachter & Latané, 1964). Subjects whose arousal was artificially increased by an experimentally administered dose of epinephrine reported and expressed more enjoyment of a slapstick movie than subjects given a placebo injection. Those whose arousal had been depressed by chlorpromazine had the least enjoyment. This depressant was also used to decrease anxiety about cheating and thus to increase the incidence of cheating. Of subjects on whom the drug worked (measured by pulse rate decrease), about 40 percent cheated on an experimental test, compared to about 20 percent of the subjects given a placebo. Thus, emotions may vary with arousal level.

A distinction must be made, however, between the reported *experience* of emotion and emotional *behavior*. Certainly in familiar circumstances, one can *act* emotional without *feeling* emotional. An overt response is given to the stimulus without a concomitant body response and feeling. Arousal does not appear to be necessary for the occurrence of overt emotional responses which have been learned previously in an aroused state. This is shown by experimental studies of dogs given a sympathectomy (a severance of nerve fibers of the sympathetic part of the autonomic nervous system) (Wynne & Solomon, 1955) and by observation of human beings who have had accidental sympathectomies. Patients who had accidental sympathectomies continued to act emotional after their accident but did not feel emotions as intensely as they had before the accident (Hohmann, 1962): ". . . it's sort of cold anger . . . a mental kind of anger"; "Seems like I get thinking mad, not shaking mad"; "I say I am afraid but I don't really feel afraid." Furthermore, the decrease in intensity of feelings, compared to the intensity remembered as typical before the injury, varied with the height of the lesion and therefore the amount of arousal still possible; the higher the lesion, the less the arousal and the greater the decrease in intensity of feelings of fear, anger, sexual excitement, and grief (Figure 14–3).

Thus, the evidence suggests that autonomic arousal facilitates the acquiring of emotional behavior but is not necessary for the behavior to be maintained and performed. The behavior that appears emotional in the absence of arousal is not accompanied by a full emotional experience. Without arousal, emotions are "cold." One may appear to be emotional because of his behavior, but not feel emotions.

Cognitive labels for arousal. Physiological states, as we have studied them so far, are not sufficient conditions for feeling emotional or for feel-

**FIGURE
14–2**

The "Jukebox" Theory of Emotion.

To hear music from a
jukebox, you must

ACTIVATE   and   SELECT   = Music

To experience emotion
you must have

BODY RESPONSE   and   COGNITIVE   = Emotion
                               INTERPRETATION
                               of BODY RESPONSE

                               —Perception of
                                 body change
                               —Label for body
                                 change

A body change (arousal)   A body change (arousal)
is necessary: alone is not sufficient:

An emotional behavior   Arousal without an
acquired with arousal may   emotional label may be
continue without arousal,   perceived as an "as if"
but the experience of   emotion.
emotion is "cold."

                               Aroused subjects with a
                               nonemotional interpretation
                               for their arousal were
                               not emotional.

                               Arousal may not be labeled
                               as emotional; the individual
                               does not appear emotional and
                               does not seem to be emotional
                               (repressor, psychopath).

FIGURE
14–3

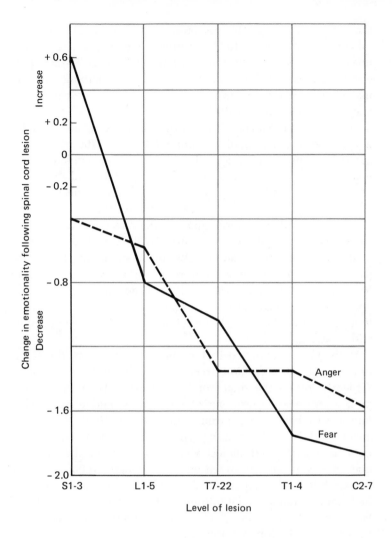

Changes in Emotionality as Related to Height of Spinal Cord Lesion.

Source: Adapted from Hohmann, 1962.

ing a specific emotion. Without a specific emotional label, the emotional state is empty—"as if" emotion (Marañon, 1925): "I feel as if I were upset, but I can't see what I have to be upset about." In such cases we are likely to search for an explanation of our feelings, and we typically look to the current situation or immediately preceding one for the explanation and label for the arousal. Sometimes, of course, the realistic explanation for the bodily state may be a nonemotional one: "I just finished exercising." Often, particularly in familiar circumstances, arousal and the emotional labeling of it may occur nearly simultaneously with each other and with the appraisal of the environment, which itself may have triggered the arousal. The cognitive response of a label, rather than different physiological states, serves to differentiate one emotion from another: "I'm uneasy about something. Oh, I'm anxious because I think I wrote a bad check yesterday." Or: "I'm uneasy about something. My roommate is making fun of me for not being able to keep my checkbook balanced, and I'm getting angry with him."

Schachter and Singer (1963) experimentally demonstrated the role of a cognitive evaluation of an aroused bodily state in determining what emotion, if any, is experienced. Arousal was manipulated by injection of epinephrine or a placebo. Cognitive interpretation of the resulting bodily state was manipulated by instructions to the subject about what side effects to expect from the injection and by the environmental situation to which the subjects were exposed after the injection. Some subjects injected with epinephrine were correctly informed about the side effects of the injection: heart palpitations, blood pounding, flushed face, sweaty palms. Misinformed subjects were given false information about what to expect: numb feet, itching, slight headache. Ignorant subjects (two epinephrine groups and the placebo group) were not given any instructions about the effects of the injection. After the injection, subjects waited with a stooge.

With subjects assigned to the euphoria condition, the stooge behaved in a very slapstick fashion, freely availing himself of the play props conveniently left in the room for that purpose. He sailed paper airplanes, built a cardboard tower out of file folders, and tossed crumpled paper into a wastebasket in a joyous game of basketball. With subjects in the anger condition, the stooge's prop was a very personal questionnaire that both he and the real subject were filling out for the experimenter. The questions were very personal and intentionally annoying, such as "What is your father's annual income?" "With how many men has your mother had extramarital sex relationships?" "How many times each week do you have sexual intercourse?" The stooge complained loudly, angrily, and consistently, as probably any real subject would.

The informed subjects, who had been correctly told of the effects to be expected from the injection, had an adequate nonemotional explanation of their bodily state and were less emotional (by self-reports and observed behavior while waiting) than those who had been misinformed or were told nothing about the likely effects (Table 14–1). Of the aroused groups, the misinformed and ignorant had increased arousal without an explanation and so were more susceptible to the emotional labels suggested by the behavior of the stooge. Whether they were euphoric or angry after the epinephrine injection varied with the behavior of the stooge. An emotional label is not only necessary for an emotion, but serves to differentiate one emotion from another when the underlying physiological arousal is presumably the same. (Only pulse rate was measured, so it is impossible to determine whether different physiological reactions were induced in different subjects by the drug or by the situations which they later encountered.) The results for the placebo group indicated that the

TABLE 14–1　Self-Report and Behavioral Ratings of Euphoria

Predictions of intensity of euphoria	Epinephrine Misinformed ≥ (Epi-Mis)	Epinephrine Ignorant > (Epi-Ign)	Epinephrine Informed = (Epi-Inf)	Placebo Ignorant (Placebo)
Self-reports				
	Epi-Mis 1.90	Epi-Ign 1.78	Placebo 1.61	Epi-Inf .98
Behavior Euphoric acts				
	Epi-Mis 22.56	Epi-Ign 18.28	Placebo 16.00	Epi-Inf 12.72
Euphoric acts Initiated				
	Epi-Mis .84	Epi-Ign .56	Placebo .54	Epi-Inf .20

Results for subjects exposed to the anger condition were similar, though in reverse order. The inversion in prediction for epi-inf and placebo groups was apparently due to the fact that some subjects in the placebo group became aroused in the situation. Analysis of placebo subjects in the euphoric condition showed that the average number of euphoric acts for those whose pulse rate decreased (n = 14) was 10.67, while the average number for subjects whose pulse increased or stayed the same (n = 12) was 23.17; the difference was significant, $p < .02$. The average number of euphoric acts for anger subjects whose pulse decreased (n = 13) was 0.15, while for those whose pulse increased or stayed the same it was 1.69 (n = 8): a significant difference, $p. < .01$.

SOURCE: Data from Schachter, S., & Singer, J.

same event may both trigger the bodily response and provide the label for it. Although the pulse rate of some placebo subjects dropped during the experiment as expected, that of others did not. The emotionality of those who were at relatively increased arousal levels was greater than that of those with lower arousal. (Expectation of increased arousal with a placebo can also induce emotionality, according to Dienstbier and Munter [1971].) Apparently for the former, the environmental situation increased their arousal, which was labeled in accordance with that event which increased it, a likely occurrence in real-life experience also. Whether they occur simultaneously or sequentially, both a bodily change and a label of it as an emotional one are necessary for experienced emotion.

Individual Differences in the Emotional Chain

The body change and the emotional label of it—both of which are necessary conditions for an emotional experience—occur within the context of a response chain, a sequence of stimuli and responses (Figure 14–4).

FIGURE 14-4

$$S \xrightarrow{\quad} r = s \xrightarrow{\quad} r = s \xrightarrow{\quad} r = s \xrightarrow{\quad} r = s \xrightarrow{\quad} R$$

ENVIRONMENTAL EVENT	APPRAISAL OF ENVIRONMENTAL EVENT	BODY CHANGE, AROUSAL	PERCEPTION OF BODY CHANGE	LABEL FOR BODY CHANGE	BEHAVIOR
Pain	An emotion-arousing situation may not be appraised as emotion-arousing, and vice versa	Genetic and acquired body reactivity	Reinforcement community may encourage or discourage attention to body	Reinforcing community may encourage or discourage the use of emotional labels, or may encourage the use of particular kinds of labels	Self-report of feeling
Response indecision —difficult discrimination —conflict —interruption			One may learn to ignore over-reactivity, to not pay attention		Facial, vocal, body expressions of emotions
Threat —symbolic —anticipation of pain —ego threat —death			One may learn to exaggerate body activity		Defense to block the development of the emotional sequence at the appraisal, body reactivity, perception, labeling, or behavioral stages Punishment for emotional behavior may inhibit the manifestation of the emotion and spread back to previous stages

Steps in the Sequence of Emotional Behavior.

The sequence is begun when the person perceives and appraises an external event and, later, the internal stimuli of thoughts and feelings (Dollard & Miller, 1942). Because of innate reasons or prior conditioning, the perception and appraisal of the event are followed quickly by a bodily response which is perceived and labeled. With repeated experience, the events in the chain may occur simultaneously, and some may be short-circuited; for example, the environmental stimulus may simultaneously trigger its appraisal, the bodily response, and the label, as happened for some placebo subjects in the experiment just discussed. Individual variation in intensity and content of emotions and in methods of dealing with emotions might be explained in terms of any or all of these events. Defense mechanisms may operate at any point in the sequence. Differences in body reactivity patterns and intensity in combination with different learning experiences in the world lead to emotional diversity among people, and to emotional richness or poverty, adequacy or inadequacy, within people.

The stimuli. A complete mapping of exactly what emotions are innately elicited by what stimuli has not yet been accomplished. For purposes of discussion, it is safe to think at least of feelings such as fear, anxiety, or distress as elicited by unexpectedness, pain, or scenes of mutilation. Other major classes of events likely to be associated with anxiety are discussed in Chapter 15. With maturation and learning, previously neutral events come to be effective in eliciting emotions, in initiating the emotional chain. Because of environmental differences in what stimuli are associated with enough contiguity for conditioning, people come to differ in what events—previously neutral—become emotional ones for them. It is assumed that major learning mechanisms in emotional development include classical conditioning and stimulus generalization because of similarity. For example, Little Albert became afraid of a white rat (cs) which had been paired with a sudden loud noise (ucs) that was originally effective in eliciting fear, and the fear generalized to objects similar to the rat (Chapter 5).

The classical conditioning model of emotional behavior is essentially a valid one. However, our understanding of it is incomplete, despite numerous studies since Pavlov's day. Moreover, conditioning of strong emotional responses differs in important respects from conditioning of other kinds of responses. Generally, strength of conditioning increases with the number of cs-ucs pairings, and withholding the ucs leads to extinction. However, emotional responses are very resistant to extinction, and when a stimulus is intense enough, one pairing may be enough to establish an emotional response that defies conventional extinction procedures (Campbell, Sanderson, & Laverty, 1964). In one piece of research, subjects experienced only one pairing of a tone (cs) with Scoline (ucs), a fast-acting drug that induces intense fear by producing a state of complete paralysis in which the subject is unable to move or breathe for almost two minutes. After one pairing, the subjects were tested with the tone (cs) only; all five showed a conditioned fear reaction, complete with the autonomic changes characteristic of acute traumatic neurosis. Three of the subjects showed no extinction after 100 presentations of the tone alone. Although the other two subjects showed extinction within ten trials of the cs only, they also showed spontaneous recovery and then no further extinction in 100 trials of the cs only. Such resistance to extinction is also characteristic of the anxiety attacks which continue to occur upon encountering stimuli similar to those present during traumatic combat experiences or civilian emergencies. In one experiment, about seven out of ten men who had supposedly been cured of combat neurosis experienced in World War II had clear symptoms of jumpiness, irritability, restlessness, and depression twenty years later (Archibald & Tuddenhan, 1965).

The applicability of the classical conditioning model for human emotions is extended by the fact that the aversive ucs need not be physically painful. Photographs of victims of a violent death were quite effective as a ucs (Geer, 1968). Consistent with the classical conditioning model, a response (skin conductance change) came to be given to the cs (a tone), and these responses were stronger for a forward conditioning (cs-ucs sequence) group of subjects than for a backward (ucs-cs sequence) conditioning group. However, a group which saw the photos and heard the tones randomly rather than in a systematic pairing were also responsive to the cs (Figure 14–5). The arousal of the random group to the cs probably reflects the lack of predictability about the occurrence of the aversive ucs.

There is also increasing reason to suppose that autonomic responses may function according to principles of instrumental conditioning as well as classical conditioning principles, and perhaps can be voluntarily controlled (Chapter 5). If a bodily response is part of a rewarded sequence of emotional behavior in a particular situation, the likelihood of its occurrence increases in that kind of situation. If the emotion is punished, one can learn to inhibit an intense bodily response in that situation. A particular kind of situation becomes a controlling, discriminative stimulus in the presence of which the body response is more or less likely to occur. This fact has important implications for the acquisition and treatment of psychosomatic disorders. If one can escape an unpleasant situation, or gain desired attention and nurturance, because of feeling weak or having high blood pressure, then the weakness or blood-pressure increases are likely to become more frequent, and perhaps to be controlled by the discriminative stimulus of whatever the person considers unpleasant situations. Hopefully, instrumental conditioning principles may be applied to the treatment of psychosomatic disorders, though this is still speculation rather than fact. Considering the many variations in environmental response to emotions, as well as in what stimuli have been associated with initially effective emotion-inducing cues, people become vastly different in what objective stimuli make them emotional. The content of emotion-

**FIGURE
14–5**

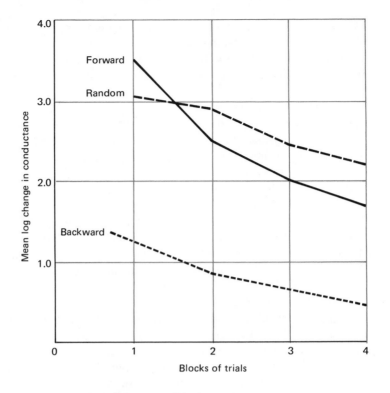

Response to CS during Conditioning.

Source: Geer, J. H. A test of the classical conditioning model of emotion: The use of nonpainful aversive stimuli as unconditioned stimuli in a conditioning procedure. *Journal of Personality and Social Psychology,* 1968, 10, 148–156.

eliciting stimuli as a source of individual differences is further widened by the fact that the meaning of objective environmental stimuli is appraised.

Appraisal. For many kinds of stimuli, it is necessary that they be appraised, that their significance be determined. Particularly in ambiguous situations, the effectiveness of a stimulus in eliciting an emotional response will differ greatly from one person to another because they have different habits of interpreting the environment (Arnold, 1970b; Lazarus, Averill, & Opton, 1970; Schachter, 1970). As discussed in Chapter 15, people have markedly different inclinations to perceive threat, and they see different things as threatening. The appraisal may be the result of a well-learned habit that occurs relatively automatically in some situations, or it may follow quickly, and equally automatically, after one has had a signal that anxiety is likely to develop. This is partly a matter of perceptual style. Generally, people who use sensitizing kinds of defenses seem prone to "see" threatening events in the environment, while repressors are inclined to avoid noticing or attending to problem areas

(Chapter 11). Faced with the same situation, one will appraise the situation as anxiety-arousing while the other will appraise it more positively or neutrally. Each will label the same situation in his characteristic fashion, if he has an opportunity to do so without committing an extreme violation of reality.

Appraisals of the environmental event may serve to increase or decrease the bodily response to the event. The effectiveness of appraisal in dampening physiological responsiveness was experimentally shown by accompanying a movie of accidents in a woodshop with different sound tracks (Lazarus et al., 1965). An "intellectualizing" version gave a detached view of the technical aspects of the accidents. A "denial" version emphasized that the people in the film were just actors pretending to have their fingers cut off, and the blood was just catsup. A brief description of the film was used as a control commentary. Subjects who heard the denial and intellectualizing commentaries had lower arousal than those in the control conditions, though all the groups had peak responses at the time of the accidents (Figure 14-6). Similar results were obtained with another film accompanied by either an intellectualizing or a reaction-formation commentary; subjects who heard the "trauma" version, emphasizing the horror of the situation and the pain and harmful consequences, had the greatest arousal (Speisman, et al., 1964b). The same stimulus leads to different reactions, depending on the nature of the appraisal. Although appraisals are often shared with others because they have grown in a common culture, there is ample room for the develop-

FIGURE
14–6

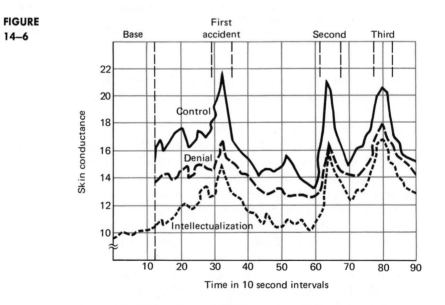

Group Average Skin Conditions for Three Orientation Treatments during the Accident Film.

Source: From Lazarus et al., 1965.

ment of individual differences in interpreting the environment, particularly when the behavior of other people is involved (Chapter 13).

The use of specific labels for environmental events may facilitate adjustive responses, or it may lead to unrealistic and maladaptive ones. Labels may be given to a variety of events one has not directly experienced, because the label serves as a mediating stimulus. Whether or not the result is adaptive depends upon the pattern of generalization and differentiation (Dollard & Miller, 1942). With strong conditioning—"Just thinking about it upsets me"—the person may come to avoid anxiety by repressing associated thoughts or by avoiding circumstances in which they would be elicited. If one had an unpleasant experience that was also dangerous—riding with an inexperienced stunt pilot, for example—avoiding the situation again because even thinking of it is disturbing would be adaptive behavior. With the use of the instruction, "Avoid inexperienced pilots," one may avoid even those with whom one has not flown as long as they are known to be inexperienced. All inexperienced pilots are labeled "dangerous." However, if one becomes upset when seeing or thinking about *any* pilot or *any* airplane trip, the generalization from the actual threatening event is unrealistic and maladaptive. This inappropriate anxiety could be controlled by acquiring relevant discriminations and more accurate use of the label of "dangerous"—that is, by labeling inexperienced flyers in airplanes "dangerous" but not so labeling thoroughly trained pilots (Figure 14–7). Often people do not use verbal labels in controlling their emotional response—they do not think. A person who becomes jittery as he takes a friend to the airport may become more relaxed if he realizes that he is responding to the nonverbal cues relevant to airplanes and then brings the response under control by appropriate use of the labels "dangerous" or "safe."

Variations in the frequency and intensity of bodily responses connected to emotions are due both to genetic predispositions to respond physiologically and to acquire and maintain conditioned responses, and to the content of learning experiences which influence how a person labels or interprets the environment. Closely associated with the interpretation of the environment are the cognitive responses to body activity.

Cognitive responses to bodily state. The cognitive activities of having perceptions about body responses and of labeling or explaining the body responses are important sources of differences in emotionality. The labels for the environmental events often affect the interpretation of the body response. Any of these may be vehicles for the operation of defenses or, more generally, for determining the extent and content of emotional experiences.

People have ideas about their body's activities, and what they think is going on can be important determinants of overt behavior and conclusions about one's emotional states. This is not to say that the viscera themselves necessarily provide direct cues for the discrimination of emotional states. When one labels a remark as an insult, he may assume that

FIGURE
14–7

Overresponsiveness with lack of label:

Unpleasant experience
with inexperienced ⟶ Strong emotional response
stunt pilot

All pilots and all
objects or thoughts
related to flying

Overgeneralization in use of "Danger" label:

The inexperienced pilot ⟶ "Danger" ⟶ Cognitive and/or
previously encountered   Physical avoidance
All pilots and all
objects or thoughts
related to flying

Appropriate generalization and discrimination:

The inexperienced pilot ⟶ "Danger" ⟶ Cognitive and/or
previously encountered   Physical avoidance
Any inexperienced pilot
or unfit airplane
Experienced pilot
Safe airplanes
Other nonverbal stimuli ⟶ "Safe" ⟶ OK to approach
and thoughts related
to flying

Generalization and Discrimination in Appraisal Labels.

his heart is pounding, whether or not it is. We use information about ourselves to make conclusions about ourselves, even if the information is not correct. For example, a rather peculiar relative insists that he is too hot or too cold, but can easily be persuaded otherwise by an incorrect thermometer whose needle points to the temperature at which he is perfectly comfortable. Similarly, Russian experimenters brought urinary urges under external control by pairing the UCS of actual bladder fullness (controlled by a tube in the bladder) with a CS, a meter giving an external display of the bladder fullness (Razran, 1961). When the meter was later rigged to falsely indicate a full bladder, or an empty one, the reported urges were consistent with the *false* meter reading, the CS, rather than with the actual bladder condition. By an analogous process, cues relevant to internal body changes which have been previously associated with stimuli considered emotional can lead one to conclude that an object or event in the environment is an emotional one (Figure 14–8).

FIGURE
14–8

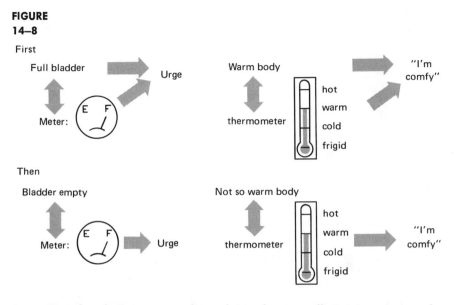

First

Full bladder — Urge

Meter: (E F)

Warm body — "I'm comfy"

thermometer [hot / warm / cold / frigid]

Then

Bladder empty

Meter: (E F) — Urge

Not so warm body

thermometer [hot / warm / cold / frigid] — "I'm comfy"

Perception of Body State as Conditioned Stimulus Controlling Interpretation of Body State.

People are often responsive to the cues they have about their body activities, whether or not the cues are a correct mirror of reality, and some people are more responsive than others. False feedback about heart-rate changes was used to create preferences for pictures of attractive females from *Playboy* magazine (Valins, 1966, 1967; Barefoot & Straub, 1971; Stern, Botto, & Herrick, 1972). College males gave higher attractiveness ratings to pictures presented while they thought their heart rate had changed markedly than to pictures presented without a perceived heart-rate change. The false heart-rate feedback may be given by a verbal report from the experimenter, or by a tape recording of what the subjects thought were their own heart sounds. Subjects were also more likely to choose gift copies of pictures which had been accompanied by heart-rate change, and the preference differential was still present when, six weeks later, they again chose among pictures in another context. Information about the internal event of heart rate did affect the reactions to the stimuli. Perhaps more important is that the effect of perceived heart-rate change was greater for subjects independently classified as relatively emotional than for the relatively unemotional subjects—the unemotional were less responsive to the information about their internal reactions than were the more emotional (Figure 14–9). Additional work using the same general procedure indicates that the emotionality engendered by the feedback is shown also in TAT projective measurements (Nuttall & Barclay, 1973) and that the false feedback may instigate changes in actual arousal which are necessary for reported emotionality, at least in highly emotional situations (Goldstein, Fink, & Mettee, 1972).

FIGURE
14–9

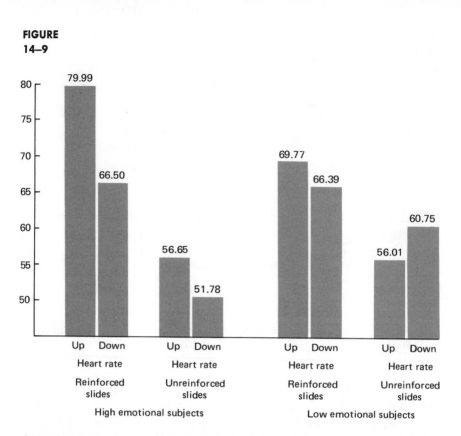

Attractiveness Ratings of Slides of Playmates Presented during Perceived Heart-Rate Increase or Decrease (Reinforced) Compared with Those of Slides for Which Heart-Rate Change Was Not Contingent upon Slide Presentation, for Subjects Independently Classified as High or Low Emotional.

Source: Valins, S. Emotionality and information concerning internal reactions. *Journal of Personality and Social Psychology,* 1967, *6,* 458–463.

Individual differences in emotionality are determined partly by differences in the *use* of information about oneself; and habitual distortions, internally rather than externally induced, in the perception of body cues may function defensively. People differ in the extent to which they use information about body states and in the kinds of errors they are likely to make in perceiving their body states. People high in manifest anxiety tend to *over*estimate their body responses in stressful situations in the laboratory, while those low in anxiety tend to *under*estimate their actual responsiveness (Mandler, Mandler, & Uviller, 1958; Mandler & Kremen, 1958a,b).

Once perceived, accurately or not, the body response must be labeled. As discussed previously, a label for arousal is necessary for an emotional experience and serves to differentiate one experience from another. The labels for arousal are often chosen on the basis of the environmental situation in a way others consider realistic. Most people would not label arousal in response to an insult as joy, nor the arousal occurring during a surprise birthday party as anger. We use cues from the environment to explain our feelings in ways that we, as well as others, consider appropriate—we have "normal" feelings. However, while there is a core of relative agreement, there is ample opportunity during the course of emotional socialization to acquire habits of using favorite labels, and sometimes inappropriate ones. Habits of cognitive labeling are an important source of individual differences in emotionality. Some people may have only a very small number of labeling responses so that they experience mainly, say, anger or happiness, but have no acquaintance with fear, depression, pride, sorrow. Others have a broader range of labels and a richer emotional life, with much more nuance and subtlety of feeling. Often, people do not know what they are feeling; they persistently have "as if" emotions. In a similar spirit, it has been suggested that individual differences, on a continuum from superficial though often intense emotional episodes to profound, deeply felt emotion, are of great importance for personality assessment (Wellek, 1970).

People differ also in the extent to which they use *any* emotional label for their arousal. Repressors, who avoid anxiety, tend to underuse emotional labels. Sensitizers, who defend by approaching anxiety, tend to overuse emotional labels in describing themselves or others. For example, repressors consistently reported less distress than did sensitizers while watching a stressful film of adolescent male aborigines subjected to crude genital operations (Weinstein et al., 1968). The effect of differences between groups was due primarily to the effect of defensive style as seen in self-reports and *not* to differences in autonomic reactivity. (Some studies have found greater arousal for one group, some for the other, but few differences approached significance.) There have also been some suggestions that sociopaths, who do not appear to experience anxiety, do not label as emotional the body states that would be considered emotional by other people (Schachter & Latané, 1964). Thus far, there is only speculation about how people develop predispositions to use emotional or nonemotional cognitive labels. Have some people failed to learn to use emotional labels? Or have they learned not to use them in order to avoid overemotionality? Or are they unaware of body responses or underestimate them? Different answers may be correct for different people, depending upon genetic predispositions and learning experiences.

Problems of emotional socialization. Genetic factors predispose autonomic reactivity and emotionality—certainly fearfulness—to some kinds of events, and individual differences in conditionability lead to differences in the range of events which will elicit body responses. Within broad but firmly set limits, experiences fill in the details of our emotional lives. The reinforcing community, beginning with the parents, can encourage or discourage attending to body states and labeling body sensations as emotional ones. By their responses to verbal reports and other overt expressions about emotions, and by their interpretation of the situation in which they occur, they help to shape the emotional habits developed by the child. In the kinds of labels and interpretations they use about themselves and provide to the growing child, they can encourage some emotional labels over others, or encourage the use of non-emotional labels for the same external and internal events. Extreme concern about and extensive positive reinforcement for the use of body cues, emotional labels, and expressions may facilitate what others will consider overemotionality. Punishment, either direct ("Boys don't cry!") or implicit in the lack of agreement by others ("Why are you so upset by that?"), may dampen whatever capacity for feeling emotions, generally or in specific situations, would otherwise develop. If one is repeatedly punished for verbalizing and expressing emotion, he learns to inhibit the overt manifestation of emotions. More subtly, expressions of emotion which are ignored by others and thus do not serve a communicative function in interpersonal interaction may drop down in the hierarchy of facial, vocal, and gestural habits (Chapter 13). It is unfortunately not always a very long step to the inhibition of the underlying thoughts, and perhaps the body responses and label of the environment, as emotion-provoking. Emotional thoughts and responses may be punished out, just as any other kinds may be.

With emotions as with other areas of individual differences, most people are considered "normal" for their social group. Their emotional socialization history shares much with that of other people (Chapter 13). We learn to discriminate between those kinds of occasions on which it is or is not considered appropriate to feel emotional or to show overt expressions of emotion. However, the job of providing adequate socialization of emotions is not an easy one (Skinner, 1963). Even a very sensitive mother cannot do a perfect job of leading a child to detect and interpret body and feeling states when she must infer the nature of those events. When the child says "chair" as he is sitting in what mother considers a chair, there is little problem. When the child is fretful without an obvious cause and can only cry or mutter, "I not right," his mother is in the awkward position of having to guess at the internal events she, and later the child, must label. Given the private nature of the body and feeling states upon which reinforcement must be contingent, it is surprising that we develop as much commonality in emotional habits as we apparently do. Given the reliance upon others for obtaining labels for private events and therefore for understanding of them, it is indeed surprising that we "know" ourselves as well as most of us do. If it is true that feelings and emotions are the basic modes of experience and the ground of all knowledge of ourselves and others (Strasser, 1970), then it is important indeed to ponder the adequacy of our emotional socialization.

SUMMARY

Human emotions clearly illustrate that man is a psycho-biological organism whose behavior and internal experiences are influenced by both genetic and experiential factors. Within broad but firm limits set by genetic factors, experience fills in the details of our emotional lives. Through physical and cognitive maturation, the infant's small repertoire of emotional behavior becomes differentiated and extended as he interacts wtih people who respond to his behavior and later help him to interpret his own feelings. With maturation, he becomes more sensitive to the environment and more knowledgeable about what to expect in it; the range of emotion-evoking stimuli increases because of his growing sensitivity, and spontaneous fears emerge. Individual differences in emotionality are partly attributable to genetic influences not completely understood, but probably involving at least differences in ANS and CNS processes. The outcome, though, varies also with the stresses encountered in the environment and with what traits are rewarded or punished in the environment. With enough stress, even someone with a very stable personality may have a temporary breakdown.

Both genetic and experiential factors, and both mind and body interact in determining emotions. There are distinct physiological responses involved in some emotional states. Epinephrine seems associated with fear while with anger the role of norepinephrine is more noticeable. Distinctive physiological patterns accompany different sets of problems of handling emotional needs, as seen in psychosomatic disorders. However, differences in physiological response patterns do not seem capable of accounting for all individual differences in emotionality or for the whole range of human emotion. A view of emotions as involving general physiological arousal and cognitive labels is more capable of accounting for emotional variation between people and differences between emotions. Without arousal, or without an emotional label for the arousal, the result is a "cold" emotion, or "as if" emotion, respectively. Emotions are a sequence of internal events in response to external or internal stimuli. Some events seem innately effective in eliciting an emotional response. Many more become so by generalization and conditioning. Body responses may also be instrumentally conditioned and come under the control of discriminative stimuli in the environment. Many stimuli are ones which must be appraised, and people differ in their appraisal habits. In addition, individual differences also occur in the perception of the body response; what a person thinks to be his body state can influence his conclusions about himself and his reactions to the environment. People differ also in their use of emotional or nonemotional labels for their body state and probably in the range and variety of labels they have and thus in their emotional richness.

Problems of overemotionality may occur at any of the steps in the sequence of emotions and corrective attempts may be directed at any of these points, probably with differential effectiveness for different individuals or for different kinds of problems. People do develop perceptual habits which are not always completely accurate views of reality and can to some extent replace them with more realistic appraisals of the environment and themselves. ANS responses may be voluntarily controlled or subject to some modification by conditioning procedures. Or one can learn to ignore or underestimate his perception of the extent of his body response, or teach himself to respond to his genetically influenced physiological overreactivity with "That's a normal reaction for me because I'm 'wired' that way," rather than "Gee, I'm upset." Or nonemotional labels may be substituted for emotional ones, "I'm not anxious about the exam. My body is jumpy because I've been drinking coffee and then rushed over to the exam."

While some people have problems of being too emotional too much of the time and at inappropriate times, an equally pervasive problem is a deficiency in the completeness of emotional experiences. Social pressures encourage inconsistency in the occurrence of components of emotions and encourage emotional control and suppression rather than acceptance and enjoyment of complete emotional experiences and expressions. The pressures may be one manifestation of cultural tendencies to define reality in terms of the external world to the neglect of the equally real internal world (Chapter 9). One cannot then know himself and is alienated from himself by virtue of neglect of himself or of behaving inconsistently with his feelings (Chapter 12). Some emotions are unpleasant, but all are real experiences of a totally functioning person who knows and accepts himself. To block emotional experiences is to lose information about oneself and to endanger the effectiveness and pleasantness of living with and knowing other people (Chapter 13). Anxiety may be unpleasant and sometimes debilitating, but, as will be discussed in the following chapter, it can be used effectively in efficient and realistic interaction with the world.

15

anxiety

Most research and theory about emotional behavior has focused on anxiety. Anxiety, and the methods used for dealing with it, have obvious implications for the individual's comfort with himself. They also influence relations with others and ability to perform at chosen or assigned tasks. Reference has been made previously to anxiety in connection with fantasy, motivation, perception of self and others, and to the role of anxiety in eliciting perceptual defense mechanisms. Here, we will take a more careful look at some of the causes and effects of anxiety and raise issues about the unconscious processes which supposedly help in controlling anxiety. How much anxiety one experiences and how he controls it have important correlates in the effectiveness of attentiveness to the world and ability to learn and perform in it. The amount of anxiety elicited in any situation varies with personal predispositions and with the situation as the subject perceives it. The behavioral effects of anxiety vary with the requirements of the situation. Anxiety is not always unrealistic, and defenses to handle anxiety are not always debilitating or always beneficial.

Anxiety states are the subjective, consciously perceived feelings of tension and apprehension associated with arousal (Spielberger, 1966, 1972). Although terminology varies, anxiety as a state (A-state) is often considered synonymous with fear and caused by stress. A stressful situation is one in which the organism is unable to produce an appropriate response to avoid or escape a noxious state of affairs (e.g., Shapiro & Crider, 1969; Lazarus, 1966). Anxiety as a state is a *response*. It is also an *energizer* and a *stimulus* with important pervasive effects on cognitive and behavioral efficiency. Anxiety as a personality trait (A-trait) is a predisposition to respond with greater anxiety state reactions than expected on the basis of the objective situation. People high in trait anxiety may have learned to appraise events as more stressful more often than those lower in the trait anxiety. Or, they may have greater emotionality in any other component of the emotional sequence, for example, autonomic responsivity, or perception and labeling of body activities (Chapter 14). As a personality trait, anxiety is usually measured by self-report tests of manifest anxiety, such as the Taylor Manifest Anxiety Scale. * Selected items from this scale follow:

1. I do not tire quickly.
2. I have very few headaches.
3. I cannot keep my mind on one thing.
4. I frequently notice my hand shakes when I try to do something.
5. I sweat very easily even on cool days.
6. I have a great deal of stomach trouble.
7. I am easily embarrassed.
8. I cry easily.
9. I am happy most of the time.
10. It makes me nervous to have to wait.
11. Sometimes I become so excited that I find it hard to get to sleep.
12. I have been afraid of things or people that I know could not hurt me.
13. I certainly feel useless at times.
14. I find it hard to keep my mind on a task or job.
15. At times I think I am no good at all.

Trait scores and self-reports about current anxiety states are sometimes related to measures of autonomic responses (an index of A-state) but not always, which is little wonder in view of the number of factors which affect self-reports of manifest anxiety. However, some classes of events seem to be sufficiently pervasive and effective in eliciting anxiety specifically and/or arousal that they can be considered relatively basic and common determinants of anxiety. People differ in how frequently they are exposed to these kinds of situations and in the specific content of the situations they have come to find stressful. People differ also in their characteristic styles of dealing with anxiety. These phenomena are illustrated in an overview of inducers and effects of anxiety shown in a chart on the facing page (355).

DETERMINANTS OF ANXIETY

The view that physical pain as an innate experience is the basic anxiety-evoking event from which other anxieties are built by conditioning has been the most popular one with learning theorists. As noted, humans do condition to painful stimuli (Chapter 14). How-

* Answers: Point for each item answered as keyed: 1. False; 2. false; 3. true; 4. true; 5. true; 6. true; 7. true; 8. true; 9. false; 10. true; 11. true; 12. true; 13. true; 14. true; 15. true. The large number of items keyed "true" is typical of the scale, and is one methodological criticism of it. Adapted from Taylor, J. A. A personality scale of manifest anxiety. *Journal of Abnormal and Social Psychology*, 1953, **48**, 285–290.

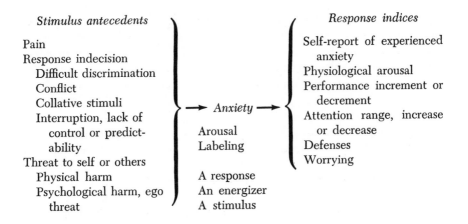

Stimulus antecedents		Response indices
Pain		Self-report of experienced anxiety
Response indecision		Physiological arousal
Difficult discrimination		Performance increment or decrement
Conflict	→ Anxiety →	Attention range, increase or decrease
Collative stimuli		Defenses
Interruption, lack of control or predictability	Arousal	Worrying
	Labeling	
Threat to self or others		
Physical harm	A response	
Psychological harm, ego threat	An energizer	
	A stimulus	

ever, pain seems to be neither the basis of all anxiety nor invariant with experience. Congenital analgesics (people who, from birth, are insensitive to what others would call pain) do develop anxiety (Kessen & Mandler, 1961). And pain experience seems to be susceptible to modification by experience and the use of nonpainful labels. Scenes of mutilation elicit anxiety. Fears of mutilation of one's own body as well as a fear of death itself probably run deep for most people. But it is unlikely that in the lives of most people physical pain and mutilation are crucial determinants of their recurring, everyday anxieties. Other kinds of stressful events are more likely to be important. These kinds of stresses seem to fit roughly into two categories: those which lead to response indecision, or those which are threatening. They characteristically induce arousal which is often accompanied by an experience of anxiety and may instigate processes for coping with anxiety. Although the situations which induce arousal or anxiety specifically are probably not necessarily stressful ones, they do seem to be pervasively occurring situations of helplessness. It may well be that they are associated with special evolutionary dangers (Chapter 14). In both cases one is momentarily helpless in the face of a noxious state of affairs. Helplessness as a chief cause of anxiety is a repeated theme in psychoanalytic and existentialist theory, and its effectiveness in eliciting arousal and anxiety is substantiated by a vast research literature only sampled here.

Response Indecision

When one is indecisive about what to think or how to behave, he is, for the moment, helpless. The indecision and momentary or extended helplessness may occur because one is unsure about the stimulus to which he must respond (a difficult discrimination is required or the meaning of the stimulus is unclear), because he is in conflict about how to respond, or because he has little control over what happens or insufficient information to predict what will happen.

Difficult discrimination. When a difficult discrimination is required, one has a response for each of two or more stimuli, but is unsure about what to do because he is not sure what the stimulus is. The problem lies in the stimulus uncertainty. Pavlov found that neurotic-like behavior was induced in dogs by requiring a difficult discrimination of them (e.g., by requiring different responses to a circle and to an ellipse which became progressively like the circle). Similarly, human subjects who had to make increasingly difficult discriminations between tone series of differing rates (until the rates of the stimulus series became in fact exactly alike, though no subject detected this) showed continual increases in physiological arousal and self-reports of bodily harm anxiety (Johnson, 1963). The increased arousal was not due to punishment (shock) received for mistakes; yoked control subjects who did not have to make the decisions but were shocked the same as an experimental subject did not show the arousal increase.

Analogous situations occur in everyday life when, for example, a student can write either a lengthy flowery paper or a tight concise one but cannot tell whether a particular professor is the kind who prefers one or the other; or when we could easily leave a friend alone or try to console him, but we are unsure about the signals he is giving about which response he wants. Part of our discomfort in such situations is due simply to the difficulty of the decision itself because of stimulus uncertainty, apart from any punishment anticipated from the professor or the friend.

Conflict. A conflictful situation is one in which the nature of the stimuli is clear, but the response tendencies elicited by simultaneous, multiple aspects of the same stimulus are incompatible. Conflict is maximum when two competing response tendencies are at exactly equal strength, and decreases as the difference between the response tendencies increases (Chapter 6). The response incompatibility may be due to the fact that one cannot *approach* both of the two objects or events (approach-approach conflict), cannot *avoid* both of the two objects of events (avoidance-avoidance conflict), cannot avoid the negative features of an object or event and at the same time approach its positive features (approach-avoidance), or may be due to the joint occurrence of these conflicts about more than one goal. Epstein (1967; Epstein & Fenz, 1962) modified Miller's model of conflict to make a variety of predictions about the anxiety generated by the approach-avoidance conflict experienced by sports parachutists—a valuable demonstration of the applicability of models derived in the experimental laboratory (with rats) to naturally occurring behavior. It was assumed first that there are approach and avoidance drives associated with jumping and that the approach drive is greater than the avoidance drive, because the parachutists do make the goal response of jumping (Figure 15–1a). Further, the magnitude of the approach response is the net result of subtracting the avoidance drive from the approach drive (Figure 15–1b), and the total arousal induced by the conflict is represented by the absolute *sum* of the magnitude of the approach and avoidance drives (Figure 15–1c). Thus, there is an inverted V pattern in the approach response, and a sharp increase in drive as the goal approaches, as seen best in the figures. Consistent with the model, novices reported eagerness to jump before the scheduled event, then second thoughts once aboard the aircraft. Tension and behavioral disorganization increased sharply as the moment of the jump arrived. The dimension of nearness to the goal may be one of time from the goal action or a symbolic dimension operationalized by the researchers in terms of words of varying degrees of relevance to the goal activity. For precise measurements of arousal as a function of nearness to the goal on both the temporal and symbolic dimensions, GSR was measured during presentation and association to words of low relevance to parachuting (sky, land), of intermediate relevance (fall, float), and high relevance to the goal activity (bail-out, ripcord); neutral words (salt, quiet) were also used for comparison purposes. Arousal increased with goal relevance and temporal closeness to the point of jumping (day of the jump compared with two weeks before or after). Additionally, the arousal *increase* as a function of the stimulus relevance was greater on the day of the jump than at some time away from the jump (Figure 15–2), as predicted by the assumption noted in Figure 15–1. How the anxiety is coped with is treated later in this chapter.

Collative stimuli. Features of difficult discrimination and conflict situations are combined in collative stimuli. Collative stimuli are those with properties of novelty, surprisingness, complexity, puzzlingness, and ambiguity (Berlyne, 1960, 1968). They are called collative because they involve the collation or comparison of stimuli and are defined with respect to the degree to which a particular environmental feature is similar to or different from others presented at the same time or in the past. What they have in common is that they are closely bound up with how much uncertainty is associated with the stimulus. One does not know what to do because one is unsure about what the stimulus is. One is unsure about how to classify the stimulus, what its hidden characteristics are, or what is to come next. No one predominant reaction comes immediately to the fore. Competing responses are evoked by different aspects of the stimulus, or at worst, no responses are evoked. Although mild deviation from the usual or expected is often pleasing, extreme deviation is likely to elicit arousal and anxiety (Chapter 22). The anxiety may be reduced by withdrawal of attention from the stimulus, such as a physical turning away or rejection, or by the operation of defenses to reduce the amount of perceived deviation. People may be collative stimuli because of their deviance from the expected. Thus, the perception of similarity between self and others may function to reduce or avoid anxiety (Chapter 13). Deviation by someone else from what is expected of them may increase anxiety and lead to unjustified or irra-

FIGURE
15–1a

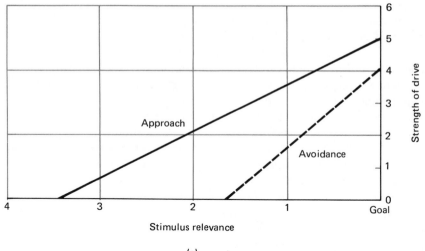

Strength of drive

Approach

Avoidance

Goal

Stimulus relevance

(a)

Strength of Approach and Avoidance Drive as a Function of a Stimulus Dimension.

tional behavior, such as derrogation and maltreatment. Anxiety at the deviance from what is expected has much in common with the spontaneous fears previously discussed (Chapter 14) and may be an important reason for pressures to get other people to conform to the group majority (Chapter 17).

Interruption, control, and predictability. Mandler (1964, 1968; Mandler & Watson, 1966; Sher, 1971) has theorized that a prime determinant of emotional behavior is the interruption of a plan of behavior. The plan of action may be as molar and abstract as a plan to achieve in a distant career, or as concrete and specific as opening a door. Interruption of a plan produces arousal which is labeled in terms of the conditions of arousal. The arousal caused by a telephone call which interrupts dinner will be labeled negatively when the call is from an insistent salesman of an unwanted product and labeled positively when it is from a long-lost friend. Anxiety specifically is likely when the person does not feel that he can control the onset and offset of arousal. That is, he does not think he has enough control of the situation to avoid possible interruption, or has been interrupted and has no alternative behavior with which to continue his plan. He does not know what to do. He is helpless. One can plan for the occurrence of events which would otherwise provide an unexpected interruption and anxiety. This requires having alternative plans of action effective for working toward the goal. For example, rejection by the college or graduate school of one's choice need not interrupt the plan for getting a degree if one has alternative

FIGURE
15–1b

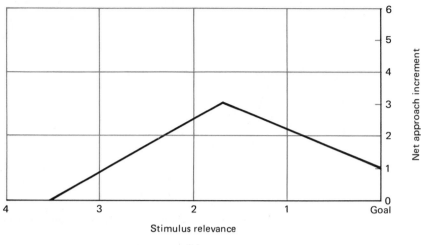

(b)

Net Approach Increment as a Function of a Stimulus Dimension.
Gradient is the result of subtracting avoidance drive from approach drive.

FIGURE
15–1c

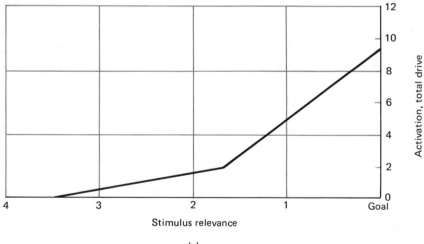

(c)

Activation as a Function of a Stimulus Dimension.
Gradient is the result of adding approach and avoidance drives.

Source: Epstein, S., & Fenz, W. D. Theory and experiment on the measurement of approach-avoidance conflict. Journal of Abnormal and Social Psychology, 1962, 64, 97–112.

ANXIETY
359

FIGURE
15–2

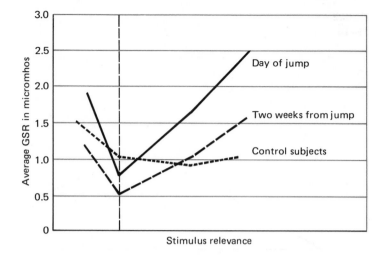

GSR of Parachutists and Controls to a Stimulus Dimension and to Anxiety Words.

Source: Epstein, S., & Fenz, W. D. Theory and experiment on the measurement of approach-avoidance conflict. *Journal of Abnormal and Social Psychology*, 1962, 64, 97–112.

schools in mind. Nor does lack of a degree need to interrupt plans for a happy life.

Unpleasant events need not be interrupting or anxiety evoking if one has control over them and has incorporated them into a plan. Although it is not always clear that a plan is necessarily involved, having control does minimize the disruption of behavior likely to accompany anxiety and having information about an unavoidable unpleasant event makes it more bearable. In one study suggesting this, subjects who had felt that they could have terminated a loud noise if they wished (though no subject did) were able to persist longer on a frustrating puzzle than were subjects who had not had the opportunity to end the noise (Glass, Singer, & Friedman, 1969). Further, those who had control over the noise rated it as less irritating and distracting than did those who had no control (Figure 15–3). Similarly, subjects told that they could not avoid or terminate shock (external control) reported greater anxiety (although they showed less arousal) than did subjects who expected to be able to avoid it (internal control) (Houston, 1972; Elliott, 1969). Also, subjects took more shock, in a series of increasingly intense shocks, before reporting discomfort and before terminating the session when they themselves could control the increment in intensity and onset of each shock than when they could not (Staub, Tursky, & Schwartz, 1971). Consistent with this view that lack of control is associated with anxiety, scores on Rotter's Locus of Control Inventory (Chapter 12) are correlated with several measures of frustration and anxiety. The

more people feel that outcomes are not contingent upon their own behavior (external control), the greater the self-reported trait anxiety and
the greater the hostility and aggression (Watson, 1967; Williams & Vantress, 1969). Thus, people like to feel that they are free and are in control
of what happens to them (Chapters 12, 17) and they relate better to
the unpleasantness of the environment when they feel this way.

What if we cannot avoid or control an unpleasant stimulus? In that
case, we are better off if we have some information about it, so that
the experience is somewhat understandable and predictable. Perhaps
this allows some cognitive control by enabling the unpleasant event to
be built into a plan of anticipation. In any case, information and predictability reduce stimulus uncertainty. Knowing how shocks were to be
delivered (apparatus information) and having information about what
they would be like (via a sample shock) decreased worry about the
shock effects (Staub & Kellett, 1972; Elliott, 1966).

Which is more important, having direct control or the ability to predict by having information about what will happen, a predictability
possible when one has control? Probably both are important, and ultimately may not be separable: ". . . control and predictability may function interchangeably as safety signals that reduce threat and the impact
of aversive stimuli; when the ability to terminate aversive stimuli is
lacking, predictability may reduce impact, and when the ability to pre-

**FIGURE
15–3**

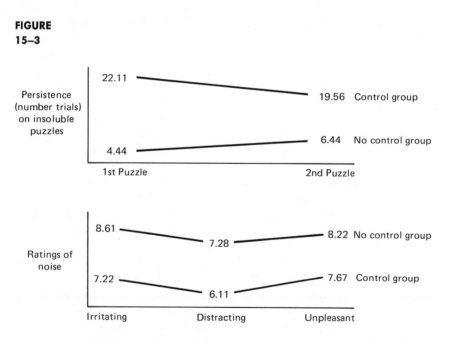

Adaptation to Stress.

Source: Glass, D. C., Singer, J. E., & Friedman, L. N. Psychic cost of adaptation to an environmental stressor. *Journal of Personality and Social Psychology,* 1969, 12 (3), 200–210.

dict is lacking, perceived ability to terminate aversive stimuli may have a similar effect" (Staub, Tursky, & Schwartz, 1971, pp. 161–162).

We all probably endure more anxiety than we need to simply because we lose sight of the fact that often we *do* have control. Often, we can choose simply to walk away from an unpleasant event, whether a boring lecture, a dry textbook, or an unsatisfying love affair. You may find your roommate's choice of music much less annoying, and perhaps even enjoyable, if you are aware of the fact that you do have some control— you could ask him to turn off the radio or you could go somewhere else to study. If the consequences of taking action to terminate the unpleasant situation would be even more undesirable than enduring the situation itself so that we elect not to use our control to avoid it, we are still better off if we stop to realize that it is by our own choice that we are exposed to it, not by the force of others. Often we are victims, not of others, but of our own neglect to exercise our right to choose. Often, of course, in exercising choice, we are faced with difficult decisions or conflict.

Threat

The other major class of events which trigger anxiety includes those that elicit the perception of threat. When a person *anticipates* an unpleasant state of affairs, particularly physical or psychological harm to himself or to others, he is said to be threatened. He expects a stressful situation to occur and is helpless to avoid it. Individuals differ even more in their anticipations than in their interpretations of an immediate reality. Notice that the person himself need not be directly threatened, but may observe someone else in threatening circumstances.

Vicarious reactions. Because of the empathic response of reacting to the threat affecting another person, we have another source of anxiety with which to deal. We "feel" for others and the feelings are not necessarily pleasant ones. Lazarus (1966; Lazarus & Opton, 1966; Averill, Olbrich, & Lazarus, 1972) has found that threat may be induced vicariously by the use of films. Some of his work on appraisal was mentioned in the previous chapter. He has used, as stressors, films about accidents in a woodshop or about genital operations (subincision) performed with crude stone instruments as part of initiation rites in primitive tribes. Arousal increased sharply during critical scenes in which operations were performed or accidents occurred, and decreased during neutral scenes. The physiological reaction to the vicarious threat of a film was similar to a direct threat induced by telling subjects that they would be shocked. Direct observation of another person being shocked or about to be shocked also produces an empathic arousal response (see Shapiro & Crider, 1969). The amount of empathy and the people for whom one is most likely to feel empathic vary from person to person. Because of responsiveness to others, we may also develop a conditioned reaction such that we respond anxiously to a formerly neutral stimulus. Thus, because of empathy, the range of situations evoking anxiety is extensive indeed, a price we pay for living with others. Empathy is also a source of similarity that enables understanding of other people (Chapter 13).

Ego threat. Consistent with the views of both Freud and Rogers, ego threat or threat to one's self-esteem induces anxiety. The circumstances in which one experiences anxiety may be ones which other people can easily detect and readily understand as threatening. However, the relevant stimuli may also be internal ones, for example, a thought or body feeling associated with "feeling angry" when one has been taught not to be angry. The perception that one has an impulse to think or act in violation of one's standards or in a way inconsistent with one's view of self is a covert event which elicits anxiety and may elicit coping responses which inhibit knowledge of one's angry feelings or fantasy expression of them (Chapters 9, 14). Thus in some situations, the objectively observable environment may be one which others cannot understand as an appropriate setting for an anxiety response if they do not understand the individual's frame of reference.

Differential frequency and intensity of A-state reactions between people varying in A-trait seem likely for ego-threatening situations because of the heavy role that learning plays when one is developing habits of appraising stimuli as threatening. In relative contrast, with an event such as physical pain, there is less variability in appraisal and, consequently, less differences between people in A-state response. Thus, people differing in A-trait would not necessarily respond differently to the threat of objective physical pain, but would be expected to differ in response to events suggesting failure, a threat to self esteem (Hodges, 1968; Hodges & Felling, 1970). Subjects high and low on the Taylor Manifest Anxiety Scale, a frequent measure of A-trait, were told that they had not done well on a short intelligence test (failure threat) and should try harder on the coming tests, or that they had done well and would receive shock during the coming series of items (shock threat), or simply that they had done well (no threat). Heart rate and affect adjective check list (AACL) measures were taken before and after the threat instructions. In the shock-threat and no-threat conditions, the heart rate increase and report of anxiety of high and low A-trait subjects were about the same. However, the high A-trait subjects in the failure-threat condition reported greater anxiety than did those in the shock-threat condition, and were more anxious than low anxiety-trait subjects under failure-threat, shock-threat, and no-threat (Figure 15–4).

More generally, most of the conditioning and verbal learning data to date can be accounted for by the hypothesis that high anxious subjects show disrupted behavior under failure-induced stress but not necessarily under pain-induced stress; while low anxious people are disrupted under pain-induced stress but not necessarily under failure (Saltz, 1970). Thus, individual differences on a measure of trait anxiety, such as the MAS, may be reflecting not differences in susceptibility to stress, but suscepti-

FIGURE
15–4

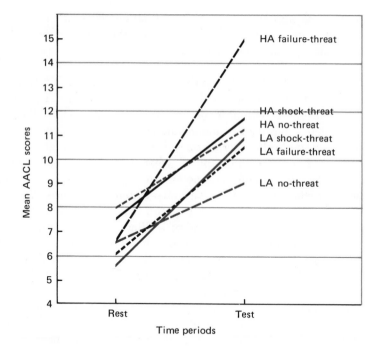

Mean AACL scores

HA failure-threat

HA shock-threat
HA no-threat
LA shock-threat
LA failure-threat

LA no-threat

Rest   Test

Time periods

Effects of Failure-Threat, Shock-Threat, and No-Threat Conditions on AACL Scores for High A-Trait (HA) and Low A-Trait (LA) Subjects.

Source: Hodges, W. F. Effects of ego threat and threat of pain on state anxiety. Journal of Personality and Social Psychology, 1968, 8 (4), 364–372.

bility to different kinds of stressors, namely painful ones and ones suggestive of failure.

Interpersonal anxiety. Many sources of threat exist in explicit interpersonal relations. One is afraid of "failing" in dealings with other people. Other people may be the ones from whom we anticipate physical harm or the ego threat of criticism. The threat of rejection by others is a powerful motivator of conformity to the wishes of others, and anxiety about the evaluations of others is an important determinant of performance before other people. Other people may also be the "content" of the difficult discriminations we face or the conflicts we find ourselves in. We may have to decide whether they really like us or are being hypocritical. Is he an important enough friend that I am willing to change my behavior the way he wants me to? Was the "insult" a sign of rejection or a careless remark made under distraction? Needless to say, other people often interrupt a plan of action and often deviate from what is expected of them. If we have not learned to understand their assumptions about the meaning of interpersonal behavior and expressions, they will seem unpredictable and we may feel that we are living in a world in which we have little control over the outcomes of our own behavior. In fact, blockage of interpersonal communication is a potent stimulus for stressful reactions (Grinker, 1966).

BEHAVIORAL EFFECTS OF ANXIETY

One noticeable effect of anxiety, as seen in previous chapters, is the defenses which an individual develops as a mode of dealing with anxiety. The defense mechanism may operate through selective responses to external stimuli (Chapter 11) or may function anywhere within the emotional sequence (Chapter 14). Anxiety, and the characteristic defense styles for dealing with it, also have important effects on performance. The physiological arousal or general drive that is likely to occur in stressful situations may affect behavior even if it is not labeled and felt as anxiety. Anxiety as a correlate of performance is considered as a response and as an *energizer* and *stimulus* eliciting responses, including defensive ones, that distract one from the task at hand. Often, it is difficult to know for sure whether the variable responsible for behavioral effects is simply physiological arousal or drive as an energizer, the thoughts and feelings associated with anxiety specifically, or both kinds of components.

Anxiety as an Energizer

Performance effectiveness is related to physiological arousal which may or may not be labeled anxiety. Generally, there is an optimum level of arousal for effective performance; as arousal decreases or increases from that level, one is "too motivated" or not motivated enough, and performance declines (Yerkes-Dodson law). The optimum varies with the task and how well one has mastered it; a higher level of arousal is necessary for simple tasks than for complex ones and deviation from the optimum is less disrupting when the task is well learned than when it is weakly learned. Although support is not unanimous in all details, the basic inverted-U relationship described by the Yerkes-Dodson law has been supported by a variety of data from humans and others animals, and has been said to be one of psychology's closest approximations to a true scientific principle (Malmo, 1959; Duffy, 1957; Levitt 1967; Hokanson, 1969). For example, performance varies in the predicted manner when arousal is manipulated in rats by hours of water deprivation (Belanger & Feldman, cited by Malmo, 1959, 1962) and in humans by the simple means of having them pull weights at varying proportions of their capacity (Wood & Hokanson, 1965).

The curvilinear relationship between arousal as a general construct and performance also seems to hold when measures of trait anxiety are used rather than physiological indices of arousal, or when arousal is presumably manipulated by motive-arousing instructions (see Sarason & Smith, 1971). The arousal level for a person is a joint function of his general predisposition to become aroused in the situation and the situation itself. The effects of the situation depend on the person; the performance of a person depends on the situation. For example, threatening instructions (arousal inducing) increased the performance of low test-anxious subjects but impaired it for high test-anxious subjects (Figure 15–5; Sarason, 1961).

The relationship between arousal and performance is often discussed in terms of the Hull-Spence formulation in which anxiety is conceptualized as a component of drive (Spence & Spence, 1966a, 1966b). Source of the drive makes no difference; whatever drive currently is aroused will energize any habits elicited by the environmental cues (thus, the term "generalized drive," or Big-D). Drive is hypothesized to energize all relevant responses, although the stronger habits gain more than do weaker ones: For a given increase in drive in the same individual (or differences in drive between two people, often inferred from MAS scores), the response with the stronger habit strength benefits more than the one of lesser strength, and the relative gain of the stronger habit increases with an increase in drive levels (Table 15–1). In easy tasks, or very well learned ones, the dominant response is the correct one; in difficult tasks, or ones in early states of acquisition, the dominant response

FIGURE 15–5

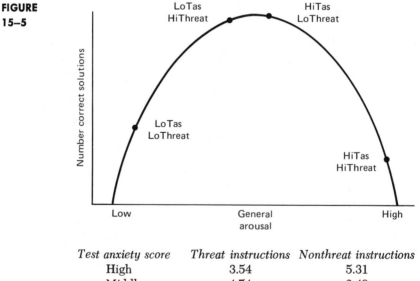

Test anxiety score	Threat instructions	Nonthreat instructions
High	3.54	5.31
Middle	4.74	3.49
Low	4.92	4.04

Performance of Subjects High and Low in Test Anxiety under High and Low Threat Instructions.

Source: Sarason, I. G. The effects of anxiety and threat on the solution of a difficult task. *Journal of Abnormal and Social Psychology*, 1961, 62, 165–168.

TABLE 15–1   Some Implications of Drive Theory

DRIVE	×	HABIT STRENGTH	=	RESPONSE POTENTIAL	DRIVE	×	HABIT STRENGTH	=	RESPONSE POTENTIAL	DIFFERENCE IN RESPONSE POTENTIAL DUE TO HABIT STRENGTH DIFFERENCE
D	×	H	=	R	D	×	H	=	R	DIFFERENCE
5	×	5	=	25	5	×	10	=	50	25
8	×	5	=	40	8	×	10	=	80	40
3				15	3				30	

> Stronger habits benefit more from an increase in drive than do weaker habits. In both examples, the increase in drive (for one person from time to time, or the difference between two people at the same time) is 3, but the effect of those 3 units of drive increase is greater for a habit of strength 10 (30) than one of strength 5 (15). The difference between the response potential of two habits of unequal strength (5 and 10) is increased (25 to 40) by an increase in drive.

is an incorrect one. Thus, increased drive (or high trait anxiety) is beneficial for easy tasks and detrimental for difficult ones. If you are high in trait anxiety (particularly test anxiety), you will do better on an easy test than will a fellow student of equal ability and preparation with low anxiety, though the results will be reversed for a difficult test unless you know the material very well. A highly anxious person will be at an initial disadvantage on complex tasks, but if he can persist in attempts to master the task, he may turn his disadvantage into an advantage as the correct response comes to be the dominant one. Unfortunately, many life circumstances require complex performances rather than simple ones, difficulty itself is likely to increase arousal, and we do not always have time to work toward mastery on all complex tasks we must deal with. Thus, high test-anxiety students tend to be inferior in performance and make lower grade point averages than students low in test anxiety (see Ray, Katahn, & Snyder, 1961), though this is not true for students with very high or very low scholastic ability (Spielberger, 1966; Figure 15–6).

Although the Hull-Spence formulation takes account of anxiety only as an energizer, it is also likely that anxiety functions as a stimulus for task-irrelevant responses which interfere with the correct one (e.g., Child, 1954). The interfering role of task-irrelevant responses associated with test anxiety is shown by the facts that high test-anxious students, relative to those low in test anxiety, report an inability to organize while studying, lack of rehearsal of material while reading assignments, and have more rumination, self-deprecation, and negative affect to distract them (see Ray, Katahn, & Snyder, 1971).

For many important life performances (including classroom examinations), we have to perform in front of other people, along with them, or

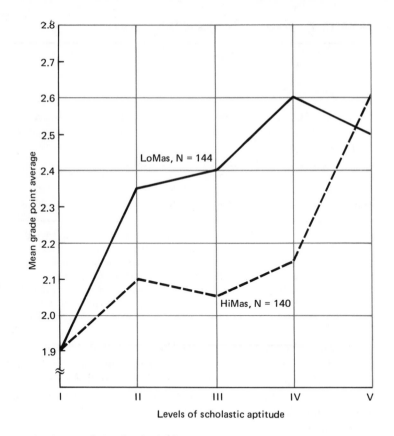

FIGURE 15–6

Anxiety and Academic Achievement.

Source: Spielberger, C. D. The effects of manifest anxiety on the academic achievement of college students. *Mental Hygiene*, 1962, 46, 420–426.

in order to be evaluated by them. Thus, we will discuss audience anxiety particularly as a long neglected but important example of the study of the relationship between anxiety and performance in which anxiety can be seen as an energizer but also probably as a stimulus eliciting interfering responses.

Audience Anxiety

Any time we are interacting with other people and it is our turn or responsibility to speak or otherwise perform, we have an audience. "In fact, one can think of social life as a series of entrances on different stages where lines are recited before audiences that vary in degree of expertness, or of size, or of importance for the actor" (Lambert & Lambert, 1964, p. 93). Sometimes people have difficulty speaking with other people or "clutch" up and become clumsy, unable to concentrate or remember, because of the presence of the others. On the other hand, people are sometimes "turned on" by other people, and perform best in their presence, whether the performance involves thinking, working out problems, showing off a skill, or being witty. It is to the question of when performance is facilitated and when impaired that much of the research on audience anxiety, or social facilitation and inhibition, is addressed. The answer seems to require consideration of anxiety as an energizer and as a stimulus eliciting distracting responses.

Energizing with others. Zajonc (1965, 1968) has attempted to specify when the presence of others is facilitating and when it is debilitating by application of the Hull-Spence drive theory. He hypothesized that the function of the presence of others is to increase general drive (not necessarily anxiety) and thereby enhance the probability of emission of dominant responses relative to subordinate ones, or of easy responses relative to difficult ones. Social effects on performance may be either facilitory or inhibitory depending on whether the dominant response is correct or incorrect. In one of his studies, using a pseudo-recognition task, he experimentally manipulated response strength by presenting nonsense words varying numbers of times (one to sixteen). When asked to recognize the words on a perceptual task, in which the stimuli were actually other words, subjects gave more dominant responses, words previously presented, when an audience was present than when there was no audience. The prediction that the presence of others increases drive and the probability of the dominant response also holds when the task is a motor task requiring fine perceptual/motor coordination (Martens, 1969). Subjects had to carefully accelerate a cursor in an elaborate game so that it reached a predetermined point at the exact time required to strike another object. During learning, when the correct response was not yet dominant, the subjects working while being watched by ten spectators made more errors than those working alone, with greater effects in the initial learning trials. However, after the task had been well learned, when the correct response was of greater strength, those performing in the presence of spectators did better than those who performed alone, and they were more consistent in their responses. If you want to learn to play pool or become a master of a Labyrinth game, start alone; after you master the skill, you can do a better job if others are watching. This advice is probably just as sound for many other kinds of motor and cognitive skills.

Distraction and evaluation. The mere presence of others seems to increase drive level, with beneficial or disadvantageous results depending on the task. Is that all there is to audience anxiety? Probably not. Audiences are people and performers are people. What significance the performer attaches to the audience, how he interprets the meaning of their presence, and what he expects of them influence drive level or audience anxiety specifically. The anxiety energizes *and* distracts. First, it seems necessary that the performer perceive the others as attentive to him if they are to influence his performance. The mere presence of others thought not to be interested in watching the subject (and who were even wearing blindfolds) did not enhance the emission of dominant responses in a pseudo-recognition task; but when the others were thought to be interested in watching the experiment, their presence did influence performance (Cottrell, Wack, Sekerak, & Rittle, 1968). When one is too anxious about giving a speech to a class, perhaps he would do well to convince himself that the class isn't really very interested!

The effect of an audience may be to distract one from his task (Jones & Gerard, 1967). Subjects learning in the presence of an audience did just as well as a group who learned in the presence of a distracting bell or flashing light. One may be distracted simply because the other catches his attention, as with a ringing bell or a noisy roommate when one is trying to study. Often the distraction is due to worrying about or being concerned about what the others are doing and thinking. This is particularly likely when one expects to be evaluated by the others and fears the evaluation. Anxiety elicits a distracting "worry response." One anticipates positive or negative outcomes as a result of performing in front of the audience (Cottrell et al., 1968). Heightened drive with an audience, then, is partially attributable to apprehension about evaluation. When subjects were observed by spectators presented as "experts" in perception and human learning, the increase in the probability of the dominant response (pseudo-recognition task) was greater than when the subjects thought the others were nonexpert students from a neighboring college (Henchy & Glass, 1968). When subjects were working alone or with the nonevaluative observers, the probability of the weaker response was greater.

Individual differences. People certainly differ in what kind of evaluation they expect from other people and the importance they attach to the reactions of others. They learn to anticipate or expect positive or negative reinforcement from others. Other people may acquire generalized rewarding or aversive properties depending on an individual's social reinforcement history (Paivio, 1964, 1965). Prior negative experiences with evaluating others increase sensitivity to an audience as a specific kind of trait anxiety. Social situations in general may become anxiety arousing if parental punishments have been severe, inconsistent, or nondiscriminating with respect to behavior. Audience anxiety in children is associated with unfavorable parental evaluations of the child's social behavior and achievements, and frequent punishment for failure to meet parental standards. On the other side of the coin, other people provide directive functions as well as reinforcing ones; one learns from watching others (Chapter 18). Children of sociable parents, who were rewarding and rewarded models in social interactions, have less fear of performing in front of others than children of less sociable parents. The effects of early interaction with parents persist. Self-reports of audience anxiety in high school and university students were negatively related to reports of frequency of public speaking experiences, parental encouragement of conversation and public performing, and the importance of speaking ability during childhood.

(Child-rearing practices appear to be *antecedents* rather than consequences of audience sensitivity.) The effect of an audience on drive and
performance will depend upon the individual's predisposition to appraise
the audience and expect a positive or negative evaluation from them
related to success or failure on the task. The total drive in any one situation varies with what the individual brings to the situation and his reaction to what he finds there. Boys low in test anxiety had an increased
response rate when an observer was present, but boys high in test anxiety
had a decreased rate while being watched (Cox, 1966, 1968). College
females who were learning a complex list while supposedly being watched
by a male observer behind a one-way vision screen were less efficient
than were those who did not think that they were being observed
(Ganzer, 1968). However, the observer was more detrimental for subjects with high or average test-anxiety scores than for those with low
scores. In fact, the low anxious group learned at a somewhat better rate
during the later trials when they were being observed than when they
were not being observed. Reactions to an authority figure evaluating
someone else also differ as a function of test anxiety (Sarason, 1972b).
Seeing a model authoritatively failed by the experimenter improved the
performance of subjects low in test anxiety while it was detrimental to
subjects high in test anxiety.

In sum, the results suggest that an audience increases anxiety, or simply drive or arousal; the effect on performance depends on the drive the
subject brings to the situation, his reactivity to drive-inducing situations, and the nature of the task. Perception of the audience as evaluative
may add to the drive induced by their presence.

Anxiety and Attention

Anxiety may facilitate or impair response acquisition and performance.
Anxiety, or drive generally, also influences interaction with the world in
the very basic sense of affecting patterns of attention deployment, that
is, how one directs attention and retains in usable form the information
about what he sees. In fact, evidence from a large number of studies
suggests that persons differing in test anxiety differ largely with respect
to the degree to which they attend to environmental stimuli and how they
use the cues in problem solving (Sarason, 1972c).

Attention deployment is often measured in incidental learning paradigms. Incidental learning occurs in the absence of formal instructions to
learn, though there is no reason to maintain that it occurs without awareness of the stimulus materials or without a self-induced intent to learn
(Postman, 1964; McLaughlin, 1965). For example, subjects are told to
learn one list of words (focal task) and then are tested for learning other
words also present during the focal learning (peripheral or incidental
task). Because the situation allows so much room for subject-induced
(rather than experimentally induced) variation in what material is attended to, incidental learning paradigms are very sensitive to individual

differences (Mendelsohn & Griswold, 1964, 1966, 1967; Dewing & Battye, 1971). Doubtless, a large share of what we notice and learn occurs without anyone instructing us to do so, and the more of the environment a person is able to attend to and keep available for use, the more effectively he can learn and profit from his interactions in social and nonsocial events.

Defenses. Patterns of attention deployment seem related to broad cognitive styles which are evident even when the material of concern is not threatening, but they are associated with defensive styles and their effect is accentuated under threat. Repression tends to be correlated with a narrow scanning of the environment, while sensitizing defenses are correlated with a wider range of looking (Luborsky, Blinder, & Schimek, 1965). The scanning styles are well suited for the defensive styles accompanying them. The narrowed range of attention may function to protect the effectiveness of repression as a defense style. If a stimulus unmistakably relevant to conflict themes comes to attention, it may be impossible to maintain a repressing defense. By looking around less, having a narrow attention range, the repressor decreases the probability of encountering potentially threatening material which may challenge the repression. The sensitizer, in contrast, is more comfortable with a broad scanning range which enables him to quickly notice problem material. Consistent with this reasoning, repression (repression scale from the MMPI) was clearly associated with minimal use of incidentally presented cues in solving anagrams but was not related to anagram-solving ability, as inferred from the number of solutions to the neutral anagrams, which had not been cued (Figure 15–7).

The differences in attention deployment of sensitizers and repressors are accentuated under threat (Markowitz, 1969). Repressors, who tend to look around little anyway, respond to threat with a narrowed attention. Sensitizers tend to look around more and respond to threat with increased vigilance and broader attention. Extreme repressors and sensitizers (Byrne R-S scale) were told that learning trigrams (three-syllable nonsense syllables) was related to mental abilities (high threat) or that the experi-

TABLE 15–2 Solution Means for Neutral, Focal, and Peripheral Anagrams

ANAGRAM	MALES			FEMALES		
		Repression			Repression	
	Low	Middle	High	Low	Middle	High
Neutral	3.35	3.65	3.52	3.91	4.00	3.52
Focal	5.74	5.00	4.57	6.17	5.22	4.61
Peripheral	4.22	3.78	2.83	3.70	3.17	3.48

SOURCE: Mendelsohn, G. A., and Griswold, B. B. Anxiety and repression as predictors of the use of incidental cues in problem solving. *Journal of Personality and Social Psychology,* 1967, **6**, 353–359.

FIGURE
15–7

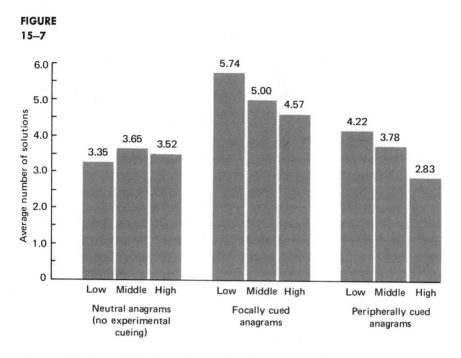

Average Number of Solutions of Uncued (Neutral), and Focally and Peripherally Cued Anagrams for Low, Middle, and High Scorers on Repression Scale.

Source: Mendelsohn, G. A., & Griswold, B. B. Anxiety and repression as predictors of the use of incidental cues in problem solving. *Journal of Personality and Social Psychology*, 1967, 6, 353–359.

menter was interested only in average performance of groups of subjects (low threat). Incidental stimuli were words also on the cards with the trigrams to be learned. Incidental learning was greatest for positive affect words (love, peace, kiss) and least for neutral words (older, sigh, wear), with recall of negative words intermediate (kill, fail, worry). More to the current point, sensitizers had greater incidental learning under high threat than under low threat. In contrast, repressors had lower incidental learning under high threat than low threat (Figure 15–8). The differences were not due to differences in intellectual or learning ability.

In sum, defense modes are associated with cognitive orientation in responding to and dealing with environmental stimuli, and their effects are accentuated under threatening conditions. The person who uses repression minimally is at an advantage when attending to a variety of stimuli can facilitate the task performance. However, when some of the stimuli present elicit responses competitive with the correct one, as on the Stroop color naming test, being able to ignore the distracting stimuli is advantageous (Chapter 11). We shall later see in another context that anxiety is also likely to be involved in determining the range of stimuli about other people which one attends to, with effects varying with what one needs to learn about other people (Chapter 18).

FIGURE
15–8

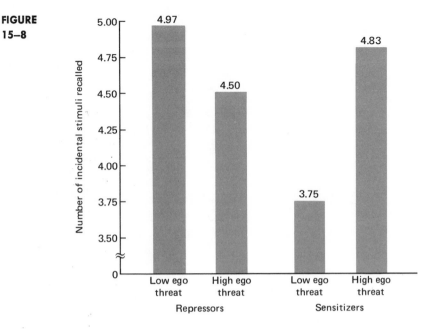

Recall of Incidental Stimuli under Low and High Ego Threat by Repressors and Sensitizers.

Source: Markowitz, A. Influence of the repression-sensitization dimension, affect value, and ego threat on incidental learning. *Journal of Personality and Social Psychology*, 1969, 11, 374–380.

Differential Learning and Recall

Repression effects. A repressive response elicited by anxiety can prevent wide attention deployment and accurate interpretation of the environment. Bigots, for example, can filter out or repress sound arguments against their irrational prejudices. Repression has been cited as responsible for differential learning and recall of information which is unpleasant, threatening, or incongruent with self-view and attitudes (see Eriksen & Pierce, 1968; Jones & Gerard, 1967). For example, repressors (high Hy-Pt) took relatively longer to relearn paired associates when the stimulus word had been associated with failure in the experiment than when it was a neutral word (Truax, 1957). In contrast, sensitizers learned the pairs with failure words more quickly than the neutral pairs. When later told that their supposed failure was a hoax, the differences disappeared. Whether differences in recall are due to differences in speed or accuracy of initial learning or to memory processes occurring after learning is not always clear; probably the effect occurs at both levels. In any case, there seems to be no reason to evoke a mysterious Freudian censoring mechanism to explain the results. To demonstrate dynamic repression, it is necessary to show that the material is available to consciousness (is learned) before the threat occurs, that the removal of threat results in its restoration to consciousness, and that alternative explanations about why threat-related material is not recalled are ruled out (see Zeller, 1950a, 1950b).

Many studies claiming repression do not meet these basic criteria. Why does the repression effect occur? In many situations where there is ambiguity about the meaning of an event, a repressing (or sensitizing) response may occur as an automatic and well-learned perceptual response. However, when a threat is unquestionably present so that denial of it would necessitate too great a distortion of reality, the reduced recall of threat-associated material appears attributable to factors other than a Freudian censor. The anxiety response to the material may increase arousal beyond an optimum necessary for adequate recall and is likely to elicit responses which distract one from careful attention to the details of the threatening material. Impaired recall of threatening material in such situations is in large part due to interference by task-irrelevant responses. Thus, repression may be a matter of distraction:

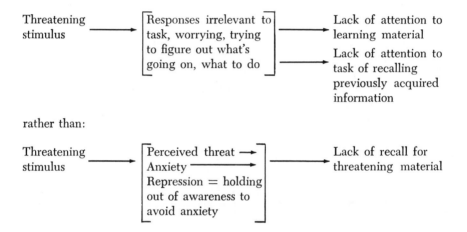

Distraction of worry. In one study about the effects of threat on recall, presumed anxiety about homosexuality appeared to lead to repression, as shown by an inability to recall material experimentally related to homosexuality (D'Zurilla, 1965). The subjects' task was to select one of a pair of words presented with inkblots that best described the blot. Experimental subjects were told that, for nine of the ten inkblots, they had selected the descriptive words characteristically chosen by homosexuals; control subjects were told they had picked normal words. When tested for recall of the words after receiving the false report, the experimental subjects had impaired recall of the stimulus words. When tested again after the falsity of the information was explained—to remove threat and lift repression—the experimental and control groups did not differ in their recall scores. Previously learned material was not "remembered" when it became associated with threat, but was available to conscious recall after the threat was removed (Figure 15–9).

Unfortunately for defenders of dynamic repression, the simple device

FIGURE
15–9

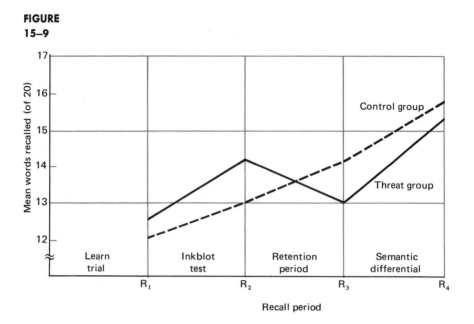

Trends in Mean Number of Words Recalled over Four Recall Trials by a Group Which Was Given Threatening Information and a Control Group.

Source: D'Zurilla, T. J. Recall efficiency and mediating cognitive events in "experimental repression." *Journal of Personality and Social Psychology,* 1965, 1, 253–257.

of asking subjects what they had been thinking about during the post-stress retention interval showed that the experimental subjects were worrying and thinking about the problem rather than avoiding it! Of the threatened subjects, 62 percent reported thinking about things related to the task (inkblots, homosexuality) but irrelevant to the specific job of recalling the stimulus words. Only 24 percent of the control subjects reported having the distracting thoughts. Interference from task-irrelevant responses appears responsible for what otherwise would seem to be a firm laboratory demonstration of repression. That is, quite possibly the experimental subjects were not repressing the "homosexual responses" when they were tested for recall while still under threat, but rather were distracted by thoughts about homosexuality which were irrelevant to the specific task of recalling stimulus words.

That apparent repression in such cases may be attributed to response competition rather than repression was more firmly demonstrated by providing control subjects with nonthreatening interfering material (Holmes & Schallow, 1969; Holmes, 1972). Subjects were led to believe that their choice of words to describe inkblots indicated that they were normal, or maladjusted and needing corrective steps (ego threatening), or that they were outstanding in some respect (ego enhancing). If dynamic repression is operating, subjects in the maladjusted feedback groups should show less recall of the words associated with the inkblots than the neutral or enhancement groups. If interference rather than repression is responsible for reduced recall of threatening material, then both the enhancement and the maladjusted feedback groups should show reduced recall of the relevant words relative to the neutral feedback group. The results clearly supported interference rather than repression as the mechanism. The subjects who had been given ego-threatening and those given ego-enhancing feedback had reduced recall of the words after the feedback; both groups showed a recall equal to that of the neutral feedback group after the debriefing about the hoax of the feedback (Figure 15–10). Results similarly indicated interference rather than repression when the recall of a threatened group was compared with that of a group who had had the experimentally induced distraction of having the inkblot description task interspersed between short movie clips of random scenes (Holmes & Schallow, 1969). The results cannot prove that repression generally, or reduced recall in the threat groups specifically, is due only to response

FIGURE
15–10

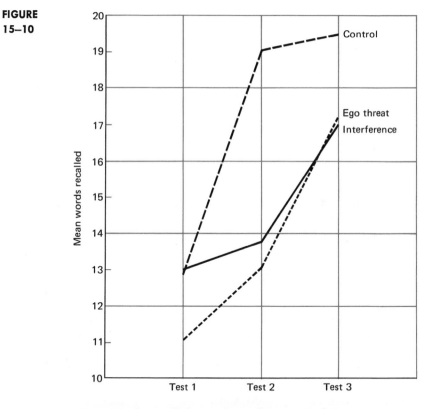

Mean Words Recalled in Each Condition on Each Test.

Source: Holmes, D. S., & Schallow, J. R. Reduced recall after ego threat: Repression or response competition? *Journal of Personality and Social Psychology*, 1969, 13 (10), 145–152.
Test 1: Pretest. Initial recall, immediately after presentation of words.
Test 2: Post-treatment. Immediately after Rorschach cards.
Test 3: Post-debriefing. Immediately after hoax explained.

competition. However, the fact of no difference between ego-enhancing and ego-threatening or between threat and interference groups suggests that previous conclusions attributing reduced recall with threat to dynamic repression should be called into serious question.

Certainly the effects attributed to repression exist—after threat induction, anxiety-related material is not effectively recalled. However, this is likely due to the distracting response of worrying about the problem, which prevents attending to the job of recalling the material. In real life, the hoax often is not revealed, or is not a hoax at all! The worry might continue, increasing one's inability to recall the specific events associated with why one is worrying. And repressors would be likely to call avoidance and denial mechanisms increasingly into play as the memory of reality fades. Sensitizers might increasingly exaggerate the severity of the problem. Either reaction in extreme distorts reality.

Realism: The Work of Worrying

Anxiety can either facilitate or impair performance. It is not always detrimental. Realistic anxiety which leads one to seek information about an unavoidable event can facilitate both physical and psychological adjustment to the event, as seen with surgery patients. Moreover, experience with anxiety-eliciting circumstances can enable a realistic recognition of danger and an increasingly effective control of anxiety with defenses which involve relatively minimal reality distortion, as illustrated by sports parachutists.

Surgery. Surgery provides an interesting naturalistic situation for the study of reactions to a kind of meaningful stress that cannot be studied easily in the laboratory. Janis (1958) found that more than 75 percent of the patients anticipating operations had moderate to high preoperative anxiety, by self-report, with the peak response in the operating room, the point of maximum danger. There were, of course, individual differences of emotional response before surgery, and these were associated with emotional symptoms after surgery. Those with high anticipatory fear were constantly worried and sought reassurances for their extreme feelings of vulnerability. They seemed to be people with a chronic disposition toward anxiety. After surgery, they continued to be disagreeable and extremely fearful that they had been permanently injured, despite the claims of the doctors. Patients with low anticipatory fear were cheerful and optimistic, and entertained themselves before surgery without signs of tension. However, they too showed more poor emotional adjustment after surgery. Apparently, they had used denial defenses unrealistically before surgery. Thus, the actual post-operative suffering they experienced was a shocking surprise that could not be denied. Because they were not prepared for the suffering, they blamed their post-operative discomfort on the incompetent and malevolent personnel. The best recovery was shown by patients who had experienced moderate anticipatory fear.

Before the operation, they were tense about the details of the operation, but their concerns were realistic. They were basically stable people who admitted to the anxiety-evoking realities of the situation, followed directions, and trusted the information they asked for and received. The information the patient had before the operation appeared to be an important variable associated with pre- and post-operative adjustment. The well-informed reported more worry before the operation and less anger and emotional upset during the post-operative period (Table 15–3). Additional research has shown that people scoring at intermediate levels on the repression-sensitization dimension show the most adaptive reactions, particularly when provided with information about the operation (Andrew, 1970). Anxiety or an internal control orientation (Chapter 12) can lead one to take an active part in obtaining realistic information about the circumstances so that one can deal with the reality. Internal control subjects do influence their care more and get more needed analgesics; however, recovery is also influenced by birth order and manifest anxiety scores (Johnson, Leventhal, & Dabbs, 1971).

The value of information per se was shown by experimentally manipulating the amount of information given (Egbert, Battit, Welch, & Bartlett, 1964). During the five days after surgery, those patients who had been given the additional information about what to expect after surgery required only half as much sedation as did patients who received only the routine information. Janis hypothesized that if fear is not aroused beforehand, the person will not build up an inner preparation and will thus have lower stress tolerance when the crisis is at hand. Obtaining information about an unpleasant event and realistically facing fear has beneficial effects. The work of worrying is important. One can deal best with the environment and himself if he knows both as they are and will be. This requires accepting and actively controlling the anxiety that may accompany unpleasant information or events.

Experience with danger. With sports parachuting, a person wants to experience what can easily be a very dangerous event (Epstein, 1967). The danger is strong enough that it cannot be denied. The fear of both novice and experienced parachutists reaches a peak at some point of varying nearness to the goal. *Where* the peak occurs varies with experience. The self-reported fear of novice parachutists steadily increased from the week before a jump to a maximum at the ready signal before jumping, and then consistently decreased through the period of waiting to jump until the landing. Their maximum fear did *not* correspond with the point of maximum danger, the period of falling before the chute opens; rather, it corresponded to the decision point where the novices committed themselves to the jump. In contrast, for the experienced jumpers, fear rose from a week before the jump to the maximum on the morning of the jump, when the decision to jump was made. Fear then declined until the points at which the chute opened and the jumper landed—the points of maximum danger. For the experienced jumpers, the decision

TABLE 15–3 Comparison of Informed and Uninformed Groups on
Preoperative Fear and Post-operative Adjustment

PREOPERATIVE FEAR

Duration of fear on the day before the operation

	Unaware of operation	Low	Moderate	High fear
Informed (N = 51)	27%	12%	32%	29%
Uninformed (N = 26)	31%	31%	11%	27%

Intensity of fear on the day before the operation

	No answer	Unaware of operation	None	Slight	Severe fear
Informed		27%	12%	37%	24%
Uninformed	8%	31%	23%	19%	19%

Intensity of fear during the hour before the operation

	None	Slight	Severe
Informed	8%	62%	30%
Uninformed	35%	38%	27%

POST-OPERATIVE ADJUSTMENT

Current emotional disturbance when recalling the operation

	Disturbed	Not Disturbed
Informed	14%	86%
Uninformed	38%	62%

Anger reactions on day of operation

	High	Moderate	Low
Informed	4%	12%	84%
Uninformed	23%	4%	73%

Confidence in the surgeon at the present time

	Low	Intermediate	High
Informed		2%	98%
Uninformed	19%	12%	69%

SOURCE: Janis, I. L. *Psychological stress: Psychoanalytic and behavioral studies of surgical patients.* New York: John Wiley, 1958. Pp. 356, 358.

point is the morning of the jump; if they decide to go ahead and jump, they then do so without question. The anxiety of both novice and seasoned parachutists reached a peak at the point of decision making, a point at which anxiety as a stimulus can influence the outcome. With experience the peak in the inverted V, relating nearness to goal and anxiety, moves, *away* from the goal activity of jumping. Epstein (1967) theorized that with experience, two developments take place. The gradient of anxiety *increases* and a gradient of inhibition of anxiety develops. As anxiety mounts, it becomes inhibited at increasingly earlier points in the approach sequence; the peak in the V pattern moves *away* from the goal activity of jumping. The expanding gradient of anxiety allows increasingly early and efficient warning signals at increasingly low levels of arousal until the anxiety is displaced almost out of existence. The defenses of the experienced parachutists involved early inhibitory reactions applied to low intensities of anxiety or arousal. The fear of the inexperienced jumpers, on the other hand, is more localized. Because they lack the early warning the experienced jumpers have, they have to resort to drastic, all-or-none defenses, such as perceptual denial and distortion, to control the intense anxiety that develops near the goal; for example, hearing "guy" rather than "sky," not responding physiologically at the point of maximum danger. The "after discharge" of fear increase during chute opening and landing indicates that the experienced chutists have not simply adapted to the situation and experienced no fear; rather, their diminished anxiety before the jump involves an *active emotional control.*

Other evidence, from the experimental laboratory, also suggests that autonomic reactivity on the initial exposure to more benign stressors may be correlated with active engagement leading to mastery of the imposed stress (see Shapiro & Crider, 1969). The *absence* of autonomic reactivity to stress can be a useful criterion of psychological maladjustment. Normal subjects were more responsive autonomically than psychiatric patients, and among psychiatric patients, those with some autonomic reactivity to the experimental threats were not as emotionally disturbed as were those with little responsiveness. Not recognizing and responding to perceived stress may be an unrealistic and ineffective response. To deal with the environment, one must know it, and this often means living with anxiety at least temporarily. To face the anxiety of the frightening, the strange, the deviant, and the unfamiliar allows becoming familiar with it as it is, rather than as we need to see it. To respond realistically with anxiety enables coping with anxiety about an event one cannot or does not wish to avoid.

SUMMARY

Anxiety is a personality trait predisposing one in varying degrees to respond to situations with the perception that they are stressful and with a resulting state of anxiety. Anxiety as a state is a response, an energizer, and a stimulus for other overt or covert responses. Pervasive inducers of anxiety include situations in which there is response indecision or helplessness; one has to make a difficult discrimination, face a conflict, deal with collative stimuli; or one does not feel in control. Anxiety is elicited also when one anticipates a stressful event, such as physical or psychological harm to others or ego threats to oneself, and people differ markedly in their responses. Anxiety as an energizer may impair or facilitate performance, depending upon the task requirements with respect to one's initial predispositions to respond. Anxiety, as energizer or as stimulus, may increase or decrease attention range, depending upon one's characteristic styles for coping with anxiety; again, the effect varies with the situation. As a stimulus, anxiety may elicit explicitly defensive reactions or simply other responses which distract one from the task at hand. The effect of distracting worrying responses may give the appearance of dynamic repression of threatening material. However, the response of worrying or of actively dealing with threatening situations may have beneficial effects; for example, realistically dealing with concerns about surgery enables more efficient recovery than unrealistic worry or lack of concern; experience with danger enables effectively mastering the anxiety it elicits. Responding anxiously to actual threat is associated with adjustment rather than maladjustment. The organism actively attending to his environment cannot be an organism at rest.

SOCIAL INFLUENCE

PART V

16

the social setting
for individual behavior

No one is alone in the world. Each person is a figure against a ground of other people and can be seen and understood only in relation to the total perceptual field of which he is a part (Figure 16–1). Thus, our study of personality development must go beyond a consideration of the psychodynamic processes which operate *within* each individual to include a look at man within the broader perspective of his overall social setting.

The concept of *social influence*, central to this and future chapters, refers to the fact that within the field of other people the behavior of an individual varies as a function of the behavior of another person or group of people. Other people can exert this influence partly because of the early and continuing development of social responsiveness (Chapter 19). If socialization agents have done their job well, we are fairly comfortable with ourselves and with other people. Correlatively, the more we deviate from societal norms, the greater our problems are likely to be in living with others.

Parents are the initial and very crucial socialization agents. However, neither the personality of the child nor that of the adult he becomes is entirely shaped by parental attitudes and behavior. Individuals differ at birth, and physical maturation makes a continuing contribution to personality development. In addition, other people encountered throughout life function as agents of socialization. Thus, consistency of personality is partly a matter of the consistency of the content and force of the social pressures which we experience. These vary with the particular people we encounter and the positions we occupy in the social system.

To an extent, living in a social world restricts freedom. Much as we strive to "do our own thing," we are necessarily influenced by our past and continuing associations

FIGURE
16–1

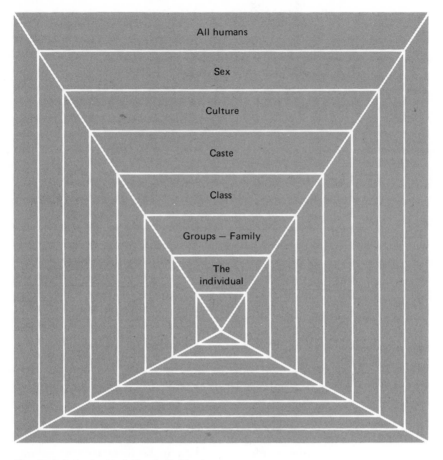

The Social Context of the Individual.

Suggested by Queener, E. L. *Introduction to social psychology*. New York: Dryden Press, 1951.

with other people. However, it is clear that these very associations enable us to effectively develop notions about what reality is and our place in it. We develop a shared perspective; that is, an organized concept of what is plausible and possible in life. This perspective is the matrix through which we perceive the environment. As with personal constructs (Chapter 13), perspectives limit experience and awareness but enable us to predict and control the events we experience. Association with others facilitates the development of shared perspectives, and shared perspectives facilitate associations with others. Indeed, the civilization developed by people living together may well be a psychological necessity for emotional survival. Modern man is more susceptible to emotional disturbance than other animals, but he has become reasonably adept at using civilization as a protective cocoon which conceals his emotional weaknesses (Hebb, 1955). Thus, he survives . . . so far.

CULTURAL GROUPINGS

Basic Themes

All people are like some other people (Chapter 1). What others they are like is largely a function of those with whom they grow and experience in a common social field. For practical purposes, the social field is divided into segments such as culture, caste, social class, sex, and special small groups. Any group of people associating with each other will develop a culture—that is, ways of coping with common problems such as living with each other and living in contiguity with other cultures. Perspectives develop prescribing what people should be like, and what they can expect in the world. Smaller groups, subcultures within a larger one, may have other perspectives, and the individual may sometimes have a choice about what smaller group he associates with, whose standards he adopts, and who he is. But in general, members of a cultural group embrace at least some similar societal values and strive to pass these values on to their children. Sharing perspectives and being part of a social group does, to an extent, limit personal freedom. But it also enables communication between people, and acts as a shield against the trauma of loneliness.

Culture

Specifically, the culture of a group ". . . consists of the modes of acting, knowing, and feeling customary in the group" (Child, 1968, p. 83). These customary modes of action are *socially learned* and reflect *socially shared* perspectives and expectations of behavior. Although the perspectives themselves exist in people's minds, they are manifested in observable behavior and often tangible products.

Culture has been defined in terms of content, tradition, values, rules, and patterns of adjustment.* When the emphasis is on content, we find broad definitions:

> Culture, or civilization, is that complex whole which includes knowledge, belief, art, law, morals, custom, and any other capabilities and habits acquired by man as a member of society (Tylor, 1871).

* Organizational scheme adapted from Kroeber, A. L., & Kluckhohn, C. [with Untereiner, J., & Meyer, A. G.] *Culture: A critical review of concepts and definitions.* New York: Vintage Books, Random House, 1952.

. . . that complex whole which includes all the habits acquired by man as a member of society (Benedict, 1929).

. . . the sum total of ideas, conditioned emotional responses, and patterns of habitual behavior which the members of that society have acquired through instruction or imitation and which they share to a greater or lesser degree (Linton, 1936).

The various industries of a people, as well as art, burial customs, etc., which throw light upon their life and thought (Murray, 1943).

The historical perspective emphasizes social heritage or tradition:

. . . culture, that is, . . . the socially inherited assemblage of practices and beliefs that determines the texture of our lives (Sapir, 1921).

. . . "culture" is not a state or condition only, but a process . . . what remains of men's past, working on their present, to shape their future (Myers, 1927).

. . . the social heredity is called *culture*. As a general term *culture* means the total social heredity of mankind, while as a specific term a *culture* means a particular strain of social heredity (Linton, 1936).

Culture . . . consists in those patterns relative to behavior and the products of human action which may be inherited, that is, passed on from generation to generation independently of the biological genes (Parsons, 1949).

The normative approach emphasizes rule or way, ideals or values:

. . . the total way of life of any society (Linton, 1945a).

Culture is . . . a set of ready-made definitions of the situation which each participant only slightly re-tailors in his own idiomatic way (Kluckhohn & Kelly, 1946a).

"A culture" refers to the distinctive way of life of a group of people, their complete "design for living" (Kluckhohn, 1951a).

Culture is the dissipation of surplus human energy in the exuberant exercise of the higher human faculties (Carver, 1935).

The psychological approach emphasizes adjustment and culture as a problem-solving device:

A culture is a common way of life—a particular adjustment of a man to his natural surroundings and his economic needs (Dawson, 1928).

. . . in brief, culture consists of learned problem-solutions (Ford, 1942).

. . . shared patterns of learned behaviour by means of which their fundamental biological drives are transformed into social needs and gratified through the appropriate institutions, which also define the permitted and the forbidden (Gorer, 1949).

It also emphasizes learning and habit:

> Culture . . . is a statement of the design of the human maze, of the type of reward involved, and of what responses are to be rewarded (Miller & Dollard, 1941).
> . . . Culture consists in all transmitted social learning (Kluckhohn, 1942).
> . . . all behavior learned by the individual in conformity with a group (A. Davis, 1948).
> Culture is the rationalization of habit (Tozzer, 1930).

And the purely psychological:

> . . . the sum of all sublimations, all substitutes, or reaction formations, in short, everything in society that inhibits impulses or permits their distorted satisfaction (Roheim, 1934).
> Society refers to the common objective relationships (non-attitudinal) between man and man and between men and their material world. It is often confused with culture, the attitudinal relationship between men . . . Culture is to society what personality is to the organism. Culture sums up the particular institutional content of a society. Culture is what happens to individuals within the context of a particular society, and . . . these happenings are personal changes (Katz & Schanck, 1938).

Cultures provide for the *organization of diversity;* part of the shared perspective of a culture is that some members of the group behave differently from others. A man does not expect his bride or her parents to behave the same way he does at the marriage ceremony. Rather, the ceremony requires that different people behave in different but interacting and complementary ways. Further, cultures tend to be *self-perpetuating* and *adaptive*. That is, in coping with common problems, members of a society try various solutions, some of which become established and are transmitted to successive generations (Kretch, Crutchfield, and Ballachy, 1962).

Biology.   No two cultures have exactly the same problems, nor do they necessarily attempt to solve what appear to be similar problems in the same ways. Some of the problems posed for a group of people are a function of the ecological system in which they live. The climate and geography of the environment influence the survival problems to be solved and the ways in which biological survival is attempted (Kluckhohn & Murray, 1964; Aronoff, 1967). For instance, John W. M. Whiting (1964) presents a convincing argument that the danger of protein deficiency is the root of complicated patterns of sleeping arrangements, residency, and sexual anxieties and behavior in rainy tropical climates where protein deficiency is the source of an often fatal tropical disease. A new mother must avoid getting pregnant so that her milk will remain rich in protein for the child she is already nursing. Since modern contraceptive techniques are largely unknown, pregnancy is prevented by abstaining from intercourse. There is a long-lasting sexual taboo after birth. The husband looks for another woman during the time of the taboo, and marries her to keep his activities "in the family." His relatives, who live nearby, give him help in keeping his co-wives in line. An unusually close attachment develops between mother and child during the sexual taboo, which presumably leads to latent conflict about sexual identity. Rituals, including circumcision rites, then follow to handle the anxiety and break the strong emotional ties a son develops from the early exclusive attention given him by his mother. These elaborate cultural practices are simply attempts by a group of people to adjust to the climate in which they live in order to meet the biological demands of the body. This is not to say that biology and climate exclusively determine cultural patterns; the pattern that emerges is probably dependent on other facets of the social system as well.

Child-rearing practices.   Cultural perspectives and solutions to problems tend to be self-perpetuating because of the continuing demands of the environment, and because of the child-rearing practices which socialize the child into an adult. Parents attempt to prepare their children for life in the world as they know it. The world they know and their perceived requirements for surviving in it reflect their own prior experiences. Thus, the experiences of children shape the expectancies and perspectives they have as adults, and these in turn influence the way they treat their own children.

The kind of behavior for which a child is punished or frustrated is often associated with adult anxieties about that kind of behavior (Whiting & Child, 1953). For example, many children are punished for masturbating by parents who in their ignorance fear that such behavior will lead to blindness or insanity. These children, in adulthood, may perpetuate this fear by establishing a similar sexual taboo for their own offspring. This child-rearing practice is a consequence of the behavior of other adults. Similarly, beliefs about the malevolent nature of deities are interpreted as both an antecedent and a consequence of a particular pattern of child-rearing practices (Lambert, Triandis, & Wolf, 1959). In societies in which deities are viewed as malevolent (causing trouble), children receive violent beatings from their otherwise affectionate parents as well as extensive positive rewards for being self-reliant and showing independent behavior. The punishment experiences supposedly prepare the child to expect a world of malevolent forces. The reward pattern teaches him to be self-reliant in the face of that world so that he will be able to survive.

These child-rearing practices exemplify one of the ways in which the shared perspectives of a culture manifest themselves in observable behavior. In addition, they illustrate a primary means by which these shared perspectives are perpetuated (and sometimes modified) from generation to generation.

Norms

The shared perspectives of a culture are codified into what is termed a set of norms. Specifically, norms are the *shared standards* or *expectations* against which perceptions, feelings, and behavior are evaluated. They provide frames of reference for ordering and evaluating the world. Further, they have an *obligatory* quality in that the people for whom the norms are held are expected to behave consistently with them. It is easy to object to the existence of norms on the grounds that they limit personal freedom. But indeed, it would be quite difficult to exist without them. Norms provide a perceptual structure within which we can order our concept of reality. They contribute to the emotional cocoon. They reduce the confusion, uncertainty, and interpersonal conflict that would otherwise disrupt social interaction.

As *rules of behavior,* they tell us what can be legitimately expected of us and what we can expect from others. Because they are relatively *stable* standards based on *agreement* or consensus, we can count on the fact that what is expected today will be expected tomorrow and that other people will follow the same norms with only *minimal surveillance.* As established rules of behavior, norms have the practical advantage of minimizing the necessity of constant decision making about day-to-day events (Thibault & Kelly, 1957). Because norms imply *impersonal values,* and are based on consensus, we need not regard compliance with them as giving in to another, more powerful person.

For instance, the norms of most of the working world dictate that people work during the hours of daylight and sleep during the hours of darkness, unless there is clear reason for norm violation. On any one day, the boss does not have to worry about deciding what time to open for business; nor does he have to constantly negotiate with employees about whether to work during the day, sunny and pleasant as it is, or during the night. The norm also protects the employee by assuring him that he can legitimately question a boss who arbitrarily decides to have his staff work on Mondays from midnight to 6 A.M. and on Tuesdays from 7 A.M. to 6 P.M. The employee who obediently goes to work from 9 A.M. to 5 P.M. has not "given in" to a more powerful other; he is simply following the norm.

In introducing the concept of the *generalized other,* Mead (1925, 1934) refers to the fact that we all come to our social world from the standpoint of the culture of our group. Because we share a perspective with others of our culture, we hold the same standards for others that we have for ourselves, and we expect others to hold the same standards. This enables us to anticipate life from a general standpoint of how other members of the culture perceive it. We can understand the boss's confusion if we come to work as he is closing the doors at the end of the day, and he can understand our frustration if he changes his mind and wants us to work at night. More generally, because we share a perspective with others, we can understand them, at least in part, even if we do not know them. If on a bus or subway we see someone push another person aside to get the seat he was about to occupy, we can react to the situation much as the victim does; we can feel an annoyance. at what we both consider rudeness, and we are likely to lament, "What's the world coming to!"

Reference groups. While some norms are generally held by the majority of members of a culture, others are specific to individual groups or sub-cultures within the culture, and particular groups translate dominant cultural values in their own way. The norms a person internalizes and responds to are those of his reference group or groups. He assumes the reference group's perspectives as his frame of reference (Sherif, 1953). Any group, real or imaginary, may be a reference group when (1) the group perspective is assumed by the person, (2) he defines himself as a group member or would like to be a member, and (3) he feels that the others in the group are emotionally or cognitively significant to him (Kiesler & Kiesler, 1969). If these conditions are not met, a group is only a *membership group.* For example, the reference group of professional actors may mean more to the star of the high school play than his membership group of high school students. At least part of his energies are directed toward achieving what he perceives to be the professional's standards and way of life, and he may identify more with that way of life than with the way of life of his fellow students.

Roles

Social structure and the individual. When a person adopts a reference group, he may be said to be adopting a role, or mode of behavior, appropriate for that group. Roles are norms which specify the behavior of people who occupy different positions, or collectively recognized categories of people (e.g., man, woman, doctor, scholar) in a social system. Some roles—sex roles, for example—are *ascribed* to us without any particular effort on our part. Others, such as scholar or doctor, must be *achieved.* In either case, we may internalize a role as a persistent part of our self-concept—that is, we see ourselves as not only behaving like a male or female, but as *being* a male or female—or we may "play the role" without any great affinity for the part. It is questionable whether a person can be defined entirely in terms of the roles he plays. The concepts of roles and personality cannot be entirely separated any more than the individual can be divorced from the social field of which he is a part. When we internalize a role, it does become an integral part of our personality. On the other hand, when we persist in playing a set of roles without comfort or satisfaction, our sense of individuality becomes lost in the social structure (see Jung, Chapter 4). We are then, in effect, "behavior without personality."

Social interaction. When people are occupying clearly defined positions in social systems, knowledge of role expectations allows each person in the system to know what he is expected to do and what he may expect of others. Some of the expectations associated with a role specify behavior toward *role partners* (Secord & Backman, 1964)—mother and child, teacher and student, husband and wife. The systems of mutual expectations enable social interactions to proceed relatively smoothly. Each partner knows what is required to receive reinforcement and avoid punishment from the other. When people know role systems, they need not infer the strategies, intentions, or preferences of their particular role partner. They need only perform appropriately and can count on the other person to respond predictably and appropriately.

Roles, of course, are not consistently performed. Cues of anger may signal that a man refuses to perform his usual acts of chivalry, or the boss's grin may signify that he has temporarily dropped his expectation that his employees keep their noses to the grindstone. Perceptual sensitivity is often necessary to detect a suspension of role performance or a change of roles (Sarbin, 1964).

Much of the interaction between role partners is evaluated against a *norm of reciprocity* which morally obliges each one to reciprocate (Goulder, 1960). Each of the role partners has both rights and duties in the relationship. For instance, a husband has traditionally had the right to expect his wife to perform her duty to keep the house clean; she has had the right to expect him to fulfill his duty to provide the house.

Role strain. Despite the advantages of roles, they are not without costs to the individual and to society. It takes effort to "fit in," to "play the proper role." The mere fact that roles exist and that any one person is likely to have several roles may induce role strain. For every role he has, the individual must possess or acquire the required set of responses. Furthermore, he must learn to discriminate the occasions on which they are appropriate. Thus, he has a perceptual and learning task which may require difficult discriminations that can be a source of anxiety (Chapter 14). What does it mean to be a college student? To be a twenty-year-old son or daughter? In dealing with parents, one may have difficulty in deciding whether to take the role of college student, of son or daughter, or of young friend.

Lack of clarity of the role is another dominant source of role strain; one is indecisive about how to act because the role itself is not well defined. This is particularly the case with new roles (member of a new kind of group or new occupation), or with old ones in the process of change (sex roles).

In some instances, a person may know the role expectations but find the demands of the role excessive, or incongruent with other roles he must perform. A time-consuming or irregularly scheduled job may make excessive demands which conflict with a man's role as husband and father. Role incongruence also arises when one does not yet have the necessary skills for a particular role. For instance, a role may require certain modes of performance, such as assertiveness, which are incompatible with a person's disposition: The new wife does not like to clean the house and does not know how to cook. If a person finds himself in an incompatible position, he may choose to change himself by seeking additional training; he may choose to try to change the requirements of the position; or he may relinquish the position.

Many roles are assigned because of membership in a subculture, and role strain may also occur when one is evaluated against stereotyped expectations with which he or she is not comfortable. A woman may be more comfortable with the role of Mr. Fixit than with the assigned one of Mrs. Cook. It is unlikely that society will quickly alter role demands or suspend them entirely, but we can hope that individuals will adapt their own expectations and behavior to allow greater freedom to the specific role partners they encounter.

Subcultures

Subcultures are specific smaller cultures necessitated by the particular features of biology or environment characteristic of a group of people who participate in or react from a more general cultural base. Ethnic groups, social classes, males and females, and families and other small groups all fall into the category of subcultures. Each subculture shapes the world the individual is exposed to and his experiences in it; moreover, each is likely to have its own norms and role demands to which he must respond, and each has its own ways of operating on dominant cultural values.

Caste Systems

A caste is "a group of people assigned opportunities on the basis of criteria over which they have no control" (Queener, 1951, p. 171). The criteria may be the religious, political, or military power of one's ancestors, or simply the antiquity of the family in a particular locale. Of all the subcultural groupings, castes are most likely to have their social worlds limited by other groups, frequently more powerful or larger.

The most conspicuous castes in the United States are ethnic groups. An ethnic group is composed of people who share a subculture based on similarities of racial, religious, or national origin (Hollander, 1967). Blacks are a painful example, but by no means are they the only victims of caste discrimination. People often attempt to justify prejudice and mistreatment of ethnic groups on the basis of their biological characteristics. However, the social heritage and social worlds of ethnic groups are so vastly different that attempts to rationalize caste systems on the basis of innate differences are hazardous at best. Even racial classifications themselves, which seem so obvious on the surface, are only rough approximations of some biological differentiation with an assumed genetic origin in the distant past (Tyler, 1965). It remains to be shown that the biological differences that exist between groups of people necessarily make a difference in social interactions and personality functions. There *are* important social differences between races, but most that have been studied so far can be more validly explained in terms of cultural experiences rather than innate determinants (Dreger & Miller, 1968; Council of the Society for the Psychological Study of Social Issues, 1969). Culturally induced differences function to perpetuate the caste system in this country. Much hope for the future lies with the possibility of changing the social class structure in which the problems are embedded.

Social Class

A social class is the largest group of people whose members have intimate access to each other (Davis, Gardner, & Gardner, 1941). Social environments and cultural opportunities for personal development vary with social class. People in the same occupational, financial, or educational group are likely to live in the same kind of neighborhood, join the same clubs, and have similar interests, attitudes, and values. Interaction with members of other classes is restricted and not expected to be on an intimate or equal-status basis. Notable differences between classes, as between ethnic groups, occur particularly in those abilities, experiences, and values which facilitate the perpetuation of differences. Academic achievement, college attendance, and level of occupational aspiration all tend to be positively related to social class (Gross, 1959). Classes also differ in what they consider a good job. People at lower class levels seem more concerned with security than those of higher classes, and are less willing to try for higher status jobs which involve risk along with the opportunity for advancement. Having a "good job" may be a cultural norm, but what kind of job is considered good and what constitutes job satisfaction vary among social classes. Overall, job satisfaction tends to increase with job status for people strongly identified with the white-collar middle-class culture. The higher status jobs provide the middle-class workers with the opportunity to satisfy their middle-class need to achieve. However, the reverse is true for blue-collar workers (Hulin & Blood, 1968), who often prefer their work because it is simple and carries little responsibility. Apparently, the middle-class notion that anyone would find repetitive tasks boring and monotonous is a mistaken assumption that overlooks class differences in motivations and value systems.

Many of the differences in occupational patterns and other concomitants of social class are partly attributable to child-rearing patterns which differentially affect development of occupationally relevant personality characteristics and abilities. Members of lower classes are more likely to attribute success to luck rather than to hard work. Thus, they are lower in achievement motivation. Unfortunately, the disillusionment of the lower classes is not without a realistic base, and is likely to be passed on to future generations. Even when members of different classes have the same education and enter the same occupations, occupational advancement is correlated with social class (West, 1953).

The loosening of class boundaries and the reduction in social-class handicaps has not yet led to the emancipation of the lower-lower classes. People of the lowest classes are subject to a cultural deprivation that perpetuates lack of specific values, goals, and abilities which could prepare them for success in the middle-class world that so often controls opportunity. Local and national efforts are increasingly directed toward such problems. If they are successful, "the United States may move much closer to its ideals of equal opportunity for all and develop a class structure that gives structure and diversity to society and yet does not prevent the full development of individuals" (Tyler, 1965, p. 363).

Sex Roles

Biology and culture. As with ethnic groups, it remains to be shown that the biological differences between the sexes necessarily make the differences in social interaction and personality function that are often attributed to these differences. People are categorized as male and female because of primary sex characteristics (genitals) and secondary sex characteristics (body size and proportions, breast development, etc.). This dichotomous categorization is not easily defensible (Money, 1970; Hatton, 1973), for it ignores the wide range of individual differences within any one sex as well as the similarities between members of the two sexes. Certainly men and women as groups differ in some dominant abilities and personality characteristics (Tyler, 1965; Maccoby, 1966; Sherman, 1971; Donelson & Gullahorn, 1973a). We have already noted as examples sex differences in achievement and affiliation motives, and in self-concept (Chapters 10, 12). However, it is not clear that existing differences are inherent, or that they justify the construct of masculinity-femininity as it now exists. (For a radically different view, see Nash, 1970.) Cultural anthropological work shows some similarities in sex roles across cultures (Barry, Bacon, & Child, 1957; Chodorow, 1972; Leavitt, 1972). However, it also clearly shows a greater variation in male and female roles from culture to culture than is consistent with the assumption of an exhaustive and exclusive biological determination of sex differences. Margaret Mead (1963) studied three cultures in the small geographical area of New Guinea, and she found societies that by Western standards are "feminine" or "masculine," and one with roles reversed. Among the "feminine" Arapesh, both men and women are cooperative and gentle. In the "masculine" Mundugumor culture, both sexes are arrogant, violent, and individualistic, with women continually fighting with their husbands and teaching their sons to taunt their fathers with irritating names. In the Tchambuli culture, the roles are reversed. The men are artists who spend much time decorating themselves and playing parts in ritual dramas. They gather to gossip, and their feelings are easily hurt. The Tchambuli women do the work, gather the food, and enjoy seeing the men's artistic productions. Similarly, in the Iranian culture the roles are generally reversals of those in our own culture (Hall, 1959). The men are expected to show emotions, throw tantrums, be sensitive and intuitive and not particularly logical. Women are expected to be hardheaded and coldly practical. Thus, there is no reason to reject the conclusion that "behaviors *peculiarly human* would be equally congenial to either sex if social objectives did not decree otherwise" (Queener, 1951, p. 229).

Role strain. No matter to what extent sex roles are necessary or justifiable in any form, they do exist; and with sex roles as with any other societal expectation, the more ways in which a person deviates, the more likely he is to have adjustment problems. Although there are suggestions that, in some segments of society, sex roles are becoming less rigid than formerly, the effect so far has been to *increase* role strain. For example, more than ever before, women now have the choice of a career, but because it is not yet a well-understood or clearly acceptable choice, their current problem is worse than if they were not allowed to be tempted. Discrimination against women in professions does, thus far, exist (Gullahorn, 1973; Willett, 1971). When they are in the working world, they are typically subordinate to men and motivated to work to provide better for the family (Hartley, 1960b). In addition, even though many women enter the working world for the sake of their children, they often continue to feel guilty about leaving them (Kagan, 1964). Perhaps psychologists have done too good a job of informing the public of mother's importance to the child, but too poor a job of clarifying exactly *why* she is important (Chapter 19).

The male, too, experiences role strain. He too has demands placed upon him that limit his freedom and often make him uncomfortable. For men as for women, occupations traditionally considered appropriate for the opposite sex, such as nursing, are opening up without clear societal approval for the choice. At a more basic level, a young man has little choice but to prepare himself to earn money in some way. A young woman may decide to do her life's work at home and be financially supported by a man, or she may elect to try for financial independence. A man is denied this choice. The anxiety about making decisions could be reduced if choices which are equally desirable to the chooser were not differentially rewarded or punished by others. Men and women must both be able to make individualized, rather than socially imposed "choices," if they are to achieve the maximum of personal growth and satisfaction.

The Family Group

The societal norms and values we have been discussing, including those attendant upon racial and sexual labels, are first learned in the home. A family's social class determines the social world to which a child is exposed, and shapes the abilities and traits which will influence his later choice of his own social world. Moreover, each family is a unique sub-culture which develops its own norms and roles (Henry, 1963). The nuclear family (biological mother and father and their children) is typical in the United States, but by no means universal. In many societies the family unit is an extended family with adults other than parents (aunts, uncles, grandparents, etc.) and perhaps the children of other adults. The value of the nuclear family can be questioned: the child is more susceptible to the perspectives of only *two* people and the victim of their deficiencies, which others in the home might compensate for. Both children and adults experience a large proportion of their satisfactions and frustrations within the family group, and both have roles to learn and perform (Ferguson, 1973). Adults must assume the role of directing the world of the family. If they do not, problems are likely. For example, in families in psychotherapy, the older children were the most influential members of the family. In a control group of families not seeking psychotherapy, the parents were the most influential (Murrel & Stachowiak, 1967).

Within the family, the child first develops concepts of roles. A psychoanalytical developmental approach to personality may be seen in terms of family role differentiation (Parsons et al., 1955). During the preoedipal phase, the child differentiates self and other and learns a two-role system. Differentiation by sex follows later, during the phallic stage, and the child views himself as a son or daughter and his mother as the mother of a son or daughter. Differentiation of view of self and others becomes increasingly complex until he learns the kinds of role relations possible in a family (Figure 16–2).

Perhaps more important than the learning of specific roles is the fact that in the family the child learns that social interaction patterns are a system of mutual expectations. To become socialized, the child has to learn the criteria by which to differentiate roles and how to behave in social systems. The family unit provides a learning program for the child by allowing him to observe the regularities of interaction between adults and the interactions of adults with him. Without this early training in detecting and responding to expectations and contingencies of behavior, social development is hampered (Chapter 19).

FIGURE
16–2

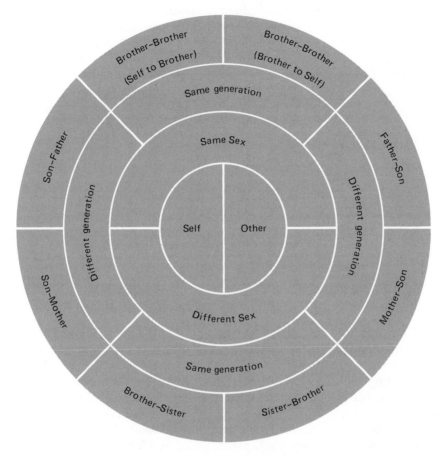

Stages of Role Differentiation in the Family of Orientations of a Male Child.

Source: Foa, U. G., Triandis, H. C., & Katz, E. W. Cross-cultural invariance in the differentiation and organization of family roles. *Journal of Personality and Social Psychology,* 1966, 4 (3), 316–327.

Group Membership

Membership in a group, formal or informal, expands our social world and broadens our horizons. It also increases the complexity of our lives, the number of role positions we have to fill, and the number of social influence pressures exerted upon us. The ways in which groups exert pressure and some of the conflicts of multiple group membership are discussed in Chapter 17. Here, we will be concerned with some of the basic implications of being part of a group, namely ingroup-outgroup bias and the effect of the number of other people in a group on the behavior of the individual.

Ingroup-outgroup bias. Some social scientists believe that attitudes toward an *outgroup* may be positive or neutral (Merton, 1957). Others contend that consciousness of group membership entails ethnocentric attitudes and rejection of people not members of the group, a position consistent with the tendency to label other people as "same" or "different" (Chapter 13). Intergroup antagonism occurs quickly, in natural situations or in experimental ones, when children or adults are placed in competitive situations. Well-developed laboratory groups working face-to-face on a cooperative task also become antagonistic, and groups of strangers can be moved to mutual antipathy by the simple flipping of a coin to decide the allocation of a scarce resource. In an experiment announced as a study of first impressions, two groups of four teenagers participated in each session. Each member of one of the groups in the session was to be given a transistor radio as a reward for participation in the research; supposedly because of limited funds, the other group was to be denied. The decision about which group to reward was apparently to be determined by the chance event of flipping a coin. "Although the subjects had no prior experience with anyone in the room, the flip of the coin was sufficient to shape their views of the outgroup members as less friendly, less familiar, less considerate, and less desirable as associates than ingroup members" (Rabbie & Horwitz, 1969, p. 276).

The suggested interpretation was that the chance win-loss situation created group bias by leading subjects to anticipate better outcomes from association with ingroup members than with outgroup members. When interacting with members of the losing group, winners would need to suppress their satisfaction over winning lest they imply pleasure at the other's loss; losers would have to suppress their dissatisfaction lest they suggest displeasure at the other's gain. The different experiences blocked comfortable communication between members of the two groups. Supporting this interpretation was the fact that the strength of ingroup preference was greater among winning girls than winning boys, but greater among losing boys than among losing girls (Table 16–1). Other evidence suggested that girls tended to be more compassionate than boys and strove for fair outcomes rather than winning at another's expense. Thus, winning girls discriminated against losers out of sympathy for those whom they had beaten, whereas the pride of losing boys led them to avoid those who had beaten them. The outcome was the same: discrimination against an outgroup.

It is not difficult to think of analogous real-life phenomena—phenomena which need not occur if there is enough freedom of choice for the ways in which one may find his route for personal development without doing so at the expense of another.

Ingroup-outgroup distinctions and biases are not limited to specific small face-to-face groups, but apply also to larger and more abstractly defined groups. Cultures differ in their perception of what kind of peo-

TABLE 16–1 Mean Ratings of Personal Attributes

DECISION MADE BY:	CHANCE		EXPERIMENTER		GROUP MEMBER	
	Own members	Other members	Own members	Other members	Own members	Other members
Reward						
Boys	5.04	4.93	4.41	4.40	4.31	4.37
Girls	5.10	4.35	4.66	4.71	4.40	4.06
Deprivation						
Boys	4.84	4.57	4.87	4.31	4.76	4.20
Girls	4.63	4.50	4.25	4.55	4.86	4.68
Overall M	4.90	4.58	4.55	4.50	4.58	4.32

SOURCE: Rabbie, J. M., & Horwitz, M. Arousal of ingroup-outgroup bias by a chance win or loss. *Journal of Personality and Social Psychology*, 1969, 13, 269–277.

ple belong to the ingroup. For example, Greeks define their ingroups in terms of family, friends, and friends of friends (Triandis, Vassiliou, & Nassiakou, 1968). Americans define ingroup members as "people like me." Thus, Greeks may treat friends of friends who are unlike them as members of the ingroup, while Americans would insist on similarity for acceptance.

Presence of others. People in groups exert pressure for conformity to their expectations about how members of the group are to behave. There is an even more basic phenomenon, however, which does not require that other people attempt, knowingly or otherwise, to control our behavior. The mere presence of others influences feelings and behavior. We saw one facet of this problem in the discussion of audience anxiety (Chapter 15). In view of concerns about overpopulation and urban living, psychologists are becoming increasingly interested in crowding (Dreson, 1972; Smith & Haythorn, 1972). It is certainly true that the number of other people in a group affects the behavior of each of its members. When a voluntary group has a small membership, members participate in a wider range of group activities, assume more positions of responsibility, and are more active in recruiting and accepting new members (Barker, 1968). Students in small high schools are more active in extracurricular activities than those in large schools. New members are more quickly assimilated into smaller groups. New members of a small church (338 members) felt more welcome and obligated to participate in a wide range of activities than new members of a larger church (1,599 members). The size of the church even influenced the size of

THE SOCIAL SETTING FOR INDIVIDUAL BEHAVIOR

contributions of each member (Table 16–2; Wicker, 1969). These results do not appear to be due to differences in socioeconomic status among membership groups. Rather, the behavior of the individual appears to vary with the situational variable of the number of others in the group.

Diffusion of responsibility in emergencies. The norm of social responsibility is assumed to be a deeply ingrained one (e.g., Berkowitz, 1970; Krebs, 1970). However, in some emergency situations the norm is not directly reflected in behavior, and one reason is that a diffusion of responsibility occurs simply because other people are present at the scene of the emergency (Latané & Darley, 1970). Several years ago, a young woman, Kitty Genovese, was stalked and finally stabbed to death on a dark street in an outlying section of New York City. At least thirty-eight witnesses saw the attack or heard the victim's cries for help, but no one attempted to intervene and no one even called the police during the more than half an hour that the attacker took to kill her. Preachers, news commentators, and other guardians of public morality quickly reached

TABLE 16–2   Behaviors in Support of Church Behavior Settings

	LARGE CHURCH (n = 34)	SMALL CHURCH (n = 30)	t
Sunday worship service attendance	15.8	24.8	3.30***
No. behavior settings entered	7.4	9.2	1.11
No. kinds of behavior settings entered	4.6	6.2	1.81**
No. behavior settings in which S was a worker or leader	2.6	4.0	1.35*
No. behavior settings in which S was a leader	.2	1.1	3.00****
No. hours spent in behavior settings	29.2	43.5	1.90**
Amount of money pledged, 1966–1967	$128	$214	2.92****
Amount of money given, 1966–1967	$111	$187	2.53***
Amount of money pledged, 1967–1968	$137	$255	2.83****

Note: All *t* tests are one-tailed. The time periods for the above behaviors were as follows: Sunday worship service attendance, September 1966, through May 1967 (39 Sundays); participation in church behavior settings, January 1, 1967, through April 15, 1967 (15 weeks); contributions to the church, June 1, 1966, through May 31, 1967 (52 weeks).
*   p < .10
**   p < .05
***   p < .01
**** p < .005

SOURCE: Wicker, A. W. Size of church membership and members' support of church behavior settings. *Journal of Personality and Social Psychology,* 1969, 13, 278–288.

conclusions about moral decay, alienation, existential despair, and dehumanization. However, the explanation in fact involves not apathy and indifference, but conflict and confusion about the nature of the unexpected event, and a diffusion of responsibility. Unexpected tragedies violate our assumptions about reality. They easily elicit a frantic, irrational, or freezing behavior, and a sense of disbelief. In public tragedies such as the Genovese case, we look to other people for an interpretation of reality and help in facing it, and the more people we can look to, the more easily we can assume that others will act and we may avoid the possible problems of acting ourselves. For example, in one study of a mock emergency situation created in a laboratory (Darley & Latané, 1968), subjects heard what they thought to be a seizure of a person in another room, with the final words of the victim, "I'm . . . gonna die —er—help—er—seizure [chokes]." Eighty-five percent of the subjects who thought they were the only ones who knew of the emergency reported it within 125 seconds, whereas only 31 percent of those who thought that there were four other bystanders did so (Figure 16–3). The subjects who did not respond within six minutes of the onset of the seizure were not indifferent, but rather were undecided about how to resolve an avoidance-avoidance conflict. They wanted to avoid the guilt and shame of not helping, but they also wanted to avoid the possibility of making fools of themselves by overreacting to what might be a minor event. Unfortunately, self-protection concerns *are* relevant in natural emergencies. Involving oneself may bring on physical danger, public embarrassment, or work days lost in legal procedures. Our society is not geared to facilitate action consistent with the norm of helping in emergencies.

COMMUNICATION AS THE SOCIAL SETTING

Communication is the vehicle we use to establish connections with other people. Communication requires a shared interpretation of symbols (words, gestures, nonverbal expressions, behaviors), which requires shared experiences. In turn, it perpetuates the shared view of reality and sense of belonging that define a culture. Communication with others is satisfying. The inability to communicate, especially with someone close to us, can lead to feelings of isolation and despair.

Meanings and Experiences

One person does not respond to another person as he is, but rather to his own *inferences* about what the other person is, is feeling, and is intending (Chapter 13). For real communication to occur, the inferences of one must match the reality of the other. Then there is true meeting of minds,

FIGURE

16–3

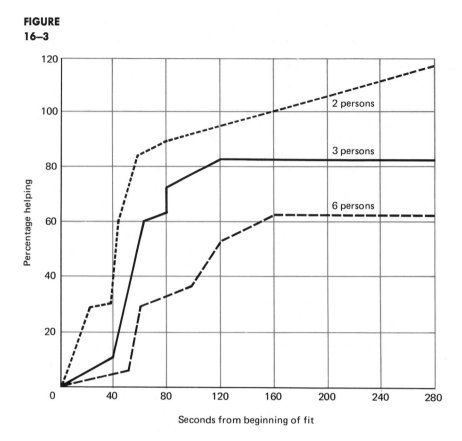

Percentage helping (y-axis)

Seconds from beginning of fit (x-axis)

Cumulative Distributions of Helping Responses.

Source: Darley, J. M., & Latané, B. Bystander intervention in emergencies: Diffusion of responsibility. *Journal of Personality and Social Psychology*, 1968, 8 (4), 377–383.

and perception and experience are shared. Unfortunately, we often assume that communication is occurring when in fact we are not correctly perceiving what the other person is thinking and feeling. This *pseudo-communication* may occur without either party being aware of it until they feel the impact of its consequences. People may agree on the *denotative* meaning of a word (the literal or observable referent) but not on the connotative meaning (what is indicated or implied along with the literal meaning). When there is an obviously shared denotative meaning, discrepancies in connotative meaning may not be easily discovered. Connotative communication becomes critical in close personal relationships. When two people agree that they want a home with each other, years of marriage may pass before they realize that by "home" he meant a place to take his shoes off and she meant a showcase for her esthetic values. Behavior, other than words, is also a communication vehicle. That is, we not only learn to behave appropriately, we also learn interpretations of behavior; when the interpretations are shared, we can "read" the behavior of others and know how they will read our behavior. We see as a generalized other. Numerous conflicts between ethnic and social-class groups within a culture doubtless result from differences in behavior patterns and associated interpretations (e.g., Aiello & Jones, 1971).

A common base of experience is necessary for common reactions to behavior, including verbal behavior. Communication "is possible to the degree to which individuals have common cognitions, wants, and attitudes" (Krech, Crutchfield, & Ballachy, 1962, p. 275). "Hunger" means almost the same in any language, for everyone has experienced the biological need it refers to. The meanings of "food" vary more widely from culture to culture. More complex concepts such as "home," "family," "work," "truth," and "beauty" have even wider ranges of meanings among individuals with different experiences and background. The successful adjustment of a traveler in a foreign country is likely to depend upon the background factors that facilitate or impede communication (Brein & David, 1971). Communication between members of different generations is also impaired by the lack of common experiences. What was "far away" to our parents has become "nearby" to us, with the advent of speedier automobiles, rapid transit, and air travel. "Since one generation cannot outlive the effects of the technological conditions of its youth, it cannot readily communicate on a basis of equal understanding with members of the generation who have been accustomed from infancy to a different technology" (Hartley & Hartley, 1961, p. 141).

The social forces that create the subcultures previously discussed limit the experiences of the subgroups and therefore interfere with effective communication between them. Caste and class lines particularly prevent contact with members of other groups, and the problem is compounded by the vast differences in experience which prevent the shared perspective necessary for communication. Technology has been steadily increasing the radius of contact possible between cultures and subcultures through radio, television, and newspapers. However, many advantages allowed by the mass media are still denied to members of the lower-lower classes. Movies and television sets cost money. Thus, the mass media that may facilitate communication between many otherwise segregated segments of society also can serve to further polarize the "haves" from the "have-nots."

Social Connections

Contact. Neither communication and its advantages nor pseudocommunication and its disadvantages may occur without contact. Although contact need not be either face-to-face meeting nor verbal exchange, those are the most easily and frequently studied. Physical nearness facilitates contact, which enables the verbal exchanges from which communications and friendships are developed. In turn, friendship and shared experiences reinforce meaningful communication and encourage further contact. The fact that physical proximity encourages communication was illustrated by a study of the residents of a housing development: people living near the mailboxes of the apartment buildings had more friendships with other apartment dwellers, and the friendship choices actually decreased as physical distance between apartments increased (Festinger, Schachter, & Back, 1950).

Restrictions on the channels of communication allowed and the content of communications within those channels are often intimately involved with roles and status, either explicitly recognized or not. Large organizations are particularly noted for rigidity in enforcing communication through prescribed channels. The system often works satisfactorily and effectively. However, the danger of elaborate communication channels is that those of low status, such as line workers or foremen, may feel that their ideas are being lost in a bureaucratic hierarchy, and they may miss the satisfaction of direct communication with those of higher status. The inability to communicate is frustrating. The greater our opportunity to share thoughts and experiences with others, the better we like it. In laboratory studies, communication channels are frequently manipulated by requiring the subjects to communicate via written notes which may be delivered only in preassigned ways (Leavitt, 1951). Results show that those members who can receive and send the most messages are more satisfied and more likely to emerge as leaders than those who are more peripheral and can communicate little. Within small face-to-face groups observed, verbal exchange nourishes group cohesion and feelings of friendship between participating members (Bales, 1950).

Solidarity and Loneliness

Communication not only requires the shared experiences which reflect a basic solidarity between communicators, it also increases solidarity and reduces loneliness. Special languages, sometimes called jargon or argot, develop from the common experiences of group members and facilitate communication about issues of common concern while reinforcing group solidarity. The language may be an occupational one, such as psychological jargon, or the slang of teenagers or students or any other group of people similar to each other in some way. It is an adaptation of a generally shared language to the functions of the particular group and expresses the distinctive experiences and thoughts of group members. Groups in special circumstances, such as military service, are especially inclined to develop special languages.

In sharp contrast to the sense of belonging that can be fostered by special languages, psychological isolation can result from lack of physical or communication contact. Physical loneliness, according to reports of hermits, explorers, and prisoners, is the negative condition predicted by Fromm (Chapter, 4; Haggard, 1964). Perhaps equally devastating is the loneliness that occurs because of lack of communication with others who are physically present. Helen Keller, deprived of sight and hearing in infancy, reported an almost intolerable sense of frustration during early childhood before she learned to communicate by the use of the manual alphabet. While most of us will be spared the persistent and intense loneliness caused by such extreme inability to communicate, we have all probably experienced some of the frustrations which come with an inability to make ourselves understood. A breakdown of communication with a good friend, parent, or spouse can easily lead to traumatic feelings of uselessness and despair. Sometimes the blockage may be a partial, temporary one because of a tragic experience which another person cannot understand. In other cases, the inability to communicate about a topic may be responsible for interpersonal friction and prolonged emotional maladjustment (Newcomb, 1947). One need not be a Freudian to know that sex remains an area about which communication is limited. Consequently, it is a source of personal and interpersonal conflict (Chapter 21), which often leads to feelings of isolation and despair.

Barriers

Individual rather than social barriers form the ultimate bulwark against persistently complete communication. Some of these communication barriers are the internal ones that prevent a person from accurately perceiving another person as he *is*. Perception is selective; we often "see" what we want to see and are used to seeing, and often process information to erroneous conclusions (Chapter 13). Personal anxieties and insecurities and the defenses for controlling them prohibit complete communication. Perhaps, we cannot exist without the defenses that keep anxiety from mounting to intolerable proportions. But in protecting ourselves, we isolate ourselves. What we need is the relative openness best articulated by Rogers and Fromm (Chapters 5, 22). If we are aware of the deficiencies that limit openness, we can attempt to compensate for them as we try to understand another person. In addition, we can attempt to remedy the reasons for the defenses and enjoy those few moments in which minds and lives meet and experience is shared.

Another major kind of individually located barrier to communication is the lack of completely shared experiences. Despite broad common bases of experience, no two people have exactly the same experiences in the world, nor do they enter the world with exactly the same biological equipment for receiving and processing information about the world. Some isolation, with its attendant anxiety, is a current fact of Western life. Perhaps this isolation is necessary if we are to achieve and retain individuality. If we are to reap whatever benefits we see implied by the concept of our individuality, we must also be prepared to face the challenges of standing as a solitary individual, and the loneliness and the responsibility for the individuality that is ours alone (Kierkegaard, 1938; Moustakas, 1972).

Summary

In this chapter we have been looking at the individual as an element in the social field. In this field, he grows and has experiences, he perceives, he reacts, he acts. Because of his susceptibility to the influences upon him as a member of that field, it plays a large part in affecting who he is and who he tries to become. He participates in a culture which has evolved distinctive ways of attempting to meet common problems and provide satisfactions for its members. As a member of given cultures and subcultures, he shares with the similar others in that portion of the social field certain perspectives, including norms and roles governing behavior, through which he can structure his environment and establish his place in the existing social order and know the expected places of others. Subcultures, such as castes, social classes, sex groups, family groups, and other kinds of groups also have their own norms and role expectancies and their own ways of expressing dominant cultural values.

However, we must not lose sight of the individual as he conforms to the norms and fulfills the role expectancies applied to him. Roles can cause role strain, simply because they exist; they are sometimes ill-defined or malfitting to the specific individual, and they pose dangers. If an individual becomes only a role or a set of roles, his individuality becomes lost in the social structure to which he has conformed. What one may gain as a member of a social structure is a perceptual framework for viewing the world that would otherwise be chaos, and the attendant possibility of communication.

Membership in a subculture or small group enables communication with those of the group, and communication increases group cohesion and personal satisfaction. However, group membership may lead to antagonism or rejection of those not a member of the group. Because of similar experiences in a social world shared with others, we can communicate. Because we can communicate, we can become increasingly connected with others in a bond that at least temporarily transcends some loneliness. How can we understand other people not of our own group with whom we lack a base of shared experiences, and whom we are too often inclined to reject?

While we cannot hope to understand a person's behavior without understanding his place in the social setting, neither can we look exclusively to social phenomena to explain the behavior of each person. Every person is like all, some, and no other person. We cannot be all-knowing experts about all people, and we cannot share all experiences with all people. What we can do is attempt to work toward an openness to learn about other people as they are, rather than as we need or expect them to be. We can go far in overcoming the inherent difficulties of interpersonal communication. In the face of impossibilities of bridging the gap, we can realize the reasonableness of the perspectives taken by others rather than evaluating them solely from our own frames of reference. To do this, we must have knowledge, strength, tolerance, and respect for the freedom of another individual.

17

social influence pressures

Man is a social animal. As such, he cares about the opinions others hold of him, and modifies his thoughts and actions to educe favorable response from those with whom he wishes to associate. He thus tends to conform to the needs and expectancies of various reference groups with whom he wishes to identify, and develops his attitudes about the world and his particular place in it as a function of prior learning experiences in social situations.

This is not to say that a person is simply the sum of the various social influence pressures exerted upon him. Biological factors, as we have said, also play an important part in personality development. However, the internal attitudes and the overt behavior of any individual are in large part the manifestation of his attempts to achieve and maintain a sense of individuality while being socially responsive. Thus, a careful look at the ways in which influence pressures occur in group interaction and in the processes of attitude formation and change will enable us to see more clearly the ways in which man adapts to meet both a need for a sense of personal freedom and the demands of his social environment.

Group Pressure to Conformity

The pressure to conform to group standards is exerted by individual members of the group interacting with each other, and is felt internally by all. This pressure is mutually applied; that is, those who expect others to conform to group standards are expected to conform also. Conformity to group standards is necessary if group members are to experience the satisfactions possible with group membership. The satisfaction may be the emotional comfort of receiving approval and acceptance from others, or it may be the satisfaction of arriving at a solution to a common problem and achieving a goal. In either case, these satisfactions reflect the basic notions that people are helpful, that their approval is reinforcing, and that loneliness is anxiety provoking. Thus, we become instrumentally and emotionally *dependent* upon people and seek and enjoy associations which meet these dependency needs.

Group Norms

Group standards, or expectations, are codified into a set of *norms* against which perceptions, feelings, and behavior are evaluated (Chapter 16). However, not *all* kinds of behavior are subject to group norms. The norms must be salient to group concerns if they are to be considered legitimate. For example, a group formed to work on a class project could not legitimately attempt to regulate the sexual behavior of its members unless sexual behavior were interfering with the group task.

The most important norms that develop are those which function to hold the group together and facilitate interpersonal interaction and communication (Kiesler & Kiesler, 1969). They increase security, help to define the group, and give it a sense of uniqueness. Such seemingly meaningless rituals as secret handclasps, passwords, or bagels in the morning and pizza at midnight help to serve these functions. Deviation from group norms is disruptive, because it destroys the similarity that is necessary for communication and solidarity and threatens group effectiveness in meeting dependency needs. Thus, pressure is exerted to maintain conformity within the group, and members respond in degrees varying with the situation and their own personality characteristics. For one person to "give in" to the group after an initial disagreement is reinforcing to other group members, and, in fact, is a more effective reinforcer than continual agreement; conversely, withdrawal of agreement is an aversive stimulus (Lombardo, Weiss, & Buchanan, 1972).

The conforming response may be only a publicly stated agreement without a private agreement (compliance), a public change of position accompanied by a private change, or simply the adoption of a realistic position in the light of the information one has, including the opinions of other people. Although "group" typically implies three or more people, the same phenomena are often typical of dyads (groups of two). Thus, understanding the social pressure that occurs in groups should illuminate our understanding of interpersonal relationships generally.

Roles and Enforcement

The number and kind of roles that emerge within a group depend upon the needs of the group as well as on the characteristics of individual members. However, at least two kinds of roles meeting two kinds of group functions seem necessary: *task functions,* and *social maintenance func-*

tions. Task functions are the role activities required to ensure group survival, achievement, and rewards from outside sources (Thibault & Kelley, 1957). They help the group to satisfy instrumental dependency needs. Social maintenance functions are necessary to deal with problems *within* a group, that is, to keep members in a stable interdependence of mutual satisfaction. They help the individuals to meet emotional dependency needs, and enable effective instrumental group functioning. Members tend to acquire distinctive task-related or social maintenance roles. One person is rarely both a task and a maintenance leader. Typically, the two leaders fall into a pattern of complementary and mutual support, such as in a family where often the husband is the task leader and the wife the social maintenance leader. The Bales (1950) Interaction Process Analysis (IPA) is frequently used as an observation instrument in studies of roles in groups (Figure 17-1).

Conformity reduces internal friction and frees energy for group members to use on tasks and work for the purpose of receiving external rewards. If pressures to conform to norms and fulfill group roles are to be effective, the group must be a reference group. Without the psychological involvement characteristic of a reference group, it is only a membership group which cannot successfully exert pressure. However, the ease with which relatively artificial groups assembled for research purposes can induce conformity in a deviant member suggests that a conforming response is a very strong one indeed. Generally, the greater the group attractiveness, the more strongly the group can influence a person, and the more likely the change is to be one of private acceptance of the group position rather than overt compliant behavior without an underlying change (Hare, 1962).

However, if a person is somehow committed to the group, he may conform with either high or low attraction to the group. This was shown in a study in which attraction was manipulated by false ratings about how the subjects were liked by other group members, and conformity was measured as a change of opinion about ratings of abstract paintings in the direction of perceived group norms (Kiesler & Corbin, 1965). The low-attracted subjects conformed when they expected to have additional interaction with the group and they increased their liking for the group (Figure 17-2). Apparently, they worked toward psychological comfort by conforming and becoming more attracted to the group to which they were committed.

Rewards for Conformity

Studies of a variety of natural and laboratory groups support Homans' (1950) hypothesis of an association between high rank and acceptance within a group and conformity to the group norms. Groups tend to reward those who abide by its norms, and persons of higher status tend to have stronger tendencies to conform. Correlatively, low popularity is associated with nonconformity. However, there are some interesting qualifications

FIGURE

17–1

PROBLEM AREAS	OBSERVATION CATEGORIES
Expressive-integrative social-emotional area: Positive reactions	1. Shows solidarity, raises others' status, gives help, reward 2. Shows tension release, jokes, laughs, shows satisfaction 3. Agrees, shows passive acceptance, understands, concurs, complies
Instrumental adaptive task area: Attempted answers	4. Gives suggestion, direction, implying autonomy for others 5. Gives opinion, evaluation, analysis, expresses feeling, wish 6. Gives orientation, information, repeats, clarifies, confirms
Instrumental adaptive task area: Questions	7. Asks for orientation, information, repetition, confirmation 8. Asks for opinion, evaluation, analysis, expression of feeling 9. Asks for suggestion, direction, possible ways of action
Expressive-integrative social-emotional area: Negative reactions	10. Disagrees, shows passive rejection, formality, withholds help 11. Shows tension, asks for help, withdraws out of field 12. Shows antagonism, deflates other's status, defends or asserts self

a. b. c. d. e. f.

Roles in Groups.

a. Orientation
b. Evaluation
c. Control
d. Decision
e. Tension-management
f. Integration

Source: Bales, R. F. A set of categories for the analysis of small group interaction. *American Sociological Review*, 1950, 15, 257–263.

to this principle. First, what is considered expected and acceptable behavior varies with one's role in the group. Groups expect diversity just as cultures do, and conformity is evaluated against the standard held for the individual. For example, some group members are expected to perform at a *low* level (Klinger & McNelly, 1969). One boy in a street gang bowled quite well when he was alone but did very poorly when the members of the gang were present (Whyte, 1943). He had been assigned a low status in a group in which bowling was important and was therefore expected

FIGURE
17–2

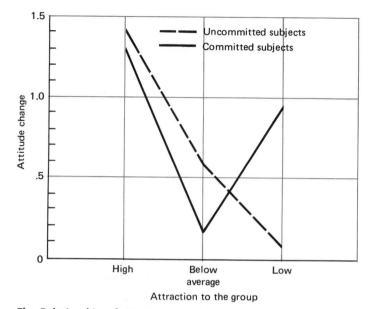

**The Relationship of Attraction to the Group and Commitment to
Continue in the Group to Conformity to Group Norms.**

Source: Kiesler, C. A., & Corbin, L. H. Commitment, attraction, and conformity.
Journal of Personality and Social Psychology, 1965, 2 (6), 890–895.

to be a poor bowler. His reward for appearing to be a poor bowler, as
his role required, was continued group membership and acceptance.

Second, high status persons are expected to innovate and to deviate
from existing norms if the group is wrong in its consensus or is not functioning well (Kiesler & Kiesler, 1969). Status hierarchies tend to be
changed if a group is failing at a task, as if the group were searching for
a new leader to cope with the situation (Hamblin, 1958). And in fact,
the most preferred members of fraternities were significantly less conforming to a clearly wrong group judgment in a laboratory task than were
the least preferred members (Feshbach, 1967).

Last, leaders are freer to deviate because of their previous conformity.
Hollander (1958, 1967) theorizes that as status is built up, so are *idiosyncrasy credits* which are drawn against by deviation from group norms.
Conformity, competency, and seniority all contribute to status. However,
even a person perceived as very competent can increase his ability to
change norms by early conformity to the norms. A low status member
must "toe the line," or "prove himself," to accrue credits before he may
deviate and still be accepted. One of higher status is free to be eccentric
as long as his credits last. If he deviates too much too often, his credit
balance will approach zero. Conformity is evaluated in terms of the specific
person and his credits.

In sum, groups evolve salient norms and exert pressure for conformity
to them. Conformity helps to maintain the group and is generally re-

warded with a high status which brings with it the responsibility of deviance when necessary for group effectiveness, and the privilege of nonconformity.

Individual Susceptibility

Conformity to group norms contributes to group maintenance and the ability to provide dependency gratification for the members. Pressure to conform is exerted, deviants are rejected, and conformers are rewarded by the group. However, a conforming response can also occur when there is no group need for it and when no direct pressure aimed at changing his views or behavior is exerted on the individual by other people. Some psychologists reserve the term conformity for agreement with others in this kind of situation (McGuire, 1968).

Sometimes the reason for a conforming response is simply that it is expedient. The issue is irrelevant to one's interests or it does not warrant the expenditure of effort necessary to make a decision on one's own. Sometimes, a conforming response is very realistic and adaptive: There occasionally is good reason for a person to believe that other people know more than he does about the issue. However, often conformity is motivated by anxiety. The individual may want to "save face" or avoid the possibility of rejection for nonagreement with others. That is, the anxiety may be due to his own perceived deviance from the rest of the group and may be concomitant with the fear of censure or rejection for the nonagreement. Perhaps a more basic reason for conformity is that it can prevent or terminate anxiety about uncertainty. The individual himself has a predisposition to make a response, to hold an opinion about what is correct, to make a judgment about a given course of action—to interpret reality in a given way. When others hold a different view, there is conflict or response indecision (Chapter 14). Conformity may resolve the problem by enabling a feeling that one has the correct view of reality because of consensus.

People vary in their tendencies to be anxious about perceived deviance, possible rejection, and uncertainty (which may be conceived as specific varieties of A-trait, Chapter 14). But the situation also certainly affects the likelihood of such feelings, and conforming responses are subject to laws of reinforcement operating in the situation.

"The Conforming Personality"

The general picture of the person likely to resist conformity pressures is that of a mature, capable person who realizes his competency; thinks well of himself; deals effectively with anxiety generated by the perception of deviance, and holds others responsible for the discrepancies; and does not have inferiority feelings, rigid and excessive self-controls, or intense needs for social approval (McGuire, 1968; Marlowe & Gergen, 1969). Conformers are more anxious and timid, have conventional and moralistic attitudes, less ability to cope with threatening situations, and tend to blame the discrepancies between group consensus and their own opinions on themselves. Consistent with the view that one function of conformity is to handle the anxiety of threat of rejection, conformers have extreme concern about social approval. Subjects high on the need for social approval conform most; those high on the need for self-approval conform least. Although there is a tendency for an individual to behave similarly across different conformity situations and issues, this is a *limited* tendency and the exact nature of the personality dispositions and their relation to conformity are not clear or consistent in all studies. For example, conservatism is frequently positively correlated with conformity, but there is no one measure of conservatism which predicts conformity in all situations (Mann, 1959).

Conforming behavior is controlled both by personality traits and by the situation. Personality factors are likely to interact with situational factors rather than dominate them. We would probably achieve a greater understanding of personality if we could give more accurate definitions of the essential stimulus conditions to which defined groups of people respond. To identify personality correlates which tend to be associated with conformity is a step along the way. However, "the conforming personality" is a label, not an explanation, and is not a consistently useful label at that. The specific antecedents which predispose people to conform under certain conditions must be specified. They are likely to include experiences which heighten anxiety about loss of status and acceptance, ability to do a job, and about uncertainty of what is correct. The specific situations which maximally elicit these feelings will vary from person to person, but overall there is a large uniformity in responding to perceived deviation with anxiety.

Anxiety at Deviation

When people are aware that others do not agree with them, anxiety is likely. In a series of dramatic pioneering experiments which gave impetus to modern conformity research, Solomon Asch (1956) asked subjects to report judgments, such as which of three lines is the same in length as another, after hearing the obviously erroneous judgments of several confederates. (The Crutchfield technique is a modification of the Asch technique in which subjects report their judgments via an electric panel which also reports the judgments supposedly made by other subjects but actually manipulated by the experimenter.) The discriminations were not difficult. Reports of subjects in a control group without confederates were almost free of error. However, only about one-fourth of Asch's original experimental subjects gave errorless reports after they heard the confederates' false reports, and the size of errors was proportional to the size of errors reported by the confederates. Some effects of the group pressure persisted when subjects later made judgments privately. Most of the subjects who yielded reported later that they believed that their own opinions were inaccurate and that those of the majority were correct. Others reported that they felt they were correct but yielded in their oral reports because they did not want to appear different from the other people.

When faced with the discrepant opinions of the other group members, subjects often show signs of distress, make comments of disbelief or annoyance, or seek reassurance from the experimenter, as did the subjects in Asch's studies. They appear to be in conflict. Even those subjects who remain independent in the face of group pressure show agitation and signs of anxiety. Physiological responses measured during conformity studies also indicate that deviance is anxiety provoking and conforming is anxiety reducing. Arousal (skin conductance) increased as subjects listened to a majority disagree with them, and the greater their confidence and perceived ability, the greater the conflict and the arousal increase (Gerard, 1961). Arousal (plasma-free fatty acid, an index of central nervous system arousal) stayed high for subjects who remained independent, but decreased for subjects who yielded to the perceived group consensus; amount of conformity and decrease in arousal with conformity were highly correlated (Back & Bogdonoff, 1964).

In short, the perception of deviance from the majority induces anxiety and conformity reduces anxiety. Exactly why deviation is anxiety arousing is seldom clear. It may imply the felt possibility of rejection by those immediately present or evoke anxiety about former rejection. Or it may be the result of uncertainty. Indeed, in real life, the bases for anxiety, or the kinds of dependency relationships threatened, are often intertwined. It is clear, however, that a person strives to be accurate. Thus, uncertainty about what is correct increases conformity and support from others for expressing one's own opinion decreases it.

Uncertainty

An individual's susceptibility to social pressure varies with the degree of confidence he has in his own solution to the problem (Walker & Heyns, 1962). Certainty is a function of the individual's self-judged competence, particularly relative to the perceived competence of relevant others (Ettinger et al., 1971). Any factor which reduces a person's perceived competence will make him more likely to conform (Marlow & Gergen, 1969). Few people feel incompetent in all situations, and few never see others as more competent than themselves. Thus, lack of a large personality consistency in conforming responses across situations is no surprise. However, some situational factors stand out as salient in predicting conformity. The judgment of one's own relative competence in the task at hand is likely to be influenced by the difficulty and ambiguity of the task, one's self-esteem, and the encouragement one has from other group members or authorities for making independent judgments.

Task difficulty and self-esteem. Generally, conformity varies positively with the complexity and difficulty of the task (Asch, 1958; Deutsch & Gerard, 1955; Crutchfield, 1955). If a task is extremely easy, most people will feel confident in handling it and will not need the opinion of others. However, it is also true that if a task is exceedingly difficult, the instrumental value of outside opinion may be nullified by the fact that the individual views those others as being as incompetent as himself. Self-esteem influences the judgment of task difficulty. In an experiment, subjects made judgments of low, moderate, or high difficulty about a series of pairs of paintings; conformity was measured as the change in judgment between the subjects' first impression, which they believed to be privately stated, and their "considered" judgment which they knew would be public both to the experimenter and to the other subject, an accomplice introduced as an art major (Gergen & Bauer, 1967). Change of opinion in the direction of the other person was greater on the medium difficult task than on the others, and was greater for medium self-esteem subjects than for those of higher or lower self-esteem (Figure 17–3). The high self-esteem subjects did not generally feel the need to rely on the opinions of others, and they seemed to see the task labeled by the experimenters as "very difficult" as being of only moderate difficulty for them. The relative underconformity by the low self-esteem subjects in the face of divergent opinions probably reflects defensiveness. Low self-esteem females, and possibly males, seem to be interpersonally defensive and rigid when confronted with opinions differing from their own.

Support for own opinion. People generally conform relatively easily when they are uncertain about what is correct. However, they are also quickly responsive to minimal cues that they may be correct and the rest of the group wrong. Certainly, or felt competence with the task, is increased if there is some objective evidence that one is correct and competent in the matter at hand. This evidence may be provided by the agreement of someone else in the group or by an authority. Asch reported that with the help of even only one other person as an ally, a subject can stand against the false judgments of seven or eight other people (also see Allen & Newtson, 1972). The ally provides support for viewing one's own position as valid; he reduces conflict and increases certainty. However, if one has already decided, as it were, that the group is correct and changed his opinion in the direction of group consensus before learning of a deviant ally, the deviant poses a *new* conflict rather than a means for resolving the first conflict. Subjects who did not learn of a supposed deviant ally until after they had conformed did not "undo" their conformity response, though they did show less final conformity than those who never were supported by a deviant (Figure 17–4; Kiesler, Zanna, & DeSalvo, 1966). Further, subjects who knew of the deviant ally early in the session liked him better than did those who did not "discover" him until after they had changed their opinion.

Support from authority. Frequently, an outside expert—whether a dictionary, encyclopedia, or experimenting psychologist—is available to clarify what is "correct." Proven accuracy of judgment increases felt com-

FIGURE
17–3

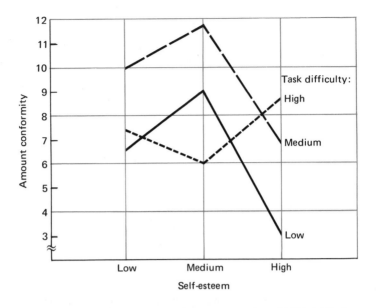

Conformity as a Function of Self-Esteem Level and Task Difficulty.

Source: Gergen, K. J., & Bauer, R. A. Interactive effects of self-esteem and task difficulty on social conformity. *Journal of Personality and Social Psychology,* 1967, 6 (1), 16–22.

petence and the tendency to make independent responses which may deviate from a group consensus. Evidence of consistent inaccuracy increases the tendency to conform to group opinion (Marlowe & Gergen, 1969). Conformity is a learned response. Like other responses, it follows reinforcement laws. The more frequently subjects received reinforcement (100 percent, 50 percent, 5 percent, or 0 percent of sixteen trials) from the experimenter for making responses agreeing with a contrived group consensus, the more conformity increased (Endler, 1966). With reinforcement for disagreeing with the group, conformity decreased. The amount of conformity varied over trials as a function of the reinforcement. The effect of reinforcement was still apparent two weeks later when the subjects did not think that others knew of their answers, although the level of conformity was reduced (Figure 17–5). Reinforcement can increase or decrease the subject's willingness or need to rely on his own independent judgment.

In sum, conformity is a socially learned response which can reduce anxiety by minimizing the threat of rejection and maximizing the feeling of accuracy and certainty. Nonconformity is likely when one does not accept or need the opinions of others, because of defensiveness, self-esteem, or reinforcement for independent responding in the specific case at hand. Much the same can be said as a partial introduction to the study of attitudes. The phenomena of conformity and nonconformity as discussed in this section are involved in the processes of attitude formation

FIGURE
17–4

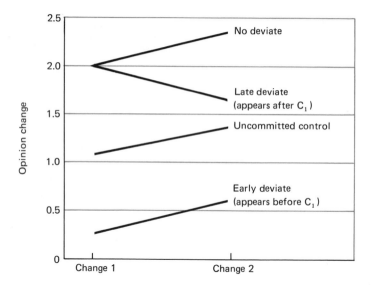

Opinion Change as a Function of Experimental Condition for Change 1 and Change 2.

Source: Kiesler, C. A., Zanna, M., & DeSalvo, J. Deviation and conformity: Opinion change as a function of commitment, attraction, and presence of a deviate. *Journal of Personality and Social Psychology*, 1966, 3 (4), 458–467.

and change or resistance to pressure for change. However, the concepts which fall under the general heading of attitudes give a broader perspective of the total individual forming perspectives within the social setting, and the person acting as a complete individual trying to come to terms with himself and his social environment.

ATTITUDES

Most simply, attitudes are learned predispositions to respond. They are relatively enduring and general predispositions which influence a fairly large class of evaluative responses directed toward some object, person, or group. Attitudes are crucial to the understanding of personality, and are in many ways difficult, if not impossible, to distinguish from personality. Through the study of the development and change of a person's attitudes, we may gain a glimpse of what his important needs are and who the important others are in his life. Obviously, one of the most important people in a person's life is himself. The person strives to behave consistently with his view of himself, and to obtain rewards for himself. These two goals are sometimes in apparent conflict. Paradoxically, a person's attitudes are likely to shift toward the position someone else wants him to hold when he is free to do what others request of him; yet he is capable of reacting against reasonable requests as he attempts

to maintain his perceived freedom. Thus, the dilemma for the individual
is how to feel free while being socially responsive, and how to maintain
a sense of individuality in interaction with other people.

The Nature of Attitudes

Definition. A person's attitudes, or predispositions to respond, are an
outcome of his previous learning experiences from and with others, and
often about others. In turn, attitudes fashion further learning, leading
people to expose themselves selectively to life experiences, and to selectively perceive, interpret, and respond to what is going on in any given
situation. Because attitudes, like norms, provide an orientation toward
the environment, they may be considered motivational-perceptual states
which direct perceptions and predispose a person to act in accordance
with his perceptions (F. H. Allport, 1955). In fact, norms may be considered shared attitudes. However, the term attitude is usually reserved for
issues about which individuals within a culture are expected and allowed
to differ; conformity is not essential for the protection of self or others.
Nonetheless, conformity is frequent, and social pressures are endless.

According to widespread usage, attitudes have three components: a
cognitive component (opinion, information, or stereotype) of belief or
disbelief, an *affective* (or emotional) component of like or dislike, and

**FIGURE
17–5**

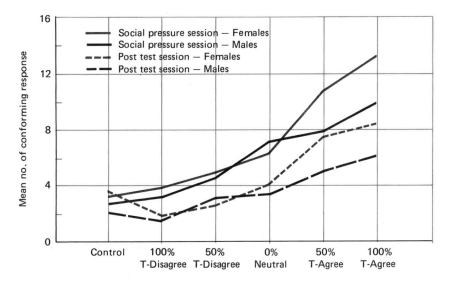

**The Effects of Different Reinforcement Conditions on Conforming Responses
for Social Pressure and Posttest Nonpressure Sessions.**

Source: Endler, N. S. Conformity as a function of different reinforcement schedules. *Journal of
Personality and Social Psychology,* 1966, 4, 175–180.

FIGURE
17–6

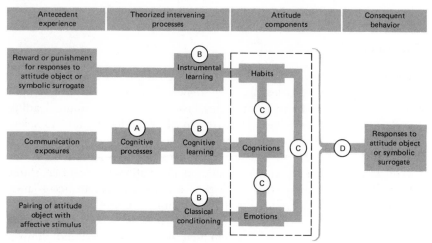

Schematic Framework for Analysis of Attitude Theory.
The four areas of attitude theory discussed in the text are identified by letters as follows:
A, theory of cognitive information processing; B, learning theory; C, theory of attitude
component interaction; D, behavior theory. Attitude is identified as a complex consisting
of the three intervening constructs enclosed in the dashed rectangle. These component
constructs are assumed to be acquired through learning processes from a variety of
categories of antecedent experience and, in combination, to determine subsequent performance relating to the attitude object.

Source: Greenwald, A. G. On defining attitude and attitude theory. In Greenwald, A. G., Brock,
T. C., and Ostrom, T. M. (Eds.), *Psychological foundations of attitudes.* New York: Academic
Press, 1968.

an *action* (or conative, behavioral, habit) component of readiness to respond. Thus, attitudes are the particular ways in which a person thinks,
feels, and acts (Figure 17–6). The affective component can be measured
by physiological responses or verbal statements of like or dislike. The
cognitive component may be measured by self-ratings of beliefs or by
the amount of knowledge a person has about a relevant topic. The behavioral component can be measured by direct observation of how the
person behaves in a specific situation, but it is most often measured by
his self-report of how he would or does behave. The most frequently used
measures are self-report attitude scales, questionnaires, or standard interviews such as those below.

> *Thurstone scale.* Samples from an equal-appearing interval
> scale by Thurstone and Chave. Scale values derived from
> judges' ratings of favorability of item. Subject's score is sum of
> scale values of items which he checks as ones with which he
> agrees.
>
> (0.4) I believe the church is the greatest influence for good
> government and right living.
> (3.1) I do not understand the dogmas or creeds of the church

but I find that the church helps me to be more honest and credible.

(5.7) I do not receive any benefit from attending church services but I think the services help some people.

(7.5) I believe too much money is being spent on the church for the benefit that is being derived.

(9.5) I believe the church is hundreds of years behind the times and cannot make a dent in modern life.

Likert scale. Samples from a Likert scale on internationalism. Each statement clearly represents a favorable or unfavorable attitude. The subject indicates his amount of agreement or disagreement.

We should be willing to fight for our country whether it is in the right or in the wrong.

Strongly approve	Approve	Undecided	Disapprove	Strongly disapprove
5	4	3	2	1

Our country should never declare war again under any circumstances.

Strongly approve	Approve	Undecided	Disapprove	Strongly disapprove
1	2	3	4	5

Bogardus social distance scale. Subjects indicate the degree of relationship to which they would admit members of a given group. A person who accepted statement 1 would accept all others; one who accepted 3 would not accept 1 and 2 but would accept statements 4, 5, 6.

I would willingly admit foreigners:
1. to close kinship by marriage.
2. to my club as personal chums.
3. to my street as neighbors.
4. to employment in my occupation.
5. to citizenship in my country.
6. as visitors in my country.

Although researchers often design instruments to measure separate components, they are highly correlated (McGuire, 1969). Everyday behavior is likely to be a synthesis of all three components, although the consistencies between thinking, feeling, and behaving are not always obvious at first glance.

Attitudes and Behavior

Early mention should be made of the fact that apparent inconsistencies between verbally expressed attitudes and actual behavior have been noted frequently, and cited as evidence against the efficacy of attitude measurement and the construct of attitudes. In a dramatic demonstration of such inconsistency, La Pierre (1934) and his Chinese traveling companions were refused service only once in over 250 hotels and restaurants. However, when he later wrote the establishments asking their policy regarding Chinese clients, over 90 percent of the replies stated a policy of nonacceptance. More recent studies have shown a lack of any simple relationship between stated attitudes toward members of another race and willingness to pose for photographs with them (Linn, 1965; Green, 1972). That is, some white students who stated intolerant attitudes toward blacks were nonetheless willing to be photographed with a black, while some who had expressed tolerant attitudes were unwilling.

Rokeach (1968; Rokeach & Kliejunas, 1972) has contended that the lack of correspondence between the verbalized attitudes and actual behavior is due to the fact that people have a variety of attitudes which influence any one behavior. For example, the previously cited restaurant owners had attitudes toward Chinese *and* attitudes about running a business. Behavior is always a function of at least two attitudes, one toward the object or event and one toward the situation in which the object or event is encountered at a particular time. When the situation varies, so too does the attitude toward it and the resulting behavior. In the case of posing with blacks, the perceived intimacy to be displayed in the anticipated photograph and its exposure (ranging from the front page of *Life* magazine to use in a textbook in underdeveloped countries) affected the willingness to pose with a black (Green, 1972).

Another way to view the complexities of relating behavior to attitudes is in terms of the situational hurdles which differ in their levels of difficulty (Campbell, 1963). For instance, it is easy to express prejudice on a questionnaire or through the mail, but more difficult in the very different situation of an actual face-to-face confrontation. Situations vary in their difficulty level. For example, in a coal-mining community, the mines were integrated but the town was not. Some miners were either friendly toward the blacks in both settings or in neither setting. Others (60 percent) were friendly to blacks in the mines but not in town (Figure 17–7). Inconsistency would have been shown by friendliness in town, the more difficult hurdle, but not in the mines, the easier hurdle. There was no case of this.

Thus, behavior toward an object reflecting a specific attitude occurs in a situation about which one also has a specific attitude. When verbal statements do not predict actual behavior, it may be because insufficient information has been considered and the situation as seen by the individual has not been completely specified. As we shall see, behavior discrepant from an underlying attitude may instigate a change of the attitude. We must first consider the basic issues of attitude development and change.

Development and Change

The fact that people have so many attitudes, even about objects of which they have little knowledge, suggests that attitudes satisfy important needs in the psychological economy (McGuire, 1969). Attitudes are the indi-

FIGURE
17–7

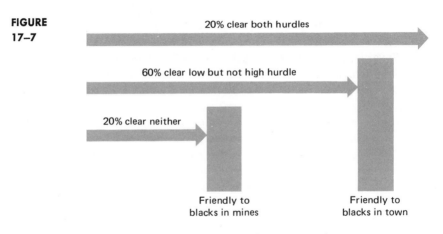

20% clear both hurdles

60% clear low but not high hurdle

20% clear neither

Friendly to
blacks in mines

Friendly to
blacks in town

Relationship of Situational Hurdles to Attitudes.

Source: Campbell, D. T. Social attitudes and other acquired behavioral dispositions. In S. Koch (Ed.), *Psychology: A study of a science.* Vol. 6. New York:
McGraw-Hill, 1963.

vidualized expressions of one's own needs and thus important keys to
understanding personality. However, these individualized expressions in
large part occur within the context of relationships with other people.
It is within this context that the individual comes to be who he is and
learns how he wishes to express himself, how to see the world, and how
to deal with his sense of personal freedom.

Attitudes often develop in the service of pleasing significant others.
More specifically, we are susceptible to the influence of specific significant
others, and of reference groups. We tend to conform to their views, as
discussed earlier in this chapter; their approval and disapproval can
function as reinforcers and punishers for our behavior, our verbal statements, and our emotional responses. Thus, attitudes are both individualized expressions *and* a reflection of the influence of significant others
in one's life. The significant others are a manifestation of whom one
identifies with, as discussed in the following chapter.

Functions of Attitudes

The functional approach to the study of attitudes emphasizes the psychodynamic motivational factors involved in attitude formation and change
(McGuire, 1969; Smith, 1968; Katz, 1960, 1968). Attitudes become established to serve at least one of four functions, and are changed when
they fail to do so. The extent of the change depends on the extent to
which an attitude fails to serve its function—or functions, since many
attitudes have more than one.

An individual receives positive responses from other people because
of attitudes which serve an *instrumental function*, also called a utilitarian,
adaptive, or adjustive function. An attitude which serves an instrumental

function helps to maintain satisfying relationships with significant others. For example, one may express anti-Semitic attitudes not because of hostility toward Jews, but because prejudice statements facilitate acceptance in an anti-Semitic environment. Such attitudes may be changed by changing the person's feelings about the other person(s) he is trying to please or his perceptions of their positions.

Attitudes serving a *knowledge function,* or economy function, represent a way of seeking predictability, consistency, and stability in the perception of the world. They give coherence and direction to experience. They are a "manual" of how to behave toward specific objects. Because they simplify a complex world, they give a feeling of competency in being able to deal with experience. (Notice the similarity to the concept of personal constructs, Chapter 13.) Ideally, an attitude is an informal theory based on information and is susceptible to change with new information. Unfortunately, attitudes are often resistant to change. This may be necessary in order to give stability to one's ideology.

Expressive, or *self-realizing,* attitudes are means of openly expressing and acknowledging cherished values and commitments. They may also be ways of presenting the positive aspects of one's self-concept which may bring social reward (instrumental function). The gratification is of a more emotional type than with the above functions. The attitude may provide a cathartic acting-out of tensions, or it may provide the opportunity for self-assertion. One justifies his behavior by adopting attitudes which bolster it, or one creates an identity for himself by taking a stand. Providing another outlet for expression could change the attitude. It has been suggested that on the island of Truk, baseball was substituted for intertribal warfare; perhaps in this way competition in sports was substituted for destructive, hostile expressions.

Prejudice attitudes illustrate those serving *ego-defensive functions:* They allow the individual to avoid knowledge about himself or to defend rather than reveal his self-concept. Their function is to help deal with inner conflicts rather than to respond to the object of the attitude as it is. Prejudice may be self-sustaining when it hides one's own weaknesses and gives a false sense of superiority over others. These kinds of attitudes require self-insight, catharsis, or cognitive reorganization if they are to be changed.

Any one attitude may serve more than one function, and probably many serve all. For example, a prejudice may develop initially to serve an ego-defensive function, but it can easily become a self-assertive attitude and a favored means of imposing order on the world. Such an attitude would likely lead to selection of acquaintances with similar attitudes and serve the utilitarian function. Thus, attitude change is no simple matter. To disturb a deeply held attitude is to shake the dynamic equilibrium of personality coherence and organization. Deeply held attitudes are intricately intertwined with many aspects of one's personality and contribute to the security or stability of one's position in interpersonal space.

Reference Groups and Attitudes

Reference groups influence the specific content of one's needs and the attitudes which will serve those needs, and constitute the social setting within which attitudes develop and perhaps change. The family is typically the first reference group, and parents provide the genesis of attitudes which may be maintained into adulthood. For instance, attitudes toward public affairs and political party affiliation of adults are consistently found to be very similar to those of the parents. Similarly, attitudes toward organized religion are likely to be much like those of the parents. However, it is at best an oversimplification and at worst an outright error to maintain that adult attitudes are simply imitations of parental views. An attitude is likely to be associated with a wide range of experiences which maintain and support each other. The child's social world, in which attitudes are initiated, is shaped and controlled by the parents (Chapter 16). A child whose parents have positive attitudes toward organized religion is likely to be sent to Sunday school, to eat only after saying grace, to donate part of his allowance to church, to have other Sunday school attenders at his birthday party, and to see attending church committee meetings as an expected activity of adults. In view of the pervasive encouragement to act, feel, and think pro-church, it is "logical" that the child develop the same preference as his parents, who have shaped the world he experiences. The same is true, though perhaps to a lesser extent, for other reference groups the child and adult later adopt.

Peer groups become increasingly important to the growing child as reference groups, and may become more important anchor points on some issues than the family group (Chapter 21). The Bennington study, a classic study of attitudes in real-life situations, illustrates the interplay of family and college reference groups and individual differences in reconciling conflicting social pressures (Newcomb, 1943, 1963). The typical freshman at Bennington College in 1935 was from a wealthy northeastern family with very conservative political attitudes. However, Bennington was noted for very liberal attitudes. Generally, students became progressively more liberal as they went through college. There was little reversion to conservative attitudes after about twenty-five years, for the graduates had selected as husbands men who were more liberal than other men of the same socioeconomic level. For those who changed toward liberalism, the college community replaced the family as a reference group for the attitudes in question. Specific motivations for the change varied widely, and included a need for approval of the college community ("I became liberal at first because of its prestige value") and a need to achieve independence from parents (". . . the vehicle for achieving independence from my family"). For some, both kinds of motivations were obvious ("Every influence I felt tended to push me in the liberal direction: my underdog complex, my need to be independent of my parents, and my anxiousness to be a leader here."). For students who did not change, the college community was only a membership group or was a negative reference group, which defines what position will not be taken. However, those who resisted the college norms were not without conflict: "I wanted to disagree . . . but I was afraid. . . . So I built up a wall inside me. . . . I decided to stick to my father's ideas." "Family against faculty has been my struggle here."

In short, attitude development and change is a function of the way the individual relates to particular groups of other people. Reference groups may shift throughout life, with resulting implications for attitude change. Similarly, with attitude change, reference groups may change, and with reference group change, there is a change in whose approval will be reinforcing.

Learning Mechanisms in Attitude Development

Both classical conditioning and instrumental conditioning concepts are appropriate for describing some mechanisms in attitude development. Some theorists maintain that the crucial feature of an attitude is the emotional component and the important principle in the formation of attitudes is that of classical conditioning, by which emotional responses are acquired or transferred to formerly neutral cues. The cognitive and behavioral components are thought of as later developments in attitude formation. Staats (1968, 1969) first demonstrated that a word stimulus (conditioned stimulus, cs) paired with an aversive unconditioned stimulus (ucs) came to elicit emotional responses (galvanic skin response, gsr), and the subjects rated the word as more unpleasant than did control subjects who did not have the pairing. Then he paired national or personal names (cs) with a variety of words (ucs) to which a positive or negative attitudinal response was already attached, that is, good, bad, and so on. Names which had been paired with negative attitudinal re-

> Words may come to elicit emotional reactions, which then can be reflected in self-report affect ratings of the words.
>
> UCS   shock ⟶ Emotional response
> CS   word
>
> then: word ⟶ Emotional response: affective rating
>
> Some words in our culture come to elicit a general positive, or negative, emotional response. These may then function as unconditioned stimuli and be paired with names of specific people or groups of people (as conditioned stimuli) which come by themselves to elicit the positive, or negative, emotional response. Notice that the cs is presented not with one word repeatedly, but with each of several words, on separate occasions, and all the words elicit the positive, or negative, emotional response.

UCS ────────→ Positive emotional   UCS ────────→ Negative
    happy   response   ugly   emotional
    beautiful   sad   response
    glad   bad
CS   CS
    Jim   Bill

then: Jim ──→ positive attitude   Bill ──→ negative attitude

sponses were rated as unpleasant, while those paired with a positive response were rated as pleasant. The strength of the effect is a function of the number of pairings, and the conditioning generalizes to synonyms of the cs word. Similarly, the extremity of a newly acquired attitude (toward a fictitious group) increased with reinforcement schedules, increasing from 50 percent to 100 percent during acquisition trials (Kerpelman & Himmelfarb, 1971).

Reinforcement by others.   Generalizing from this research, one can suggest that if a child notices that mother always smiles (ucs) when she sees an American Indian (cs) but frowns when she sees a Puerto Rican, he is likely to feel the warm glow that is a response to mother's smile when he sees Indians and feel the unpleasantness previously associated with her frown when he sees a Puerto Rican. Modification of action and

Mother's behavior (or that of other significant people) is an effective elicitor (UCS) of emotional reactions, and these often occur in the presence of particular kinds of people, or along with words or pictures of them (the other is symbolically presented).

UCS Mother smiles   Positive   UCS Mother   Negative
  CS American Indian ──→ emotional   frowns ──→ emotional
                          response   CS   Puerto   response
                                             Rican

The behavior of others comes to be a discriminative stimulus (S^D) signaling that positive, or negative, behavior toward a given target will be rewarded with approval and agreement.

S^D Mother smiles ●   R Positive ──→ S$_+$ Mother's ──→ R Self-
     at American   ●   actions   approval,   approval
     Indians   agreement

Mother's approval tends to elicit self-approval and thus comes to occur contiguous with self-approval. The response then can be maintained by the reinforcer of self-approval long after mother's approval is withdrawn, or is no longer immediately present or immediately relevant.

     R   Positive actions toward ──→ S$_+$ Self-approval
         American Indians

cognitive components of attitudes toward the groups are likely to be not far behind, and supporting responses and attitudes developed. Mother's smile, and later Indians alone, will come to function as a discriminative stimulus (s^D) signaling that positive statements and behavior will be rewarded. Her frown, and later Puerto Ricans alone, signal that negative statements will be rewarded. The young child is likely to modify his behavior accordingly and receive the reinforcement of mother's approval. If mother reinforces one kind of response, she is also likely to reinforce functionally similar responses. The mother who smiles at Indians and rewards her son's positive statements about them will also approve when he chooses an Indian classmate as a playmate. Because mother's approval is associated with approval of self, the attitudes become self-reinforcing and perpetuated without mother's continued surveillance and reinforcement. The responses may be acquired with awareness of the stimulus contingencies and of mother's expectancies, but awareness is not necessary for the performance of well-learned responses. Nor is it necessary that the person, child or adult, remember the ways in which the response was acquired. The attitude may persist and automatically direct behavior long after the time of acquisition.

The kinds of statements and other behavior that will be reinforced and the kinds of events that will be reinforcing vary with the functions served by the attitudes and with the person's reference groups. If another person is not a "desirable other" or is not salient for the issue at hand, responsiveness to his attempts at social influence is minimal. With personality development and reference group change, there is a change of the people who are reinforcers for given kinds of attitudes, and attitudes may in turn change, as shown in the Bennington study. Attitudes, or specific components of attitudes, may also come under the control of discriminative stimuli. In such cases, the individual learns that a statement or behavior is rewarded in one situation, but not in another. In other terms, role behavior changes with the situation. Although attitudes may change because of shifting needs and reference groups, early learned and deeply held attitudes are likely to have a strong emotional component not easily subject to change.

Attitudes as inferences. Attitudes may also develop from behavior without there having been an obvious initial emotional base or cognitive concomitant of the behavior. The attitude as an internalized principle is a later development. With the Skinnerian framework developed by Bem (1967, 1968, 1969), an attitude is seen as a self-description about preferences for aspects of the environment. The individual himself may infer his attitude from his own observable behavior. Bem's famous recurring example is brown bread. "Do you like brown bread?" "I guess so, I'm always eating it." The individual's overt behavior, in this case eating the bread, is the stimulus controlling the attitudinal statement. This is the same stimulus used by others in inferring his attitude. If someone asks a woman if her husband likes brown bread, she might answer for him,

"I guess he does, he is always eating it." Thus, the attitudinal statement occurs *after* the behavior when one attempts to describe what he thinks of the person, himself, who is acting in a given way. Self-descriptions may also come as *directives* of behavior. Parents often incorporate attitudinal statements in their comments about behavior, such as saying to a child: "You don't like dogs. Leave him alone!" Bem speculates that attitudes, as self-descriptions, become internalized variants of the attitudinal descriptions used by parents to instruct their children and to control their behavior. The internal components of attitudes may come to be antecedents as well as consequents of behavior. Going beyond Bem, it may be suggested that, given a strong statement of like or dislike, an emotional component may occur because of the controlling functions that words and perceptions of the environment come to have over emotional responses (Chapter 14).

Bem's reasoning has important implications for procedures of attitude change, and for behavior therapy. As discussed in a following section, manipulation of behavior is highly effective in changing attitudes. Techniques which deal only with observable behavior can be effective in changing underlying attitudes or conflicts as consequents of the behavioral change rather than as antecedents, as is the case in conventional attitude change techniques and conventional psychotherapies.

Persuasibility

Persuasibility is the term used to describe attempts to change attitudes in situations in which a source, or communicator, gives his position on an issue and presents emotional or rational arguments about why his position is correct (McGuire, 1968). Political advertising and indoctrination campaigns, and attempted face-to-face personal influence are persuasibility situations. The effectiveness of persuasion attempts varies with a host of variables associated with the perceived characteristics of the source, the nature of his message, and the recipient of the message (see Zimbardo & Ebbesen, 1969; McGuire, 1969; Triandis, 1971). We will mention only selected facets of individual differences in persuasibility. Persuasibility on one issue in one circumstance tends to be positively related to persuasibility on other issues in other circumstances. As with conformity, people with low self-esteem, feelings of inadequacy, and social inhibitions are likely to be susceptible to social influence. However, again the conclusions are weak and the "persuasibility trait" is far from strong or unitary. People respond in situations, not in vacuums. Their response varies with their own personality characteristics and with the characteristics of the situation, as shown in the case of fear appeals.

Many would-be persuaders assume that heightened emotionality will facilitate acceptance of their communications: Scare the public into buying your brand of deodorant, show gory pictures of the horrors of war, dramatize the dangers of electing the opposing candidate or of not wearing a seat belt. The tactic sometimes works. But not always. Consider the inverted U relating arousal and performance and the logic of defense mechanisms. An hypothesized curvilinear relation seems to describe the results. It suggests that acceptance of the recommendations of a fear-arousing communication is more likely if the total fear operative is slight or moderate, and less likely if fear is strongly or only weakly aroused (McGuire, 1969; Janis, 1967, 1969; Janis & Leventhal, 1968). The fear is a function of how much the communication dramatizes dangers and the predispositions of the subjects to react to it emotionally. In one study, a strong threat version of a film of a young smoker included a sequence showing the surgical removal of the man's cancerous lung; the sequence was not included in the mild threat version (Niles, 1964). Both the strength of the film's fear appeals and the subjects' feelings of susceptibility or vulnerability to illness affected their intention to decrease cigarette smoking and obtain chest X rays. Subjects of low vulnerability changed more if they saw the strong threat film, while those of high vulnerability changed more with the mild threat than with the strong threat film (Figure 17–8). Similarly, a high threat increases the persuasibility of peo-

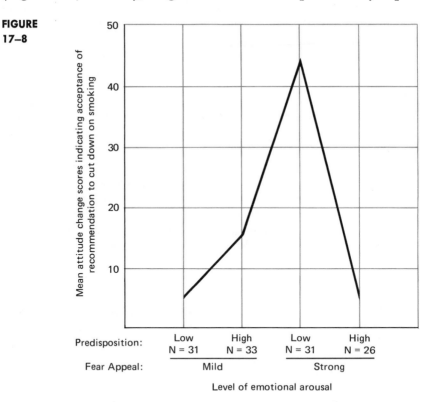

FIGURE 17–8

Relation between Level of Emotional Arousal Evoked by an Anti-Smoking Communication and Acceptance of the Recommendation.

Source: Based on data from Niles, P. The relationship of susceptibility and anxiety to acceptance of fear-arousing communications. (Unpublished doctoral dissertation, Yale University, 1964.)

ple chronically low in anxiety and decreases it for people high in chronic anxiety. Behavior, in this case attitude change, results from the interaction of the personality dispositions and the stimulus of the moment.

The inverted U is likely due to two aspects of anxiety (Chapter 15). On the one hand, anxiety is conceptualized as an energizer which facilitates performance, at least up to a point, and thus may be associated with increased attention paid to the message because of ego involvement or because of its relevance. However, anxiety also has cue functions of eliciting responses. As fear increases, distracting responses are increasingly elicited, including aggression and defenses which distort or induce resistance to the unpleasant message. The intense fear interferes with the acceptance of the rational arguments about the benefits of giving up smoking or otherwise taking the protective steps advocated in the message. Consistent with this interpretation, higher fear arousal is optimal for those whose typical response to fear is avoidance rather than approach.

ATTITUDE AND BEHAVIOR INCONGRUITIES

"One of the most effective ways to change a person's attitudes is to induce him to engage in behavior inconsistent with those attitudes" (Carlsmith, 1968, p. 803). Because of pervasive societal norms and roles and the never-ending pressures from other people, we are often induced into behaving differently from the way we think we want to behave or should behave. Our compliant behavior may be appropriate to a role with which we are not yet comfortable, or it may be a statement of agreement with a specific view with which we internally disagree. The ultimate effect may be to change our attitudes. Once our attitudes are changed, the new ones will presumably come to control behavior in the absence of surveillance or social pressure. Attendant upon this fact are some interesting implications about the relative interaction of thought and behavior.

Thus, successful tactics of manipulating behavior pose poignant, often disguised, threats to freedom. However, the possibility of change of attitude by induced compliance does not necessarily mean that an individual is merely a pawn easily pushed around by others. His concepts of self and perceived freedom of choice about his compliant behavior affect the conditions in which attitude change will or will not occur. Nevertheless, one chooses and acts in environments which others may control, and one is subject to pressures in that environment. Thus, maintaining effective freedom and control of self in a world of other people is no easy matter.

Induced Compliance

Compliant behavior may be elicited from another person in several ways. Group pressure and persuasibility efforts previously discussed may be effective in getting a person to "go along" when his heart isn't really in it, when he has not made an initial change of attitude. The techniques discussed in this section essentially involve asking or telling a person to do something, to "role play," to be a subject in an experiment, or, when one has sufficient legal power, changing his environment so that he is forced to make contact with targets of his prejudice.

Role playing. With role-playing techniques, the subject plays the "role" of someone else, often someone with attitudes different from his own, with a frequent outcome that he "persuades himself" to change his opinion to be more in line with that which, as part of his role, he is publicly advocating in a speech or debate. The effectiveness of the technique requires an active participation of the subject, in which he thinks about the material he is delivering, contemplates the issue, and generally plays the role of the "sincere advocate" (Janis, 1968). In developing his own views or in thinking through the arguments contained in a provided script, the subject feels as though he is expressing his own ideas. As is true also for other techniques of attitude change, subjects with an initial extreme attitude are likely to be less responsive to influence than are those with moderate opinions. Data from a study in which whites were asked to give arguments why blacks moving into white neighborhoods would protect rather than damage property prices are shown in Figure 17–9.

FIGURE 17–9

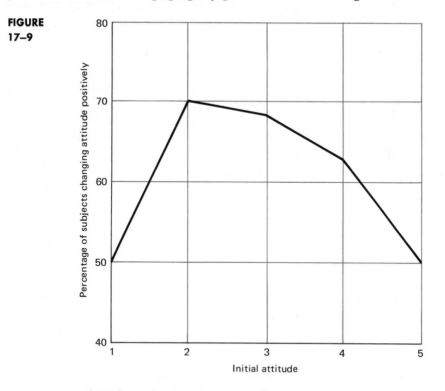

The Relationship between the Original Attitude and Amount of Attitude Change.

Source: Carlson. Attitude change through modification of attitude structure. *Journal of Abnormal and Social Psychology,* 1956, 52, 256–261.

Emotional role playing is even more effective than the cognitive role playing of making speeches. In one study, experimental subjects played the role of a medical patient being told by a doctor that she has lung cancer (Janis & Mann, 1965; Mann & Janis, 1968). Observation and self-reports suggested that the role playing in this psychodramatic situation was a very disquieting experience for the subjects. Subjects who role played reported a sharper reduction in number of cigarettes smoked daily than did control subjects who simply listened to a tape recording of a role-playing session. The effects of the short role-playing session were still observable eighteen months later. During this time, the Surgeon General's Report on Smoking and Health was published. Although both the role playing and the control subjects reacted to the report, the prior effect of the emotional role playing held up (Figure 17–10). Janis (1969) suggested that emotional role playing enables a "repackaging" of information in a way that leads to a change in one's self-image of personal vulnerability to health hazards. It reduces psychological resistances so that one can tolerate a higher level of fear without becoming defensive. Apparently, the role playing makes the threat real enough that defenses are not attempted. Most people will not use extreme distorting defenses in the face of unambiguous information, even though that information may be unpleasant or threatening (Chapter 11).

Emotional role playing is also being used in psychotherapy. For example, it may lessen a "generation gap" problem between parents and children. If father and son are each willing to "step into the other's shoes," so to speak, the perspectives of each may be broadened and the attitudes of each modified as they feel somewhat as the other feels.

Induced Contact

Effectiveness. The bit of common sense folklore that "stateways cannot change folkways" is often advanced in criticism of civil rights legislation against discrimination. However, research evidence about enforced integration contradicts this proposition. Increased interaction of an *egalitarian* nature lowers the prevalence of ethnic prejudice. Black-white relations were improved by integrated housing (Deutsch & Collins, 1951). Living close together in integrated units (random assignment without consideration of race) was associated with more frequent and intimate interpersonal relations with members of the other race than was living in segregated projects (assignment, based on race, to specific buildings or wings of a building). The increased contact led to a marked decline in prejudiced attitudes and the changes were much more dramatic for the residents living in integrated projects than in segregated ones (Table 17–1). The attitude change was not due to those residents with initially favorable attitudes. Similar results were reported about the attitudes of black and white soldiers during World War II; the greater the proximity, the greater the contact, and the greater the attitude change (Star, Williams, & Stouffer, 1949). The effectiveness of enforced contact may be due in part to the role-playing phenomenon; some people will act posi-

**FIGURE
17–10**

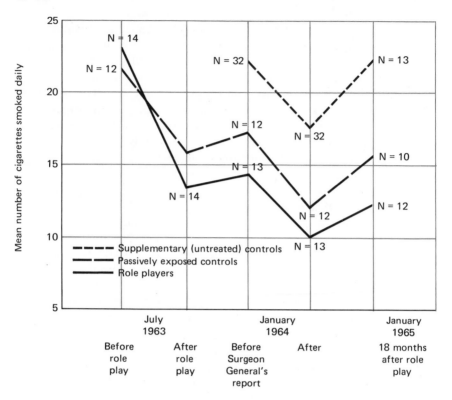

Long-Term Effects of Emotional Role Playing on Cigarette Smoking.

Source: Mann, L., & Janis, I. L. A follow-up study on the long-term effects of emotional role playing. *Journal of Personality and Social Psychology,* 1968, 8, 339–342.

tively in face-to-face contact although they initially want to act negatively. Probably just as potent is the communication enabled by contact (Chapter 16). With communication, members of each race may discover common interests that had previously been overshadowed by the presumed differences. There is strong evidence that racial attitudes are modifiable, particularly when people of different races interact under conditions favoring the perception of similar beliefs (Dreger & Miller, 1968).

Cautions. Although there is evidence that forced contact may lead to positive attitude change towards members of a prejudiced outgroup, there are limitations in the technique. First, the development of positive attitudes may be highly specific to the situation of contact. For example, department store employees who had worked with blacks were more willing to do so again than were those who had not, but there were no changes in other action tendencies toward blacks (Harding & Hogrefe, 1952). Second, people with extreme attitudes may selectively perceive and remember characteristics of the group to which they are exposed and gain "evidence" for their position. This is most likely when the duration of contact is relatively short. The immediate effect of contact is to *strengthen* existing attitudes: The hostile become more hostile, those favorably predisposed become more favorable (McGuire, 1969). Another factor germane to some situations is the question whether the controlling group holding the norm of equality is a positive or a negative reference group. Some boys at an integrated summer camp showed increased prejudice toward blacks during the summer (Mussen, 1950). Those who accepted the norm of equality and became less prejudiced found camp a rewarding experience. Those showing increased prejudice rejected the norm; they had needs to defy authority and strong aggressive feelings. Enforced contact may also elicit the perception that one's freedom is threatened, with a resulting reaction against social influence pressures, as discussed shortly.

Obedience to Authority

Milgram (1963, 1965) has offered provocative evidence of the extent to which normal adults will comply with the commands of an authority figure even when doing so violates their norms and generates intense conflict. The subject's task was to act as a "teacher" and shock the "student" subject (actually a confederate in an adjoining room) for errors, increasing the intensity of the shock with each error. Thirty voltage levels were clearly marked on the shocking apparatus and identified with verbal labels ranging from "Slight Shock" to "Danger," "Severe Shock" and finally "XXXX." If the teacher hesitated to deliver shock, he was

TABLE 17–1 Changes in Attitudes of Residents (Percent Net Gain) Living in Segregated or Integrated Units of Housing Projects

Initial attitude	INTEGRATED HOUSING PROJECTS		SEGREGATED HOUSING PROJECTS	
	Koaltown	Sacktown	Bakerville	Frankville
Highly unfavorable	71	78	26	19
Moderately unfavorable	46	61	18	2
Favorable	13	28	15	−18

Net gain in percent of favorable attitudes toward blacks expressed by the residents. The somewhat derogatory names given the integrated projects and the "All-American" names given the segregated projects appeared in the original research project; they were not chosen by the author of this book.

SOURCE: Deutsch, M. & Collins, E. *Interracial housing: A psychological evaluation of a social experiment.* Minneapolis: University of Minnesota Press, 1951.

urged by the experimenter to continue. As the shock level got higher and higher, the confederate made increasingly agonizing sounds until, at 180 volts, he cried that he couldn't stand the pain, and, at 300 volts, refused to answer. Forty psychiatrists had previously predicted that only 0.1 percent of the subjects would give the maximum shock. In the original study, 62 percent (26 of 40 subjects) actually did so. The earliest point at which teachers refused to continue was after delivering 300 volts (Figure 17-11). Control subjects permitted to select whatever shock levels they desired typically selected mild levels. Conformity to the experimenter's commands was not without conflict and discomfort for the subjects. As the shock got stronger, they showed increasing signs of tension and emotional strain. A mature and poised businessman within thirty minutes "was reduced to a twitching, stuttering wreck, who was rapidly approaching a point of nervous collapse . . . he pushed his fist into his forehead and muttered, 'Oh, God, let's stop it.'" However, he continued, and gave maximum shock. In a later study, 30 percent of the subjects went so far as to physically hold the hand of the victim on a shock plate to receive a shock marked "Danger," although proximity to the victim generally decreased the aggressive obedience.

What, if any, are the lingering effects on the subjects? The answer is not known. Some psychologists think that procedures which lead grown men to tears exceed tolerable bounds of professional ethics (e.g., Baumrind, 1964). Milgram's (1964) reply is that on a post-experimental questionnaire, only 1.3 percent of the subjects indicated that they were sorry to have participated, while 80 percent indicated that further similar experiments should be done. However, one cannot help wondering about the responsibilities of researchers and the implications of their behavior, even in an "artificial experiment," on the self-concepts of the subjects.

In any case, the willingness to inflict harm on others at the command of another person is demonstrated, and we know more about human behavior than we did before, although it is not very satisfying knowledge. As some recent investigators, who replicated the results, concluded, "One implication [of these results] is that our society tends to produce individuals who act contrary to their conscience when faced with even mildly compelling situations" (Larsen, Coleman, Forbes, & Johnson, 1972, p. 287).

FREEDOM AND SELF

So far we have seen that people comply with requests even at the perceived harm of another person, that being "forced" to have contact with targets of prejudice may diminish prejudice, and that playing the role of someone with a view different from one's own may change attitudes in the direction advocated by that other person. However, situational variables effect the likelihood that one will make the "internal adjustments" to maintain a consistency between behavior and attitudes. These involve concepts of one's view of himself and of one's perceived freedom for action.

FIGURE

17–11

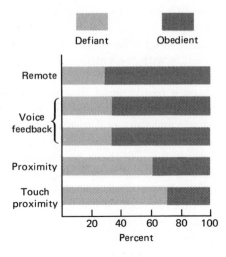

| Defiant | Obedient |

The effect of proximity on the percentage of subjects who were defiant at any point in the experiment, as a function of proximity to "victim."

DISTRIBUTION OF BREAKOFF POINT	
Verbal designation and voltage indication	*Number of subjects for whom this was maximum shock*
Slight shock	
15	0
30	
45	
60	
Moderate shock	
75	
90	
105	
120	0
Strong shock	
135	
150	
165	
180	
Very strong shock	
196	
210	
225	
240	
Intense shock	
255	
270	
285	
300	5
Extreme intensity shock	
315	4
330	2
345	1
360	1
Danger: severe shock	1
375	
390	
405	
420	
XXXX	
435	0
450	26

Response to Authority.

The number of people who refused to continue after each shock level.

SOURCES: Milgram, S. Behavioral study of obedience. *Journal of Abnormal and Social Psychology*, 1963, **67**, 371–378; Some conditions of obedience and disobedience to authority. *Human Relations*, 1965, **18**, 57–76.

Consistency

Consistency theory, particularly Festinger's cognitive dissonance theory (Chapter 12), has been a popular one for interpreting the attitudinal changes that often occur with an induced compliance to behave incongruently with one's attitudes (see Abelson et al., 1968). The inconsistency between "I think X" and "I behaved as if I think non-X" creates an unpleasant motivational state of dissonance which one attempts to reduce. However, the magnitude of the dissonance is markedly less if there is an adequate external justification for the inconsistent action. Pleasing a pleasant person rather than an unpleasant one, or eating a disliked food because it is nutritious are circumstances in which there is external justification for a behavior inconsistent with one's attitude. A large incentive, rather than a small one, also provides such a justification. Thus, the dissonance is greater if one commits himself to comply for a small incentive than for a large one. For example, saying that a dull task is interesting creates less dissonance and resulting attitude change if one is offered twenty dollars than if he is offered only one dollar for doing it (Festinger & Carlsmith, 1959). The incentive changes the situation and one's feelings about it. People apparently like to see themselves as behaving consistently with their attitudes, and, when necessary, will change attitudes to match their inconsistent behavior, for example, if there is little external justification for the attitude-discrepant behavior.

However, for consistency to be an issue, for dissonance to be aroused, the individual must feel that he has *personal responsibility* in the situation, by having free choice and knowledge of the likely outcomes (Cooper, 1971). In attitude change situations, the individual must feel that he has freely chosen to behave in a way inconsistent with his view of himself as a fairly decent human being who does not harm himself or others—the counterattitudinal behavior must threaten the individual's self-concept or produce objective negative consequences for the self or the audience (Aronson, 1968, 1969; Collins, 1968; Bramel, 1968). If one sees himself as having relatively little choice about what to do, then the behavior discrepant with his private attitude does not arouse much dissonance. When one tells a lie because the experimenter tells him that this is the rule of the game, the act is not as likely to threaten self-esteem as when he himself chooses to tell a lie. There is an external justification for the behavior in the social pressure of another person.

Perceived freedom about compliance with another's request affects the role of the incentive offered for the discrepant behavior. There is more dissonance and greater attitude change if one feels relatively free and is offered a low incentive, say fifty cents, than when offered a higher one, say $2.50, for compliance (Linder, Cooper, & Jones, 1967). With minimal perceived freedom to comply, attitude change is greater if one is offered a large rather than a small incentive. It is as if, with minimal involvement of self because of the pressure to comply, the importance of external reward, as a justification, is maximized. With greater self-involvement because of perceived freedom of choice, the inconsistency between attitude and behavior becomes important and a dissonance effect is created.

The crucial inconsistency necessary for attitude change because of dissonance appears to be between the cognitions, "I am a good human being," and "I have misled another." Choosing to mislead another person in a harmful way apparently is a violation of a strongly internalized norm, which creates a dissonance. A lie is "white" if it helps rather than hurts someone, and we are likely to be pleased with the success of our thoughtfulness, without necessarily coming to believe the lie. If the lie is likely to produce results we consider harmful, our own self-esteem is threatened. Similarly, making a speech counter to one's own attitude should not be particularly dissonance arousing if the audience is already committed to the position we publicly espouse but privately disfavor. If they are not already committed one way or the other, one's own behavior would be expected to have maximal effect on them. If they are committed to a position counter to the one we publicly favor (though in agreement with the privately held position) there should be less effect, but the effect that would occur would be detrimental. This reasoning was confirmed in a study in which subjects who were strongly opposed to the legalization of marijuana were offered fifty cents or five dollars for making a video recording in which they advocated a position favoring the legalization (Nel, Helmreich, & Aronson, 1969). Subjects who expected a neutral audience to see the tape and who were offered fifty cents changed their own position to a degree which was 73 percent of the possible change. This amount of change was greater than that of subjects with other combinations of incentive level and expectations regarding the audience (Figure 17–12). Consistent with the interpretation given, there was greater attitude change, presumably because of greater dissonance to be reduced, for those speaking to the neutral or committed con audience when offered only fifty cents rather than five dollars. The crucial variable then "seems to be in the consequences of the compliant behavior and the concomitant effect on the individual's self-concept" (Nel, Helmreich, & Aronson, 1969, p. 123).

When faced with requests to comply with the wishes of another, individuals probably differ in their tendency to feel coerced and in their willingness and ability to consider the implications of their behavior for others, as well as in their experiences of dissonance and level of self-esteem. It is somewhat paradoxical that when people feel "free" to choose an alternative, and when their choice is one which implies an inconsistency with a basic view of themselves as "good," their compliant behavior at the request of another has such a large impact on their privately held convictions.

The explanation of the paradox may be quite simple. It makes sense if we assume that people need and want to view themselves as having personal freedom (as de Charms does, Chapter 12) and as competent to use their freedom (as an Adlerian, such as White, would, Chapter 4). When one feels free and competent, he is vulnerable to perceived threats to his

FIGURE
17–12

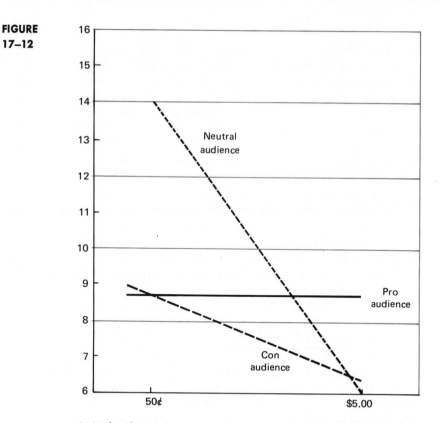

Attitude Change.
Higher scores represent agreement with the counterattitudinal position.

Source: Nel, E., Helmreich, R., & Aronson, E. Opinion change in the advocate as a function of the persuasibility of his audience: A clarification of the meaning of dissonance. *Journal of Personality and Social Psychology,* 1969, 12, 117–124.

freedom and competence. Changing one's views about what is a proper course of action or a correct view provides an internal justification for one's actions which enables the maintenance of a view that one has used his freedom competently as a well-intentioned human being. A person changes his attitude to allow a feeling of competence. People also change their views and behavior to allow a perception of themselves as free. This brings us to another attempt to understand the freedom that people like to think they have in the midst of the social pressures attendant upon interaction with others.

Psychological Reactance

People change their views and behavior when they think they are free. They like to feel that they have freedom to behave as they wish and that they themselves control their behavior. Thus, they also change their views and their behavior to allow a perception of themselves as free. The changes sometimes seem defensive and irrational. Jack Brehm (1966, 1968) has suggested that psychological reactance is a motive state that is aroused when an individual perceives that his freedom is restricted or threatened about an *important* matter on which he thinks himself *competent* to make a choice among *distinguishably different* alternatives. The reactance may be triggered by events which obviously curtail freedom of choice, and by any perceived social influence attempt which the individual feels is a force pushing him one way or the other. It motivates efforts to restore the lost freedom or prevent the loss of other freedoms. A well-meaning friend or adviser may suggest taking one psychology course rather than another, and this advice may be construed as social pressure. Choosing another alternative can reduce the reactance, even if the suggested course was the one initially preferred. One reasserts freedom, but the result is a pyrrhic victory. If one maintains his own position, he may reassert freedom by derogation of the adviser, thinking, "He doesn't really know anything" (Pallack & Heller, 1971). If one does not see himself as competent to make the choice, the advice may be welcomed (Wicklund & Brehm, 1968). If there seems to be no meaningful difference between the available courses, the advice is generally followed. Similarly, if having freedom of choice is not important, threats to freedom are ignored.

When it is important to be free, reactance can be intense enough to motivate a violation of the strongly held cultural norm of reciprocity (Chapter 16). For instance, a favor received places the recipient under the obligation to provide a right for the donor. The obligation restricts freedom. When it is important to be free of the obligation, the favor arouses a reactance which may be reduced by refusing to provide a right, refusing to return the favor (Brehm & Cole, 1966). Subjects who had been given a Coke by a confederate were likely to return the favor by helping him to stack some papers when it was not particularly important that they have the freedom to be objective in their ratings of him for experimental purposes. When the importance of objective ratings was emphasized, those whose freedom had been threatened by the favor were likely to reassert freedom by not helping their benefactor with a task the experimenter requested of him (Figure 17–13). Control subjects who had not been given a Coke were not under an obligation to the confederate and were not affected by the perceived task importance; the rate of helping was the same when the task was seen as important as when it was seen as unimportant.

Brehm's theory and supporting evidence begins to provide documentation of anecdotal evidence of the obstinacy and rebelliousness in children and in adults who do the opposite of what they are supposed or expected to do. A child who is himself tired of his bedwetting may persist because of, rather than in spite of, his parents' pleas and offered reward for conformity. Brehm's theory also serves as a warning about procedures for norm enforcement; social influence attempts may boomerang (Sen-

**FIGURE
17–13**

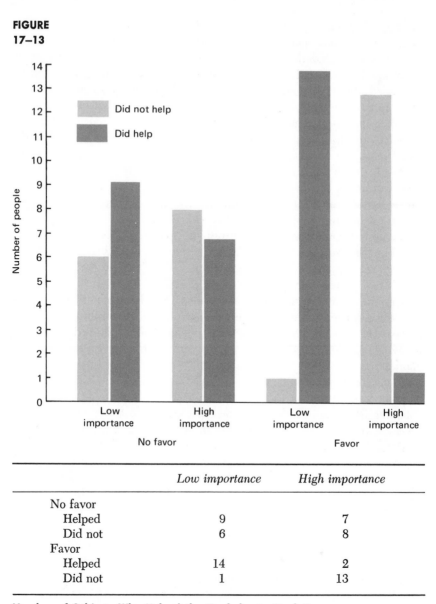

	Low importance	*High importance*
No favor		
Helped	9	7
Did not	6	8
Favor		
Helped	14	2
Did not	1	13

Number of Subjects Who Helped the Confederate Stack Papers.

Source: Brehm, J. W., & Cole, A. H. Effect of a favor which reduces freedom. *Journal of Personality and Social Psychology,* 1966, 3 (4), 420–426.

senig & Brehm, 1968). Stubbornness can reassert freedom, and it can be called "courage" in the face of adversity or unjustified conformity pressures. But it can also be defensive and motivate unwise behavior. The ability to recognize advice as advice rather than pressure, and to detect areas of personal incompetence in decision making, may make the difference between behavior choices that lead to positive versus negative results for the individual as well as for others.

Complete freedom is not possible when living with others; how we adjust to this fact and negotiate within the social matrix to maintain a desired sense of individuality makes the difference between happiness and malcontent.

The many personal and societal protests we all experience, alone or with the help of others, against large segments of society or against a particular person, demonstrate the crucial role that a perception of freedom plays as we strive for our sense of satisfaction with ourselves and the world in our everyday lives. They may stem not from a lack of freedom but from an attempt to reassert important freedoms in the face of perceived threats. Certainly, complex societies with elaborate norm and role systems exert control and limit freedom of action, and smaller groups, of two or more, do also. Oddly enough, the social system that restricts freedom, whether a matter of society as a whole or a particular interpersonal relation, can also provide the conditions in which people can develop reactance.

The restrictions on complete freedom imposed by norm prescriptions and interpersonal expectancies cannot lead to reactance if the individual is not aware that they are restrictions. The *awareness* is a sign that knowledgeability has replaced ignorance. Reactance also implies a feeling of competence to make decisions among meaningful alternatives. The price of being and feeling competent and having meaningful alternatives is concern about the protection of freedom. Unfortunately, the decision-making responsibility itself and the need to protect freedom engender anxiety which may be relieved by denying the possibility of freedom of choice and leaving the decision to someone else. Without freedom, one has neither vulnerability to threats to freedom nor the responsibility for competent use of it. People often seek to escape from freedom, as Fromm suggested (Chapter 4).

SUMMARY

Behavior control is essential for the maintenance of any social system. Groups exert pressures to enforce conformity to the norms which they evolve for their own protection and maintenance; they reward conformity with status. Individuals tend to comply. People become anxious at the perception that their own view is deviant from that of other people, perhaps because of an implicit fear of rejection by others, perhaps because the conflicting views induce uncertainty about what is "accurate" or "real." Their uncertainty may be reduced and their independent responses increased when they have been given support from authority or the group, and when they see themselves as competent for the task at hand. In interaction with important others, people develop attitudes, or ways of thinking, feeling, and acting, which serve the important functions of getting along with others, defending and expressing self, and imposing order on the world. They acquire attitudes to meet these functions by learning from others, responding to reference groups, and observing their own behavior.

However, people may change their attitudes when they are at deviance with those of important others, or when they are asked to behave incongruently with them. When a person is induced to play a role which is incongruent with his privately held attitudes, he often changes or modifies his attitudes to be consistent with his compliant behavior. Resistance to attitude change varies with external justification for inconsistent behavior and with the extent to which he feels his self-concept and personal freedom are threatened. The perception of deviance increases anxiety, but so does the feeling that one is not free to deviate if he wishes. Thus, the problem of how to maintain a sense of individuality in a social environment is the problem of both the individual and his society. Society must resolve how it is to maintain structure while encouraging diversity and freedom. The individual must resolve how he is to be free enough to be "I" rather than "We," yet "We" enough to be bound with others in harmony and freedom. This is partially a matter of identification, as we shall see in the following chapter.

18

imitation and identification

Two of the most important social-influence mechanisms by which personality development occurs are identification and imitation. They determine, to a great extent, the values and attitudes a child internalizes as he becomes socialized into adult life, and the behaviors he displays; they may well be basic mechanisms underlying the effectiveness of other social-influence procedures such as group pressures, role playing, persuasibility efforts, and social reinforcement.

Identification is an ongoing developmental process whereby an individual takes on the characteristics or behavior patterns of another person until he has actually incorporated aspects of that person into his own personality (Ferguson, 1970). *Imitation* is more specific; it refers to the reproduction of a particular response made by another person rather than to the general internalization of another's characteristics on a long-term basis. Thus, a child may be said to *identify* with his father when he takes on the attitudes, values, and responses of his father. The fact that this same child *imitates* the way his father walks and imitates his father's habit of slamming his fist on the table to emphasize a point may be indicative of an actual or growing identification, but as isolated instances these acts of copying do not constitute identification.

The identification and imitation habit patterns initiated in younger years tend to be maintained over the course of a lifetime, as are many responses and values acquired through them. Identification and imitation determine the extent and content of continuing responsiveness to other people, instrumental and emotional dependence upon them, and internalization of their evaluative frames of reference, attitudes, and other attributes. Therefore, we will be concerned in this chapter with identification as a social-influence process of continuing importance rather than as

449

a term describing only the socialization experiences of childhood. We will look first at characteristics of models likely to elicit identification, then at individual differences in identification patterns. Finally, we will relate identification to previously discussed social-influence concepts and elaborate on the notion that identification is an ongoing process which affects the personality development of the adult as well as the child. Because of the difficulty of elucidating the intricate relationship between the concepts of identification and imitation, more attention than usual will be given here to theoretical statements, in the hope of providing the perspective into which to place research on imitation and the other mechanisms of social influence.

Model Characteristics

Theories of identification have been focused on the issue of the characteristics of the model who is most likely to elicit identification. The most general and crucial characteristic of an effective model is that it be *salient*. The salience may be due to the fact that the model is perceived as *powerful* or as *similar* to the learner, although much greater theoretical attention has been given to the specific characteristics associated with power than to the determinants and effects of perceived similarity (Figure 18-1). *Power* is used here in a general sense, meaning that the model can somehow *control* the long-term fate of the learner or his attainment of immediate rewards and punishments. That is, the learner is *dependent* upon the model, either by choice or by necessity. The rewards and punishments controlled by the model may be intangible resources such as the approval or disapproval of a parent or employer, or tangible resources such as the bicycle at Christmas or the paycheck at the end of the week. Because power can be used to provide both positive or negative results for the recipient, some theoretical positions emphasize a positive-negative or rewarding-punitive distinction. However, people seldom act to produce only rewards or only punishments for another person. Rather, it is likely that identification always involves some *ambivalence*, implicitly if not explicitly, toward the model (Ferguson, 1970). A model perceived as similar to oneself can be neither wholly positive nor wholly negative unless one sees oneself as all good or all bad; such a view of self is unlikely in normal populations (Chapter 12).

Power

Many of the current theoretical and research orientations concerning identification are elaborations of and modifications on Freudian themes. Freud originated the term *identification* to refer to the process whereby a person molds his own ego upon that of another (Freud, 1948). This process, Freud suggested, is particularly important if a child is to acquire the appropriate sex role, self-control, morality, and attitudes generally considered necessary for a healthy adult life. Although we are concerned here with identification as a continuing developmental process, we should

FIGURE
18–1

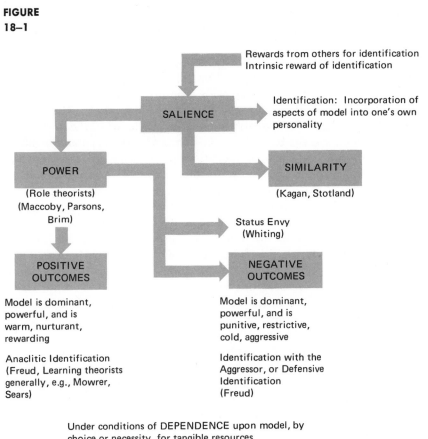

Schematic Outline of Variables Which Facilitate Identification and the Results or Indicants of Identification.

Aspects of identification:

1. Increased actual or perceived similarity to other.
   Imitation of behavior.
   Conformity in views.
   Assumption of similarity in attitudes, traits.
2. Responsiveness to the approval, disapproval of other.
3. Generally adopting the views of other, e.g., norms, values.
4. Resistance to separation from other.
5. Adopting evaluative frame of reference of other for oneself—evaluate self in terms of other.
6. Define self only through other.
7. Feel that one *is* the other.

Identification enables love and understanding of the other, communication, accurate interpersonal perception, attraction, learning from others. The danger is increasing dependence upon the other and exclusive definition of self in terms of others, i.e., lack of identity and individuality.

keep in mind that many theorists still consider the Oedipal situation the prototypical one for the occurrence of identification.

Positive outcomes. Freud's theory is essentially a power theory, emphasizing the actual or anticipated use of power for both positive and negative outcomes. Identification with a positive warm, nurturant figure is *anaclitic identification* (dependent upon, leaning upon). Whether girl or boy, the child's first identification is anaclitic with the mothering figure, because she has been the main source of sustenance and comfort, although there is some anaclitic identification with father also. Anaclitic identification depends upon desire for the mother's love and is motivated by fear of loss of it and the resulting frustration and deprivation. The child copes with experiences of loss of attention as he grows older by taking on aspects of mother's behavior, which indirectly serve to reinstate some of the gratification previously experienced with her. For the young girl, the intensity of identification with mother is increased because of the additional threat of loss of mother's love in response to the girl's rivalry for father's attention (Chapter 3).

Social-learning elaborations of anaclitic identification emphasize the dependence of the learner on the model, and the reinforcing effect of imitation when the care and attention of the mothering figure are withdrawn. Mowrer's (1950) formulation was originally developed to account for verbal behavior specifically but has been extended to cover all imitative acts and is a leading theory of identification. His original example was teaching birds to talk. One of the first prerequisites for teaching a bird to talk (there is no evidence of an innate mimicry drive) is that the bird must like the teacher, who must feed it, tend it, and caress it. These caretaking activities (ucs) result in a pleasant state of affairs (ucr) for the bird. All the stimuli associated with the trainer, his appearance and his noises (cs) occur along with the caretaking activities. As a result of the cs-ucs pairing, the sights and sounds of the trainer become capable of eliciting a "happy" response and become rewarding in themselves. The bird makes the sounds of the trainer because they have acquired a secondary reinforcing value. The bird rewards himself by making trainer-like sounds.

UCS   Caretaking activities, feeding, petting ⟶ R   Pleasant feelings
                                                                   HAPPY BIRD

     CS   Stimuli associated with the caretaker, appearance, gestures, vocalizations

     CS   Caretaker-like stimuli ⟶ R   HAPPY BIRD

     R   Imitation of caretaker: ⟶ S+   HAPPY BIRD *
          caretaker-like stimuli
          produced by the bird

* Theoretical diagram of Mowrer's explanation of identification, using the example of teaching birds to talk.

Similarly, with children, the affection and nurturance of the mother establishes a *dependency* on her (Sears, Maccoby, & Levin, 1957; Sears, Rau, & Alpert, 1965). After dependency is established, the child is frustrated when the mother is not there and tries to reproduce bits of the desired parent by imitation of parental behavior. The dependency is strengthened by periodic withdrawal of the affection and nurturance. If the mother is always present and nurturant, there is no need to copy her actions, and no chance for the child to practice the parental behavior and obtain self-reinforcement for imitation.

Naturalistic and experimental studies do support the contention that a warm, positive, emotionally tinged relationship is a factor of considerable importance in facilitating identification (see Bandura, 1969). Nurturance by a model, or a parent specifically, is positively related to the child's acquisition of parental characteristics. Boys of warm, affectionate fathers have a greater masculine identification than boys with relatively non-nurturant fathers. They play with a father doll rather than a mother doll, have more masculine vocational interests, show a greater similarity to the father on a personality inventory, assume the father role in play activities, and see themselves as thinking and acting like their fathers. Nursery-school children are also more likely to imitate the novel verbal and motor responses of a strange model who has been warm and nurturant with them than to imitate responses of one who has not. Imitation is increased when the nurturance is withdrawn.

Negative outcomes. The experiences of the young boy in the phallic stage exemplify the other major kind of identification Freud postulated, identification with the aggressor, sometimes called *defensive identification.* The father is seen as a rival who obstructs the expression of love for the mother, but one far too powerful to be openly attacked. The boy copes with the anxiety aroused by the threat of loss of his father's love and of punitive retaliation from the powerful authority by incorporating some of the authority's actions and attitudes. Identification with father allows the boy to reduce the fear of him and to enjoy vicariously the special, envied relationship father has with mother. It enables the boy to say, as it were, "If I am he, he cannot hurt me, and I may enjoy Mother." Identification thus functions as a defense mechanism to reduce anxiety and provide the immediate side benefit of vicarious satisfaction. Identification with the aggressor is possible, with children or adults, any time there is a powerful, aggressing other who threatens safety or a love object. Emotional distress disappears with identification. Physical features, values and criticisms, or a symbol of the strength of the aggressor may all be imitated. One of Anna Freud's (1936) examples is that of a little girl afraid to cross a dark hall for fear of meeting a ghost. She resolved the fear by making peculiar gestures as she ran across the hall. As she explained to her brother, there is no need to be afraid; "you just have to pretend that you're the ghost who might meet you." The fear was dissipated by imitation of the aggressor's imagined physical characteristics and gestures. To explain more parsimoniously: Imitation reduces anxiety by making the unfamiliar familiar, the novel less novel (Chapters 14, 22).

Much of the empirical evidence for aggressive identification is anecdotal and is often criticized as inadequate for demonstrating identification. Nonetheless, people do imitate others whose punitive features are more evident than any rewarding ones they may have. The most dramatic example was reported by Bruno Bettelheim (1943), a Jewish Viennese psychoanalyst who was imprisoned in 1938 in Nazi concentration camps. He noted that prisoners who had been there more than a year attempted to cope with the situation by incorporating some of the actions and attitudes of the powerful, threatening Gestapo in authority. The older prisoners used the Gestapo vocabulary, aped the behavior of the guards, cherished old pieces of Gestapo uniforms, and tried to change their own clothes to resemble Nazi dress. They treated other prisoners as did the Gestapo, and with slow and cruel torture killed prisoners they thought to be traitors. The identification was not complete, however, as the same old prisoners also sometimes acted with courage in defying the Gestapo. Similar, though less extreme, phenomena have been claimed for other groups who are subject to maltreatment and discrimination at the hands of a more powerful majority. Some blacks identify with the values and behavior of whites. They abandon black values and culture and may try to copy the appearance of whites, by hair straightening and skin bleaching (K. Clark, 1965; Friedman, 1966; Newfield, 1966). Identification with the aggressor may also be involved in the dynamics of anti-Semitic Jews (Sarnoff, 1951) and women who are prejudiced against other women (Goldberg, 1968).

Dependency is necessary for identification with the aggressor as well as for anaclitic identification. The victim must not only be dependent upon the aggressor in some way but must be unable to escape the perceived hostility of the aggressor. Because of the dependency, the aggressor is, and remains, a salient figure. A home in which the parents are in high conflict with each other and are both low in warmth is a case in which the child is dependent, and only punitive others (parents) are salient. Studies of nursery-school children revealed that both boys and girls from such homes imitated the dominant parent, regardless of the sex of that parent (Hetherington & Frankie, 1967). Because there was no warm parent to turn to for support, the child minimized his insecurity by identifying with the more powerful parent. If the nondominant parent was *warm*, or there was less conflict between the parents, the trend to imitate the aggressive dominant parent was reduced but not eliminated.

For the child, powerful parents are salient. For minority groups, majority groups are salient; for prisoners, guards are salient. Why some adults will focus attention on a majority group of which they are not a member, or on guards rather than fellow prisoners, while others direct attention to the presumably more benevolent similar others is not clear.

We shall later suggest roots in the earlier identification patterns acquired in childhood.

Role dominance and envy. Some modern elaborations of Freud by sociological and social-psychological role theorists focus explicitly on the power of the modeled figure rather than on the use of power in providing positive or negative outcomes (Maccoby, 1959; Parsons, 1955). Father's *power* as he plays the father's *role* and the child's *envy* of father's role status are seen as the crucial features of the prototypical oedipal situation. The learner practices the role of the enviable powerful model and adopts the role. Identification becomes a matter of role playing and role adoption. Again, dependency on the model is crucial in that the child is helpless before the power of the father to fend off any who attempt to usurp his position. The son identifies with the father because he is both a powerful punishing agent, an attribute which facilitates aggressive identification, and a powerful rewarding agent, an attribute which facilitates anaclitic identification. One identifies with powerful figures because it is important to predict their behavior (Brim, 1958). One has much to gain from their beneficence and much to lose from their antagonism. The behavior of the powerful other may be best predicted if one, in some sense, is that other person so that the behavior principles followed by the other are internalized and ever present. The child rehearses both the rewarding and the punitive characteristics of the model, since both are relevant to him in guiding his behavior. This idea is basically a derivative of Freud's contention that the superego was in part due to the ineffectiveness of the ego to predict when parents would reward and when they would punish.

A major variant of the power position emphasizes the function of power to allow enjoyment of desired resources. According to Whiting's (1959, 1960) *status-envy* theory, identification is the outcome of rivalrous inter-action between two people for limited resources. Status envy produces identification with the *recipient* (consumer) of resources. Freud's concern was with the mother's sexual and affectional attention as resources enjoyed by the father. In Whiting's theory, another person is envied when he is perceived as enjoying resources of any variety, including food, water, rest, information, freedom, love, praise. When a child envies the status of another who is controlling resources and depriving him of them, he covertly practices the role of the controlling other. He indulges in fantasy in which he sees himself as the envied person, controlling and consuming the valued resources of which he has been deprived. He will not envy the status of another person who shares the resources with him because then he himself is the consumer of the resources and occupies the envied status. Only when mother refuses to give him a cookie will the child envy the control of the cookie jar and fantasize himself controller of the cookie jar. If she gives him a cookie, he himself is the consumer; if she gives sister a cookie, the sister is envied and her role covertly practiced. Without deprivation, there is no envy of the status of the other, no role practice and role acquisition. Notice that the relationship with the model is ambivalent; the learner is dependent upon the model for desirable resources which he withholds from the learner.

Research comparisons. The power of a model in controlling and enjoying tangible and intangible resources and in providing positive or negative outcomes for the learner have all been suggested as model characteristics which facilitate identification. Which use of power is most important? What is most important in increasing model salience? Overall, the simple fact of having power or being dominant seems the critical feature. The use of power in being nurturant, generous, and warm with the learner is a close second, and often a concomitant of power which increases its effectiveness. Although highly masculine boys perceive their fathers as rewarding and nurturant, they also see them as stronger and more powerful than the less masculine boys see their fathers to be (Mussen & Distler, 1960). The sex typing of male college students tended to correspond to the sex of the dominant disciplinarian, mother or father, especially when that person was high in affection (Moulton, et al., 1966).

Experimental evidence also shows the efficacy of power in promoting imitation, and the greater susceptibility to the influence of a powerful model perceived as kind in contrast to one not seen as so benevolent (Bandura, Ross, & Ross, 1963a). Nursery-school children, about four and a half years old, were placed in a play situation with an adult male and an adult female, an approximation of a typical nuclear family. The adults alternated between playing roles of a *controller* of resources (attractive toys, cookies) and a rival of the child as *consumer* of the resources. In the adult consumer condition, the controlling adult gave the resources to the other adult but ignored the child. In the child consumer condition, the child received the resources and attention while the other adult was ignored. Each of the models exhibited distinctive motor and verbal behavior patterns during a later task, then left the room while the children were observed for imitation of the behaviors. The findings clearly support the power theory of identification, in that the model who had controlling power over the resources was most imitated, regardless of whether the resources were given to the other adult (the child's rival) or to the child himself while the other adult was ignored. Secondary-reinforcement theory comes out second best. Children who had been rewarded by being given the resources (child as consumer) showed significantly more imitation, of both adult models, than children who were ignored while an adult had the enviable status of being the consumer of the resources. Notice, however, that although children imitated the controlling model most, they also imitated the subordinate model. They were not junior-sized replicas of only one model.

Although there was a tendency for the rewarding model to be imitated, the children were also responsive to how the other adult was treated. Even at their relatively young age, the subjects seemed to have adopted the norm of sharing and objected to violation of this norm. They negatively evaluated the rewarding model who did not share the rewards with the other adult as well as with the child himself. Boys particularly were critical of the controlling female who did not share with the ignored male—for example, "She's a bit greedy." When the controlling female offered to share the toys with the neglected male as well as with the child, she was imitated about four times as much as when she ignored the other adult. It is not just the absolute magnitude of reward received from a model that is important, but the total image of the model behaving in a social context in a way that the child labels positively.

Similarity

Antecedents of identification. The other major variable which increases the salience of a model is the perception by the learner that the model is similar to him. Perceived similarity to a model is a likely manifestation of identification *and* a possible contributor to identification. The power of the model in attaining desired goal states may also be relevant. The child who sees adults, namely, parents, as having the power to attain desirable goals—such as a feeling of mastery and power over the environment, or love and affection—can enjoy the goal states by perceiving himself as similar to the parents. Any behavior that confirms or enhances the child's perceived similarity with the parental model becomes intrinsically rewarding (Kagan, 1958, 1967). Adopting the behavior of powerful models increases the perceived similarity with them and *motivates* the search for and adoption of other similarities. The perception that one is similar to the model in one respect strengthens the belief that one must also possess other similar characteristics, including covert ones, and allows one to vicariously share more of the positive experiences of the model.

Perceived similarity to another person may also increase the salience of the model without the help of the model's power to attain desirable ends. Quite simply, when a person conceives of himself as similar to another person in some way, he believes himself also similar in other ways (Stotland, 1969). If the relevant traits are not incongruous with one's self-concept, the perception of similarity leads to the perception or creation of additional similarities. There need be no particular relationship between the two traits, no obvious need for the observer to identify, and no emotional relationship with the model. It is likely that the perception of one dimension of similarity establishes the model as a *relevant* other for comparison and for approaching, and as one who very well may be like self in other ways (Chapters 10, 13). People similar in one respect are often similar in others; traits are correlated or assumed correlated. Given that similar people are attracted to each other, the perception of a similarity may function as a signal that one may find the other person rewarding and accepting, which in turn increases the importance of attending to the other person. The perception of similarity itself is also likely to be rewarding, because it is a cue that one is, after all, not so deviant oneself, there are others who share one's tastes and traits. A snowball effect is likely—the more similarity one perceives, the more important it is to perceive additional similarities to avoid a possible deviance and risk of rejection by the other who is important because of his similarity. The perception of similarity captures attention and motivates the search for additional similarity. And people are in fact more responsive to similar others than dissimilar others.

The influence of similar others. People perceived as similar to oneself are more effective as imitation models than are those perceived as dissimilar (Stotland, 1969). The influence is shown in preferences, attitudes, self-ratings, and overt imitative behavior. College women who thought that another subject had music preferences similar to their own later expressed a preference in nonsense syllables closer to that of the other subject than when the musical preferences were dissimilar. Preadolescent Boy Scouts imitated more behavior of a film-presented model playing a game when the model was presented as very similar to them than when he was not. The similar model was said to live in the same area, enjoy Scouting activities, and have the same specific interests and skills as the subjects. When introduced as very dissimilar to them, he was described as one who lived in another state and did not share any interests with the subjects. The effects of perceived similarity were much stronger than the effects of whether the model in the film received praise, criticism, or no response from the male experimenter in the film (Figure 18–2).

The tendency of adults to imitate similar others affects even the norm of being helpful to others. The altruism of New Yorkers was influenced by the feelings of another person only when he was perceived as an American (Hornstein, Fisch, & Holmes, 1968). A letter enclosed with wallets left in various areas of midtown Manhattan indicated that the wallet had been lost by a previous finder before he had returned it to the original owner. The letter was written either in good "American" English or in the broken English characteristic of a foreigner who had just arrived in this country. It expressed the previous finder's pleasure at being able to perform the favor of returning the wallet, or his annoyance at the owner's carelessness in causing him the inconvenience of having to return it. When the model, the previous finder of the wallet, was thought to be an American, more wallets were returned intact by subjects who found the positive letter with the wallet than by those who found the negative letter with it. When the model was dissimilar, a foreigner, his feelings as expressed in the letter made no difference in the number of intact returns of the wallet (Figure 18–3). Ingroup-outgroup, similar-dissimilar distinctions are relevant even when it comes to the supposedly strong cultural norm of being helpful. The unwitting subjects were not responsive to the feelings of another person who was unlike themselves.

FIGURE
18–2

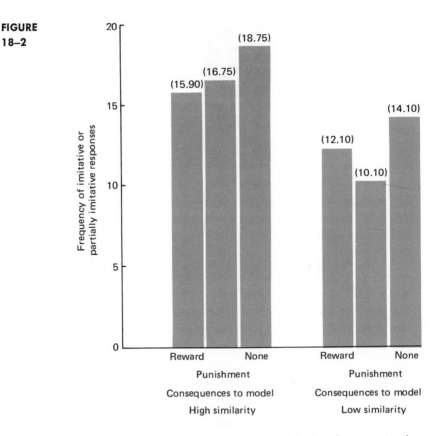

Frequency of Imitative Responses of Model of High or Low Similarity to Subjects, When the Model Received Reward, Punishment, or No Consequences for His Actions.

Source: Rosenkrans, M. A. Imitation in children as a function of perceived similarity to a social model and vicarious reinforcement. *Journal of Personality and Social Psychology*, 1967, 7 (3), 307–315.

Learning Processes in Identification

Learning interpretations of identification tend to equate identification with imitation and emphasize the necessity of positive outcomes for the learner, not necessarily from the model, if imitative responses are to be acquired and performed. The effective model is one whom the learner can imitate and therefore receive rewards. Although it may not be desirable to define identification only as imitation, these positions serve to suggest specific learning processes which contribute to the occurrence of imitative responses. The previously mentioned theories of secondary reinforcement (Mowrer) and dependency (Sears) are of course learning interpretations. As with the s-r and Skinnerian positions discussed here, they attempt to account for the self-reinforcing nature of imitation and the acquisition of a generalized habit of imitation as an identification

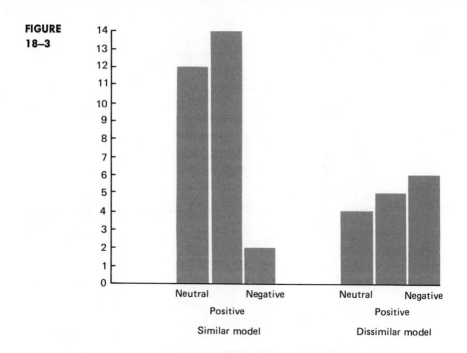

FIGURE 18-3

CONDITION	TOTAL RETURNS	NO. RETURNS		
		Total no. returns	*Returned but not intact*	*No return*
Similar model				
Neutral	12	8	1	7
Positive	14	6	2	4
Negative	2	18	6	12
Dissimilar model				
Neutral	4	11	5	6
Positive	5	10	5	5
Negative	6	9	5	4

Helpful Responses to Similar and Dissimilar Others.
Return rates for neutral, positive, and negative letter conditions for similar and dissimilar models.

Source: Hornstein, H. A., Fisch, E., & Holmes, M. Influence of a model's feeling about his behavior and his relevance as a comparison other on observers' helping behavior. *Journal of Personality and Social Psychology*, 1968, 10 (3), 222–226.

response. The observational-learning viewpoint stresses the specific conditions under which a learner acquires and performs a given specific imitative response. Actually, there is no good account of why imitation occurs at all. It first occurs toward the end of the first year of life and may be maintained because it elicits the attention of caretakers. However, it seems that as the child grows older, the tendency to imitate is certainly strengthened and directed toward specific kinds of people; the child is rewarded for imitation of them, and the perception of similarity with them becomes intrinsically reinforcing and self-maintaining.

The generalized response of imitation. Miller and Dollard (1941) conceptualize imitation as a special case of instrumental conditioning in which social cues serve as a discriminative stimulus and the learner's responses are rewarded if they match those made by the model. In their original example, a young boy learns to imitate his big brother and obtain the candy reward brought home by their father (Figure 18–4). The younger boy cannot read the clock to know for himself when his punctual father will arrive at the door with candy in his pocket for whoever greets him. He can, however, see his brother begin to run, and can learn that if he runs to the door when his big brother does, he as well as his brother may get some candy. More formally, the learner, or follower, observes a response of the leader which is followed by a reward desired by the learner. The response of the leader is a discriminative stimulus such that when the follower makes the same response, he is rewarded. The response of the imitator is *matched* with that of the leader and is *dependent* upon it. However, let us quickly note that the drive and the reward need not be the same for both leader and follower. The follower may not know the motivation of the leader (Figure 18–5). Nor is it necessary that the reward be one which reduces a biological drive. The only requirement is the follower's discovery, by one means or another,

FIGURE 18–4

	LEADER		FOLLOWER
Drive	Get candy		Get candy
Cue	Clock says 6:05, time of father's arrival home	*Dependency*	Brother runs to the door
Response	Run to door to greet father	*Matches*	Run to door to greet father
Reward	Candy		Candy

Miller and Dollard's Formulation of Matched-Dependency Imitation.
The leader can discriminate an environmental cue which the follower cannot. The follower is *dependent* upon the leader to provide a cue. Social cues serve as discriminative stimuli.
The follower's response is differentially rewarded or not according to whether it *matches* or fails to match that of the leader.
If matched-dependency imitation is regularly rewarded in a variety of situations, a generalized tendency for imitation may develop.

FIGURE
18–5

	LEADER		FOLLOWER
Drive	?		Social approval for being properly dressed
Cue	?	Dependency	He is putting on a tie
Response	Put on a tie	Match	Put on a tie
Reward	?		Social approval for being properly dressed

Drives and Rewards for Leaders and Followers.
It is not necessary that the drive and the reward be the same for leader and follower. The follower may not know the motivation of the leader, the cues to which he responds, nor the reward he receives. All that is necessary for matched-dependency imitation to be effective is that the follower discover that by matching his response with that of the model, he may receive a reward he desires.

that by matching his response with the model's, he may receive a reward he desires. If matching is regularly rewarded, a secondary tendency to match may be developed and imitation become a general drive. Thus, the response of imitation may become autonomous of extrinsic rewards and rewarding in and of itself. A young boy comes to imitate his big brother in a variety of situations, because doing what big brother does is itself rewarding. The matched-dependency model seems particularly applicable whenever people find themselves in situations where they are unfamiliar with the reinforcement contingencies or cannot "read" the cues of the environment to know what response will be rewarded. In such situations, they find a leader who seems an effective model to imitate. This behavior is likely when one moves into a new social class or an unfamiliar peer group. Matched dependency may substitute for an internalization of the norms of a subculture. Without knowing about the "rules" of the subculture for oneself, one may attain rewards by imitation. The imitation may also promote internalization of norms as one gradually learns what responses will be rewarded and acquires discriminatory capacity for oneself. Thus, imitation may lead to independence of a specific model.

A position very similar to Miller and Dollard's is derived within a Skinnerian operant analysis. Imitative responses develop through a learning history in which reinforcement has been contingent upon a response similar to one of a model; similarity of behavior becomes a reinforcer itself. An example from this tradition shows that a generalized imitation response may acquire secondary-reinforcement characteristics (Baer & Sherman, 1964). Similarity of responding between a puppet and the child became a reinforcing stimulus dimension. Nursery-school children imitated the head nodding, mouthing, and strange verbalizations of

Jimmy, a cowboy puppet, when those responses were followed by social approval from Jimmy. Jimmy also occasionally pressed a bar, and the children imitated this response also, although it was *never* reinforced specifically. When reinforcement for the other responses was withdrawn, imitative bar pressing decreased, and then increased again when reinforcement was reinstated (Figure 18–6). Imitation was controlled by reinforcement, and the specific response of bar pressing, not itself reinforced, was also imitated. In some real-life situations, a child must reproduce a response highly similar to that of a model if he is to attain a success (e.g., opening a latched door). However, given enough such situations, the stimulus of *perceived similarity* between the model's and one's own response can become a discriminative stimulus for reinforcement. Since a discriminative stimulus for reinforcement becomes a secondary reinforcer in its own right, responses which produce a similarity of behavior will be strengthened. Hence, the learner becomes an imitator, and the imitation can become apparently autonomous. One learns to imitate and to "reward oneself" because one's response matches that of someone else.

Learning by observation: imitation in action. The theoretical viewpoints previously discussed attempt to explain the acquisition of the general response of imitation, or identification generally. The observational-learning emphasis of Bandura and Walters (1963; Bandura, 1965, 1969) is concerned with aspects of a model and a situation which affect the acquisition and performance of specific imitative responses and similar responses after the child already knows how to imitate; that is, after the general response of imitation is already strongly in his response repertoire (Ferguson, 1970). Some of Bandura and Walters' work has already been

FIGURE
18–6

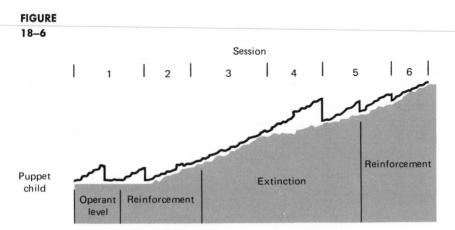

The Effects of Extinction of Previously Reinforced Imitation on Generalized Imitative Bar Pressing (Subject 1).

Source: Baer, D. M., & Sherman, J. A. Reinforcement control of generalized imitation in young children. *Journal of Experimental Child Psychology*, 1964, 1, 37–49.

cited. Here we will be concerned with the basic conditions under which imitative responses are performed. Observation alone is not necessarily an effective eliciting agent (e.g., White, 1972).

Observing the model punished for his responses decreases the probability of the learner's imitating those responses, and observing the model rewarded increases the probability of imitation. (However, it is probably the model's affective response, of pleasure or displeasure, to the reward that is critical [Lerner & Weiss, 1972].) The models may be actually present or presented on film. Models in films are capable of evoking a wide range of responses, from motor actions to verbalized preferences, from aggression to courage and self-sacrifice (see Bryan & Schwartz, 1971). In one of the early studies using aggressive filmed models, nursery-school children observed adult models playing with toys in a highly aggressive manner (Bandura, Ross, & Ross, 1963b). When Rocky, the aggressive model, was refused permission to play with Johnny's toys, he started throwing darts, kicking, making a general fuss, and emitting what were euphemistically called "distinctive verbalizations." In the punishment version of the film, Rocky fell and Johnny managed to get hold of him and spank him. In the reward version, Rocky was the victor, who hit Johnny and got the toys, Coke, and cookies; with a bag of toys in his hand, he triumphantly rode a rocking horse into the sunset singing, "Hi ho, hi ho, it's off to play I go." In a control condition, two male adults engaged in vigorous but nonaggressive play. Children who had seen the aggressive model rewarded displayed more imitative aggressive behaviors during a play period with the toys that had been in the film than children who had seen him punished for his aggression. They also showed more *non-imitative* aggression. The aggressive model's reward elicited or released aggressive responses which were presumably already in the response repertoire (Figure 18–7). Children who saw Rocky rewarded also selected him as the one of the two models they wanted to be like, even though they evaluated him negatively. They described him as "rough and bossy, mean, wicked, he whack people"; "Rocky is harsh, I be harsh like he was." The authors suggested that the film was analogous to many television programs in which the bad guy gains rewards by his aggressive behavior and is not punished until immediately before the last commercial. The delayed punishment may not be effective in counteracting the rewards the bad guy receives during the whole show.

The effect of punishment, however, is not to prevent response *acquisition* but to inhibit response *performance*. If the model is punished, the probability of the child's performing his responses is reduced, but he acquires them nevertheless. Children who observed a model punished showed fewer imitative responses than children who had seen him rewarded or receive no particular consequences. However, when a positive incentive, a treat, was offered for reproducing the model's behavior, the differences attributable to the model's outcome disappeared. All groups of children had learned the punished responses equally well. The consequences of the model's behavior apparently serve as cues to

FIGURE
18–7

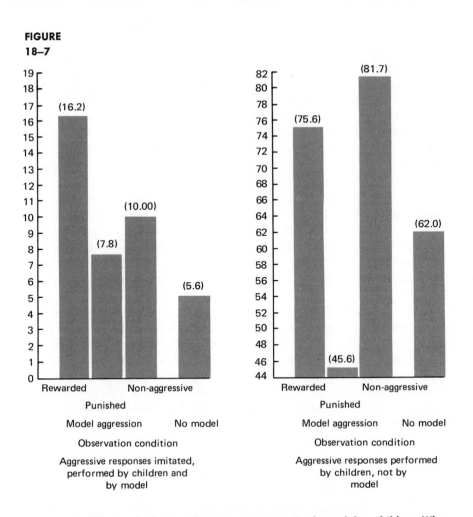

Imitative and Nonimitative Aggressive Responses Performed by Children Who Saw an Aggressive Model Rewarded or Punished, a Nonaggressive Model, or No Model.

Source: Bandura, A., Ross, D., & Ross, S. A. Vicarious reinforcement and imitative learning. Journal of Abnormal and Social Psychology, 1963, 67, 601–607.

indicate the permissibility or nonpermissibility of reproducing his behavior (e.g., Grusec, 1972; Flanders, 1968; Krebs, 1970). The effects of punishment in reducing the likelihood of performance of acquired responses can have useful results in real-life situations; after a child observes a model punished for disapproved behavior, there typically is a period of time during which he does not have a specially introduced incentive to perform such acts. During this time, other responses, frequently pro-social ones, can be practiced and strengthened. Punishment, to self or model, can be an effective training technique (Chapter 5). The responses nevertheless are acquired and are available for later use if the incentive occurs (Chapter 20).

The fact that observers are exposed to a model is no guarantee that they will be affected by his behavior. The model must be sufficiently salient for the observer to actively watch him. Symbolic or representational responses in the form of images and verbal associates of a model's behavior are crucial for observational learning, whether or not the responses observed are performed immediately, or ever (Bandura, Grusec, & Menlove, 1966). Any stimulus situation which produces the mediating responses is sufficient for observational learning to occur. Thus, verbal description of behavior is a representation of the behavior and can function as a "model" which the individual imitates as he carries out the verbally described behavior. For example, a verbal description of how to open a combination lock is not essentially different from a visual demonstration of opening the lock. What kind of model—live or symbolically presented—is attended to and imitated may reflect the kind of people (e.g., parents) with whom one has identified, in conjunction with one's own socialization history for the kind of responses performed by the model.

In sum, models effective in inducing imitation and identification are those who are salient because of their power, whether negatively or positively used, or because of their similarity to the learner. Power used to provide rewards for the observer seems more effective in eliciting imitation than power used punitively. The perception of similarity to a model becomes reinforcing in its own right. Once acquired, the imitative response occurs as one acquires responses by observation and learns what responses are likely to be permissible. The effectiveness of a model, however, varies with individual differences in the learner.

INDIVIDUAL DIFFERENCES IN IDENTIFICATION PATTERNS

There has been surprisingly little systematic attention given to the development and implications of individual differences in identification patterns, that is, what kind of person is likely to identify to what extent with what kind of model under what circumstance. This unfortunate neglect may be due partially to the obviously heavy weight exerted by situational variables in affecting adult responses to social-influence attempts (Chapter 17). Some work with children shows individual differences in the kind of person imitated and in the kind of responses imitated. There is also reason to suppose that differences in selection of targets for identification and in intensity of identification in adults is a result of early experiences with the parents.

Susceptibility to Identification

Relevant variables. If we assume that identification and imitation responses are learned, and contribute to further learning, we can expect that individual differences in learning abilities and patterns will be relevant. Intelligence is one correlate (Nash, 1970). Children in the educable range of mental retardation have greater appropriate sex-role preference than retardates in the lower trainable range, and the brighter children among normals are developmentally more advanced in sex-role identification than children of average intelligence. Given the relevance of perceived power, nurturance, punishment, and similarity as aspects of the interpersonal situation in which identification is instigated, a variety of variables other than intelligence are expected to be relevant. While such variables have not been well studied systematically under the rubric of identification, the chief among them is probably anxiety, particularly about dependency. The anxiety may occur in the context of interpersonal relationships in which one fears rejection, or it may be about one's perceived helplessness and powerlessness in moving effectively and happily through the world of people. Anxiety can increase the salience of a modeling figure from whom one hopes for acceptance but fears rejection, or from whom one hopes for help in increasing mastery and effectiveness to acquire desirable outcomes. As will be clarified later (Chapters 19, 20), dependency and anxiety about acceptance are increased by punishment or by withdrawal of nurturance from an otherwise attentive and rewarding important other.

Dependency. Dependency appears to be an essential condition for identification, or at least a pervasive feature for children. Children are typically dependent upon their parents, presumably the first identification figures, but children as well as adults differ in their dependency needs, which affect responsiveness to nonparental as well as parental figures. Dependent people, children and adults, are more responsive than less dependent subjects to social reinforcers for instrumental behavior and to social-influence pressures in conformity and persuasibility settings (Chapter 17); they also show greater imitation than less dependent subjects. However, there is a momentary paradox in that much of the learning that enables *independence* is observational learning which contributes to and results from identification. The resolution appears to be that high-dependent children seem to attempt to pay attention to everything a model is doing, while low-dependent children are more selective in what they pay attention to and are likely to concentrate on the specific task at hand. Because they are trying to learn less than the high-dependent children, they learn a focal task of immediate importance better. Because they are not particularly attending to behavior irrelevant to the task, they learn less of the task-irrelevant behaviors than do the high-dependent children. That is, high- and low-dependent children differ in how much of the situation they are trying to take in and therefore in what they learn. Dorothea Ross (1966) tested this reasoning by running a play post office as the focal learning task, specifically dealing with money, letter regulations, and telephoning. While demonstrating the task-relevant responses, the female model also gave incidental cues irrelevant to the main task, tapping a balloon while talking, doodling on a scratch pad, throwing paper wads, and so on. The subjects observed her, then served as a postman to teach another child the postman's role. As predicted, low-dependent children, classified on the basis of observer ratings, had higher focal but lower incidental imitation scores than the high-dependent children (Table 18–1). The learning pattern may reflect a greater anxiety of the high-dependent children in the specific interpersonal learning situation, or a more pervasive concern with social stimuli generally. The behavior of the children and parental reports indicated that the high-dependent children were socially oriented with little concern for achievement, preferred the passive role of being customer to the active one of being postman, and were rewarded at home for social-interaction skills more than for achievement behaviors. The general picture is consistent with that of the subjects high on field dependence (Chapter 11) having a diffuse deployment of attention and concern with social stimuli of the field rather than focusing on those aspects of the field immediately relevant for the task at hand. As is true of sensitizers, the dependent children "look around more," to be alert to the possibilities in the environment (Chapter 15). The results suggest that high-dependent people will be more likely to notice and imitate a wide range of behavior of a model, and their awareness and imitation are more likely to be attributed to identification because the behavioral similarity is more pervasive than is true of the low-dependent. Many of the important behaviors acquired by imitation, particularly the little touches of masculinity or femininity, are not central to an ongoing activity, fixing the car or baking a cake, but are incidental expressions performed during the focal task. Children and adults differ in their attentiveness to social stimuli, and also in what kind of people they are most responsive to as models.

TABLE 18–1 Learning Scores for High- and Low-Dependent Children

	INTENTIONAL LEARNING				INCIDENTAL LEARNING		
	N	M	SD	p.	M	SD	p.
Boys							
Low-dependent	10	37.6	9.04	$< .05$	12.7	6.12	$< .005$
High	10	31.0	6.26		29.5	12.92	
Girls							
Low	10	41.8	6.76	$< .025$	12.1	5.95	$< .025$
High	10	34.4	6.68		23.5	14.61	
All low-dependent	20	39.7	8.39	$< .01$	12.4	6.06	$< .0005$
All high-dependent	20	32.7	6.80		26.5	14.11	

SOURCE: Adapted from Ross, D. Relationship between dependency, intentional learning, and incidental learning in preschool children. *Journal of Personality and Social Psychology,* 1966, 4, 374–381.

Model Preferences

Social reinforcement history. One tends to identify with the kind of models one is used to, when the model is behaving as expected. The kind of target with whom one is familiar may be either nonrewarding—increasing or sustaining anxiety which motivates imitation—or rewarding —one with which identification is intrinsically reinforcing. The model's use of power to provide positive or punitive outcomes can contribute to the perception of similarity with previously relevant models. An experiment with children which cleverly combined naturalistic and experimental techniques illustrates the effect of the learner's social-reinforcement history on differential imitation of rewarding or nonrewarding peer models (Hartup & Coates, 1967). Observers watched preschool children in natural interaction and classified them as high or low in the total number of reinforcements (attention, approval, affection, acceptance, submission, or tangible objects) they received from their peers. For each child, either a rewarding peer, who had given the subject the most social reinforcements, or a nonrewarding one, who had never given the subject reinforcement, served as a "model" in the experimental session. The model worked on puzzles and "gave away" the trinket prizes awarded for solving the puzzles. The subject then played the games by himself; the number of trinkets the subject put in the "others" bowl rather than in his own was the dependent measure of imitative altruism. Subjects who had received frequent reinforcement from peers imitated a rewarding peer more frequently than they imitated a nonrewarding one (Figure 18–8). In contrast, subjects who had a nonrewarding model imitated him more if they had had infrequent social reinforcement than if they had had frequent reinforcement.

Matching the behavior of a rewarding model has greater incentive value than matching a nonrewarding model when the subject is accustomed to frequent reinforcement from peers. However, when one is not used to reinforcement from the model and others similar to him (peers), the nonrewarding model may increase or sustain anxiety, which motivates imitation; a rewarding model reduces the anxiety and motivation for imitation. The dual theory advanced by the authors is a parallel to psychoanalytic theories in that nurturant models are said to be emulated when the previous interpersonal relations are characterized by reward (anaclitic identification), whereas anxiety-eliciting figures are defensively emulated (defensive identification). The theory suggests that one originally learns to identify with whoever was present and salient enough to be identified with. The predisposition to identify with that kind of person persists. (Because giving and receiving reinforcements in peer groups is high, the results are also consistent with similarity theory.)

Socialization severity. Parents, as well as peers, differ in the amount of rewards and punishments they provide, with effects which persist and

FIGURE
18–8

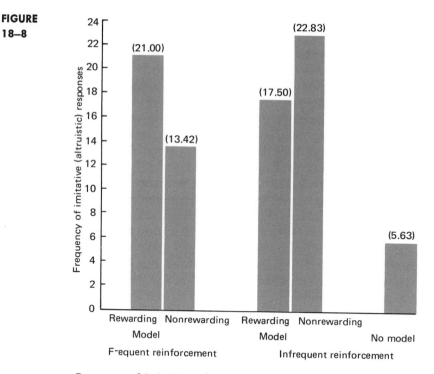

Frequency of imitative (altruistic) responses

24
22 (21.00)
20
18 (17.50)
16
14 (13.42)
12
10
8
6 (5.63)
4
2
0

(22.83)

Rewarding Nonrewarding   Rewarding Nonrewarding
Model   Model   No model

Frequent reinforcement   Infrequent reinforcement

Frequency of Imitative (Altruistic) Responses by Children Who Had Received Frequent or Infrequent Reinforcement from Peers, When Peer Model Was Rewarding or Nonrewarding in the Modeling Situation (First Five Trials).

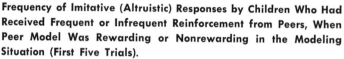

Source: Hartup, W. W., & Coates, B. Imitation of a peer as a function of reinforcement from the peer group and rewardingness of the model. *Child Development,* 1967, 38 (4), 1003–1016.

may in fact influence whether the child will receive reinforcements from his peers. Children from homes in which parents are punitive and restrictive are expected to identify especially with models who are threatening (Balint, 1945). Jewish college students who were anti-Semitic, presumably indicating identification with the "aggressor," reported seeing their parents as more rejecting, hostile, and frustrating than those who were not anti-Semitic (Sarnoff, 1951). Those not antagonistic to Jews reported love-oriented and accepting parents. Subject reports of severity of childhood socialization are also related to patterns of identification with peers (Baxter, Lerner, & Miller, 1965). The ruse of a learning experiment was used to place the subject in a dependent relationship with his "teacher" for the study. The teacher, supposedly in an adjoining room, was to be a punitive one who would give shock for errors, a rewarding one who would give quarters for correct answers, or an informative one, who would simply announce right or wrong. After hearing a four-minute tape of conversation of the alleged teacher, the subject rated the teacher, himself, and the average male at the university. Subjects whose responses to a questionnaire about their parents indicated that they had had a highly restrictive socialization background had an unusually high degree of identification (perceived similarity) with a punitive teacher, and very little with a rewarding or informative one. (Similarity to the average university male was statistically parceled out.) In contrast, those with a less severe background tended to identify more with the rewarding and informative figure than with the punitive one (Figure 18–9). Assuming that the subjects had identified with their parents, the evidence is consistent with the view of maintaining into adulthood the kind of identification patterns experienced in childhood.

Implications. The effects of earlier childhood experiences with parents persist and predispose selective identification in adults. The overall picture, then, is that negative experiences with parents or peers seem to encourage identification with punitive figures, while positive experiences seem to facilitate identification with rewarding figures. This picture may reflect the fact that the person originally had little choice, as a de-

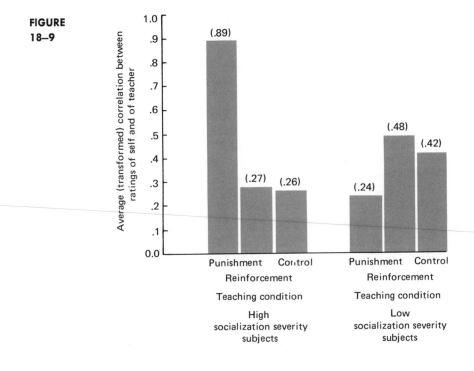

FIGURE 18–9

Average (Transformed) Correlation between Ratings of Self and of Teacher for Subjects of High and Low Socialization Severity, under Conditions of Expecting Punishment (Shock), Reinforcement (Money), or Verbal Statements about Correctness from Teacher.

Source: Baxter, J. C., Lerner, M. J., & Miller, J. S. Identification as a function of the reinforcing quality of the model and the socialization background of the subject. *Journal of Personality and Social Psychology,* 1965, 2 (5), 692–697.

pendent child largely confined to home, about whether he was to identify with a positive or a negative figure. The parent is a salient figure for whom an identification response is developed. The established pattern tends to be maintained; one continues to identify as one did in early years. Why an adult continues to identify with punitive figures is puzzling. The reason probably involves a low self-esteem and perhaps a diffuse, indefinite sense of self. The severity and inconsistency of socialization with parents which increases identification with the aggressor or with negative, punitive people generally is likely to be a background which also inhibits the development of a sense of self as an acceptable and competent person on his own, who can act effectively from an internal locus of control and evaluation (Chapter 12). It has been suggested that identification is "a desperate attempt to deal with a crisis involving the self" (Sanford, 1955, p. 111). Thus, one is more *dependent* on other people for self-evaluation and definition. With diffuse sense of self, the approval and acceptance of other people, both positive and punitive, is excessively important. Identification with punitive people is more likely than with positive ones for several reasons. Punitive people are more likely to be salient than rewarding ones because of similarity to parents. With negative view of self, it is more reasonable to assume that others also labeled negatively are like self. With perceived incompetence, it is important to carefully observe others who have sufficient power to be punitive. However, when a person of low self-esteem is convinced that someone else does accept him, attachment to that person is likely to be intense, and the consequences of possible rejection more acute and damaging to one's whole view of the world and self. One is dependent and anxious in social situations, ever scanning the environment for social cues in hopes of finding acceptance and in fear of finding rejection; focusing intently upon the negative and clinging to the positive when one thinks one has found it.

In relative contrast, sometimes sharp, the positive experience with parents, which favors continuing identification with positive figures such as the rewarding teacher or the rewarding peer, also favors the development of a firm sense of self and a reasonably high self-esteem. The person develops into a competent individual who thinks well of himself and can act effectively and independently. With a positive view of self, it is reasonable to assume similarity with others also labeled positively. With positive view of self and a feeling of competence, there is no reason to expose oneself or be susceptible to the pressures or presence of a punitive other. The approval of others is not a desperate need; in the face of rejection, one recuperates and surges forward. There is less need to identify with others in any pervasive way, nor to be overly responsive to their presence and pressures. Social responsiveness is directed toward positive others and kept within bounds. (Notice the lower assumed similarity for subjects with low socialization severity, whatever the target.)

However, the mature adult will certainly not be without imitation of others or identification with them. He will continually be responsive to other people, other people will be important to him, and their wishes taken into account in his own behavior. But his identification with any one person functions as a beneficial social-influence mechanism rather than as a desperate defensive need for self-definition and protection.

SOCIAL INFLUENCE AS IDENTIFICATION

At the outset of this chapter—a chapter usually expected in a section on child psychology rather than social-influence mechanisms—imitation and identification were said to be the most important social-influence mechanisms in child and adult, and were named as processes underlying the effectiveness of other mechanisms. Basically, the reasons involve three kinds of issues. First, identification and imitation are obviously important mechanisms in the acquisition of norms, including but not limited to the all-important ones governing aggressive, sex-typed, and moral behavior, which will be discussed in their own right in a later chapter (Chapter 20). Study of imitation may elucidate the circumstances of norm acquisition and of performance in accordance with the norms, and may illustrate the problems of norm conflict. Second, the conditions in which models are successful in eliciting the identification response or specific imitation responses have much in common with the successful operation of other social-influence mechanisms, which, in fact, may be seen in terms of identification. Third, when considering identification and imitation, as with other social-influence mechanisms, one must deal with the relationships between overt behavior and internal cognitive principles, and the related issue of how people come to differ, are allowed to differ, when social and intrapersonal pressures to conformity are so pervasive and so effective in changing a person's attitudes and behavior. The point of ultimate importance behind all is that all mechanisms of social influence, if they are to be successful, require not certain model characteristics so much as certain *learner* characteristics—particularly the characteristics of being socially responsive, of having learned to care what other people do, think, feel; of finding their approval reinforcing and their disapproval punitive. Learning occurs in the learner, not in the teacher. Much of the value of social influence in adults as well as in children requires that the individual learner be able to adopt some features of others for his own use and enjoyment, that is, that he have the ability to identify.

Imitation and Norms

The necessity and efficiency of observation. Observational learning is an effective vehicle for the transmission of normative behavior of all sorts—sex-role behavior, moral standards and values, aggression inhibition, and routine skills—as implicit in examples previously given. Some socially desirable behaviors contributing to child or adult socialization are learned mainly by observation or by direct training made more efficient because of previous observational learning (Bandura, 1969b). Observational learning is a more *efficient* way of acquiring behavior patterns than is possible on the basis of conditioning and reinforcement of trial-and-error responses. It eliminates much of the need for direct training of each individual for each kind of response. Part of the efficiency is attributable to the fact that the model need not be one with whom the learner has direct face-to-face contact; the model may be symbolically presented. In some cases, observational learning is *necessary* for the immediate security of society. Models serve to accelerate the learning process and become essential means of behavioral transmission where errors are dangerous or costly. Firearms are not trusted to an armed-services recruit without a demonstration of how they should be handled. Nor does one permit a teenager to learn to drive a car by means of trial-and-error learning in which one hopes that he may fairly quickly emit a response likely to be followed by the positive reinforcement of a sigh of relief at a safe return. If learning were dependent only upon trial and error, most people would not survive their own socialization process.

Observational learning also extends the range of parental effectiveness and helps to overcome the consequences of the parents' deficiencies as models themselves. Parents cannot be expected to be the primary sources of many of the skills appropriate at different stages of social development. They are no longer children who are well acquainted with the acceptable behavior in their children's peer groups, and they do not themselves behave appropriately for younger age brackets. Although parents are continually important agents in the socialization process, with increasing social complexity and mobility, they can no longer be adequate models themselves for all areas of importance to the socialization of their children. Parents frequently use exemplary models, ranging from national heroes to members of the family or even the neighbors' children. Exemplary models are chosen to reflect social norms and provide a means of describing in varying degrees of detail the approved conduct for given situations more efficiently and more thoroughly than parents themselves often can. The value of nonparental models is particularly clear in families of low educational and financial attainment. The parents themselves do not have the habits, skills, and attitudes required for successful upward mobility. They may encourage their children to have high aspirations, but other socialization agents must be the models for the complex behaviors necessary for attaining the desired status and class-associated habits of speech and customs. The attitudes and values of models the children sometimes select may be discrepant from the norms they have been taught at home, and even parents may behave differently and hold different expectations for the child. As the individual develops, the important responses for him to have and the important people who have those responses vary. Identification is a continuous process involving multiple modeling, with targets changing as the individual's needs change; his needs change with age and with shifts in his social world and therefore with shifts in the people important to him.

Conflict in observational learning. As is true with other forms of social influence, there are often conflicting pressures on the person observing others. People do not behave consistently with each other or with cultural norms, and these inconsistencies are observed. One kind of incongruity is the norms-model discrepancy reflected in the parental maxim, more often acted upon than verbalized, "Do as I say, not as I do." In such cases, direct training demands one kind of behavior, but the trainer himself behaves (models) otherwise. Another kind of incongruity occurs when two models display different behaviors in the same situation, either simultaneously or successively (model-model discrepancy). Parents often behave differently from each other, or behave like each other but differently from other adults and peers whom the child also observes. The latter is a case of conflict between the family and the peer-reference group, such as in the case of the Bennington students (Chapter 17).

Norms are preached but not always practiced by the preachers. Consequently, children not only learn norms, they learn by observation to either deviate or conform to them. If rules are made to be broken, children learn by observation when to break them. A discrepancy between the model's behavior and a stated norm decreases the likelihood that the observer will abide by the norm, and the resulting behavior is a compromise adjustment (Mischel & Liebert, 1966). Fourth-grade boys and girls played what was supposedly a game of skill in a miniature bowling alley, with instructions to reward themselves with a poker chip, to be exchanged for a prize, only for the highest possible score, twenty points. They played the game first with an adult model, who consistently imposed the twenty-point rule for both himself and the subject, or who imposed it only on the subject but rewarded himself for lesser scores. When the subjects then bowled by themselves and rewarded themselves, there were significantly fewer incidences of self-lenient behavior when the training agent had himself followed the stringent rule he imposed on the subject (average about one deviation from the norm per twenty trials) than when he was lenient with himself (more than four deviations). Subjects who then played with a second model whose behavior was discrepant from the norm were the most self-lenient in rewarding themselves on the second test; 90 percent violated the standard at least once. Subjects who observed the two models *both* behaving consistently with the rules were most in conformity to it. Those who observed one model conform to the norm and one deviate were intermediate in self-leniency. The behavior of the most recently observed model was the most important (Table 18–2, Figure 18–10). Social injunctions not followed by models may have little efficacy unless maintained by direct

TABLE 18–2 Mean Self-Leniency Scores for All Subjects during Test 1

CRITERION IMPOSED BY 1ST AGENT	CRITERION MODELED BY 1ST AGENT	MEAN SELF-LENIENCY SCORE
Stringent (20 only)	Stringent (20 only)	1.83 (Boys) .25 (Girls) 1.04 (Total)
Stringent (20 only)	Lenient (20 and 15)	4.91 (Boys) 4.04 (Girls) 4.33 (Total)

constraints. A social norm loses much effectiveness if children observe others who are not consistent in their observances of it.

As a child grows older, peers do become salient figures and increasingly powerful as a social-influence group. Learning from peers is as necessary for successful development as learning from parents. However, the parent-peer conflict is popularly overdramatized. The selection of peer models is greatly influenced by values and attitudes learned in the home, so that children tend to choose as friends those who share values and therefore are more likely to *complement* parental influence pressures than to detract from them (Bandura, 1969b). Furthermore, when there is conflict for the child between parents and peers, the parents are likely to have the longer-lasting influence in many matters. For example, children (aged four to six) who had observed any model, peer or adult, behaving aggressively were more aggressive in their own play immediately after the observation than were children who had not seen a model, and a peer male model was more effective than other models in releasing aggression (Hicks, 1965). However, after six months, only the prior exposure to the adult-male model was relevant to the child's incidence of aggression (Table 18–2; Figure 18–11). The greater effectiveness of male models, both peer and adult, probably is due to the fact that aggressive behavior is stereotypically a masculine rather than a feminine behavior. The greater long-term effect of the adult probably reflects the greater salience of adults than of peers in the life of a young child. Peers are more salient for adolescents than they are for young children, and conflicts between peers and adults more frequent and poignant. However, again, the conflicts are often overdramatized in lay views and are not resolved so simply as by a complete identification with parents *or* with peers (Chapter 21). While high-school adolescents desire to avoid being different from or separated from peers, they are aware of the ways in which they differ from peers and are similar to their parents (Brittain, 1963, 1967). The more important and difficult a choice is perceived to be, the more likely high-school students are to resolve the parent-peer conflict by complying with parental preference rather than peer preference.

Identification in the Social Context

Imitation is itself an important method for acquiring social norms. In addition, other social-influence processes are in many ways sophisticated forms of imitation and identification, and are probably called by other names simply because they are studied in adult rather than in child populations. More generally and more importantly for continuing socialization, the acquisition and operation of imitative and identificatory mechanisms are necessary for the other social-influence processes to be effective. If one is to interact effectively with others, one must have learned to attend to other people as salient parts of the environment and to internalize some of their views of the world. This essential learning apparently passes through a critical phase during the Oedipal years, as Freud suggested. The relevance of the learning at that stage continues, not only in the form of the specific prosocial responses acquired then, but in the form of the process itself—learning to respond *to* other people and learning to learn *from* them and to incorporate some features of them as one's own. This process requires the previous development of attachment

FIGURE 18–10

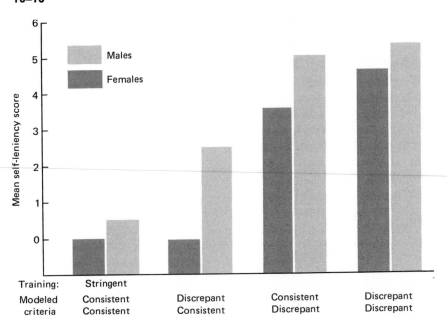

Mean Self-Reward Leniency Scores during Test 2 as a Function of the Consistency or Discrepancy of the Self-Reward Criteria Modeled by Two Successively Presented Social Agents.

Source (for both table and figure): McMains, M. J., and Liebert, R. M. Influence of discrepancies between successively modeled self-reward criteria on the adoption of a self-imposed standard. *Journal of Personality and Social Psychology*, 1968, 8 (2), 166–171.

and social responsiveness, discussed in the following chapter. It is continually operative in social-influence mechanisms discussed in previous chapters.

Norms and conformity. To internalize a norm is to see from the perspective of a group of people, be it society at large, the hometown folks, or the smaller but salient work and friendship groups (Chapter 16). The views of others become one's own. Reference groups are those which are salient and important. A change of reference groups is a shift in who and what are salient. It is possible progressively to identify with one after another of specific people within a group, until by generalization the identification extends to all group members (Nash, 1970). One may also abstract for himself, or have presented to him in exemplary form, a "typical person" of the group, or the generalized other. Although that person is hypothetical in terms of objective reality, an individual may nevertheless have a very real sense of such a person as a model and a goal for himself—the ideal business executive, the typical fraternity man, the average American, the blue-collar solid citizen, the good student. He strives to attain maximum similarity with him, to "incorporate" him, to be him, just as the child tries to walk in his father's shoes. And each evaluates himself in terms of approaching that goal. Similarity is reinforcing.

To conform is to agree with the group, an adult version of the child imitating the behavior of a model, and increasing his similarity to it. One states an opinion that one would not otherwise state because it is consistent with the perceived group majority (Chapter 17). For the group to have maximal effectiveness in inducing conformity, it must be of psycho-

TABLE 18–3   Mean Imitative Aggression Scores for Experimental and Control Groups

	EXPERIMENTAL CONDITIONS				
Response category	*Adult male*	*Adult female*	*Peer male*	*Peer female*	*Control*
Initial imitative aggression	9.58	16.33	22.75	13.42	.00
Boys	14.00	27.50	29.83	20.33	.00
Girls	5.17	5.17	15.67	6.50	.00
Subsequent imitative aggression	8.92	3.92	6.42	4.33	.33
Boys	7.33	7.17	5.17	6.50	.67
Girls	10.50	.67	7.67	2.17	.00

SOURCE: Hicks, D. J. Imitation and retention of film-mediated aggressive peer and adult models. *Journal of Personality and Social Psychology*, 1965, **2** (1), 97–100.

FIGURE
18–11

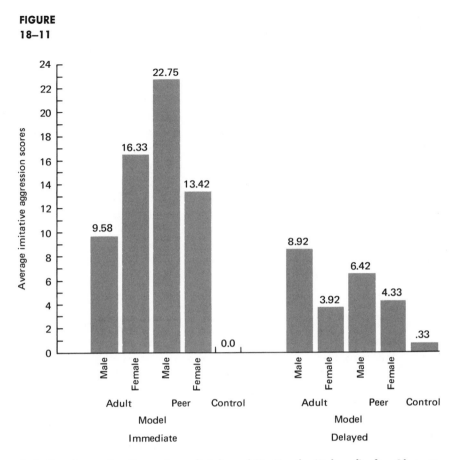

Imitative Aggression Scores Immediately and Six Months (Delayed) after Observation of Adult or Peer Male or Female Models.

Source: Hicks, D. J. Imitation and retention of film-mediated aggressive peer and adult models. Journal of Personality and Social Psychology, 1965, 2 (1), 97–100.

logical importance (a reference group), and its demands must be relevant to its perceived function for the individual (legitimate expectations). That is, it must be salient in the matter at hand. The salience is most clearly seen as due to the power of the group to reward the individual with the benefits of continued membership and acceptance and to its power in reducing uncertainty. The attractiveness of acceptance is often enhanced because the members are seen as similar to self. Similarity is increased because of the group's successful conformity pressures. One is dependent upon the group because of the external and internal rewards that membership in it brings. However, if one must stay in an initially unattractive group, it elicits conformity and becomes increasingly attractive. This is not very different from the situation in which, when one is forced to be exposed to a punitive other, he imitates to defend. In both cases, one learns to live with the situation by increasing similarity. Conformity in groups is rewarded by acceptance and status, just as the child's conformity to parental expectations brings rewards. The individual acquires idiosyncracy credits which decrease his dependence on group approval for continued acceptance and give him power over the group to deviate from its expectancies. He is himself the envied powerful other, the idealized group member, or, in other terms, he is rewarded by others for his successful imitation of the "ideal member." It is somewhat noteworthy also that conformity to a group is likely when one feels uncertain about reality; specifically, one feels incompetent in the face of a difficult task and is instrumentally dependent upon others. The same conditions likely to elicit conformity in the adult are those pervasively characteristic of the child, who can easily observe the greater competence of adults to master the world and move freely in it, and is dependent upon them for social acceptance and knowledge about the world and what is correct. Conformity and the perception of similarity with the relevant others reduces anxiety about uncertainty in what to do or think, deviance of self and others, and the threat of possible rejection and social failure (Chapters 13, 15, 17).

Behavior and labels: role acquisition. To induce in an adult behavior which is discrepant from his attitude is one of the most effective ways of changing his attitude (Chapter 17). To manipulate the behavior of the child is similarly effective. However, the child, in relatively frequent contrast with the adult, may not be behaving in contradiction to his internalized principles or self-view, so much as he is trying to find, develop, and clarify the principles and self-view. One can observe one's own behavior and make conclusions from it (Chapters 12, 17). The conclusions influence later behavior. Behavior is an important antecedent as well as a consequence of internalized principles about what is culturally approved behavior, about individualized norms—which is what attitudes are—and of the self-located view of self. This principle is seen particularly clearly through the concept of role playing.

The child who may not yet have a coherent comprehensive view of masculinity or femininity, of right or wrong, of approved or unapproved behavior works toward such views, and toward the important view of who he is and how he thinks, by first behaving in a way that others expect and command. The child complies; he "plays the role" of boy or girl, or of one who knows right from wrong. The appropriate role behavior often is observed *in* others. The little boy observes and imitates his father's swaggering walk, the college freshman observes and imitates the behavior of seniors. Each by imitation is enacting a role he may not yet understand. Each is making unfamiliar behavior familiar by imitation. Imitation is one vehicle by which appropriate behavior "gets going" and allows the learner to "try on" the responses and become familiar and comfortable with them. The behavior is observed *by* others. If the imitated responses are considered appropriate for the individual, they are encouraged and rewarded by the benefits that occur when one is behaving acceptably.

Reinforcement for imitation increases recall of the model's behavior and thus extends the power of observational learning (Grusec & Brinker, 1972). Social-influence mechanisms seldom work in isolation from each other, except perhaps in the experimental room. Imitation is an effective means for the initiation of role playing, for learning and becoming comfortable with the behavior appropriate for the many roles one plays and is throughout life. Associated with behavior changes are likely to be cognitive labels of one's behavior as appropriate and desirable. One comes to think of oneself as a person who "should" or wants to act as he is acting. Such a person attempts to behave more like he thinks he should and is attentive to others who can be helpful in the pursuit. In short, the result of a behavior change induced by role playing or other social-influence mechanisms is often a consistency between the behavior and an internalized statement of what is appropriate for oneself, about who one is. The result is a feeling that the role behavior is behavior freely chosen and comfortable. One has internalized the views of others via behavior. He has imitated and identified. At least part of one's individuality is other people.

Imitation, Identification, and Individuality

Relative distinctions. Despite the intricate relationship between the concepts of identification and imitation, it is important to articulate a meaningful difference between them, particularly for adults, for whom the distinctions are more crucial. One may think, first, of identification in terms of degree of imitation, or more broadly, degree of perceived or actual similarity with a model; and, second, in terms of what is accomplished by the imitation. There is little need for the term *identification* as long as the imitation is not pervasive. Identification becomes a more relevant concept when a perceived or actual similarity with the model becomes important in and of itself and is an internal reinforcer. One approves of oneself for being similar to the model; the model's behavior and attitudes "feel right." In the extreme case of obvious pathology, one thinks one *is* the other person. In less extreme, but also maladjusted, individuals, the identification may be shown in intense concern for the other person, or groups of persons, and evaluation of self is from the perspective of the other. The other's frame of reference is used as one's own base for evaluating himself. The self is invested in the other. One *is* only as the other is; separation from the other is separation from self. This often occurs when married couples become so identified with each other that neither can stand alone. Less obviously dramatic, perhaps because they are numerous, are people who are largely externally defined in terms of their relationships with others. They strongly identify with the profession, the social group, the family, or the home town. They are nothing but a psychologist, a student or fraternity man, or member of the Jet Set, a wife or father or son. The perception or accusation of deviation from the ideal of these groups or threat of rejection is traumatizing, a threat to the existence of self. The more pervasive the imitation and conformity to one person or one set of perspectives, the greater the identification and the less the individuality. In normal adult form, identification is selective and various, occurring against a background of a firm sense of self and individuality. One has partial identification with various groups of people, idealized normative principles and stereotypes, and selected other people. The normal person has identifications, but he is not defined exclusively in terms of any one of them. He is internally rather than externally defined and need not conform or identify to have an identity.

The benefit and the problem. Conformity to societal regulations is necessary. Role behavior is necessary for social interaction. Similarity with others is necessary for communication, accuracy of interpersonal perception, attraction, and living meaningfully and comfortably with other people. "The common basis of loving and of understanding is identification, and without it both would be impossible" (Balint, 1945, p. 321). There is no necessary reason that identificatory mechanisms or conformity need destroy individuality or produce a mass of identical citizens. Children learn from observation of adults. But they are not junior-sized replicas of one model. They are exposed to many models and may imitate some features of all. Their overall behavior pattern is a relatively novel combination of selected responses of the models to whom they are exposed. Children within the same family may be quite different because they have imitated different elements of their parents' response repertoires. Within the same society, people adopt and conform to different norms and reference groups. Children seem to spontaneously generate cognitive principles from the collection of specific rules and responses they observe in themselves and others, a relatively natural event in the course of cognitive development (Chapter 20). The potential for novelty of behavior or individuality is minimized when one is dependent upon only a small range of salient others. This may occur because of unusual circumstances; for example, if the parent does not let the child out, psychologically or physically, or, more generally, when the environmental pressures are so intense that one must conform to stay alive, again, psychologically or physically. The adult most likely to succumb to pressures is likely to be one of low perceived competence and self-esteem, who feels he can succeed at achieving his personal goals only by imitating, conforming, and pleasing another. He is dependent upon others for himself. Such a situation need not occur. That it does or does not reflects the relative adequacy or inadequacy of other people as socialization agents, as powerful controllers who do or do not use their power for the mutual benefit of themselves and the other people over whom they have control. The initial agents in the process of identification are the parents, and the central point of the following chapter is that the development of attachment and social responsiveness with them is a crucial ingredient of the "normal" socialization we often take for granted.

Whether the targets of immediate concern are parental or nonparental figures, one cannot escape the fact that one is simultaneously a result of other people and a recipient of their views of himself and the world; that one is as he is because of others, and at the same time acts upon others and has the potential for freedom and individuality within the social system of which he is a part.

SUMMARY

Identification and imitation are social-influence mechanisms which enable a person to internalize values and attitudes normative in his culture. Although *identification* is a term most often associated with childhood socialization experiences, the identification habit patterns formed in younger years tend to be maintained over the course of a lifetime.

One identifies with those who are salient in one's perceptual field. The salience may be due to the perception of a model as either similar or powerful to the learner, although power seems to be the most critical feature in facilitating identification with model characteristics. The kind of socialization history one experiences in childhood determines, to a great extent, whether one will tend to identify with models who use power positively and nurturantly or with models who use power aversively. Thus, although nurturance certainly increases the effectiveness of power, the simple fact of having power or being dominant is a more crucial determinant of identification than whether the power is used positively or negatively.

Identification and imitation permit the acquisition of norms and specific responses which can be used in instrumentation of one's values and pursuit of goals. One can achieve his own individuality when he is exposed to a broad array of others and can choose identification objects for his own benefit. Identification allows the similarity which makes possible accurate interpersonal perception and communication (Chapters 13, 16). It permits learning from others for one's own benefit. It facilitates the effective development of self and the acquisition of competence in expression and additional development of self. Responding *because* of others is a fact of life. Responding *to* others and enjoying the benefits of association with them can also be a fact of life. This requires the self that develops in the biological organism which interacts with others, a self aware of its separateness and of its belongingness.

DEVELOPMENT
OF PERSONALITY

PART VI

19
early parental influences

Is a human being born with a personality? If not, at what point does personality begin? The problem with answering such questions is that personality is not something which *is* or *is not*. Personality is process, a developmental phenomenon. We are likely to use the term "personality" when we observe responsiveness and individual differences in responses, which reflect the ongoing developmental processes within the organism.

Although we may not be eager to say that the newborn infant has a personality, infants certainly do differ from each other, in obvious ways such as the type and intensity of responsiveness and in activity levels, and probably in many more subtle ways we do not yet know much about. Anyone who has observed a nursery full of newborns can attest to the fact that babies do not come into the world as behavioral blank slates. They are not empty containers into which the environment pours a content, a "personality." Anyone who has listened to the comments of parents and friends watching at the nursery window will be even more aware that these babies will turn out differently from one another. The social worlds into which they are born and in which they will grow vary, as do the infants themselves.

Certainly the personality of the mature adult seems quite different from that of the infant. However, the personality of the adult is a development from the initial base which nature has provided within the infant himself, a development occurring in an environment. Behavioral patterns observable at birth and the predispositions toward behavior will be differently encouraged, modified, and changed by the family into which the child is born, the parental attitudes and behavior, interactions with other people, and ongoing maturation processes.

Socialization, maturation, and personality development

are continual. The growing child has important socialization tasks to master, with the help of parents, peers, and other adults: He acquires ways of handling aggression and dependency. He develops standards of behavior and the sex identity considered necessary in our society (Chapter 20). He confronts the upheaval of adolescence and enters the world of adulthood only to find that he has new positions in the social system to fill, continuing needs to meet, new behaviors to acquire—all sources of new satisfactions and new conflicts (Chapter 21). In the course of development from infancy to old age, of interacting with the world, the individual may evolve an open, creative posture toward the world, or a closed, fearful, unproductive one (Chapter 22).

Personality is shaped by early experiences, and by later ones, too. Personality is dynamic as well as consistent. Development is continual rather than achieved.

The burden of reacting to the newborn's behavioral patterns and of directing the initial steps in the socialization process lies with the parents, and it is with these important people that we shall begin our examination of the development of personality.

FAMILY INTERACTIONS

It is in the home that the child has very crucial early experiences which influence the course of the development of traits and abilities. In the home he develops as a biological and social organism, and the adequacy of his development depends upon whether the parents give him the "raw materials" necessary for each.

Some broad outlines of a child's path of development are sketched before the child is himself aware of them. There is a shape and a content to the world that is to be his, before his birth and even before his conception.

Before Infancy

Before conception. Often, because of the impending birth of a child, people speed up marriage plans or make them where none had existed before. The child influences his parents long before he enters the world, and in a way they may or may not appreciate! Even when marriage is planned, it is often motivated by the desire to have a child, and the child may have the extra task of proving to be a good reason for marriage.

In any case, parents are likely to have preconceptions about what they expect of a child. In a study of about two hundred college students, in which all but two expected to have children after marriage, Rabin (1965) found that some students valued the potential child as an end in himself, while others wanted a child as a means to their own ends. College women saw having children as being natural, the fulfillment of a basic need or their role and purpose in life. Both men and women saw the motives of men to be ones of proving their masculinity, wanting their names carried on, showing others that they were capable of reproducing.

Children may be rejected if they do not serve the functions the parents intended. This was dramatically illustrated in a study of sixty-four *planned* but rejected children who were referred to the Institute of Juvenile Research in Chicago (Sloman, 1948). Children were most often rejected because they were not the desired sex or because they did not save the marriage. The mothers tended to be compulsive and perfectionistic; they had planned their child's arrival just as they planned everything else, and had rejected the child when he did not fit the preconceived picture. The mothers had rigid moral attitudes and strict religious training which prevented them from adapting to any negative behaviors the children developed.

Case studies of unsuccessful adoptions also revealed that the children were expected to be instrumental in achieving other goals (Ross & Anderson, 1965). One mother wanted a child to help her avoid situations she feared; another, when she became bored with antiques as a hobby, intended for the child to become a new hobby to keep her from becoming an alcoholic; another wanted to adopt a child because she thought a natural pregnancy might follow adoption. Whatever the reasons, expectations are held for the child before he arrives, and he is evaluated according to how well he meets these expectations.

Pregnancy and birth. The mother's psychological and physiological condition during pregnancy and birth may have immediate and long-term effects on the child. Inadequate diet during pregnancy is associated with complications during birth, with the health of the baby after birth, and with some forms of mental retardation in the child.

Although there are complications in only about 10 percent of the births in the United States, the actual number of babies affected is not small. Some birth defects and accidents are fatal; nonfatal damage during birth may result in mental retardation, epilepsy, cerebral palsy, and even hyperactivity and reading problems (Knobloch & Pasamanick, 1958, 1960). Irritability, lower pain thresholds, visual deficit, insufficient muscle tension, and defects in general maturation are greater in children who experience problems at birth than in those with unremarkable deliveries (Graham, Matarazzo, & Caldwell, 1956). Premature babies are more likely than full-term ones to be retarded in physical and cognitive development, a condition that might continue until about five or six years of age.

The mother's and the fetus's nervous systems are *not* directly connected, but the mother's emotional experiences, as well as her physical condition, can nevertheless influence the fetus via chemicals released into her bloodstream. Fetal body movements increase several hundred percent while mothers are in emotional stress.

Infants whose mothers had experienced the prolonged, severe stress of wartime conditions during pregnancy were hyperactive, irritable, squirmy, cried and emptied their bowels frequently, spit up much of their feedings, and were generally a nuisance. "He is to all intents and purposes a neurotic infant when he is born—the result of an unsatisfactory fetal environment" (Sontag, 1944, p. 4). Less severe emotionality in the mother also has its effect. Mothers of colicky babies were more tense and anxious during pregnancy and had more doubts about their ability to care for the child than did mothers of noncolicky babies. Women who had abnormal or complicated deliveries were more anxious (on the Taylor MAS) during pregnancy than those with normal deliveries (Davids, deVault, & Talmadge, 1961). (The anxiety scale was given on the first visit to the doctor, so that it seems unlikely that the anxiety was triggered by cues from the obstetrician that he expected complications.)

Even for a physically healthy mother, pregnancy is a developmental crisis which makes demands for adjustment requiring emotional maturity. There are also demands on the future father and on the marriage relationship. Marital conflict is a major concomitant of rejecting attitudes toward pregnancy. Although both the conflict and rejection probably reflect a basic problem in the mother's emotional maturity, the conflict can intensify the rejection, with possible effects on the fetal environment and the birth process itself.

The changing family environment. The mother, of course, is not the only significant other in the early life of the child. The child typically enters a group, a social environment called the family. Like other social environments, the family is continuously shifting and sifting, changing or becoming less changeable. Because of this constant change, no two children born of the same biological parents and reared in the same household will experience the same environment. Parents' attitudes, emotional development, and financial security, as well as the children's birth order, affect the family experiences of each child.

Children are born at different times in their family's development as a social structure, and to parents who have reached different stages of their personal development. The attitudes and behaviors of each parent and their relationship with each other also vary as the parents grow. A firstborn child experiences parental attitudes, family size, and often family status different from those experienced by his siblings who are born later (Warren, 1966). Even identical twins may be reacted to differently by their parents (see Chapter 14).

The financial security of the family and the desirability and comfort of living arrangements also vary from year to year, often with important consequences for the child. A large proportion of schizophrenic subjects in one study were born at financially unusual or desperate times, and at times of conflict between the parents (Lu, 1962). Although the implications for being born at unfortunate times are not so extreme for all children, this fact does underscore the principle that the initial condition of the family social system can prompt interpersonal expectations and behaviors which, in combination with other developmental factors, can have tremendous impact on the personality of the child.

The Infant as Participant

Adults approach parenthood with preconceived expectations and attitudes which affect the social world into which the child is born, as well as influencing their behavior toward the child. However, the newborn infant, and later the growing child, is himself an active participant in this social world (Bell, 1968; Rheingold, 1969). Congenital differences in temperament and behavioral patterns between infants influence parental reactions. It is easier to care for and interact with a child who is generally positive in mood, adaptable, moderately active, highly rhythmic (and therefore predictable) than it is to care for a child who is arrhythmic and unpredictable, persistent, nonadaptable, and generally negative in mood (Thomas et al., 1963)—all characteristics of infant reactivity identifiable as early as three months of age and consistent for at least the first two years of life. Of course, exactly how the baby is reacted to depends on the parents, their own personalities and expectations, and the life style they have established or expect. While an active, restless baby is likely to get into more mischief and meet with more discipline than the placid baby, the active, noisy one might fit better into an emotionally unrestrained family than the quieter one. Indeed, in the home in which emotions are labile and easily expressed, the quiet baby may arouse concern or disappointment.

Through his actions and reactions—his perceptual activity and his responsiveness—the infant makes an impact on his world and the people in it. He has some awarenesses of his world and talents for acting and communicating in it and is sometimes in control of his parents rather than only being controlled by them.

Infant perceptual activity. Neither the newborn nor the world he experiences is an amorphous blob. The newborn has far greater sensory discrimination capacity and response capability than most of us imagine (see Hartup & Yonas, 1971; Kessen, 1963). Because of his sensory competence, the infant can attend to the world and respond to events in it. While apparently lying helpless, he can actively watch and listen and achieve active sensory interaction with people and events. He makes clearly different responses to variations in light, odors, noise, and other stimulus changes. He is capable of accurate visual tracking and approach. For instance, when an adult moves a finger around a baby's head, the baby turns his head to reduce the distance between his mouth and the finger; that is, he "picks up" an approaching stimulus and attempts to "approach" it.

True, such sensory and response skills are hardly impressive by adult standards. However, they illustrate the precision with which newborns can interact with the environment and the extent to which they can be active participants in the world, receiving at least some of its "messages," and reacting to definable, observable events.

The infant is more responsive to social than to nonsocial stimuli

(Fantz, 1958) and also very early comes to discriminate between his mother and strangers. When the mother and strangers are present and talking, he can make the discrimination as early as six weeks of age, and by four months he can respond differentially to a television display of mother's face and strangers' faces (Fitzgerald, 1968).

Discriminative selectivity between mother's voice and strangers' voices, as well as a preference for the mother's voice compared to music, has also been shown. The early appearing discriminative and response capacities, particularly the early discrimination of mother's appearance and voice, obviously has adaptive significance. Much of the infant's behavior is shaped by conditioning, and mother's attention, even simply her presence, may be a reinforcing stimulus and an eliciting stimulus. Without awareness of her, the infant could not respond to her attempts to act toward him and respond to his actions. Another element in the facilitation of mother-child interaction is the fact that the newborn has reasonable visual acuity at distances of up to 19 centimeters—a typical distance between mother's breast and her face (Haynes, 1962).

Infant responsiveness. The child is a stimulus which from earliest days controls parental behavior. The cry of the young is, in all species, an aversive stimulus whose termination is reinforcing. Infant and parental behavior are both "outcomes" of the behavior of each of them in interpersonal *interaction* with each other. This is well illustrated in a careful study of infant activity levels.

While some infants sleep quietly, others restlessly thrash around, and still others lie awake peacefully. Moss (1967) observed thirty firstborn children in their homes at three weeks and at three months of age. The variations in infant behavior and in maternal behavior were striking. For example, infant sleep time ranged from 25 percent to 75 percent of the eight-hour observation periods. The amount of time the mother spent holding the infant varied from 38 to 218 minutes. The simple fact of number of waking hours may have important implications for the infant's amount of experience and contact with the environment. The more waking hours, the greater the experience and contact with mother. Greater learning opportunities facilitate the development of the infant's perceptual discriminations and the quality of his cognitive organization. Some effects of contact with mother, however, depend upon the *kind* of contact and her expectations; these in turn vary with the sex of the child.

Differential treatment of male and female children begins in early infancy and reflects parental expectations and infants' behavior patterns (Fitzgerald, 1973). Moss (1967) found that boy babies generally are awake more, cry more, and have more vigorous activity levels than girl babies. They initially receive more maternal contact, stimulation, and arousal, and the maternal responses are likely to be ones stressing musculature. In relative contrast, the mothers' responses to girls are more likely to be ones of imitation of the infants' vocalizations, a possible precursor of the greater verbal ability of girls relative to boys. However, boy babies are less easily calmed than girl babies. Males seem more subject to inconsolable states, indicating that they have less well organized physiological reactions and are more vulnerable to adverse conditions than are females.

The female's more efficient functioning contributes to a more favorable response to maternal intervention; that is, the mother is more successful in her attempts to calm the female baby (Moss, 1967). The girl babies who cried more got more attention and handling than the girl babies who did not cry so much. Mothers attending to crying girl babies were positively reinforced for their attention to the child by the success of terminating the aversive stimulus of crying.

In contrast, by the time they were three months old, the more irritable boys were handled *less* than the less irritable. Moss hypothesized that the mothers were negatively reinforced for their responses to the boys' cries—the crying and the irritability of the boys continued in spite of maternal attention. A mother's growing lack of responsiveness to the boy's irritability may reflect not only *his* inconsolability but also *her* expectation that boys will be more aggressive and less responsive to socialization pressures. Thus, the mother who is unable to soothe her upset male infant may eventually come to classify his intractable irritability as an expression of expected "maleness" and let him be. These early interpersonal events may have important implications for children's responsiveness to later socialization attempts and for resulting social behavior patterns.

Data on older children do indicate that girls learn social responses earlier and more easily than do boys (Becker, 1964). Notice that for both boys and girls, the final behavior pattern of mother and of infant is attributable to the interaction of mother and infant, and to the combined effects of the infant's congenital differences and his experience in the environment because of them. Mother responds to child, child responds to mother, mother responds to the child's responses, etc. The child's initial responses are mainly of biological origin; later responses are a product of these biological predispositions and his mother's responses to them.

Parental Attitudes and Behavior

Because of their practical importance in our culture and their importance in the Freudian theory which initially inspired much developmental research, techniques of feeding and toilet training have been thoroughly investigated. In both of these areas, as in others, the success of the socialization attempt is a *joint* outcome of the behavior of parents and child.

The major importance of feeding and toilet-training situations to the child's personality development appears to be that they are settings for interaction between parent and child within which the personality of parents is demonstrated and their attitudes toward the child expressed and communicated to him. Parental attitudes and personality are more important determinants of the effects of the techniques than are the techniques per se.

The most important parental characteristic for successful socialization appears to be a willingness and ability to recognize and adapt to the child's reaction patterns. Not all children respond in the same way to a given environmental event or parental action. A procedure effective for training one child may be ineffective, perhaps damaging, for another. The parents' adaptability or lack of it will likely have consequences far beyond the child's eating and eliminating habits.

Feeding. Freud assumed that during the first year of life, an innate oral drive to gain pleasure through sucking is the dominant one; excessive gratification or frustration of oral impulses will lead to oral fixation and result in oral character traits throughout life. The evidence does favor the view that sucking is an innate response, possibly strengthened by the reward of hunger reduction. However, effects of experiences during the oral stage have not been shown to be as dramatic and far-reaching as Freud claimed (Zigler & Child, 1969; Caldwell, 1964).

There is no evidence of consistent stable relationships between early oral training and later behavior. The attitudes of parents and their effectiveness in detecting and responding to the child's needs are cited as the most crucial variables operative in feeding practices, particularly as they are or are not effective in making contact with the child and responding to his needs. For example, it is not the breast or the bottle that consistently influences later adjustment. Any apparent effects of breast or bottle feeding are likely to be due to the mother's personality, which will influence many of her interactions with the child, beyond those attendant upon feeding.

In one study, bottle-feeding mothers were found to be more anxious and modest about sexuality, more dependent, more rejecting of the child, more dissatisfied with their own sex role, and generally less mature than breast feeders (Sears, Maccoby, & Levin, 1957)—a collection of maternal characteristics whose effects are not likely to be limited to the use of bottle rather than breast! Although the breast-feeding mothers in this study proved to be mature, loving, and well adjusted, there is no reason to believe that *all* mothers with these qualities will elect, or be able to provide, breast feeding; nor is there reason to assume that *all* breast-feeding mothers have these qualities. A warm, accepting mother may accompany bottle feeding with closeness and vocal interchange, just as a cold, hostile mother may offer no soothing touch or word with the breast.

In addition to providing opportunity for closeness, the feeding situation is one in which the mother may demonstrate that she is or is not accepting the child as he is. Whatever the feeding technique, the scheduling procedures reflect the degree of her sensitivity to the child's needs in contrast to her own need for rigidity or for arbitrarily scheduled feedings. "In general, one could say that those mothers who could see things from the baby's point of view tended to adopt infant-care practices which led to harmonious interaction not only in feeding but generally" (Ainsworth & Bell, 1967, p. 21). And those babies whose behavior elicited consistently gratifying or interesting feedback from mother tended to cry less and to gain more frustration tolerance and more regular and predictable rhythms than babies whose behavior made little difference in determining what happened to them. The feeding situation apparently is a highly sensitive reflection of the mother's predispositions in ways to interact with the child as another person. The same is true of elimination training.

Toilet training. A heavy cultural emphasis on cleanliness often leads to intense parental concern about toilet training the child. The emphasis, of course, stems from the ways in which the parents themselves were socialized (Chapter 16). To master this major socialization task, the child must learn to delay the gratification of tension release to conform to the rules practiced by parents. This requires enough physical maturation to control the relevant muscles and enough cognitive maturation to understand the rules and the relationship between the sensations of his body and parental behaviors.

Parents' overeagerness to put a stop to the child's messiness may prevent them from understanding the intensity of the demands they place on the child. Generally, the earlier toilet training is started, the longer it takes to complete; the more severe the training, the more upset the child is by it (Sears, Maccoby, & Levin, 1957; Heinstein, 1966).

Predispositions of the child and of the parents affect the toilet-training process. Rhythmic infants, who have relatively stable body processes, can easily recognize the connection between their bodies and toilet-training attempts, and they are fairly easily taught (Thomas et al., 1963). In contrast, arrhythmic infants usually cannot be successfully trained until they can speak well enough to be informed of the aim of toilet training and can communicate their needs. And children who are relatively insensitive to unpleasant odors are most difficult to toilet-train! (Burton, 1969). Lack of recognition of the child's physical dispositions may make the socialization of the bowel and bladder habits more severe than it need be.

What are the effects of toilet training on the child's later behavior and personality characteristics? There are clusterings of personality traits suggestive of a Freudian anal character, both in terms of specific symptoms of difficulty of elimination control and in terms of traits such as orderliness, parsimony, and obstinacy (Ferguson, 1970; Zigler & Child, 1969; Bishop, 1967; Grygier, 1956). Again, however, the effects of parental characteristics far outweigh the effects of specific techniques. Mothers who severely train their children also put a variety of other pressures on them, such as pressures for good table manners, neatness, care about furniture, being quiet, doing well in school. But severity is not necessarily damaging. Mother's warmth can overcome the negative effects of her severity in toilet training. Fewer children severely trained by warm mothers showed emotional upset over toilet training than children severely trained by relatively cold mothers. Parental behavior may be of great importance in the development of personality traits, including those Freud called oral and anal, but the techniques of socialization thus far studied have not been shown to be of special importance themselves. Future research may be able to detect those specific parental responses most effective for the child's development, responses perhaps now used intuitively by sensitive parents (Fitzgerald, 1973).

Successful outcomes in all areas of training depend upon parental recognition of the child's needs and natural disposition and upon their willingness and ability to adapt to those in the context of respect for the child as a person. With this overview of parent-child interactions in mind, we will turn to the most basic outcome of successful interactions—attachment to people.

ATTACHMENT AND SOCIAL RESPONSIVENESS

The most important single process occurring within the interaction of parents and child is the attachment response, or the beginning of filiative behavior—also called infant dependency, or simply dependency. Attachment is the tendency of the young to seek the proximity of certain other members of the species (Schaffer & Emerson, 1964a; Bowlby, 1969). This response has immense survival value for the young, as the young come to care about other members of the species and to interact successfully with them.

Without the social responsiveness inherent in attachment, identification mechanisms could not occur in full form, nor could the child respond positively to continuing pressures throughout adulthood to socialize him in other ways. Relationships with other people would be unsatisfactory, and socialization of the child into an adult considered mature in his social group would be impossible.

Formation of the Attachment Response

In their natural environments, animals, including humans, typically become attached to their mothers. To dismiss this obvious fact with "That's nature" is an admission of ignorance rather than an explanation. Knowing *how* nature sees to it that attachment occurs should put us in a much better position than we now are to understand the normal course of human development and to minimize the occurrence or severity of some major personality disturbances.

The critical ingredient for the formation of an attachment response is that the attachment object, usually the mother, and the subject (the infant) "make contact." More formally, the mother is *salient* in the infant's environment, and the infant *acts toward* the mother and is *responded to* by her. Through this process, the mother provides the sensory and social stimulation that is necessary for adequate biological and psychological growth.

Feeding is one of the ways in which the mother can be salient to the infant, can be acted upon by him, and can respond contingently to his needs and behavior. But with feeding, as with all areas of interaction, it is stimulation and attention to the infant that elicit attachment, not merely the satisfaction of obvious physical needs.

If other animals, or objects, are more conspicuous because mother is absent or does not respond to the infant, the attachment is likely to be developed for those other objects. This view of how the attachment response is acquired has several bases of theoretical and empirical support which help to illuminate critical features of the social environment and the features inherent in the biological organism which facilitate infant love.

Comfort and punishment. The salience of the mothering one necessary for attachment, as for the identification mechanism that appears later, may be due to either the pleasurable or aversive stimulation she provides the infant, or, often, to both. However, pleasure is more than just a matter of need satisfaction.

The research of Harry Harlow and his associates has shown that mother preferences are *not* made on the basis of her association with primary need reduction (Harlow & Zimmerman, 1959; Harlow, 1958; Harlow & Harlow, 1966). They provided some monkeys with a wire-mesh mother with a bottle attached to her "chest." Other monkeys were supplied with a similar but nonfeeding mother covered with terry cloth. When given a choice about which mother to approach and spend time with, the monkeys preferred the cloth mother, even though the wire mother fed them. The wire mother was approached only to obtain food and then ignored in favor of the cloth mother.

Why was the cloth mother more desirable? Harlow suggested that it was because of the tactile stimulation she provided, that is, *contact comfort.* Although only another monkey offers full contact comfort—is "best" for clinging—the cloth surrogate offers sensations more similar to those of a real monkey than does a wire substitute and is probably a more effective stimulus for the infant's action of clinging.

The importance of contact is illustrated by the fact that even negative stimulation by mother can elicit attachment; in fact, punishment from a parent can sometimes *increase* attachment. Monkeys continued to cling to or return to a mother substitute after she gave them a noxious air blast, and they held onto her more strongly than they did before the punishment (Harlow, 1962). Similarly, young chicks shocked by the wings of a model chicken followed it more than did control chickens which were not shocked (Kovach & Hess, 1963).

One explanation for a child's approaching a punitive parent is that, because of the pain, the child is more motivated than usual to seek the pleasant feelings that the parent also produces, and therefore attaches more strongly (King, 1966). The more someone important to you rejects you, the more you need their acceptance. Perhaps a more basic reason for attachment to a punitive parent is that punishment by the parent makes that parent a salient feature of the environment (Cairns, 1966).

Imprinting and critical periods. The importance of the mere presence and salience of the mothering object is shown in the work of Konrad Lorenz (1935). Lorenz was the first to use the term "imprinting" to refer to attachment phenomena. He hatched goslings in an incubator and exposed them to himself and not to their mother. He got down on his haunches and waddled around in a reasonably close approximation of a goose's walk. The goslings imprinted on Lorenz rather than on the mother goose. When geese reared by Lorenz and those reared by their natural mother were intermingled, they immediately unscrambled themselves and headed for their respective "parents."

Unlike conventional learning processes, imprinting is facilitated by punishment from the model and by the effort involved in following the model—conditions which increase the salience of the object and the infant's involvement with it. It also seems essential for the formation of an attachment that exposure to the object occur within a *critical period*, which varies from species to species and seems to be a function of neural maturation (Figure 19–1). At least the effect of an exposure within the critical period is maximal. This has been demonstrated under laboratory conditions in which the attachment cannot be attributed to reinforcers such as food which are supplied by the imprinting object, or to other traditional learning mechanisms (Hess, 1959a, b, 1964; Scott, 1963).

Scott (1963) has suggested that an animal, and perhaps a person, of any age who is exposed to certain individuals or even physical surroundings for any length of time will become attached to them. The general adaptive nature of this mechanism may be that the survival of any member of a highly social species depends upon rapid development of social relationships so that inhibition of the formation of social bonds may be almost impossible.

Psychologists are well aware of the hazards of generalizing to humans from research with other animals. Nevertheless, many are intrigued by the possible applicability of the imprinting and critical periods concepts to the attachment process in humans (Gray, 1957, 1958; Scott, 1963; Caldwell, 1962; Bowlby, 1958, 1969). Estimates of the critical time for the human attachment response vary widely, with guesses as low as six weeks and as high as three years; the most reasonable guess seems to be between the fourth month and the twelfth month. A recent theory of early infantile autism holds that fetuses with inherited high potential for intellectual superiority are developmentally ready for imprinting with human behaviors much before birth, so that they become imprinted on the restricted uterine environment, thus accounting for the autistic child's

**FIGURE
19–1**

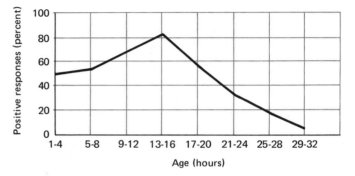

Attachment during the Critical Period.
The critical age at which ducklings are most effectively imprinted;
average test score of ducklings imprinted at each age group.

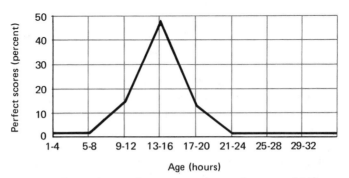

Percentage of animals in each age group that made scores of 100 percent in testing.

Source: Adapted from Hess, E. H. Imprinting. *Science,* 1959, 130, 133–141.

fascination with inanimate things and lack of responsiveness to people
(Moore & Shiek, 1971).

Whether or not the imprinting concept turns out to be an appropriate
one for human infants, contact with a mothering one and social stimulation are as essential for the development of infant love of mother as they
are for animal imprinting.

"Making contact" with human infants. Because human infants do not
have the motor ability to seek a cloth mother rather than a wire one or
to follow a mother figure around a laboratory, we must look for other
clues to their predisposition to make contact with the mother figure. As
noted earlier, infants' visual discrimination and visual pursuit abilities are
fairly precise and efficient, and their preference for perceiving social objects is fairly clear. In addition, human infants are able to suck and
cling, to smile and cry—all responses which elicit caretaking activities
and help to ensure contact that enables attachment to another human
being (Bowlby, 1969).

The stimulation of close contact does facilitate the development of the attachment response; however, there is no one mode by which parent and child must interact. Much depends on the personality of the parent and the temperament of the child.

Not all infants are "cuddlers" who enjoy close physical contact (Schaffer & Emerson, 1964a, 1964b). Non-cuddlers, who struggle, squirm, and whimper when held closely, develop initially less intense attachments than cuddling babies, but the difference is a temporary one found only in the beginning stage of the attachment formation. Mothers of non-cuddlers report alternative ways of relating to the child: rough play, jostling, tossing the infant in the air, walking about. Resistance to close physical contact need not be considered a social rejection of mother; it appears to be a primitive and general aspect of the infant himself.

It is important that the mother not interpret the non-cuddler's behavior as a rejection of her and that she look for ways to create a warm interaction that is consistent with the child's temperament. If the mother is too rigid in her insistence that the infant "snuggle," and if she fails to try alternative methods for making contact, she will be taking the first step toward the development of a pathological relationship.

The *amount* of time the mother spends with her child is not as important to the development of attachment as the *quality* of the interaction. The mother—or any other adult who is the primary caretaker of the infant—must respond to the child in a way that is clear and meaningful to him. Thus, even if mother is around all day, the child's attachment may be directed to others who are around less but are more effective in interacting with the child in a way that is meaningful to him. Infants differ in the kinds of contact they find compatible, in the age at which they form attachments, in the strength of the attachments they form, and certainly in their favorite people for attachment. These differences influence others' responses, which in turn further influence personality development.

Immediate Implications of Attachments

Anxiety and anxiety reduction. As the infant develops an attachment to mother, or to some other person or object, he finds her absence anxiety-provoking and her presence anxiety-reducing. When human infants protest strongly and show distress at mother's absence, they are said to have *separation anxiety*. This response serves to keep the infant close to mother and out of danger when he is young and most vulnerable. The phenomenon is not limited to humans, nor to animate mothering objects, for that matter: lambs reared with a television set formed a strong attachment to it and became agitated when the set was removed (Cairns, 1966).

Separation anxiety about the absence of a particular person seems to peak between seven and ten months, and diminishes around eighteen months (see Mussel, Conger, & Kagan, 1969). Previously, the attachment response was not strong enough for the separation to be disturbing. It takes time for the attachment to be developed. During this time, the infant is being exposed to the mothering object, a necessary but not sufficient condition for the formation of the attachment response. Cognitive maturation is also occurring, however, and this enables the formation of the attachment response because of the development (around eight months of age) of *object permanence* (Piaget, 1950)—an awareness that an object or person exists even when it cannot be seen. An infant cannot miss mother's presence if he has no concept of her existence apart from him (Schaffer, 1958).

A corollary of the attachment response is the occurrence of *fear of the novel*. When the young organism has had enough experience and maturation, he learns what is familiar. Strange and novel objects elicit fear, a spontaneous fear which emerges in all animals studied (King, 1966; Bronson, 1968). Of course, there is an obvious survival value in this reaction because strange objects in an infant's environment very well may be dangerous ones.

The mother, a familiar stimulus, is able to reduce fears about novel objects that might be in her presence. When Harlow's monkeys were placed in a strange environment or confronted with novel objects such as a large wooden spider, they huddled in a corner if just the wire mother was present. When the cloth mother was present, the infants clung to her and gradually began to explore the room, returning to her for occasional reassurance. Similarly, the human infant first hides behind his mother when a stranger is present, and then cautiously ventures forth, frequently "checking back" with mother to gain courage from her familiarity.

With the development of attachment to mother and the fear of the novel, the infant exhibits *stranger anxiety*, which, although given a different name, is not much different from separation anxiety. Both are aspects of the same dynamic, namely, the dependent attachment to mother.

Responsiveness to others. Because of the same attachment response that at one time led to stranger anxiety, the infant can come to respond positively to people other than his mother. The realm of what is familiar and safe becomes extended partially because of the principle of stimulus similarity and generalization. Members of the same species as the mothering object are more similar to her than are members of other species. Thus, there is a greater approach response to other members of the species of the mothering one, whether or not they are of the same species as the infant himself. For example, Harlow found that monkeys reared by humans spent more time with humans than with other monkeys, while those reared by their natural mothers approached other monkeys in preference to humans.

What is familiar, safe, and approachable is extended also because of the infant's having had increasing experience so that less of the world of objects and people is novel—that is, the idea of novelty becomes less novel. Development of the fear of novelty depends upon prior experience, which determines what is familiar. What if an infant is exposed, more or less simultaneously, to more than one caretaker, so that a larger number of objects are similar to the familiar caretakers? Will there then be less fear of strangers? In a study instructive on this point, litters of kittens, beginning at five weeks of age, were handled by only one person or by five different persons, or not handled at all (Collard, 1967). Those kittens usually handled by five different people had much less fear of a strange person than those handled by one person or by no one, and the fear of strangers of the latter groups increased over the four weeks of testing (Figure 19–2). However, the one-person kittens were much more playful and affectionate than the other kittens (Figure 19–3). A similar deficit in play activities occurs in institutionalized infants, compared to infants reared at home.

Thus, the development of a strong attachment to one person temporarily increases fear of strangers but also is associated with successful social and emotional development as defined in our culture (e.g., play, affection). The long-term effects of having one or several caretakers during early life are not known. However, if the caretaker, one or many, is caretaker in name only, disastrous effects are evident. Lack of continuing

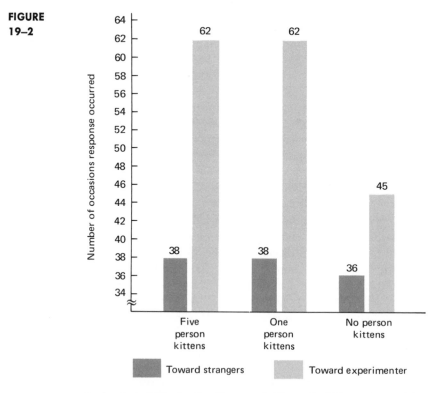

FIGURE 19–2

Exploratory Behavior (Looking at, Sniffing at) of Kittens Reared by Five People, One Person, or No One.

Source: Collard, R. R. Fear of strangers and play behavior in kittens with varied social experience. *Child Development,* 1967, 38 (3), 877–891.

FIGURE
19–3

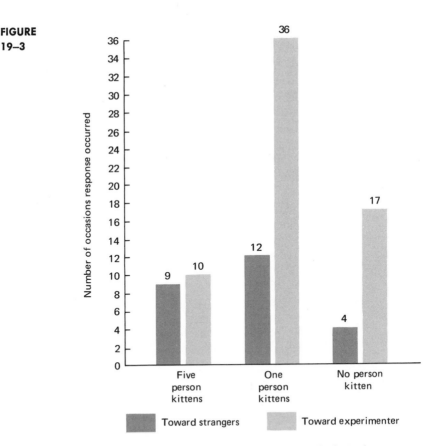

Playful, Affectionate Behavior (Pawed, Mouthed, Body Contact, Purring) toward Experimenter and Strangers of Kittens Reared by Five People, One Person, or No One.

Source: Collard, R. R. Fear of strangers and play behavior in kittens with varied social experience. *Child Development*, 1967, 38 (3), 877–891.

attachment with any mothering figure(s) and the social deprivation likely without mother will prevent normal social and emotional development.

Social Deprivation

Social deprivation is a general term used to describe impoverished environments in which a child or adult is prevented from having the contact with other members of his species that he would ordinarily have. It is a form of sensory deprivation in which one is deprived particularly of social stimuli. The absence of social stimuli may also imply a reduction in other forms of sensory stimulation typically provided by other animate objects. In a socially deprived environment there is no one for the infant to make contact with and form an attachment for. Social stimulation and learning in interaction with others continue to be necessary beyond the formation of the attachment response. Other people teach

EARLY PARENTAL INFLUENCES

TABLE 19–1 Social Behavior of Kittens

Behavior	FIVE-PERSON KITTENS				ONE-PERSON KITTENS				NO-PERSON KITTENS			
	No. of occasions response occurred		No. Ss making responses		Occasions		Ss		Occasions		Ss	
	Strangers	Exp.	Strangers	Exp.	Strangers	Exp.	Strangers	Exp.	Strangers	Exp.	Strangers	Exp.
Exploratory												
Looked at	20	35	10	10	20	44	9	10	22	28	10	9
Sniffed	18	27	7	10	18	18	9	9	14	17	7	9
Playful, affectionate												
Pawed	3	0	2	0	1	4	1	3	0	0	0	0
Mouthed	0	5	0	3	3	14	3	9	1	3	1	2
Body contact *	3	4	1	3	2	8	2	5	2	9	2	4
Purred	3	1	3	1	6	10	5	4	1	5	1	4
Total playful or affectionate	9	10			12	36			4	17		

* Climbed on, rubbed against, snuggled, or treaded.

SOURCE: Collard, R. R. Fear of strangers and play behavior in kittens with varied social experience. *Child Development*, 1967, 38 (3), 877–891.

social skills and provide circumstances for the development of impersonal skills. Consideration of extreme cases of social deprivation highlight the necessity of social interaction for normal development, for man and for other animals, and perhaps may sensitize the reader to the deprivation that may occur in what appears to be a satisfactory environment for adequate development—in other words, a "normal home."

Stimulation and social learning. Informal accounts of unusual cases of human children having been kept in an attic for years or left alone in the wilds to be tended by animals indicate the stunted physical, cognitive, and social development likely when humans are deprived of early contact with other humans. More systematic evidence is available from laboratory animal research. Animals which have been reared in complete or partial social isolation show marked social and emotional disturbances upon being removed from isolation (Mason et al., 1968; Harlow & Harlow, 1966).

Generally, the longer and more complete the isolation, the more intense and long lasting the disturbance. Monkeys socially deprived for only three months were able to establish effective social relationships rapidly. In contrast, those isolated for six months clutched at themselves, crouched, and avoided all social contact when they were removed from isolation. Isolates did show some small gain in social interactions when placed with other isolates, but not when they were placed with normal animals. After twelve months of deprivation, the isolates would not interact with others at all, and were intensely afraid of other monkeys, but showed no aggression, apparently because of inhibitory fears.

In addition to providing stimulation, normal mothers teach their young some fundamentals of social interaction. Learning to interact with others is an important process that is expected to occur in the family (Chapter 16). Although Harlow's infant monkeys formed attachments with the cloth mother and found her an effective fear reducer, the cloth mother was *not* as effective as a real mother (Harlow, 1961, 1962). When infants of the cloth mother grew up, they showed more aggressiveness, poorer social adjustment, and less effective heterosexual behavior than did monkeys reared by real mothers. They mated only with difficulty and coaching. When they could be made to mate and bear infants of their own, they were markedly ineffective as mothers themselves: they both avoided their babies and beat them so savagely they had to be separated from them. The babies, however, continued to approach them—an example of an approach response to negative stimulation, discussed above.

Peers also participate effectively in early social learning. Harlow's monkeys raised by surrogate mothers which were allowed adequate peer contact did not show such extreme adult maladjustment as those deprived of peer contact as well. Play experience in social groups of emotional (rather than chronological) peers also proved an effective behavior modification procedure for socially deprived monkeys (Missakian, 1972). The only monkey who did not improve was one who did not engage in social play. Play with peers also seems beneficial for the human young (Klinger, 1969; Chapter 22).

The implications for personality development are clear and frightening, especially because the conditions of social isolation in which Harlow's monkeys were raised are often closely approximated in institutions such as orphanages, and are approximated in homes more often than is pleasant to contemplate.

Institutions for children. The critical damaging feature of most institutions is not necessarily that the child living there is deprived of his biological mother, but that he is deprived of the stimulation that other species members typically provide (Casler, 1961, 1965).

While the caretakers in institutions may attend adequately to the physical needs of the child, they are not likely to have time to provide him with social attention. The kinesthetic, tactile, social, and affective stimulation usually provided by adults is therefore lacking. Affective blandness is characteristic; the child is exposed to a small variety of emotions only weakly expressed. Even the attention to physical needs is likely to be on an arbitrary, perhaps unpredictable schedule rather than to be contingent upon the child's needs. With frequent turnover of personnel, the institutionalized child has little opportunity to know one person and to become able to predict the reactions of those with whom he interacts.

With the absence of the attention of others, normal development is unlikely. Retardation is common among institutionalized children, and the amount of retardation tends to increase with the length of time spent in the institution (Yarrow & Goldfarb, 1964). Late adolescents who have been reared in institutions may show the simple and unrefined behavior typical of preschool children (Goldfarb, 1945). Their general personality pattern is impoverished, meager, undifferentiated, and deficient in inhibition and control. Impulsive behavior and overt antisocial and aggressive behaviors occur frequently and without anxiety and guilt. Frustration tolerance and achievement motivation are low, and there is minimal goal directedness.

Two prominent patterns of social maladjustment observable in institutionalized children are social apathy and affect hunger (Yarrow, 1961). The *social apathy* pattern consists of withdrawal and apathy when others make social approaches, lack of attachment to caretakers, and lack of appropriate response to different kinds of emotional expression. *Affect hunger* is continual and insatiable seeking for attention and affection. The child is "exacting, demanding, apparently passionate, but always disappointed in new attachments" (Freud, A., & Burlingham, 1944, p. 58). Apathy is likely if separation (without replacement) occurs *before* the attachment response develops, hunger if it occurs *after* the child learns to need people. In the one case, he has not learned to need people; in the other, he has. In Horney's terms, the dominant patterns are moving away from people or toward people (Chapter 4). In both cases, however, the strategy is more compulsive and pervasive in institutionalized children than in children living in families.

Less extreme parental deprivation. The fact that a child is reared by both parents does not mean that life automatically goes smoothly. The same lack of stimulation and unpredictability that can interfere with the cognitive, motor, and personality development of the institutionalized child may also occur in less noticeable form with children living with both parents. The fact that two people had the biological capacity and willingness to produce a child does not by itself mean that their behavior will be adequate for eliciting attachment and identification responses or that they will be effective teachers of the social norms and skills needed by a mature, adjusted adult.

Social apathy and affect hunger may occur in less obvious but just as certain forms in children who have lived with their parents if the parents have not been socially responsive to the child. Social apathy in mild or more obvious forms may occur if there has been early neglect and if the attachment response has been weakly formed. Reduced imitation learning and identification as the child gets older, and reduced care about other people and responsiveness to them, may occur in the child reared at home just as in the child reared in an orphanage. Affect hunger may occur in children who have managed to form the attachment response but do not later receive the kind or amount of social stimulation they need. Nurturance withdrawal and perhaps direct punishment for bids for attention will increase the dependency on the adult figure and make him or her a more desirable and salient other to approach, to want the approval of, to imitate, and to identify with. The child may then always be hungry for affection but never satisfied.

The women's liberation movement has brought with it an increase in discussions about the effects on the child of a mother's employment. "If a woman is going to have children, she should stay home and take care of them," maintain the traditionalists; "otherwise, they will grow up maladjusted, or even delinquent." "Not so," contend the liberated mothers; "a mother who stays at home when she would rather be working will not necessarily attend to her children or behave predictably or sensitively with respect to them."

Who is right? It is impossible to say whether the working mother or the nonworking mother *in general* has a more salutary effect on the personality development of her children, since the outcome is dependent on the *quality* of the mother-child interaction rather than the *quantity*. It is interesting, however, that often when maternal employment in the background of disturbed or delinquent children is cited as evidence of the disastrous effects to be expected when women leave home, the subjects are drawn from a population characterized by broken homes, poverty, racial discrimination, and marital conflict (Yarrow & Yarrow, 1964). It is little wonder that mothers in such a population are likely to work and that the children in such a population are likely to have behavioral disturbances.

It is unrealistic and inaccurate, however, to claim that the disturbances of the children are attributable solely to the mother's employment outside the home (see Nye & Hoffman, 1963).

Until recent years, the role of the father in child development was relatively neglected. However, when the available evidence is examined, he emerges as an extremely important figure in the social and emotional development of both females and males among both humans and other primates (Nash, 1952, 1965, 1969; Mitchell, 1969). For example, Peterson and his associates (1961), in studying groups of maladjusted young boys, found the effects of the fathers to be crucial. In this study, a pattern emerged in which the fathers were found to be "cold, maladjusted, punitive . . . lacking the human kindness shown by the fathers of the relatively well-adjusted . . . children" (p. 157). More recently, significant differences were found between the fathers, but not between the mothers, of normal and disturbed (aggressive, socially withdrawn, or distractible) children (Bugenthal, Love, & Kaswan, 1972). The fathers of the normal children were evaluatively neutral and nondirecting (i.e., low attempts to control) and relatively untalkative (i.e., social independence).

With mothers and fathers alike, an awareness of *why* parents are important, rather than just that they are important, can enable a more satisfactory parent-child interaction which contributes to the child's growth into an independent, competent adult.

SUMMARY

The infant, and later the adult, is a biological organism living in an environment in which he is influenced by other people and in which he influences them. The influence of others begins before birth in the form of genetic heritage, the parents' reasons and expectations for the child, and the parents' personality development and maturity during pregnancy, at birth, and later. The child is, from his earliest days, an active participant in the social system into which he is born. Nature has planned well to make it likely that human infants, as well as those of other species, survive and develop into healthy adults. A critical feature for normal development is sensory stimulation, and particularly the stimulation inherent in interaction with other members of the species. The human infant has early appearing capacities to observe and respond to environmental events, to prefer social objects over nonsocial ones, and to discriminate mother from strangers. In the natural course of events, he develops an attachment for the mothering one because of her salience created by her attentiveness to him and responsiveness to his bids for social attention—and the stimulation she provides. Because of the infant's attachment to her, the mother's absence becomes anxiety inducing, and her presence anxiety reducing. Because of the attachment, the infant comes to fear others who are not her, but later becomes able to respond positively to them also. The development of responsiveness to mother and others enables learning from and with them in the continuing process of socialization. When there is a disruption in "the way things usually are," the infant may attach to an object other than mother, or form no attachment to an animate object at all. Continued social deprivation impedes development, particularly social-emotion development.

It is not enough that the infant simply be around other people. They must be attentive to him and sensitive to his needs and predispositions. He is not, after all, an empty organism, even at birth. It appears to be essential that the parents "make contact" with the infant as he is and take him into account in their interaction with him rather than arbitrarily imposing their own demands and expectations. The adult is happier with other people if he feels that they are responding to him rather than ignoring his preferences, intentions, feelings, and thoughts; he likes to make contact with others. So too, the infant functions and develops better when the environment is attentive and responsive to him.

In the process of making contact with the child, the parents are not just responders or stimulators, but are people whose personality influences the kind of interaction that will take place, including that interaction which occurs during feeding and elimination training. Their presence and their personality make continuing contributions to the child's own development and personality as he grows, identifies with them, and acquires their attitudes, values, and expectations, which he applies to his own behavior as well as that of others.

20

socialization requirements

The rewards and punishments a child receives, the anxiety he experiences, the biological predispositions with which he is born, and the subcultural influences and expectations with which he is faced all contribute to his social development. While all human beings are biological organisms whose thinking and behavior are influenced by the social system in which they live, not all people behave as society requires or expects—and what is expected varies with subcultural and familial influences and the sex of the individual.

The early development of social responsiveness is essential to effective socialization. As the child comes to pay attention to other people and is responsive to their attempts to control his behavior, he begins to understand what behavior is necessary to meet their requirements and expectations. Conformity to expectations is rewarded; deviancy is punished. Thus, reward comes from knowing the parental and subcultural requirements for aggressive, dependent, sex-typed, and moral behavior and from controlling responses accordingly.

AGGRESSION

When Is Aggressive Behavior Aggressive?

Despite the pervasiveness of aggression in our society, or perhaps because of it, aggression remains one of the most difficult behavior systems to explain from any theoretical position (Baldwin, 1967). While there is no particular evidence favoring a view of an innate drive in man to destroy other species members, responses likely to be considered aggressive occur frequently enough that some attention must be given to their control.

Attention to feelings that may accompany aggressive responses varies with the orientation of the commenting psychologist. At one extreme is a behavioristic, purely external view: an aggressive response is one which delivers a harmful stimulus to another person (Buss, 1961). At the other extreme is an internal view: the focal point for the study of aggression is the inner state of hostility which motivates injury or destruction of some object (Saul, 1956). A person *intends* to be injurious to someone else.

Intent, and the underlying motive, must be inferred, by professional and layman, from the situation in which the behavior occurs and from whatever we can find out about the individual's perception of the situation. In many situations the judgment of intent is difficult. When a waiter drops a plate on a complaining customer, does he intend to be aggressive, or is it an accident? When a teacher does not get examinations graded for several weeks, is it aggression against the students or simply the result of overwork? Either teacher or waiter may not intend to hurt, but may be judged by others as aggressing; or he may have an intent to harm but conceal it in an ambiguous expression. Whether or not the individual actually intends to express aggression is often irrelevant to the consequences of his behavior. For instance, if the customer concludes that the waiter is aggressive, he will not leave a tip; if the students conclude that their teacher's laxity is aggressively motivated, the class will give the instructor a negative evaluation.

The individual who does not use the same system that others use to interpret behavior will often find himself misunderstood and may also be unable to understand the behavior of others (Chapter 13). In view of the complexity of making inferences about the intent of others, it is a wonder that we develop as much agreement as we do about the meaning of behavior. "Strictly speaking . . . it is not 'aggressive' responses that are learned, but only classes of responses that are labeled as aggression on the basis of social judgments that themselves must be learned" (Bandura & Walters, 1963, p. 114). Because of these considerations, attention here will focus mainly on the variables that affect the occurrence or nonoccurrence of responses which are likely to be considered aggressive, with examples mainly of physical aggression.

Biological Bases of Aggressive Behavior

Innate predispositions. There is an abundance of evidence substantiating the existence of instinctual bases for aggressive behavior in animals other than man (Lorenz, 1950, 1966; Tinbergen, 1953). Although Lorenz and others have suggested that serious attention be given to discovering the innate mechanisms which activate aggression in human beings, instinctual bases for human aggression are often denied in favor of viewing aggression as acquired responses. However, it may be premature to disregard totally the claim of the ethologists (Chapter 10).

It is probable that there are innate predispositions to social behavior, including aggression, in man, but they are flexible enough to be molded into a variety of forms through learning, making it difficult to discern them, even though they may play crucial roles in molding socially relevant behavior (Miller, 1964). For example, pain elicits reflexive fighting in animals which is not dependent upon prior conditioning, and it increases the incidence of aggressive responses even when nonaggressive responses would terminate the pain (Zigler & Child, 1969; Ulrich & Craine, 1964). A fixed stare is often an expression of aggression that may elicit attack or submission, in man as well as in other primates (Ekman, 1972; Ellsworth, Carlsmith, & Henson, 1972). True, humans may learn not to attack the fellow bus passenger who steps on their toes or the dentist whose drill slips or the stranger who stares persistently, but this does not preclude instinctual bases for aggression.

Biological predispositions have a role in shaping interpersonal behavior, including aggressive behavior. However, for neither man nor other animals are aggressive responses completely instinctual, mechanistic acts which occur regardless of experience and the nature of the current environment. For both, the behavior that develops is a complex interaction of genetic makeup and early experience (Chapter 14). The role of frustration in eliciting aggression is a relevant case in point for indicating both innate and learned components of human aggression.

Frustration. The view expressed in the frustration-aggression hypothesis is that aggression is an innate response to frustration—a universal and natural response (Dollard et al., 1939, 1944; Miller, 1941). Frustration results from an interruption of a goal-directed behavior so that rewards are not attained or are delayed in coming. The barrier to goal attainment may be tangible or intangible. A train blocking an intersection (tangible) makes you late for a date with a friend, and then the friend is not there when you do arrive; attainment of the goal of association (intangible) is prevented. Aggression is not always directed toward the appropriate frustrating object, but may be displaced to an "innocent" object or person (Chapter 5). We pound the steering wheel of the car while waiting for the slow train to pass, or we kick the lamp post on the corner where the friend was supposed to meet us. A pigeon denied a reinforcer previously given for pecking a button attacks another pigeon rather than the button (Azrin, Hutchinson, & Hake, 1966).

Frustration is certainly a major instigator of aggression in humans as well as in other animals. However, psychologists no longer maintain that aggression is the only response that occurs to frustration. They have modified the frustration-aggression hypothesis: Although aggression is probably a natural and highly probable response to frustration, aggression can be replaced, or displaced, if aggressive responses have previously been followed by punishment or lack of reward, or if other types of responses to frustration have been rewarded. Similarly, reward of aggressive responses may increase their incidence, with or without an immediately obvious frustration and often without an intent to harm.

Thus, the study of human aggression has focused most extensively on aggression as an acquired response and one whose occurrence varies with present circumstance and past experience. Much of the research can be seen as offering specifications of how particular aggressive responses are acquired and how the disposition to respond aggressively in the face of frustration is enhanced or dampened. Such research certainly shows that aggressive behaviors are modifiable, or that they have learned determinants. It does not show that aggression has no innate determinants. There seems to be no reason to deny either the innate or learned components of aggressive responses. In any case, the growing child must learn how to deal with frustration effectively and must know what responses in what situations others will consider aggressive, so that he may behave in ways that bring rewards and avoid punishments.

Aggression as a Learned Response

Reinforcement. It is tempting to underestimate the efficacy of aggressive responses. Aggressive behavior may be strengthened because it is successful in overcoming barriers and because it is rewarded by other people. One mechanism by which frustration leads to aggression is by increasing drive, which increases the organism's pool of generalized arousal (Chapters 10, 14, 15), and therefore is likely to increase the vigor of the response (compare with Mandler's interruption theory, Chapter 14).

Intense responses are likely to be labeled aggressive, and because they often are effective, their probability of occurrence increases. An intense response often works when a milder one does not—we "try harder" and succeed in the face of immediate frustration. Shoving a door open with a foot is not aggressive; kicking the same door open with the same foot when the attempted shove is unsuccessful is likely to be perceived as aggressive and may well succeed in opening the door. Neither blockage nor response intensity need be a physical matter. Overly intense attempts to gain acceptance into a higher social class or college clique of special importance are often thought of as aggressive responses, and the extra effort used in trying to gain acceptance may be rewarded.

Intense responses, with or without intent to harm, may be developed and maintained because they are instrumentally effective in acting upon the objects which cause frustration or pain or upon those people who have the power to remove objectionable objects or assist in goal attainment. A violent outburst of crying may attract parental attention when a gentle whimper or polite tug at mother's skirts would be easily ignored. Temper tantrums are effective means of getting the reinforcement of parental attention. By ignoring responses to mild bids for attention, parents unwittingly shape more undesirable responses of greater intensity. The child keeps trying to attract parental attention with increasing intensity, and he is finally successful. Because an intensified response is reinforced by goal attainment and by the reduction of the frustration-produced or conflict-produced drive, the aggressive behavior takes on characteristics of a secondary reinforcer and aggression becomes an acquired drive (Sears et al., 1953; Sears, Maccoby, & Levin, 1957). The aggressive response itself becomes reinforcing.

Because of the secondary reinforcement principle, the young child may become sadistic. Frequently, mother expresses her own pain at the child's aggression, or she expresses anger at being interrupted to attend to the infant's needs. Her expressions occur in contiguity with the child's tension reduction and reinforcement. Thus, the expression of pain in others acquires reinforcement value, and the incidence of aggressive responses effective in eliciting those expressions increases. By the second year of life children do show aggression which seems to have no reason other than that of eliciting pain cues from another person. Young children sometimes laugh when their victims cry, a response considered sadistic in adults.

If aggressive responses are successful in attaining desired reinforcers, the child does not have the need or the opportunity to practice prosocial responses and receive reinforcement for them. When the child, or adult, who has used aggressive behavior effectively encounters a situation in which aggression is not effective, he will be at a loss. He will have few prosocial responses to fall back on. Although he may be asking for something in the only way he knows, his behavior will be reacted to negatively by other people, who may intend to refuse the reinforcer until there is a prosocial response, "Please . . . may I?" If prosocial responses have so little strength that they cannot be elicited, the result is extreme frustration and possibly a violence so intense that the other people will do anything to stop it, or if they have no responsibility toward the person, they will ignore the outburst—and thus a vicious circle is established.

The reinforcement for aggressive behavior may be due to the instrumental effectiveness of the response, or the praise of those who reward aggression—that is, aggression toward others, not toward themselves. Aggressive responses increase as a function of positive reinforcement and are more resistant to extinction under intermittent reinforcement schedules than under continuous ones. Further, generalization is evident: responses which are initially directed toward inanimate objects come to be directed toward personal targets as well, and reinforcement for verbal aggression increases nonverbal aggression (see Bandura & Walters, 1963).

Social groups vary markedly in their rewards for aggression and, accordingly, in the amount of aggression of their members. Among the headhunting Iatmul, scalping enemies is rewarded by prestige and celebrations. On the other hand, children of the Hutterites show virtually no interpersonal aggression because aggressive behavior is not rewarded; this occurs even though the children are subjected to severe and frustrating socialization procedures. In the United States, social class and ethnic group differences probably reflect reinforcement practices, among other things. Lower-class parents reward physical aggression much more than do middle-class parents. In fact, for lower-class males and for delinquent subcultures, a certain amount of physical aggression is given a prosocial label. Middle-class boys are expected by their parents to avoid direct physical aggression, but they are also expected to be assertive, competitive, and able to stand up for their rights—which requires discriminations between unacceptable and acceptable aggression that may be difficult and anxiety-provoking for the young child (Ferguson, 1970). Children who show the most antisocial aggression in later childhood and adolescence may have been punished severely for aggression toward the parents but encouraged and even rewarded for aggression toward peers and perhaps other adult authorities (Bandura & Walters, 1959).

Parental punishment and permissiveness. Parents may unwittingly increase their child's aggressive, or simply intense, responses by ignoring milder prosocial ones, and they may actively encourage and reward aggression toward others. Aggressive responses may also be acquired and maintained because parents punish them *or* because they permit them.

With aggressive behavior, the problems of punishment are more complicated than with other types of behavior. The effect of punishment in suppressing the response often is outweighed by the effect of observing the parental aggression inherent in the punitive act and by the child's increased feelings of frustration and hostility that occur with punishment, particularly physical punishment (Sears et al., 1953; Bandura & Walters, 1963). Parental punitiveness tends to *increase* the child's aggression rather than decrease it. However, the aggression is likely to be directed away from the punishing parent himself. Miller's conflict analysis suggests that when expression of the response toward the desired target is inhibited, the response is displaced toward objects similar to the goal target (Chapter 5). Generally, punishment by an authority figure inhibits aggression in his presence but may be associated with high aggression toward other targets. The more parental punishment for aggression, the more aggression outside the home. Children whose mothers disapproved of aggression and physically punished it were likely to be very aggressive at nursery school (Sears, Maccoby, & Levin, 1957).

Permissiveness toward aggression is also positively associated with aggression. Mothers who were permissive regarding aggression directed toward them had more aggressive boys than did nonpermissive mothers (Bandura & Walters, 1959). The *combination* of permissiveness and punitiveness results in the *greatest* aggression (Sears, Maccoby, & Levin, 1957; Becker, 1964). Some mothers, or fathers, are permissive and tolerant of aggressive behavior for a while, but when their tolerance is passed, they physically punish the child. In other families, there is a general laxity, especially by the mother, and high punitiveness, especially by the father. The conjunction of permissiveness and punishment for the same kind of responses is likely to be a confusing and frustrating state of affairs for the child. The rules are not clear. He does not know what to do.

If both punishment and permissiveness of aggressive responses increase their incidence, what is a poor parent to do? The *least* aggressive children come from homes where aggression is *clearly* and *consistently* disapproved and stopped immediately when it occurs, but stopped by techniques other than physical punishment (Sears, Maccoby, & Levin, 1957; Becker, 1964). Restriction of aggression by warm parents has very different results than does restriction by cold, punitive, or hostile parents. Control of aggression may be enhanced when parents take time to teach and to explain. If the child is taught and encouraged to make prosocial responses incompatible with aggressive ones, his need for intense aggressive responses decreases. Reasoning and explanation are generally effective in promoting internal control of aggression, and other unacceptable behaviors, perhaps because reasoning generally involves fairly explicit labeling of what is acceptable and unacceptable and thus facilitates internalization (Ferguson, 1970). The use of these effective control procedures requires that parents be able to notice the positive as well as the negative in their child's behavior, that they take time to communicate their expectations to the child, and that they be consistent in their expectations and behavior toward the child.

Observation and Catharsis

Because television and movies depict so much aggression and violence, there has been increasing concern, both practical and theoretical, about determining the extent to which observation of aggression increases or decreases aggression in the viewers (U.S. National Commission on the Causes and Prevention of Violence, 1970). Children do learn by observation, but what they learn, how they learn, and the relationship between what they learn and what they do are complicated considerations (Chapter 18).

Observation may provide the means whereby the child notices inconsistency between norm prescriptions and the behavior of others, and it may thus detract from the effectiveness of direct instruction. Even though he has been told that aggression is forbidden, he may observe that aggressive responses are often effective in obtaining rewards; if the model is not rewarded or is punished for the aggressive responses, the tendency for imitation is reduced. However, in either case, the child has observed the responses and may use them, immediately or later, with or without an accompanying intent to harm. Generally, observing other people's aggressive behavior in a situation such as a movie tends to increase aggressiveness (Berkowitz, 1970). However, simply being exposed to models does not automatically increase imitation of them (Chapter 18). There are wide variations in children's responses to models. Biological predispositions and previous learning experiences (many associated with sex-role socialization) are probably important sources of differences in attentiveness to aggressive models and in performance of the observed responses.

On the other side of the coin, the catharsis principle holds that observation of other people's aggression, or one's own actual or fantasied aggression, should reduce one's need to feel or act aggressively; that is, the aggression is "drained off" (Chapter 9). Research is not yet definitive enough to allow a firm statement of the conditions under which observation or fantasy of aggression increases or decreases the probability of aggressive feelings and behaviors, in children or in adults. The state of the viewer (thoughtful, angry, or excited), his identification with film characters, his previous reinforcement for aggression, and the specific content of the behavior sequence observed (justification of the aggression, consequences of aggression, emphasis on aggressive responses of the attacker or on pain reactions of the victim, similarity of victim to someone who has frustrated the viewer, etc.) are all important variables mediating the effect and increasing or decreasing the viewer's aggressive responses (Berkowitz, 1970 ; Turner & Berkowitz, 1972; Dobb & Wood, 1972).

Juvenile delinquents who watched a film that focused on the aggressive responses (hitting, kicking, etc.) became more aggressive; aggression was inhibited when they watched a similar film which vividly portrayed the pain of the victim (Hartman, 1969). However, if the subjects had been angered before watching the films, the pain cues of the film victim enhanced their later aggressiveness. Generally, the subjects with longer records of antisocial behavior were more punitive than those with less extensive records, particularly when they had been angered and then observed the pain film; presumably they had a longer history of association of reinforcement with the pain cues of others, the victims of aggression. This and other work suggests that observation of aggression is likely to increase aggressiveness in subjects who are themselves angry or who have a long history of reinforcement for aggression.

However, there are situations in which catharsis does occur (Chapter 9). One of these occasions is when the viewer sees something harmful happening to a particular person who has frustrated him, especially if he himself causes the harm; the probability of later aggression against the annoyer is sharply decreased (Doob & Wood, 1972; Konečni & Doob, 1972). Under these conditions at least, displaced aggression also is cathartic.

Individual and Situational Differences

Sex differences. The kinds of responses that come to be elicited by frustration are determined in part by socialization history—the ways in which the parents dealt with the child's aggressive responses. The child develops habits of responding to frustration cues. In our culture, but not in all others (Chapter 16), child-rearing practices are likely to accentuate aggression in males more than females, particularly physical aggression. Fighting, quarreling, destructiveness, and temper tantrums—all are more common among boys than girls (Maccoby, 1966a; McCandless, 1967; Feshbach, 1970). Certainly there are biological contributions to sex differences in aggression; for example, boy babies are more active and inconsolable than girl babies (Chapter 19). However, it is clear that norms prescribe sex differences, and the differential socialization of boys and girls begins quite early.

Parents expect their sons to be more aggressive than their daughters. Boys and girls expect greater aggression in adult males than in adult females. They respond with behavior consistent with the cultural expectations and are shaped by their parents' reinforcement patterns. At two years of age, hitting, screaming, and crying occur with equal frequency in boys and girls; by age four, sex differences in aggressive responses, particularly hitting, have appeared.

Boys perform more imitative aggression than do girls after being exposed to aggressive models (Chapter 18; Bandura, 1965). However, this does not necessarily mean that girls are inattentive to aggressive models or are incapable of behaving aggressively. Sex differences in imitative aggression are markedly reduced when a positive incentive is provided for demonstrating the model's aggressive responses. Third-grade girls were just as aggressive as boys when they had been assured that no one would find out about it (Mallick & McCandless, 1966). However, females are continually subjected to more severe socialization pressures regarding aggression than are males and, in the middle class especially, are expected to refrain from any physical aggression—whereas men are taught to redirect it to socially acceptable forms (competitive sports, defense of self and family under attack).

Anxiety about aggression is generally higher among girls than among boys (Ferguson, 1970). By the time some females reach adulthood, the anxiety has become so intense that they cannot act assertively when the situation demands it, even for their own protection, and they may even become incapable of being aware of the desire for aggressive behavior. They become passive and dependent creatures.

Although anxiety about aggression is lower for males, the socialization of aggressive behavior is not simple for them. They are not allowed unbridled expression of aggressive feelings and are often required to make difficult discriminations in order to determine which forms of "masculine vigor" are acceptable and which are not.

Situational differences. Although aggressive responses are relatively consistent within individuals, they, like any other response, are the product of an individual's behaving in a given situation; there is both organismic and situational variance. Children frequently respond to the frustration of having attractive toys or candy taken away or having a movie stopped with less constructiveness and more immaturity in their play than they showed before the frustration (sometimes called regression; Baker, Dembo, & Lewin, 1941). However, the arousal presumably induced by frustration need not intensify aggressive responses if cues for nonaggressive responses are salient. Children (aged seven to nine years) who had just been verbally rewarded for constructive, cooperative responses continued to behave constructively in a free play situation immediately following a frustration (Davitz, 1952). Those who had been rewarded for aggressive, competitive responses before the frustration were not so constructive after frustration. Children who were participating in an experiment with a good friend showed increased cooperation and decreased aggression after frustration (Wright, 1943).

On the other hand, aggressiveness may be increased if there are cues that aggression is justified or will not be punished. When a permissive adult was present who allowed aggressive behavior to occur or continue once it had begun, the aggression of children playing with dolls or with each other increased within sessions and from one session to another; aggression did not increase when the adult was absent (see Bandura & Walters, 1963). When the adult is present, it seems, the child abides by the adult's standards as he perceives them to be because aggression is allowed; when the adult is absent, he relies on his internalized standards of the inhibition of aggression (Siegel, 1957). Thus, frustration may predispose a person to respond aggressively, but whether or not aggressive responses occur depends in large part on the circumstances and the perceived consequences (Berkowitz, 1964, 1965, 1969, 1970).

The Victim

The victim, or target, of aggressive behavior is an important and often overlooked feature of situations to which people respond aggressively. Individuals toward whom aggression may be directed with instrumental effectiveness seem to make the most likely targets. Nursery school children repeated aggressive responses directed toward another child who had previously responded to attacks by withdrawing, crying, or giving in to the aggressor's demands (Patterson, Littman, & Bricker, 1967). If the victim responded with retaliation or attempts to recover property from the aggressor, the aggressor was likely to change his target. Well-learned habits of estimating the success of aggression toward some people may increase the likelihood that these people will elicit aggression. Members of minority groups, who are often victims, are perceived to have low power of retaliation and so are ideal victims for displaced aggression. It is also likely that people who appear to be low in self-esteem and high in guilt attract aggressive behavior; often they seem to ask for punishment. There are doubtless many learning bases in the selection of a victim.

However, perhaps we should keep our minds open to the ethologist's concept of innate releasing mechanisms. For other species studied, specific cues and characteristics of the situation or of other animals elicit attack behavior. Perhaps humans have at least the vestiges of similar mechanisms. Such a conceptual open-mindedness might be particularly useful in analyzing situations in which one finds himself wanting to behave aggressively toward another person or object without rational justification, and sometimes without the inner feelings that usually are said to accompany aggression. People can be observed to kick a can on a sidewalk because "it's there to be kicked." As we saw, the steady gaze of a stranger has aversive qualities which often induce tension or a feeling of being threatened. It seems well worth the effort to invest time and thought in determining whether characteristics and behavioral cues of other people (or nations?) tend to elicit aggressive responses. Perhaps there is something we have been missing in our intense concern with the learning experiences of man the domesticated animal.

DEPENDENCY

Superficially, dependency is the opposite of aggression in that one "clings" to others rather than harming them. However, the two kinds of behavior have much in common. Both may be successful in attaining goals. Both may occur appropriately or inappropriately. Both are strongly shaped by early experiences with the parents, by parental reward and punishment patterns. Severe socialization may induce anxiety which sometimes increases, sometimes decreases the probability of dependency as well as aggression. And aggression and dependency may interact psychodynamically so that the same response may be both aggressive and dependent, or appear to be one when it is the other.

The Concept

Dependency usually refers to those responses which are directed toward obtaining the satisfactions of contact with or nurturance from other people, specifically the responses of seeking intricate, supportive, affectionate relationships with others (Hartup, 1963; Maccoby & Masters, 1970). A dependent response is an "approach" response; it may be instigated by anxiety which can be reduced by the presence of others, or it may be instigated by an affiliative wish for help, advice, support, or affection. Some facets of dependency have been discussed previously, under the rubrics of affiliation motive, conformity, identification, and infant attachment (Chapters 10, 17, 18, 19). What is of concern in all cases is approaching other people: While approach does not *always* reflect dependency, dependency *does* require approach.

It is from early attachment that dependency is differentiated. Dependency allows identification, and identification increases dependency. Dependency needs are reflected in adult conformity and affiliation. While it does not seem appropriate to speak of an innate drive to be dependent, there are biological components of the basic attachment response, and biological needs are served by it (Chapter 19).

Here we will focus on some specific functions and content of dependent behavior, particularly in children, and on specific ways in which dependency is increased or decreased by parental reinforcement patterns. Although the layman often uses the word "dependency" to describe childish and inappropriate behavior that needs to be replaced, severe socialization can inhibit the development of the mature dependency of the normal adult. One must be dependent upon others, in some sense, in order to learn from them, live with them, and enjoy them.

Functions. Successful instrumental (or task-oriented) dependency directed toward a specific person or group of people helps us in the pursuit of a goal not directly connected to the other person (Heathers, 1955). With emotional (or person-oriented) dependency, we approach the other person for the intrinsic value of his social responses—love, approval, respect, a smile, a pat on the back. Both functions may be served simultaneously, in child or adult. The young infant is dependent both instrumentally and emotionally. With increasing age, there is a tendency for an increasing divergence between the two kinds of dependent responses (Emmerich, 1966); they become more differentiated. Instrumental dependency (e.g., seek *assistance* from the teacher) was found to be highly related to emotional dependency (seeking *affection* from the teacher) during the first year of nursery school but not during the second year. With cognitive and physical growth, the child distinguishes between the perceived importance and interpersonal significance of each form of dependency. He also comes to make a distinction between self-reliance and help-seeking as means of solving problems and attaining goals. The rapid development of skills during this time makes possible the diminution of instrumental dependency.

Content and evaluation of behavior. In child or adult, the content of behavior likely to be called dependency, and to serve either of its functions, falls into three main classes (Baldwin, 1967). The first is *attention-seeking* behavior. The child begs a peer or an adult to look at him or notice his activities; he approaches his teacher, wants to sit in father's lap, shows mother his finger painting. The teenager wants his parents to listen with him to his newest record. The adult searches for a witticism to draw attention to himself. Second, dependency is inferred when social attention or approval is *reinforcing*. If the approval of another person functions as a reinforcer in learning situations, the learner is assumed to want or to value the attention and approval of the reinforcing person, that is, to be dependent upon him, perhaps to have identified with him. The effectiveness of approval as a reinforcer is especially marked in individuals who are more dependent or anxious than others. Similarly, dependency appears frequently in lists of attributes of people who are most likely to conform under group pressure or be persuaded by exposure to attitudes other than their own. The third indicator of dependency is *anxiety in the absence of others* and seeking the company of others in time of stress (Chapter 10; compare with separation and stranger anxiety, Chapter 19). Both instrumental and emotional dependency may be shown in each of these ways, and in many real-life situations both dependency functions may be served simultaneously.

Attention may be sought for its own sake or as a vehicle for gaining other goals (Chapter 10). The child may value both the teacher's attention and her help on a task. The approval of a boss who controls one's professional prospects may be as reinforcing as that of a good friend regardless of the potential extrinsic reinforcement it may foreshadow or its meaning that one has accomplished a step along the way. One may approach another in times of stress because of the intrinsic anxiety-reducing properties of another person, and because "two heads are better than one." There may be more than one kind of reinforcement for any behavior.

Approaching other people for attention, approval, or anxiety-reduction, in the service of emotional or instrumental dependency, can be observed in normal children and adults, and the absence of such approaches may indicate an inhibition or a lack of normal development of dependency responses. Dependent behavior may be appropriate or inappropriate; lack of dependent responses may be appropriate or inappropriate. Not to approach other people for comfort, affection, or help is as maladjustive as is excessive reliance on them for any purpose. However, dependent responses are more likely to be noticed and labeled as dependent when they are judged, against society's standards, to be excessive, directed toward inappropriate objects, or directed toward appropriate objects in inappropriate circumstances. An adult may turn inappropriately to his mother, rather than to his wife, for a decision about when to have the next child, or to his wife instead of his boss for help with decisions on the job. Or he may depend on his wife to make decisions that adults typically make for themselves—when to take a bath, whether or not to have dessert. With dependency, as with aggression and most other responses, the ideal is neither "too much" nor "too little." Whether one is dependent too often or too seldom is influenced by early experience and by the extent to which anxiety is attached to dependent responses.

Nurturance, Inconsistency, and Anxiety

Increasing dependency. Parental nurturance is the central variable studied in the socialization of dependency. Nurturance involves positive reinforcement coupled with the active eliciting of dependent responses, and the conditioning of positive emotional responses to the nurturant figure (Bandura & Walters, 1963). It is usually inferred from emotional demonstrativeness and warmth (Maccoby & Masters, 1970). From early childhood through adolescence, there are positive correlations, though not always high ones, between parental warmth and the dependent behavior of the child. Warm parents increase dependency in their children by giving direct encouragement for dependent responses and reinforcing them when they occur. Parents of highly dependent adolescent and pre-adolescent boys were warm and affectionate, spent a lot of time caring for them, and rewarded their sons' dependency (Bandura & Walters, 1959; Bandura, 1960).

Experimental evidence also shows the effectiveness of reinforcement in increasing dependency. Children who had been reinforced for dependency in an experimental session were subsequently more dependent on the experimenter in a *different* situation, and they learned more rapidly in a task in which the reinforcement was the verbal approval of *someone else* than did children who did not have prior experimental reinforcement for dependent responses (Nelsen, 1960; Cairns, 1962). The approval of others became more significant because of the experimenter's nurturance. Thus, warmth of the parents, or important others, increases their ability to control the child.

A pervasive immature and excessive dependency continuing into later years occurs when parents are overprotective. The child does not have the opportunity or need to learn to act for himself, to accomplish developmental tasks, to achieve for himself, or to learn how to request attention in acceptably mature ways. Overprotection, sometimes called "smother love," leads to passivity and submissiveness, an overdependence that precludes normal growth and inhibits effective social interaction (Levy, 1943).

Without initial nurturance, of course, early responsiveness and dependency are unlikely. However, once the minimum conditions for socialization are present, active dependent behavior is *increased* by *inconsistency* in parental reaction to the child's dependent behavior. The inconsistency may take the form of occasionally withholding reinforcement previously given or using both reward and punishment for dependent behavior (see Parke, 1969). According to one interpretation, dependency acquires motivational characteristics (as does aggression) because of the conflict induced by the parental inconsistency (Sears et al., 1953). The inconsistency causes a greater need for nurturance and promotes more intense efforts to obtain rewards by dependent behavior.

As the child gets older, some inconsistency occurs fairly naturally; adult tolerance for childish dependency decreases and expectations for the child's independence and more mature forms of dependency increase. The result may be a beneficial one. On the one hand, the withdrawal of nurturance allows practice of identification responses while it increases the salience of the parents and their ability to teach the child. The prior nurturance and reward of dependency increase susceptibility to the withdrawal of nurturance or punishment for dependence, and dependency increases. Thus, when dependency has been previously rewarded, rejection is positively related to dependency (Sears, Maccoby, & Levin, 1957). Similarly, a period of nurturance withdrawal after a period of freely given nurturance was found to increase the effectiveness of adult approval as a reinforcer in an experimental situation (Hartup, 1955, 1958). On the other hand, withdrawal of reward for childish dependence requires the child to begin learning to fend for himself and to be comfortable with a lack of consistent attention and the help of other people. If more mature prosocial responses, both dependent and independent, come to be rewarded, the overall result is an adaptive one.

Conflict. If dependency-related punishment and conflict are too intense and the child is not led to develop effective independent responses and mature dependent ones, two responses are likely: increased childish dependency, or inhibitory anxiety. A vicious cycle may be established. The inconsistency increases the need for nurturance and the intensity of efforts to obtain rewards by dependent behavior; the greater the punishment from the previously nurturant figure, the greater the need for nurturance, the more punishment, etc. As with aggression, intense responses, rather than more socially appropriate, milder ones, may be rewarded. The mother first ignores or punishes mildly dependent behavior, but ultimately gives in to more intense demands. A greater drive has been built up to be reduced, and intense, highly persistent dependent responses are selectively reinforced, while less intense responses are ignored or punished.

Severe socialization of dependency by intense punishment and conflict, particularly with lack of attention to the development of prosocial responses, may lead to dependency anxiety which *inhibits* the occurrence of the prosocial dependent responses that would otherwise develop (Baldwin, 1967). The child becomes anxious or ashamed of normally acceptable, active, dependent responses or overly sensitive about the rejection implied by lack of positive parental responses. He may then take unusual routes to secure attention. The child is mischievous and disobedient in ways obvious enough to ensure adult attention, even though the attention is likely to be disapproving. The request for attention is disguised so that anxiety about being dependent is avoided.

As the child grows, his bids for attention may become dramatic and socially damaging. Indeed, delinquent behavior is often viewed as an extreme manifestation of inhibited anxieties about dependence (Bandura & Walters, 1959). Overly aggressive adolescent boys, who had experienced a large amount of parental rejection, showed much less dependent behavior than a control group of nonaggressive boys, who had more accepting parents. The aggressive boys refused to seek the advice of others, talk over problems with parents, or behave affectionately toward their parents. Anxiety about showing dependence on others apparently inhibited the normal, prosocial manifestations of dependency. Thus, aggression may be dependency in disguise.

Dependency may also disguise aggression. Dependency anxiety may inhibit aggression because the individual fears that it would threaten relationships with others. Under mild frustration, preschool children dependent on the teacher were found *less* likely to show aggression than those who were not so dependent (Otis & McCandless, 1955). A dependent child or adult, eager to have the attention and approval of others, may be passive when an aggressive reaction would be justified. The importance of maintaining acceptance is too intense to allow risk of rejection because of aggression. One possible correlate of the inhibition of aggression is ulcers (Chapter 14); another is the passive-aggressive pattern in which the aggression is expressed subtly or indirectly or the passivity itself functions to anger others.

In most normal adults, there is enough dependency on others to enable reasonable enjoyment of and interaction with them. Anxiety about dependency, lest one receive censure for being too dependent, may be present, but not in enough quantity to inhibit appropriate dependency or to inhibit appropriate aggression.

The difficulty of discriminating between the appropriate and inappropriate is complicated by the sex-role prescriptions allowing greater dependency in women than in men, and greater aggressiveness in men than in women. Thus, while women have greater anxiety about aggressiveness than do men, men have greater anxiety about dependency than do women. Accordingly, aggression is more stable in boys than girls, while dependency responses are more stable in girls than boys (Kagan & Moss, 1952).

SEX-ROLE IDENTITY AND BEHAVIOR

Sex Standards

A major task for the child is to learn to adhere to a complex network of sex standards against which people are evaluated. A sex-role standard is a public consensus about the characteristics appropriate to males and females—a learned association between the concepts of masculinity and femininity, on the one hand, and the chosen attributes and behavioral patterns, on the other (Kagan, 1964).

Expectations. Sex-role standards contain a number of expectations, or preconceptions, about both the physical and psychological attributes of males and females. Physically, females are expected to be pretty, small, attractive, and smooth skinned; males are expected to be large and strong and to have hair on face and body. Males are expected to be aggressive and dominant. Girls are expected to be more dependent, passive, and conforming, and more concerned with social affiliation and nurturance, than are males. Socialization patterns tend to prepare each sex to conform to these expectations.

Males and females are also expected to have covert feelings and predispositions compatible with their externally observable behaviors. Females are expected to be emotional and motherly. Males are expected to be pragmatic, and to hide fear and control emotions (see Kagan, 1964). Although the data about feelings are less clear than those for overt behavior, by and large societal expectations seem to be met. However, there are wide individual variations, and few people can consistently meet all expectations and be ideal males or females in all respects. As in any case in which preconceptions are applied to an individual, they may not fit his predispositions because of innate incompatibilities, or because of some deviance in socialization experiences. Such generalized preconceptions often result in conflicts between identity, preference, and current characteristics and behavior.

Preference and identity. An individual may accept as personally relevant the cultural expectations of appropriate characteristics for males and females without necessarily believing that he himself possesses those expected traits or that he even wants to have them. The degree to which an individual regards himself as masculine or feminine is his sex-role identity (Kagan, 1964). Belief about one's sex-role identity is one part of the complex of attitudes that form the self-concept (Chapter 12). Masculinity-femininity is different from many other aspects of the self-concept in that it is apparently mandatory in our culture that the individual evaluate himself against culturally defined maleness or femaleness.

As with any part of the self-concept, one's self-perceptions may not match perfectly with the evaluations made by others. An individual may have inaccurate perceptions of cultural standards, of his own behavior, or of the discrepancy between the standards and his behavior. For example, a girl may think that she is feminine but actually have many characteristics considered masculine. She may have acquired sex-role standards for femininity different from the cultural norms, or she may have developed distortions in her perception of the norms or of her own behavior and feelings. Or she may underestimate the size and significance of the discrepancy between the ideal and herself for defensive reasons or because of idiosyncrasies in basic perceptual processes.

Another complication is that one's sex-role *preference* may not necessarily be consistent with one's sex-role identity or behavior (Lynn, 1959; Mussen, 1969). Social pressures may prevent a little boy from allowing his "feminine" preferences to control his behavior. Or a little girl may prefer to be a boy, but nevertheless attempt to guide her behavior by cultural standards of femininity in conjunction with the knowledge that she is classed by society as a girl. In sum, the effect of sex-role standards is to encourage males and females to behave and feel and think in ways that have been established without reference to the individual himself.

The sex-role system is a caste system (Chapter 16). Until recently, it has been a relatively unobtrusive one, because socialization efforts tend to fit people to the system without their questioning the adequacy of the fit or the appropriateness of the social pressures toward it. Cultural pressures tend to shove people toward a congruence between sex-role identity and sex-role preference and behavior. However, much incongruence probably goes unnoticed by others because the overt behavior is appropriate. People generally learn to behave as expected, but they are not necessarily happy doing so.

Acquisition of Sex-Role Behavior

Labels. Identification with the same-sex parent may facilitate or impair the development of sex-appropriate behavior and identity. However, that identification is not necessary, though it may be frequent, and both parents contribute to sex-role development. Essentially, sex-role development begins when the child first becomes aware of sex roles and of how he himself is categorized (Kagan, 1964; Kohlberg, 1966, 1969). By about two or three years of age, the child has realized that people are either male or female and labels himself appropriately. Then, he wishes to believe that his actions, attitudes, and feelings are consistent with the sex-role standards, both because he wants to be rewarded and accepted by others and because he values acts and objects consistent with the categorization of himself as a male or female simply because they *are* consistent.

The sex-role label increases the similarity of the same-sex parent to the child, and this similarity may motivate additional imitation and identification with the parent. The same-sex parent is a similar other who is more competent in being a male or female than is the child himself. The child is rewarded for imitation of same-sex models. By observation, he increases his understanding of sex-role content and extends his repertoire of appropriate behavior. Any factor which helps to accentuate the content of the sex-role standards and allows encouragement and reward for behaving consistently with the standards facilitates the development of sex-typed behavior and, hopefully but not necessarily, of an identity and preference consistent with the behavior. The clarity of standards and methods of enforcement vary with social groups and with the sex-role involved.

Cultural and social class differences. The content of sex-role expectations and the techniques for enforcing them vary from culture to culture, and within the United States social classes differ in the extent to which they have clear-cut expectations of differential behavior and in their methods of inculcating the differences (Mussen, 1969; McCandless, 1967).

The general content of sex-role standards is fairly consistent among classes, but the stereotypes are more sharply drawn and enforced in the working class than in the middle and upper classes. Lower-class mothers encourage sex typing more consistently than do middle-class mothers. Children respond. When asked to pick the toys they liked best, lower-class boys made stable masculine choices by age five, while middle-class boys were six before they did so (Rabban, 1950). Lower-class girls made sex-appropriate choices by age six, but middle-class girls had not done so by age eight. Apparently, the middle-class girl has the most freedom in sex-related behavior, at least for a while.

The class differences may reflect the greater tolerance and permissiveness in the application of sex-role standards that are likely with education, which increases with social class. The "masculine" activities engaged in by girls increase with educational level of the family. The class differences also may be reflecting the related fact that the sex-roles practiced by the parents are more distinct among lower- and working-class populations. Working-class men are more likely to have obviously masculine jobs involving heavy work and are less likely to perform caretaking activities and other domestic chores. The employed mother is likely to have a traditionally feminine job, such as housekeeper or laundress.

Among middle-class people, overlaps in the occupations and domestic activities of mothers and fathers are more typical. Both may be teachers or doctors. Both may handle finances, drive the car, do some grocery shopping, bathe the children, and help with the dishes.

Sex differences in acquiring sex-roles. The young boy must shift some of his attention from mother to masculine models. However, overall, the process of masculinization of boys is less complex and difficult than is feminization of girls. This seems to be because the male role is both more highly valued and better defined than is the female role in middle-class American culture (Mussen & Rutherford, 1963). Concomitant with the value and consistency of definition is greater censure for deviation in the male than in the female. Because of this, the little boy has an extra incentive to acquire and maintain sex-appropriate behavior. Tomboys have an easier time than sissies. A woman wearing a tailored pantsuit is more easily accepted than a man wearing a dress.

Because of the greater and more pervasive role clarity, the boy's parents have help in his sex-role socialization. The same-sex models he observes are likely to be more similar to each other than is true for girls. Other people's expectations of him and their reward for his behavior are also more consistent, because of the greater clarity and sharper definition of the set of sex-role expectations to which they respond in guiding their interaction with him.

As a result of the greater and clearer pressure, boys generally show earlier and sharper awareness of sex-role behavior than do girls (see Mussen, 1969; McCandless, 1967). Age trends for females are more variable and less clear-cut, but the overall picture suggests a marked resistance to developing a stable, complete feminization. Boys adopt sex-role-appropriate responses more quickly and show them more consistently than do girls. Among kindergartners, 75 percent of the boys preferred boys' toys to girls' toys, and 77 percent preferred the father's role to the mother's role; the percentages were in the 90's from the second grade on (Brown, 1957). While most little girls are well enough socialized that they are physically and psychologically recognizable as girls rather than boys, between the ages of three and ten they definitely prefer masculine games, activities, and objects. By the fifth grade, 37 percent of the girls still preferred masculine toys, and 21 percent preferred to be a father rather than a mother. The moderate preference for the conventional female role that had occurred earlier changed to a rejection of it in elementary school—four-year-old girls were more feminine than ten-year-old girls! (Brown, 1957; Hartup & Zook, 1960).

The rejection and variability of feminine behavior probably stem from the girls' recognition of the greater cultural value placed on males relative to females, the attractiveness and even necessity of behavior labeled masculine, and her growing realization of the relative ambiguity of the female role. Early in life, the mother is the main female model available to the girl. As the girl grows older, she observes—through reading, television, and direct observation—females in a variety of activities not engaged in by her mother, including activities which are either conventionally labeled masculine or at least not unanimously considered appropriate for females. The social system imposes more role strain on the girl than on the boy (Chapter 16). The girl is not as severely punished for sex-deviant behavior and interests as is her male counterpart, but neither are the numerous alternatives within the ambiguous female role so clearly rewarded. Even if she has female identity and preference, she may not know exactly how to direct it. How she comes to be relatively self-accepting remains a mystery.

The People Involved

Mother, father, and others. No one doubts the importance of the mother, or of the same-sex parent, as a socialization agent. However, there has been accumulating evidence of the importance of the opposite-sex parent and increased emphasis on the father as important for the sex-typing of *both* boys and girls (see, for example, Heilbrune, 1968). In fact, father may be *more* important than mother for sex-typed behavior in both sexes (Johnson, 1963). Mothers report less concern about their child's appropriate sex-typing than do fathers and less active involvement and conscious attempt to implement sex-typing of their children than do fathers (Goodenough, 1957). The expectations that are acted upon by the mother are more similar for boys and girls because so much of the mother's interaction with her children involves caretaking activities in which the child's sex is not relevant. Because of social pressures about the male role, masculinity is a more important personal construct to fathers than femininity is to mothers, and an area of concern about which there is greater cognitive complexity and polarization of attitudes (Chapter 13).

That the father contributes to sex-role socialization is most clearly seen in the effects of his absence. Generally, the absence of the father for long or short periods during a boy's early childhood decreases the boy's masculinity and his general social adjustment, with some of the effects persisting into adulthood (Hartup & Jonas, 1971). A frequent pattern is compensatory masculinity in the sons—the occurrence of intense, overly masculine behavior along with some femininity. It is as if the young boy knows that he is a boy and wants to adopt appropriate masculine behavior, but is not sure of himself and has few masculine responses in his repertoire, so that he overuses those he does have. (However, the absence of the father need not always retard the young boy's masculinization.)

It is also true that the father's masculinity, and his presence, can accentuate the girl's sex-typing (Hetherington, 1965, 1967, 1968; Mussen & Rutherford, 1963). Highly feminine girls were found to have more masculine fathers who urged them on in feminine activities than was true for the less feminine. The sex-typing of preschool and preadolescent girls was not disrupted by the absence of the father. However, girls with absent fathers did have deviant heterosexual patterns during adolescence (Hetherington, 1973). They showed either accelerated dating and sexually provocative behavior or, in contrast, were retarded in dating and very shy and anxious about heterosexual situations.

Emphasis on the parents should not detract from the contribution made by other children. Older siblings are particularly salient as models and as reinforcers for appropriate behavior. A younger child's interests and abilities vary with the sex of an older sibling, and the presence of an opposite-sex older sibling generally leads to interests and abilities more similar to the other sex than would otherwise occur (Rosenberg & Sutton-Smith, 1964). Peers use all the social pressures toward sex-role conformity that adults do and provide a social context in which the individual child observes and practices sex-appropriate responses. Play activities during middle childhood particularly are segregated by sex and often organized around sex-typed activities. Boys are building forts while girls are playing house and gossiping. Boys' activities emphasize mastery and competition, while the goal in girls' groups is affiliation and acceptance (see Ferguson, 1970). As discussed in Chapter 21, popularity with the peer group is positively related to the match of the individual with sex-role stereotypes.

What the people do. Sex-typed behavior and identity provide a particularly good illustration of the multitude of ways in which general societal norms guide social interactions and are transmitted and enforced through them. The people with whom the child, and later the adult, associates are models from whom he can extend the range of his acceptable behavior and learn by observation the details of sex-role content. Once the child labels himself sexually, he becomes more attentive and responsive to same-sex models, inside and outside the home.

Perhaps the most critical feature for the development and maintenance of appropriate sex-role identity and behavior is that other people have sex-related expectations for the individual. People direct their own behavior in part on the basis of what they expect of others and what they think others expect of them. Much behavior in interpersonal interactions is sex-role related, although it is so well learned and practiced that the central position of sex-roles often goes unnoticed. The set of expectations and perceptions held by other people helps to elicit appropriate sex-typed behavior and contribute to sex identity (Colley, 1959). Other people, peers and adults, tell the young boy by their own behavior that he is a male and is expected to behave like one, to respond to them as a male responds to another male or to a female, as the case may be (similarly for the female). Faced with the perception of him held by others, the boy comes to think of himself as a male (identity) and to behave like one. Other people encourage and reward the behavior that meets their expectations. Thus, the masculine father is an appropriate model for his son and one who interacts with his son on a male-to-male basis. He is also one who expects and rewards his daughter's femininity in interaction with males. With him, she may acquire and practice feminine social behavior. Thus, sufficient identification with father so that he is a salient and important figure for the girl as well as for the boy facilitates feminization. The absence of same-sex parents, or lack of strong identification with them if they are present, need not deter appropriate sex identity development if other models are available and if the opposite-sex parent is secure enough in his own identity to operate on the basis of it and encourage the appropriate behavior in the child. Women seem to relax encouragement of masculinity in their sons when the father is present, but when father is absent, maternal encouragement for masculinity in their sons is positively related to the child's sex-role orientation (Biller, 1969).

What is necessary for the development of appropriate sex-role behavior, and for a congruent preference and identity, is that the role be clear and that the child be rewarded for performing the role. This does not require identification with a same-sex parent; identification with both parents can promote appropriate identity and preference as well as behavior.

MORAL DEVELOPMENT

The psychologist's concept of moral behavior is much like the layman's and psychoanalyst's concept of conscience or moral character. Morality is inferred from a person's intrinsically motivated resistance to temptation and from his guilt feelings which follow acts of transgression when he understands and accepts prevailing standards of morality (Kohlberg, 1963a, 1964). Moral behavior is internally controlled rather than dependent upon monitoring by other people. The source of internal control may exist because of previous learning experiences in similar situations or because of a personal evaluative standard; that is, one may behave morally because of moral principle or because behavior labeled moral has been reinforced by other people or is expected to be. Fully developed morality implies behavior controlled by one's own principle. We will look first at the development of moral behavior and then at moral judgment.

The Behavior

By imitation and identification, children can and do acquire and practice stable moral responses without direct external reinforcement (Chapter 18). However, some forms of internal control over behavior are established by direct reinforcement and punishment of overt responses in ways that are not easily translated into modeling or cognitive concepts. Reinforcement mechanisms exercise a high degree of control over behavior, regardless of the complex cognitive events that may also occur.

Many of the phenomena of internalized control may be explained by relationships between responses and external events: reinforcement of a response increases the response strength. More interesting is the role of punishment, and the anxiety it presumably elicits, in the acquisition and maintenance of moral behavior.

Anxiety. Punishment can elicit an aversive affective state which may take various specific forms—guilt, fear, shame—but may be broadly considered anxiety. Anxiety seems to be involved in two mechanisms important in moral development (Aronfreed & Reber, 1965). First, anxiety comes to be elicited by the environmental cues and warning signals and also by the internal stimuli that have been associated with the punished act. The internal stimuli include those cues elicited by the response itself (response-produced stimuli), and the verbal representations of the act, such as intentions. Because internal cues become conditioned eliciters, anxiety is evoked before the forbidden act is carried out, when the child is only thinking of it or is just beginning to perform it (Figure 20–1a). Second, and complementary to the first, the reinforcement of anxiety avoidance or anxiety reduction accompanies responses other than the forbidden, previously punished one (Figure 20–1b). Thus, alternative responses which are not punished, and their internal correlates, acquire the instrumental value of anxiety avoidance. With continued operation of these mechanisms, suppression of the forbidden behavior and of thoughts of the behavior becomes automatic. The effectiveness of the punishment, which may be physical or verbal, in inducing

FIGURE 20–1

a. *Anxiety is attached to intrinsically produced stimuli.*

Forbidden act ⟶ Response-produced s ⟶ Anxiety (fear, guilt, shame)

Environmental cues, warning signals, cognitive representation of the act ⟶

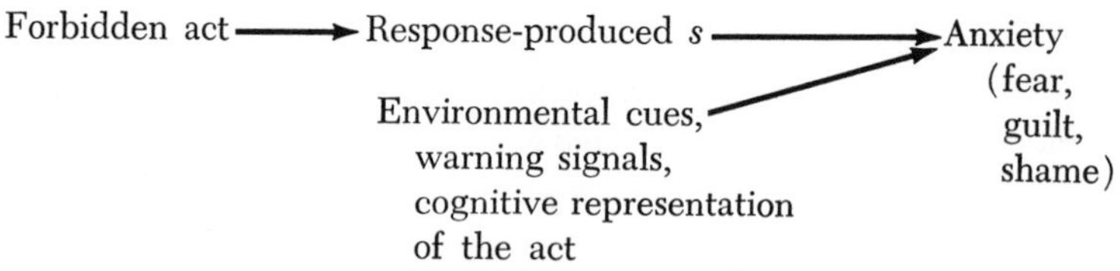

b. *Anxiety reduction is attached to intrinsically produced stimuli.*

Acts other than the forbidden one ⟶ Response-produced s ⟶ Anxiety avoidance and reduction

Cognitive correlates of response suppression ⟶

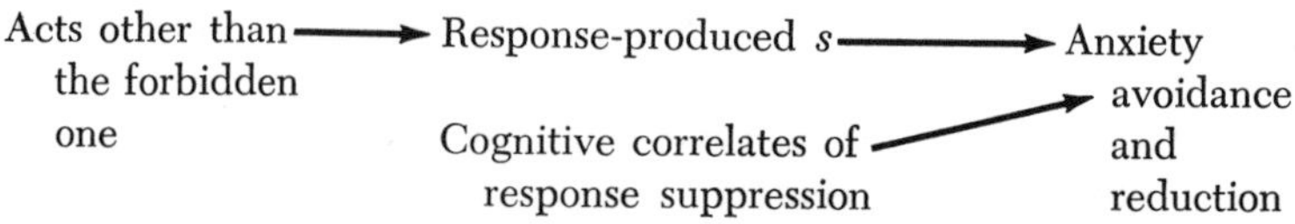

Anxiety and Intrinsic Stimuli.

Source: Adapted from Aronfreed & Reber, 1965.

anxiety will depend on the value of the punitive agent to the child and on the meaning attached to the punishment. Whether the immediate effect of punishment is resistance to temptation or guilt at transgression depends upon the timing of punishment and thus upon where in a behavior sequence punishment is given and where, therefore, anxiety is initially attached.

Punishment given at the start of a forbidden act is more effective in producing *resistance to temptation* than punishment given during or at the end of the act (Figure 20–2a). Further, simple instructions about what is forbidden are not always enough to suppress behavior that has otherwise attractive consequences. One sometimes has to learn by getting punished instead of merely being informed (Aronfreed & Reber, 1965). Fourth- and fifth-grade boys were trained to select the less attractive of two toys and not to touch a more attractive one. When they were left alone, only 26 percent (9 of 34) of the boys who had been verbally reproved as they had reached for the forbidden toy during training touched another attractive toy. Of those who had been reproved *after* they had picked up the forbidden toy, 71 percent (24 of 34) transgressed. Of the control group, who had only preliminary instruction not to select the attractive toy and no punishment if they did, 80 percent transgressed (16 of 20) in the absence of surveillance. Thus, the transgression had to be specifically punished, in this case by verbal reproval, to lead to internalized suppression.

On the other hand, punishment given *after* the completion of an act (Figure 20–2b), rather than at the beginning of it, is more effective in developing *guilt* reactions about committed transgressions—that is, self-criticism, reparation, apology, confession (Aronfreed, 1964). The experimenter punished some acts, called "blue acts," by verbally reproving the child and depriving him of candy. Children who had been told at the *offset* of a buzzer that they had been "blue" were more self-critical (labeled themselves "blue") than children who had been reproved with "blue" at the *onset* of the buzzer. The self-criticism appeared to be an anxiety-reducing instrumental response.

Thus, the characteristic patterns of the socialization agents in timing punishment affect whether the child will be more likely to learn resistance to temptation, or to feel guilt about a completed transgression. After a child has learned to feel guilt for his transgressions, he will probably learn fairly quickly to avoid guilt by resisting temptation, because the anxiety spreads backward (Levin & Fleischman, 1968). He will learn to resist temptation, but when he does succumb, he will feel guilty. However, if he has first learned to resist temptation, guilt about transgressions that do occur may be long in coming.

If the socialization of resistance to temptation could be complete, there would be little reason to be concerned about the presence or absence of guilt responses. However, temptations are numerous, new, and alluring. Transgression is likely when the temptation situation is markedly different from those previously encountered, there is uncertainty about

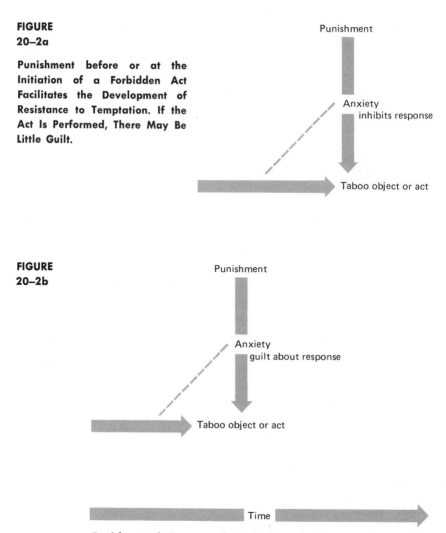

FIGURE 20–2a

Punishment before or at the Initiation of a Forbidden Act Facilitates the Development of Resistance to Temptation. If the Act Is Performed, There May Be Little Guilt.

Punishment

Anxiety inhibits response

Taboo object or act

FIGURE 20–2b

Punishment

Anxiety guilt about response

Taboo object or act

Time

Punishment during or at the End of a Forbidden Act Facilitates the Development of Guilt Responses after a Forbidden Act Has Been Performed.
The effect of anxiety may spread backward, so that resistance to temptation develops.

what is appropriate, or the forbidden act is highly attractive. The benevolent or malevolent effect of guilt as a possible condition of life is not entirely a matter for psychology. However, at least we may say that guilt often functions to calm the waters of social interaction troubled by transgression.

Guilt may prompt one to attempt to undo his wrong, do a victim the social courtesy of apology and explanation, or be self-critical, as others expect of him. People expect guilt and often temper their censure and condemnation when they see evidence of it: "At least he's sorry." One little boy supposedly escaped parental punishment for chopping down a cherry tree by his honest confession. Perhaps if his parents had shouted at him as he reached for the ax, today's children might be deprived of the exemplary model of the honest father of our country.

On the other hand, many people probably suffer guilt when it is not warranted, because they do not distinguish between situations in which they previously received punishment and the one they now face, or because their emotional responses do not "catch up" with the fact that as adults they do not consider the rules applied to them in childhood appropriate for them. Strong emotional responses are amazingly resistant to modification, and rules about how to behave do transfer inappropriately (Chapters 14, 15). Presumably, humans have the ability to make sophisticated distinctions between situations and to make moral judgments which vary with the situation. However, their anxiety often continues to reflect their prior training rather than their current, mature judgment.

The verbal and the social. The control of moral behavior by punishment does not rule out the contribution of other more sophisticated factors. Both cognitive labels and the nature of the relationship with the socializing adult may enhance or detract from the effectiveness of punishment. The extensive verbal mediation and reasoning used by parents is probably the component of socialization that most effectively leads to internalization of resistance to temptation (Aronfreed, 1969; Aronfreed & Reber, 1965; Hoffman, 1970). Verbal punishment and reasoning make it easier for the child's anxiety to be monitored by cognitive processes such as intentions and conceptual labels. The cognitive processes can bridge the separation of events. For example, when a verbal rationale is given to the child for the rule he is to obey, delayed punishment can be just as effective in inhibiting forbidden behavior as punishment given earlier (Aronfreed, 1965).

The degree of cognitive structure in the situation and the degree of control the child feels also affect guilt reactions to transgression (Aronfreed, 1963). Children who had been given the cognitive label, "Be careful," were most likely to criticize themselves when led to think they had been careless with a toy than did the subjects who had not been given the extra cognitive structuring of the label (Table 20–1). Subjects who had been given high control over the consequences of their transgression of breaking the toy (deciding how many Tootsie Rolls they should lose) were more likely to make suggestions for repairing the toy than were those whose consequences were under the exclusive control of the experimenter. Notice that the two indices of guilt, self-criticism and reparation, had different antecedents.

Naturalistic evidence also indicates the effectiveness of verbal techniques. Mothers' reports of using reasoning techniques were positively correlated with a global measure of conscience in their children (Sears, Maccoby, & Levin, 1957). Middle-class parents are likely to use reasoning and explanation rather than direct punishment alone, and they are responsive to signs of internal control in their children. The methods of

TABLE 20–1   Frequency of Self-Critical and Reparative Responses under Four Conditions of Cognitive Structure

TYPE OF RESPONSE	HIGH COGNITIVE STRUCTURE		LOW COGNITIVE STRUCTURE	
	HIGH CONTROL	LOW CONTROL	HIGH CONTROL	LOW CONTROL
Self-criticism				
Present	11	10	5	4
Absent	6	7	12	13
Reparation				
Present	14	4	10	6
Absent	3	13	7	11

N = 7 in each experimental group. Frequencies represent number of subjects who show any instance (one or more) of a given response and number of subjects who show no evidence of the response.
SOURCE: From Aronfreed, J. The effects of experimental socialization paradigms upon two moral responses to transgression. *Journal of Abnormal and Social Psychology*, 1963, 66 (5), 437–448.

working-class parents are more direct and less verbal; they react more to the visible consequences of the act and sensitize their children to threat of punishment. In turn, middle-class children show more *internal* controls of their behavior and report guilt for deviations, while working-class children show an external orientation and relative absence of guilt.

Positive value of the teaching agent usually increases the effectiveness of that person's approval as a reward and of his disapproval as an anxiety-eliciting punishment. In fact, it has been suggested that the effectiveness of punishment lies in the withdrawal of approval it implies (Walters & Parke, 1968). And the value of reinstatement of approval or love varies with the value of the teacher. However, some reinforcement and punishment procedures are more effective than others and can enhance the effectiveness of the teacher. Self-criticism was most likely when a child had previously had a rewarding interaction with an adult teacher, and the punishment for a violation in the experimental game was withdrawal of love which was reinstated as soon as the child criticized himself (Grusec, 1966). Delayed reinstatement (the teacher's response not immediately contingent upon the child's self-criticism), diminished the effectiveness of withdrawal of love as a punishment. The least effective technique was withdrawal of love by a model with whom the child had had a low-rewarding interaction, and the love was not reinstated until some time after the child had been self-critical. In this situation, punishment as withdrawal of a material reward was not affected by the rewardingness of the model or the model's response contingency. Thus, the value of the relationship with the training agent, the method of punishment, and the timing of reinstatement of reward all influence the occurrence of the guilt reaction of self-criticism.

The nonunitary conscience: ego. Both Freudian theory and conventional thought suggest that moral behavior is controlled by the conscience, a superego component. One knows right from wrong and therefore acts accordingly—internalized principles guide behavior. There is some kernel of truth in this view, but by and large it is a simpleminded one. As we have seen, two chief manifestations of "conscience"—resistance to temptation and guilt—have different antecedents in punishment timing and different patterns of accompanying emotional reactions. Confession, apology, self-criticism, reparation—all presumably observable responses accompanying guilt—are not necessarily highly correlated, and each occurs *without* evidence of internal self-evaluation of processes (Aronfreed, 1961, 1969; Kohlberg, 1963; Hoffman, 1970).

The moral behavior of the child indicates an external orientation rather than an internal one and often is initiated by the demands of others or the anticipation of avoiding disapproval. Although some relationship comes to develop between indices of conscience in middle childhood, the unity of moral behavior is popularly overestimated. For example, honesty is not consistent across situations, but is heavily influenced by the nature of the situation (Hartshorne & May, 1928; see Hartup & Jonas, 1971). The individual makes a decision in a particular situation. The decision-making is an *ego* function; indices of moral character are more indicative of ego strength than of superego strength (Kohlberg, 1963, 1964, 1969). Both individual and situational factors affect the decision. Individual ego factors include intelligence, anticipation of future events, control over fantasy, capacity for delayed reward, self-esteem, and attention level. Situational factors include risk of detection, attractiveness of the incentive, the effort required to cheat, and the level of interest of the task.

Any situation may have different effects on the behavior of different individuals. For example, sixth-grade boys were classed as preferring a delayed, larger reward—$.30 a week later—or an immediate, smaller one—$.15 right away (Mischel & Gilligan, 1964). When placed in a rigged shooting gallery game, those who preferred the delayed but larger gratification cheated much less in reporting their scores to win a prize than did those who preferred the immediate but smaller reward. And cheating was influenced by the relevance of the incentive to the subject's motivation. Boys who had achievement imagery in TAT stories falsified their scores as being high enough to merit an achievement reward for marksmanship more than did boys without achievement imagery (Table 20–2).

Perhaps the underlying factor basic to cheating is attention, which varies with individual predispositions and the situation (Grim, Kohlberg, & White, 1968). Cheating often results from not maintaining attention to the task at hand. Stability of attention to the task promotes honesty because of a higher threshold for distracting thoughts about the possible benefits of cheating or about the greater interest of cheating activities—cheating can shortcut a monotonous task. The importance of

TABLE 20–2 Relation between Achievement Motivation and Cheating to Obtain Achievement Rewards

Number of subjects reporting scores:	ACHIEVEMENT MOTIVATION IMAGERY	
	Absent	Present
Falsified high enough to get reward	14	15
Not falsified enough to get reward	3	16

Chi square = 5.29, p = .05.
SOURCE: From Mischel & Gilligan, 1964.

attentional factors probably decreases as moral values become more mature and stable and the situation more structured. However, distractibility probably increases cheating even in adulthood. Are you more likely to cheat on a boring assignment or an interesting one? When the task is interesting, concern about your grade or awareness of the opportunities for cheating are not attended to. Your honesty is not the result of a moral decision alone, but is at least partly the result of the direction and stability of attention. When the rational, problem-solving, perceiving ego is hard at work, questions of morality are irrelevant.

Internal moral values do develop, but they occur relatively late compared to the moral behavior that develops from external rewards and punishments. The development of moral standards of evaluation is a particular area of concern of cognitive theories of moral judgment, notably those of Piaget and Kohlberg.

Moral Judgment

Piaget and Kohlberg. One of Piaget's techniques for studying the moral judgment aspect of cognitive development was to present the child with a pair of stories in which the nature of the content is the same, but the motivation, intention, and consequences vary. For example, a child in a story steals a pretty ribbon for a dress or steals a roll for a hungry friend. The subject judges which story character is the naughtiest and why, the likelihood of punishment, the appropriate punishment, etc. Responses are used to infer what stage the child has reached in developmental maturity of moral judgments rather than whether he is moral or not. Maturity is defined in terms of the age sequence of the appearance of methods of judgment. (Piaget, 1948).

Piaget hypothesizes three main stages of moral development. At first the child automatically obeys adults' rules without reasoning; judgment is *heteronomous*, dependent upon external standards and mores. Moral rules are seen as absolute, and violation of them invariably brings punishment by human or supernatural forces. This is a stage of *moral realism* in which the content and severity of the punishment vary with the objective consequences of the act, regardless of the motive for the act.

Between the age of six or seven and adolescence, there is a stage of *transition* during which the trend is away from the stage of moral realism to the third stage, one of *moral relativism*. The child gains the cognitive capacities to take the role of others, to appreciate their motives and intentions. Rules are seen as manmade, capable of being changed, and instrumental in maintaining social order rather than based on universal absolutes. The young person's judgments become *autonomous* as he develops his own law based on an increasing awareness of the needs of social cooperation, respect for the viewpoint of others, and the realities of social situations. While Freud maintained that the superego is acquired from others, Piaget hypothesizes that autonomous morality results from the child's *spontaneous* efforts to organize a moral code. In making moral judgments, the child no longer appeals to an externally enforced absolute law but to internal and self-generated concepts of mutual respect and equity in which circumstances of the behavior are taken into account in evaluating the behavior and recommending punishments. The *intent* behind an act is evaluated, not just the consequences of the act.

Thus, the immature pole of intentionality is objectivity, judging an act bad because of the objective, physical damage done. The mature pole is subjectivity, judging an act on the basis of the subjective intention of the agent. Piaget's efforts have been judged as the single greatest influence in the psychological study of moral values. His basic methods are continually used and his general hypotheses find a wide base of general support, particularly those which primarily reflect cognitive development (see Bronfenbrenner, 1962; Hoffman, 1963; Levin & Fleischman, 1968; Pittel & Mendelsohn, 1966).

Kohlberg (1963a, 1963b, 1964, 1969) elaborated Piaget's theory to postulate and demonstrate moral development as a continuing process more complex than Piaget theorized. Using Piaget's procedures with ten- to sixteen-year-old boys, he identified three major levels, each with two types (Table 20–3). Each stage of thought depends upon the attainment of a preceding stage and then the restructuring and displacement of it, as shown by age trends across subjects (Figure 20–3) and by patternings within individuals. If the level of judgment is mainly at one stage of thought, the rest of the boy's thinking would be at stages immediately above and below that stage. Displacement of former stages is shown by the fact that children will accept moral reasoning at a *higher* stage than their own current one more readily than reasoning at a lower stage. Maturity of moral judgment is correlated with intelligence but is related to age even when intelligence is statistically controlled.

The principles evolved at each stage are spontaneous products of the child, and not just learned patterns of verbalization. When one boy was asked whether it was better to save one important person or lots of unimportant people, he indicated that preference should be given to lots

TABLE 20–3 Kohlberg's Stages of Moral Development, with Definitions for the Aspect of Motivation for Moral Action

---

LEVEL I. PREMORAL

Type 1. Punishment and obedience orientation

Obey rules to avoid punishment.

Age 10: (Should Joe tell on his older brother to his father?) "In one way it would be right to tell on his brother or his father might get mad at him and spank him. In another way it would be right to keep quiet or his brother might beat him up."

Type 2. Naive instrumental hedonism

Conform to obtain rewards, have favors returned.

Age 13: (Should Joe tell on his older brother to his father?) "I think he should keep quiet. He might want to go someplace like that, and if he squeals on Alex, Alex might squeal on him."

LEVEL II. MORALITY OF CONVENTIONAL ROLE-CONFORMITY

Type 3. Good-boy morality of maintaining good relations, approval of others

---

Conform to avoid disapproval, dislike by others.

Age 16: (Should Joe keep quiet about what his brother did?) "If my father finds out later, he won't trust me. My brother wouldn't either, but I wouldn't have a conscience that he (my brother) didn't."

Type 4. Authority-maintaining morality

Conform to avoid censure by legitimate authorities and resultant guilt.

LEVEL III. MORALITY OF SELF-ACCEPTED MORAL PRINCIPLES

Type 5. Morality of contract, of individual rights, and of democratically accepted law

---

Conform to maintain the respect of the impartial spectator judging in terms of community welfare.

Type 6. Morality of individual principles of conscience

Conform to avoid self-condemnation.

Age 16: (Should the husband steal the expensive black-market drug needed to save his wife's life?) "Lawfully no, but morally speaking I think I would have done it. It would be awfully hard to live with myself afterward, knowing that I could have done something which would have saved her life and yet didn't for fear of punishment to myself."

SOURCE: From Kohlberg, 1964, pp. 400–401.

of people: ". . . a whole bunch of people have an awful lot of furniture. . . ." Kohlberg suggests that the boy's concern with furniture probably reflects his parents' concern, but deriving the value of life from furniture is a spontaneous product of the boy himself.

DEVELOPMENT OF PERSONALITY

**FIGURE
20–3**

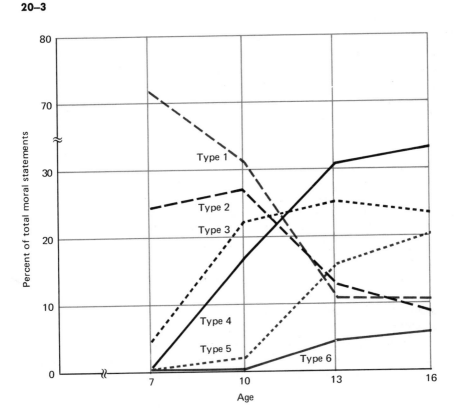

Development of Moral Character.

Mean percent of total moral statements of each of six moral judgment types at four ages.

Source: Kohlberg, L. Development of moral character and moral ideology. In M. F. Hoffman & L. W. Hoffman (Eds.), *Review of child development research.* New York: Russell Sage Foundation. Pp. 383–431.

Social influences in the developmental trend. Exactly how values develop and control behavior is not clear. It appears that the child evolves for himself abstractions and generalizations based upon what he observes and knows about himself and other people. Both Piaget and Kohlberg imply that the emergence of the moral stages is a product of the child's interactions with other people, including peers, rather than the automatic unfolding of neural structures. However, the child does not simply adopt the values of others; he operates on those values in his own way, as shown by the boy who equated furniture with the value of life. He relates the social values expressed by others to his own goals and thus incorporates them and makes them his own. The kind of mental operations he can perform on the information he has varies with age.

Specific social factors may stimulate or retard the age trends of development, but do not seem to cause the trends (Kohlberg, 1964, 1969).

The developmental sequence occurs in Western cultures regardless of nationality (Swiss, English, Belgian, Spanish, American), social class, religion, or the parental use of physical punishment. Middle-class and working-class children in the United States both move through the sequences, although middle-class children move farther and faster; the class differences in moral judgments do not seem to reflect differences in the content of cultural values or beliefs. Thus the development of maturity in moral judgments results from both social experiences and maturational factors.

The contribution of both social experiences and developmental readiness is shown in a study of social influence among junior high school students (Le Furgy & Woloshin, 1969). Students about thirteen years old who had been assessed as realistic or relativistic in their judgments were placed in a conformity situation (Crutchfield situation, Chapter 17) in which they thought that their peers were making the opposite kinds of judgment; control subjects did not hear the supposed responses of others. Those who were initially relativistic showed changes in the direction of social influence, to the lower stage of realism, at an immediate and a one-week post-test, but the effects had dissipated after 100 days so that the final change was essentially zero. However, the movement from the original position of the realistic subjects in the direction of social influence to the more advanced stage of relativism was not diminished over 100 days. Social influence pressures have long-lasting effects only if the pressures are in the direction of developmental *advancement*, not if they are in the direction of developmental regression.

SUMMARY

The development of social responsiveness in the areas of aggression, dependency, sex-role identity, and moral behavior and judgment is a critical socialization task. Although socialization requirements extend far beyond those regulating the selected behavior systems discussed in this chapter, adequate socialization in these particular areas is necessary if a person is to relate effectively to others and be in harmony with himself. The person who is aggressive, overly dependent, lacking appropriate sex-role identity, or unable to make mature moral judgments is likely to be uncomfortable. The ability to behave appropriately in these respects is an interpersonal skill with developmental antecedents in interactions with parental figures, complemented later by peer pressures and the internalization of cultural norms containing prescriptions about behavior.

The occurrence or nonoccurrence of aggressive responses is contingent upon a complex interaction of biological predispositions and early learning experiences. The role of frustration in eliciting aggression illustrates both the innate and learning components of human aggression. Sex differences and situational determinants are important variables which affect the occurrence of aggressive responses. Dependency, like aggression, has antecedents in both biological components (of the basic attachment response for dependency) and early interactions with parental figures. Parental nurturance is the central variable in the socialization of dependency. Excessive dependency in later years occurs when parents are overprotective.

A major socialization task for a child in contemporary American society is to achieve an appropriate sex-role identity. While there is abundant evidence supporting the importance of the mother and the same-sex parent as socialization agents, increasing emphasis is being placed on the father as an important influence in the sex typing of both boys and girls. Sex-typed behavior and identity provide a particularly good example of the ways in which general societal expectations guide social interactions. The sex-role related expectations others hold for the individual contribute greatly to the development and maintenance of appropriate sex-role behavior, and, hopefully but not necessarily of congruent sex-role identity and preference.

Moral development, like the other behavior systems discussed in this chapter, begins at home. Parents initially control the development of stable moral responses through external rewards and punishment, and through extensive verbal mediation and reasoning. The way in which the child then develops his own set of moral standards is not entirely clear. In part, the emergence of mature moral judgment is a product of a child's interaction with other people, including peers. In part, it is contingent on maturational factors. Thus, the development of maturity in moral judgments results from both social experiences and developmental readiness.

Adequate socialization in the areas of aggression, dependency, sex-role identity, and moral development implies the internalization of socially shared interpretations of behavior as well as the acquisition of appropriate responses. If socialization agents have done their job well, the individual will generally behave in ways others consider appropriate and will feel comfortable with himself. However, to behave consistently appropriately and to be consistently comfortable with one's behavior is an idealized goal few, if any, can attain. In view of the rigidity, and often the inconsistency and unreasonableness, of some normative standards and of the tremendous variety among people—who they are and who they want to be—this is little wonder. The extent to which a person can cope with his inhibitions, anxiety, and discomfort, and manage to achieve feelings of freedom, comfort, and personal centeredness is itself an index of socialization adequacy and of personal adequacy reflecting mechanisms that we do not yet understand well.

Thus, socialization requirements embrace all facets of continual personality development and all requirements relevant to becoming adjusted and comfortable with oneself and with others. In Chapter 21 we will look at social relationships, which are themselves a socialization requirement and a source of socialization, and at sexuality, which poses socialization demands and reflects the appropriateness or inappropriateness of attempts to meet previous socialization tasks.

21

development through the life span

In this chapter, we shall use interpersonal relations and sexuality as topics with which to illustrate the continual development of personality, and the participation of biological factors in that development as the individual human being grows in a social environment. There are, of course, other facets to personality development and many ways in which biological maturation and processes influence the course of personality development and functioning. However, these seem appropriate topics because of the extent to which social relations influence the course of life.

To a great extent, personality development is affected by a person's relationships with other people. In turn, his relationships with others are shaped by who he is. The physical development of the organism places limits on how he can interact with the animate and inanimate world, predisposes him to act in certain ways, and influences how others will react to him. External appearance and internal physiological processes must be accepted, understood, and incorporated into one's view of self.

Along with physical development goes psychological development, which, hopefully, prepares one to accept the changing societal expectations accompanying development from infancy to old age. Patterns of attachment to other people vary in terms of the targets of the attachment, the reasons for the attachment, and the stability of the attachment. The attachment pattern reflects an individual's level of cognitive maturity, his interests and personality needs as they develop, and his prior socialization, as seen particularly in terms of differences between the sexes. Some of the important attachments made in life are sexual ones. The nature of specifically sexual attachments is influenced by previous and other current social relations. Attachment patterns, sexual and nonsexual, are often forced on one by the expectations of others. Nevertheless, the individual—biological and psychological being that he is—must find himself and negotiate himself within the social system in which others too are attempting to find themselves. In this search for self-identity, the potential is present for communicating with and benefiting from the presence of others.

SOCIAL RELATIONSHIPS

As the normal individual progresses from infancy to his final years, other people are major targets of attention, major sources of satisfaction, and often major sources of frustration and anxiety. Early socialization efforts are designed largely to enable the individual to live in peace and enjoyment with others, to have a mature dependency upon them for emotional and instrumental purposes (Chapter 20). The development and maintenance of meaningful contacts with others is itself a socialization task, and one which presupposes the mastery of others. Unfortunately, the social system does not always provide adequate conditions for easy or full development and expression of the individual as a social and sexual being attempting to find himself in the interpersonal matrix within which he lives.

Childhood

Friendships. Peer relations assume an increasingly important role in determining the content of the growing child's activities and in providing information about himself and the world (Campbell, 1964; Ferguson, 1970). Within the peer group the child practices interpersonal skills and begins forming attachments with friends. The nature of interpersonal interaction changes from the *parallel play* typical of three-year-olds, who seem to enjoy being with each other but generally pursue separate activities, to cooperative activity in middle childhood. However, before preadolescence, there is little emotional investment in friendship, perhaps because capacities for empathy and appreciation of the rights of others are not sufficiently mature. Choice of friendship is largely a matter of ease of association due to physical availability and similarity of interests. Because of the rapid fluctuations of interests and needs, friendships are relatively unstable. By the sixth grade, personal characteristics such as friendliness and cheerfulness have become important in selection of friends (Austin & Thompson, 1948), but there is a strong tendency for friends to be selected on the basis of similarity in intelligence, socioeconomic status, race, ethnic subculture, and sex.

During preadolescence, the increased capacity to understand the feelings of others and the social skills developed earlier allow more meaningful and stable friendships, which appear to be the first real occurrence of interpersonal intimacy, or love (Sullivan, 1953; Douvan & Adelson, 1966; Strommen, 1973). The intense friendship is almost exclusively with members of one's own sex, but is typically preparatory to the establishment of heterosexual rather than homosexual intimacy. Self-exploration and acquisition of a sense of personal identity are more likely to occur in interaction with a same-sex friend than with an opposite-sex friend.

Peer group functions. When parents are absent, there may be unusually intense attachment to the peer group (A. Freud & Dann, 1951). German-Jewish orphans lived together in a concentration camp during World War II from the time they were a few months old. When they were taken to an English country house between three and four years of age, they did not, during a year's time, form any close ties with adults. The attachment usually directed toward mothers and other adults was directed toward each other. Completely lacking were the jealousy, rivalry, and competition that are typical among siblings or peers from normal families.

More typically, attachments to the family continue to be the most important ones, but peer group identification contributes to modifications in those attachments and enables the child to work safely toward autonomy and emancipation from the parents. The child's peers supply both support and pressure. Identification with peers allows enough security for the child to risk the moderate parental rejection that may accompany each small step in his development to independence. From his peers, he gets pressure to stick to the timetable used by age mates of the same sex—or, more simply, to grow. The child who is clinging to parental restrictions against venturing to the movies with other children is pressured by his friends and thus pressures his parents until a concession is made: "He has thus taken one more step toward autonomy as a result of the combined coercion and support received from the peers with whom he identifies" (Johnson & Medinnus, 1965, p. 332). From acceptance by the peer group, the child also gains increased self-esteem, greater realism about groups and other people, and the opportunity to practice social skills.

The peer group is in many ways a microcosm of society at large, in which cultural norms are transmitted, pressures for conformity exerted, and conforming behavior practiced and rewarded (Chapters 17 and 18). However, it is also a distinct subculture, with rituals and rules of its own. Because of its relative separation from the world of adults, particularly the child's own family, the child must "go it on his own." In the typical family, the child is accepted without any particular effort on his part, and is viewed and reacted to as a child. In the peer culture, he is evaluated as a person. He is expected to learn the rules of the game practiced by the group and is evaluated on the basis of what he can contribute to the group and how enjoyable he is to have around. He has to learn to get along with people other than his parents and siblings.

Adolescence

Physical maturation. Adolescence is both a physical and a social phenomenon. Although the period of adolescence cannot be precisely defined, it is generally regarded as the time between the onset of puberty and the attainment of adult status. The onset of puberty in girls is marked by the beginning of menstruation (the menarche), at around age thirteen for American girls (Kinsey et al., 1953). Puberty in boys is defined as beginning with the appearance of pigmented pubic hair (Tanner, 1955) or at the slightly later time of the first ejaculation (Kinsey et al., 1948), both typically occurring at age thirteen or fourteen. During puberty there is rapid acceleration in skeletal and muscular growth, extensive hormonal changes, changes in body and facial proportions, and less obvious internal changes in fatty tissue, heart rate, and lymphoid activities (Figure 21–1). These external and internal body changes must be interpreted and integrated into one's image of himself, a large adjustment demand, considering their number and scope. The job is unnecessarily intensified by

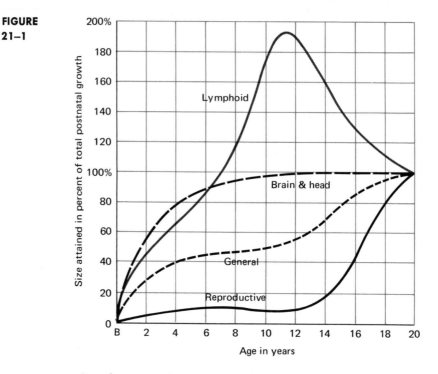

FIGURE 21–1

Growth Curves of Four Different Parts and Tissues of the Body. All the curves are of size attained (in percent of the total gain from birth to maturity) and plotted so that size at age 20 is 100 on the vertical scale.

Lymphoid type: thymus, lymph nodes, intestinal lymph masses.
Brain and head type: brain and its parts, dura, spinal cord, optic apparatus, head dimensions.
General type: body as a whole, external dimensions (except head), respiratory and digestive organs, kidneys, aortic and pulmonary trunks, musculature, blood volume.
Reproductive type: testis, ovary, epididymis, prostate, seminal vesicles, Fallopian tubes.
Source: Tanner, J. M. *Growth at adolescence.* Oxford: Blackwell Scientific Publications, 1955. Suggested by Scammon, R. E., 1930.

both adults and peers who increase the adolescent's self-consciousness and evaluate him against standards of physical appearance and capabilities. An adolescent who deviates markedly from cultural ideals is likely to have to cope with feelings of inadequacy and with his body as a source of dissatisfaction (Chapter 12). The acceptance of cultural norms demanding physical prowess in boys and attractiveness in girls is shown in the teenagers' concern with body appearance. Physical characteristics have been cited more often than intellectual or social characteristics as what teenagers most like or would prefer to change about themselves (see Mussen, Conger, & Kagan, 1969).

Although the physical changes are convenient, gross landmarks of adolescence, it is the cultural response to the changes which gives them the ambiguous significance and creates the social phenomena of adolescence (Eisenberg, 1965). The storm and stress we have come to expect in adolescence is not a necessary concomitant of physical changes and is not expected in all cultures. In some societies, puberty is immediately followed by rituals which confer adult status. In Western cultures, recognition as an adult is prolonged, and the adolescent has to work into adulthood by means not always clear either to him or to his parents. Adolescence is a time of indeterminant status whose termination is ambiguous because there is no single criterion by which the adolescent and others can know that he is perceived as an adult (Stone & Church, 1957). Consider the variation in the legal ages required for marriage, driving, voting, buying alcohol, military draft. Small wonder the adolescent has ambiguous views of himself and is sometimes in conflict with the "system" which forces the ambiguity on him. Although a time of apprenticeship seems necessary for preparation for the complexities of adult life, it is not clear that the procedures currently followed are the most efficient ones for helping a child transform himself into an adult.

Individual differences in maturation rate take on added impact during adolescence because of the importance attached to physical appearance by adolescents and adults alike. Early-maturing boys have advantages in social relations during adolescence, some of which persist into adulthood (Jones & Bayley, 1950). The early maturers, who were of the same chronological age but about two years ahead of the late maturers in skeletal growth, were rated superior in physical attractiveness and good grooming, and tended to be well built, muscular, and athletic. They were considered by adults and peers as more mature than the average and were easily accorded status. Late maturers were relatively unattractive, slender, poorly muscled (Figure 21–2a). They had many forms of relatively immature behavior and seemed to need to compensate for their relative immaturity by seeking attention. They were relatively uninhibited, though tense, in social situations (Figure 21–2b), and tended to be considered by peers as restless, talkative and bossy, less grown-up, and less good looking. Some of the late maturers attained some personal security and status which balanced their temporary physical inadequacies, and some early maturers had disturbing accompaniments of rapid growth

FIGURE
21–2a

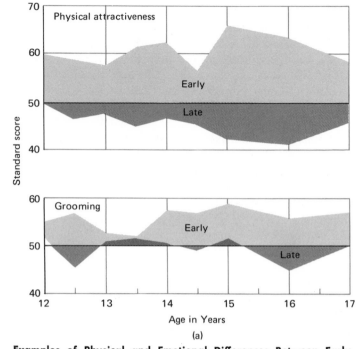

Examples of Physical and Emotional Differences Between Early- and Late-Maturing Adolescent Boys.
Mean standard scores for early- and late-maturing groups, in physical appearance.

(e.g., severe acne) which offset other advantages. However, overall, the early maturers were much more likely to achieve and maintain the kind of prestige given to athletes and office holders. When the subjects were studied again at about age thirty-three, differences in physical characteristics were slight, while some psychological differences persisted. Early maturers presented a consistently favorable picture on social variables (on the CPI, Chapter 7) such as making a good impression, socialization, dominance, self-control, and responsibility, though the differences from the late maturers were not great. Late maturers still tended to strive for attention, were impulsive, and had a greater need for succorance. There was also some indication that more of the early maturers than the later ones had attained satisfying and status-conferring vocational goals. Better physique and greater strength may fairly directly determine competence in some activities. However, some of the effect of maturation rates is likely due to the fact that a more mature appearance encourages the expectation, in adults and peers alike, of more mature behavior, which in turn may stimulate more mature efforts and accelerate psychological growth.

The effect of maturation rate is more variable in girls than in boys. The social implications of developmental stage vary with the age and values of other girls (Faust, 1960). In the sixth grade, being prepuberal meant being in phase with the rest of the girls and was a social asset, as seen in peer ratings of prestige-related traits. However, in the seventh grade, most girls were puberal and began to value those who were developmentally ahead of them. As the average girl advanced into a postpuberal stage, girls in the late adolescent stage of physical development were given most prestige. The prestige of the prepuberal girls consistently declined; being physically immature became increasingly undesirable (Figure 21–3).

Family relations. In the intense period of adolescence, relationships with parents have to be negotiated, friendships become more intense, and heterosexual adjustment becomes a major hurdle. The adolescent apparently recognizes the necessity and desirability of breaking and remolding the ties that formerly bound him to his family, yet he is in need of the support of other people. He seeks autonomy and his own identity, but an identity and autonomy which are legitimized by a realistic contact with the norms of relevant social groups. Peers, who are also attempting to cope with rapidly changing bodies and social perspectives, are a relevant comparison group which provides information and emotional support in the struggle for autonomy.

It has been a popular theme that the adolescent's search for autonomy

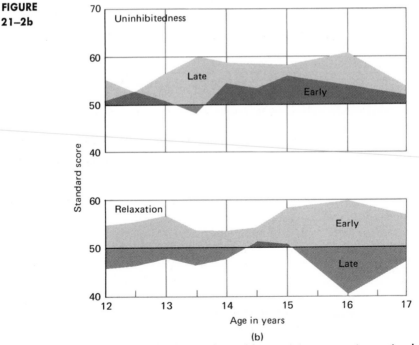

FIGURE 21–2b

Mean standard scores of early- and late-maturing groups, in emotional patterning.

Source: From Jones, M. C., & Bayley, N. Physical maturation among boys as related to behavior. *Journal of Educational Psychology,* 1950, 41, 129–148.

**FIGURE
21–3**

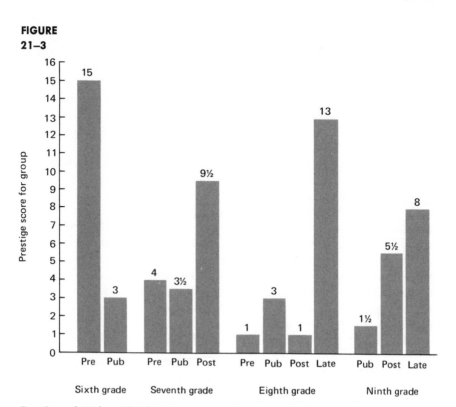

Prestige of Girls with Their Peers as a Function of Their Developmental Level and Grade.

Developmental Levels:

Pre   Prepuberal: Had not yet reached menarche at time of study.

Pub   Puberal: Had reached menarche within a year of time of study.

Post   Postpuberal: Had reached menarche more than one year, less than three years prior to study.

Late   Late adolescent: Had reached menarche three years or more prior to study.

Source: Faust, M. S. Developmental maturity as a determinant in prestige of adolescent girls. Child Development, 1960, 31, 173–184.

is a struggle of dominance, self-definition, and integrity which he can win only by rebellion and flight into his own culture. Research findings do *not* support such a view (Douvan & Gold, 1964). Apparent support of the idea seems due to highly visible but atypical groups such as delinquents and the introspective upper-middle-class adolescents who seek professional help. "In large-scale studies of normal populations, we do not find adolescents clamoring for freedom or for release from unjust constraint. We do not find rebellious resistance to authority as a dominant theme" (Douvan & Gold, 1964, p. 485).

Behavioral autonomy does increase sharply during adolescence, but is not paralleled by an equally dramatic increase in emotional autonomy (Douvan & Adelson, 1966). Compared to preadolescent years, there is an increase in the percentage of both boys and girls who date, have jobs outside the home, have independent financial support, and spend leisure time with nonfamily members. However, the emotional detachment from the family is a modest one and behavioral independence is achieved before the emotional independence and the associated independence of morals and values. Girls particularly are encouraged to cling to emotional ties with parents.

The important conditions that encourage effective autonomy and self-direction in adolescents are parental warmth and concern, democratic control, and consideration and consistency in rule enforcement (Bronfenbrenner, 1961; Elder, 1962, 1963, 1965). With democratic control, the children are involved with their parents in an interchange of reasoning and decision making. This provides the opportunity to learn skills of responsible independence and the training in self-reliance that are essential for the successful development of competent autonomy. Children of very autocratic or very lenient parents are likely to be low in self-confidence and either rebellious or dependent (Douvan & Adelson, 1966; Elder, 1962). In the autocratic situation, there is no opportunity for the child to express his opinions or show initiative in self-direction; he is told what to do, usually without reasons or explanations, and may receive harsh punishment for deviation from parental dictums. In the face of this treatment, he rebels, often with strong underlying feelings of dependency (Chapter 20). If parents are excessively lenient, permissive, or negligent, it is as if the child were cast out to make decisions before he is ready to; he must venture out into the world on his own without a firm base of emotional support and without the benefit of whatever wisdom the parents could provide to help him make his own decisions.

Peer acceptance. Although adolescents do seek the advice of their parents about important decisions, the values and norms of the peer group are felt in everyday matters. Adolescents of various social classes differ in many ways, but they are much alike in a desire for popularity and a need to conform to the peer group (Remmers & Radler, 1957; Douvan & Adelson, 1966). During childhood, the child more or less accepts himself as he is, as popular or unpopular. As he enters adolescence, he becomes conscious of himself as a social stimulus and eager to develop friendships and change himself to make good on the social scene. Adolescents who are not part of the "leading crowd" typically know it, and frequently wish they were (Coleman, 1961). Acceptance and popularity in a group is easier if one is a member of the culturally dominant majority in terms of ethnic groups and social class; members of minorities are less likely to be accepted by the majority *or* by other minority group members (see Mussen, Conger, & Kagan, 1969). Conformity to sex-role standards is expected and rewarded. Popular boys are more masculine, popular girls are more feminine, than the less popular (e.g., Tuddenham, 1952). Conformity is also expected to the group norms that develop concerning appearance and behavior. The distinctive dress, special language, and fads that appear bizarre to the adult eye and fall heavily on the adult ear are distinctive expressions which contribute to group identity and solidarity; conformity to them heightens feelings of group belongingness and acceptance (Chapter 16).

The personal characteristics typical of the adolescent who is likely to be accepted by his peers read much like the caricature of the "all-American." He is viewed by his peers as liking others, being tolerant, flexible, sympathetic, lively, cheerful, good-natured, having a sense of humor, acting naturally and with self-confidence but without conceit, and having initiative, enthusiasm, drive, and plans for group activities. Adolescents favored by others "tend to be those who contribute to others—by making them feel accepted and involved, by promoting constructive interaction with peers, or by planning and initiating interesting or enjoyable group activities" (Mussen, Conger, & Kagan, 1969, p. 663). An adult with such characteristics would probably not find himself unpopular; adolescents and adults do not live in completely different worlds. The unpopular person may get caught in a vicious circle. Peer group rejection because of lack of self-confidence lowers his already low self-esteem, which makes it likely that he will continue to be rejected.

Friendship. Attachment to particular people rather than the group as a whole also becomes intensified, and adolescence is a critical time in the development of the capacity for intimate friendships. Between the ages of about eleven and eighteen, the nature of friendship changes from a parallel partnership centered around a common activity to a mutual emotional relationship valued in and of itself. The mere sharing of activities is displaced by an emotional interdependence in which the personality of the other and the other's response to self are central themes (Douvan & Gold, 1966; Douvan & Adelson, 1966). Thus, friendships become more stable (Figure 21–4).

Sex differences in prior socialization experiences become apparent in the pattern of social relations of adolescents. Girls tend to be more advanced in interpersonal development than boys and to have more crystallized ideas about the nature of mature friendship. They seek more intimate and dependent relations with friends, a reflection of their greater dependency and concern with love and nurture as major motives. The fourteen- to sixteen-year age range is a particularly crucial time for same-sex friendships characterized by loyalty, security, and need for similarity with friends. For girls, the group is a setting in which to seek targets for close dyadic relationships; they show few signs of a true gang spirit. The social patterns of males, on the other hand, are consistent with their typical motives for autonomy, independence, and achievement. Although boys do have intimate friendships, group attachments are more important to them than individual attachments. In the group, they find support without the threat to independence that intimate relations with specific individuals might bring. The group supports the boys' move toward independence by asserting its influence through norms and demands for loyalty. In return for the support and structure provided by group norms,

FIGURE
21–4

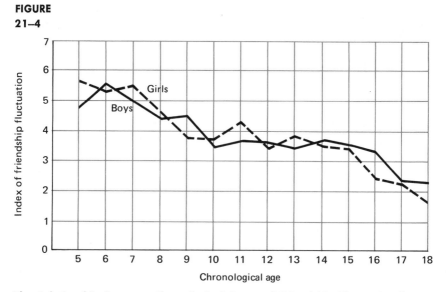

The Relationship between Chronological Age and Friendship Fluctuation for an Urban Sample of 585 Boys and 647 Girls.

The friendship fluctuation index was calculated by assigning a score of 1 for each differ-ence in rank of a choice between the initial statement of choice and the second state-ment two weeks later. If a friend not previously chosen was listed as one of three best friends in the second situation, a score of 2 was given if that person was listed as third-best friend, 3 for second-best, and 4 for best friend. Thus, a ten-year-old girl had a friendship fluctuation index of 3:

	First choice situation	Second choice situation
Best friend	Mary	Mary
Second-best friend	Patricia	Jane
Third-best friend	Jane	Doris

One point is assigned for the shift of Jane from 3rd to 2nd place, and two points for the new appearance of Doris on the list. If Doris had moved to "best friend," a score of 4 would have been assigned for her appearance on the second list.

Source: Horrocks, J. E., & Buker, M. E. A study of the friendship fluctuations of preadolescents. Journal of Genetic Psychology, 1951, 78, 131–144.

boys respond with loyalty and intense gang spirit. For boys and girls, dating is an important influence in the development of interpersonal skills.

Dating. The date is a characteristically American adolescent phenom-enon, with specific norms which are middle class (Smith, 1962). Its specific function is to provide an approved outlet for heterosexual in-terests at a time when adult status is denied; it is a transition institution which fills the gap between the time of play and the time of marriage. Parents frequently do not understand dating because they view it as courtship, which is oriented toward ultimate commitment and marriage.

In the broadest perspective, the final goal in dating is also to select and win a mate; but to overemphasize this final goal is to misunderstand its intermediate effects (Douvan & Adelson, 1966). Although dating may lead to courtship, the norms governing dating behavior often function to *inhibit* the development of mutual affection. Dating has both advantages and disadvantages.

One advantage of dating is that because of its highly prescribed role system, the adolescent may be introduced to heterosexual social life with some protection from failure. Errors are less costly in the transitory dating situation than in more prolonged contact. The structure provides security of rules of behavior; some of the rules provide for the easy termination of relationships without loss of face. Within dating, the adolescent may be able to resolve some confusions he has developed about the opposite sex, and he is required to acquire valuable ego skills and habits of impulse control in social interactions. The successful dater also reaps the important gains of increased status and peer acceptance because of success in a salient expected activity. Among girls particularly, an increase in dating is associated with increasingly mature conceptions of interpersonal relationships. With greater dating experience they develop a greater awareness of the individuality of both male and female friends.

However, the protection of the highly prescribed role system has a price. The disadvantage is that it fosters a superficiality of interpersonal interactions which may damage rather than assist the development of the ability to engage in mature social relationships. Douvan and Adelson (1966) cite the case of a Finnish girl who spent a year in this country and reported that she had been unable to come to feel comfortable about dating because she was not allowed to be herself; she was expected to be a "social role." She suggested that an American boy takes out a date the way he takes out a pair of skis. That is, he regards her as a necessary piece of equipment, and values her more for her ability to perform as expected than for whatever personal attributes she might possess. The researchers suggested that though the Finnish visitor's newness to the date role may have made it difficult for her to be comfortable with it, more sensitive American girls agree with her; some adolescents have grown into the role so much that role and personality are hard to separate.

The early age at which dating is begun, about fourteen for girls and a year or so later for boys, increases the possible damage. American youths learn from an early age to be socially suave and sexually superficial. They acquire *exterior* graces. Dating does sometimes result in intimate physical relationships, but the regulating norms control intimacy. In the absence of external controls of chaperones, personal inhibitions operate. The dating person engages in only token sexuality, and that more to fulfill obligations than to express erotic interests. What is learned is "only manner-deep . . . the deeper bewilderments go untouched" (Douvan & Adelson, 1966, p. 208). The adolescent retreats into the skilled manner of the social persona to minimize the anxieties of sexuality and self. Hiding behind the face of the date role protects the "true self" from exposure to a failure that could be interpreted as an omen of eternal heterosexual failure. The danger is that the retreat may become permanent and the commitment to the social style may serve to delay and distort psychological adjustment, with serious consequences for interpersonal relations in marriage.

Unfortunately, it is not apparent that the role prescriptions of dating are any different from those occurring in adult interactions. Social intercourse, for adolescents or adults, is regulated by norm systems demanding some behaviors and prohibiting others. While we often refrain from being totally frank with others at the risk of hurting their feelings, such socially acceptable inhibitions as "the little white lie," when generalized and well practiced, often come to preclude the possibility of meaningful communication. As the adolescent loses childhood innocence, he learns to perform in the ways considered socially proper. The point at which tact and self-control become cynical deceits and self-distortion is not clear. Sensitivity to the differences between the maturity of the one and the immature defensiveness of the other must be acquired in painful and confusing steps.

Social Patterns and Adjustments in Adulthood

Marriage. Although an increasing number of people today are questioning the necessity of legitimizing an intimate relationship with an official document, marriage is still a dominant interpersonal relationship and a major source of adjustment demands for a large majority (about 90 percent) of men and women. Certainly, personality factors are significantly related to dimensions of marital interaction (Barton & Cattell, 1972). However, compared with other small groups, the interaction of two people in marriage is simplified only by the fact that husband and wife are usually of the same generation and thus have a core of some common interests and experiences (Hill & Aldous, 1969). Complications are more the rule.

Despite the complexities inherent in marriage, it remains a popular institution, and one with apparently high psychological and physical survival value, at least for men. Married people generally have higher death ages and better health records than do single people; they have a lower incidence of mental disorders, are less likely to be admitted to mental hospitals, and are more likely to report themselves very happy than are single people (see Crago, 1972; Bernard, 1971). Although some selection may occur so that the less healthy do not marry, marriage itself has an effect. Even those who have had relatively unhappy marriages, as indicated by divorce, apparently find marriage desirable; a high proportion of those who divorce marry again, and most find at least average success in remarriage. Although marriages before age twenty are especially vulnerable to divorce, young marriages too can be advantageous. Married male college students tend to make better grades than the unmarried, and the same tends to be true for student wives if they do not have children (Medialia, 1962; Jensen & Clark, 1958).

However, marriage is not as consistently, thoroughly, or obviously beneficial for women as for men. Married women report themselves happy more often than single women, but there is just as much reason to conclude that this report is the result of reconciliation and a conformity adjustment to the assigned role for which they have been socialized than it is a reflection of the mental health of full maturity and expressiveness of personal growth. Certainly, the benefits of marriage are not as obvious for women as for men. The transition into marriage, and later parenthood, is more difficult for the wife than for the husband (Barry, 1970). Women are repeatedly found more dissatisfied with marriage than are men, while a wife's general life happiness and overall well-being is more dependent upon marital happiness than is her husband's (e.g., Burr, 1967; Renne, 1970; Bradburn, 1969).

Oddly enough, the single male is generally assumed to be unmarried by choice, while the unmarried woman often is still assumed to be unmarried because she is undesirable and has not been asked (Donelson, 1973; Donelson & Gullahorn, 1973c). The truth is that the single woman is in many ways better off than her married sister while the single man is the worst off of all sex-marital status combinations. Examinations of specific personality and behavioral items in surveys of mental health impairment indicate that married women are more damaged than are single women or married men, and single men are consistently shown to suffer the greatest deficit (see reviews by Bernard, 1971; Donelson, 1973b). Overall, married women are more likely than single women to feel that they are about to go to pieces, to be depressed, passive, and phobic about a number of things ranging from death to windstorms. Among nonhospitalized populations, it is single women who report a greater sense of well-being than do married men or women or single men (Gurin et al., 1960). Meanwhile, social pressures upon the unmarried female continue, as she is thought to be miserable and lonely and often a threat to the marriages of her friends, both male and female, while she may be happier than either of them. However, increasing numbers of young women, particularly college women, are considering a single life as a viable and desirable alternative for themselves, and these are more likely to be from the ranks of the very desirable and competent than from the ranks of the undesirable and incompetent (Adams, 1971; Donelson, 1973b; Bernard, 1964).

In sum, the evidence suggests the advice: If you are a man, get married, by all means! If you are a woman, be prepared. Both singleness and marriage may take their toll if you are not careful.

Parenthood. It has been suggested that parenthood rather than marriage is the crucial point which signals entrance into adult status in our society, but is also a time of major crises and conflict possibly more demanding and damaging than is marriage (Hill & Aldous, 1969; Laws, 1971; Meyerowitz, 1970; Rossi, 1968; Cohen, 1966; LeMasters, 1957). The appearance of a child does seem to impose a stability on the marriage which supplements the sometimes fleeting passionate involvement, and forces a married couple into accepting the domestic responsibilities expected of adults (Renne, 1970). In fact, children are sometimes planned to save a marriage (Chapter 19), and are often (for 63 percent of couples surveyed) the *only* satisfaction listed by unsatisfied married couples (Luckey & Bain, 1970). However, a child, even if much loved and desired, can easily cause marital conflict. Three-person groups of almost any description are likely to break down into a dyad and an isolate (Simmel, 1964). The husband is likely to be the isolate. A mature man may be jealous of the child who now receives the attention that was formerly exclusively his and fear loss of self-esteem (Meyerowitz, 1970; Dyer, 1963). The sexual relations and other intimacies that could function to strengthen the husband-wife relationship may be reduced because of the wife's fatigue at her new caretaking responsibilities. (Oddly, husbands take *decreased* responsibility for household work with the birth of the first child [Heer, 1958; Blood & Wolfe, 1960; Campbell, 1967].) Both spouses show an abrupt decline in marital satisfaction when there are young children in the home (Burr, 1970). However, the husband is not as tied to the home by the child as is his wife, and his socialization history and occupational concerns encourage an extrafamilial orientation. Thus, it is women rather than men for whom satisfaction with marriage varies more markedly with number and age of children, and women who have the more noticeable increase in marital satisfaction after the children leave home (Hill & Aldous, 1969; Rollins & Feldman, 1970):

> Thus, parenthood may require a longer period of adjustment than did marriage. The new parental roles must be learned and somehow reconciled with pre-existing marital patterns in a context where adult domestic responsibilities can no longer be shirked. It is well that our society places such a high valuation on the achievement of parenthood status within marriage as this valuation may serve to soften some of its attendant trials (Hill & Aldous, 1969, p. 925).

Sociability needs: speculations. Despite its prominence in the lives of most people, marriage is by no means the only social interest of adults or necessarily an effective vehicle for meeting all of their social needs. The commonsense hypothesis about sociability needs is the simplest one: people who have lost a marriage partner or mothers whose children have left home are advised to get out and meet people, join clubs, etc., to compensate for the loss of a loved one. The underlying assumption is that a large number of relationships of low intensity should yield the same total satisfaction as a few intense ones. However, the assumption of a common pool of sociability is probably erroneous (Weiss, 1969). It seems more likely that there are specific sociability needs such that satisfaction of any one is no substitute or little compensation for the lack of gratification of another.

Four kinds of sociability needs have been suggested: need to express feelings (intimacy), to share common concerns and relevant information and ideas (social integration), to have evidence of competence in a role of central importance (reassurance of worth), and to receive assistance (Weiss, 1969). There are certainly individual differences in the ability to withstand the absence of any of these kinds of relationships and in the strength of the relationships required to serve the functions. Although it intuitively seems that the intimate relation, often provided by marriage, should be the most important one, it is impossible to say that a deficiency in intimacy is more serious than other deficits. Nor is marriage required for intimacy. Nor does a happy marriage, in which intimacy needs may be met, necessarily imply that the marriage is sufficient for meeting all sociability needs. For example, happily married women who moved with their husbands to new communities became unhappy and developed feelings of social isolation (which the husbands did not understand) because of the absence of old friends and the difficulty of establishing new attachments. Probably more severe and permanent than the frustrations imposed by moving to new communities are those that accompany moving into a new age and becoming what society euphemistically calls a "senior citizen."

Later years. Older people tend to elicit negative stereotypes in the United States. They are seen as withdrawn, uncaring, uninvolved, socially incompetent, more to be occasionally indulged and often forgotten than as suitable targets for interpersonal interactions involving love and respect. There are general kinds of age changes which offer support for these perceptions. From the forties on, there is a shift from active to passive mastery, from an outer-world to an inner-world orientation, from active direct gratification of needs to indirect and vicarious gratifications, particularly through identification with one's children (Neugarten, 1963; Kuhlen, 1964). The social interest dominant during adolescence and early adulthood declines and there is a change in the nature of interaction patterns. The decline is shown in self-reports on scales of sociability, social responsibility, and introversion. There is also a shift from interactions with large numbers of people to close relationships with a few people. Along with decreases in sociability goes an apparent increase in concern with self, though the evidence is mainly from groups who were available as subjects because they had sought psychiatric or medical attention (see Chown & Heron, 1965). There is also an apparent reduction in drive level or ego involvement in life. TAT stories of older people compared to middle-aged people were less complex, involved fewer people and less conflict, and had fewer assertive activities and emotions (Rosen & Neugarten, 1960). Rigidity also increases with age (Figure 21–5).

Thus, the aging process is marked by an increasing disengagement from

FIGURE

21–5

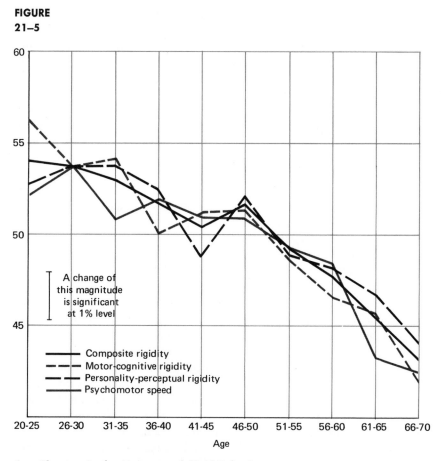

Age Changes in the Measures of Rigid Behavior.

Source: Schaie, , K. W. Rigidity-flexibility and intelligence: A cross-sectional study of the adult life span from 20 to 70 years. *Psychological Monographs,* 1958, 72 (9), No. 462, 26 pp.

life. It has been suggested that this disengagement results from the *need* people have to withdraw from life as they face the inevitability of death (Cumming, 1963; Cumming & Henry, 1961; Cumming et al., 1960). However, whether this withdrawal is voluntary, necessary, desired, or productive of happiness is very much open to question.

The evidence suggests that although older people do by and large become disengaged, they *prefer* and have greater life satisfaction with active engagement (see Kuhlen, 1964; Havighurst & Albrecht, 1953). For example, residents in a Veterans Administration domicile who were encouraged to make useful contributions to the residence area had a greater increase in adjustment compared to a control group (Filer & O'Connel, 1962). Inability to remain engaged in life apparently is a source of unhappiness.

Why, then, does withdrawal occur? Old age brings rapid changes in physical capacities, which began a gradual decline in the thirties, including glandular involution, impairment of sense organs, hardening of the arteries, wasted musculature, and along with these, general decrements in sensory, motor, and symbolic functions (see Munn, 1965). However, the withdrawal and personality problems do not appear to be inevitable consequences of the psychological and biological phenomena inherent in aging. Rather, they result from the situations in which the aging people find themselves and their reactions to the situations (see Tyler, 1965). They are reasonable reactions of anyone who is experiencing a deficit in the number and kind of their relationships with people, a deficit forced on the older person by the social structure. Withdrawal is predictable from social structure, apart from any organic or personality changes in the aging individual himself (Riley et al., 1969). Socialization occurs *within* the individual and also *between* the individual and the social system. Older people must learn to give up old roles for new ones. However, the new roles that they are to learn are often ambiguously defined and have few positive incentives offered for involvement in them. It is rather difficult to reward conformity to role expectations when the role is ambiguous. "In effect, withdrawal from many past involvements—without full opportunity for replacement—seems to be *socially imposed* upon the aging individual" (Riley et al., 1969, p. 970, italics added). Retirement and widowhood illustrate these points.

An adequate pension for expected retirement is probably not sufficient compensation for the problems it evokes. Even before retirement, the aging worker is expected to be inadequate in his job and because of his age and impending retirement is bypassed for promotions he deserves. He is deprived of an important source of self-esteem. Men do encounter occupational crises in their fifties (Bossard & Boll, 1955). Things do not improve after receiving the gold watch. Retirees do pursue short-term goals, usually derived from previous interests, and spend much time in simply taking it easy, as they are expected to do. However, the retiree is not expected to intrude himself as an active member of society. In a society in which usefulness, productivity, and achievement are valued, the retiree is given a "roleless role" in which there is no clear correspondence between the behavior expected of him and dominant societal values.

Because of advancing death ages, the problem of widowhood has become largely a problem of the aged. The widowed individual can no longer administer to the physical or emotional needs of a spouse, and no longer has needs attended to by a spouse. The widow is expected to continue her previous activities rather than withdrawing; friends tell her to get out and do things. But the goals are no longer clearly a part of society's goals. Support given early in the mourning period quickly disappears. Warm relationships with grandchildren are often denied lest the grandparent usurp parental prerogatives. Independence is expected and activities are focused on the self rather than another person. Society becomes indifferent.

DEVELOPMENT OF PERSONALITY

In sum, the learning tasks assigned to the mature individual in contemporary society are great. As early as his middle years, he must begin to face the loss—threatened or actual—of dependent children and the function of rearing them, of job, of spouse, and finally of life itself. Furthermore, many of the new roles he must learn are themselves shut off from society. In effect, he is often required to learn to withdraw. Hence his very success in learning often constitutes deviation from our dominant value patterns, depriving him at once of the goals invested with wider social meaning and of esteem in his own eyes and in the eyes of others. Yet, according to the evidence, the spirit of many older people is indestructible; typically, they withdraw with grace (Riley et al., 1969, p. 979).

With age, and retirement or widowhood likely, an individual is robbed of the satisfactions of needs for intimacy, social integration, reassurances of worth, opportunity for nurturant behavior and assistance. Some needs are met through peer support, which becomes important in facilitating role transfer in old age. But by and large the aging person loses the sense of being essential. "The aged, therefore, are vulnerable to relational losses, boredom, and worthlessness, and a sense that they are no longer of critical importance to anyone else" (Weiss, 1969, p. 43). Many disturbances can be remedied by relationships which meet the sociability needs. However, the remedies are not totally under the control of the aging person himself. Although he must look for and develop potential relationships, social relations do require more than one person. His search for effective treatment for his social malady requires the participation of others, who are not always inclined to care.

SEXUALITY

No other set of behaviors or feelings is so susceptible to the total impact of biological, psychological, and sociological pressures as the sexual ones. Sex is a set of physiological processes typically finding expression in psychologically defined relationships between people who occupy defined social roles. We have biological tensions; equally important, we have roles and identities, feelings and fears, perceptions of ourselves and others. In sexuality, our membership in the animal world is apparent. Equally apparent is our ability to communicate deeply with other human beings. This communication requires knowledge, acceptance, and sensitivity—about ourselves and about another person. It is interfered with by cultural restrictions which often serve to take sexual functioning out of its natural context. Inhibiting fears and distorting perceptions prevent total appreciation and acceptance of one's body and its use in free expression and discovery of feeling.

Sex Education

In recent years, much public, private, and professional discussion has focused on sexual behavior (see, for example, the 1969 issues of *Time* and *Psychology Today*). Two related themes are evident in long overdue professional discussions: a concern about exactly what sexuality is and an increasing recognition of the need of sex research and education. Laymen often assume that sexuality is a matter only of that behavior which directly leads to, and immediately involves, the physical act of intercourse between a male and a female, and that this act requires no special educative efforts. Evidence does not support these views, although professionals have been delinquent and reluctant in gathering the evidence, a neglect now starting to be corrected.

Kinsey and his co-workers and Masters and Johnson have made notable contributions to the objective study of human sexuality, and there is increasing concern about sex research and education. Nevertheless, some questions are still well asked: "How can biologists, behaviorists, theologians, and educators insist in good conscience upon the continued existence of a massive state of ignorance of human sexual response, to the detriment of the well-being of millions of individuals? Why must the basics of human sexual physiology create such high levels of personal discomfort among the very men and women who are responsible for guiding our culture?" (Masters & Johnson, 1966, pp. vi-vii). The sexual taboos of our society, especially severe in relation to children, must be blamed.

As a result, sex education is haphazard and more effective in promoting maladjustment than adjustment. Although Freud pointed out that childhood sexuality is not confined to a few evil children, parents still punish or ignore the sexuality of children, and often of adults. ". . . we have been very busy pretending that the sexuality of children does not exist when in actuality it is our relegation of it to nonexistence that is the cause of distortions and difficulties in later sexuality" (Calderone, 1966, p. 270). Few parents or teachers can talk about sexuality without fear or embarrassment; they have not accepted and understood their own sexuality. The child is left free to educate himself by imagination, bathroom talk with other children, and pornography. What he does learn easily from adults is that sexuality is something about which to have fear and embarrassment. Elaborate defenses result.

One advantage to be expected of sex education is an increased ability to discuss sex as a natural body function and a set of social-psychological attitudes and behavior not limited to explicitly genital acts. Sex education, it is hoped, will prepare people emotionally and intellectually to be able to make personal decisions. Sexuality is not well defined by statements of physiological processes, though knowledge about those is essential for consistently informed action and mature choice. The concern with sexuality in recent years reflects an awareness that much more is required for knowledgeability about sexuality than the details of anatomy and techniques of genital hygiene. The shift in thinking is away from considering sex as a genital act to sex as an interpersonal relationship (Kirkendall & Libby, 1966). The change in sexual morality that is developing is a change from evaluation of the morality of sexual behavior in terms of abstinence from nonmarital intercourse to one in which morality is defined in terms of responsible behavior and a sincere regard for others. In the words of one prominent sex educator, "morality is a question of how one human being deals responsibly with another human being" (Calderone, 1966, p. 271). To deal responsibly with another human being, one must have the freedom of knowledge to deal responsibly with oneself. Sexuality is an expression of personality which allows communication with another person and also discovery and growth, for the relationship as well as for each of its participants separately.

Male and Female

A communications problem. "Vive la difference" is a romantic slogan likely to elicit laughter that often serves to reduce tension and change the topic in informal discussions that threaten to raise matters of sexuality too quickly or too poignantly. The underlying assumption is that the greater the difference, the greater the normalcy and mutual attractiveness of the two who are so different and the greater the enjoyment of flirtation and intercourse. However, remember that communication is facilitated by the mutual understanding enabled by similarity of experience (Chapter 16). The fact that males and females are as successful as they are in their sexual relations is somewhat amazing. Some of the basic inhibitors of communication are inherent in biological differences; others result from extensive socialization experiences: ". . . no man will ever fully understand woman's sexual function or dysfunction. What he does learn, he learns by personal observation and exposure, repute, or report, but if he is at all objective he will never be sure in his concepts because he can never experience orgasm as a woman" (Masters & Johnson, 1970, p. 4). Conversely, a woman may learn to conceptualize male sexual functioning but can never fully understand it because she can never experience ejaculatory demand or the release of semen. A man can never know the experience of menstruation or childbearing, or a woman know the embarrassment of an ill-timed erection. More generally, early and extreme differentiation of sex roles limits the ability of a member of one sex to understand a member of the other. Most women do not really understand the need of men to avoid displays of dependency or the pressures they feel to achieve and to protect the family. Men have difficulty understanding women's apparent lack of assertiveness and their relatively freely expressed emotionality in the face of day-to-day frustrations. The facts of biological differences and socialization differences make mandatory increased attempts to communicate openly and honestly. Impairment in sexual functioning often reflects the partners' inability to communicate with one another (Masters & Johnson, 1970). The problems resulting from both kinds of differences are unnecessarily exaggerated by fear and embarrassment about talking about sexuality and resistance in admitting one's own feelings.

Socialization experiences.　Although parents differ in their permissiveness, a child is rarely rewarded and more often punished for fondling his genitals, or manually or visually exploring those of his parents or of other children. Even the most liberal father does not find it pleasant when his daughter enthusiastically tugs at his penis. The sexes do differ of course in the ways in which many other behavior systems are socialized —aggression, achievement, dependency—and these all contribute to self-concepts and help mold one's identity as a male or female (Chapters 12, 20). Pressures to adopt extremely differentiated sex-role behaviors and to evaluate oneself as masculine or feminine accentuate problems of understanding the other sex. One of the dominant effects of differential socialization practices for sexual behavior specifically is the development of much more intense and pervasive anxiety about sexuality in females than in males, and, concomitantly, a greater sexual freedom in males. Both sexes have sexual anxiety and restriction from early ages, but sex differences are still apparent. The differential sex anxiety and freedom affect the stability of sex-related behavior in boys and girls and the nature of the variables which are associated with their sexual activity before and during adulthood. The pervasive cultural norms that are expressed in socialization activities establish a strong link of sexuality with dependency and passivity for females, and with aggression, competence, and conquest for males, but the links are much stronger and consistent for males than for females (Kagan & Moss, 1962; Table 21–1).

Adolescence.　During adolescence, with increased biological urges and cultural expectations, the problem of accepting one's own sexuality and the necessity of understanding the other sex often take dramatic forms. Both males and females are in the rather awkward position of experiencing physical maturation, and the increase in sexual drive that go with it, without having immediate access to the adult status that would permit marriage, the only sexual outlet consistently approved in our culture. Further, the adolescent confronts his rising sexual interest with minimal information about the biological facts of his body and a history of viewing sex as a taboo, so that his emotional preparation for the acceleration of sexual development is likely to be even less than his intellectual preparation. At the same time, cultural demands are intensified for evidence of masculinity and femininity, as shown particularly in heterosexual behavior. During childhood, masculinity or femininity could be demonstrated and popularity assured by appropriate sex-typed behavior, mainly in interaction with a same-sex group. At puberty, more becomes required for convincing others and oneself that one is not deficient on the all-important dimension of masculinity-femininity. Boys are subjected to propaganda from peers, and sometimes from their fathers and other

TABLE 21–1   Relations between Childhood Behavior and Adult Indices

Childhood variable	ADULT AVOIDANCE OF PREMARITAL SEXUALITY		ADULT SEXUAL CONFLICT		OPPOSITE SEX ACTIVITIES IN ADULTHOOD	
	Males	Females	Males	Females	Males	Females
Heterosexual interaction						
Age 6–10 years	.06	−.27	.15	−.34*	.35	−.04
10–14 years	−.47**	−.06	−.39*	.15	−.05	−.32
Opposite sex activities						
Age 3– 6 years	.49***	−.14	.41**	−.23	.54***	.10
6–10 years	.65****	.13	.61****	−.11	.63****	.44***
10–14 years	.35*	.22	.18	−.01	.57***	.10

    *   p = .10
    **   p = .05
    *** p = .01
    **** p = .001

Heterosexual interaction: Amount of contact with opposite sex peers.
Masculine activities: Interest in athletics, mechanical objects, highly competitive activities.
Feminine activities: Interests in gardening, music, cooking, and noncompetitive activities.
Adult avoidance of premarital sexuality: Reluctance to establish heterosexual relationships during late adolescence and early adulthood, and degree of inhibition in erotic behavior (necking, petting, coitus).
Adult sexual conflict: Anxiety over anticipation or commission of sexual behavior.
SOURCE: Kagan, J., & Moss, H. A. *Birth to maturity: A study in psychological development.* New York: John Wiley, 1962. Pp. 159 and 168.

adults, that their masculinity depends upon their sexual experience and prowess. A large proportion of 100 virgin college males reported feeling insecure about their virginity and pressured by peers to gain experience (Tebor, 1957). Significant adults—teachers and parents—were meanwhile unaware of the dilemma of these young men and were offering them no support for their chastity.

Girls are urged to be sexy and appealing, to look and act provocative, and to prove their attractiveness by acquiring dates. Yet they are expected to control their sexual desires and are assigned the responsibility for prohibiting sexual intimacies. Thus, they have to face the *double standard*, which generally assigns greater dominance, superiority, and freedom to the male than to the female. The adolescent boy who boasts of his sexual conquests is generally admired by his peers; the teenage girl who sleeps around is considered a tramp. The sex-differentiated perception of the relationship between love and sex is also relevant. Female sexual expression is often intimately intertwined with being in love; for the male, sexuality is less exclusively attached to romantic concepts. Therefore, the young woman may have less problem controlling her sexual impulses in the absence of a genuine relationship than the adolescent male. However, when she does participate in sexual intimacies as an expression of her sincere commitment, she often runs into complications. Although the young man may have been sincerely convinced of their "meaningful relationship," he may nonetheless come to feel guilty about his conquest and quickly drop her because of his own guilt (see McCary, 1967). Or he may misinterpret her responsiveness to his sexual advances as the sign of a morally loose girl, lose his respect for her, and reject her.

Long-term implications of the double standard are even more disturbing. The girl may maximize her chances of avoiding sexual intimacy by preventing the development of genuine emotional involvement. Or she may form a deep attachment, and marry, but the anxiety about either sexual desire or sexual behavior may continue long after the societal prohibitions have been removed by a marriage ceremony. She becomes a frigid wife.

> It is obvious that man has had society's blessing to build his sexual value system in an appropriate, naturally occurring context and woman has not. . . . During her formative years the female dissembles much of her developing functional sexuality in response to societal requirements for a "good girl" façade. Instead of being taught or allowed to value her sexual feelings in anticipation of appropriate and meaningful opportunity for expression, thereby developing a realistic value system, she must attempt to repress or remove them from their natural context of environmental stimulation under the implication that they are bad, dirty, etc. . . . In short, negation of female sexuality, which discourages the development of an effectively useful sexual value system, has been an exercise of the so-called double standard and its sociocultural precursors (Masters & Johnson, 1970, pp. 215–216).

The double standard has tended to be self-perpetuating. Females are rewarded by masculine acceptance and cultural approval for acting subserviently, and come to expect subservience in themselves, thus reinforcing the perception that they are inferior. Females who have learned to control sexual feelings, even to the point of frigidity, reinforce the perception that females have lower sexual desire and so should have the responsibility of controlling male desire before marriage and submitting as a gratification object afterward. However, there does seem to be a shift in male attitudes about the appropriateness of double standards and their traditional role as the dominator of subservient woman. Males seem to be becoming more equalitarian in their attitudes about women and are attempting to take more careful account of the feelings and desires of the women they associate with, either inside or outside of marriage. At the same time, they are more desirous of expressing sexual tenderness rather than unquestioned mastery. One of the dramatic aspects of youth movements is a unisex approach to interpersonal relations in which each sex is accepted equally, as people to be loved. Our comments below about data gathered longer ago than yesterday should be interpreted with such a change in mind. Still, it will be many years before concepts of masculine superiority are not at least in the background of male, and often female, thoughts. The double standard is falling, but has not yet fallen (Smigel & Seiden, 1968).

Sexual Activities before Marriage

Sexual activities are far more varied and extensive than considered appropriate by overt cultural norms. The incidence of various activities varies greatly with religion, social class, conservative vs. liberal attitudes, and education and age, including age at time of marriage. However, overall, the double standard is apparent in the greater sexual activity of males. One qualification to this pattern is that once females participate in a kind of sexual activity, they are likely to continue it, sometimes at a rate increasing with age and sometimes with greater frequency than men.

Masturbation and petting. One common sexual outlet in adolescence— though it is certainly not limited to adolescents or to unmarried people— is masturbation, that is, any type of self-stimulation, including fantasy stimulation, that produces erotic arousal, with or without orgasm. Masturbation frequently causes extreme guilt feelings in the teenager because of punishment for masturbation in infancy and perhaps simply because of the strangeness of his newly developed sexuality. Contrary to folk tales, masturbation is a normal and frequent activity which does not lead to insanity, impotence, or telltale signs in one's eyes. Our population would be a strange one indeed were these tales true.

By their tenth birthday, about 13 percent of both sexes have masturbated, and by age twenty, about 40 percent of females and 95 percent of males (Reevy, 1961; Kinsey et al., 1953). Female genitals are less prominent than those of males, so that females are slower to discover the efficacy of masturbation. Once they do, they continue its practice, and the incidence increases with age and is still high in the sixties. The initial lack of masturbation also probably results from prohibitive sexual anxiety. About one-third of women without prior masturbation experience did not reach orgasm in the first year of marriage, in contrast to only about 15 percent of those who had masturbated (Kinsey et al., 1953).

Another common outlet for unmarried couples is petting, which may or may not result in an immediate orgasm for either partner. Petting may be an avenue of expression for a deeply devoted couple. It is also a frequent activity of young people who are attempting to be good dates. By age twenty-five, 89 percent of males and 90 percent of females have petted (Kinsey et al., 1953).

Premarital intercourse. Despite the popular misconception, the current incidence of premarital sexual activity is not indicative of a revolution. The rebels of the revolutionary change in American sexual behavior were those of one of today's "older generations." About two and a half times as many women born between 1900 and 1910 had premarital intercourse as those born before 1900. The incidence of virginity in college women has been relatively stable since then, with 80 percent as a low estimate of college virginity (Corry, 1966).

What *is* different is our more open *attitude* toward premarital sex. The fact that society has come to accept premarital sex, if not to condone it, is evidenced by the ease with which single women can now obtain birth-control pills and legal abortions. Interestingly, a study of unmarried college students revealed that only 59 percent of those who approved of premarital intercourse had actually experienced a sexually intimate relationship (Bell, 1966; Kirkendall & Libby, 1966). This discrepancy between attitude and behavior may represent a basic personality conflict, or it may reflect the fact that the approving students had not found the emotional commitment that would, by their standards, justify intercourse.

Guilt about premarital intercourse is possible. Rejection by a male who accepts the double standard may not only reveal his own guilt but also lead the girl to feel guilty. The locale in which premarital intercourse often occurs (a cramped car, a sleazy motel) is more conducive to anxiety about violating a culturally pronounced standard than to physical and emotional satisfaction. Intellectually based decisions are often ineffective in counteracting the strong emotional responses built up over the years. However, the occurrence of intense guilt about premarital intercourse is popularly overestimated to be consistent with cultural prohibitions. Clinical and survey evidence consistently shows the *absence* of guilt about most premarital relationships (e.g., Freedman, 1965; McCary, 1967). The low incidence of premarital intercourse and absence of remorse about it may mean simply, and encouragingly, that people *think* before committing themselves to the emotional investment that sex demands, and having made the commitment are willing to stand by it without shame. In fact, "psychotherapists have long detected more regret among women who were virgins at marriage for *not* having experienced premarital coitus than among those women who did experience it" (McCary, 1967, p. 207). Ironically, although women who were not virgins at marriage maintain that they would do the same thing over, they generally hold much more conservative attitudes and expectations for their daughters. Perhaps this is because the mother who feels she had a strong emotional commitment to her affair cannot identify sufficiently with her daughter to realize that she, too, may have an intense emotional attachment.

Marriage

Marital sex. After the magic of a marriage ceremony, the couple is expected by cultural ideals of romanticism to reach the pinnacle of sexual bliss. Unfortunately, the few moments it takes to say "I do" cannot always overcome a lifetime of emotional conditioning. About 10 percent of husbands and 26 percent of wives enter marriage with attitudes of disgust, aversion, or indifference to sex (Burgess & Wallin, 1953). Even when attitudes are positive, the first attempts at sexual union are generally awkward (Hill & Aldous, 1969). Women who have had premarital coitus do enjoy intercourse more during the early part of marriage than those who have not, but the difference between virgins and nonvirgins diminishes fairly quickly. About 20 to 25 percent of middle-class American women report having orgasm infrequently or never during marriage (Clark & Wallin, 1965). It has been conservatively estimated that sexual relations in about one-third of all marriages are somewhat inadequate (see McCary, 1967), and sexual inadequacies have been cited as a leading cause of divorce.

Male-female interaction. When couples marry in the early or mid-twenties, in the first years of marriage the sex drive of men is somewhat greater than that of women, though each sex overestimates the drive of the other (Burgess & Wallin, 1953). The peak of the male's drive occurs between the late teens and age twenty-five, declining thereafter (Kinsey et al., 1948). Women reach the peak between ages thirty-one and forty, and decline at a much slower rate than men. Given these differences in sex drive, many couples work out compromise arrangements about the frequency of intercourse, but these arrangements often do not meet the needs of either partner (Bell, 1963). The reason women in their forties show less marital satisfaction may not be because their children are growing up, as is popularly assumed, but because their sexual disinhibition coincides with their husbands' loss of power or interest (Bossard & Boll, 1955). The sex drives of men and women also differ in that the drive of women is likely to be cyclic. Added to the problems posed by socialization and biological differences is the fact that even in their most intimate moments, many marital partners are frequently unable to communicate and express their desires. A woman hesitates about telling her husband explicitly where his touch will most excite her; a husband avoids suggesting variations on normal intercourse such as oral-genital contact and anal insertion of the penis for fear that his wife will be shocked by his "unnatural" desires. The hesitancy of married couples to communicate with each other is of course only one reflection of cultural reluctance to appreciate and enjoy one's own body and the body of another. Unfortunately, ". . . the failure of communication in the bedroom extends rapidly to every other phase of the marriage. When there is no security or mutual representation in sexual exchange, there rarely is freedom of other forms of marital communication" (Masters & Johnson, 1970, p. 15).

Sex and marital adjustment. How is sexual adjustment related to general marital adjustment? Among the middle-class respondents typically used in studies relating sexual behavior to marital satisfaction, two factors have been shown related to marital satisfaction: the frequency of orgasm in the wife, and the equality of sexual desire (see Udry, 1968). Greater marital satisfaction is expressed by men who *report* that their wives enjoy sex as much as they do, and by couples who report that both husband and wife nearly always have an orgasm in their sexual relations. Further, those couples who state that they are highly satisfied with their sexual relationships are more satisfied with other aspects of their relationships than couples reporting sexual dissatisfaction. Some of the satisfaction is based on distorted views: Agreement with the spouse is overestimated. Couples who report being satisfied with their marriages are likely to see themselves as equal in the frequency of sexual activities desired even when this is *not* the case. Distortion in the direction of agreement occurs with a variety of perceptions, including attitudes toward family life, the relative importance of communication topics, real and ideal behavior in task performance, decision making, frequency of communication, social-emotional supportiveness, and frequency of sexual relations (Levinger & Breedlove, 1966). Overall, assumed agreement with the spouse exceeds actual agreement, and is positively associated with general marital satisfaction (Figure 21–6; Table 21–2). Correlations of satisfaction and *actual* agreement were statistically insignificant but positive. Definitive research about which causes which is

FIGURE 21–6

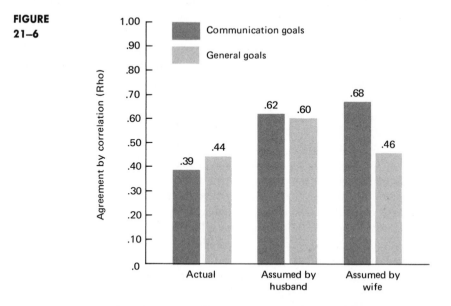

Actual and Assumed Agreement about Marital Goals.

Source: Levinger, G., & Breedlove, J. Interpersonal attraction and agreement: A study of marriage partners. *Journal of Personality and Social Psychology,* 1966, 3 (4), 367–372.

TABLE 21–2   Correlations between Marital Satisfaction and
Assumed Agreement

Topics	Husbands	Wives
Communication goals	.39***	.19*
General goals	.45***	.29**

  *   p = .08
  ** p = .02
***p = .01

SOURCE: Levinger, G., & Breedlove, J. Interpersonal attraction and agreement: A study of marriage partners. *Journal of Personality and Social Psychology*, 1966, 3 (4), 367–372.

lacking—does general marital satisfaction cause sexual satisfaction, or vice versa? Or do both forms of satisfaction stem from other factors? Evidence is weak, but there is some reason to suspect that for men at least, sexual adjustment causes marital adjustment, rather than the reverse: "There is nothing in the male value system which says that in order to enjoy sex with a woman you must have a satisfying affectional relationship with her" (Udry, 1968, p. 32). In apparent contrast, sexual behavior for women is intimately related with emotional commitment. Sex derives from love rather than love from sex. For women, there is some evidence that a satisfying marriage encourages sexual responsiveness and that unsatisfying marital experiences lead her to move from sexual responsiveness to unresponsiveness (Clark & Wallin, 1965). It is also true that for women, outside sources of satisfaction and involvement (e.g., religion) may compensate for lack of sexual satisfaction in marriage, whereas this does not seem to be true for men (Wallin, 1957; Wallin & Clark, 1964). Failure to recognize these differences is often the cause of day-to-day friction.

The statements about the association of marital and sexual satisfaction must be qualified by considerations of the expectations about the role of sex in the marriage and the intensity of the double standard. If the couple has not internalized reciprocal norms that imply sexual equality, the perception that the wife's sexual interest and satisfaction do not match those of her husband does not disturb the marital relationship. When there is extreme segregation of the sexes, as is likely in lower classes—men live in a man's world, women in a woman's world—there is less interest and enjoyment in marital sex than when there is less segregation. Middle-class husbands complain more about sexual incompatibility than lower-class husbands, while the relationship is reversed among wives (Levinger, 1966). With high segregation, "sex is stripped of its interpersonal significance, and does not become the important source of satisfaction that it is in more emotionally intimate marriages" (Udry, 1968, p. 34). This analysis is consistent with previous comments about sex-differentiated experiences and communication.

Sex and aging. Cultural stereotypes lead to unnecessary restriction of sexual enjoyment in older people. Sexual interest and capability of men and women are assumed to cease in their later years, but this is far from true (see McCary, 1967; Kinsey et al., 1948, 1953; Masters & Johnson, 1970). Seven out of ten healthy couples are sexually active past age sixty. More could be if they did not assume that they could not be, or should not be. Sexual enjoyment is not impaired by menopause or by total hysterectomy (removal of the uterus, Fallopian tubes, and ovaries), though women may become depressed if they think that their usefulness is over. The sexual drive of women remains about the same between ages thirty and sixty. By age seventy, only about a quarter of the male population is impotent. There are of course physiological changes in both males and females, but they are not changes which need prohibit intercourse. They are changes to accept and understand in oneself and one's partner. When impotence does occur, it is likely to be because neither husband nor wife understands the natural changes that aging imposes on their previous patterns of sexual functioning. Older men believe that they are unable to perform. What is perhaps worse, they feel guilty about having sexual needs at their age. They feel like "dirty old men." Meanwhile, their wives' sexual desire is nearly as high as it was at age thirty. The internalization of cultural assumptions prohibits knowledge and acceptance of self and the natural sexual functioning and mutual enjoyment that would otherwise occur.

The Forbidden

Adultery. If premarital sexual intercourse is disapproved in our society, postmarital sex with someone other than one's spouse is doubly condemned. In this respect, we are more in tune with other societies; adultery is condemned in almost all Western cultures (Harper, 1961). Therefore, anyone who is married is expected to find nonsexual ways of expressing affection and concern for someone of the opposite sex who is not his spouse. The implications of the prohibition against adultery for the development of mature social relations with people of the opposite sex have not been thoroughly considered. In spite of cultural dictums, adultery occurs. A conservative estimate of married men who have had extramarital relations by the time they are forty is 50 percent (see McCary, 1967). About one-fourth of white American married women have extramarital relations by age forty; for 41 percent of those, the activity is limited to a single partner. For women, the incidence of adulterous relationships increases with age, whereas it declines for men. As with other sexual activities, the double standard is evident. Although adulterous women no longer have to wear the scarlet "A" of Hawthorne's time, they continue to be chastised, while adultery among men is tolerated and sometimes expected. Wives at every social level are more accepting of their husbands' affairs than husbands are of their wives' affairs (Kinsey et al., 1948). While slightly more than a quarter (27 percent) of women would consider adultery by their husbands as grounds for divorce, about half (51 percent) of men see infidelity in their wives as destroying their marriage. However, erring wives typically do not say that they would not repeat the experience in similar circumstances. There has been some liberalization in husbands' attitudes. About half the adulterous wives in Kinsey's sample thought their husbands knew about their affairs and in almost half (42 percent) of those cases, the husbands posed no difficulty. In fact, in some cases, the husband encouraged his wife to have affairs, sometimes to excuse his own behavior but more commonly to provide her with additional sexual satisfaction.

Homosexuality. The consistent negative evaluation of homosexual relationships in our society is at odds with some other cultures (see Ford & Beach, 1951), and with the history of Western civilization. The Greeks not only did not condemn homosexuality, they preferred it. To the male leaders of the society, women were to bear children, men were to love. Plato maintained that homosexuals were homosexuals because of their strong souls, manly courage, and virile characters—quite a different view from our contemporary one. In spite of cultural dictates, homosexuality is not uncommon, though it is more seldom acted upon than thought about, and the incidence of homosexual relations increases with both age and education. Among white males, 50 percent have had some form of homosexual experience, as have about 28 percent of women (Kinsey et al., 1948, 1953). The percentage of women who have experienced orgasm in homosexual relations increases from 6 percent for those with grade school education to 10 percent for those with college education, and 14 percent for women who have attended graduate school. Only 20 percent of women with extensive homosexual experience regret it.

Laymen erroneously assume that if one indulges in homosexual activities, he does not engage in heterosexual ones, and is immoral and psychologically unhealthy. These conceptions have far from unanimous support. Although 50 percent of the white male population has had some homosexual activity, only about 4 percent of men in Kinsey's sample are exclusively homosexual for all their sexual lives, and some men continue to have homosexual experiences after marriage (Kinsey et al., 1948). Some estimates range as high as 50 percent of all women who have felt "intense feelings" for another woman or women, though most sexologists make a more conservative estimate of 28 percent (see McCary, 1967). Some women (3 percent) have homosexual activity after marriage and may even terminate a marriage of long standing, with children, to make a commitment to another woman (Kinsey et al., 1953; Magee, 1966; Abbott & Love, 1972).

Evidence of the emotional maladjustment of homosexuals comes mainly from the highly biased samples of people who are studied because they have made themselves conspicuous by getting into trouble with the law or by appearing in a clinic for emotional problems. It is not warranted to argue from this kind of evidence that homosexuality necessarily implies maladjustment, though some writers seem to (e.g., Bergler, 1957; Bieber et al., 1962; Doidge & Holtzman, 1960). The personality structures of homosexuals vary as much among themselves as they vary from comparable heterosexuals, and the assumptions that as a group they are generally pathological or feel sexually inadequate are not supported by evidence from inconspicuous samples (e.g., De Luca, 1966). In a thorough study of inconspicuous samples, Hooker (1957) compared non-clinic male homosexuals and heterosexuals. Judges, chosen for clinical expertise, were unable to distinguish between the two samples on the basis of the time-honored projective tests, the Rorschach, the TAT, and the Make-A-Picture Story Test. Whatever the latent maladjustment characteristic of homosexuals, it was well concealed in those tests generally relied on to detect the most subtle nuances of psychodynamics. Nor is it evident on self-report measurements (e.g., self-concept and ideal-self ratings; the Sixteen Personality Factor Questionnaire; adjective check lists; semantic differential) (Chang & Block, 1960; Evans, 1970; Thompson, McCandless, & Strickland, 1971). In fact, the male homosexuals in one sample were *less* defensive and female homosexuals *more* self-confident than their respective heterosexual controls (Thompson, McCandless, & Strickland, 1971).

Nor is it true that male homosexuals are feminine in appearance and female homosexuals masculine. In fact, in some male interpersonal networks, the members take obvious pride in masculinity of appearance, and some homosexual bars actively exclude men of feminine appearance (Hooker, 1965).

Homosexuals, like other minority groups, are slowly emerging as an organized and vocal force to be reckoned with by society. Through the Gay Liberation Front and other such organizations, they are exerting pressure on city and state legislatures to extend antidiscrimination statutes governing jobs, housing, and public accommodations to include homosexuals. Thus far, they have been less than successful. But the emancipation of a minority group has never happened overnight. Perhaps with time, and with a more sexually enlightened public, the same tolerance and encouragement which is tentatively, and in some cases only vocally, being extended to women and blacks will be extended to homosexuals as well.

Summary

Personality development is a continual process which occurs in a social system. Within the system, the individual seeks rewarding relationships with others which are shaped by, and which shape, his personality. As we follow a person's development from childhood through adolescence, adulthood, and old age we can appreciate the influence of social relations on personality development as one attempts to find his social and sexual identity within an interpersonal matrix.

Throughout life, the family can provide a social security which can foster the development of competent individuality. Similarly, peer groups provide a social setting in which the individual may find support for being as he is and developing a sense of self. However, conformity pressures in the peer group of both the adolescent and the adult may exert a negative influence by encouraging superficiality and retarding the achievement of identity.

Such societal institutions as marriage and parenthood pose particular developmental tasks for any individual. Although many sociability needs of the adult can be met within the natural family unit, marriage is neither necessary nor sufficient for meeting all social needs. Furthermore, the adequacy with which social needs are met is likely to decline with advancing years, because of death of loved ones and simply because the older person is erroneously assumed to be incapable of participating actively in life.

Along with a person's social development goes the development of sexuality, which allows deep and physical communication with other human beings. Sexuality is a matter of personal development into an individual who is effective in touching others as he expresses himself, without fear of censure from himself or from others. Sexual relationships, like other social relationships, provide the individual with an avenue of self-expression and discovery, and a means of communicating with other human beings.

The social and sexual relationships a person forms throughout his lifetime allow the potential for developing a sense of self-awareness and individuality. However, the course of development is often impeded by the lack of realism in societal expectations and the lack of personal understanding of human sexuality. Specifically, there must be greater recognition of the problems posed in adolescence by societal expectations, of the difficulties of socialization into marriage and parenthood, and of the desire of older people to continue functioning as active participants in life. Similarly, there must be greater understanding of human sexuality if man is to know himself and realize his individual potential in a social environment.

22

creativity

What shapes a creative personality? What basic perceptual, cognitive, and emotional predispositions lead a Picasso to produce artistic masterpieces, an Einstein to develop scientific theories, or a Freud to discover new ways of viewing human development? Research into creativity as a *process* has uncovered a host of variables which effect the likelihood that a person will be creative—that he will evolve a process for producing tangible constructions which others regard as creative. Among the variables which have been suggested as relevant to the development of a creative personality are: tolerance for ambiguity, or even a desire for it; openness to experience; childlike traits; self-expression; and independence of judgment (Golann, 1963; Dellas & Gaier, 1970).

But creativity is more than a process in which materials are reorganized into tangible products considered unique to civilization. Creativity, in the broadest sense, is growth. It is a *life style*, a stance toward oneself and the world which allows one to realize his fullest potentials in interaction with the environment (Figure 22–1). The personality variables which enable this life style should form the criteria for defining creativity. Thus, creativity is relevant even to those who have neither the intent nor the ability to produce masterworks of theater or advances in nuclear physics or great musical compositions. A person may be creative in his outlook on himself and life, and this outlook will be reflected in his own personal growth and, at the same time, in the interpersonal relationships which link him with his fellow man.

Understanding creativity as a life style must involve all the psychodynamic and external considerations related to personality. This chapter may serve as a useful springboard for reviewing and partially integrating many of the conceptual approaches discussed in preceding chapters.

**FIGURE
22–1**

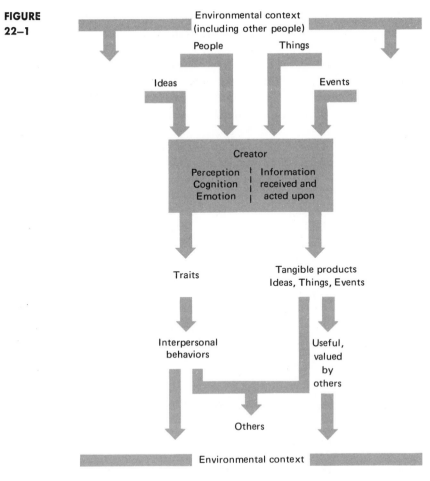

Interaction of Self with Environment.

THEORETICAL ORIENTATIONS

Personality theorists, though often starting from markedly different assumptions about the nature of man, all seem to recognize two factors or modes of functioning in the creative process. One mode *revises the known*, explores the speculative, and perceives and produces the unusual and unexpected; it is open to internal and external events as they are and as they may become. The other *retains the known*, conserves and perpetuates what is, and perceives and produces the usual and expected.

Freudian Views

Freud (1940a, b, 1949, 1959) thought that creativity, and indeed all civilization, is the result of sublimation of instinctual drives and unconscious conflicts which cannot be directly expressed. More specifically, he postulated that artistic achievements are attributable to the temporary loosening of repression and a regression to infantile primary process modes of thought and experience. When the behavioral expression is compatible with ego standards, the result is creative; when it is not acceptable, it will lead to neurotic or psychotic behavior. For Jung (1928), the wellspring of creativity is in the collective unconscious. When only the personal unconscious is involved, the art is symptomatic. But when an archetype is raised from the collective unconscious and brought into relation with conscious ideas, the art is symbolic and of universal significance because it develops material common to all men.

Regression in the service of the ego. One of the most important developments within the basic Freudian framework is the position evolved by ego psychologist Ernst Kris (1952, 1953). In the *inspiration phase* of the creative process, according to Kris, the ego regresses to primary process thought and allows the expression of repressed impulses. However, the regression is in the service of the ego; the ego is active in creative regression, while it is passive in defensive regression. In the *elaboration phase*, the primary process material is reorganized into secondary process form and tested against reality. Secondary processes translate the primitive—actually psychotic—thought into logical forms of expression and subject this thought to synthesis, criticism, and integration for constructive use. Ego control differentiates the socially valued, creative product from the drive laden and original but bizarre psychotic product.

Openness to experience. Schachtel's (1959) modification of Freudian thinking brings him very close to the fulfillment theorists. Creative experience is an open encounter of the total person with some part of the world. Schachtel sees this as moving forward rather than backward: Rather than regressing, the person who is open to experience *progresses* to encounter experience and all of its possibilities. Man needs to be creative because he needs to relate to his world, not because he needs to satisfy internal drives. He goes beyond the familiar and routine to relate fully to another object, and in this relatedness finds both the world and himself. With the openness of creativity, man is object-centered and seeks to grasp things as they are (allocentric perception). When he sees things only in terms of his own personal habits and interests (autocentric perception), he is closed to the experience of things as they are in their fullness and cannot be creative. Openness is a major theme in fulfillment theories and in empirical approaches.

Fulfillment Positions

Carl Rogers. For Rogers, as for others in the fulfillment tradition, the motivation for creativity is concentric with the basic motivation central to human nature, namely, the tendency to actualize oneself. Creative behavior is self-actualizing behavior. We grow and create because it is satisfying to do so. The fundamental necessity is that the locus of evaluation be internal:"No outside evaluation can change the " 'feel' of being 'me in action' " (Rogers, 1959, p. 76). Another major condition is openness to experience, the opposite of psychological defensiveness. One is alive to experiences which fall outside the usual categories. Ambiguity is tolerated. Conflicting information is received without a simplifying distortion. One toys spontaneously and exploratively with ideas, colors, shapes, relationships. The likelihood that constructive creativity will emerge is maximized by psychological safety and freedom; the individual is accepted as unconditionally worthy, external evaluations are absent, and empathic understanding is present. The individual has freedom to think, feel, and be whatever is in himself. Although evaluation is internal, the creator also desires to communicate with an understanding group. He wants to share a newly discovered aspect of *himself-in-relation-to-his-environment*.

Erich Fromm. Although Fromm was previously discussed as a Freudian descendent, his position on creativity emphasizes his compatibility with fulfillment theorists. He sees creativity as ". . . the ability to *see* (or to *be aware*) and *to respond*" (Fromm, 1959, p. 44). Perceptions of others are often superficial and unrealistic, the product of our own needs and perceptual categories, rather than creative. To see creatively means to see without projections and distortions. This requires overcoming in oneself the neuroticism which leads to distortions. A creative attitude requires also the surprise, wonder, and puzzlement that come easily to the child but are feared by the adult as signs of ignorance. One must have courage and faith, a certainty and trust in the reality of one's own experience. One must be able to accept conflict and have the willingness to be born every day. This allows a full commitment to experience here and now, including the experience of self. "I" can be experienced only in relatedness to others, that is, on the basis of a creative attitude. When one responds creatively, he responds as a whole person; he thinks with his belly, he sees with his heart, and the "object ceases to be an object." There is a ". . . complete relatedness, in which seer and seen, observer and observed, become one, although at the same time they remain two" (Fromm, 1959, p. 48).

Abraham Maslow. Maslow (1954, 1959) blends both Freudian and fulfillment positions in his emphasis on self-acceptance. Improvisations in jazz and childlike paintings are primary process creativity. Secondary process creativity includes production-in-the-world: the building of bridges, the design and execution of scientific experiments. Integrated creativity, which produces the great works of art, philosophy, and science, uses both types of process in a productive fusion. After the inspiration of voluntary regression comes activity, control, work. Secondary processes take over from the primary. The deliberate follows the spontaneous, criticism follows total acceptance, rigorous thought follows intuition, caution succeeds daring, reality testing succeeds fantasy and imagination. Maslow's main concern has been with primary creativity, a spontaneous expression of an integrated, self-actualized person. The self-actualized people he studied had a special kind of perceptiveness which allowed them to see the fresh and raw as well as the abstract and categorized, to live in the real world of nature more than in the verbalized world of conceptions, expectations, and stereotypes. Like happy, secure children, they were spontaneous and expressive, natural and uninhibited in their behavior. However, their innocence was combined with sophisticated minds. They did not deny or run away from the unknown, nor did they have an overwhelming need for certainty and safety. Further, any two opposite aspects of their personalities were *fused* together in a sensible dynamic unity. They had reconciled dichotomies: cognition and co-nation, instinct and reason, duty and pleasure, work and play. They were selfish and unselfish; they had strong egos, but could easily be ego-less and self-transcending. Basic to the integration of these otherwise contradictory elements seemed to be the relative absence of fear. Self-actualized people had less need of others. Thus, they could be less afraid of other people and less afraid of being laughed at by their peers. More important, they were not afraid of their own emotions and thoughts. They were self-accepting and therefore wasted less of their energies protecting themselves against themselves. When a person turns his back on aspects of himself that are dangerous he is protected from underlying conflicts, but he is also cut off from much of importance to himself. As Maslow suggests, "By protecting himself against the hell within himself, (a person) also cuts himself off from the heaven within" (Maslow, 1959, p. 91).

Problem-Solving Approaches

Others, who are not always defined as personality theorists specifically, have also developed approaches to creativity which are of major importance (see Anderson, 1959). Theory and research are much more explicitly and closely related than is true for theories of creativity derived from personality theory. In one important research tradition, creativity is a matter of being able to achieve a successful solution to a problem, often including the process of detecting or formulating the problem itself.

Factor analysis: J. R. Guilford. Guilford (1950, 1959, 1963, 1967) views creativity in terms of his theory of the structure of the intellect, derived with factor analytic procedures (Chapter 8). Creativity is not a unitary trait, but rather a collection of interacting and complementary, component abilities, all of which may enter into creative thinking. All genuine problem solving is creative and most, if not all, creative thinking is problem solving. Both problem solving and creativity are productive thinking, which includes both convergent and divergent abilities. With *convergent thinking*, the product of thought converges toward the accepted, conventional answer; the thinker is able to produce the answer considered correct by his social group. With *divergent thinking*, the product of thought diverges from the usual and conventional; it is typical of the creator specifically rather than of his social group. Divergent thinking tends to occur when there is no set way of solving a problem, or when the problem has not been discovered. Divergent thinking abilities which are involved in creative productions are flexibility, fluency, and originality (Figure 22–2). Creative thinking and problem solving are characterized primarily by divergent productive thinking but are by no means limited to that kind of functioning. They involve an initial sensitivity to a problem (a cognitive ability, sometimes referred to as an evaluative ability), followed by a search for stored information and redefinition of the problem (convergent ability). Evaluation abilities are everywhere present—in sensitivity to the problem, selection of the best information from memory or the environment, addition of details to produce information, and acceptance of the finished product. Although present at all steps, evaluative judgment is frequently relaxed in order to obtain a large quantity of ideas with which to work. There are parallel sets of abilities dealing with verbal material, visual-figural (perceived) content, letters or numbers (symbolic content), and, theoretically, behavioral content.

**FIGURE
22–2**

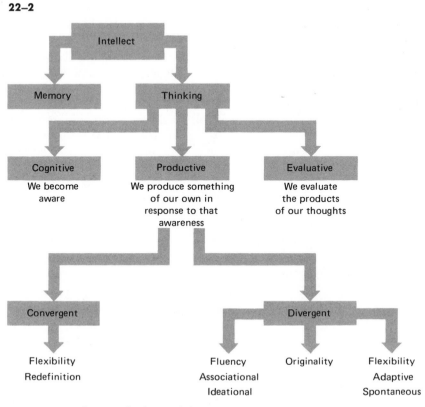

Divergent Productive Thinking Abilities.

Creativity may be expressed in a variety of ways, varying with the abilities of the individual; the underlying general abilities are currently assumed the same regardless of the method of expression. Because the abilities important for creative expression were not represented in conventional intelligence tests, Guilford devised several test procedures to measure these abilities. His procedures for measuring the divergent abilities are widely used and have been incorporated into other tests (e.g., Torrance, 1966).

Associationistic view: Sarnoff Mednick. What one concept links *rat, blue,* and *cottage?* To produce a fourth word which can serve as an associative link connecting three other words is the task posed by Mednick's Remote Associations Test (RAT), designed as an operationalization of his (1962) associationistic theory of creativity. He sees creative thinking as the process of forming associative elements (ideas) into new combinations which are in some way useful in meeting specified requirements or in solving a problem. To be creative, a product must be useful as well as original. The more remote the elements, the more creative the process of using them in new combinations. Associative elements may be brought into ideational contiguity by serendipity (chance association, analogous to pulling two balls at random from a hat full of balls), by the similarity of the elements or of stimuli eliciting them, and by mediation using common elements, which is the main concern in Mednick's approach.

Mednick's mediational theory is based on the concept of response hierarchies (Chapter 5), of associations to a stimulus element. The likelihood of achieving creative solutions by mediation is a function of the number of associations to any one element (size of the associative hierarchy), and the accessibility of associative elements (shape of association gradients). The individual with steep gradients, or small hierarchies, will have only a small number of associations available to the ideas *rat, blue, cottage,* and will be relatively unlikely to arrive at an association common to all (Figure 22–3 and Figure 22–4). With a steep gradient, he will fixate on

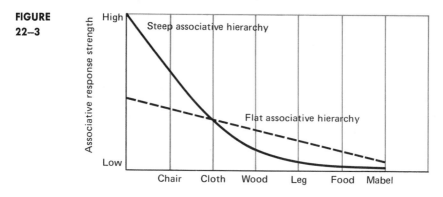

FIGURE
22–3

Associative Hierarchies around the Word "Table."

Source: Mednick, S. A. The associative basis of the creative process. *Psychological Review*, 1962, 69, 220–232.

one or a few associations to each of the words; he cannot do much besides the usual and expected. In contrast, an individual with characteristically flatter gradients will more likely have the concept *cheese* in his hierarchy as an available associate for each of the words, *rat, blue,* and *cottage.* Cheese mediates the concepts, brings them into contiguity. However, the person likely to consistently produce creative solutions will have hierarchies in which the association of maximum probability is the same as that of most other people—his associative gradient is flatter ("divergent") but peaks at a common point ("convergent"). This is a statement in learning theory terms of the view that a creative person is "in touch" with socially defined reality but not bound by it. If the dominant associative response is not the typical one, the individual may be the one-time novelist who can write one and only one good book, or if his peak point is deviant enough, he may be unable to make any societally useful products. His products will be original, but not useful, realistic, or accepted. *Mother* as an associative link between *rat, blue,* and *cottage* would not be accepted as creative because its associations with the stimulus concepts are not understood by others. Although creativity involves the original and unusual, the individual must be enough in contact with socially defined reality to allow communication with others and relatedness to them.

Consensus: Two Factors

A careful review of the theoretical positions just discussed will illuminate the amazing consensus among theorists that there are two factors, or modes of functioning, in the creative process. Whether they call these

**FIGURE
22–4**

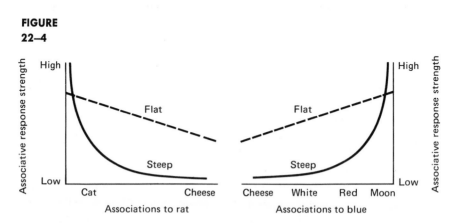

Associative Hierarchies around the Words "Rat" and "Blue."
The person with flat hierarchies will be more likely than one with a steeper hierarchy to mediate the concepts rat and blue with the concept cheese. A person who had not heard of blue cheese would be unlikely to associate cheese to blue.

Source: Mednick, 1962.

factors an inspiration and elaboration phase, primary and secondary process functioning, a progression from the familiar to the unexplored, or divergent and convergent thinking, the theorists all seem to agree that the creative person is socialized into the modes of perception and thinking typical of his social community, but is open enough to feel free to explore the unknown of the world and of himself. The creative personality has mastered the old, but develops the new from it. He has freedom and originality, but also control. He is in touch with a reality he shares with others, but he is not victimized by it. He can wander with ease from the well-worn path, but he can use that path without feeling threatened by conformity pressures.

Research generally substantiates the existence of and necessity for both factors, or modes of functioning, in the creative process. More specifically, there is a recurring emphasis on childlike qualities of openness to external and internal experience, tolerance for the inconsistencies that realistically exist in the world, and willingness to deviate from accepted standards and make independent judgments not necessarily in accord with the status quo. Concurrent with these qualities is repeated evidence that the creative adult is a socially mature person as well. He addresses his talents to the requirements of the situation, and he adapts to and lives within the realities of his environment. However, before looking at the evidence which substantiates these qualities, we must ask how creativity can be measured.

MEASUREMENT

The Criteria Problem

How can we ascertain an individual's creative potential? How can we evaluate the originality of his responses on a creativity test? Obviously, some criteria must be established for defining what shall be considered creative.

Restrictions on originality. Originality, a prime component of creativity, may be quantified by defining it statistically in terms of the frequency of a response in a particular sample being studied or in a larger normative sample. For example, an original response may be defined as one which occurs less than 10 percent or only 1 percent of the time. However, an original response is not always necessarily a creative one. Typically, creativity is defined as originality that is adaptive to a problem and acceptable to some group of people at some point in time. Therefore, researchers as well as theorists often put a restriction, implicitly or explicitly, on the unusualness that they will consider creative. Beyond originality, they require a response they consider to be *correct* in terms of socially agreed upon perceptions of reality.

The limitations of using such criteria to define a person's creativity are obvious. One has only to consider the lives of many of the great creative thinkers throughout history whose thoughts, or works, were considered blasphemous or, at best, strange in their own time, to realize the disadvantage of using social valuations to judge creativity. However, despite the fact that the objectivity of creativity tests is limited by the subjective criteria imposed by the tester (who is not necessarily creative), these quantitative evaluations of creativity can help us define more accurately at least some of the many elusive components of the creative personality.

Variety in response methods.   A more specific form of the criteria problem is that creativity may be expressed in a number of ways. We do not expect the successful artist to produce prize-winning novels, nor the creative scientist to compose symphonies, yet any one test may tap only limited methods of expression. Tests have method variance. They require set kinds of responses. A test requiring verbal responses may not always correlate highly with one requiring a choice between two drawings. In fact, small correlations between some tests using different methods made possible the separate factors in Guilford's classification. The solution to the problem of formulating a general evaluation lies in continued work to define the basic variables (general factors) which influence creativity and to develop measures which are relatively free of method variance and which, for example, would enable both a creative architect and a creative scientist to score well. Currently, many researchers use a battery of tests to identify those they call creative. However, with or without such "pure" tests, creativity may still be understood as a construct.

The Construct

Creativity, like any construct, is defined by interrelationships among a variety of concepts and by the results of different kinds of relevant measurements. Thus, objective tests are useful in helping us to define creativity as a construct, even when any one of them taps only a single domain of creativity such as verbal abilities, because they allow us to make explicit statements about a variety of aspects of creativity. Collectively, these statements should give us a more complete and definitive picture of what we wish to study under the label of creativity than would collections of unverifiable intuitive judgments.

As with other constructs, the measures of creativity need not only be test instruments; they may be experimental procedures as well, as shown in the following examples. Studies of select groups (artists and architects are frequently used) have given valuable leads and provide easy first steps at construct validation of measuring procedures (known groups method, Chapter 7). The next step must be the study of those characteristics associated with creative performance, rather than simply the prediction of who is or will be a successful artist or scientist. This implies a shifting of the locus of the criteria of creativity from a product or a kind of occupational activity to the psychological processes which collectively may define a creative life style. It enables the use of normal samples (people not noted for their creative achievements) in which there is subject variability on the relevant measures. More important, it also may enable a clearer understanding of the view that creativity is relevant to all aspects of the life of the inconspicuous man on the street. Thus, our next consideration will be the intellectual and psychodynamic factors which so far seem distinctive to recognized creators and most helpful in pointing the way to what is meant by a creative life style.

INTELLECTUAL AND PSYCHODYNAMIC FACTORS

Intelligence

Intelligence is a *necessary* condition for the demonstration of creative potential in ways that society is likely to recognize. (This may reflect society's limited view about what is to be valued, i.e., attention to the external and tangible to the neglect of the internal and interpersonal.) However, intelligence alone is not a sufficient condition for creative productions; the highly creative are likely to be highly intelligent, but *high intelligence does not by itself ensure creative production.* The ability to produce recognized creative products does require a requisite level of intelligence; the most popular estimate is an IQ of 120 (Torrance, 1964; Barron, 1963a). Above that level, however, personality factors such as those discussed later are more important determinants of creativity than intellect per se.

The necessity for a distinction between creativity and intelligence is buttressed by the personality and stylistic differences noted between groups selected for their high intelligence but not creativity, and vice versa (Barron, 1957). Getzels and Jackson (1962) compared high school students shown by several measures to be *high* (top 20 percent of the sample) in either intelligence *or* creativity and *low* (bottom 20 percent of the sample) in the other. (However, the average IQ of the high creativity-low intelligence group was high, 127, compared with the general population.) One of several kinds of differences between the two groups was the greater spontaneity and unconventionality in TAT stories of the high-creative than in those of the low-creative or less creative children. The two stories which follow were told by high-creative and low-creative students:

> The man in the foreground is the leader of a counterfeiting ring. They have abducted the older man in the background. The older man is an excellent artist. They have kidnapped him so that they can force him to engrave the plates. He is very reluctant but they threaten to harm his wife and children so he gives in. But he draws George Washington cross-eyed and the counterfeiters are captured and he is released.

This is the story of counterfeiters. The man with the hat is the printer. The other man is the big boss. They are in danger of being captured by the police. They want to get out of the house. The police will arrive too late. The men and the evidence will be gone (Getzels & Johnson, 1962, p. 107).

Evidence from a similar study suggested that children high in creativity but low in intelligence were in angry conflict with themselves and their school environment, and had feelings of unworthiness and inadequacy (Wallach & Kogan, 1965). Those low in creativity but high in intelligence were "addicted" to school achievement and strove for academic excellence to avoid a failure that would be catastrophic for them. Those low in both dimensions were bewildered and defensive, with defenses ranging from useful adaptations of intensive social activity to regressions of passivity and psychosomatic symptoms. Those high in both had both adultlike and childlike behavior; they behaved with both control and freedom. Intelligence is an asset for the high creative, but it is not a sufficient criterion for defining creativity.

Flexibility in Cognitive Functioning

Shifting. Creativity requires the ability to use and control the immature modes of functioning characteristic of primary process thinking, or to engage in unregulated thinking more generally. To be creative, one must feel free to indulge in the primitive and the unconventional, and be open to encounters with the new, unusual, and complex. Rorschach testing shows that normals, relative to recognized creators (artists), have rigid, self-limiting controls that prevent primitive functioning and openness (e.g., Hersch, 1962). However, creativity is not just a matter of feeling free to indulge in unconventional thought processes. It requires also the ability to *shift* between the two modes of functioning generally evidenced as necessary for creativity: the divergent or personalized mode and the convergent or socialized mode, the sophisticated and the primitive, the mature and immature.

The ability to shift between the two modes of functioning is a form of cognitive flexibility. The correlation between the shifting ability and creativity was shown in studies in which subjects were required to think as a person described as highly regulated, and then as one described as highly unregulated (Wild, 1965; Fitzgerald, 1966). The regulated person was described as a conventional, cautious, reliable person who values good common sense, is suspicious of unusual ideas, and does not allow his thoughts to wander from ordinary routes. The unregulated person was described as having novel thoughts and whimsical but acute perceptions that startle other people, enjoying fanciful speculations, and

---

* The first paragraph is a story of "Counterfeiters" given by a high-creativity child; the second is by a high-IQ child.

pointing to contradictions in experience. As predicted, artists had a greater *difference* in the originality of their responses on a word-association test and object-sorting task under the regulated and unregulated conditions than did teachers and schizophrenics. The artists could be just as conventional under regulated instructions as the control subjects, but they were able to become more unconventional under unregulated instructions. They were able to shift more easily from convergent to divergent thinking. Similar results were obtained for undergraduates high and low on a measure of openness to experience which is presumed essential for originality; those high in openness were able to become more original than were those low in openness, but were able also to become very conventional (Table 22–1). The openness which allows encountering the strange and bizarre, either in oneself or in the world, requires minimal use of the repressive defenses which block out or distort the frightening. It also requires strong ego control and security with self to deal with any anxiety that may result and to maintain realistic perspective about the realm of the novel.

Ego control. Ego control is necessary if one is to indulge in unconventional thinking. Without such control, there would be anxiety about the danger of loss of control that accompanies psychotic primitization of thought. Ego control is again necessary for the primitive to be molded into the sophisticated, for the private inspiration to be elaborated into

TABLE 22–1 Originality Scores on the Word Association and Object-Sorting Tests for Subjects High and Low on the Experience Inquiry

Spontaneous condition	Highs [a]	Lows [b]	t
Word association	5.16	1.86	2.42*
Object sorting	3.26	1.07	3.24**
Shift scores			
Word association	5.16	1.86	2.42*
Object sorting	2.11	0.64	2.23**
Unregulated			
Word association	12.74	6.50	3.85***
Object sorting	4.63	2.36	3.29**
Regulated			
Word association	7.26	5.57	1.14
Object sorting	2.53	1.71	1.48

[a] $N = 19$
[b] $N = 14$
  * $p < .05$
 ** $p < .01$
*** $p < .001$

SOURCE: Fitzgerald, E. T. Measurement of openness to experience: A study of regression in the service of the ego. *Journal of Personality and Social Psychology*, 1966, 4 (6), 655–663.

a realistic form to be communicated to others. Factors of ego control have emerged as clear correlates of creativity (Barron, 1963a). For example, the quality of responses to the Rorschach and TAT tests are related to the effectiveness with which primary process and unconscious material is controlled and adapted to reality. The literary quality of TAT stories can be rated in categories such as figures of speech, vocabulary, variety of sentence construction, continuity, genuineness, originality (Pine, 1957). Literary quality is positively correlated with the amount of drive content present and incorporated into the main theme of the story, and negatively correlated with the use of drive material in ways extraneous to the story content. Subjects with high-quality productions channel drive energies into the constructive ego activity involved in creating a story, rather than discharging all such drive energies in the direct pursuit of immediately gratifying goals. The role of ego control is also apparent in openness.

Openness

Empirical evidence points to openness, or an awareness of and receptiveness to both the outer world and the inner world of self, as a characteristic pattern in creative functioning (see Dellas & Gaier, 1970). The evidence takes diverse forms. For example, students classified as high creative (RAT) or high in verbal or nonverbal fluency made better use of incidental cues (Chapter 15) in solving anagram problems than did low scorers (Mendelsohn & Griswold, 1966; Dewing & Battye, 1971). That is, they were more aware of and receptive to stimuli initially incidental to their task, and were able to draw on this stored information in solving the anagrams.

In a quite different kind of study, perceptual openness was revealed as a relatively stable predisposition of creative writers and architects (MacKinnon, 1961). The high-creative subjects differed from both their less creative colleagues and the general population in being perceptual rather than judgmental in their orientations (in terms of Jungian functions, measured by the Myers-Briggs inventory). They were flexible, spontaneous, and openly receptive to internal and external experience, rather than attempting to carefully plan and structure their lives.

Such openness requires a strong ego which can forego the security of being conventional and rational in order to face and enjoy the unconventional and the unexplored. Openness implies a relative lack of avoidance defenses such as suppression and repression, which can inhibit primitive exploration and the spontaneous expression of impulses. Suppression and repression as mechanisms for impulse control are infrequent among creative people, and are negatively related with scores on an openness to experience inquiry (Barron, 1955, 1963a; Fitzgerald, 1966). Although the avoidance of repression may be accompanied by anxiety, the anxiety does not cause insurmountable problems for a relatively strong ego (Helson, 1971; Barron, 1968; MacKinnon, 1962). In fact, the anxiety can help to provide energy for creative activity, and the material associated with the anxiety can provide inspiration for the content of the activity.

Complexity and the Need for Order

The world of people and objects is a complex one. When thoughts and perceptions are characterized by a style of openness and wander from the path of the well structured and the usual, they are likely to encounter disorder and confusion. Creative people, regardless of their field of expression, are distinguished by a preference for the novel and unexpected, and the ambiguous and complex, and work to be exposed to such stimulation (see Dellas & Gaier, 1970).

Paradoxically, the same creative people who seem so willing to seek out the confusion of the complex and improbable in life also appear to have a strong need for order (Barron, 1963b). Does this paradox result from the necessity of dealing with and "conquering" the complexity they expose themselves to? Or is exposure to the complex necessary to allow active expression of the need for order? Barron (1963b) suggests the latter alternative: The highly creative need the challenge of making new order out of apparent chaos by using their own abilities and experiences. Concomitantly, the creative person is willing to take more risks than other people when his *own* efforts and abilities will make a difference in the odds (Torrance, 1962a; McClelland, 1955, 1963). The faith which creative people possess in their ability to discover order in the world and the intensity of efforts to discover or impose order are reflected in their persistent devotion to long-range goals. Barron posits a moral attitude reflected in commitment to the aesthetic and philosophical meanings expressed in the work. The creator is involved in creating his own private universe of meaning. "Without this cosmological commitment no amount of mental ability will suffice to produce a genuinely creative act" (Barron, 1963a, p. 243).

Basic Psychodynamic Processes

Highly creative people prefer, or even need, variety and complexity in their lives. Expressing these preferences requires ego control, openness, and minimum repression, and is, perhaps, a manifestation of a need to impose order on the world. The basic psychodynamic factors enabling this pattern of preferences or needs are likely to be basically matters of how one reacts to uncertainty and deviation, and how one handles the anxiety that may be induced.

Reactions to collative stimuli. The term *collative stimulus properties* refers to the novelty, surprisingness, complexity, puzzlingness, and ambiguity inherent in things or events (Berlyne, 1960, 1966, 1968). These properties all involve the collation of stimuli, and are defined with respect to the degree to which a particular environmental feature is similar to or different from others presented at the same time or in the past. The stimulus induces conflict, uncertainty, and arousal (Chapters 10, 14, 15). The subject is unsure about how to classify the stimulus or what to anticipate next. When the stimuli are very different from those to which one is accustomed, they are disliked, but if they do not induce extreme fright they are approached and explored. People spend more time looking at novel stimuli than at familiar ones, at the complex and incongruous rather than at the simple and congruous (Berlyne, 1963; Harrison, 1968). The combination of dislike and desire to explore very novel stimuli may well have a survival value and a genetic base. An instinctive fear reaction to a stimulus presented for the first time has been observed in a variety of animals (Bronson, 1968). Similarly, the human infant is also made anxious by new situations and maternal absence (Chapter 19). However, if no negative consequences come from the first encounter with the novel stimulus, the avoidance reaction will be weaker on the second exposure. With increased familiarity, the extremely novel becomes somewhat less novel and better liked. For instance, people initially find unusual color combinations, unfamiliar rhythms, and modern music unpleasant, but come to like them increasingly as they are repeatedly presented (see Zajonc, 1968; Berlyne, 1960, 1970). An experiment with rats suggests that one may even get used to novelty itself, regardless of its content (Hudson, 1950). Rats initially avoided a novel visual pattern. However, after members of one group had been exposed to miscellaneous novel objects in their cages before being introduced to the novel test object, their avoidance of the test object was reduced, although the objects in the cage resembled it only in having the property of novelty.

Encounters with novel stimuli may at first induce uncertainty and anxiety—but on the other hand we are bored by unchanging routine and complete predictability in the world. Thus, the overall relationship between liking and amount of exposure to or familiarity with stimuli is an inverted-u function (Zajonc, Shaver, Tavrix, & van Kreveld, 1972; Harrison & Crandall, 1972; Berlyne, 1970). The extremely novel is disliked, though perhaps explored; as it becomes somewhat less novel and more familiar, it is liked and perhaps sought. When we encounter almost no variation from the usual or expected, we are bored; further, we may become aroused and tense because of our boredom. We often seek the moderately deviant in order to increase arousal to an optimum associated with pleasant experiences.

We also seek and enjoy *arousal jags*, which temporarily increase arousal above the usual optimum (Berlyne, 1960, 1963). For an enjoyable arousal jag to occur, the arousal increase must be *moderate* and *temporary*, and one must be *secure* in the knowledge that it will end shortly. A small child first shudders with fear when tossed in the air, but the toss becomes pleasurable as he realizes the adult will catch him. The security required for exploration and enjoyment of the novel is probably the same security needed to loosen the boundaries of self in intrinsically motivated endeavors (Chapter 12). We enjoy the brief ride on a roller coaster or Ferris wheel when we trust the operator and the equipment, but we are glad when the ride is over and we are once again on familiar ground.

In short, moderate amounts of collative stimulation may be sought and enjoyed when the arousal increase they induce does not result in a total of too much arousal, and when there is security that the arousal will be quickly reduced. However, the arousal induced by collative stimuli may be a physiological base for anxiety.

Emotionality and defense. This basic formulation of reactions to collative stimuli sheds some light on the close relationship between creativity and emotions, which have an arousal base, and can help to identify some sources of individual differences in creative functioning. Individuals differ in the absolute level of the optimum amount of arousal, in their chronic arousal level and their physiological reactivity to stimuli, and in the degree of collative properties which will put them at their optimum or produce an arousal jag. Arousal level at any one time is a joint result of organismic and situational variables. How intense the collative properties and induced arousal must be to produce a pleasant experience or a satisfactory arousal jag, rather than a negative or neutral experience, varies from time to time and from person to person. The arousal induced by one kind of event is assumed to add to the arousal present for other reasons. The collative event which at one time produces the right amount of arousal to be enjoyed may at other times produce more arousal than can be enjoyed; this is likely to be so if the initial arousal level is high enough that additional arousal results in a total exceeding the limits of comfort.

People differ, of course, in their general tendencies to feel insecure and in their sensitivity to collative and other anxiety-inducing cues. How they deal with anxiety when faced with ambiguity and deviance from the usual will in large part determine whether their life style is an open creative one or a closed defensive one. The psychodynamic aspects of creative functioning may then be seen as a matter of emotionality. At one extreme, one may be closed to his own feelings and to external events that may induce emotionality. At the other, one may be open to himself and to the world.

The Closed and the Open

An emotionally closed person keeps arousal and anxiety low by physically avoiding collative stimuli, or by ignoring or distorting them so that they are perceived as familiar and congruent with expectancies (i.e., the assimilation effect, Chapters 11, 13). Such a person selects and remembers only the familiar and the commonplace, and prematurely imposes a safe structure when others might respond positively to the new and challenging. He won't try snails, regards foreigners with suspicion, and generally attempts to associate himself with a world in which every-thing is "just like me." In Jungian terms, he reacts with preconceived judgments rather than perceiving the stimulus as it is or may be (also compare with Schachtel's autocentric versus allocentric perception, Fromm's defensive seeing versus creative seeing, Rogers' openness versus defensiveness). He is closed to the world as it is, and sees the world only as he needs it to be. Another means of coping with the anxiety induced by uncertainty about external stimuli is simply to block out one's awareness of this anxiety (e.g., repress). The anxiety-arousing stimuli are not limited to external ones with collative properties, but include the fact of the existence of one's own memory, experience, and capacity for childlike exploration of self and environment. A person learns to defend even at the fantasy level, a level which might otherwise furnish inspiration or allow one to uncover his internal conflicts or un-conventional impulses (Chapter 9).

Those who have difficulty tolerating anxiety have difficulty admitting to the complexity and ambiguity in themselves and in their environment; they become cognitively and emotionally closed. It is as if they have a relatively high level of arousal so that additional arousal, which might be tolerated or enjoyed by others, elicits blocking defenses. Authoritarians are a good case in point. For the authoritarian personality, "too much existing emotional ambiguity and ambivalence are counteracted by denial and intolerance of cognitive ambiguity. It is as if everything would go to pieces once the existing discrepancies were faced" (Frenkel-Brunswik, 1949, p. 134). The background of such people is antithetical to the de-velopment of openness. They received severe punishment for expressing sexual and aggressive impulses; this punishment presumably led to the in-tense use of denial of impulses and repressions and to their need to keep the world and themselves compartmentalized into neat, simple, and safe categories. They structure situations in cognitively consistent and simple ways, and they reject, distort, deny, and ignore inconsistent stimuli (Miller & Rokeach, 1968). Because of high intolerance of ambiguity, they prefer the familiar, the symmetrical, the definite. When faced with a stimulus likely to arouse conflicting emotions or one which does not fit neatly into an existing category, they react with prejudice, stereotyping, and all-or-none thinking.

In contrast to the defensive modes of experiencing and behaving, the open modes which characterize creative functioning are marked by a relative lack of anxiety about the unfamiliar and the unconventional. The person with the openness to experience which is necessary for the development of creative potential can explore the unusual in the world and in himself without using distorting defenses to make internal and external events appear safer and more orderly than they really are. He may experience anxiety as he faces the complex and ambiguous, but he has sufficient ego strength to control his anxiety and perhaps use it to good end. His security and confidence in dealing with the collative stimuli of the world and of himself will be at least partly rooted in his early experiences and in his current interaction with his social environment. (Remember Rogers' emphasis on the necessity of a safe and accepting environment to foster openness [Chapter 5].) Unfortunately, experiences in the social setting in which people develop often inhibit openness and discourage exploration of the unknown and tolerance for the unusual in oneself or others.

DEVELOPMENT OF CREATIVITY IN THE SOCIAL SETTING

Despite the lip service society gives to the value of creativity, many of the normative values of our culture actually work to inhibit creative growth. Although there are doubtless biological determinants in both the intellectual and psychodynamic components of creativity, socialization variables have been more thoroughly discussed and researched. The inhibiting cultural forces are in large part mediated by teachers, parents, and peers, and generally result from a pervasive underlying pressure to conformity. Conformity and similarity with others are necessary ingredients for accurate social perception and communication and for social responsiveness in normal social emotional development (Chapters 13, 16, 18). However, the problem of socialization is that conformity easily becomes an all-pervasive pattern of life. Such oversocialization leads to intolerance and rejection of deviation, and a loss of spontaneity, fascination, and experience of personal freedom. The societal pressures which encourage conformity are not always necessary for the good of society, and are often too intense to allow identification *and* individuality (Chapter 18). Indeed, it is rather amazing that creative potential ever develops and flourishes within the sociocultural limitations man has imposed on himself and allowed to endure.

Inhibiting Cultural Forces

Torrance (1964, 1967) has listed several specific features of cultural thinking and behaving that discourage the development of creative potential. First, divergence tends to be equated with *abnormality*. Although theorists and researchers in creativity no longer think genius and creativity are associated with madness, a milder but insistent popular belief is that those who deviate from norms are somehow unhealthy or immoral (Chapters 13, 17, 21). *Peer pressures* against deviance, even outstanding performance, are exerted at early ages. A child who is definitely superior to others of his group in creative abilities experiences pressures to reduce his productivity and originality. Among adults, conformity is also negatively related with creativity (Crutchfield, 1959, 1962).

Further, cultural pressures encourage people to act and think in strict accordance with their societal *roles*. For instance, children quickly learn to inhibit interests and abilities not consistent with their sex roles. Even though Timmy wants a doll for Christmas, he is given a catcher's mitt; if Susie asks for a tool box, she receives a set of cooking utensils. *Sanctions against questioning and exploration* also operate to dampen curiosity and the production of novel ideas. Concomitant with this is a pressure to *achieve success* in conventionally defined ways, producing a realistic fear of censure for failing at an unconventional task.

Furthermore, achieving success is thought of as serious work, not play. The prevailing culture fosters a *work-play dichotomy.* Play is to be enjoyed; work is to be disliked. Those who enjoy work, including the work of school, make others uneasy because of their deviant pleasure. Teachers see highly creative students as less ambitious and hard-working than other students although the creative students often do just as well on standardized achievement tests as their classmates (Torrance, 1964). The creative children learn while appearing to the teachers to be playing around. Not only are play and work separated in cultural thinking, but the value of play and fantasy is minimized (Chapter 9). Work is valuable, and we are not always comfortable with leisure nor do we know how to use it well. Fantasy is for children, realism for the adult. Dutiful parents and teachers too quickly start training the child to work and think realistically. Even children's stories are changing from the fancy of Goldilocks to earthbound accounts of industrious, pragmatic, drab figures of a technological age, in the form of Nurse Nancy and Mr. Fixit (Kneller, 1965). The task of parents and teachers of keeping alive the child's spontaneous capacity for fantasy is a difficult one when they themselves may have an impoverished fantasy life.

Creativity in the Classroom

Developmental patterns. At what point do the openness and spontaneity of childhood responses give way to the inhibitions of the adult world? Evidence shows that there are definite periods of decline in creative growth which are most likely due to the cultural pressures that become particularly salient at certain ages. Creative thinking (on tests similar to Guilford's) declines around ages five, nine, thirteen, and seventeen (Torrance, 1962b). Around age five, concerns about sex appropriateness assume tremendous inhibiting proportions (Chapter 20). In the first three grades, creative children, especially boys, often get a reputation among other children for silly or naughty ideas. They learn to keep their thoughts to themselves, with a consequent loss of some of the spark of originality. In the fourth-grade classroom, activity becomes more organized, teachers are more concerned with correctness, and students receive credit only for what they put on paper. Upon entering the seventh grade the child must deal with emphasis on promptness, discouragement of deviations in appearance, concern with approval from the opposite sex, and an intensified pressure to be well rounded. At the end of high school, students are faced with the necessity of transition to college, work, or military service, and face new demands to behave "grown-up" and put behind their childish thinking and behavior. For originality to persist and creativity to mature, the demands imposed by socialization agents must be integrated into a pattern of discipline *and* freedom, restraint *and* expression.

The teacher. Social pressures against creative functioning are brought into the classroom via the teacher as an adult representative of society. Sad to say, her values are generally not compatible with those of creative children and she does not encourage traits that facilitate creative development. The values of students who were the highest in their class in intelligence but not creativity were positively correlated with their perception of the teacher's values (Getzels & Jackson, 1958). However, the relationship was negative for students who were highest in creativity but not intelligence. Members of the creative group were aware of cultural values and the teacher's values, but did not adopt them. The high-IQ students were success- and grade-oriented, and teacher-oriented, while the high-creative students were neither. Further, teachers ranked being courageous and having independent judgment—traits intimately associated with creativity—low on a list of characteristics to be encouraged in their students (Torrance, 1962a). Considering the creative children's lack of concern with achieving conventional success and getting the teacher's approval, and their self-direction and autonomy, it is no wonder that they do not get high grades, or that creativity and grades often are negatively related (Mednick, 1962). However, high RAT scorers tended to get higher grades from flexible teachers than from dogmatic ones, while low scorers received higher grades from dogmatic than from flexible teachers. Not surprisingly, college grades do not do very well in predicting the future creativity of such people as architects and research scientists (MacKinnon, 1960, 1961).

In fairness to teachers, it should be pointed out that permitting spontaneity, initiative, and creativity in an often crowded classroom is no easy task (J. Henry, 1959). Teachers have a responsibility to help children conform in many ways, for the child's own good and for the good, and order, of the classroom. Creative children do present problems. They propose unexpected solutions and disrupt the routine of the classroom by proposing novel possibilities in the face of boredom. Girls high in both creativity and intelligence were overeager and enthusiastic; those high in creativity but low in intelligence showed disruptive attention-seeking behavior as a protest against their frustration and lack of confidence (Wallach & Kogan, 1965). Even when teachers want to reward creativity in their students, they may be hampered by their own personal limitations and the limitations imposed upon them by others (Torrance et al., 1964). Teachers are inhibited from carrying out creative thinking activities when the principal does not give his direct approval. Just as student grades correlate negatively with creativity, so too do the principal's ratings of teachers correlate negatively with the teacher's creativity. Such evidence reminds us ". . . that teachers themselves work in social systems and the degree to which their own creativity is rewarded may affect the degree to which they stimulate and reward the creativity of their students" (Stein, 1968, p. 906).

Creativity in the Family

Different family patterns may be related to different styles of creativity, and evidence is sometimes contradictory. However, a key feature repeatedly found in the families of creative people—adults and children—is that the interaction patterns in the family serve to counteract general cultural forces and to encourage autonomy and independence (Roe, 1952; MacKinnon, 1962; Stein, 1957; R. Helson, 1971). The immediate family, or relatives and teachers, provides emotional support, encouragement, and respect. Direction is provided in terms of generalized values and in disciplinary actions that function to *guide* rather than to punish. Parents permit the freedom necessary for development of independence and self-exploration. More specifically, the typical family of highly creative high school students was seen to be one in which individual divergence was permitted and risks were accepted, and parents emphasized their children's values, interests, and responsiveness to experience (Getzels & Jackson, 1961). In contrast, parents of less-creative children were concerned about financial security, class status, and their child's perseverance for high academic achievement. Parents of gifted children or adults are themselves good models for independent behavior and open expression (MacKinnon, 1962; Weisberg & Springer, 1961). Both mother and father have independent interests and do not depend on others to provide their own security as individuals; that is, they do not overly identify with spouse or child (Chapter 18). They often freely express stormy feelings without fear of losing control. All in all, parents of gifted children seem to have largely settled the question of who and what they are. Although self-knowledge is sometimes painful and anxiety-provoking, they do not turn aside from it. With the secure parent, the children themselves may be both secure and free.

Sex Roles and Creativity

The social pressures exerted against creative functioning, and the creative person's independent response to these pressures, are clearly seen in the case of sex roles. "Feminine" characteristics and interest patterns are typical in creative men; this has been found with architects, research scientists, military officers, and artists, through the use of measuring instruments including projective instruments, self-report measures, and observational assessments (see Dellas & Gaier, 1970; Nash, 1970). However, creative men are *not* effeminate. The "feminine" traits of sensitivity and intuition are blended with "masculine" traits of purposive action, determination, assertiveness, confidence, and independence. Similarly, creative women have masculine characteristics but are at the same time feminine. In fact, among a sample of female mathematicians, excessive masculinity was characteristic of the low and moderately creative rather than the highly creative (R. Helson, 1967, 1971). Although high-creative young college women reported having rejected conventional feminine patterns, they apparently did not need to go overboard to don armor in a masculine protest (Chapter 4).

The integration of opposite-sex characteristics reflects the creative person's openness to experience and tolerance for complexity (Barron, 1957; MacKinnon, 1962). The creative male is open and willing to reveal his feelings and emotions; he has self-awareness, and is sensitive and open to wide-ranging interests, including many labeled feminine. Women must develop masculine characteristics if they are to effectively use their creative potential, and in their openness will encounter, admit, and enjoy masculine interests. Barron (1957) suggests that the openness is associated with the basic predisposition to allow complexity and contradictions into consciousness; tabooed interests and impulses are allowed into awareness and integrated into the complex whole personality. He assumes an initial biological bisexual disposition claimed by Freud and Jung. Barron's thinking is also reminiscent of Jung's contention that all opposites must be developed and integrated to achieve self-actualization; in this case, the masculine and feminine traits we all have.

The creative are independent, complex, and open enough to express opposite-sex characteristics. However, they are not immune to the fact of their deviation. Males who were highest in openness to experience described themselves as relatively feminine *and* had higher anxiety scores than males lowest in openness; they did not repress the anxiety (Fitzgerald, 1966). Senior college women nominated by the faculty for creative potential had higher ego-strength, more personal effectiveness, more independence, and greater flexibility than the control group, but reported in an interview that they cried more often than the control group (R. Helson, 1961). Further, of the creative group, four-fifths reported experiences of overwhelming feelings of emptiness, desolation, and aloneness, compared with one-third of the controls. Thoughts of death and suicide were common. This may reflect a greater emotional intensity, "but perhaps also they tell us something of the existential reality deeply experienced by young women who sense their own potential and yet despair at the prospect before them when they move out into a world which demands that they sacrifice either their femininity or their intellectual creativity" (Barron, 1965, p. 96).

Prognosis

Are we living in a plastic and tinfoil society? Have the technological advances of the past decade so dulled our human sensitivities that we are a machine-, rather than person-oriented, society? Perhaps. But so long as we are a society of individuals, there will be those among us who possess the inner freedom to pursue a creative life style. How they develop this inner freedom is an enigma. Perhaps a parent, a teacher, or a friend has encouraged it in some subtle, undetected ways. Perhaps they made a sort of personal decision, as Third Force spokesmen suggest is possible. Perhaps in a moment of distraction or emotional crisis their defenses fell and they caught a glimpse of the potential that is theirs. The task for the individual is to be able to open up to himself and move with freedom and control even when others attempt to limit or eliminate his freedom. The challenge for society is to foster the development of inner freedom, so that the individual may evolve from a conforming world a style of life in which he may realize his fullest potentials.

SUMMARY: THE CREATIVE PERSON

What is a "creative personality"? In brief, it is a felicitous combination of perceptual, cognitive, and emotional predispositions which enable a person to be open and responsive to the realistic complexities, novelty, deviance, and disorder of himself and the world. From the new and complex comes the familiar and simple, from the disorder comes an order which may be embodied in artistic masterpieces, scientific discoveries, or in the meaningful interpersonal relationships which link the creatively functioning individual with his fellow man in the growth that characterizes a creative life style.

There is general agreement among the personality theorists of the necessity for both a personalized and socialized, an idiosyncratic and a communal, mode of functioning in creative expressions. The socialized mode retains the known and produces the usual and expected. The personalized mode revises the known and produces the unusual and unconventional. Evidence indicates that the creative person is capable of both modes of functioning and, furthermore, possesses the cognitive flexibility to shift between the two modes of functioning with relative ease. Ego control and openness have also been positively correlated with creativity; they allow the creative person to wander from the security of familiar paths and to exploit positively the potential consequences of his intellectual and emotional peregrinations in the search for order.

Societal pressures to conform to existing norms often inhibit the development of creativity. The home and school, two primary learning environments, play a crucial role in discouraging unconventional thinking as they attempt to mold the child into societal perceptions of a proper, albeit stagnant and personally thwarting, life style. Despite these pressures, people have shown that they can transcend their environment and attempt to realize their creative potential. Such inner freedom requires openness to the complexity of self, and energy and direction in working with the complexity to find order.

Our knowledge of the world of things, people, and events will probably always be shaped and limited by the nature and complexity of the personal constructs we use in ordering the world of discrete sensations. And for most of us, there will probably always be some need to see others as we wish them to be. However, while we may not be able to achieve a perfect openness, we can be aware of the kinds of distortions we are likely to have, and we can attempt to make corrections for the distortions we cannot overcome. We can work toward knowledge of self and of others, and make some headway in admitting the unfulfilled potentials that characterize human beings as we now know them. When these potentials, unknown as they may be today, can be recognized and realized, we may be able to find a kind of human being we have thus far seldom seen. And, for this author, that is what being a psychologist is all about.

BIBLIOGRAPHY

Abelson, R. P., et al. 1968. *Theories of cognitive consistency: a sourcebook.* New York: Rand McNally.

Abbott, S., and Love, B. 1972. Is women's liberation a lesbian plot? In Gornick, V., and Moran, B. K. (Eds.), *Women in sexist society, studies in power and powerlessness.* New York: Signet, New American Library (paperback edition).

Adams, D. 1954. *The anatomy of personality.* New York: Doubleday.

Adams, M. 1971. The single woman in today's society: A reappraisal. *American Journal of Orthopsychiatry,* 41, 5, 776–786.

Adey, W. R., Kado, R. T., and Rhodes, J. M. 1963. Sleep: Cortical and subcortical recordings in the chimpanzee. *Science,* 141, 932–933.

Adler, A. 1926. *The neurotic constitution.* New York: Dodd, Mead.

Adler, A. 1930. Individual psychology. In Murchison, C. (Ed.), *Psychologies of 1930.* Worcester, Mass.: Clark University Press.

Adler, A. 1957. *Understanding human nature.* New York: Fawcett Publications, Premier Books. (Originally published, 1927)

Adler, A. 1964. *Social interest: A challenge to mankind.* Trans. by J. Linton and R. Vaugh. New York: Capricorn Books.

Adler, A. 1973. *Superiority and social interest, a collection of later writings.* Third Revised Edition. Edited by H. L. Ansbacher and R. R. Ansbacher. New York: Viking.

Aiello, J. R., and Jones, S. E. 1971. Field study of the proxemic behavior of young school children in three subcultural groups. *Journal of Personality and Social Psychology,* 19, 3, 351–356.

Ainsworth, M. D. S., and Bell, S. M. 1969. Some contemporary patterns of mother-infant interaction in the feeding situation. In Ambrose, A., *Stimulation in early infancy.* New York: Academic Press.

Allen, V. L. 1966. Effect of knowledge of deception on conformity. *Journal of Social Psychology,* 69, 101–106.

Allen, V. L., and Newtson, D. 1972. Development of conformity and independence. *Journal of Personality and Social Psychology,* 22, 1, 18–30.

Allport, F. H. 1955. *Theories of perception and the concept of structure.* New York: Wiley.

Allport, G. 1937. *Personality: A psychological interpretation.* New York: Holt, Rinehart and Winston.

Allport, G. 1955. *Becoming: Basic considerations for a psychology of personality.* New Haven: Yale University Press.

Allport, G. 1961. *Pattern and Growth in Personality.* New York: Holt, Rinehart and Winston.

Allport, G. 1962. The general and the unique in psychological science. *Journal of Personality,* 30, 405–422.

Allport, G. 1965. *Letters from Jenny.* New York: Harcourt Brace Jovanovich.

Allport, G., and Pettigrew, T. F. 1957. Cultural influence on the perception of movement: The trapezoidal illusion among Zulus. *Journal of Abnormal and Social Psychology,* 55, 104–113.

American Psychological Association. 1965. Testing and public policy. *American Psychologist,* 20, 857–993 (Special Issue).

American Psychological Association. 1966. *Standards for Educational and Psychological Tests and Measurements.* Washington, D.C.: American Psychological Association.

Anastasia, A. 1968. *Psychological Testing.* New York: Macmillan.

Anderson, H. H. (Ed.). 1959. *Creativity and its cultivation.* New York: Harper & Row.

Angyal, A. 1941. *Foundations for a science of personality.* New York and

Cambridge, Mass.: Commonwealth Fund and Harvard University Press.

Ansbacher, H. L. 1964. Introduction to Adler, A. *Problems of neurosis*. New York: Harper & Row, Torchbook Edition.

Ansbacher, H. L. 1965. The structure of individual psychology. In Wolman, B. B., and Nagel, E. (Eds.), *Scientific psychology*. New York: Basic Books.

Antrobus, J. S. 1963. The effects of varied and repetitive talking on visual vigilance performance under reduced external stimulation. Doctoral dissertation, Teachers College, Columbia University.

Antrobus, J., Dement, W., and Fisher, C. 1964. Patterns of dreaming and dream recall: An EEG study. *Journal of Abnormal and Social Psychology*, 69, 341–344.

Archibald, H. C., and Tuddenhan, R. D. 1965. Persistent stress reaction after combat. *Archives of General Psychiatry*, 12, 475–481.

Argyle, M. 1967. *The psychology of interpersonal behavior*. Baltimore: Penguin.

Argyris, C. 1968. Some unintended consequences of rigorous research. *Psychological Bulletin*, 70, 185–197.

Arnold, M. B. (Ed.). 1970a. *Feelings and emotions, The Loyola symposium*. New York: Academic Press.

Arnold, M. B. 1970b. Perennial problems in the field of emotion. In Arnold, M. B. (Ed.), *Feelings and emotions*. New York: Academic Press.

Aronfreed, J. 1961. The nature, variety, and social patterning of moral responses to transgression. *Journal of Abnormal and Social Psychology*, 63, 223–240.

Aronfreed, J. 1963. The effects of experimental socialization paradigms upon two moral responses to transgression. *Journal of Abnormal and Social Psychology*, 66, 5, 437–448.

Aronfreed, J. 1964. The origin of self-criticism. *Psychological Review*, 71, 193–218.

Aronfreed, J., and Reber, A. 1965. Internalized behavioral suppression and the timing of social punishment. *Journal of Personality and Social Psychology*, 1, 3–16.

Aronoff, J. 1967. *Psychological needs and cultural systems: A case study*. Princeton, N.J.: Van Nostrand, Insight.

Aronfreed, J. 1969. The concept of internalization. In Goslin, D. A. (Ed.), *Handbook of socialization theory and research*. Chicago: Rand McNally.

Aronson, E. 1969. The theory of cognitive dissonance: A current perspective. In Berkowitz, L. (Ed.), *Advances in experimental social psychology*, Volume 4. New York: Academic Press.

Asch, S. E. 1946. Forming impressions of personality. *Journal of Abnormal and Social Psychology*, 41, 258–290.

Asch, S. E. 1956. Studies of independence and conformity: I. A minority of one against a unanimous majority. *Psychological Monographs*, 70, 9 (Whole No. 416).

Asch, S. E. 1958. Effects of group pressure upon the modification and distortion of judgements. In Maccoby, E. E., Newcomb, T. M., and Hartley, E. L. (Eds.), *Readings in social psychology*. New York: Holt, Rinehart and Winston.

Atkins, A. L. 1966. Own attitude and discriminability in relation to anchoring effects in judgement. *Journal of Personality and Social Psychology*, 4, 5, 497–507.

Atkins, A. L., and Bieri, J. 1968. Effects of involvement level and contextual stimuli on social judgement. *Journal of Personality and Social Psychology*, 9, 2, 197–204.

Atkinson, J. W. 1957. Motivational determinants of risk-taking behavior. *Psychological Review*, 64, 359–372.

Atkinson, J. W. 1964. *An introduction to motivation*. Princeton, N.J.: Van Nostrand.

Atkinson, J. W. (Ed.). 1958. *Motives in fantasy, action, and society*. Princeton, N.J.: Van Nostrand.

Atkinson, J. W., and McClelland, D. C. 1948. The projective expression of needs. II. The effect of different intensities of the hunger drive on thematic apperception. *Journal of Experimental Psychology*, 38, 643–658.

Auld, F., Jr., and Murray, E. J. 1955. Content-analysis studies of psychotherapy. *Psychological Bulletin*, 52, 377–395.

Austin, M. C., and Thompson, G. G. 1948. Children's friendships: A study of the bases on which children select and reject their best friends. *Journal of Educational Psychology*, 39, 101–116.

Ausubel, D. P., et al. 1954. Perceived parent attitudes as determinants of children's ego structure. *Child Development*, 1954, 25, 173–183.

Averill, J. R., Olbrich, E., and Lazarus, R. S. 1972. Personality correlates of differential responsiveness to direct and vicarious threat: A failure to replicate previous findings. *Journal of Personality and Social Psychology*, 21, 25–29.

Ax, A. F. 1955. The physiological differentiation between fear and anger in humans. *Psychosomatic Medicine*, 15, 433–442.

Ayllon, T. 1963. Intensive treatment of psychotic behavior by stimulus satiation and food reinforcement. *Behavioral Research and Therapy*, 1, 53.

Ayllon, T., and Azrin, M. 1968. *The token economy: A motivational system for therapy and rehabilitation.* New York: Appleton-Century-Crofts.

Azrin, N. H., Hutchinson, R. R., and Hake, D. F. 1966. Extinction-induced aggression. *Journal of Experimental Analysis of Behavior*, 9, 191–204.

Azrin, N. H., and Lindsley, O. R. 1956. The reinforcement of cooperation between children. *Journal of Abnormal and Social Psychology*, 52, 100–102.

Back, K. W., and Bogdonoff, M. D. 1964. Plasma lipid responses to leadership, conformity, and deviation. In Leiderman, P. H., and Shapiro, D. (Eds.), *Psychobiological approaches to social behavior.* Stanford, Calif.: Stanford University Press.

Baer, D. M., and Sherman, J. A. 1964. Reinforcement control of generalized imitation in young children. *Journal of Experimental Child Psychology*, 1, 37–49.

Bagby, J. W. 1957. A cross-cultural study of perceptual predominance in binocular rivalry. *Journal of Abnormal and Social Psychology*, 54, 331–334.

Bakan, D. 1966. The test of significance in psychological research. *Psychological Bulletin*, 66, 423–437.

Baldwin, A. L. 1942. Personal structure analysis: A statistical method for investing the single personality. *Journal of Abnormal and Social Psychology*, 37, 63–183.

Baldwin, A. L. 1948. Socialization and the parent-child relationship. *Child Development*, 19, 127–136.

Baldwin, A. L. 1967. *Theories of child development.* New York: Wiley.

Bales, R. F. 1950. A set of categories for the analysis of small group interaction. *American Sociological Review*, 15, 257–263.

Balint, A. 1945. Identification. In Lorand, S. (Ed.), *The Yearbook of Psychoanalysis*, Volume 1. New York: International University Press.

Bandura, A. 1960. Relationship of family patterns to child behavior disorders. Progress Report, U.S.P.H. Research Grant M-1734. Stanford, Calif.: Stanford University Press.

Bandura, A. 1965. Influence of models' reinforcement contingencies on the acquisition of imitative responses. *Journal of Personality and Social Psychology*, 1, 589–595.

Bandura, A. 1969a. *Principles of behavior modification.* New York: Holt, Rinehart and Winston.

Bandura, A. 1969b. Social learning of moral judgements. *Journal of Personality and Social Psychology*, 11, 275–279.

Bandura, A. 1969c. Social-learning theory of identificatory processes. In Goslin, D. A. (Ed.), *Handbook of socialization theory and research.* Chicago: Rand McNally.

Bandura, A., and Menlove, F. L. 1968. Factors determining vicarious extinction of avoidance behavior through symbolic modeling. *Journal of Personality and Social Psychology*, 8, 99–108.

Bandura, A., and Walters, R. H. 1959. *Adolescent Aggression.* New York: Ronald.

Bandura, A., and Walters, R. H. 1963. *Social learning and personality development.* New York: Holt, Rinehart and Winston.

Bandura, A., Grusec, J. E., and Menlove, F. L. 1966. Observational learning as a function of symbolization and incentive set. *Child Development*, 37, 499–506.

Bandura, A., Grusec, J. E., and Menlove, F. L. 1967. Vicarious extinction of avoidance behavior. *Journal of Personality and Social Psychology*, 5, 16–23.

Bandura, A., Ross, D., and Ross, S. A. 1963a. A comparative test of the status envy, social power, and secondary reinforcement theories of identificatory learning. *Journal of Abnormal and Social Psychology*, 67, 6, 527–534.

Bandura, A., Ross, D., and Ross, S. A. 1963b. Imitation of film-mediated aggressive models. *Journal of Abnormal and Social Psychology*, 66, 3–11.

Barclay, A. M. 1971. An overview of central processes affecting the expression of sexual and aggressive behaviors. Paper presented at American Association for the Advancement of Science, Philadelphia, December 30, 1971.

Barclay, A. M. 1973. Social and biological foundations of human sexuality. In Donelson, E., and Gullahorn, J. (Eds.), *Women: A psychological perspective*. In press.

Bardwick, J. M. 1971. *Psychology of women: A study of bio-cultural conflicts*. New York: Harper & Row.

Barefoot, J. C., and Straub, R. B. 1971. Opportunity for information search and the effect of false heart-rate feedback. *Journal of Personality and Social Psychology*, 17, 154–157.

Barker, R. G. 1963. *The stream of behavior: Explorations of its structure and content*. New York: Appleton-Century-Crofts.

Barker, R. G. 1968. *Ecological psychology: Concepts and methods for studying the environment of human behavior*. Stanford, Calif.: Stanford University Press.

Barker, R. G., and Wright, H. F. 1951. *One boy's day*. New York: Harper & Row.

Barker, R. G., Dembo, T., and Lewin, K. 1941. Frustration and regression: An experiment with young children. *University of Iowa Studies in Child Welfare*, 18, No. 1, 1–314.

Baron, R. M., and Ganz, R. L. 1972. Effects of locus of control and type of feedback on the task performance of lower-class black children. *Journal of*

Personality and Social Psychology, 21, 124–130.

Barron, F. 1953. Complexity-simplicity as a personality dimension. *Journal of Abnormal and Social Psychology*, 48, 163–172.

Barron, F. 1955. The disposition toward originality. *Journal of Abnormal and Social Psychology*, 51, 478–485.

Barron, F. 1957. Originality in relation to personality and intellect. *Journal of Personality*, 25, 730–742.

Barron, F. 1963a. *Creativity and psychological health*. Princeton, N.J.: Van Nostrand.

Barron, F. 1963b. The needs for order and for disorder as motivation in creative activity. In Taylor, C. W., and Barron, F. (Eds.), *Scientific creativity: Its recognition and development*. New York: Wiley.

Barron, F. 1965. The psychology of creativity. In Barron, F., et al., *Directions in psychology*, Volume II. New York: Holt, Rinehart and Winston.

Barron, F. 1968. *Creativity and personal freedom*. Princeton, N.J.: Van Nostrand.

Barry, W., Bacon, M. K., and Child, I. L. 1957. A cross-cultural survey of some sex differences in socialization. *Journal of Abnormal and Social Psychology*, 55, 327–332.

Barry, W. A. 1970. Marriage research and conflict: An integrative review. *Psychological Bulletin*, 73, 41–54.

Barthell, C. N., and Holmes, D. S. 1968. High school yearbooks: A nonreactive measure of social isolation in graduates who later became schizophrenics. *Journal of Abnormal Psychology*, 73, 313–316.

Barton, K., and Cattell, R. B. 1972. Marriage dimensions and personality. *Journal of Personality and Social Psychology*, 21, 3, 369–375.

Baughman, E. E. 1971. *Black Americans: A psychological analysis*. New York: Academic Press.

Baughman, E. E. 1972. *Personality, the psychological study of the individual*. Englewood Cliffs, N.J.: Prentice-Hall.

Baughman, E. E., and Welsh, G. S. 1962. *Personality: A Behavioral Science*. Englewood Cliffs, N.J.: Prentice-Hall.

Baumrind, D. 1964. Some thoughts on

ethics of research: After reading Milgram's Behavior study of obedience. *American Psychologist*, 19, 421–423.

Baxter, J. C., Lerner, M. J., and Miller, J. S. 1965. Identification as a function of the reinforcing quality of the model and the socialization background of the subject. *Journal of Personality and Social Psychology*, 2, 692–697.

Becker, W. C. 1964. Consequences of different kinds of parental discipline. In Hoffman, M. L., and Hoffman, L. W. (Eds.), *Review of child development research*, Volume I. New York: Russell Sage Foundation.

Bell, R. Q. 1968. A reinterpretation of the direction of efforts in studies of socialization. *Psychological Review*, 75, 81–95.

Bell, R. R. 1963. *Marriage and family interaction*. Homewood, Ill.: Dorsey Press.

Bellak, L. 1971. *The T.A.T. and C.A.T. in clinical use*, Second Edition. New York: Grune and Stratton.

Bem, D. J. 1965. An experimental analysis of self-persuasion. *Journal of Experimental Social Psychology*, 1, 199–218.

Bem, D. J. 1966. Inducing belief in false confessions. *Journal of Personality and Social Psychology*, 3, 707–710.

Bem, D. J. 1967. Self-perception: An alternative interpretation of cognitive dissonance phenomena. *Psychological Review*, 74, 183–200.

Bem, D. J. 1968a. Attitudes as self-descriptions: Another look at the attitude-behavior link. In Greenwald, A. G., Brock, T. C., and Ostrom, T. M. (Eds.), *Psychological foundations of attitudes*. New York: Academic Press.

Bem, D. J. 1968b. Dissonance reduction in the behaviorist. In Abelson, R. P., et al., *Theories of cognitive consistency: A sourcebook*. New York: Rand McNally and Co.

Bem, D. J. 1970. *Beliefs, attitudes, and human affairs*. Belmont, Calif.: Brooks-Cole.

Benedict, R. 1929. The science of custom. Reprinted in Calverton, V. F. (Ed.), *The Making of Man*. New York: Greenwood.

Bennett, E. M., and Cohen, L. R. 1959. Men and women: Personality patterns

and contrasts. *Genetic Psychology Monographs*, 59, 101–155.

Bentler, P. M., Jackson, D. N., and Messick, S. 1971. Identification of content and style: A two-dimensional interpretation of acquiescence. *Psychological Bulletin*, 76, 3, 186–204.

Bentler, P. M., Jackson, D. N., and Messick, S. 1972. A rose by any other name. *Psychological Bulletin*, 77, 2, 109–113.

Berger, R. J. 1969. Oculomotor control: A possible function of REM sleep. *Psychological Review*, 76, 144–164.

Berger, R. J. 1970. Morpheus descending. *Psychology Today*, 4, 1, 33–36, 70.

Berger, R. J., and Oswald, I. 1962. Effects of sleep deprivation on behavior, subsequent sleep and dreaming. *Journal of Mental Science*, 108, 457–465.

Bergler, E. 1957. *Homosexuality: Disease or way of life?* New York: Hill and Wang.

Berkowitz, L. 1964. *The development of motives and values in the child*. New York: Basic Books.

Berkowitz, L. 1965. The concept of aggressive drive: Some additional considerations. In L. Berkowitz (Ed.), *Advances in experimental social psychology*. New York: Academic Press.

Berkowitz, L. 1969. Social motivation. In Lindzey, G., and Aronson, E. (Eds.), *The handbook of social psychology*, second edition, Volume III. Reading, Mass.: Addison-Wesley.

Berkowitz, L. 1970a. The contagion of violence: An S-R mediational analysis of some effects of observed aggression. *Nebraska Symposium on Motivation*, 18, 95–135.

Berkowitz, L. 1970b. The self, selfishness, and altruism. In Macaulay, J., and Berkowitz, L. (Eds.), *Altruism and helping behavior*. New York: Academic Press.

Berkowitz, L. 1972. Social norms, feelings, and other factors affecting helping and altruism. In Berkowitz L., *Advances in experimental social psychology*, Volume 6. New York: Academic Press. Pp. 63–108.

Berlyne, D. E. 1960. *Conflict, arousal, and curiosity*. New York: McGraw-Hill.

Berlyne, D. E. 1963. Motivational problems raised by exploratory and epistemic behavior. In Koch, S. (Ed.),

Psychology: A study of a science, Volume 5. New York: McGraw-Hill.

Berlyne, D. E. 1966. Curiosity and exploration. *Science*, 153, 23–33.

Berlyne, D. E. 1968. The motivational significance of collative variables and conflict. In Abelson et al., *Theories of cognitive consistency: A sourcebook*. New York: Rand McNally and Co.

Berlyne, D. E. 1970. Novelty, complexity and hedonic value. *Perception and Psychophysics*, 8, 279–286.

Bernard, J. 1972. The paradox of the happy marriage. In Gornick, V., and Moran, B. K. (Eds.), *Woman in sexist society, studies in power and powerlessness*. New York: Signet, New American Library.

Berscheid, E., and Walster, E. H. 1969. *Interpersonal attraction*. Reading, Mass.: Addison-Wesley.

Bettelheim, B. 1943. Individual and mass behavior in extreme situations. *Journal of Abnormal and Social Psychology*, 38, 417–452.

Bexton, W. H., Heron, W., and Scott, T. H. 1954. Effects of decreased variation in the sensory environment. *Canadian Journal of Psychology*, 8, 70–76.

Bieber, I., et al. 1962. *Homosexuality: A psychoanalytical study*. New York: Basic Books.

Bieri, J. 1955. Cognitive complexity-simplicity and predictive behavior. *Journal of Abnormal and Social Psychology*, 51, 263–268.

Bieri, J. 1968. Cognitive complexity and judgement of inconsistent information. In Abelson, et al., *Theories of cognitive consistency: A sourcebook*. New York: Rand McNally.

Bieri, J., et al. 1966. *Clinical and social judgement: The discrimination of behavioral information*. New York: Wiley.

Biller, H. B. 1969. Father absence, maternal encouragement, and sex role development in kindergarten-age boys. *Child Development*, 40, 539–546.

Birney, R. C. 1968. Research on the achievement motive. In Lambert, W. W., and Borgatta, E. F. *Handbook of personality theory and research*. Chicago: Rand McNally.

Bishop, F. V. 1967. The anal character: A rebel in the dissonance family. *Journal of Personality and Social Psychology*, 6, 23–36.

Block, J. 1961. *The Q-sort method in personality assessment and psychiatric research*. Springfield, Ill.: Charles C Thomas.

Block, J. 1971. On further conjectures regarding acquiescence. *Psychological Bulletin*, 76, 205–210.

Block, J., and Thomas, H. 1955. Is satisfaction with self a measure of adjustment? *Journal of Abnormal and Social Psychology*, 51, 254–259.

Blood, R. O., and Wolfe, D. M. 1960. *Husbands and wives: The dynamics of married living*. Glencoe: Free Press.

Blum, G. S. 1950. *The Blacky pictures and manual*. New York: The Psychological Corporation.

Bokert, E. 1965. The effects of thirst and related auditory stimulation on dream reports. Presented to the Association for the Psychophysiological Study of Sleep. Washington, D.C.

Bonarius, J. C. J. 1965. Research in the personal construct theory of George A. Kelly: Role Construct Repertory Test and Basic Theory. In Maher, B. A. (Ed.), *Progress in experimental personality research*, Volume 2. New York: Academic Press.

Bonner, H. 1965. *On being mindful of man*. Boston: Houghton Mifflin Co.

Bossard, J. H. S., and Boll, E. S. 1955. Marital unhappiness in the life cycle of marriage. *Marriage and family living*, 17, 10–14.

Bovard, E. W. 1959. The effects of social stimuli on the response to stress. *Psychological Review*, 66, 267–277.

Bowlby, J. 1958. The nature of the child's tie to his mother. *International Journal of Psychoanalysis*, 39, 350–373.

Bowlby, J. 1969. *Attachment and loss*, Volume 1. New York: Basic Books.

Brackbill, Y. 1958. Extinction of the smiling response in infants as a function of reinforcement schedule. *Child Development*, 29, 115–124.

Bradburn, N. M. 1963. Achievement and father dominance in Turkey. *Journal of Abnormal and Social Psychology*, 67, 464–468.

Bradburn, N. M. 1969. *The structure of psychological well-being*. Chicago: Aldine.

Bradbury, R. 1968. A conversation with Ray Bradbury and Chuck Jones, by Hall, M. H. *Psychology Today*, Volume 1, No. 11, Pp. 28–37.

Brady, J. V. 1958. Emotional behavior and the nervous system. Transactions of the New York Academy of Science, 18, 601–612.

Braithwaite, R. B. 1960. *Scientific explanation: A study of the function of theory, probability and law in science.* New York: Harper and Brothers.

Bramel, D. 1962. A dissonance-theory approach to defensive projection. *Journal of Abnormal and Social Psychology*, 65, 192–202.

Bramel, D. 1963. Selection of a target for defensive projection. *Journal of Abnormal and Social Psychology*, 66, 318–324.

Bramel, D. 1968. Dissonance, expectation, and the self. In Abelson, et al., *Theories of cognitive consistency: A sourcebook.* New York: Rand McNally and Co.

Breger, L. 1967. Functions of dreams. *Journal of Abnormal Psychology Monograph.* 72, 5, Part 2 (Whole No. 641). Pp. 1–28.

Breggin, P. R. 1964. The psychophysiology of anxiety. *Journal of Nervous and Mental Diseases*, 139, 558–568.

Brehm, J. W. 1966. *A theory of psychological reactance.* New York: Academic Press.

Brehm, J. W. 1968. Attitude change from threat to attitudinal freedom. In Greenwald, A. G., Brock, T. C., and Ostrom, T. C. (Eds.), *Psychological foundations of attitudes.* New York: Academic Press.

Brehm, J. W., and Behar, L. B. 1966. Sexual arousal, defensiveness, and sex preference in affiliation. *Journal of Experimental Research in Personality,* 1, 195–200.

Brehm, J. W., and Cole, N. H. 1966. Effect of a favor which reduces freedom. *Journal of Personality and Social Psychology*, 3, 4, 420–426.

Brein, M., and Dovid, K. H. 1971. Intercultural communication and the adjustment of the sojourner. *Psychological Bulletin,* 76, 3, 215–230.

Bridges, K. 1932. Emotional development in early infancy. *Child Development,* 3, 324–341.

Briggs, K. C., and Myers, I. B. 1957. *Myers-Briggs Type Indicator.* Privately printed.

Brigham, J. C. 1971. Ethnic stereotypes. *Psychological Bulletin,* 76, 1, 15–38.

Brim, O. 1958. Family structure and sex role learning in children. *Sociometry,* 21, 1–16.

Brittain, C. V. Adolescent choices and parent-peer cross pressures. *American Sociological Review,* 28, 385–391.

Brittain, C. V. 1967. An exploration of the bases of peer-compliance and parent-compliance in adolescence. *Adolescence,* 2, 445–458.

Broadbent, D. W. 1957. A mechanical model for human attention and immediate memory. *Psychological Review,* 64, 205–215.

Brodbeck, M. 1959. Models, meaning, and theories. In Gross, L. (Ed.), *Symposium on sociological theory.* Evanston, Ill.: Row, Peterson and Company.

Bronfenbenner, U. 1961. Some familial antecedents of responsibility and leadership in adolescents. In Petrullo, L., and Bass, B. (Eds.), *Leadership and interpersonal behavior.* New York: Holt, Rinehart and Winston.

Bronfenbrenner, U. 1962a. The role of age, sex, class, and culture in studies of moral development. *Religious Education,* 57, 3–17.

Bronfenbrenner, U. 1962b. Soviet methods of character education: Some implications for research. *American Psychologist,* 17, 550–564.

Bronson, G. W. 1968. The fear of novelty. *Psychological Bulletin,* 69, 350–358.

Bronson, G. W. 1970. Fear of visual novelty: Developmental patterns in males and females. *Developmental Psychology,* 2, 33–40.

Brown, D. G. 1957. Masculinity-femininity development in children. *Journal of Consulting Psychology,* 21, 197–202.

Brown, J. S. 1969. Factors affecting self-punitive locomotor behavior. In Campbell, B. A., and Church, R. M. (Eds.), *Punishment and aversive behavior.* New York: Appleton-Century-Crofts.

Brown, J. S., and Jacobs, A. 1949. The role of fear in the motivation and acquisition of responses. *Journal of Ex-*

perimental Psychology, 39, 747–759.

Bruche, H. 1961. Transformation of oral impulses in eating disorders: A conceptual approach. Psychiatric Quarterly, pp. 35, 458–481.

Bruner, J. S. and Goodman, C. D. 1947. Value and need as organizing factors in perception. Journal of Abnormal and Social Psychology, 42, 33–44.

Bruner, J. S. and Tagiuri, R. 1954. The perception of people. In G. Lindzey (Ed.), Handbook of social psychology. Vol. 2. Reading, Mass.: Adison Wesley, Publisher.

Bryan, J. H. and Schwartz, T. 1971. Effects of film material upon children's behavior. Psychological Bulletin, 75, 50–59.

Bugenthal, D. E., Love, L. R., and Kaswan, J. W. 1972. Videotaped family interaction: Differences reflecting presence and type of child disturbance. Journal of Abnormal Psychology, 79, 3, 285–290.

Burgess, E. W., and Wallin, P. 1953. Engagement and marriage. Chicago: Lippincott.

Burlingham, D., and Freud, A. 1943. Young children in war-time. London: Allen and Unwin.

Burnstein, E., and Zajonc, R. B. 1965. Individual task performance in a changing social structure. Sociometry, 28, 16–29.

Buros, O. K. (Ed.). 1970. Personality tests and reviews. Highland Park, N.J.: Gryphon.

Burr, W. R. 1970. Satisfaction of various aspects of marriage over the life cycle: A random middle class sample. Journal of Marriage and the Family, 32, 29–37.

Burris, R. W. 1958. The effect of counseling on achievement motivation. Unpublished doctoral dissertation, Indiana University.

Burton, R. V. 1969. Socialization, Psychological Aspects. In Sills, D. L. (Ed.), International encyclopedia of the social sciences. New York: Crowell-Collier. Vol. 14; 534–545.

Buss. 1961. The psychology of aggression. New York: Wiley.

Butcher, J. N. (Ed.). 1969. MMPI: Research developments in clinical applications. New York: McGraw-Hill.

Butler, J. M. and Haigh, G. V. C. 1954. Changes in the relation between self-concepts and ideal concepts consequent upon client-centered counseling. In Rogers, C. R., and Dymond, R. F. (Eds.), Psychotherapy and personality change: Co-ordinate studies in the client-centered approach. Chicago: University of Chicago Press. pp. 55–76.

Butler, R. A. 1953. Discrimination by Rhesus monkeys to visual-exploration motivation. Journal of Comparative and Physiological Psychology, 46, 95–98.

Byrne, D. 1961. The Repression-Sensitization Scale: Rationale, reliability, and validity. Journal of Personality, 29, 334–349.

Byrne, D. 1964. Repression-sensitization as a dimension of personality. In Maher, B. A. (Ed.), Progress in Experimental Personality Research. Vol. 1. New York: Academic Press.

Byrne, D. 1966. An introduction to personality. Englewood Cliffs, N.J.: Prentice-Hall, Inc.

Byrne, D. 1969. Attitudes and attraction. In L. Berkowitz (Ed.), Advances in experiment social psychology. Volume 4. New York: Academic Press.

Byrne, D., and Clore, G. L. 1967. Effectance arousal and attraction. Journal of Personality and Social Psychology (Monograph), 6, No. 4, Part 2.

Cairns, R. B. 1962. Antecedents of social reinforcer effectiveness. Unpublished manuscript. Indiana University. Cited in Bandura, A., and Walters, R. H., Social learning and personality development. 1964. New York: Holt, Rinehart and Winston.

Cairns, R. B. 1966. Attachment behavior of mammals. Psychological Review, 73, 409–426.

Calderone, M. S. 1966. Sex education for young people—and for their parents and teachers. In Brecher, R. and Brecher, E. (Eds.), An analysis of human sexual responses. New York: New American Library.

Caldwell, B. M. 1962. Assessment of infant personality. Merrill-Palmer Quarterly, 8, 71–81.

Caldwell, B. M. 1964. The effects of infant care. In Hoffman, M. L., and

Hoffman, L. W. (Eds.), *Review of child development research*, Volume 1. New York: Russell Sage Foundation. Pp. 9–87.

Cameron, N. 1947. *The psychology of behavior disorders*. New York: Houghton Mifflin.

Campbell, D. T. 1957. Factors relevant to the validity of experiments in social settings. *Psychological Bulletin*, 54, 297–312.

Campbell, D. T. 1960. Recommendations for APA test standards regarding construct, trait, or discrimination validity. *American Psychologist*, 15, 546–553.

Campbell, D. T. 1963. Social attitudes and other acquired behavioral dispositions. In S. Koch (Ed.), *Psychology: A study of a science*. Vol. 6. New York: McGraw-Hill.

Campbell, D. T. 1964. Distinguishing differences of perception from failures of communication in cross-cultural studies. In F. C. S. Northrop and H. H. Livingston (Eds.), *Cross-cultural Understanding: Epistemology in Anthropology*. New York: Harper and Row.

Campbell, D. T., and Stanley, J. C. 1963. Experimental and quasi-experimental designs for research on teaching. In Gage, N. L. (Ed.), *Handbook of research on teaching*. Chicago: Rand McNally. pp. 171–246.

Campbell, D. T., and Stanley, J. C. 1966. *Experimental and quasi-experimental designs for research*. Chicago: Rand McNally and Co.

Campbell, D., Sanderson, R. E., and Laverty, S. G. 1964. Characteristics of a conditioned response in human subjects during extinction trials following a single traumatic conditioning trial. *Journal of Abnormal and Social Psychology*, 68, 627–639.

Campbell, F. L. 1967. Demographic factors in family organizations. Unpublished PhD. dissertation, University of Michigan.

Carlsmith, J. M. 1968. Varieties of counter attitudinal behavior. In Abelson, et al., *Theories of Cognitive Consistency: A Sourcebook*. New York: Rand McNally and Co.

Carlson, E. R. 1956. Attitude change through modification of attitude structure. *Journal of Abnormal and Social Psychology*, 52, 256–261.

Carlson, R. 1971. Where is the person in personality research? *Psychological Bulletin*, 75, 203–219.

Carrigan. 1960. Extraversion-introversion as a dimension of personality: A reappraisal. *Psychological Bulletin*, 57, 329–360.

Carter, L. F. and Scholler, K. 1949. Value need and other factors in perception. *Psychological Review*, 56, 200–207.

Cartwright, R. D. and Monroe, L. J. 1968. Relation of dreaming and REM sleep: The effects of REM deprivation under two conditions. *Journal of Personality and Social Psychology*, 10, 69–74.

Carver, T. N. 1935. The essential factors of social evolution. Cambridge.

Casler, L. 1961. Maternal deprivation: A critical review of the literature. *Monographs Social Research and Child Development*, 26, No. 2 (Whole No. 80).

Casler, L. 1965. The effects of extratactile stimulation on a group of institutionalized infants. *Genetic Psychology Monographs*, 71, 137–175.

Cattell, R. B. 1950. *Personality*. New York: McGraw-Hill.

Cattell, R. B. 1957. Personality and motivation: Structure and measurement. New York: Harcourt, Brace & World.

Chance, J. E. and Meaders, W. 1960. Needs and interpersonal perception. *Journal of Personality*, 28, 200–210.

Chang, J. and Block, J. 1960. A study of identification in male homosexuals. *Journal of Consulting Psychology*, 24, 307–310.

Chapanis, A. 1961. Man, machines, and models. *American Psychologist*, pp. 16, 3, 113–131.

Chapanis, A., Garner, W. R., and Morgan, C. T. 1949. *Applied experimental psychology*. New York: Wiley.

Chess, S., Thomas, A., and Birch, H. G. 1965. *Your child is a person*. New York: Viking.

Child, I. L. 1954. Personality. *Annual Review of Psychology*, 5, 149–170.

Child, I. L. 1968. Personality in culture. In E. F. Borgatta and W. W. Lambert, *Handbook of personality theory and research.* Chicago: Rand McNally and Co.

Child, I. L., Frank, K. F., and Storm, T. 1956. Self-ratings and TAT: Their relation to each other and to childhood background. *Journal of Personality*, 25, 96–114.

Church, R. M. 1969. Response suppression. In Campbell, B. A. and Church, R. M. (Eds.), *Punishment and aversive behavior.* New York: Appleton-Century-Crofts.

Clark, A. L. and Wallin, P. 1965. Women's sexual responsiveness and the duration and quality of their marriages. *American Journal of Sociology*, 71, 2, 187–196.

Clark, K. B. 1965. *Dark ghetto, dilemmas of social power.* New York: Harper & Row.

Clark, K. B., and Clark, M. P. 1958. Racial identification and preference in Negro children. In Maccoby, E. E., Newcomb, T. M., and Hartley, E. L. (Eds.), *Reading in social psychology,* Third Edition. New York: Henry Holt.

Clark, R. A. 1952. The projective measurement of experimentally induced levels of sexual motivation. *Journal of Experimental Psychology*, 1952, 44, 391–399.

Clark, R. A., and Sensibar, M. R. 1956. The relationships between symbolic and manifest projections of sexuality with some incidental correlates. *Journal of Abnormal and Social Psychology*, 50, 327–334.

Cline, M. G. 1956. The influence of social context on the perception of faces. *Journal of Personality*, 25, 142–158.

Clore, G. L. and Byrne, D. 1971. The process of personality interaction. In Cattell, R. B. (Ed.), *Handbook of modern personality theory.* Chicago: Aldine.

Cohen, D. B. 1970. Current research on the frequency of dream recall. *Psychological Bulletin*, 73, 433–440.

Cohen, M. B. 1966. Personality identity and sexual identity. *Psychiatry*, 29, 1, 1–14.

Cole, D., Jacobs, S., and Zubok, C. B. 1962. The relation of achievement imagery scores to academic performance. *Journal of Abnormal and Social Psychology*, 65, 208–211.

Coleman, J. S. 1961. *The adolescent society.* New York: Free Press of Glencoe.

Collard, R. R. 1967. Fear of strangers and play behavior in kittens with varied social experience. *Child Development*, 38, 877–892.

Colley, T. 1959. The nature and origins of psychological sexual identity. *Psychological Review*, 66, 165–177.

Constantinople, A. 1969. An Eriksonian measure of personality development in college students. *Developmental Psychology*, 1, 357–372.

Cooper, J. 1971. Personal responsibility and dissonance: The role of foreseen consequence. *Journal of Personality and Social Psychology*, 18, 3, 354–363.

Coopersmith, S. 1967. *The antecedents of self-esteem.* San Francisco: Freeman.

Coopersmith, S. 1968. Studies in self-esteem. *Scientific American*, 218, (2), 96–106.

Corry, J. 1966. Current sexual behavior and attitudes. *The New York Times,* July 11, 1966.

Cottrell, N. B., et al. 1968. Social facilitation of dominant responses by the presence of an audience and the mere presence of others. *Journal of Personality and Social Psychology*, 9, 245–250.

Couch, A., and Keniston, K. 1960. Yea-sayers and naysayers: Agreeing response set as a personality variable. *Journal of Abnormal and Social Psychology*, 60, 151–174.

Cowen, E. L., and Beier, E. G. 1950. The influence of "threat-expectancy" on perception. *Journal of Personality*, 19, 85–94.

Cowles, J. T. 1937. Food-tokens as incentives for learning by chimpanzees. *Comparative Psychology Monographs*, 14, No. 71.

Cox, F. N. 1966. Some effects of test anxiety and presence or absence of other persons on boy's performance on a repetitive motor task. *Journal of Experimental Child Psychology*, 3, 100–112.

Cox, F. N. 1968. Some relationships between test anxiety, presence or absence of male persons, and boys' performance on a repetitive motor task.

Journal of Experimental Child Psychology, 2, 1–12.

Crago, M. A. 1972. Psychopathology in married couples. Psychological Bulletin, 77, No. 2, 114–128.

Crandall, V. J. 1963. Achievement. In Stevenson, H. W. (Ed.), Child Psychology, Yearbook of the National Society for the Study of Education. 62, 1, 416–459.

Crandall, V. J., Katkovsky, W., and Preston, A. 1962. Motivational and ability determinants of young children's intellectual achievement behaviors. Child Development, 33, 643–661.

Crockett, W. H. 1965. Cognitive complexity and impression formation. In B. Maher (Ed.), Progress in experimental personality research, Vol. 2. New York: Academic Press.

Cronbach, L. J. 1957. The two disciplines of scientific psychology. American Psychologist, 12, 671–684.

Cronbach, L. J. 1960. Essentials of psychological testing. New York: Harper & Brothers.

Cronbach, L. J. and Meehl, P. E. 1955. Construct validity in psychological tests. Psychological Bulletin, 52, 281–302.

Crowder, J. E., and Thornton, D. W. 1969. Effects of systematic desensitization, programmed fantasy, and bibliotherapy on reduction of fear. Paper presented at the 1969 Midwestern Psychological Association Convention, Chicago, Illinois.

Crowne, D. P. and Marlowe, D. 1964. The approval motive: Studies in evaluative dependence. New York: Wiley.

Crutchfield, R. S. 1955. Conformity and character. American Psychologist, 10, 191–198.

Crutchfield, R. S. 1959. Personal and situational factors in conformity to group pressure. Acta Psychologica, 15, 386–388.

Crutchfield, R. S. 1962. Conformity and creative thinking. In H. E. Gruber, G. Terrell, and Wertheimer, M. (Eds.), Contemporary approaches to creative thinking. New York: Atherton Press.

Cumming, E. 1963. Further thoughts on the theory of disengagement. UNESCO International Social Science Journal, 15, 377–393.

Cumming, E. and Henry, W. 1961. Growing old. New York: Basic Books.

Cumming, E., et al. 1960. Disengagement: A tentative theory of aging. Sociometry, 23, 23–35.

Daniel, W. J. 1942. Cooperative problem solving in rats. Journal of Comparative Psychology, 34, 361–368.

Darley, J. M. and Latané, B. 1968. Bystander intervention in emergencies: Diffusion of responsibility. Journal of Personality and Social Psychology, 8, 377–383.

Darlington, R. B., and Macker, C. E. 1966. Displacement of guilt-produced altruistic behavior. Journal of Personality and Social Psychology, 4, 442–443.

Davids, A., deVault, S., and Talmadge, M. 1961. Anxiety, pregnancy and childbirth abnormalities. Journal of Consulting Psychology, 25, 74–77.

Davidson, P. O. and Costello, C. G. 1969. N = 1; experimental studies of single cases. New York: Van Nostrand Reinhold Company.

Davis, A. 1948. Social class influences upon learning. Cambridge.

Davis, A., Gardner, B. B., Gardner, M. R. 1941. Deep south: A social anthropological study of caste and class. Chicago: University of Chicago Press.

Davitz, J. L. 1952. The effects of previous training on post-frustration behavior. Journal of Abnormal and Social Psychology, 47, 309–315.

Davitz, J. R. 1964. The communication of emotional meaning. New York: McGraw Hill.

Dawson, C. 1928. The age of the gods: A study in the origins of culture in prehistoric Europe and the ancient east. London.

De Charms, R. 1968. Personal causation, the internal affective determinants of behavior. New York: Academic Press.

Dellas, M. and Gaier, E. L. 1970. Identification of creativity: The individual. Psychological Bulletin, 73, 55–73.

De Luca, J. N. 1966. The structure of homosexuality. Journal of Projective Techniques and Personality Assessment, 30, No. 2, 187–191.

Dement, W. 1960. The effect of dream deprivation. Science, 131, 1705–1707.

Dement, W. C. 1965. An essay on dreams: The role of physiology in understanding their nature. In Barron, F., et al., *New Directions in Psychology II.* New York: Holt Rinehart Winston.

Dement, W., and Kleitman, N. 1957a. The relation of eye movements during sleep to dream activity: An objective method for the study of dreaming. *Journal of Experimental Psychology,* 53, 339–346.

Dement, W., and Wolpert, E. A. 1958. The relation of eye movements, body motility, and external stimuli to dream content. *Journal of Experimental Psychology,* 55, 543–553.

De Ropp, R. S. 1969. *Sex energy.* New York: Delacorte Press.

Desor, J. A. 1972. Toward a psychological theory of crowding. *Journal of Personality and Social Psychology,* 21, 79–83.

Deutsch, M. and Collins, E. 1951. *Interracial housing: A psychological evaluation of a social experiment.* Minneapolis: University of Minnesota Press.

Deutsch, M. and Gerard, H. B. 1955. A study of normative and informational social influences upon individual judgement. *Journal of Abnormal and Social Psychology,* 51, 629–636.

Dewing, K., and Battye, G. 1971. Attention deployment and nonverbal fluency. *Journal of Personality and Social Psychology,* 17, 214–218.

DiCara, L. V., and Miller, N. E. 1968. Changes in heart rate instrumentally learned by curarized rats as avoidance responses. *Journal of Comparative and Physiological Psychology,* 65, 8–12.

DiCara, L. V., and Miller, N. E. 1969. Transfer of instrumentally learned heart-rate changes from curarized to noncurarized state: Implications for a mediational hypothesis. *Journal of Comparative and Physiological Psychology,* 68, 159–162.

DiCara, L. V., and Weiss, J. M. 1969. Effect of heart-rate learning under curare on subsequent noncurarized avoidance learning. *Journal of Comparative and Physiological Psychology,* 69, 368–374.

Dienstbier, R. A., and Munter, P. O. 1971. Cheating as a function of the labeling of natural arousal. *Journal of Personality and Social Psychology,* 17, 208–213.

DiGiusto, E. L., Cairncross, K., and King, M. G. 1971. Hormonal influences on fear-motivated responses. *Psychological Bulletin,* 75, 432–444.

Doidge, W. T. and Holtzman, W. H. 1960. Implications of homosexuality among Air Force trainees. *Journal of Consulting Psychology,* 24, 9–13.

Dollard, J., and Miller, N. E. 1950. *Personality and psychotherapy.* New York: McGraw-Hill.

Dollard, J. et al. 1939. *Frustration and aggression.* New Haven: Yale University Press.

Donelson, E. 1973 a. Development of sex role behaviors and self concept. In Donelson, E., and Gullahorn, J. (Ed.), *Women: A psychological perspective.* In press.

Donelson, E. 1973 b. Social responsiveness and sense of separateness. In Donelson, E., and Gullahorn, J. (Eds.), *Women: A psychological perspective.* In press.

Donelson, E. 1973 c. The single woman. In Donelson, E., and Gullahorn, J. (Eds.), *Women: A psychological perspective.* In press.

Donelson, E. and Gullahorn, J. (Eds.). 1973 a. *Women: A psychological perspective.* In press.

Donelson, E. and Gullahorn, J. 1973 b. Achievement motivation and career orientation. In press. In Donelson, E., and Gullahorn, J. (Eds.), *Women: A psychological perspective.* In press.

Donelson, E. and Gullahorn, J. 1973 c. Sex role pressures and life plans. Unpublished manuscript, Michigan State University.

Donelson, F. E. 1966. Discrimination and control of human heart rate. Doctoral dissertation, Cornell University.

Doob, A. N., and Wood, L. 1972. Catharsis and aggression: The effects of annoyance and retaliation on aggressive behavior. *Journal of Personality and Social Psychology,* 22, 156–162.

Douvan, E. and Adelson, J. 1966. *The adolescent experience.* New York: Wiley.

Dreger, R. M. and Miller, K. S. 1968.

Comparative psychological studies of Negroes and Whites in the United States: 1959–1965. *Psychological Bulletin Monograph Supplement*, Vol. 70, No. 3, Part 2.

Duffy, E. 1941. An explanation of "emotional" phenomena without the use of the concept "emotion". *Journal of General Psychology*. 25, 283–293.

Duffy, E. 1949. A systematic framework for the description of personality. *Journal of Abnormal and Social Psychology*, 44, 175–190.

Duffy, E. 1951. The concept of energy mobilization. *Psychological Review*. 58, 30–40.

Duffy, E. 1957. Psychological significance of the concept of "arousal" or "activation." *Psychological Review*, 64, 265–275.

Dukes, W. F. 1965. $N = 1$. *Psychological Bulletin*, 64, 74–79.

Dulaney, D. E., Jr. 1957. Avoidance learning of perceptual defense and vigilance. *Journal of Abnormal and Social Psychology*, 55, 333–338.

Duncan, S., Jr. 1969. Nonverbal communication. *Psychological Bulletin*, 72, 118–137.

Duncan, S., Jr. 1972. Some signals and rules for taking speaking turns in conversations. *Journal of Personality and Social Psychology*, 23, 2, 283–292.

Dyer, E. D. 1963. Parenthood as crisis: A restudy. *Marriage and Family Living*, 25, 196–201.

D'Zurilla, T. J. 1965. Recall efficiency and mediating cognitive events in "experimental repression". *Journal of Personality and Social Psychology*, 1, 253–257.

Eagly, A. H. 1967. Involvement as a determinant of response to favorable and unfavorable information. *Journal of Personality and Social Psychology Monograph*, 7, Part 2, 15 pages.

Eagly, A. H. and Whitehead, G. I. 1972. Effect of choice on receptivity to favorable and unfavorable evaluations of oneself. *Journal of Personality and Social Psychology*, 22, 2, 223–230.

Edlow, D. W., and Kiesler, C. A. 1966. Ease of denial and defensive projection. *Journal of Experimental Social Psychology*, 2, 56–69.

Edwards, A. L. 1953a. *Edwards Personal Preference Schedule*. New York: Psychological Corporation.

Edwards, A. L. 1953b. The relationship between the judged desirability of a trait and the probability that the trait will be endorsed. *Journal of Applied Psychology*, 37, 90–93.

Edwards, A. L. 1957. *The social desirability variable in personality research*. New York: Dryden.

Edwards, A. L. 1959. *Manual for the Edwards Personal Preference Schedule*. New York: Psychological Corporation.

Edwards, A. L. 1961. Social desirability or acquiescence in the MMPI? A case study of the SD scale. *Journal of Abnormal and Social Psychology*, 63, 351–359.

Edwards, A. L. 1970. A *manual for the Edwards Personality Inventory*. Chicago: Science Research Associates.

Egbert, L., et al. 1964. Reduction of postoperative pain by encouragement and instruction of patients. *New England Journal of Medicine*, 270, 825–827.

Eisenberg, L. 1965. A developmental approach to adolescence. *Children*, 12, 131–135.

Ekman, P. 1972. Universals and cultural differences in facial expressions of emotions. In Nebraska Symposium on Motivation.

Ekman, P., and Friesen, W. V. 1968. Nonverbal behavior in psychotherapy research. In Shlien, J. (Ed.), *Research in psychotherapy*. Volume 3. Washington, D.C.: American Psychological Association.

Ekman, P., and Friesen, W. V. 1971. Constants across cultures in the face and emotion. *Journal of Personality and Social Psychology*, 17, 124–129.

Ekman, P., Sorenson, E. R., and Friesen, W. V. 1969. Pan-cultural elements in facial displays of emotion. *Science*, 164, 86–88.

Elder, G. W., Jr. 1962. Structural variations in the child-rearing relationship. *Sociometry*, 25, 241–262.

Elder, G. W., Jr. 1963. Parental power legitimation and its effect on the adolescent. *Sociometry*, 26, 50–65.

Elder, G. H., Jr. 1965. Role relations,

sociocultural environments, and autocratic family ideology. *Sociometry*, 28, 173–196.

Elliott, R. 1966. Effects of uncertainty about the nature and advent of a noxious stimulus (shock) upon distress. *Journal of Personality and Social Psychology*, 3, 353–356.

Elliott, R. 1969. Tonic heart rate: Experiments on the effects of collative variables lead to a hypothesis about its motivational significance. *Journal of Personality and Social Psychology*, 12, 211–228.

Ellsworth, P. C., Carlsmith, J. M., and Henson, A. 1972. The stare as a stimulus to flight in human subjects: A series of field experiments. *Journal of Personality and Social Psychology*, 21, 302–311.

Emmerich, W. 1966. Continuity and stability in early social development: II. Teacher's ratings. *Child Development*, 37, 17–27.

Endler, N. S. 1966. Conformity as a function of different reinforcement schedules. *Journal of Personality and Social Psychology*, 4, 175–180.

Ephron, H. S., and Carrington, P. 1966. Rapid eye movement sleep and cortical homeostasis. *Psychological Review*, 73, 500–526.

Epstein, S. 1967. Toward a unified theory of anxiety. In Maher, B. A. (Ed.), *Progress in experimental personality research*. New York: Academic Press.

Epstein, S. and Fenz, W. D. 1962. Theory and experiment on the measurement of approach-avoidance conflict. *Journal of Abnormal and Social Psychology*, 64, 97–112.

Epstein, S., and Smith, R. 1957. Thematic apperception, Rorschach content, and ratings of sexual attractiveness of women as measures of the sex drive. *Journal of Consulting Psychology*, 21, 473–478.

Eriksen, C. W. 1960. Discrimination and learning without awareness: A methodological survey and evaluation. *Psychological Review*, 67, 279–300.

Erikson, C. W. 1963. Perception and personality dynamics. In Heine, R. W., and Wepman, J. M. (Eds.), *Perspectives in personality theory*. Chicago: Aldine Publishing Co.

Erikson, C. W. 1966. Cognitive responses to internally cued anxiety. In Spielberger, C. D. (Ed.), *Anxiety and behavior*. New York: Academic Press.

Eriksen, C. W. and Kuethe, J. L. 1956. Avoidance conditioning of verbal behavior without awareness: a paradigm of repression. *Journal of Abnormal and Social Psychology*, 53, 203–209.

Eriksen, C. W. and Pierce, J. 1968. Defense mechanisms. In Borgatta, E. F., and Lambert, W. W. (Eds.), *Handbook of personality theory and research*. Chicago: Rand McNally.

Erikson, E. H. 1956. The problem of ego identity. *Journal of American Psychoanalytic Association*, 4, 56–121.

Erikson, E. H. 1959. Identity and the life cycle. *Psychological Issues*, 1, 1–171.

Erikson, E. H. 1963. *Childhood and society*, Second Edition. New York: W. W. Norton.

Escalona, S. K. and Heider, G. M. 1959. *Prediction and outcome*. New York: Basic Books.

Ettinger, R. F., et al. 1971. Effects of agreement and correctness on relative competence and conformity. *Journal of Personality and Social Psychology*, 19, 2, 204–212.

Evans, E. D. (Ed.) 1970. *Adolescents: Reading in behavior and development*. Winsdale, Ill.: Dryden Press.

Eysenck, H. J. 1947. *Dimensions of personality*. London: Routledge and Kegen Paul.

Eysenck, H. J. 1953. *The structure of human personality*. London: Mathuen.

Eysenck, H. J. 1959. *Maudsley Personality Inventory*. London: University of London Press.

Eysenck, H. J. (Ed.). 1961. *Handbook of abnormal psychology*. New York: Basic Books.

Fantz, R. L. 1958. Pattern vision in young infants. *Psychological Record*, 8, 43–47.

Farber, I. E. 1964. A framework for the study of personality as a behavioral science. In Worchel, P., and Byrne, D. (Eds.), *Personality change*. New York: Wiley.

Farina, A., Chapnick, B., and Chapnick, J. 1972. Political views and interpersonal behavior. *Journal of personality and Social Psychology,* 22, 3, 273–278.

Farina, A., Holland, C. H., and Ring, K. 1966. Role of stigma and set in interpersonal interactions. *Journal of Abnormal and Social Psychology,* 71, 421–428.

Faust, S. 1960. Developmental maturity as a determiner in prestige of adolescent girls. *Child Development,* 31, 173–184.

Feather, N. T. 1967. Valence of outcome and expectation of success in relation to task difficulty and perceived locus of control. *Journal of Personality and Social Psychology,* 7, 372–386.

Feigl, H. 1945, 1952. Operationism and scientific method. In W. S. Langfeld (Ed.) *Symposium on operationism. Psychological Review,* pp. 250–259, 284–288.

Fenichel, O. 1945. *The psychoanalytic theory of neurosis.* New York: Norton.

Ferguson, L. R. 1970. Personality development. Belmont, California: Brooks/Cole Publishing Company, A Division of Wadsworth Publishing.

Ferguson, Lucy Rau 1973. The woman in the family. In Donelson, E., and Gullahorn, J. (Eds.), *Women: A psychological perspective.* In press.

Feshbach, N. D. 1967. Nonconformity to experimentally induced group norms of high-status versus low-status members. *Journal of Personality and Social Psychology,* 6, 55–63.

Feshbach, S. 1970. Aggression. In Mussen, P. H. (Ed.), *Carmichael's manual of child psychology,* Third Edition. New York: Wiley.

Feshbach, S. and Singer, R. 1957. The effects of personal and shared threat upon social prejudice. *Journal of Abnormal and Social Psychology,* 54, 411–416.

Festinger, L. 1954. A theory of social comparison processes. *Human Relations,* 7, 117–140.

Festinger, L., and Carlsmith, J. M. 1959. Cognitive consequences of forced compliance. *Journal of Abnormal and Social Psychology,* 58, 203–210.

Festinger, L., Schachter S., Back, K. 1950. *Social pressure in informal groups: A study of a housing project.* New York: Harper.

Field, W. F. 1951. The effects on thematic apperception of certain experimentally aroused needs. Unpublished doctoral dissertation, University of Maryland.

Filer, R. N., and O'Connell, D. D. 1962. A useful contribution climage for aging. *Journal of Gerontology,* 17, 51–57.

Fillenbaum. 1966. prior deception and subsequent experimental performance: The "faithful" subject. *Journal of personality and social psychology,* 4, 537.

Fisher, C. 1960. Subliminal and supraliminal influences on dreams. *American Journal of Psychiatry,* 116, 1009–1017.

Fisher, C. 1967. Psychological significance of the dream-sleep cycle. In Witkin, H. A., and Lewis, H. B., *Experimental studies of dreaming.* New York: Random House.

Fisher, C., and Dement, W. 1963. Studies of the psychopathology of sleep and dreams. *American Journal of Psychiatry,* 119, 1160–1168.

Fisher, S. 1967. Projective methodologies. *Annual Review of Psychology,* 18, 165–190.

Fisher, S. 1970. *Body experience in fantasy and behavior.* New York: Appleton-Century-Crofts.

Fisher, S. and Cleveland, S. E. 1965. Personality, body perception, and body image boundary. In Wapner, S., and Werner, H. (Eds.), *The body percept.* New York: Random House.

Fisher, S., and Cleveland, S. E. 1968. *Body image and personality.* New York: Dover. 2nd revised edition.

Fishman, D. B. 1966. Need and expectancy as determinants of affiliative behavior in small groups. *Journal of Personality and Social Psychology,* 4, 155–164.

Fiske, D. W., and Maddi, S. R. (Eds.) 1961. *Functions of varied experience.* Homewood, Ill.: Dorsey Press.

Fitzgerald, E. T. 1966. Measurement of openness to experience: A study of regression in the service of the ego. *Journal of Personality and Social Psychology,* 4, 655–663.

Fitzgerald, H. E. 1968. Autonomic pupillary reflex activity during early infancy and its relation to social and nonsocial visual stimuli. *Journal of Experimental Child Psychology*, 6, 470–482.

Fitzgerald, H. E. 1973. Socialization during infancy: A psychobiological perspective. In Donelson, E. and Gullahorn, J. (Eds.), *Women, a psychological perspective*. In press.

Flanagan, J. C. 1954. The critical incident technique. *Psychological Bulletin*, 51, 327–358.

Flanders. 1968. A review of research on imitative behavior. *Psychological Bulletin*, 69, 316–337.

Fletcher, R. 1966. *Instinct in man, in the light of recent work in comparative psychology*. New York: Schocken Books.

Foa, U. G., Triandis, H. C., and Katz, E. W. 1966. Cross-cultural invariance in the differentiation and organization of family roles. *Journal of Personality and Social Psychology*, 4, 316–327.

Ford, C. S. 1942. Culture and human behavior. *Scientific Monthly*, 55, 546–557.

Ford, C. S. and Beach, F. A. 1951. *Patterns of sexual behavior*. New York: Harper.

Forehand, G. A. 1964. Comments on comments on testing. *Educational and Psychological Measurement*, 24, 853–859.

Forgus, R. H. 1966. *Perception: the basic process in cognitive development*. New York: McGraw-Hill.

Foulkes, D. 1966. *The psychology of sleep*. New York: Charles Scribners.

Foulkes, W. D., and Rechtschaffen, A. 1964. Presleep determinants of dream content: effects of two films. *Perceptual and Motor Skills*, 19, 983–1005.

Freedman, J. L. 1965. Confidence, utility, and selective exposure: A partial replication. *Journal of Personality and Social Psychology*, 2, 778–780.

Freedman, J. L. and Doob, A. N. 1968. *Deviancy*. New York: Academic Press.

French, E. G., and Lesser, G. D. 1964. Some characteristics of the achievement motive in women. *Journal of Abnormal and Social Psychology*, 68, 119–128.

Frenkel-Brunswik, E. 1949. Intolerance of ambiguity as an emotional and perceptual personality variable. In Bruner, J. S., and Krech, D. (Eds.), *Perception and personality: A symposium*. Durham: Duke University Press.

Freud, A. 1937. *The ego and the mechanisms of defense*. London: Hogarth.

Freud, A. 1946. The ego and the mechanisms of defence. New York: International Universities Press.

Freud, A., and Burlingham, D. 1943. *War and children*. New York: International Universities Press.

Freud, A., and Burlingham, D. T. 1944. *Infants without families*. New York: International Universities Press.

Freud, A., and Dann, S. 1951. An experiment in group upbringing. In *The psychoanalytic study of child*, Vol. 6. New York: International University Press.

Freud, S. 1925. Mourning and melancholia. *Collected Papers*, Vol. 4. London: Hogarth Press.

Freud, S. 1933. *New introductory lectures*. New York: W. W. Norton.

Freud, S. 1948 a. "Civilized" sexual morality and modern nervousness. Trans. J. Riviere. In *Collected papers*, Vol. 2. London: Hogarth Press.

Freud, S. 1948 b. The relation of the poet to daydreaming. Trans. J. Riviere. *Collected papers*, Vol. 4. London: Hogarth Press.

Freud, S. 1949. *A general introduction to psychoanalysis*. Trans. J. Riviere. New York: Simon & Schuster.

Freud, S. 1950. *Totem and taboo*. New York: W. W. Norton.

Freud, S. 1957. Instincts and their vicissitudes. In Strachey, J. (Ed.), *Standard edition of the complete psychological works of Sigmund Freud*, Vol. 14. London: Hogarth Press.

Freud, S. 1959 a. *Beyond the pleasure principle*. Trans. J. Strachey. New York: Bantam Books.

Freud, S. 1959 b. *Collected papers of Sigmund Freud*. Vol. 5 (Ed. Ernest Jones). New York: Basic Books.

Freud, S. 1959 c. Creative writers and day-dreaming. In Strachey, J. (Ed.), *Standard edition of the complete psychological works of Sigmund Freud*, Vol. 9. London: Hogarth Press.

Freud, S. 1962. *The ego and the id*. Trans. J. Riviere; rev. and ed. J. Strachey. New York: W. W. Norton.

Freud, S. 1963. *An outline of psychoanalysis.* Trans. J. Strachey. New York: W. W. Norton.

Freud, S. 1964. *New introductory lectures on psychoanalysis.* Trans. and ed. J. Strachey. New York: W. W. Norton.

Frijda, N. W. 1970. Emotion and recognition of emotion. In Arnold, M. (Ed.), *Feelings and emotion.* New York: Academic Press.

Fromm, Erich. 1941. *Escape from freedom.* New York: Rinehart.

Fromm, Erich. 1947. *Man for himself.* New York: Rinehart.

Fromm, Erich. 1955. *The sane society.* New York: Holt, Rinehart & Winston.

Fromm, E. 1956. *The art of loving, an enquiry into the nature of love.* New York: Harper.

Fromm, E. 1959. The creative attitude. In Anderson, H. H., *Creativity and its cultivation.* New York: Harper & Row.

Funkenstein, D. H. 1955. The physiology of fear and anger. *Scientific American,* 192, 5, 74–80.

Gale, A. 1969. "Stimulus hunger": Individual differences in operant strategy in a button-pressing task. *Behavior Research and Therapy,* 7, (3), 265–274.

Gamow, G. 1947. *One, two, three . . . infinitely.* New York, Viking Press.

Gantt, W. H. 1944. Experimental basis for neurotic behavior. *Psychosomatic Medicine Monographs.* 3, (3–4).

Ganzer, V. J. 1968. Effects of audience presence and test anxiety on learning and retention in a serial learning situation. *Journal of Personality and Social Psychology,* 8, 2, 194–199.

Garai, J. E. 1970. Sex differences in mental health. *Genetic Psychology Monographs,* 81, 123–142.

Gardner, R. W. 1962. Cognitive controls in adaptation: Research and measurement. In Messick, S., and Ross J. (Eds.), *Measurement in personality and cognition.* New York: Wiley.

Geer, J. H. 1968. A test of the classical conditioning model of emotion: The use of nonpainful aversive stimuli as unconditioned stimuli in a conditioning procedure. *Journal of Personality and Social Psychology,* 10, 148–156.

Gellhorn, E. (Ed.). 1968. Biological foundations of emotion, research and commentary. *Scott, Foresman Physiological Psychology Series.*

Gerard, H. B. 1961. Disagreement with others, their credibility, and experienced stress. *Journal of Abnormal and Social Psychology,* 62, 559–564.

Gerard, H. B. 1963. Emotional uncertainty and social comparison. *Journal of Abnormal and Social Psychology,* 66, 568–573.

Gerard, H. B., and Rabbie, J. M. 1961. Fear and social comparison. *Journal of Abnormal and Social Psychology,* 62, 586–592.

Gergen, K. J. 1965. Interaction goals and personalistic feedback as factors affecting the presentation of self. *Journal of Personality and Social Psychology,* 1, 413–424.

Gergen, K. J., and Bauer, R. A. 1967. The interactive efforts of self-esteem and task difficulty on social conformity. *Journal of Personality and Social Psychology,* 6, 16–22.

Gergen, K. J., and Morse, S. J. 1967. Self-consistency: Measurement and validation. *Proceedings of the American Psychological Association,* 207–208.

Getzels, J. W., and Jackson, P. W. 1961. Family environment and cognitive style: A study of the sources of highly intelligent and highly creative adolescents. *American Sociological Review,* 26, 351–359.

Getzels, J. W., and Jackson, P. W. 1958. The meaning of "giftedness"—an examination of an expanding concept. *Phi Delta Kappan,* 40, 75–77.

Getzels, J. W., and Jackson, P. W. 1962. *Creativity and intelligence.* New York: Wiley.

Gibson, E. J. 1969. Principles of perceptual learning and development. New York: Appleton-Century-Crofts.

Giddan, N. S. 1967. Recovery through images of briefly flashed stimuli. *Journal of Personality,* 35, 1–19.

Gilchrist, J. C., and Nesberg, L. S. 1952. Need and perceptual change in need-related objects. *Journal of Experimental Psychology,* 44, 369–376.

Glass, D. C. 1964. Changes in liking as a means of reducing cognitive discrepancies between self-esteem and aggression. *Journal of Personality, 32,* 520–549.

Glass, D. C. (Ed.). 1967. Neurophysiology and emotion. Proceeding of a conference under the auspices of Russell Sage Foundation and The Rockefeller University, the Rockefeller University Press and Russell Sage Foundation.

Glass, D. C. 1968a. Theories of consistency and the study of personality. In Lambert, W. W., and Borgatta, E. F. (Eds.), *Handbook of personality theory and research.* Chicago: Rand McNally.

Glass, D. C. 1968b. Individual differences and the resolution of cognitive inconsistencies. In Abelson, R. P. et al. (Eds.), *Theories of cognitive consistency: A sourcebook.* Chicago: Rand McNally.

Glass, D. C., Singer, J. E., and Friedman, L. N. 1969. Psychic cost of adaptation to an environmental stressor. *Journal of Personality and Social Psychology,* 12, 3, 200–210.

Gleser, G. C. 1963. Projective methodologies. *Annual Review of Psychology,* 14, 391–422.

Golann, S. E. 1963. Psychological study of creativity. *Psychological Bulletin,* 60, 548–565.

Goldberg, L. R. 1968. Simple models or simple processes: Some research on clinical judgements. *American psychologist,* 23, 483–496.

Goldberg, L. R. 1970. Man vs. model of man: A rationale, plus some evidence for a method of improving on clinical inference. *Psychological Bulletin,* 73, 422–432.

Goldberg, L. R. 1972. Man versus mean: The exploitation of group profiles for the construction of diagnostic classification systems. *Journal of Abnormal Psychology,* 79, 2, 121–131.

Goldberg, P. 1968. Are women prejudiced against women? *Trans-action,* 5, 28–30.

Goldfarb, W. 1945. Psychological privation in infancy and subsequent adjustment. *American Journal of Orthopsychiatry,* 15, 247–255.

Goldman, R., Jaffa, M., and Schachter, S. 1968. Yom Kippur, Air France, dormitory food, and the eating behavior of obese and normal persons. *Journal of Personality and Social Psychology,* 10, 2, 117–123.

Goldstein, D., Fink, D., and Metee, D. R. 1972. Cognition of arousal and actual arousal as determinants of emotion. *Journal of Personality and Social Psychology,* 21, 41–51.

Goldstein, K. 1939. *The organism.* New York: American Book.

Goldstein, K. 1963. *The organism.* Boston: Beacon Press.

Goodenough, D. R. 1967. Some recent studies of dream recall. In Witkin, H. A., and Lewis, H. B. (Eds.), *Experimental studies of dreaming.* New York: Random House.

Goodenough, D. R. et al. 1965. Dream reporting following abrupt and gradual awakenings from different types of sleep. *Journal of Personality and Social Psychology,* 2, 170–179.

Goodenough, E. W. 1957. Interest in persons as an aspect of sex differences in the early years. *Genetic Psychology Monographs,* 55, 287–323.

Goodstein, L. D., and Lanyon, R. I. (Eds.). 1971. *Readings in Personality Assessment.* New York: Wiley.

Gorer, G. 1949. *The people of great russia.* London.

Gottesman, I. I. 1966. Genetic variance in adaptive personality traits. *Journal of Child Psychology and Psychiatry,* 7, 199–208.

Gough, H. G. 1957. *California psychological inventory manual.* Palo Alto: Consulting Psychologists Press.

Gough, H. G. 1960. The Adjective Check List as a personality assessment research technique. *Psychological Reports,* 6, 107–122.

Gough, H. G. 1968. An interpreter's syllabus for the California Psychological Inventory. In P. McReynolds (Ed.), *Advances in psychological assessment,* Volume 1. Palo Alto, Calif.: Science & Behavior Books.

Gough, H. G., and Heilbrun, A. B. 1965. *Joint manual for the Adjective Check List and the ACL Need Scales.* Palo Alto, Calif.: Consulting Psychologists Press.

Goulder, A. W. 1960. The norm of reciprocity: A preliminary statement.

American Sociological Review, 25, 161–179.

Graham, D. T. 1962. Some research on psychophysiologic specificity and its relation to psychosomatic disease. In Roessler, R., and Greenfield, N. S. (Eds.), *Physiological correlates of psychological disorder*. Madison: University of Wisconsin Press.

Graham, F. K., Matarazzo, R. G., and Caldwell, B. M. 1956. Behavioral differences between normal and traumatized newborns. *Psychological Monographs*, 70, No. 5.

Gray, J. A. 1971. *The psychology of fear and stress*. New York: McGraw-Hill.

Gray, P. H. 1957. Theory and evidence of imprinting in human infants. Student Research, University of Chicago.

Gray, P. H. 1958. Theory and evidence of imprinting in human infants. *Journal of Psychology*, 46, 155–166.

Green, J. A. 1972. Attitudinal and situational determinants of intended behavior toward blacks. *Journal of Personality and Social Psychology*, 22, 1, 13–17.

Greenwald, A. G. 1968. On defining attitude and attitude theory. In Greenwald, A. G., Brock, T. C., and Ostrom, T. M. (Eds.), *Psychological foundations of attitudes*. New York: Academic Press.

Grim, P. F., Kohlberg, L., and White, S. H. 1968. Some relationships between conscience and attentional processes. *Journal of Personality and Social Psychology*, 8, 239–252.

Grinker, R. R. 1966. The Psychosomatic aspects of anxiety. In Spielberger, C. D. (Ed.), *Anxiety and behavior*. New York: Academic Press.

Gross, N. 1959. The sociology of education. In R. K. Merton, et al., (Eds.), *Sociology today: Problems and prospects*. New York: Basic Books.

Grummon, D. L., and Barclay, A. M. (Eds.) 1971. *Sexuality: A search for perspective, based on a colloquy held at Michigan State University*. New York: Van Nostrand.

Grusec, J. E. 1966. Some antecedents of self-criticism. *Journal of Personality and Social Psychology*, 4, 244–252.

Grusec, J. E. 1972. Demand characteristics of the modeling experiment:

Altruism as a function of age and aggression. *Journal of Personality and Social Psychology*, 22, 139–148.

Grusec, J. E., and Brinker, D. B., Jr. 1972. Reinforcement for imitation as a social learning determinant with implications for sex-role development. *Journal of Personality and Social Psychology*, 21, 149–158.

Grygier, T. G. 1956. *Dynamic personality inventory*. London: National Foundation for Educational Research in England and Wales.

Guilford, J. P. 1950. Creativity. *American Psychologist*, 5, 444–454.

Guilford, J. P. 1959. Traits of creativity. In Anderson, H. H. (Ed.), *Creativity and its cultivation*. New York: Harper.

Guilford, J. P. 1963. Intellectual resources and their values as seen by scientists. In Taylor, C. W., and Barron, F. (Eds.), *Scientific creativity: Its recognition and development*. New York: Wiley.

Guilford, J. P. 1967. Intellecutal factors in productive thinking. In Mooney, R. and Razik, T., *Exploration in creativity*. New York: Harper & Row.

Guilford, J. P. and Zimmerman, W. S. 1956. Fourteen dimensions of temperament. *Psychological Monographs*, 70, No. 10.

Gullahorn, J. 1973. The Professional Woman. In Donelson, E. and Gullahorn, J. (Eds.), *Women: A psychological perspective*. In press.

Gump, J. P. 1972. Sex-role attitudes and psychological well-being. *Journal of Social Issues*, 28, 79–92.

Gunderson, E. K. E. 1965. Body size, self-evaluation, and military effectiveness. *Journal of Personality and Social Psychology*, 2, 902–906.

Gurin, G., et al. 1960. *Americans view their mental health*. New York: Basic Books.

Haggard, E. A. 1964. Isolation and personality. In Worchel, P., and Byrne, D. (Eds.), *Personality change*. New York: Wiley.

Hall, C. 1966. *The meaning of dreams*. New York: McGraw Hill.

Hall, C. S. and Lindzey, G. 1970. *Theories of personality*, Second Edition. New York: Wiley.

Hall, C. S., and Van de Castle, R. L. 1966. *The content analysis of dreams.* New York: Appleton-Century-Crofts.

Halvorson, L. F., and Shore, R. E. 1969. Self-disclosure and interpersonal functioning. *Journal of Consulting and Clinical Psychology,* 33, 213–217.

Hamacheck, D. E. 1971. *Encounters with self.* New York: Holt, Rinehart and Winston.

Hamblin, R. L. 1958. Leadership and crisis. *Sociometry,* 21, 322–335.

Hamilton, D. L. 1969. Responses to cognitive inconsistencies: Personality, discrepancy level, and response stability. *Journal of Personality and Social Psychology,* 11, 351–362.

Hamsher, J. H., Geller, J. D., and Rotter, J. B. 1968. Interpersonal trust, internal-external control and the Warren Commission Report. *Journal of Personality and Social Psychology,* 9, 210–215.

Harding, J. and Hogrefe, R. 1952. Attitudes of white department store employees toward Negro co-workers. *Journal of Social Issues,* 8, 18–28.

Hare, A. P. 1962. *Handbook of small group research.* New York: Free Press.

Harlow, H. F. 1950. Learning and satiation of response in intrinsically motivated complex puzzle performance by monkeys. *Journal of Comparative and Physiological Psychology,* 43, 289–294.

Harlow, H. 1961. The development of affectional patterns in infant monkeys. In Foss, B. (Ed.), *Determinant of infant behavior.* London: Methuen.

Harlow, H. F. 1962b. The heterosexual affectional system in monkeys. *American Psychologist,* 17, 1–9.

Harlow, H. F. 1958. The nature of love. *American Psychologist,* 13, 673–685.

Harlow, H. F. and Harlow, M. K. 1966. Learning to love. *American Scientist,* 54, 244–272.

Harlow, H. F., and Zimmermann, R. R. 1959. Affectional response in the infant monkey. *Science,* 130, 421–432.

Harper, R. A. 1961. Extramarital sex relations. In Ellis, A. and Abarbanel, A., (Eds.), *The encyclopedia of sexual behavior,* Volume I. New York: Hawthorn Books.

Harrison, A. A. and Crandall, R. 1972. Heterogeneity-homogeneity of exposure sequence and the attitudinal effects of exposure. *Journal of Personality and Social Psychology,* 21, 234–238.

Hartley, R. E. 1960. Some implications of current changes in sex role patterns. *Merrill-Palmer Quarterly,* 6, 153–164.

Hartley, E. L. and Hartley, R. E. 1961. *Fundamentals of social psychology.* New York: Alfred A. Knopf.

Hartman, E. 1969. The biochemistry and pharmacology of the D-state (dreaming sleep). *Experimental Medicine and Surgery,* 27, 1–2, 105–120.

Hartmann, H. 1958. *Ego psychology and the problem of adaptation.* New York: International Universities Press.

Hartshorne, H., and May, M. A. 1928. Studies in the nature of character, Volume 1. *Studies in deceit.* New York: Macmillan.

Hartup, W. W. 1955. Nurturance and nurturance-withdrawal in relation to the dependency behavior of preschool children. Doctoral dissertation, Harvard University.

Hartup, W. W. 1963. Dependency and independence. In Stevenson, H. W. (Ed.), *Child Psychology, The Sixty-second Yearbook of the National Society for the Study of Education,* Part I. pp. 333–363. Chicago: The National Society for the Study of Education.

Hartup, W. W., and Yonas, A. 1971. Developmental Psychology. In Mussen, P. H., and Rosenzweig, M. R. (Eds.), *Annual Review of Psychology,* Volume 22. Palo Alto, California: Annual Reviews Inc. pp. 337–392.

Hartup, W. W., and Coates, B. 1967. Imitation of peers as a function of reinforcement from the peer group and rewardingness of the model. *Child Development,* 38, 1003–1016.

Hartup, W. W. 1958. Nurturance and nurturance-withdrawal in relation to dependency behavior of preschool children. *Child Development,* 29, 191–202.

Hartup, W. W. 1970. Peer interaction and social organization. In P. H. Mussen (Ed.), *Carmichael's manual of child psychology,* Third Edition. New York: Wiley.

Hartup, W. W., and Zook, E. A. 1960. Sex-role preference in 3- and 4-year-old children. *Journal of Consulting Psychology,* 24, 420–426.

Harvey, O. J., Kelley, H. H. and Shapiro,

M. M. 1957. Reactions to unfavorable evaluations of the self-made by other persons. *Journal of Personality*, 25, 393–411.

Hathaway, S. R. 1960. Foreword. In Dahlstrom, W. G., and Welsh, G. S., *An MMPI handbook: A guide to use in clinical practice and research*. Minneapolis: University of Minnesota Press.

Hathaway, S. R., and Monachesi, E. D. 1963. *Adolescent personality and behavior*. Minneapolis: University of Minnesota Press.

Hatton, G. 1973. Biology and Gender: Structure, sex, and cycles. In Donelson, E., and Gullahorn, J. (Eds.), *Women: A psychological perspective*. In press.

Havighurst, R. J., and Albrecht, R. 1953. *Older people*. New York: Longmans.

Haynes, H. M. 1962. Development of accommodative behavior in infants. Paper read at Conference on Theoretical Optometry and Visual Training at St. Louis.

Heathers, G. 1955. Emotional dependence and independence in nursery school play. *Journal of Genetic Psychology*, 87, 37–57.

Hebb, D. O. 1955a. Drives and the C.N.S. (Conceptual Nervous System). *Psychological Review*, 62, 243–254.

Hebb, D. O. 1946. On the nature of fear. *Psychological Review*, 53, 259–276.

Hebb, D. O. 1955b. The mammal and his environment. *American Journal of Psychology*, 111, 826–831.

Hebb, D. O. 1949. *The organization of behavior: A neuropsychological theory*. New York: Wiley.

Heckhausen, H. 1967. *The anatomy of achievement motivation*. New York: Academic Press.

Heer, D. M. 1958. Dominance and the working wife. *Social Forces*, 26, 341–347.

Heider, F., and Simmel, M. 1944. An experimental study of apparent behavior. *American Journal of Psychology*, 57, 243–259.

Heider, F. 1958. *The psychology of interpersonal relations*. New York: John Wiley.

Heilbrun, A. B., Jr. 1968. Sex role, instrumental-expressive behavior, and psychopathology in females. *Journal of Abnormal Psychology*, 73, 2, 131–136.

Heinstein, M. 1966. Child rearing in California. Berkeley: Bureau of Maternal and Child Health, State of California Department of Public Health.

Heisenberg, W. 1958. *Physics and philosophy*. New York: Harper Torch Books.

Helson, H. 1948. Adaptation level as a basis for a quantitative theory of frames of reference. *Psychological Review*, 55, 297–313.

Helson, R. 1961. Creativity, sex, and mathematics. In MacKinnon, D. W. (Ed.), *The creative person*. Berkeley: University of California Extension.

Helson, R. 1967. Sex differences in creative style. *Journal of Personality*, 35, 214–233.

Helson, R. 1971. Women mathematicians and the creative personality. *Journal of Consulting and Clinical Psychology*, 36, 210–220.

Henchy, T., and Glass, D. C. 1968. Evaluation apprehension and the social facilitation of dominant and subordinate responses. *Journal of Personality and Social Psychology*, 10, 446–454.

Hendrick, C. 1972. Effects of salience of stimulus inconsistency on impression formation. *Journal of Personality and Social Psychology*, 22, 2, 219–222.

Hendrick, C., and Brown, S. R. 1971. Introversion, extraversion, and interpersonal attraction. *Journal of Personality and Social Psychology*, 20, 31–36.

Henry, J. 1963. *Culture against man*. New York: Random House.

Henry, J. 1959. The problem of spontaneity, initiative and creativity in suburban classrooms. *American Journal of Orthopsychiatry*, 29, 266–279.

Henry, W. E. 1956. *The analysis of fantasy*. New York: Wiley.

Hersch, C. 1962. The cognitive functioning of the creative person: A developmental analysis. *Journal of Projective Techniques*, 26, 193–200.

Hess, E. H. 1959a. Imprinting. *Science*, 130, 133–141.

Hess, E. H. 1964. Imprinting in birds. *Science*, 146, 1128–1139.

Hess, E. 1959b. The relationship between imprinting and motivation. In Jones, M. R. (Ed.), *Nebraska symposium on motivation*, 7, 44–77.

Hess, E. H., Seltzer, A. L., and Shlein,

J. M. 1965. Pupil responses of hetero- and homosexual males to pictures of men and women: A pilot study. *Journal of Abnormal and Social Psychology*, 70, 165–168.

Hess, R. D. 1970. Social class and ethnic influences on socialization. In Mussen, P. H., *Carmichael's manual of child psychology*. New York: Wiley.

Hetherington, E. M. 1965. A developmental study of the effects of sex of the dominant parent on sex-role performance, identification, and imitation in children. *Journal of Personality and Social Psychology*, 2, 188–194.

Hetherington, E. M., and Frankie, G. 1967. Effects of parental dominance, warmth, and conflict on imitation in children. *Journal of Personality and Social Psychology*, 6, 119–125.

Hicks, D. J. 1965. Imitation and retention of film-mediated aggressive peer and adult models. *Journal of Personality and Social Psychology*, 2, 97–100.

Hilgard, E. 1953. *Introduction to psychology*. New York: Harcourt, Brace.

Hilgard, E. R. 1956. *Theories of learning*, Second Edition. New York: Appleton-Century-Crofts.

Hill, R., and Aldous, J. 1969. Socialization for marriage and parenthood. In Goslin, D. A. (Ed.), *Handbook of socialization theory and research*. Chicago: Rand McNally.

Hochberg, J. E. 1964. *Perception*. Englewood Cliffs, N.J.: Prentice-Hall.

Hodges, W. F. 1968. Effects of ego threat of pain on state anxiety. *Journal of Personality and Social Psychology*, 8, 4, 364–372.

Hodges, W. F., and Felling, J. P. 1970. Types of stressful situations and their relation to trait anxiety and sex. *Journal of Consulting and Clinical Psychology*, 34, 333–337.

Hoffman, L. W. 1972. Early childhood experiences and women's achievement motives. *Journal of Social Issues*, 28, 129–155.

Hoffman, L. W. 1961. Effects of maternal employment on the child. *Child Development*, 32, 187–197.

Hoffman, L. W. 1963. Research findings of the effects of maternal employment on the child. In Nye, I., and Hoffman,

L. W. (Eds.), *The employed mother in America*. Chicago: Rand McNally.

Hoffman, M. L. 1963. Childrearing practices and moral development: Generalizations from empirical research. *Child Development*, 34, 295–318.

Hoffman, M. L. 1970. Moral development. In Mussen, P. H. (Ed.), *Carmichael's manual of child psychology*, Third Edition, Volume 2. New York: Wiley.

Hohman, G. W. 1962. The effect of dysfunctions of the autonomic nervous system on experienced feelings and emotions. Paper read at Conference on Emotions and Feelings at New York School for Social Research, New York.

Hokanson, J. E. 1969. *The physiological bases of motivation*. New York: Wiley.

Hollander, E. P. 1958. Conformity, status, and idiosyncrasy credit. *Psychological Review*, 65, 117–127.

Hollander, E. P. 1967. *Principles and methods of social psychology*. New York: Oxford University Press.

Holmes, D. S. 1967. Amount of experience in experiments as a determinant of performance in later experiments. *Journal of Personality and Social Psychology*, 7, 403–407.

Holmes, D. S. 1968. Dimensions of projection. *Psychological Bulletin*, 69, 248–268.

Holmes, D. S. 1972. Repression or interference? A further investigation. *Journal of Personality and Social Psychology*, 22, 163–170.

Holmes, D. S., and Houston, B. K. 1971. The defensive function of projection. *Journal of Personality and Social Psychology*, 20, 2, 208–213.

Holmes, D. S., and Schallow, J. R. 1969. Reduced recall after ego threat: Repression or response competition? *Journal of Personality and Social Psychology*, 13, 10, 145–152.

Holt, R. R. 1958. Clinical and statistical prediction: A reformulation and some new data. *Journal of Abnormal and Social Psychology*, 56, 1–12.

Holtzman, P. S., and Gardner, R. W. 1959. Leveling and repression. *Journal of Abnormal and Social Psychology*, 59, 151–155.

Holtzman, W. H. 1958a. Holtzman Inkblot Technique. Form A. New York: Psychological Corporation.

Holtzman, W. H. 1958b. Holtzman Inkblot Technique. Form B. New York: Psychological Corporation.

Holtzman, W. H. 1959. Objective scoring of projective techniques. In Bass, B. M., and Berg, I. A. (Eds.), *Objective approaches to personality assessment.* Princeton, N.J.: Van Nostrand.

Holtzman, W. H. et al. 1963. Comparison of the group method and the standard individual version of the Holtzman Inkblot Technique. *Journal of Clinical Psychology,* 19, 441–449.

Holtzman, W. H., et al. 1961. *Inkblot perception and personality.* Austin: University of Texas Press.

Holz, W. C., and Azrin, N. H. 1961. Discriminative properties of punishment. *Journal of the Experimental Analysis of Behavior,* 4, 225–232.

Homans, G. C. 1950. *The human group.* New York: Harcourt, Brace.

Hooker, Evelyn. 1965. An empirical study of some relations between sexual patterns and gender identity in male homosexuals. In Money, J. (Ed.), *Sex Research: New Developments.* New York: Holt, Rinehart and Winston.

Hooker, Evelyn. 1957. The adjustment of the male overt homosexual. *Journal of Projective Techniques,* 21, 18–31.

Hornberger, R. 1960. The projective effects of fear and sexual arousal on the ratings of pictures. *Journal of Clinical Psychology,* 16, 328–331.

Horner, M. 1968. Sex differences in achievement motivation and performance in competitive and noncompetitive situations. Doctoral dissertation, University of Michigan.

Horner, M. S. 1972. Toward an understanding of achievement-related conflicts in women. *Journal of Social Issues,* 28, 157–175.

Horney, K. 1937. *Neurotic personality of our times.* New York: Norton.

Horney, K. 1939. *New ways in psychoanalysis.* New York: Norton.

Horney, K. 1945. *Our inner conflicts.* New York: Norton.

Horney, K. 1942. *Self-analysis.* New York: Norton.

Hornstein, H. A., Fisch, E., and Holmes, M. 1968. Influence of a model's feeling about his behavior and his relevance as a comparison other on observers'

helping behavior. *Journal of Personality and Social Psychology,* 10, 222–226.

Horrocks, J. E. and Buker, M. E. 1951. A study of the friendship fluctuations of preadolescents. *Journal of Genetic Psychology,* 78, 131–144.

Houston, B. K. 1972. Control over stress, locus of control, and response to stress. *Journal of Personality and Social Psychology,* 21, 249–255.

Houts, P. S., and Entwisle, D. R. 1968. Academic achievement effort among females: Achievement attitudes and sex-role orientation. *Journal of Counseling Psychology,* 15, 284–286.

Howes, D. H., and Solomon, R. L. 1950. A note on McGinnies' "Emotionality and perceptual defense." *Psychological Review,* 57, 229–234.

Howes, D. H., and Solomon, R. L. 1951. Visual duration threshold as a function of word probability. *Journal of Experimental Psychology,* 41, 401–410.

Hudson, B. B. 1950. One-trial learning in the domestic rat. *Genetic Psychology Monographs,* 41, 99–145.

Hulin, C. L., and Blood, M. R. 1968. Job enlargement, individual differences and worker responses. *Psychological Bulletin,* 69, 41–55.

Hunt, J. McV. 1965. Intrinsic motivation and its role in psychological development. In Levine, D. (Ed.), *Nebraska symposium on motivation.* Lincoln: University of Nebraska Press.

Hyman, R. 1964. *The nature of psychological inquiry.* Englewood Cliffs, N.J.: Prentice-Hall.

Isen, A. M. and Levin, P. F. 1972. Effect of feeling good on helping: Cookies and kindness. *Journal of Personality and Social Psychology,* 21, 384–388.

Izard, C. 1971. *The face of emotion.* New York: Appleton-Century-Crofts.

Jacobi, I. 1949. *The psychology of C. G. Jung.* London: Kegan, Paul, Trench, Trubner and Co.

Jacobs, L., Berscheid, E., and Walster, E. 1971. Self-esteem and attraction. *Journal of Personality and Social Psychology,* 17, 84–91.

James, W. 1890. *The principles of psychology.* New York: Henry Holt.

Janis, I. L. 1968. Attitude change via

role playing. In Abelson, et al., *Theories of cognitive consistency: A sourcebook*. New York: Rand McNally.

Janis, I. L. 1967. Effects of fear arousal on attitude change: Recent developments in theory and experimental research. In Berkowitz, L. (Ed.), *Advances in experimental social psychology*, Volume 3. New York: Academic Press.

Janis, I. L. 1958. *Psychological stress: Psychoanalytic and behavioral studies of surgical patients*. New York: John Wiley.

Janis, I. L. 1969. *The contours of fear*. New York: Wiley.

Janis, I. L., and Leventhal, H. 1968. Human reactions to stress. In Borgatta, E. F., and Lambert, W. W. (Eds.), *Handbook of personality theory and research*. New York: Rand McNally.

Janis, I. L., and Mann, L. 1965. Effectiveness of emotional role playing in modifying smoking habits and attitudes. *Journal of Experimental Research In Personality*, 1, 84–90.

Jasper, H. H. 1958. Reticular-cortical systems and theories of the integrated action of the brain. In Harlow, H. F., and Woolsey, C. N. (Eds.), *Biological and biochemical bases of behavior*. Madison: University of Wisconsin Press.

Jensen, V., and Clark, M. 1958. Married and unmarried college students. *Personnel and Guidance Journal*, 37, 123–125.

Johnson, H. J., and Eriksen, C. S. 1961. Preconscious perception: A reexamination of the Poetzl phenomenon. *Journal of Abnormal and Social Psychology*, 62, 497–503.

Johnson, J. E., Leventhal, H., and Dabbs, J. M., Jr. 1971. Contribution of emotional and instrumental response processes in adaptation to surgery. *Journal of Personality and Social Psychology*, 20, 55–64.

Johnson, M. M. 1963. Sex-role learning and the nuclear family. *Child Development*, 34, 319–333.

Johnson, R. C., and Medinnus, G. R. 1965. *Child psychology*. New York: Wiley.

Jones, E. E., and Gerard, H. B. 1967. *Foundations of social psychology*. New York: Wiley.

Jones, M. C. 1924. A laboratory study of fear: The case of Peter. *Journal of Genetic Psychology*, 31, 308–315.

Jones, M. C., and Bayley, N. 1950. Physical maturing among boys as related to behavior. *Journal of Educational Psychology*, 41, 129–148.

Jones, S. C., and Pine, H. A. 1968. Self-revealing events and interpersonal evaluations. *Journal of Personality and Social Psychology*, 8, 277–281.

Joy, V. L. 1963. Repression-sensitization and interpersonal behavior. Paper read at American Psychological Association, Philadelphia, August 1963.

Julian, J. W., and Katz, S. B. 1968. Internal versus external control and the value of reinforcement. *Journal of Personality and Social Psychology*, 8, 89–94.

Jung, C. G. 1928. On the relation of analytical psychology to poetic art. In Jung, C. G., *Contributions to analytical psychology*. New York: Harcourt, Brace.

Jung, C. G. 1933a. *Modern man in search of a soul*. New York: Harcourt, Brace and World.

Jung, C. G. 1933b. *Psychological types*. New York: Harcourt, Brace, and World.

Jung, C. G. 1956. *Two essays on analytical psychology*. New York: Meridian Books.

Jung, C. G. 1959a. The archetypes and the collective unconscious. In Read, H., Fordham, M., and Adler, G. (Eds.), *Collected works of Carl Jung*. Princeton: University Press.

Jung, C. G. 1959b. *The basic writing of C. G. Jung*. New York: Random House.

Kagan, J. 1958. The concept of identification. *Psychological Review*. 65, 296–305.

Kagan, J. 1964. Acquisition and significance of sex typing and sex role identity. In Hoffman and Hoffman (Eds.) *Review of child development research*. Volume 1. New York: Russell Sage Foundation.

Kagan, J. 1967. On the need for relativism. *American Psychologist*, 22, 131–142.

Kagan, J., and Moss, H. A. 1959. Stability and validity of achievement fantasy. *Journal of Abnormal and Social Psychology*, 58, 357–364.

Kagan, J., and Moss, H. A. 1962. *Birth to maturity*. New York: Wiley.

Kamiya, J. 1972. Operant control of the EEG Alpha rhythm and some of its reported effects on consciousness. In Tart, C. T. (Ed.), *Altered states of consciousness*. Garden City, N.Y.: Anchor Books, Doubleday (Originally published, 1969, Wiley).

Karabenick, S. A. 1972. Valence of success and failure as a function of achievement motives and locus of control. *Journal of Personality and Social Psychology*, 21, 101–110.

Karabenick, S. A., and Youssef, Z. I. 1968. Performance as a function of achievement motive level and perceived difficulty. *Journal of Personality and Social Psychology*, 10, 414–419.

Karp, S. A. 1963. Field dependence and overcoming embeddedness. *Journal of Consulting Psychology*, 27, 486–491.

Katkousky W., Preston, A., and Crandall, U. J. 1964a. Parents' achievement attitudes and their behavior with their children in achievement situations. *Journal of Genetic Psychology*, 104, 105–121.

Katkousky, W., Preston, A., and Crandall, U. J. 1964b. Parents' attitudes toward their personal achievements and toward the achievement behaviors of their children. *Journal of Genetic Psychology*, 104, 67–82.

Katz, D. 1960. The functional approach to the study of attitude. *Public Opinion Quarterly*, 24, 163–204.

Katz, D. 1968. Consistency for what? The functional approach. In Abelson, et al., *Theories of cognitive consistency: A sourcebook*. New York: Rand McNally.

Katz, D., and Schanck, R. L. 1938. *Social psychology*. New York.

Katz, I. 1970. Experimental studies of Negro-white relationships. In Berkowitz, L. (Ed.), *Advances in experimental social psychology*, Volume 5. New York: Academic Press.

Katz, I., Roberts, O. S., and Robinson, J. M. 1963. Effects of difficulty, race of administrator, and instructions on Negro digit-symbol performance. *ONR Technical Report*. Washington, D.C.: Office of Naval Research.

Katz, I., Roberts, S. O., and Robinson, J. M. 1965. Effects of task difficulty, race of administrator, and instructions on digit-symbol performance of Negroes. *Journal of Personality and Social Psychology*, 2, 53–59.

Keller, F. S. 1954. *Learning, reinforcement theory*. New York: Random House.

Kelley, H. H. 1967. Attribution theory in social psychology. In Levine, D. (Ed.), *Nebraska symposium on motivation*. Lincoln: University of Nebraska Press.

Kelly, G. A. 1955. *The psychology of personal constructs*, Volumes 1 and 2. New York: Norton.

Kelman, H. C. 1965. Manipulation of human behavior—an ethical dilemma for the social scientist. *Journal of Social Issues*, 21, 31–46.

Kelman, H. C. 1967. Human uses of human subjects, the problem of deception in social psychological experiments. *Psychological Bulletin*, 67, 1–11.

Kempf, E. J. 1918. Autonomic functions and the personality. *Nervous and mental disorders*. Monograph No. 28.

Kendler, H. H. 1968. *Basic psychology*. New York: Benjamin.

Kerpelman, J. P. and Himmelfarb, S. 1971. Partial reinforcement effects in attitude acquisition and counter-conditioning. *Journal of Personality and Social Psychology*, 19, 3, 301–305.

Kessen, W. 1963. Research in the psychological development of infants: An overview. *Merrill-Palmer Quarterly*, 9, 83–94.

Kessen, W., and Mandler, G. 1961. Anxiety, pain, and the inhibition of distress. *Psychological Review*, 68, 396–404.

Kety, S. S. 1967. Psychoendocrine systems and emotions: Biological aspects. In Glass, D. C. (Ed.) *Proceedings of a conference under the auspices of Russell Sage Foundation and The Rockefeller University*. New York: The Rockefeller University Press and Russell Sage Foundation.

Kierkegaard, S. 1938. *Purity of heart is to will one thing*. Translated from the Danish by D. V. Steere. New York: Harper and Brothers. First Harper Torchbook Edition, 1956.

Kiesler, C. A., and Corbin, L. H. 1965. Commitment, attraction, and conformity. *Journal of Personality and Social Psychology*, 2, 890–895.

Kiesler, C. A., and Kiesler, S. B. 1969. *Conformity*. Reading, Mass.: Addison-Wesley.

Kiesler, C. A., Zanna, M., and DeSalvo, J. 1966. Deviation and conformity: Opinion change as a function of commitment, attraction, and pressure of a deviate. *Journal of Personality and Social Psychology*, 3, 4, 458–467.

Kiesler, S. B., and Baral, R. L. 1970. The search for a romantic partner: the effects of self-esteem and physical attractiveness on romantic behavior. In Gergen, K. L., and Marlowe, D. (Eds.), *Personality and social behavior*. Reading, Mass.: Addison-Wesley.

Kimble, G. A. 1961. *Hilgard and Marquis' conditioning and learning*. New York: Appleton-Century-Crofts.

Kimmel, H. D. 1967. Instrumental conditioning of autonomically mediated behavior. *Psychological Bulletin*, 67, 337–345.

King, D. L. 1966. A review and interpretation of some aspects of the infant-mother relationship in mammals and birds. *Psychological Bulletin*, 65, 143–155.

Kinsey, A. C., et al. 1948. *Sexual behavior in the human male*. Philadelphia: Saunders.

Kinsey, A. C., et al. 1953. *Sexual behavior in the human female*. Philadelphia: Saunders.

Kintz, B. L., et al. 1965. The experimenter effect. *Psychological Bulletin*, 63, 223–232.

Kirkendall, L. A., and Libby, R. W. 1966. Interpersonal relationship—crux of the sexual renaissance. *Journal of Social Issues*, XXII, No. 2, 1–140 (whole issues).

Kissel, S. 1965. Stress reducing properties of social stimuli. *Journal of Personality and Social Psychology*, 2, 378–384.

Klein, G. S. 1954. Need and regulation. In Jones, M. R. (Ed.), *Nebraska symposium on motivation*. Lincoln: University of Nebraska Press.

Klein, G. S. 1958. Cognitive control and motivation. In Lindzey, G. (Ed.), *Assessment of human motives*. New York: Holt, Rinehart and Winston.

Kleinmuntz, B. 1967. *Personality measurement: An introduction*. Homewood, Ill.: Dorsey.

Kleitman, N. 1963. *Sleep and wakefulness*. Second Edition. Chicago: University of Chicago.

Klineberg, O. 1954. *Social psychology*, Revised Edition. New York: Henry Holt.

Klinger, E. 1966. Fantasy need achievement as a motivational construct. *Psychological Bulletin*, 66, 291–308.

Klinger, E. 1969. Development of imaginative behavior: Implications of play for a theory of fantasy. *Psychological Bulletin*, 72, 4, 277–298.

Klinger, E. and McNelly, F. W., Jr. 1969. Fantasy need achievement and performance: A role analysis. *Psychological Review*. 76, 6, 574–591.

Kluckhohn, C. 1942. Report to the sub-sub-committee on definitions of culture. Committee on conceptual integration. Mimeographed. Cited in Kroeber, A. L. and Kluckhohn, C., *Culture, a critical review of concepts and definitions*. New York: Vintage Books, Random House 1952.

Kluckhohn, C. 1951. The concept of culture. In Lerner, D. and Lasswell, H. D. (Eds.), *The policy sciences*. Stanford, California. Pp. 86–101.

Kluckhohn, C., and Kelly, W. H. 1945. The concept of culture. In Linton, R. (Ed.), *The science of man in the world crisis*. New York. Pp. 78–105.

Kluckhohn, C., and Murray, H. A. 1949. *Personality in nature, society and culture*, first edition. New York: Knopf.

Kneller, G. F. 1965. *The art and science of creativity*. New York: Holt, Rinehart and Winston.

Knobloch, H., and Pasamanick, B. 1958. The relationship of race and socioeconomic status to the development of motor behavior patterns in infancy. *Psychiatric Research Reports No. 10*.

Knobloch, H., and Pasamanick, B. 1960. Exogenous factors in infant intelligence. *Pediatrics*, 26, 210–218.

Koch, S. 1956. Behavior as "intrinsically" regulated: Work notes towards a pretheory of phenomena called "motivational." In Jones, M. R., (Ed.), *Nebraska symposium on motivation*, Volume 4. Pp. 42–86.

Kohlberg, L. 1963a. Moral development and identification. In Stevenson, H. W.

(Ed.), *Child psychology*. Chicago: University of Chicago Press.

Kohlberg, L. 1963b. The development of children's orientations toward a moral order. I. Sequence in the development of moral thought. *Vita Humana*, 6, 11–33.

Kohlberg, L. 1964. Development of moral character and moral ideology. In M. L. Hoffman and L. W. Hoffman (Eds.) *Review of child development research*. Volume 1. New York: Russell Sage Foundation.

Kohlberg, L. 1966. A cognitive developmental analysis of children's sex-role concepts and attitudes. In E. Maccoby (Ed.) *The development of sex differences*. Stanford, Calif.: Stanford University Press.

Kohlberg, L. 1969. Stage and sequence: The cognitive-development approach to socialization. In Goslin, D. A. (Ed.), *Handbook of socialization theory and research*. Chicago: Rand McNally.

Kolb, D. A. 1965. Achievement motivation training for under-achieving high school boys. *Journal of Personality and Social Psychology*, 2, 783–792.

Konecni, V. J., and Doob, A. N. 1972. Catharsis through displacement of aggression. *Journal of Personality and Social Psychology*, 23, 379–387.

Kovach, J. K. and Hess, E. H. 1963. Imprinting effects of painful stimulation upon the following response. *Journal of Comparative and Physiological Psychology*, 56, 461–464.

Kramer, E. 1963. Judgement of personal characteristics and emotions from nonverbal properties of speech. *Psychological Bulletin*, 60, 408–420.

Krasner, L. 1971. Behavior therapy. In Mussen, P. H., and Rosenzweig, M. R. (Eds.), *Annual Review of Psychology*, Volume 22. pp. 483–532. Palo Alto, Calif.: Annual Reviews Inc.

Krebs, D. L. 1970. Altruism—An examination of the concept and a review of the literature. *Psychological Bulletin*, 73, 258–302.

Kretch, D. and Crutchfield, R. 1948. *Theory and problems of social psychology*. New York: McGraw-Hill.

Kretch, D., Crutchfield, R. S., Ballachy, E. L. 1962. *Individual in society*. New York: McGraw-Hill.

Krippner and Hughes. 1970. Genius at work. *Psychology Today*, 4, 1, 40–43.

Kris, E. 1952. *Psychoanalytic exploration in art*. New York: International Universities Press.

Kris, E. 1953. Psychoanalysis and the study of creative imagination. *Bulletin of the New York Academy of Medicine*, 334–351.

Kroeber, A. L., and Kluckhohn, C. 1952. *Culture: A critical review of concepts and definitions*. New York: Vintage Books, Random House.

Kuhlen, R. G. 1964. Personality change with age. In Worchel, P., and Byrne, D., *Personality Change*. New York: Wiley.

Kukla, A. 1972. Attributional determinants of achievement-related behavior. *Journal of Personality and Social Psychology*, 21, 166–174.

Lacey, J. I. 1956. The evaluation of autonomic responses: Toward a general solution. *Annals of the New York Academy of Science*, 67, 123–164.

Lachman. 1960. The model in theory construction. *Psychological Review*, 67, 113–129.

La Forge, R. 1967. Confidence intervals or tests of significance in scientific research? *Psychological Bulletin*, 6, 446–447.

Lambert, W. W., and Lambert, W. E. 1964. *Social psychology*. Englewood Cliffs, N.J.: Prentice-Hall, Inc.

Lambert, W. W., Solomon, R. L., and Watson, P. D. 1949. Reinforcement and extinction as factors in size estimation. *Journal of Experimental Psychology*, 39, 637–641.

Lambert, W. W., Triandis, L. M., and Wolf, M. 1959. Some correlates of beliefs in the malevolence and benevolence of supernatural beings: A cross-societal study. *Journal of Abnormal and Social Psychology*, 58, 162–169.

Lana, R. E. 1969. Pretest sensitization. In Rosenthal, R., and Rosnow, R. L., *Artifact in behavioral research*. New York: Academic Press. pp. 119–141.

Lang, P. J. 1968. Fear reduction and fear behavior: Problems in treating a construct. In Shlien, J. M. (Ed.), *Research in psychotherapy*. Washington, D.C.: American Psychological Association.

Lang, P. J., and Lazovik, A. D. 1963. Experimental desensitization of a phobia. *Journal of Abnormal and Social Psychology*, 66, 519–525.

Lang, P. J., Lazovik, A. D. and Reynolds, D. J. 1965. Desensitization, suggestibility, and pseudotherapy. *Journal of Abnormal Psychology*, 70, 395–402.

Lang, P. J., Melamed, B. G., and Hart, J. 1970. A physiological analysis of fear modification using an automated desensitization procedure. *Journal of Abnormal Psychology*, 76, 221–234.

Lang, P. J., Sroufe, L. A., Hastings, J. E. 1967. Effects of feedback and instructional set on the control of cardiac-rate variability. *Journal of Experimental Psychology*, 75, 425–431.

Lanzetta, J. T. and Kleck, R. E. 1970. Encoding and decoding of non-verbal affect in humans. *Journal of Personality and Social Psychology*, 16, 12–19.

LaPierre, R. T. 1934. Attitudes vs. actions. *Social Forces*, 13, 230–237.

Larsen, K. S., et al. 1972. Is the subject's personality or the experimental situation a better predictor of a subject's willingness to administer shock to a victim? *Journal of Personality and Social Psychology*, 22, 3, 287–295.

Latané, B. 1968. Gregariousness and fear in laboratory rats. *Journal of Experimental Social Psychology*.

Latané, B., and Darley, J. M. 1970. *The unresponsive bystander: Why doesn't he help?* New York: Appleton-Century-Crofts.

Latané, B., and Glass, D. C. 1968. Social and nonsocial attraction in rats. *Journal of Personality and Social Psychology*, 9, 142–146.

Laws, J. L. 1971. A feminist review of marital adjustment literature: The rape of the locke. *Journal of Marriage and the Family*, 483–516.

Lazarus, R. S. 1966. *Psychological stress and the coping process.* New York: McGraw-Hill.

Lazarus, R. S., and McCleary, R. A. 1951. Autonomic discrimination without awareness: A study of subception. *Psychological Review*, 58, 113–123.

Lazarus, R. S., and Opton, E. M., Jr. 1966. The study of psychological stress: A summary of theoretical formulations and experimental findings. In C. D. Spielberger (Ed.), *Anxiety and behavior.* New York: Academic Press.

Lazarus, R. S., Averill, J. R., Opton, E. M., Jr. 1970. Toward a cognitive theory of emotion. In Arnold, M. (Ed.), *Feelings and emotion.* New York: Academic Press.

Lazarus, R. S., et al. 1965. The principle of short-circuiting of threat: Further evidence. *Journal Personality*, 33, 622–635.

Leavitt, H. J. 1951. Some effects of certain communication patterns on group performance. *Journal of Abnormal and Social Psychology*, 46, 38–50.

Leeper, R. W. 1963. Theoretical methodology in the psychology of personality. In Marx, M. H., *Theories in contemporary psychology.* New York: Macmillan.

Lefcourt, H. M. 1966. Internal vs. external control of reinforcement: A review. *Psychological Bulletin*, 65, 206–220.

Lefcourt, H. M. 1972. Recent developments in the study of locus of control. In Maher, B. A. (Ed.), *Progress in experimental personality research*, New York: Academic Press. Pp. 1–39.

Lefcourt, H. M., and Ladwig, G. W. 1965. The American Negro: A problem in expectancies. *Journal of Personality and Social Psychology*, 1, 377–380.

Le Furgy, W. G., and Woloshin, G. W. 1969. Immediate and long-term effects of experimentally induced social influence in the modification of adolescents' moral judgements. *Journal of Personality and Social Psychology*, 12, 104–110.

Leipold, W. D. 1963. Psychological distance in a dyadic interview as a function of introversion-extraversion, anxiety, social desirability and stress. Doctoral dissertation, University of North Dakota.

Le Masters, E. E. 1957. Parenthood as crisis. *Marriage and Family Living*, 19, 4, 352–355.

Lenneberg, 1962. Understanding language without ability to speak: A case report. *Journal of Abnormal and Social Psychology*, 51, 327–358,

Lerner, J. J., and Simmons, C. H. 1966. Observer's reactions to the "innocent victim": Compassion or rejection? *Jour-*

nal of Personality and Social Psychology, 4, 203–210.

Lerner, L., and Weiss, R. L. 1972. Role of value of reward and model affective response in vicarious reinforcement. Journal of Personality and Social Psychology, 21, 1, 93–100.

Lerner, M. J. 1971. Observer's evaluation of a victim: Justice, guilt, and veridical perception. Journal of Personality and Social Psychology, 20, 2, 127–135.

Lesser, G. S., Krawitz, R. N., and Packard, R. 1963. Experimental arousal of achievement motivation in adolescent girls. Journal of Abnormal and Social Psychology, 66, 59–66.

Levin, H., and Fleischman, B. 1968. Childhood socialization. In Borgatta, E. F., and Lambert, W. W. (Eds.), Handbook of personality theory and research. Chicago: Rand McNally.

Levinger, G. 1966. Sources of marital dissatisfaction among applicants for divorce. American Journal of Orthopsychiatry, 36, 5, 803–807.

Levinger, G., and Breedlove, J. 1966. Interpersonal attraction and agreement: A study of marriage partners. Journal of Personality and Social Psychology, 3, 4, 367–372.

Levitt, E. E. 1967. The psychology of anxiety. Indianapolis: Bobbs-Merrill.

Levy, D. M. 1943. Maternal overprotection. New York: Columbia University Press.

Lewin, K. 1951. Field theory in social science. New York: Harper.

Lewis, H. B., et al., 1966. Individual differences in dream recall. Journal of Abnormal Psychology. 1966, 71, 52–59.

Linder, D. E., Cooper, J., and Jones, E. E. 1967. Decision freedom as a determinant of the role of incentive magnitude in attitude change. Journal of Personality and Social Psychology, 6, 245–254.

Lindsley, D. B. 1951. Emotion. In Stevens, S. S. (Ed.), Handbook of experimental psychology. New York: Wiley. Pp. 473–516.

Lindzey, G. 1961. Projective techniques and cross-cultural research. New York: Appleton-Century-Crofts.

Lindzey, G. 1965. Seer versus sign. Journal of Experimental Research in Personality, 1, 17–26.

Lindzey, G., et al. 1971. Behavioral genetics. In Mussen, P. H., and Rosenzweig, M. R. (Eds.), Annual review of psychology, Volume 22. Palo Alto, Calif.: Annual Reviews, Inc. Pp. 39–94.

Linn, L. S. 1965. Verbal attitudes and overt behavior: A study of racial discrimination. Social Forces, 43, 353–364.

Linton, R. 1936. The study of man. New York: Appleton-Century-Crofts.

Linton, R. 1945. The cultural background of personality. New York: Appleton-Century-Crofts.

Lipman-Blumen, J. 1972. How ideology shapes women's lives. Scientific American, 226, 34–42.

Little, K. B., and Fisher, J. 1958. Two new experimental scales of the MMPI. Journal of Consulting Psychology, 22, 305–306.

Little, K. B., and Shneidman, E. S. 1959. Congruencies among interpretations of psychological test and anamnestic data. Psychological Monographs, 73 (6, Whole No. 473).

Livensparger, D. 1965. Empathy inventory. Unpublished manuscript. Cited by Smith, 1966, Sensitivity to people. New York: McGraw Hill.

Loehlin, J. C. 1968. Computer models of personality. New York: Random House.

Loevinger, J. 1957. Objective tests as instruments of psychological theory. Psychological Reports Monographs, No. 9.

Lombardo, J. P., Weiss, R. F., Buchanan, W. 1972. Reinforcing and attracting functions of yielding. Journal of Personality and Social Psychology, 21, 3, 359–368.

Lorenz, K. 1935. Der kumpan in der unwelt des vogels. Journal of Ornithology, 83, 137–213; 289–413.

Lorenz, K. 1943. Die angeborenen formen möglicher erfahrung. Zs. Tierpsychol., 1943, 5, 235–409.

Lorenz, K. 1950. The comparative method of studying innate behavior patterns. In Society for experimental biology, Symposium No. 4: Physiological mechanisms in animal behavior. New York: Academic Press.

Lorenz, K. 1958. The deprivation experiment; its limitations and its value as a means to separate learned and unlearned elements of behavior. Paper presented at the Downing State Hospital, Illinois. Cited by Hess, 1962.

Lorenz, K. 1966. *On aggresion.* Trans. M. K. Wilson. New York: Harcourt, Brace, and World.

Lovaas, O. I. 1967. A behavior therapy approach to the treatment of childhood schizophrenia. In Hill, J. P., *Minnesota symposia on child psychology.* Minneapolis: University of Minnesota Press. Pp. 108–159.

Lovaas, O. I. 1968. Some studies on the treatment of childhood schizophrenia. In Shlien, J. M. (Ed.), *Research in psychotherapy.* Washington, D.C.: American Psychological Association. Pp. 103–121.

Lovaas, O. I., et al. 1966. Acquisition of imitative speech in schizophrenic children. *Science,* 151, 705–707.

Lu, Yi-Chuang. 1952. Contradictory parental expectations in schizophrenia: Dependence and responsibility. *AMA Archives of General Psychiatry,* 6, 219–234.

Luborsky, L., Blinder, B., and Schimek, J. 1965. Looking, recalling, and GSR as a function of defense. *Journal of Abnormal Psychology,* 70, 270–280.

Luckey, E. G., and Bain, J. K. 1970. Children: A factor in marital satisfaction. *Journal of Marriage and the Family,* 32, 43–44.

Lundin, R. W. 1963. Personality theory in behavioristic psychology. In Wepman, J. M., and Heine, R. W. (Eds.), *Concepts of personality.* Chicago: Aldine. Pp. 257–290.

Lykken, D. T. 1968. Statistical significance in psychological research. *Psychological Bulletin,* 70, 151–159.

Lynn, D. B. 1959. Sex differences in masculine and feminine identification. *Psychological Review,* 66, 126–135.

Maccoby, E. E. 1959. Role-taking in childhood and its consequences for social learning. *Child Development,* 30, 239–252.

Maccoby, E. E. 1966. Sex differences in intellectual functioning. In Maccoby, E. E. (Ed.), *The development of sex differences.* Stanford, Calif.: Stanford University Press.

Maccoby, E. E., and Masters, J. C. 1970. Attachment and dependency. In Mussen, P. H. (Ed.), *Carmichael's manual of child psychology,* Third Edition. New York: Wiley.

MacKinnon, D. W. 1960. The highly effective individual. *Teachers College Record,* 61, 367–378.

MacKinnon, D. W. 1961. Fostering creativity in students of engineering. *Journal of Engineering Education,* 52, 129–142.

MacKinnon, D. W. 1962. The nature and nurture of creative talent. *American Psychologist,* 17, 484–495.

Maddi, S. R. 1968. The pursuit of consistency and variety. In Abelson, R. P., et al., *Theories of cognitive consistency: A sourcebook.* New York: Rand McNally.

Maddi, S. R. 1972. *Personality theories, A comparative analysis,* Revised Edition. Homewood, Ill.: Dorsey.

Magee, B. 1966. *One in twenty: A study of homosexuality in men and women.* New York: Stein and Day.

Maier, N. R. F. 1949. *Frustration, The stuly of behavior without a goal.* New York: McGraw-Hill.

Mallick, S. K., and McCandless, B. R. 1966. A study of catharsis of aggression. *Journal of Personality and Social Psychology,* 4, 591–596.

Malmo, R. B. 1957. Anxiety and behavioral arousal. *Psychological Review,* 64, 276–287.

Malmo, R. B. 1958. Measurement of drive: An unsolved problem. In Jones, M. R. (Ed.), *Nebraska symposium on motivation.* Lincoln: University of Nebraska Press.

Malmo, R. B. 1959. Activation: A neuropsychological dimension. *Psychological Review,* 66, 367–386.

Malfo, R. B. 1962. Activation. In Bachrach, A. J. (Ed.), *Experimental foundations of clinical psychology.* New York: Basic Books.

Malmo, R. B., Boag, T. J., and Smith, A. A. 1957. Physiological study of personal interaction. *Psychosomatic Medicine,* 19, 105–119.

Maltzman, I., and Raskin, D. C. 1965. Effects of individual differences in the orienting reflex on conditioned and complex processes. *Journal of Experimental Research in Personality,* 1, 1–16.

Mandler, G. 1962. From association to structure. *Psychological Review,* 69, 415–427.

Mandler, G. 1964. The interruption of behavior. In Levine, D. (Ed.), *Nebraska symposium on motivation.* Lincoln: University of Nebraska Press.

Mandler, G. 1968. Anxiety. In Sills, D. L. (Ed.), *International encyclopedia of the social sciences,* Volume 1. New York: Free Press.

Mandler, G., and Kremen, I. 1958. Autonomic feedback: A correlational study. *Journal of Personality,* 26, 388–399. Errata, 1960, 28, 545.

Mandler, G., Mandler, J. M., and Uviller, E. T. 1958. Autonomic feedback: The perception of autonomic activity. *Journal of Abnormal and Social Psychology,* 56, 367–373.

Mandler, G., and Watson, D. L. 1966. Anxiety and the interruption of behavior. In Spielberger, C. (Ed.), *Anxiety and behavior.* New York: Academic Press.

Mann, J. H. 1959. The relationship between cognitive, behavioral and affective aspects of racial prejudice. *Journal of Social Psychology,* 49, 223–228.

Mann, L., and Janis, I. L. 1968. A follow-up study on the long-range effects of emotional role playing. *Journal of Personality and Social Psychology,* 8, 339–342.

Manosevitz, M., Lindzey, G., Thiessen, D. D. (Eds.). 1969. *Behavioral genetics: Method and research.* New York: Appleton-Century-Crofts.

Marañon, G. 1924. Contribution à l'étude de l'action émotive de l'adrénaline. *Rev. Francaise Endocrinol,* 2, 301–325.

Marecek, J., and Mettee, D. R. 1972. Avoidance of continued success as a function of self-esteem, level of esteem certainty, and responsibility for success. *Journal of Personality and Social Psychology,* 22, 1, 98–107.

Markley, O. W. 1971. Latitude of rejection: An artifact of own position. *Psychological Bulletin,* 75, 5, 357–359.

Markowitz, A. 1969. Influence of the repression-sensitization dimension, affect value and ego threat on incidental learning. *Journal of Personality and Social Psychology,* 11, 374–380.

Marks, I. M., and Gelder, M. G. 1968. Controlled trials in behaviour therapy. In Porter, R. (Ed.), *The role of learning in psychotherapy.* London: Churchill.

Marlow, D., and Gergen, K. J. 1969. Personality and social interaction. In Lindzey, G., and Aronson, E. (Eds.), *The handbook of social psychology,* Second Edition. Volume 3. Reading, Mass.: Addison-Wesley.

Marshall, S. L. A. 1951. *Men against fire.* Washington, D.C.: Combat Forces Press.

Martens, R. 1969. Effect of an audience on learning and performance of a complex motor skill. *Journal of Personality and Social Psychology,* 12, 252–260.

Martin, B. 1961. The assessment of anxiety by physiological behavioral measures. *Psychological Bulletin,* 58, 234–255.

Masling, J. 1959. The effects of warm and cold interaction on the administration and scoring of an intelligence test. *Journal of Consulting Psychology,* 23, 336–341.

Masling, J. 1960. The influence of situational and interpersonal variables in projective testing. *Psychological Bulletin,* 57, 65–85.

Masling, J. 1966. Role-related behavior of the subject and psychologist and its effects upon psychological data. In Levine, D. (Ed.), *Nebraska symposium on motivation.* Lincoln: University of Nebraska Press.

Maslow, A. H. 1943. A theory of human motivation. *Psychological Review,* 50, 370–396.

Maslow, A. H. 1954. *Motivation and personality.* New York: Harper.

Maslow, A. H. 1955. Deficiency motivation and growth motivation. In Jones, M. R. (Ed.), *Nebraska symposium on motivation.* Lincoln: University of Nebraska Press.

Maslow, A. H. 1956. Personality problems and personality growth. In Moustakas, C. G. (Ed.), *The self: Explorations in personal growth.* New York: Harper & Row.

Maslow, A. H. 1959. Creativity in self-actualizing people. In Anderson, H. H.

(Ed.), Creativity and its cultivation. New York: Harper & Row.

Maslow, A. H. 1962. Some basic propositions of a growth and self-actualization psychology. In Perceiving, behaving, becoming: A new focus for education. Washington, D.C.: Association for Supervision and curriculum development.

Maslow, A. H. 1970. Motivation and personality, Second Edition. New York: Harper & Row.

Mason, W. A. 1960. Socially mediated reduction on emotional responses of young Rhesus monkeys. Journal of Abnormal and Social Psychology, 60, 100–105.

Masserman, J. H. 1943. Behavior and neurosis. Chicago: University of Chicago Press.

Masters, W. H., and Johnson, V. E. 1970. Human sexual inadequacy. Boston: Little, Brown.

Mayo, C. W., and Crockett, W. H. 1964. Cognitive complexity and primacy-recency effects in impression formation. Journal of Abnormal and Social Psychology, 68, 335–338.

McCandless, B. R. 1967. Children, behavior and development, Second Edition. New York: Holt, Rinehart and Winston.

McCandless, B. R. 1970. Adolescents, behavior, and development. Hinsdals, Ill.: Dryden Press.

McCary, J. L. 1967. Human sexuality. Princeton, N.J.: Van Nostrand.

McClelland, D. C. 1951. Personality. New York: Sloane.

McClelland, D. C. 1958a. Risk taking in children with high and low need for achievement. In Atkinson, J. W. (Ed.), Motives in fantasy, action, and society. Princeton, N.J.: Van Nostrand.

McClelland, D. C. 1958b. The importance of early learning in the formation of motives. In Atkinson, J. W. (Ed.), Motives in fantasy, action, and society. Princeton, N.J.: Van Nostrand.

McClelland, D. C. 1961. The achieving society. Princeton, N.J.: Van Nostrand.

McClelland, D.C. 1963. The calculated risk: An aspect of scientific performance. In Taylor, C. W., and Barron, F. (Eds.), Scientific creativity: Its recognition and development. New York: Wiley.

McClelland, D. C. 1965a. Achievement and entrepreneurship: A longitudinal study. Journal of Personality and Social Psychology, 1, 389–392.

McClelland, D. C. 1965b. Achievement motivation can be developed. Harvard Business Review, 6–24.

McClelland, D. C. 1965c. Toward a theory of motive acquisition. American Psychologist, 20, 321–333.

McClelland, D. C. (Ed.). 1955. Studies in motivation. New York: Appleton-Century-Crofts.

McClelland, D. C., and Atkinson, J. W. 1948. The projective expression of needs, I: The effect of different intensities of the hunger drive on perception. Journal of Psychology, 25, 205–222.

McClelland, D. C., et al. 1953. The achievement motive. New York: Appleton-Century-Crofts.

McClelland, D. C., and Friedman, G. A. 1952. A cross-cultural study of the relationship between child rearing practices and achievement in folk tales. In Swanson, G. E., Newcomb, T. M., and Hartley, E. L. (Eds.), Readings in social psychology. New York: Holt, Rinehart and Winston.

McDougall, W. 1908. An introduction to social psychology. New York: Barnes and Noble, 1960.

McGinnies, E. 1949. Emotionality and perceptual defense. Psychological Review. 56, 244–251.

McGinnis, R. 1965. Mathematical foundation for social analysis. Indianapolis: Bobbs-Merrill.

McGuire, W. 1968. Personality and susceptibility to social influence. In Borgatta, E. F., and Lambert, W. W. (Eds.), Handbook of personality theory and research. Chicago: Rand McNally.

McGuire, W. J. 1969. Suspiciousness of experimenter's intent. In Rosenthal, R., and Rosnow, R. L. (Eds.), Artifact in behavioral research. New York: Academic Press.

McLaughlin, B. 1971. Effects of similarity and likableness on attraction and recall. Journal of Personality and Social Psychology, 20, 1, 65–69.

McLaughlin, D. 1965. "Intentional" and "incidental" learning in human subjects: The role of instructions to learn and motivation. *Psychological Bulletin*, 63, 359–376.

McMains, M. J., and Liebert, R. M. 1968. Influence of discrepancies between successively modeled self-reward criteria on the adoption of a self-imposed standard. *Journal of Personality and Social Psychology*, 8, 2, 166–171.

Mead, G. H. 1925. The genesis of the self and social control. *International Journal of Ethics*, 35, 251–277.

Mead, G. H. 1934. *Mind, self, and society*. Chicago: University of Chicago Press.

Mead, M. S. 1963. *Sex and temperament in three primitive societies*. New York: Dell, Laurel Edition.

Medialia, N. Z. 1962. Marriage and adjustment: In college and out. *Personnel and Guidance Journal*, 40, 545–550.

Medinnus, G. R., and Curtis, F. J. 1963. The relation between maternal self-acceptance and child acceptance. *Journal of Counseling Psychology*, 27, 542–544.

Mednick, S. A. 1962. The associative basis of the creative process. *Psychological Review*, 69, 220–232.

Meehl, P. E. 1945. The dynamics of structure personality tests. *Journal of Clinical Psychology*, 1, 296–303.

Meehl, P. E. 1954. *Clinical vs. statistical prediction*. Minneapolis: University of Minnesota Press.

Meehl, P. E. 1956. Wanted—a good cookbook. *American Psychologist*, 11, 263–272.

Meehl, P. E. 1965. Seer over sign: The first good example. *Journal of Experimental Research in Personality*, 1, 27, 32.

Megargee, E. I. 1971. The prediction of violence with psychological tests. In Spielberger, C. D. (Ed.), *Current topics in clinical and community psychology*, Vol. 2. New York: Academic Press. Pp. 97–156.

Mehrabian, A. 1969. Some referents and measures of nonverbal behavior. *Behavior Research Methods and Instrumentation*, 1, 203–207.

Mendelsohn, G. A., and Griswold, B. B. 1964. Differential use of incidental stimuli in problem solving as a function of creativity. *Journal of Abnormal and Social Psychology*, 68, 431–436.

Mendelsohn, G. A., and Griswold, B. B. 1966. Assessed creative potential, vocabulary level, and sex as predictors of the use of incidental cues in verbal problem solving. *Journal of Personality and Social Psychology*, 4, 423–431.

Mendelsohn, G. A., and Griswold, B. B. 1967. Anxiety and repression as predictors of the use of incidental cues in problem solving. *Journal of Personality and Social Psychology*, 6, 353–359.

Merton, R. K. 1948. The self-fulfilling prophecy. *Antioch Review*, 8, 193–210.

Merton, R. K. 1957. *Social theory and social structure*. Glencoe, Ill.: Free Press.

Meyerowitz, J. H. 1970. Satisfaction during pregnancy. *Journal of Marriage and the Family*, 32, 38–42.

Michotte, A. 1954. *La perception de la causalite*, Second Edition. Louvain: Publications Universitaires de Louvain.

Milgram, S. 1963. Behavioral study of obedinece. *Journal of Abnormal and Social Psychology*, 67, 371–378.

Milgram, S. 1964. Issues in the study of obedience: A reply to Baumrind. *American Psychologist*, 19, 848–852.

Milgram, S. 1965. Liberating effects of group pressure. *Journal of Personality and Social Psychology*, 1, 127–134.

Miller, G. R., and Rokeach, M. 1968. Individual differences and tolerance for inconsistency. In Abelson, R. P., et al. (Eds.), *Theories of cognitive consistency: A sourcebook*. Chicago: Rand McNally. Pp. 624–632.

Miller, N. E. 1941. The frustration-aggression hypothesis. *Psychological Review*, 48, 337–342.

Miller, N. E. 1944. Experimental studies of conflict. In Hunt, J. McV. (Ed.), *Personality and the behavior disorders*. New York: Ronald.

Miller, N. E. 1948. Theory and experiment relating psychoanalytic displacement to stimulus-response generalization. *Journal of Abnormal and Social Psychology*, 43, 155–178.

Miller, N. E. 1958. Central stimulation and other new approaches to motivation and reward. *American Psychologist*, 13, 100–108.

Miller, N. E. 1959. Liberalization of

basic S-R concepts: Extensions to conflict behavior, motivation, and social learning. In Koch, S. (Ed.), *Psychology: A study of a science.* New York: McGraw-Hill.

Miller, N. E., and Bugelski, R. 1948. Minor studies of aggression. II: The influence of frustrations imposed by the in-group on attitudes expressed toward out-groups. *Journal of Psychology,* 25, 437–442.

Miller, N. E., and Dollard, J. 1941. *Social learning and imitation.* New Haven: Yale University Press.

Miller, N. E., and Weiss, J. M. 1969. Effects of the somatic or visceral responses to punishment. In Campbell, B. A., and Church, R. M. (Eds.), *Punishment and aversive behavior.* New York: Appleton-Century-Crofts. Pp. 343–372.

Miller, R. E., Caul, W. F., and Mirsky, I. A. 1967. Communication of affects between feral and socially isolated monkeys. *Journal of Personality and Social Psychology,* 7, 231–239.

Minard, J. G. 1965. Response-bias interpretation of "perceptual defense": A selective review and evaluation of recent research. *Psychological Review,* 72, 1, 74–88.

Mischel, W. 1968. *Personality and assessment.* New York: Wiley.

Mischel, W. 1971. *Introduction to personality.* New York: Holt, Rinehart and Winston.

Mischel, W., and Gilligan, C. 1964. Delay of gratification, motivation for the prohibited gratification, and responses to temptation. *Journal of Abnormal and Social Psychology,* 69, 411–417.

Mischel, W., and Liebert, R. M. 1966. Effects of discrepancies between observed and imposed reward criteria on their acquisition and transmission. *Journal of Personality and Social Psychology,* 3, 45–53.

Missakian, E. A. 1972. Effects of adult social experience on patterns of reproductive activity of socially deprived male Rhesus monkeys (Macaca Mulatta). *Journal of Personality and Social Psychology,* 21, 131–134.

Mitchell, G. D. 1969. Paternalistic behavior in primates. *Psychological Bulletin,* 71, 6, 399–417.

Molish, H. B. 1969. The quest for charisma. *Journal of Projective Techniques and Personality Assessment,* 33, 103–117.

Molish, H. B. 1972. Projective methodologies. In Mussen, P. H., and Rosenzweig, M. R. (Eds.), *Annual review of psychology,* Volume 23. Palo Alto, Calif.: Annual Reviews. Pp. 577–614.

Moltz, H. 1965. Contemporary instinct theory and the fixed action pattern. *Psychological Review,* 72, 27–47.

Money, J. 1970. Sexual dimorphism and homosexual gender identity. *Psychological Bulletin,* 74, 6, 425–440.

Moore, D. J., and Shiek. 1971. Toward a theory of early infantile autism. *Psychological Review,* 78, 5, 451–456.

Moreno, J. L. 1953. *Who shall survive? Foundations of sociometry, group psychotherapy, and sociodrama,* Second Edition. Beacon, N.Y.: Beacon House. Sociometry Monographs, No. 29.

Morgan, C. D., and Murray, H. A. 1938. Thematic apperception test. In Murray, H. A. (Ed.), *Explorations in personality.* New York: Science Editions, 1962. Pp. 530–545.

Moss, H. A. 1967. Sex, age, and state as determinants of mother-infant interaction. *Merrill-Palmer Quarterly,* 13, 19–36.

Moulton, R. W. 1966. Patterning of parental affection and disciplinary dominance as a determinant of guilt and sex-typing. *Journal of Personality and Social Psychology,* 4, 356–363.

Moustakas, C. E. 1972. *Loneliness and love.* Englewood Cliffs, N.J.: Prentice-Hall.

Mowrer, O. H. 1947. On the dual nature of learning—a reinterpretation of "conditioning" and "problem-solving." *Harvard Educational Review,* 17, 102–148.

Mueller, E. F., et al. 1970. Psychosocial correlates of serum urate levels. *Psychological Bulletin,* 73, 238–257.

Munn, N. L. 1965. *The evolution and growth of human behavior.* Boston: Houghton Mifflin.

Munroe, R. L. 1955. *Schools of psychoanalytic thought: An exposition, critiques, and attempt at integration.* New York: Holt, Rinehart and Winston.

Murray, E. J. 1954. A case study in a behavioral analysis of psychotherapy. *Journal of Abnormal and Social Psychology*, 49, 305–310.

Murray, E. J. 1962. Direct analysis from the viewpoint of learning theory. *Journal of Consulting Psychology*, 26, 226–231.

Murray, E. J. 1964. *Motivation and emotion*. Englewood Cliffs, N.J.: Prentice-Hall.

Murray, E. J. 1965. Sleep, dreams, and arousal. New York: Appleton-Century-Crofts.

Murray, H. A. 1938. *Explorations in personality*. New York: Oxford.

Murray, H. A. 1943. *Thematic apperception test* (set of cards and manual). Cambridge, Mass.: Harvard University Press.

Murray, H. A., and MacKinnon, D. W. 1946. Assessment of OSS personnel. *Journal of Consulting Psychology*, 10, 76–80.

Murray, R. W. 1943. *Man's unknown ancestors*. Milwaukee.

Murrell, S. A., and Stachowiak, J. G. 1967. Consistency, rigidity, and power in the interaction patterns of clinic and nonclinic families. *Journal of Abnormal Psychology*, 72, 265–272.

Murstein, B. I. 1968. Discussion for current status of some projective techniques. *Journal of Projective Techniques and Personality Assessment*, 32, 229–239.

Murstein, B. I. 1972. Physical attractiveness and marital choice. *Journal of Personality and Social Psychology*, 22, 8–12.

Mussen, P. H. 1950. Some personality and social factors related to changes in children's attitudes toward Negroes. *Journal of Abnormal and Social Psychology*, 45, 423–441.

Mussen, P. H. 1969. Early sex-role development. In Goslin, A. A. (Ed.), *Handbook of socialization theory and research*. Chicago: Rand McNally.

Mussen, P. H., and Distler, L. 1960. Child-rearing antecedents of masculine identification in kindergarten boys. *Child Development*, 31, 89–100.

Mussen, P. H., Conger, J. J., and Kagan, J. 1969. *Child development and personality, Third Edition*. New York: Harper & Row.

Mussen, P. H., and Naylor, H. K. 1954. The relationships between overt and fantasy aggression. *Journal of Abnormal and Social Psychology*, 49, 235–240.

Mussen, P. H., and Rutherford, E. 1963. Parent-child relations and parental personality in relation to young children's sex-role preferences. *Child Development*, 34, 589–608.

Myres, J. L. 1927. *Political ideas of the Greeks*. New York.

Nash, J. 1952. Father and sons: A neglected aspect of child care. *Child Care*, 6, 19–22.

Nash, J. 1965. The father in contemporary culture and current psychological literature. *Child Development*, 36, 261–297.

Nash, J. 1970. Developmental psychology: A psychobiological approach. Englewood Cliffs, N.J.: Prentice-Hall.

Nash, J. 1973. The father in child development. In Caldwell, B., and Ricciuti, H. N. (Eds.), *Review of research in child development*, Volume 3. New York: Russell Sage Foundation.

Neisser, U. 1967. *Cognitive psychology*. New York: Appleton-Century-Crofts.

Nel, E., Helmreich, R., and Aronson, E. 1969. Opinion change in the advocate as a function of the persuasibility of his audience: A clarification of the meaning of dissonance. *Journal of Personality and Social Psychology*, 12, 117–124.

Nelsen, E. A. 1960. *The effects of reward and punishment of dependency on subsequent dependency*. Unpublished manuscript. Stanford University.

Neugarten, B. 1963. Personality changes during the adult years. In Kuhlen, R. G. (Ed.), *Psychological backgrounds of adult education*. Chicago: Center for the study of Liberal Education for Adults.

Neuringer, C. 1970. Behavior modification as the clinical psychologist views it. In Neuringer, C., and Michael, J. L. (Eds.), *Behavior modification in clinical psychology*. New York: Appleton-Century-Crofts.

Newcomb, T. M. 1943. *Personality and*

social change: Attitude formation in a student community. New York: Dryden.

Newcomb, T. M. 1947. Autistic hostility and social reality. *Human Relations*, 1, 69–86.

Newcomb, T. M. 1950. Role behavior in the study of individual personality and of groups. *Journal of Personality*, 18, 273–290.

Newcomb, T. M. 1961. *The acquaintance process*. New York: Holt, Rinehart and Winston.

Niles, P. 1964. The relationship of susceptibility and anxiety to acceptance of fear-arousing communications. Doctoral dissertation. Yale University.

Nisbett, R. 1968. Taste, deprivation, and weight determinants of eating behavior. *Journal of Personality and Social Psychology*, 10, 2, 107–116.

Nissen, H. W. 1930. A study of exploratory behavior in the white rat by means of the obstruction method. *Journal of Genetic Psychology*, 37, 361–376.

Notterman, J. M., Schoenfeld, W. N., and Bersh, P. J. 1952. Partial reinforcement and conditioned heart rate response in human subjects. *Science*, 115, 77–79.

Nowlis, V., and Nowlis, H. H. 1956. The description and analysis of mood. *Annals of the New York Academy of Science*, 65, 345–355.

Nunnaly, J. C. 1955. An investigation of some propositions of self-conception: The case of Miss Sun. *Journal of Abnormal and Social Psychology*, 50, 87–92.

Nuttall, J. R., and Barclay, A. M. 1973. The effect of false feedback on cognitive and fantasy measures of emotional arousal. In Press. Michigan State University.

Nye, I., and Hoffman, L. W. (Eds.). 1963. *The employed mother in America*. Chicago: Rand McNally.

Office of Strategic Services Assessment Staff. 1948. *Assessment of men*. New York: Holt, Rinehart and Winston.

Olds, J. 1962. Hypothalamic substrates of reward. *Physiological Review*, 42, 554–604.

Olds, J., and Olds, M. 1965. Drives, rewards, and the brain. In Barron, F., et al., *New directions in psychology*, Volume II. New York: Holt, Rinehart and Winston.

Omwake, K. T. 1954. The relation between acceptance of self and acceptance of others shown by three personality inventories. *Journal of Consulting Psychology*, 18, 443–446.

Orne, M. T. 1962. On the social psychology of the psychological experiment: With particular reference to demand characteristics and their implications. *American Psychologist*, 17, 776–783.

Orne, M. T. 1969. Demand characteristics and the concept of quasicontrols. In Rosenthal, R., and Rosnow, R. L., *Artifact in behavioral research*. New York: Academic Press.

Orne, M. T. 1970. Hypnosis, motivation, and the ecological validity of the psychological experiment. *Nebraska Symposium of Motivation*, 18, 187–265.

Osgood, C. E. 1952. The nature and measurement of meaning. *Psychological Bulletin*, 49, 197–237.

Osgood, C. E., and Luria, Z. 1954. A blind analysis of a case of multiple personality using the semantic differential. *Journal of Abnormal and Social Psychology*, 49, 579–591.

Ostrom, T. M., and Upshaw, H. S. 1968. Psychological perspective and attitude change. In Greenwald, A. G., Brock, T. C., Ostrom, T. M. (Eds.), *Psychological foundations of attitudes*. New York: Academic Press.

Otis, N. B., and McCandless, B. R. 1955. Responses to repeated frustrations of young children differentiated according to need area. *Journal of Abnormal and Social Psychology*.

Owens, W. A. 1968. Toward one discipline of scientific psychology. *American Psychologist*, 23, 11, 782–785.

Page, M. M., and Scheidt, R. J. 1971. The elusive weapons effect: Demand awareness, evaluation apprehension, and slightly sophisticated subjects. *Journal of Personality and Social Psychology*, 20, 3, 304–318.

Paivio, A. 1964. Child rearing antecedents of audience sensitivity. *Child Development*, 35, 397–416.

Paivio, A. 1965. Personality and audience influence. In Maher, B. A. (Ed.), *Progress in experimental personality research*, Volume 2. New York: Academic Press.

Pallak, M. S., and Heller, J. F. 1971. Interactive effects of commitment to future interaction and threat to attitudinal freedom. *Journal of Personality and Social Psychology*, 17, 325–331.

Papanek, H. 1965. Adler's concepts in community psychiatry. *Journal of Individual Psychology*, 21, 117–126.

Parke, R. D. (Ed.). 1969. *Readings in social development*. New York: Holt, Rinehart and Winston.

Parsons, T. 1949. *Essays in sociological theory*. Glencoe, Ill.: Free Press.

Parsons, T. 1955. Family structure and the socialization of the child. In Parsons, T., and Bales, R. F. (Eds.), *Family, socialization, and interaction process*. Glencoe, Ill.: Free Press.

Parsons, T., et al. 1955. *Family socialization and interaction process*. Glencoe, Ill.: Fress Press.

Pastore, N. 1949. Need as a determinant of perception. *Journal of Psychology*, 28, 457–475.

Patterson, G. R., Littman, R. A., and Bricker, W. 1967. Assertive behavior in children: A step toward a theory of aggression. Monograph for the Society for Research in Child Development, 32, No. 5 (Whole No. 113).

Paul, G. L. 1966. *Insight vs. desensitization in psychotherapy: An experiment in anxiety reduction*. Stanford, Calif.: Stanford University Press.

Paul, G. L. 1969. Outcome of systematic desensitization. II: Controlled investigations of individual treatment, technique variations and current status. In Franks, C. M. (Ed.), *Behavior therapy: Appraisal and status*. New York: McGraw-Hill.

Peabody, D. 1967. Trait inferences: Evaluative and descriptive aspects. *Journal of Personality and Social Psychology*, Monograph 7, Part 2 (Whole No. 644).

Peterson, D. R., et al. 1959. Parental attitudes and child adjustment. *Child Development*, 30, 119–130.

Peterson, D. R., et al. 1961. Child behavior problems and parental attitudes. *Child Development*, 32, 151–162.

Phares, E. J., Wilson, K. G., and Klyver, N. W. 1971. Internal-external control and the attribution of blame under neutral and distractive conditions. *Journal of Personality and Social Psychology*, 18, 285–288.

Phillips, B. N. 1962. Sex, social class, and anxiety as sources of variation in school achievement. *Journal of Educational Psychology*, 55, 316–322.

Piaget, J. 1948. *The moral judgment of a child*. Glencoe, Ill.: Free Press. (First published in French, 1932.)

Piaget, J. 1950. *The psychology of intelligence*. London: Routledge & Kegan Paul.

Piaget, J. 1952. *The origins of intelligence in children*. New York: International University Press.

Pine, F. 1957. Thematic drive content and creativity. *Journal of Personality*, 27, 136–151.

Pittel, S. M., and Mendelsohn, G. A. 1966. Measurement of moral values: A review and critique. *Psychological Bulletin*, 66, 22–35.

Pittluck, P. 1950. The relation between aggressive fantasy and overt behavior. Doctoral dissertation, Yale University.

Poetzl, O. 1908. The relationship between experimentally induced dream images and indirect vision. *Psychological Issues*, 1960, 3, 41, 120.

Postman, L. 1964. Short-term memory and incidental learning. In Melton, A. W. (Ed.), *Categories of human learning*. New York: Academic Press.

Prince, M. 1924. *The unconscious*, Second Edition. New York: Macmillan.

Pytkowicz, A. R., Wagner, N. N., and Sarason, I. G. 1967. An experimental study of the reduction of hostility through fantasy. *Journal of Personality and Social Psychology*, 5, 295–303.

Queener, E. L. 1951. *Introduction to social psychology*. New York: Dryden Press.

Rabban, M. 1950. Sex-role identification in young children in two diverse social groups. *Genetic Psychology Monographs*, 42, 81–158.

Rabbie, J. M. 1963. Differential preference for companionship under threat. *Journal of Abnormal and Social Psychology*, 67, 643–648.

Rabbie, J. M., and Horwitz, M. 1969. Arousal of ingroup-outgroup bias by a chance win or loss. *Journal of Personality and Social Psychology*, 13, 269–277.

Rabin, A. I. 1965. Motivation for parenthood. *Journal of Projective Techniques and Personality Assessment*, 29, 405–411.

Rabin, A. I. 1968. Projective methods: An historical introduction. In Rabin, A. I. (Ed.), *Projective techniques in personality assessment*. New York: Springer.

Radloff, R. 1961. Opinion evaluation and affiliation. *Journal of Abnormal and Social Psychology*, 62, 578–585.

Rapaport, D. 1951. The autonomy of the ego. *Bulletin of the Menninger Clinic*, 15, 113–123.

Rapaport, D. 1953. A critique of Dollard and Miller's "Personality and psychotherapy." *American Journal of Orthopsychiatry*, 23, 204–208.

Rapaport, D. 1958. The theory of ego autonomy: A generalization. *Bulletin of the Menninger Clinic*, 22, 13–32.

Ratner, S. 1973. The comparative view. In Donelson, E., and Gullahorn, J. (Eds.), *Women: A psychological perspective*. In Press.

Ray, W. J., Katahn, M., and Snyder, C. R. 1971. Effects of test anxiety on acquisition, retention, and generalization of a complex verbal task in a classroom situation. *Journal of Personality and Social Psychology*, 20, 147–154.

Razran, G. 1961. The observable unconscious and the inferrable conscious in current Soviet psychophysiology. *Psychological Review*, 68, 81–147.

Rechtschaffen, A., and Foulkes, D. 1965. Effect of visual stimuli on dream content. *Perceptual and Motor Skills*, 20, 1149–1160.

Reevy, W. R. 1961. Child sexuality. In Ellis, A., and Abarbanel, A. (Eds.), *The encyclopedia of sexual behavior*, Volume I. New York: Hawthorn Books.

Regan, J. W. 1971. Guilt, perceived injustice, and altruistic behavior. *Journal of Personality and Social Psychology*, 18, 124–132.

Rehm, L. P. 1971. Effects of validation on the relationship between personal constructs. *Journal of Personality and Social Psychology*, 20, 267–270.

Remmers, H. H., and Radler, D. H. 1957. *The American teenager*. Indianapolis: Bobbs-Merrill.

Renne, K. S. 1970. Correlates of dissatisfaction in marriage. *Journal of Marriage and the Family*, 32, 54–67.

Rescorla, R. A., and Solomon, R. L. 1967. Two-process learning theory: Relationships between Pavlovian conditioning and instrumental learning. *Psychological Review*, 74, 151–182.

Rheingold, H. L. 1969. The social and socializing infant. In Goslin, D. A. (Ed.), *Handbook of socialization theory and research*. Chicago: Rand McNally.

Riley, M. W., et al. 1969. Socialization for the middle and later years. In Goslin, D. A. (Ed.), *Handbook of socialization theory and research*. Chicago: Rand McNally.

Ring, K. 1967. Experimental social psychology: Some sober questions about some frivolous values. *Journal of Experimental Social Psychology*, 2, 113–123.

Rodin, M. J. 1972. The informativeness of trait descriptions. *Journal of Personality and Social Psychology*, 21, 3, 341–344.

Roe, A. 1952. *The making of a scientist*. New York: Dodd, Mead.

Roethlisberger, F., and Dickson, W. 1939. *Management and the worker*. Cambridge, Mass.: Harvard University Press.

Roffwarg, H. P., Dement, W., and Fisher, C. 1964. Preliminary observations of the sleep-dream pattern of neonates, infants, children and adults. In Harms, E. (Ed.), *Problems of sleep and dream in children*. New York: Pergamon Press.

Rogers, C. R. 1947. Some observation on the organization of personality. *American Psychologist*, 2, 358–368.

Rogers, C. R. 1951. *Client-centered therapy*. Boston: Houghton Mifflin.

Rogers, C. R. 1959. Toward a theory of creativity. In Anderson, H. H. (Ed.),

Creativity and its cultivation. New York: Harper & Row.

Rogers, C. R. 1961. *On becoming a person: A therapist's view of psychotherapy.* Boston: Houghton Mifflin.

Rogers, C. R. 1962. The interpersonal relationship: The core of guidance. *Harvard Educational Review,* 32, 416–429.

Rogers, C. R. 1963. Actualizing tendency in relation to "motives" and to consciousness. In *Nebraska Symposium on Motivation.* Lincoln: University of Nebraska Press.

Rogers, C. R., and Dymond, R. F. (Eds.). 1954. *Psychotherapy and personality change: Coordinate studies in the client-centered approach.* Chicago: University of Chicago Press.

Roheim, G. 1934. *The riddle of the sphinx.* Translated by A. Money-Kyrle. London.

Rokeach, M. 1968. *Beliefs, attitudes, and values.* San Francisco, Calif.: Jossey-Bass.

Rokeach, M., and Kliejunas, P. 1972. Behavior as a function of attitude-toward-object and attitude-toward-situation. *Journal of Personality and Social Psychology,* 22, 2, 194–201.

Rollins, B. C., and Feldman, H. 1970. Marital satisfaction over the family life cycle. *Journal of Marriage and the Family,* 32, 20–28.

Rorer, L. G. 1965. The great response-style myth. *Psychological Bulletin,* 63, 129–156.

Rorschach, H. 1921. *Psychodiagnostik.* Bern and Leipzig: Ernst Bircher Verlag.

Rosen, B. C., and D'Andrade, R. 1959. The psychosocial origins of achievement motivation. *Sociometry,* 22, 185–218.

Rosen, J. L., and Neugarten, B. L. 1960. Ego functions in the middle and later years: Thematic apperception study of normal adults. *Journal of Gerontology,* 15, 62–67.

Rosenberg, B. G., and Sutton-Smith, B. 1964. Ordinal position and sex-role identification. *Genetic Psychology Monograph,* 70, 297–328.

Rosenberg, M. J. 1969. The conditions and consequences of evaluation apprehension. In Rosenthal, R., and Rosnow, R. L. (Eds.), *Artifact in behavioral research.* New York: Academic Press.

Rosenberg, S., and Jones, R. 1972. A method for investigating and representing a person's implicit theory of personality: Theodore Dreiser's view of people. *Journal of Personality and Social Psychology,* 22, 3, 372–386.

Rosenberg, S., Nelson, C., and Vivekananthan, P. S. 1968. A multidimensional approach to the structure of personality impressions. *Journal of Personality and Social Psychology,* 9, 283–294.

Rosenfeld, H. M., and Jackson, J. 1965. Temporal mediation of the similarity-attraction hypothesis. *Journal of Personality,* 649–656.

Rosenkrans, M. A. 1967. Imitation in children as a function of perceived similarity to a social model and vicarious reinforcement. *Journal of Personality and Social Psychology,* 7, 3, 307–315.

Rosenthal, R. 1966. *Experimenter effects in behavioral research.* New York: Appleton-Century-Crofts.

Rosenthal, R. 1967. Covert comunication in the psychological experiment. *Psychological Bulletin,* 67, 356–367.

Rosenthal, R., and Jacobson, L. 1968. *Pygmalion in the classroom: Teacher expectation and pupils' intellectual development.* New York: Holt, Rinehart and Winston.

Rosenthal, R., and Rosnow, R. L. (Eds.). 1969. *Artifact in behavioral research.* New York: Academic Press.

Ross, A., and Anderson, A. S. 1965. An examination of motivation of adoptive parents. *American Journal of Orthopsychiatry,* 35, 375–377.

Ross, D. 1966. Relationships between dependency, intentional learning, and incidental learning in preschool children. *Journal of Personality and Social Psychology,* 4, 374–381.

Rossi, A. S. 1968. Transition to parenthood. *Journal of Marriage and the Family,* 30, 26–39.

Rotter, J. B. 1966. Generalized expectancies for internal vs. external control of reinforcement. *Psychological Monographs,* 80, 1 (Whole No. 609).

Rowe, R. R. 1963. The effects of daydreaming under stress. Doctoral dissertation, Teachers College, Columbia University.

Rubin, I. 1968. The "sexless older years" —A socially harmful stereotype. *Annals of the American Academy of Political and Social Science,* 376, 86–95.

Rubovits, P. C., and Maehr, M. L. 1971. Pygmalion analyzed: Toward an explanation of the Rosenthal-Jacobson findings. *Journal of Personality and Social Psychology,* 19, 2, 197–203.

Ryckman, R. M., Gold, J. A., and Rodda, W. C. 1971. Confidence rating shifts and performance as a function of locus of control, self-esteem, and initial task experience. *Journal of Personality and Social Psychology,* 18, 305–310.

Ryckman, R. M., and Rodda, W. C. 1971. Locus of control and initial task experience as determinants of confidence changes in a chance situation. *Journal of Personality and Social Psychology,* 18, 116–119.

Saltz, E. 1970. Manifest anxiety: Have we misread the data? *Psychological Review,* 77, 568–573.

Sampson, E. E. 1965. The study of ordinal position: Antecedents and outcomes. In Maher, B. A. (Ed.), *Progress in experimental personality research,* Volume 2. New York: Academic Press.

Sanford, N. 1955. The dynamics of identification. *Psychological Review,* 62, 106–118.

Sapir, E. 1921. *Language.* New York.

Sarason, I. G. 1961. The effects of anxiety and threat on the solution of a difficult task. *Journal of Abnormal and Social Psychology,* 62, 165–168.

Sarason, I. G. 1972a. *Personality: An objective approach.* Second Edition. New York: Wiley.

Sarason, I. G. 1972b. Test anxiety and the model who fails. *Journal of Personality and Social Psychology,* 22, 410–413.

Sarason, I. G. 1972c. Experimental approaches to test anxiety: Attention and the uses of information. In Spielberger, C. D. (Ed.), *Anxiety: Current trends in theory and research,* Volume 2. New York: Academic Press.

Sarason, I. G., and Smith, R. E. 1971. Personality. In Mussen, P. H., and Rosenzweig, M. R. (Eds.), *Annual review of psychology,* Volume 22. Palo Alto, Calif.: Annual Reviews.

Sarbin, T. R. 1964. Role theoretical interpretation of psychological change. In Worchel, P., and Byrne, D. (Eds.), *Personality change.* New York: Wiley.

Sarnoff, I. 1951. Identification with the aggressor: Some personality correlates of anti-Semitism among Jews. *Journal of Personality,* 20, 199–218.

Sarnoff, I., and Zimbardo, P. G. 1961. Anxiety, fear, and social affiliation. *Journal of Abnormal and Social Psychology,* 62, 356–363.

Sattler, J. N. 1970. Racial "experimenter effects" in experimentation, testing, interviewing, and psychotherapy. *Psychological Bulletin,* 73, 137–160.

Sattler, J. M., and Theye, F. 1967. Procedural, situational, and interpersonal variables in individual intelligence testing. *Psychological Bulletin,* 68, 347–360.

Saugstad, P. 1966. Effect of food deprivation on perception-cognition. *Psychological Bulletin,* 65, 2, 80–90.

Saugstad, P. 1967. Comments on the article by David L. Wolitzky: "Effect of food deprivation on perception-cognition: A comment". *Psychological Bulletin,* 68, 5, 345–346.

Saul, L. J. 1956. *The hostile mind.* New York: Random House.

Sawyer, J. 1966. Measurement *and* prediction, clinical *and* statistical. *Psychological Bulletin,* 66, 178–200.

Scammon, R. E. 1930. The measurement of the body in childhood. In Harris, J. A., et al., *The measurement of man.* Minneapolis: University of Minnesota Press.

Scarr, S. 1966. Environmental bias in twin studies. Paper presented at the Second Invitational Conference on Human Behavior Genetics, University of Louisville.

Schachtel, E. G. 1959. *Metamorphosis, on the development of affect, perception, attention, and memory.* New York: Basic Books.

Schachter, S. 1959. *The psychodogy of affiliation: Experimental studies of the source of gregariousness.* Stanford: Stanford University Press.

Schachter, S. 1966. The interaction of cognitive and physiological determinants of emotional state. In Spielberger, C. D., *Anxiety and behavior.* New York: Academic Press.

Schachter, S. 1967. Cognitive effects on bodily functioning: Studies of obesity and eating. In Glass, D. C. (Ed.), *Proceedings of a conference under the auspices of Russell Sage Foundation and The Rockefeller University.* New York: Rockefeller University Press and Russell Sage Foundation.

Schachter, S. 1970. The assumption of identity and peripheralist-centralist controversies in motivation and emotion. In Arnold, M. (Ed.), *Feelings and emotions.* New York: Academic Press.

Schachter, S., Goldman, R., Gordon, A. 1968. Effects of fear, food, deprivation, and obesity on eating. *Journal of Personality and Social Psychology.* October, 10, 91–97.

Schachter, S., and Gross, L. P. 1968. Manipulated time and eating behavior. *Journal of Personality and Social Psychology,* 10, 98–106.

Schachter, S., and Latane, B. 1964. Crime, cognition, and the autonomic nervous system. In Levine, D. (Ed.), *Nebraska symposium on motivation: 1964.* Lincoln: University of Nebraska Press.

Schachter, S., and Singer, J. 1962. Cognitive, social, and physiological determinants of emotional state. *Psychological Review,* 69, 379–399.

Schaffer, H. R. 1958. Objective observations of personality development in early infancy. *British Journal of Medical Psychology,* 31, 174–183.

Schaffer, H. R., and Emerson, P. E. 1964a. The development of social attachments in infancy. *Moongravhs of the Society for Research in Child Development,* 29, 3, (Whole No. 94).

Schaffer, H. R., and Emerson, P. E. 1964b. Patterns of response to physical contact in early human development. *Journal of Child Psychology and Psychiatry,* 5, 1–13.

Schaie, K. W. 1958. Rigidity-flexibility and intelligence: A cross-sectional study of the adult lifespan from 20 to 70 years. *Psychological Monographs,* 72, 9, No. 462.

Schilder, P. 1950. *The image and ap-*

pearance of the human body. New York: International University Press.

Schlosberg, H. 1952. The description of facial expressions in terms of two-dimensions. *Journal of Experimental Psychology,* 44, 229–237.

Schlosberg, H. 1954. Three dimensions of emotion. *Psychological Review,* 61, 81–88.

Schopler, J., and Compere, J. S. 1971. Effects of being kind or harsh to another on liking. *Journal of Personality and Social Psychology,* 20, 155–159.

Sanford, N. 1963. Personality: Its place in psychology. In Koch, S. (Ed.), *Psychology: A study of a science,* Volume 5. New York: McGraw-Hill.

Schultz, D. P. 1969. The human subject in psychological research. *Psychological Bulletin,* 72, 214–228.

Schwitzgebel, R. L. 1967. Short-term operant conditioning of adolescent offenders on socially relevant variables. *Journal of Abnormal Psychology,* 72, 134–142.

Scott, J. P. 1963. The process of primary socialization in canine and human infants. *Monographs of Society for Research in Child Development,* 28, 1 (Whole No. 85).

Scott, W. A., and Wertheimer, M. 1962. *Introduction to psychological research.* New York: Wiley.

Sears, R. R., Maccoby, E. E., and Levin, H. 1957. *Patterns of child rearing.* Evanston, Ill.: Row, Peterson.

Sears, R. R., Rau, L., and Alpert, R. 1965. *Identification and child rearing.* Stanford, Calif.: Stanford University Press.

Sears, R. R., et al. 1953. Some child rearing antecedents of aggression and dependency in young children. *Genetic Psychology Monographs,* 47, 135–234.

Sechrest. 1968. Testing, measuring, and assessing people. In Borgatta, E. F., and Lambert, W. W. (Eds.), *Handbook of personality theory and research.* Chicago: Rand McNally.

Secord, P. F., and Backman, C. W. 1964. *Social psychology.* New York: McGraw-Hill.

Secord, P. F., Backman, C. W., and Eachus, H. T. 1964. Effects of imbalance in the self concept on the perception of persons. *Journal of Abnor-*

mal and Social Psychology, 68, 442–446.

Seeman, W. 1948. Daydreams: A study of seven types. *American Psychologist*, 3, 365.

Segall, M. H., Campbell, D. T., and Herskovits, M. J. 1963. Cultural differences in the perception of geometrical illusions. *Science*, 139, 769–771.

Segall, M. H., Campbell, D. T., and Herskovits, M. J. 1966. *The influence of culture on visual perception*. Indianapolis: Bobbs-Merrill.

Seligmen, M. E. P., Maier, S. F., Solomon, R. L. 1969. Unpredictable and uncontrollable aversive events. In Brush, F. R. (Ed.), *Aversive conditioning and learning*. New York: Academic Press.

Sensenig, J., and Brehm, J. W. 1968. Attitude change from an implied threat to attitudinal freedom. *Journal of Personality and Social Psychology*, 8, 324–330.

Shaffer, L. F., and Shoben, E. J., Jr. 1956. *The psychology of adjustment*. Boston: Houghton Mifflin.

Shapiro, D., and Crider, A. 1969. Psychophysiological approaches in social psychology. In Lindzey, G., and Aronson, E., *The handbook of social psychology*, Second Edition. Volume III. Reading, Mass.: Addison Wesley.

Shapiro, J. L. 1966. The effects of sex, instructional set, and the problem of awareness in a verbal conditioning paradigm. Master's thesis, Northwestern University.

Shaw, J. I., and Skolnick, P. 1971. Attribution of responsibility for a happy accident. *Journal of Personality and Social Psychology*, 18, 380–383.

Sheffield, F. D., and Roby, T. B. 1950. Reward value of a nonnutritive sweet taste. *Journal of Comparative and Physiological Psychology*, 43, 471–481.

Sheffield, F. D., Wulff, J. J., and Backer, R. 1951. Reward value of copulation without sex drive reduction. *Journal of Comparative and Physiological Psychology*, 44, 3–8.

Sheldon, W. H. (with the collaboration of C. W. Dupertuis and E. McDermott). 1954. *Atlas of men: A guide for somatotyping the adult male at all ages*. New York: Harper & Row.

Sher, M. A. 1971. Pupillary dilation before and after interruption of familiar and unfamiliar sequences. *Journal of Personality and Social Psychology*, 20, 281–286.

Sherif, M. 1953. The concept of reference groups in human relations. In Sherif, M., and Wilson, M. O. (Eds.), *Group relations at the crossroads*. New York: Harper & Row.

Sherif, M., and Hovland, C. I. 1961. *Social judgement*. New Haven: Yale University Press.

Sherman, J. 1971. *On the psychology of women*. Springfield, Ill.: Charles C Thomas.

Shevrin, H., and Luborsky, L. 1958. The measurement of preconscious perception in dreams and images: An investigation of the Poetzl phenomenon. *Journal of Abnormal and Social Psychology*, 56, 285–294.

Shrauger, J. S. 1972. Self-esteem and reactions to being observed by others. *Journal of Personality and Social Psychology*, 23, 192–200.

Siegel, A. E. 1957. Aggressive behavior of young children in the absence of an adult. *Child Development*, 28, 371–378.

Sigall, H., Aronson, E., and Vanhoose, T. 1970. The cooperative subject: Myth or reality. *Journal of Experimental Social Psychology*, 6, 1–10.

Silverman, I., and Shulman, A. D. 1970. A conceptual model of artifact in attitude change studies. *Sociometry*, 33, 97–107.

Silverman, I., Shulman, A., and Wiesenthal, D. L. 1972. The experimenter as a source of variance in psychological research: Modeling and sex effects. *Journal of Personality and Social Psychology*, 21, 2, 219–227.

Simmel, G. 1964. *The sociology of Georg Simmel*. New York: Free Press.

Simon, H. A., and Newell, A. 1956. The uses and limitations of models. In White, L. D. (Ed.), *The state of the social sciences*. Chicago: The University of Chicago Press.

Simons, C. W., and Piliavin, J. A. 1972. Effect of deception on reactions to a victim. *Journal of Personality and Social Psychology*, 21, 2, 56–60.

Singer, J. E., and Shockley, V. L. 1965. Ability and affiliation. *Journal of Personality and Social Psychology*, 1, 95–100.

Singer, J. L. 1961. Imagination and waiting ability in young children. *Journal of Personality*, 29, 396–413.

Singer, J. L. 1966. *Daydreaming: An introduction to the experimental study of inner experience*. New York: Random House.

Singer, J. L., and Antrobus, J. S. 1963. A factor-analytic study of daydreaming and conceptually-related cognitive and personality variables. *Perceptual and Motor Skills*, Monograph Supplement, 17, 3.

Singer, J. L., and McCraven, V. 1961. Some characteristics of adult daydreaming. *Journal of Psychology*, 51, 151–164.

Singer, J. L., and McCraven, V. 1962. Patterns of daydreaming in American subcultural groups. *International Journal of Social Psychiatry*, 8, 272–282.

Singer, J. L., and Schonbar, R. 1961. Correlates of daydreaming: A dimension of self-awareness. *Journal of Consulting Psychology*, 25, 1–6.

Singer, J. L., and Singer, D. G. 1972. Personality. In Mussen, P. H., and Rosenzweig, M. R. (Eds.), *Annual Review of Psychology*, Volume 23. Palo Alto, Calif.: Annual Reviews.

Singer, R. D. 1961. Verbal conditioning and generalization of prodemocratic responses. *Journal of Abnormal and Social Psychology*, 63, 43–46.

Skinner, B. F. 1935. Two types of conditioned reflex and a pseudo type. *Journal of General Psychology*, 12, 66–77.

Skinner, B. F. 1937. Two types of conditioned reflex: A reply to Konorski and Miller. *Journal of General Psychology*, 16, 272–279.

Skinner, B. F. 1950. Are theories of learning necessary? *Psychological Review*, 57, 193–216.

Skinner, B. F. 1961. The flight from the laboratory. *Current Trends in Psychological Theory*. Pittsburgh: University of Pittsburgh Press.

Skinner, B. F. 1963. Behaviorism at 50. *Science*.

Sloman, S. S. 1948. Emotional problems in "planned for" children. *American Journal of Psychopsychiatry*. 18, 523–528.

Smigel, E. O. and Seiden, R. 1968. The decline and fall of the double standard. *Annals of the American Academy of Political and Social Science*, 376, 6–17.

Smith, E. A. 1962. *American youth culture*. Glencoe, Ill.: Free Press.

Smtih, H. C. 1966. *Sensitivity to people*. New York: McGraw-Hill.

Smith, M. B. 1968. Attitude change. In *International encyclopedia of the social sciences*. New York: Macmillan and Free Press.

Smith, S. and Haythorn, W. W. 1972. Effects of compatibility, crowding, group size, and leadership seniority on stress, anxiety, hostility, and annoyance in isolated groups. *Journal of Personality and Social Psychology*, 22, 1, 67–79.

Snyder, F. 1967. In quest of dreaming. In Witkin, H. A., and Lewis, H. B. (Eds.), *Experimental studies of dreaming*. New York: Random House.

Snyder, R. 1963. The new biology of dreaming. *Archives of General Psychiatry*, 8, 381–391.

Society for the Psychological Study of Social Issues. 1969. SPSSI Council statement on race and intelligence. *Journal of Social Issues*, 25, 1–3.

Sokolov, E. N. 1963. Higher nervous functions: The orienting reflex. *Annual Review of Physiology*, 25, 545–580.

Solomon, R. L. 1949. An extension of control group design. *Psychological Bulletin*, 46, 137–150.

Solomon, R. L. 1964. Punishment. *American Psychologist*, 19, 239–253.

Sontag, L. W. 1944. War and fetal maternal relationship. *Marriage and Family Living*, 6, 1–5.

Speisman, J. L., et al. 1964b. Experimental reduction of stress based on ego-defense theory. *Journal of Abnormal and Social Psychology*.

Spence, K. W., and Spence, J. T. 1966. Sex and anxiety differences in eyelid conditioning. *Psychological Bulletin*, 65, 137–142.

Spence, J. T. and Spence, K. W. 1966a. The motivational components of manifest anxiety: Drive and drive stimuli. In Spielberger, C. D. (Ed.), *Anxiety and behavior.* New York: Academic Press.

Spielberger, C. D. 1972. Anxiety as an emotional state. In Spielberger, C. D. (Ed.), *Anxiety: Current trends in theory and research.* New York: Academic Press.

Spielberger, C. D. 1962. The effects of manifest anxiety on the academic achievement of college students. *Mental Hygiene,* 46, 420–426.

Spielberger, C. D. 1966. Theory and research on anxiety. In Spielberger, C. D. (Ed.), *Anxiety and behavior.* New York: Academic Press.

Sprott, D. A. and Kalbfleisch, J. G. 1965. Use of the likelihood function in inference. *Psychological Bulletin,* 64, 15–22.

Staats, A. W. 1970. Social behaviorism, human motivation, and the conditioning therapies. In Maher, B. A. (Ed.), *Progress in experimental personality research,* Volume 5. New York: Academic Press.

Staffieri, J. R. 1967. A study of social stereotype of body image in children. *Journal of Personality and Social Psychology,* 7, 101–107.

Star, S. A., Williams, R. M., Jr., and Stauffer, S. A. 1949. Negro infantry platoons in white companies. In Stouffer, S. A., et al., *The American soldier.* Princeton, N.J.: Princeton University Press.

Staub, E., and Kellett, D. S. 1972. Increasing pain tolerance by information about aversive stimuli. *Journal of Personality and Social Psychology,* 21, 198–203.

Staub, E., Tursky, B., and Schwartz, G. 1971. Self-control and predictability: Their effects on reactions to aversive stimulation. *Journal of Personality and Social Psychology,* 18, 157–162.

Stein, M. I. 1968. Creativity. In Borgatta, E. F., and Lambert, W. W. (Eds.), *Handbook of personality theory and research.* Chicago: Rand McNally.

Stein, M. I. 1957. Creativity and the scientist. In National Physical Laboratories, *The direction of research establishments,* Part 3. London: Her Majesty's Stationery Office.

Stennet, R. G. 1957. The relationship of performance level to level of arousal. *Journal of Experimental Psychology,* 54, 54–61.

Stephan, W., Berscheid, E., and Walster, E. 1971. Sexual arousal and heterosexual perception. *Journal of Personality and Social Psychology,* 20, 1, 93–101.

Stephenson, W. 1953. *The study of behavior.* Chicago: University of Chicago Press.

Stone, L. J., and Church, J. 1957. *Childhood and adolescence: A psychology of the growing person.* New York: Random House.

Stotland, E. 1969. Exploratory investigations of empathy. In Berkowitz, L. (Ed.), *Advances in Experimental Social Psychology,* Volume 4. New York: Academic Press. Pp. 271–314.

Strasser, S. 1970. Feeling as basis of knowing and recognizing the other as an ego. In Arnold, M. (Ed.), *Feelings and emotions.* New York: Academic Press.

Stricker, L. J., Messick, S., and Jackson, D. N. 1969. Evaluating deception in psychological research. *Psychological Bulletin,* 71, 5, 343–351.

Strickland, B. R. 1972. Delay of gratification as a function of race of the experimenter. *Journal of Personality and Social Psychology.*

Strickland, L. H. 1958. Surveillance and trust. *Journal of Personality,* 26, 200–215.

Stritch, T. M. and Secord, P. F. 1956. Interaction effects in the perception of faces. *Journal of Personality,* 24, 271–284.

Strodbeck, F. 1958. Family interaction, values and achievement. In McClelland, D. C., et al., *Talent and society.* New York: Appleton-Century-Crofts.

Strommen, E. A. 1973. Friendship. In Donelson, E., and Gullahorn, J. (Eds.), *Women: A psychological perspective.* In Press.

Suinn, R. M. 1961. The relationship between self-acceptance and acceptance of others: A learning theory analysis. *Journal of Abnormal and Social Psychology,* 63, 37–42.

Suinn, R. M. and Oskamp, S. 1969. *The predictive validity of projective measures: A 15-year evaluative review of* research. Springfield, Ill.: Charles C Thomas.

Sullivan, H. S. 1953. *The interpersonal theory of psychiatry.* New York: Norton.

Summers, G. F., and Hammonds, A. D. 1966. Effect of racial characteristics of investigator on self-enumerated responses to a Negro prejudice scale. *Social Forces,* 44, 515–518.

Tagiuri, R. 1969. Person perception. In Lindzey, G. and Aronson, E. (Eds.), *The handbook of social psychology,* Second Edition, Volume 3. Reading Mass.: Addison-Wesley.

Tangri, S. S. 1972. Determinants of occupational role innovation among college women. *Journal of Social Issues,* 28, 177–199.

Tanner, J. M. 1955. *Growth at adolescence.* Blackwell Scientific Publications, Oxford. Printed simultaneously in U.S., Springfield, Ill.: Charles C Thomas.

Tart, C. T. 1965. Toward the experimental control of dreaming: A review of the literature. *Psychological Bulletin,* 1965, 64, 81–91.

Taylor, J. A. 1953. A personality scale of manifest anxiety. *Journal of Abnormal and Social Psychology,* 48, 285–290.

Taylor, J. G. 1971. *The shape of minds to come.* New York: Weybright and Talley.

Tebor, I. 1957. Selected attributes, interpersonal relationships and aspects of psychosexual behavior of one hundred college freshmen, virgin men. Doctoral dissertation, Oregon State College.

Teevan, R. C., and McGhee, P. E. 1972. Childhood development of fear of failure motivation. *Journal of Personality and Social Psychology,* 21, 345–348.

Tempone, V. J. 1962. Differential thresholds of repressors and sensitizers as a function of a success and failure experience. Unpublished doctoral dissertation, University of Texas.

Thibaut, J. W., and Kelley, H. 1959. *The social psychology of groups.* New York: Wiley.

Thigpen, C. H. and Cleckley, H. 1954. A case of multiple personality. *Journal of Abnormal and Social Psychology,* 49, 135–151.

Thomas, et al. 1963. *Behavioral individuality in early childhood.* New York: New York University Press.

Thompson, N. L., McCandless, B. R., and Strickland, B. R. 1971. Personal adjustment of male and female homosexuals and heterosexuals. *Journal of Abnormal Psychology,* 78, 2, 237–240.

Thorton, J. W. and Jacobs, P. D. 1971. Learned helplessness in human subjects. *Journal of Experimental Psychology,* 87, 3, 367–372.

Thurstone, L. L. 1947. *Multiple-factor analysis, a development and expansion of the vectors of mind.* Chicago, Ill.: University of Chicago Press.

Tinbergen, N. 1953. *Social behaviour in animals.* London: Methuen.

Torgerson, W. S. 1958. *Theory and methods of scaling.* New York: John Wiley and Sons.

Torrance, E. P. 1962a. *Guiding creative talent.* Englewood Cliffs, N.J.: Prentice-Hall.

Torrance, E. P. 1962b. Cultural discontinuities and the development of originality in thinking. *Exceptional Child,* 29, 2–13.

Torrance, E. P. 1964. Education and creativity. In Taylor, C. W. (Ed.), *Creativity, progress and potential.* New York: McGraw-Hill.

Torrance, E. P., and staff. 1964. Role evaluation in creative thinking, revised summary report. Cooperative Research Project No. 725, U.S. Office of Education, Department of Health, Education, and Welfare. Minneapolis: University of Minnesota, Bureau of Education Research.

Torrance Tests of Creative Thinking. 1966. Princeton, N.J.: Personnel Press.

Toulmin, S. 1953. *The philosophy of science.* London: Hutchinson's University Library.

Traux, C. B. 1957. The repression response to implied failure as a function of the hysteria-psychasthenia index. *Journal of Abnormal and Social Psychology,* 55, 188–193.

Triandis, H. C. 1971. *Attitude and attitude change.* New York: Wiley.

Triandis, H. C., Vassiliou, V., and Nassiakou, M. 1968. Three cross-cultural studies of subjective culture. *Journal of Personality and Social Psychology Monograph Supplement,* 8, Part 2. 42 pp.

Tuddenham, R. D. 1952. Studies in reputation: I. Sex and grade differences in school children's evaluation of their peers. II. The diagnosis of social adjustment. *Psychological Monographs,* No. 333.

Turner. 1967. *Philosophy and the science of behavior.* New York: Appleton-Century-Crofts.

Turner, C. W., and Berkowitz, L. 1972. Identification with film aggressor (covert role taking) and reactions to film violence. *Journal of Personality and Social Psychology,* 21, 256–264.

Tyler, L. E. 1963. *Tests and measurements.* Englewood Cliffs, N.J: Prentice-Hall.

Tyler, L. E. 1965. *The Psychology of human differences.* New York: Appleton-Century-Crofts.

Tylor, E. B. 1871. *Primitive culture.* Boston.

Udry, J. R. 1968. Sex and family life. *Annals of the American Academy of Political and Social Science,* 376, 25–35.

Ullman, M. 1958a. Dreams and arousal. *American Journal of Psychotherapy,* 12, 222–242.

Ullman, M. 1958b. Hypotheses on the biological roots of the dream. *Journal of Clinical and Experimental Psychopathology,* 19, 128–133.

Ullman, M., and Krippner, S. 1970. ESP in the night. *Psychology Today,* 4, 1, June, 46–50, 72.

Ulrich, R. E., and Craine, W. H. 1964. Behavior: Persistence of shock-induced aggression. *Science,* 143, 971–973.

Underwood, B. J. 1966. *Experimental psychology.* New York: Appleton-Century-Crofts.

U. S. National Commission on the Causes and Prevention of Violence. 1970. To establish justice, to insure domestic tranquility: The final report. New York: Praeger.

Valins, S. 1966. Cognitive effects of false heartrate feedback. *Journal of Personality and Social Psychology.*

Valins, S. 1967. Emotionality and information concerning internal reactions. *Journal of Personality and Social Psychology,* 6, 4, 458–463.

Van de Castle, R. L. 1970. His, hers and the children's. *Psychology Today,* 4, 1, 37–39.

Vaughan, C. 1963. The development and use of an operant techniques to provide evidence for visual imagery in the Rhesus monkey under sensory deprivation. Doctoral dissertation, University of Pittsburgh, 1963.

Vernon, P. E. 1964. *Personality assessment: A critical survey.* New York: Wiley.

Veroff, J. 1965. Theoretical background for studying the origins of human motivational dispositions. *Merrill-Palmer Quarterly,* 11, 3–18.

Vidmar, N. 1972. Effects of decision alternatives on the verdicts and social perceptions of simulated jurors. *Journal of Personality and Social Psychology,* 22, 2, 211–218.

Volkmann, J. 1951. Scales of judgement and their implications for social psychology. In Roher, J., and Sherif, M. (Eds.), *Social psychology at the crossroads.* New York: Harper.

Von Bertelanffy. 1951. Theoretical models in biology and psychology. *Journal of Personality,* 20, 24–38.

Wagman, M. 1967. Sex differences in types of daydreams. *Journal of Personality and Social Psychology,* 7, 329–332.

Wakeley, J. H. 1961. The effects of special training on accuracy in judging others. Doctoral dissertation, Michigan State University.

Walker, E. L., and Heyns, R. W. 1962. *An anatomy for conformity.* Englewood Cliffs, N.J.: Prentice-Hall.

Walker, R. N. 1962. Body build and behavior in young children: I. Body and nursery school teachers' ratings. *Monographs of the Society for Research in Child Development,* 27, 3, Serial No. 84.

Wallach, M. A., and Kogan, N. 1965. *Modes of thinking in young children.* New York: Holt, Rinehart and Winston.

Wallin, P. 1957. Religiosity, sexual gratification, and marital satisfaction. *American Sociological Review*, 22, 300–305.

Wallin, P., and Clark, A. L. 1964. Religiosity, sexual gratification and marital satisfaction in the middle years of marriage. *Social Forces*, 42, 3, 303–309.

Walster, E. 1965. The effect of self-esteem on romantic liking. *Journal of Experimental and Social Psychology*, 1, 184–197.

Walster, E. 1967. "Second-guessing" important events. *Human Relations*, 20, 239–250.

Walters, R. H., and Parke, R. D. 1967. The influence of punishment and related disciplinary techniques and social behavior of children: Theory and empirical findings. In Maher, B. A. (Ed.), *Progress in experimental personality research*. Volume IV. New York: Academic Press.

Wapner, S., and Werner, H. (Eds.). 1965. *The body percept*. New York: Random House.

Warren, J. R. 1966. Birth order and social behavior. *Psychological Bulletin*, 65, 38–49.

Watson, D. 1967. Relationship between locus of control and anxiety. *Journal of Personality and Social Psychology*, 6, 91–92.

Watson, J. B. 1924. *Psychology from the standpoint of a behaviorist* Second Edition. Philadelphia: Lippincott.

Webb, E. J., et al. 1966. *Unobtrusive measures: Nonreactive research in the social sciences*. Chicago: Rand McNally.

Wegner, D. M. 1971. Self-other differentiation: Field dependence and assumed similarity to others. Master's thesis, Michigan State University.

Weick, K. E. 1968. Systematic observational methods. In Lindzey, G., and Aronson, E. (Eds.), *Handbook of social psychology*, Second Edition, Volume 2. Reading, Mass.: Addison-Wesley.

Weiner, H., et al. 1957. Etiology of duodenal ulcer: I. Relation of specific psychological characteristics to rate of gastric secretion (serum pepsinogen). *Psychosomatic Medicine*, 19, 1–10.

Weiner, M., and Schiller, P. H. 1960. Subliminal perception or perception of partial cues. *Journal of Abnormal and Social Psychology*, 61, 124–137.

Weinstein, J., et al. 1968. Defensive style and discrepancy between self-report and physiological indexes of stress. *Journal of Personality and Social Psychology*, 10, 4, 406–413.

Weisberg, P. S., and Springer, K. 1961. Environmental factors in creative function. *Archives of General Psychiatry*, 5, 554–564.

Weiss, R. S. 1969. The fund of sociability. *Trans-action*, 6, 9 (Whole No. 47), pp. 36–43.

Weitzman, B. 1967. Behavior therapy and psychotherapy. *Psychological Review*, 74, 300–317.

Wellek, A. 1970. Emotional polarity in personality structure. In Arnold, M. (Ed.), *Feelings and emotion*. New York: Academic Press.

Welsh, G. S. 1956. Factor dimensions A and R. In Welsh, G. S., and Dahlstrom, W. G. (Eds.), *Basic readings on the MMPI in psychology and medicine*. Minneapolis: University of Minnesota Press.

Wenger, M. A. A., Jones, F. N., and Jones, M. H. 1956. *Physiological psychology*. New York: Henry Holt.

White, G. M. 1972. Immediate and deferred effects of model observation and guided and unguided rehearsal on donating and stealing. *Journal of Personality and Social Psychology*, 21, 139–148.

White, R. W. 1957. Is Alfred Adler alive today? *Contemporary Psychology*, 2, 1–4.

White, R. W. 1959. Motivation reconsidered: The concept of competence. *Psychological Review*, 66, 297–333.

White, R. W. 1960. Competence and the psychosexual stages of development. In Jones, M. R. (Ed.), *Nebraska symposium on motivation*. Lincoln: University of Nebraska Press.

White, R. W. 1966. *Lives in progress: A study of the natural growth of personality*, Second Edition. New York: Holt, Rinehart and Winston.

Whiting, J. W. M. 1959. Sorcery, sin, and the superego. In Jones, M. R. (Ed.), *Nebraska symposium on motivation*. Lincoln: University of Nebraska Press.

Whiting, J. W. M. 1960. Resource mediation and learning by identification. In Iscoe, I., and Stevenson, H. W. (Eds.), *Personality development in children*. Austin: University of Texas Press.

Whiting, J. W. M. 1964. Effects of climate on certain cultural practices. In Goodenough, W. H. (Ed.), *Explorations in cultural anthropology*. New York: McGraw-Hill.

Whiting, J. W. M., and Child, I. L. 1953. *Child training and personality: A cross-cultural study*. New Haven: Yale University Press.

Whiting, J. W. M., and Mowrer, O. H. 1943. Habit progression and regression—a laboratory study of some factors relevant to human socialization. *Journal of Comparative Psychology*, 36, 229–253.

Whyte, W. F. 1943. *Street corner society: The social structure of an Italian slum*. Chicago: University of Chicago Press.

Wicker, A. W. 1969. Size of church membership and members' support of church behavior settings. *Journal of Personality and Social Psychology*, 13, 278–288.

Wickes, F. G. 1938. *The inner world of man*. New York: Henry Holt.

Wickler, W. 1967. Socio-sexual signals and their intra-specific imitation among primates. In Morris, D. (Ed.), *Primate ethology*. Chicago: Aldine.

Wicklund, R. A., and Brehm, J. W. 1968. Attitude change as a function of felt competence and threat to attitudinal freedom. *Journal of Experimental Social Psychology*, 4, 64–75.

Wild, C. 1965. Creativity and adaptive regression. *Journal of Personality and Social Psychology*, 2, 161–169.

Willems, E. T., and Raush, W. L. (Eds.). 1969. *Naturalistic viewpoints in psychological research*. New York: Holt, Rinehart and Winston.

Williams, C. B., and Vantress, F. E. 1969. Relation between internal-external control and aggression. *Journal of Psychology*, 71, 59–61.

Williams, H. J., et al. 1964. Responses to auditory stimulation, sleep loss, and the EEG stages of sleep. *EEG Clinical Neurophysiology*, 16, 269–279.

Williams, J. H. 1964. Conditioning of verbalization: A review. *Psychological Bulletin*, 62, 6, 383–393.

Winterbottom, M. R. 1958. The relation of childhood training in independence to achievement motivation. Unpublished doctoral dissertation, University of Michigan. In Atkinson, J. W. (Ed.), *Motives in fantasy, action, and society*. Princeton, N.J.: Van Nostrand.

Witkin, H. A. 1965. Development of the body concept and psychological differentiation. In Wapner, S., and Werner, H., *The body percept*. New York: Random House.

Witkins, H. A. 1969. Social influences in the development of cognitive style. In Goslin, D. A., *Handbook of socialization theory and research*. Chicago: Rand McNally.

Witkin, H. A., and Lewis, H. B. (Eds.). 1967a. *Experimental studies of dreaming*. New York: Random House.

Witkin, H., and Lewis, H. 1967b. Presleep experiences and dreams. In Witkin, H., and Lewis, H. (Eds.), *Experimental studies of dreaming*. New York: Random House.

Witkin, H. A., Goodenough, D. R., and Karp, S. A. 1967. Stability of cognitive style from childhood to young adulthood. *Journal of Personality and Social Psychology*.

Witkin, H. A., et al. 1954. *Personality through perception*. New York: Harper & Row.

Witkin, H. A., et al. 1962. *Psychological differentiation*. New York: Wiley.

Wittenborn, J. R. 1955. *Wittenborn psychiatric rating scales*. (Revised, 1964) New York: Psychological Corporation.

Wolf, S., and Wolff, H. G. 1942. Evidence on the genesis of peptic ulcer in man. *Journal of the American Medical Association*, 120, 670–675.

Wolf, S., and Wolff, H. G. 1947. *Human gastric function*. New York: Oxford University Press.

Wolfe, J. B. 1936. Effectiveness of token-rewards for chimpanzees. *Comparative Psychology Monograph*, 12, No. 60.

Wolff, P. H. 1969. The natural history of crying and other vocalizations in early infancy. In Foss, B. M. (Ed.), *Determinants of infant behavior*, Volume IV. London: Methuen.

Wolpe, J. 1952. Experimental neuroses

as learned behavior. *British Journal of Psychology*, 43, 243–268.

Wolpe, J. 1958. *Psychotherapy by reciprocal inhibition.* Stanford, Calif.: Stanford University Press.

Wolpe, J. 1962. The experimental foundations of some new psychotherapeutic methods. In Bachrach, A. J. (Ed.), *Experimental foundations of clinical psychology.* New York: Basic Books.

Wolpe, J. 1968. Behavior therapy in complex neurotic states. In Shlien, J. M. (Ed.), *Research in psychotherapy.* Washington, D.C.: American Psychological Association.

Wolpe, J., and Lazarus, A. A. 1968. *Behavior therapy techniques: A guide to the treatment of neuroses.* New York: Pergamon Press.

Wood, C. G., Jr., and Hokanson, J. E. 1965. Effects of induced muscular tension on performance and the inverted U function. *Journal of Personality and Social Psychology*, 1, 506–510.

Wright, M. E. 1943. The influence of frustration upon the social relations of young children. *Character and Personality*, 12, 111–122.

Wrightsman, L. S. 1969. Wallace supporters and adherence to "law and order." *Journal of Personality and Social Psychology*, 13, 17–22.

Wyer, R. S., Jr. 1965. Self-acceptance, discrepancy between parents' perceptives of their children, and goal-seeking effectiveness. *Journal of Personality and Social Psychology*, 2, 311–316.

Wylie, R. C. 1961. *The self concept.* Lincoln: University of Nebraska Press.

Wylie, R. C. 1968. The present status of self theory. In Borgatta and Lambert (Eds.), *Handbook of personality theory and research.* Chicago: Rand McNally.

Wynne, L. C., and Solomon, R. L. 1955. Traumatic avoidance learning: Acquisition and extinction in dogs deprived of normal peripheral autonomic functions. *Genetic Psychology Monographs*, 52, 241–284.

Yarrow, L. J. 1961. Maternal deprivation: Toward an empirical and conceptual re-evaluation. *Psychological Bulletin*, 58, 459–490.

Yarrow, L. J. 1964. Separation from parents during early childhood: Implications for personality development. In Hoffman, M., and Hoffman, L. (Eds.), Review of child development research. New York: Russell Sage Foundation.

Young, P. T. 1947. Studies of food preference, appetite and dietary habit: VII. Palatability in relation to learning and performance. *Journal of Comparative and Physiological Psychology*, 40, 37–72.

Young, P. T. 1955. The role of hedonic processes in motivation. In Jones, M. R. (Ed.), *Nebraska symposium on motivation.* Lincoln: University of Nebraska Press.

Young, P. T. 1961. *Motivation and emotion, a survey of the determinants of human and animal activity.* New York: Wiley.

Zajonc, R. B. 1965. Social facilitation. *Science*, 149, 269–274.

Zajonc, R. B. 1968. Social facilitation in the cockroach. In Simmel, E. C., Hoppe, A. A., Milton, G. A. (Eds.), *Social facilitation and imitative behavior.* Boston: Allyn and Bacon.

Zajonc, R. B., et al. 1972. Exposure, satiation, and stimulus discriminability. *Journal of Personality and Social Psychology*, 21, 270–280.

Zeller, A. F. 1950a. An experimental analogue of repression: 1. Historical summary. *Psychological Bulletin*, 47, 39–51.

Zeller, A. F. 1950b. An experimental analogue of repression. 2. The effect of individual failure and success of memory measured by relearning. *Journal of Experimental Psychology*, 40, 411–422.

Zigler, E., and Child, I. L. 1969. Socialization. In Lindzey, G., and Aronson, E. (Eds.), *The Handbook of Social Psychology*, Second Edition, Volume 3. Reading, Mass.: Addison-Wesley.

Ziller, R. C., et al. 1969. Self-esteem: A self-social construct. *Journal of Consulting and Clinical Psycholgy*, 33, 84–95.

Zimbardo, P., and Ebbesen, E. B. 1969. *Influencing attitudes and changing behavior.* Reading, Mass.: Addison-Wesley.

Zubin, J., Eron, L .D., and Sultan, F.

1956. Current status of the Rorschach test: I. A psychometric evaluation of the Rorschach experiment. *American Journal of Orthopsychiatry,* 26, 779–782.

Zubin, J., Eron, L. D., and Schumer, F. 1965. *An experimental approach to projective techniques.* New York: Wiley.

Zucker, R. A., Manosevitz, M., and Lanyon, R. I. 1968. Birth order, anxiety, and affiliation during a crisis. *Journal of Personality and Social Psychology,* 8, 354–359.

NAME INDEX

SUBJECT INDEX

CREDITS

(continued from p. iv)

Figure 2–3: From Loehlin, J. C. *Computer models of personality*. New York: Random House, 1968. Pp. 12–15 (Fig. 1).

Figure 4–1: From Jacobi, I. *The psychology of C. G. Jung*. London: Kegan Paul, Trench, Trubner and Co., 1949.

List on pp. 70–71: Reprinted from *Self-analysis* by Karen Horney, M. D. by permission of W. W. Norton and Company, Inc. Copyright 1942 by W. W. Norton and Company, Inc. Copyright renewed 1969 by Marianne Von Eckardt, Renate Mintz, and Brigitte Swarzenski.

Figure 5–1: From Kimble, G. A. *Hilgard and Marquis' conditioning and learning*. New York: Appleton-Century-Crofts, 1961.

Figure 5–4: From Azrin, N. H., & Lindsley, O. R. The reinforcement of cooperation between children. *Journal of Abnormal and Social Psychology*, 1956, **52**, 100–102.

Figure 5–6: From Brackbill, Y. Extinction of the smiling response in infants as a function of reinforcement schedule. *Child Development*, 1958, **29**, 115–124.

Figure 5–7: From Brown, J. S., and Jacobs, A. The role of fear in the motivation and acquisition of responses. *Journal of Experimental Psychology*, 1949, **39**, 747–759.

Figure 5–8: From Notterman, J. M., Schoenfeld, W. N., & Bersh, P. J. Partial reinforcement and conditioned heart rate response in human subjects. *Science*, 1952, **115**, 77–79.

Figure 5–9: From Lang, P. J., Sroufe, L. A., & Hastings, J. E. Effects of feedback and instructional set on the control of cardiac-rate variability. *Journal of Experimental Psychology*, 1967, **75**, 425–431.

Figure 5–10: From DiCara, L. V., & Miller, N. E. Changes in heart rate instrumentally learned by curarized rats as avoidance response. *Journal of Comparative and Physiological Psychology*, 1968, **65**, 8–12.

Figure 5–11: From Church, R. M. Response suppression. In B. A. Campbell & R. M. Church (Eds.), *Punishment and aversive behavior*. New York: Appleton-Century-Crofts, 1969.

Figures 5–12 and 5–13: From Miller, N. E. Theory and experiment relating psychoanalytic displacement of stimulus-response generalization. *Journal of Abnormal and Social Psychology*, 1948, **43**, 155–178.

Figure 5–14: From Murray, E. J. A case study in a behavioral analysis of psychotherapy. *Journal of Abnormal and Social Psychology*, 1954, **49**, 305–310.

Figure 5–15: From Bandura, A., & Menlove, F. L. Factors determining vicarious extinction of avoidance behavior through symbolic modeling. *Journal of Personality and Social Psychology*, 1968, 8, 99–108.

Table 5–2: From Lang, P. J., & Lazovik, A. D. Experimental desensitization of phobia. *Journal of Abnormal and Social Psychology*, 1963, **66**, 519–525.

Figure 5–16: From Schwitzegebel, R. L. Short-term operant conditioning of adolescent offenders on socially relevant variables. *Journal of Abnormal Psychology*, 1967, **72**, 134–142.

Quotation on p. 129: Reprinted from *Nebraska symposium on motivation*, M. R. Jones, Ed., by permission of University of Nebraska Press. Copyright 1963 by University of Nebraska Press.

Figures 6–2 and 6–3: From Rogers, C. R. *Client-centered therapy*. Boston: Houghton Mifflin, 1951.

Quotation on p. 137: From Rogers, C. R. On becoming a person: A therapist's view of psychotherapy. Boston: Houghton Mifflin, 1961.

Figure 8–2: From Katz, I., Roberts, S. O., & Robinson, J. M. Effects of task difficulty, race of administrator, and instructions on digit-symbol performance of Negroes. *Journal of Personality and Social Psychology,* 1965, **2,** 53–59.

Table 8–6: From Sawyer, J. Measurement *and* prediction, clinical *and* statistical. *Psychological Bulletin,* 1966, **66,** 178–200.

Figure 11–2: From Kendler, H. H. *Basic psychology.* New York: Appleton-Century-Crofts, 1968.

Figure 11–3: From Hochberg, J. E. *Perception.* Englewood Cliffs, N.J.: Prentice-Hall, 1964.

Figure 11–5: From Underwood, B. J. *Experimental psychology.* New York: Appleton-Century-Crofts, 1966.

Figure 11–9: From Ostrom, T. M., & Upshaw, H. S. Psychological perspective and attitude change. In A. G. Greenwald, T. C. Brock, & T. M. Ostrom (Eds.), *Psychological foundations of attitudes.* New York: Academic Press, 1968.

Figure 11–10: From Gilchrist, J. C., & Nesberg, L. S. Need and perceptual change in need-related objects. *Journal of Experimental Psychology,* 1952, **44,** 369–376.

Figure 11–11: From Lambert, W. W., & Solomon, R. L., & Watson, P. D. Reinforcement and extinction as factors in size estimation. *Journal of Experimental Psychology,* 1949, **39,** 637–641.

Figures 11–14 and 11–15: From Eriksen, C. W., & Kuethe, J. L. Avoidance conditioning of verbal behavior without awareness: A paradigm of repression. *Journal of Abnormal and Social Psychology,* 1956, **53,** 203–209.

Figure 12–1: From Wapner, S., & Werner, H. An experimental approach to body perception from the organismic-developmental point of view. In S. Wapner, & H. Werner (Eds.), *The body percept.* New York: Random House, 1965.

Figures 13–1 and 13–2 and Table 13–1: From Freedman, J. L. & Doob, A. N. *Deviancy: The psychology of being different.* New York: Academic Press, 1968.

Figure 13–6: From Cline, M. G. The influence of social context on the perception of faces. *Journal of Personality,* 1956, **25,** 142–158.

Figure 14–1: From Bridges, K. M. B. Emotional development in early infancy. *Child Development,* 1932, **3,** 324–341.

Figure 14–5: From Geer, J. H. A test of the classical conditioning model of emotion: The use of nonpainful aversive stimuli as unconditioned stimuli in a conditioning procedure. *Journal of Personality and Social Psychology,* 1968, **10,** 148–156.

Figure 14–6: From Lazarus, R. S. et al. The principle of short-circuiting of threat: Further evidence. *Journal of Personality,* 1965, **33,** 622–635.

Figure 14–9: From Valins, S. Emotionality and information concerning internal reactions. *Journal of Personality and Social Psychology,* 1967, **6,** 458–463.

Figures 15–1 and 15–2: From Epstein, S., & Fenz, W. D. Theory and experiment on the measurement of approach-avoidance conflict. *Journal of Abnormal and Social Psychology,* 1962, **64,** 97–112.

Figure 15–3: From Glass, D. C., Singer, J. E., & Friedman, L. N. Psychic cost of adaptation to an environmental stressor. *Journal of Personality and Social Psychology*, 1969, **12**, 200–210.

Figure 15–4: From Hodges, W. F. Effects of ego threat and threat of pain on state anxiety. *Journal of Personality and Social Psychology*, 1968, **8**, 364–372.

Figure 15–5: From Sarason, I. G. The effects of anxiety and threat on the solution of a difficult task. *Journal of Abnormal and Social Psychology*, 1961, **62**, 165–168.

Figure 15–6: From Spielberger, C. D. The effects of manifest anxiety on the academic achievement of college students. *Mental Hygiene*, 1962, **46**, 420–426.

Table 15–2: From Mendelsohn, G. A., & Griswold, B. B. Anxiety and repression as predictors of the use of incidental cues in problem solving. *Journal of Personality and Social Psychology*, 1967, **6**, 353–359.

Figure 15–7: From Mendelsohn, G. A., & Griswold, B. B. Anxiety and repression as predictors of the use of incidental cues in problem solving. *Journal of Personality and Social Psychology*, 1967, **6**, 353–359.

Figure 15–8: From Markowitz, A. Influence of the repression-sensitization dimension, affect value, and ego threat on incidental learning. *Journal of Personality and Social Psychology*, 1969, **11**, 374–380.

Figure 15–9: From D'Zurilla, T. J. Recall efficiency and mediating cognitive events in "experimental repression." *Journal of Personality and Social Psychology*, 1965, **1**, 253–257.

Figure 15–10: From Holmes, D. S., & Schallow, J. R. Reduced recall after ego threat: Repression or response competition? *Journal of Personality and Social Psychology*, 1969, **13**, 145–152.

Figure 15–11: From Janis, I. L. *Psychological stress: Psychoanalytic and behavioral studies of surgical patients.* New York: John Wiley, 1958.

Figure 16–2: From Foa, U. G., Triandis, H. C., & Katz, E. W. Cross-cultural invariance in the differentiation and organization of family roles. *Journal of Personality and Social Psychology*, 1966, **4**, 316–327.

Table 16–1: From Rabbie, J. M., & Horwitz, M. Arousal of ingroup-outgroup bias by a chance win or loss. *Journal of Personality and Social Psychology*, 1969, **13**, 269–277.

Table 16–2: From Wicker, A. W. Size of church membership and members' support of church behavior settings. *Journal of Personality and Social Psychology*, 1969, **13**, 278–288.

Figure 16–3: From Darley, J. M., & Latane, B. Bystander intervention in emergencies: Diffusion of responsibility. *Journal of Personality and Social Psychology*, 1968, **8**, 377–383.

Figure 17–2: From Kiesler, C. A., & Corbin, D. W. Commitment, attraction, and conformity. *Journal of Personality and Social Psychology*, 1965, **2**, 890–895.

Figure 17–3: From Gergen, K. J., & Bauer, R. A. Interactive effects of self-esteem and task difficulty on social conformity. *Journal of Personality and Social Psychology*, 1967, **6**, 16–22.

Figure 17–4: From Kiesler, C. A., Zanna, M., & DeSalvo, J. Deviation and conformity: Opinion change as a function of commitment, attraction, and presence of a deviate. *Journal of Personality and Social Psychology*, 1966, **3**, 458–467.

Figure 17–5: From Endler, N. S. Conformity as a function of different reinforcement schedules. *Journal of Personality and Social Psychology*, 1966, **4**, 175–180.

Figure 17–6: From Greenwald, A. G. On defining attitude and attitude theory. In A. G. Greenwald, T. C. Brock, & T. M. Ostrom (Eds.), *Psychological foundations of attitudes*. New York: Academic Press, 1968.

Figure 17–7: From Campbell, D. T. Social attitudes and other acquired behavioral dispositions. In S. Koch (Ed.), *Psychology: A study of a science*. Vol. 6. New York: McGraw-Hill, 1963.

Figure 17–9: From Carlson, E. R. Attitude change through modification of attitude structure. *Journal of Abnormal and Social Psychology*, 1956, **52**, 256–261.

Figure 17–10: From Mann, L., & Janis, I. L. A follow-up study on the long-range effects of emotional role playing. *Journal of Personality and Social Psychology*, 1968, **8**, 339–342.

Table 17–1: From Deutsch, M., & Collins, M. E. *Interracial housing*. Minneapolis: University of Minnesota Press, 1951.

Figure 17–11: From Milgrim, S. Liberating effects of group pressure. *Journal of Personality and Social Psychology*, 1965, **1**, 127–134.

Figure 17–12: From Nel, E., Helmreich, R., & Aronson, E. Opinion change in the advocate as a function of the persuasibility of his audience: A clarification of the meaning of dissonance. *Journal of Personality and Social Psychology*, 1969, **12**, 117–124.

Figure 17–13: From Brehm, J. W., & Cole, A. H. Effect of a favor which reduces freedom. *Journal of Personality and Social Psychology*, 1966, **3**, 420–426.

Figure 18–2: From Rosenkranz, M. A. Imitation in children as a function of perceived similarity to a social model and vicarious reinforcement. *Journal of Personality and Social Psychology*, 1967, **7**, 307–315.

Figure 18–3: From Hornstein, H. A., Fisch, E., & Holmes, M. Influence of a model's feeling about his behavior and his relevance as a comparison other on observers' helping behavior. *Journal of Personality and Social Psychology*, 1968, **10**, 222–226.

Figure 18–6: From Baer, D. M., & Sherman, J. A. Reinforcement control of generalization imitation in young children. *Journal of Experimental Child Psychology*, 1964, **1**, 37–49.

Figure 18–7: From Bandura, A., Ross, D., & Ross, S. A. Imitation of film-mediated aggressive models. *Journal of Abnormal and Social Psychology*, 1963, **66**, 3–11.

Figure 18–8: From Hartup, W. W., & Coates, B. Imitation of a peer as a function of reinforcement from the peer group and rewardingness of the model. *Child Development*, 1967, **38**, 1003–1016.

Figure 18–9: From Baxter, J. C., Lerner, M. J., & Miller, J. S. Identification as a function of the reinforcing quality of the model and the socialization background of the subject. *Journal of Personality and Social Psychology*, 1965, **2**, 692–697.

Table 18–2 and Figure 18–10: From McMains, M. J., & Liebert, R. M. Influence of discrepancies between successively modeled self-reward criteria on the adoption of a self-imposed standard. *Journal of Personality and Social Psychology*, 1968, **8**, 166–171.

Table 18–3 and Figure 18–11: From Hicks, D. J. Imitation and retention of film-mediated aggressive peer and adult models. *Journal of Personality and Social Psychology*, 1965, **2**, 97–100.

Figures 19–2 and 19–3 and Table 19–1: From Collard, R. Fear of strangers and play behavior in kittens with varied social experience. *Child Development*, 1967, **38**, 877–892.

Table 20–1: From Aronfreed, J. The effects of experimental socialization paradigms upon two moral responses to transgressions. *Journal of Abnormal and Social Psychology*, 1963, **66**, 437–448.

Table 20–2: From Mischel, W., & Gilligan, C. Delay of gratification, motivation for the prohibited gratification, and responses to temptation. *Journal of Abnormal and Social Psychology*, 1964, **69**, 411–417.

Table 20–3 and Figure 20–3: From Kohlberg, L. Development of moral character and moral ideology. In M. L. Hoffman, & L. W. Hoffman (Eds.), *Review of child development research.* New York: Russell Sage Foundation, 1964.

Figure 21–1: From Scammon, R. E. *The measurement of man.* Minneapolis: University of Minnesota Press, 1930.

Figure 21–2: From Jones, M. C., & Bayley, N. Physical maturation among boys, related to behavior. *Journal of Educational Psychology*, 1950, **41**, 129–148.

Figure 21–3: From Faust, M. S. Developmental maturity as a determinant in prestige of adolescent girls. *Child Development*, 1960, **31**, 173–184.

Figure 21–4: From Horrocks, J. E., & Buker, M. E. A study of the friendship fluctuations of preadolescents. *Journal of Genetic Psychology*, 1951, **78**, 131–144.

Figure 21–5: From Schaie, K. W. Rigidity-flexibility and intelligence: A cross-sectional study of the adult life span from 20 to 70 years. *Psychological Monographs*, 1958, **72**, No. 462.

Table 21–1: From Kagan, J., & Moss, H. A. *Birth to maturity: A study in psychological development.* New York: John Wiley, 1962.

Figure 21–6 and Table 21–2: From Levinger, G., & Breedlove, J. Interpersonal attraction and agreement: A study of marriage partners. *Journal of Personality and Social Psychology*, 1966, **3**, 367–372.

Figure 22–3: From Mednick, S. A. *The associative basis of the creative process. Psychological Review*, 1962, **69**, 220–232.

Table 22–1: From Fitzgerald, E. T. Measurement of openness to experience: A study of regression in the service of the ego. *Journal of Personality and Social Psychology*, 1966, **4**, 655–663.